PORTUGAL GUIDE

YOUR PASSPORT TO GREAT TRAVEL!

CRITICAL ACCLAIM FOR
OPEN ROAD TRAVEL GUIDES!

*Whether you're going abroad or planning a trip in the United States, take Open Road along on your journey. Our books have been praised by **Travel & Leisure, The Los Angeles Times, Newsday, Booklist, US News & World Report, Endless Vacation, American Bookseller, Coast to Coast**, and many other magazines and newspapers!*

Don't just see the world – experience it with Open Road!

ABOUT THE AUTHOR

Ron Charles is the author of five Open Road travel guides: Portugal, Spain, Holland, Bermuda, and The Bahamas. He lives in Montreal, Canada.

HIT THE OPEN ROAD - WITH OPEN ROAD PUBLISHING!

Open Road Publishing now has guide books to exciting, fun destinations on four continents. As veteran travelers, our goal is to bring you the best travel guides available anywhere!

No small task, but here's what we offer:

•All Open Road travel guides are written by authors with a distinct, opinionated point of view - not some sterile committee or team of writers. Our authors are experts in the areas covered and are polished writers.

•Our guides are geared to people who want great vacations, great value, and great tips for both standard tourist sights *and* fun, unique alternatives.

•We're strong on the basics, but we also provide terrific choices for those looking to get off the beaten path and *experience* the country or city - not just *see* it or pass through it.

•We give you the best, but we also tell you about the worst and what to avoid. Nobody should waste their time and money on their hard-earned vacation because of bad or inadequate travel advice.

•Our guides assume nothing. We tell you everything you need to know to have the trip of a lifetime - presented in a fun, literate, no-nonsense style.

•And, above all, we welcome your input, ideas, and suggestions to help us put out the best travel guides possible.

PORTUGAL GUIDE

YOUR PASSPORT TO GREAT TRAVEL!

RON CHARLES

OPEN ROAD PUBLISHING

This book is dedicated to José Rodrigues dos Santos and João Manuel Vieira de Castro Ribeiro, and also to José Almeida, Maria Regina Moreira, Jean Louis de Talance, Jan Willem Bos, Alfredo Jorge Pereira Santos, Martina de Almeida, António Simoes de Almeida, José Portugal Catalão, and Irene Pereira.

These are the people who have developed the business of accommodating tourists in Portugal into an art form. They have deeply inspired me throughout the years, and I certainly hope that my readers will have the privilege of benefiting from the experience and professionalism of these special hoteliers.

2nd Edition

TABLE OF CONTENTS

CONTENTS

CONTENTS

13. COSTA DE PRATA   238

CONTENTS

CONTENTS

CONTENTS

CONTENTS

MAPS

SIDEBARS

CONTENTS

ACKNOWLEDGEMENTS

I wish to thank the following people who I've interviewed for this publication. Without their help it would have taken me several more years to complete my work: Dr. Alexandre Relvas, Secretary of State of Portugal, Tourism Division, Lisbon; Maria do Carmo Sousa Dias, Portuguese National Tourist Board, Toronto; Paulo Loff, ICEP, Tourism Promotion, North American Division, Lisbon; Pedro Antunes de Almeida, Chairman of Enatur-Pousadas, Lisbon; Nuno Jardim Fernandes, Marketing Manager of Enatur-Pousadas, Lisbon; João Ricardo Alves, Director of Marketing for Europcar, Lisbon; Luís Filipe da Piedade André, Ticketing Supervisor for TAP Air Portugal, Lisbon, Paulo B. Melo, Northeast Regional Manager for TAP Air Portugal, Boston; Gloria Melo, Supervisor, TAP Air Portugal, Newark Headquarters, Artur Mc Millan, Director of Quasar Tours, Lisbon; António Morais, Director of Feriasol Viagens, Cascais; Nina Chung, Director of Public Relations, Hostelling International, Canada; Sandra Quintino da Silva, INP, Interpretor and Guide, Queluz; and Pedro Mesquita, Lawyer and Political Advisor, Porto.

And thank you also to the countless hotel managers, quinta owners, museum curators, winery staff, pousada workers, taxi drivers, tour guides, airline employees, mayors, civil servants, Turismo offices, and especially the kind and informative local residents of Portugal who have provided me with much of the material used in this book.

EXPLORE PORTUGAL'S BEAUTIFUL COAST!

1. INTRODUCTION

Portugal is a warm and mysterious country that is still largely undiscovered by the majority of travelers from North America.

In today's Europe, it is difficult to imagine a country as warm, friendly, and inexpensive to explore. While many tourists have been to the beaches of Portugal's Algarve region, few make the effort to look into the soul of Portugal. This book will help you experience the soul of Portugal: medieval walled villages, Roman temples, prehistoric megaliths, royal palaces, pristine beaches and traditional fishing villages. As you travel in any region of Portugal, you will learn to expect the unexpected and thoroughly enjoy the adventure.

You can spend your vacation in a combination of palaces, castles, romantic bed and breakfasts, oceanfront fortresses, opulent villas, turn-of-the-century spas, and resort hotels for much less money than you might imagine. The once dangerous and archaic transportation and road system is now much, much better. It is now possible to travel from one end of Portugal to the other by superhighway in less than seven hours. A large amount of the country can be experienced and enjoyed in the space of just one or two weeks.

What's there to do in Portugal? You can visit great wineries, enjoy fine gourmet meals, wander through ancient stone villages, hike through parks filled with wild horses, meet local families, take in magnificent museums, hunt for handmade local crafts and antiques, play a round of golf on a dramatic oceanside course, try your luck at a casino, shop for great bargains, experience a wonderful Fado show, and just relax and sunbathe on a magnificent beach.

This book has been designed so that you can put together your own unique itinerary. There are many recommendations included in each chapter to point you in the right direction. With a little planning and a taste for adventure and fun, your trip to Portugal will be the trip of a lifetime!

2. EXCITING PORTUGAL!
- OVERVIEW

Welcome to Portugal! Get ready for the trip of a lifetime!

Prices for accommodations, rental cars, air tickets, trains, and meals are among the lowest in all of Western Europe. The low season is an exceptional value, especially the warmer months of March and October.

Historically, Portugal was divided into 11 separate provinces – the Minho, Trás-os-Montes, Douro, Beira Alta, Beira Baixa, Beira Litoral, Estremadura, Ribatejo, Alto Alentejo, Baixa Alentejo, and the Algarve. Although these old provincial divisions still remain, these days the government has decided to consolidate these provinces into a series of six larger regions. These regions are thus called, and referred to in this publication, as the **Costa Verde**, **Montanhas**, **Costa de Prata**, **Planícies**, **Costa de Lisboa**, and the **Algarve**.

WHERE IS PORTUGAL?

Portugal rests on the westernmost point of the European continent. It is a fairly small country that occupies a little over 91,500 square kilometers (about 34,350 square miles), and has a population base of some 10 million people. The Atlantic Ocean has carved its dramatic coastlines to form the country's southern and western beach- laden borders, while Spain surrounds Portugal to the north and east. The inland sections of the country are covered with remarkable mountains, vast plains, tranquil river valleys, fish filled lakes, unpolluted rivers, and all but forgotten hamlets.

LISBON

Lisbon is a modern, vibrant city, but it is also steeped in history and tradition. Vendors will stand outside their establishments and chat with passers-by. Fishmongers can be heard in the markets extolling the virtues of the day's catch. Children walk to school clutching the bottom of their grandmothers' dresses. The old village way of life can still be found in some parts of Lisbon.

You can experience this blend of old and new in Lisbon in just a few days of wandering around the city; it is entirely possible to do some serious sightseeing, visit impressive art collections, eat inexpensive regional cuisines, shop for bargain-priced fine European goods, walk past hundreds of opulent old houses, and then spend an enjoyable late night out. Lisbon is a safe, inexpensive, and welcoming city to explore.

PORTO

The massive city of **Porto**, the second largest city in Portugal, is located on the north bank of the **Douro River's** mouth. Porto's inner beauty will become apparent to all who visit. The magnificent Gothic 14th-century **Igreja de São Fransisco** church and its unforgettable vaulted baroque interior should not be missed.

Shoppers will particularly like Porto; the famed merchant street of Rua de Santa Catarina provides the best shopping possibilities for high quality men's and women's clothing, leather goods, jewelry, and antiques.

COSTA DE LISBOA

The **Costa de Lisboa** region includes portions of southern **Estremadura** and northwestern **Baixa Alentejo**, as well as a sliver of southwestern **Ribatejo** province. This beautiful area is comprised mainly of the cities, villages, and seaside resort areas that surround the capital city of Lisbon and its southern suburbs. The majority of this area is in close proximity to the coast and the Atlantic Ocean.

COSTA DE PRATA

This relatively peaceful region, north of Lisbon, contains **Beira Litoral**, the northern section of **Estremadura**, and a small piece of western **Beira Alta** provinces. Although the **Costa de Prata** boasts some magnificent beaches, most of the region is consists of forests and countryside. Many small roads wind their way through centuries-old villages and cities, each with their own special charm.

COSTA VERDE

The **Costa Verde** region is located in the extreme northwestern section of Portugal and contains both **Douro** and **Minho** provinces as well as a tiny slice of northwestern **Trás-os-Montes**. Many mountains, valleys, and rivers surround the Costa Verde's major population areas.

The land in this region is very fertile, and much of Portugal's wine production occurs here. Within the last several years, a major increase in industry has resulted in a big increase in population.

THE MONTANHAS

The **Montanhas** - the mountainous region - is a remote section in Portugal's northeast corner, seldom visited by tourists. This region includes large chunks of the **Trás-os-Montes**, **Beira Baixa**, and **Beira Alta** provinces, and is dominated by rugged snow-capped mountains, dense pine forests, and huge boulder spiked valleys.

One of the country's oldest rituals, the **Festas dos Rapazes** during which young men dress up in bizarre masks and colorful costumes, is held during the last week of December and first week of January in small villages of the Montanhas.

THE PLANÍCIES

The **Planícies** - the plains - is the largest region in Portugal, roughly one-third of Portugal's land mass, and consists of all of **Alto Alentejo** province, as well as most of **Ribatejo** and **Baixa Alentejo** provinces. The majority of this highly agricultural and historic region is covered with cork and olive fields. Prehistoric megaliths, cave drawings, and opulent cathedrals are common sights in this vast area.

The friendly peasants who ride their oxen and donkeys down the small rural highways are happy to stop and talk to locals and tourists alike. Besides the wonderful handmade ceramics and tapestries created by local artisans, the Planícies produces several varieties of enjoyable and inexpensive table wines.

THE ALGARVE

The **Algarve** is the southernmost region of Portugal and is drenched with sunshine for almost the entire year. Surrounded by a series of mountain ranges to its north and an abundance of sand dunes and rock cliff beaches on its windswept southern coastline, this area is the most visited region in the country.

Although most of the Algarve's beautiful coast is crammed with one hotel after another, several small fishing villages and inland towns are quite secluded and full of their original historic and traditional character. Most visitors seem determined to spend their days on the vast assortment of sandy beaches (several are topless) and their nights hopping between the many pubs and loud discos in such packed resort areas as **Albufeira**, **Praia da Rocha**, and **Vilamoura**.

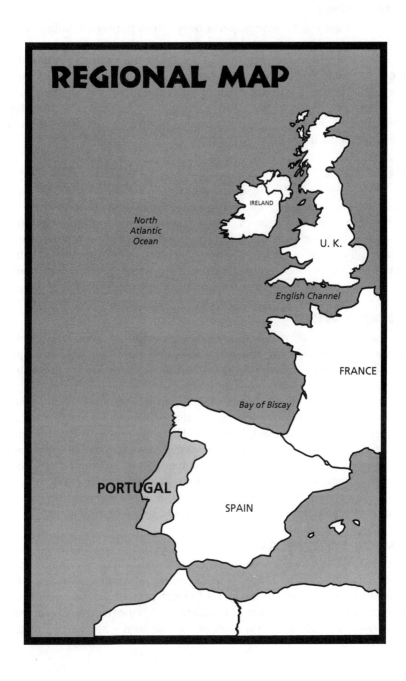

BULLFIGHTS

One of the most exciting spectator sports in Portugal is bullfighting - tourada. It has been enjoyed in Portugal since the 14th century, and is a great source of regional pride. Unlike the brutal Spanish form of the sport, in Portugal the bulls are not killed at the end of a fight. Here the sport seems much more like a test of wills rather than a grisly slaughter.

Many cities and towns all over Portugal hold weekly or monthly bullfighting events from April through October in specially designed arena-style bullrings - Praça de Touros.

SHOPPING

Every region in Portugal offers a variety of outdoor bazaar-style markets. The wide assortment of goods for sale include local cheeses, meats, live poultry, ceramics, crafts, leather jackets, shoes, clothing, tapestries, furniture, antiques, and an assortment of imported items and trinkets. Fine shoes, shirts, sweaters, dresses, handbags, belts, suits, linens, ceramics, tiles, embroidery, vintage wines, jewelry, and many other items can be found at a fraction of their export price.

FOOD & WINE

Each region of Portugal offers a large selection of unique traditional foods. While wandering through the country it is possible to enjoy sumptuous dishes in small local restaurants and adegas at reasonable prices.

Wine in Portugal is superb. Grapes are grown in almost every corner of the country. Local residents of small villages and rural hamlets commonly make their own table wines. There are now over 125 different varieties produced in Portugal. Nine special zones have been established as the finest sectors in the country for high quality wine production. These so-called **Demarcated Regions** - Regioes Demarcadas - are strictly controlled as to their exact boundaries, types of wines allowed for production, maximum yields, production methods, and length of aging.

ENJOY PORTUGAL!

My hope is that after reading this book, you will be a well-informed and culturally sensitive visitor who can travel throughout Portugal with almost no stress. The best traveler is the well prepared traveler, and that is what I am trying to achieve with this book. I hope that I will be able to assist you in creating the vacation of your dreams – at a price you can afford.

3. SUGGESTED ITINERARIES

These are just a few of the many possibilities for a great vacation in Portugal. More detailed information can be found in each regional chapter. All of these schedules can be altered to suit your specific needs, and unless otherwise noted can be followed by rental car or public transportation. Make sure to check for local markets and regional festivals that might coincide with your visit.

WEEKEND IN LISBON
(3 days/2 nights)
This tour is designed for those who have limited time in Lisbon. Travel times are minimal and flights should be via Lisbon.

Day 1 - Overnight in **Lisbon**.
Take a full day by metro, foot, or bus to see the sights in Lisbon.

Day 2 - Overnight in **Lisbon**.
Take a full day by car, train, or bus tour to see the sights in Estoril, Cascais, and Sintra.

Day 3 - No Overnight.
Last minute shopping in Lisbon before departure.

LISBON & ENVIRONS
(6 days/5 nights)
This tour is designed for those who want to see Lisbon and visit the nearby sights with minimal travel times. I suggest flights via Lisbon.

Day 1 - Overnight in **Cascais**.
If you would like to go to a beach, walk over to Cascais's fine beaches.
Take a full day by foot, car, taxi, or bus to relax and see the sights in Cascais and Estoril.

Day 2 - Overnight in **Cascais**.

If you would like to go to a beach, use a car or taxi to get to Guincho.

Take a half day by car, train, or bus to see the sights in Colares and Cabo da Rocha.

Enjoy a fine seafood meal on the Guincho waterfront or in central Cascais.

Day 3 - Overnight in **Sintra**.

If you would like to go to a beach, use a car or bus to get to Praia Grande.

Take a full day by car, bus, taxi, or foot to relax and see the sights in Sintra and Queluz.

Day 4 - Overnight in **Lisbon**.

Take a full day by metro, bus, taxi, or bus tour to see the sights throughout Lisbon.

Enjoy a fine Fado dinner and drinks in the Bairro Alto.

Day 5 - Overnight in **Lisbon**.

Take a full day by foot, metro, and taxi to relax, wander, and shop throughout Lisbon.

Enjoy a fine casual dinner in the Alfama.

Day 6 - No Overnight.

Last minute shopping in Lisbon before departure.

LISBON & THE NORTH COAST

(7 days/6 nights)

This tour is designed for those who want to see Lisbon and would like to experience a little old world culture, history, and seaside relaxation without traveling long distances. Flights should be via Lisbon.

Day 1 - Overnight in **Cascais**.

If you would like to go to a beach, walk over to Cascais's fine beaches.

Take a full day by foot, car, taxi, or bus to relax and see the sights in Cascais.

Day 2 - Overnight in **Cascais**.

If you would like to go to a beach, use a car or taxi to Guincho.

Take a full day by car, train, or bus tour to see the sights in Sintra, Queluz, and Mafra.

Enjoy a fine seafood meal on the Guincho waterfront or in central Cascais.

Day 3 - Overnight in **Óbidos**.
Take a full day by foot to relax and see the sights in Óbidos.

Day 4 - Overnight in **Óbidos**.
If you would like to go to a beach, use a car or bus to go to Praia de Santa Cruz.
Take a full day by car, train, or bus to see the sights in Peniche and Caldas da Rainha.

Day 5 - Overnight in **Lisbon**.
Take a full day by metro, bus, taxi, bus tour, or foot to relax and see the sights in Lisbon.
Enjoy a fine casual dinner in the Alfama.

Day 6 - Overnight in **Lisbon**.
Take a full day by foot, taxi or metro to shop, wander, and eat in Lisbon.
Enjoy a fine Fado dinner and drinks in the Bairro Alto.

Day 7 - No Overnight.
Last minute shopping in Lisbon before departure.

LISBON & THE SOUTH COAST
(7 days / 6 Nights)
This tour is designed for those who want to see Lisbon, but still would like to experience the dramatic seaside cliffs, beaches, and wine regions of the area. Travel times are minimal, and I suggest flights via Lisbon.

Day 1 - Overnight in **Sesimbra** or **Palmela**.
If you would like to go to a beach, drive or take a bus to Sesimbra's sandy beach.
Take a half day by foot to relax and see the sights in Sesimbra.
Take a half day by car or bus to see the sights around Cabo Espichel.
Enjoy a fine seafood dinner and drinks on Sesimbra's back-streets or seaside.

Day 2 - Overnight in **Sesimbra** or **Palmela**.
If you would like to go to a beach, use a car or bus to get to Praia do Meco.
Take a full day by car or bus to see the sights in Azeitão, Palmela, and Setúbal.
Enjoy a tour and wine tasting at the José Maria da Fonseca wine caves in Azeitão.

Day 3 - Overnight in **Estoril**.

If you would like to go to a beach, walk over to Estoril's Tamariz beach.

Take a half day by foot to relax and see the sights in Estoril.

Take a half day by car, bus, or taxi to see the sights in Guincho and Cascais.

Day 4 - Overnight in Estoril.

If you would like to go to a beach, use a car or taxi to get to Guincho.

Take a full day by car, train, or bus tour to see the sights in Sintra, Queluz, and Mafra.

Day 5 - Overnight in **Lisbon**.

Take a full day by metro, bus, taxi, bus tour, or foot to see the sights throughout Lisbon.

Enjoy a fine casual dinner in the Alfama.

Day 6 - Overnight in **Lisbon**.

Take a full day by foot, taxi and metro to shop, wander, and eat in Lisbon.

Enjoy a fine Fado dinner and drinks in the Bairro Alto.

Day 7 - No Overnight.

Last minute shopping in Lisbon before departure.

LISBON COAST & HISTORICAL PORTUGAL

(9 days/8 nights)

This tour is designed for those who want to see Lisbon, but are also interested in the Roman and Medieval sights in the plains region. Travel times are on the moderate side, and I suggest flights via Lisbon.

Day 1 - Overnight in **Cascais**.

If you would like to go to a beach, walk over to Cascais's fine beaches.

Take a full day by foot to relax and see the sights in Cascais.

Day 2 - Overnight in **Cascais**.

If you would like to go to a beach, use a car or taxi to get to Guincho.

Take a full day by car, train, or bus tour to see the sights in Sintra, Queluz, and Mafra.

Day 3 - Overnight in **Évora**.

Take a half day by foot to see the Roman and medieval sights in Évora.

Day 4 - Overnight in **Évora**.
Take a half day by foot to see the sights in Évora.
Take a few hours by car, train, or bus to see castle town of Estremoz.

Day 5 - Overnight in **Monsaraz**.
Take a full day by foot to see the sights in the medieval village of Monsaraz.

Day 6 - Overnight in **Redondo**.
Take a few hours by car, bus or foot to see the sights in Redondo.
Take a few hours by car or bus to visit the 15th century Convento de São Paulo.
Take a few hours by car or bus to see the sights in the historic villages of Vila Viçosa and Borba.

Day 7 - Overnight in **Redondo**.
Take a full day by car or bus to see the sights in the medieval towns of Elvas, Castelo de Vide, and Marvão.

Day 8 - Overnight in **Lisbon**.
Take a few hours by metro, foot, taxi, or bus to see the sights in Lisbon.
Enjoy a fine Fado dinner and drinks in the Bairro Alto.

Day 9 - No Overnight.
Last minute shopping in Lisbon before departure.

LISBON TO THE ALGARVE

(8 days/7 nights)
This tour is designed for those who want to see Lisbon, but are also interested in spending most of their time on the sunny beaches of the Algarve. The travel times are minimal, and I suggest flying into Lisbon and out of Faro.

Day 1 - Overnight in **Lisbon**.
Take a full day by metro, foot, or bus tour to see the sights in Lisbon.
Enjoy a fine Fado dinner and drinks in the Bairro Alto.

Day 2 - Overnight in **Estói**.
If you would like to go to a beach, use a car or bus and take a ferry from Faro or Olhão to get to one of the islands.
Take a full day to relax and see the sights by foot around Estói.
Enjoy a superb gourmet meal at Monte do Casal.

Day 3 - Overnight in **Albufeira**.
If you would like to go to a beach, use a car, bus, or walk to Albufeira's beach.
Take a full day to relax and see the sights by foot around Albufeira.

Day 4 - Overnight in **Albufeira**.
If you would like to go to a beach, use a car or bus to get to Praia do Falésia.
Take a full day by car or bus to see the sights in Vilamoura and Loulé.

Day 5 - Overnight in **Armaçãco de Pêra**.
If you would like to go to a beach, walk over to get to Armação de Pêra's beach.
Take a half day by foot to relax and see the sights in Armação de Pêra.
Take a few hours by car or bus to see the sights in Lagos.
Enjoy a fine seafood meal on Lagos's oceanfront.

Day 6 - Overnight in **Armação de Pêra**.
If you would like to go to a beach, take a car, bus, or walk to the beaches near Vila Lara and Vila Vita Parc.
Take a half day by car or bus to see the sights in Silves and Monchique.

Day 7 - Overnight in **Vilamoura**.
If you would like to go to a beach, walk to Vilamoura's beach.
Take a half day by foot to relax and see the sights in Vilamoura.
Take a few hours by car or bus to see the sights in Faro.

Day 8 - No Overnight.
Last minute shopping in Faro before departure.

BEST OF THE ALGARVE
(11 days/10 nights)
This tour is designed for those who want to see the sunny beaches, fishing hamlets, country villages, and historical sights of the Algarve. The travel times are in the moderate range. Flights should be via Faro.

Day 1 - Overnight in **Tavira**.
If you would like to go to a beach, take a ferry to the Ilha da Tavira.
Take a full day by foot to relax and see the sights in Tavira.

Day 2 - Overnight in **Tavira**.
If you would like to go to a beach, take a car or bus to Praia Verde.
Take a half day to see the sights by car, bus, or train in Cacela.

Take a half day to see the sights by car, bus, or train in Vila Real de Santo António.
Enjoy a fine seafood meal on Tavira's river front.

Day 3 - Overnight in **Albufeira**.
If you would like to go to a beach, take a car or bus, or walk to Albufeira's beach.
Take a full day by foot to relax and see the sights in Albufeira.

Day 4 - Overnight in **Albufeira**.
If you would like to go to a beach, take a car or bus to Praia da Falésia.
Take a half day by foot to relax in Albufeira and the beach.
Take a half day by car or bus to see the sights in Loulé.

Day 5 - Overnight in **Carvoeiro**.
If you would like to go to a beach, walk to Carvoeiro's beach.
Take an hour by car or bus to see the sights in Algar seco.
Take a half day by car or bus to see the sights in Portimão.
Enjoy a casual fish meal on Portimão's harbor-side.

Day 6 - Overnight in **Armação de Pêra**.
If you would like to go to a beach, walk over to Armação de Pêra's beach.
Take a half day by foot to relax and see the sights in Armação de Pêra.
Take a few hours by car or bus to see the sights in Lagos.
Enjoy a fine seafood meal at the Alladin Grill at Vila Vita Parc.

Day 7 - Overnight in **Armação de Pêra**.
If you would like to go to a beach, take a car or bus, or walk to the beaches near Vila Lara and Vila Vita Parc.
Take a half day by car or bus to see the sights in Silves and Monchique.

Day 8 - Overnight in **Monchique**.
Take a half day by car or foot to see the sights in Monchique
Take a half day by car or bus to see the sights in Caldas de Monchique.

Day 9 - Overnight in **Sagres**.
If you would like to go to a beach, walk over to Praia do Martinhal.
Take a half day by car, bus, or foot to see the sights around Sagres.
Take a half day by car or bus to see the sights in Vila do Bispo.

Day 10 - Overnight in **Vilamoura**.
If you would like to go to a beach, walk over to Vilamoura's beach.

Take a full day by foot to relax and see the sights in Vilamoura.
Enjoy a fine seafood meal on Vilamoura's marina area.

Day 11 - Overnight in **Estói**.
If you would like to go to a beach, use a car or bus and take a ferry from Faro or Olhão to one of the islands.
Take a half day by car or bus to see the sights in Almancil and Vale de Lobo.
Take a half day by car or bus to see the sights in Estói and Faro.
Enjoy a fine relaxed gourmet meal at Monte do Casal.

Day 12 -Overnight in **Estói**.
If you would like to go to a beach, take a ferry to get to Faro.
Take a full day by car, bus, or foot to relax and see the sights in Faro.

Day 13 - No Overnight.
Last minute shopping in Faro before departure.

CENTRAL & NORTHERN WINE REGIONS
(8 days/7 nights)
This tour is designed for those who want to see Lisbon, but are also interested in the fine wine producing regions of north and central Portugal. Travel times are moderate, and I suggest flights into Lisbon and out of Porto.

Day 1 - Overnight in **Lisbon**.
Take a full day by metro, foot, or bus tour to see the sights Lisbon.

Day 2 - Overnight in **Luso** or **Buccaco**.
Take a half day by car or bus to relax and see the sights in the Buccaco forest.
Enjoy great wine from the Palace of Buccaco's caves.
Take a half day by car or bus to the wineries of the Bairrada wine district.

Day 3 - Overnight in **Luso** or **Buccaco**.
Take a half day by car or bus to see the sights in Coimbra.
Take a half day by car or bus to the wineries of the Bairrada wine district.

Day 4 - Overnight in **Viseu**.
Take a half day by foot to relax and see the sights in Viseu.
Take a half day by car or bus to the wineries of the Dão wine district.

Day 5 - Overnight in **Lamego**.
Take a couple of hours by foot to see the sights around Lamego.
Enjoy the wineries of the Varosa wine district.
Enjoy great wine tasting at the Raposeira wine caves just outside of Lamego.

Day 6 - Overnight in **Lamego**.
Take a full day by car or bus to relax and see the sights in Peso da Regua and Vila Real.
Enjoy the wineries of the Douro (Port) wine district.
Enjoy great wine tasting at the Ramos Pinto wine caves in Peso da Regua.

Day 7 - Overnight in **Amarante**.
Take a half day by foot to relax and see the sights in Amarante.
Enjoy the wines of the Vinho Verde wine district.

Day 8 - Overnight in **Porto**.
Take several hours by foot or taxi to see the sights in Porto.
Take a couple of hours by foot to go wine tasting at the caves of Vila Nova de Gaia.
Enjoy a great evening wine tasting at the Solar do Vinho do Porto.

Day 9 - No Overnight.
Last minute shopping in Porto before departure.

BEST OF THE COSTA VERDE

(12 days/11 nights)
This tour is designed for those who wish to travel to Porto and the nearby enchanting Costa Verde region. The travel times are somewhat longer, and flights via Porto are strongly suggested.

Day 1 - Overnight in **Porto**.
If you would like to go to a beach, take a car or bus to get to Matoshinos.
Take several hours by foot to relax and see the sights in Porto.
Enjoy a glass of vintage Port wine at the Solar do Vinho do Porto.

Day 2 - Overnight in **Amarante**.
Take a full day by foot to relax and see the sights in Amarante.

Day 3 - Overnight in **Amarante**.
Take a half day by car, train, or bus to see the sights in Vila Real.

Take a half day by car, train, or bus to see the sights along the Douro River.

Day 4 - Overnight in **Guimaraes**.
Take a full day by foot to relax and see the sights in Guimaraes.

Day 5 - Overnight in **Ponte de Lima**.
Take a half day by foot to see the sights in Ponte de Lima.
Take a half day by car or bus to see the sights in Ponte de Barca.

Day 6 - Overnight in **Monção**.
Take a half day by foot to see the sights in Monção.
Take a half day by car or bus to see the sights in the Peneda-Geres National Park.

Day 7 - Overnight in **Monção**.
Take a half day by car or bus to see the sights in Melgaco.
Take a half day by car or bus to see the sights in Valenca and Caminha.

Day 8 - Overnight in **Viana do Castelo**.
If you would like to go to a beach, use a car or ferry to Praia do Cabedelo.
Take a full day by foot to see the sights in Viana do Castelo.

Day 9 - Overnight in **Viana do Castelo**.
If you would like to go to a beach, take a car or bus to Praia Moledo.
Take a half day by car or bus to see the sights in Barcelos.
Take a half day by car or bus to see the sights in Braga and Bom Jesus.

Day 10 - Overnight in **Vila do Conde**.
Take a full day by foot to see the sights in Vila do Conde.

Day 11 - Overnight in **Porto**.
Take a half day by foot, bus, taxi, or bus tour to see the sights in Porto.
Enjoy a tour and wine tasting at one of the many wine caves in Vila Nova de Gaia.
Enjoy a fine casual seafood dinner along the Cais de Ribeira.

Day 12 - No Overnight.
Last minute shopping in Porto before departure.

PORTO & THE MOUNTAINS
(15 days/ 14 nights)

This tour is designed for those who wish to see Porto as well as the seldom visited ancient castle laden villages and pristine countryside of the far north. Travel times are a bit on the long side, and I suggest flights via Porto. I do not advise following this tour in the winter.

Day 1 - Overnight in **Porto**.

If you would like to go to a beach, take a car or bus to Matoshinos.

Take several hours by foot to see the sights in Porto.

Enjoy a glass of vintage Port wine at the Solar do Vinho do Porto.

Day 2 - Overnight in **Bom Jesus**.

Take a full day by car or bus to see the sights in Braga and Bom Jesus.

Day 3 - Overnight in **Bom Jesus**.

Take a full day by car, train, or bus to see the sights in Barcelos and Viana do Castelo.

Day 4 - Overnight in the **Geres** area.

Take a half day by car or bus to see the sights in Geres.

Take a half day by car or bus to see the sights in the Peneda-Geres National Park.

Day 5 - Overnight in **Chaves**.

Take a full day by foot to see the sights in Chaves.

Day 6 - Overnight in **Braganca**.

Take a full day by foot to see the sights in Braganca.

Day 7 - Overnight in **Braganca**.

Take a full day by car or bus to see the sights in the Montezinho Natural Park.

Day 8 - Overnight in **Vila Real**.

Take a half day by foot to see the sights in Vila Real.

Enjoy great wine tasting at the Ramos Pinto wine caves in Peso da Regua.

Take a couple of hours by car or bus to see the sights in Mateus.

Day 9 - Overnight in **Lamego**.

Take a full day by foot to see the sights in Lamego.

Day 10 - Overnight in **Guarda**.
Take a few hours by foot to see the sights in Guarda.
Take a several hours by car or bus to see the sights in Monsanto and Sortelha.

Day 11 - Overnight in **Guarda**.
Take a full day by car or bus to see the sights in the Serra da Estrela.

Day 12 - Overnight in the **Manteigas** area.
Take a full day by car or bus to see the sights in the Serra da Estrela.

Day 13 - Overnight in **Viseu**.
Take a half day to relax and see the sights by foot in Viseu.

Day 14 - Overnight in **Porto**.
Take several hours by foot to see the sights in Porto.
Enjoy a fine casual seafood dinner along the Cais de Ribeira.

Day 15 - No Overnight.
Last minute shopping in Porto before departure.

DELUXE CASTLES & QUINTAS OF PORTUGAL
(12 days/11 nights)
This tour is designed for the most discriminating travelers who desire accommodations in some of the finest hotels in Portugal and fine gourmet meals. Travel times are moderate, and I suggest that you fly into Lisbon and out of Porto. This tour is not geared towards those of you who are using public transportation.

Day 1 - Overnight in **Lisbon**.
Recommend you stay in the Hotel da Lapa, Hotel Lisboa Plaza or the Hotel Metropole.
Take a full day by foot, metro, bus tour, or private sedan to see the sights in Lisbon.
Enjoy a delicious dinner at the Cervejaria da Trindade.
Stop off at the Pavilhão Chines for an after dinner cocktail.
Enjoy a fun late night Fado in the Bairro Alto.

Day 2 - Overnight in **Lisbon**.
Take a full day by foot to see the sights in Lisbon.
Enjoy a fine gourmet dinner at the Casa do Leão.

Day 3 - Overnight in **Cascais**.

Recommend you stay at the Hotel Palácio Estoril, Hotel Albatroz or the Hotel do Guincho.

If you would like to go to a beach, use a car or taxi to get to Guincho.

Take a half day by foot to see the sights in Cascais.

Take a half day by car, bus, or taxi to see the sights in Estoril and Guincho.

Enjoy a fine seafood meal at the Four Season's Grill at the Palácio Estoril.

Day 4 - Overnight in **Queluz** or **Sintra**.

Recommend you stay at the Pousada D. Maria 1 or the Palácio de Seteais.

If you would like to go to a beach, use a car or bus to get to Praia Grande.

Take a full day by car, taxi, carraige, or foot to see the sights in Sintra.

Day 5 - Overnight in **Queluz** or **Sintra**.

If you would like to go to a beach, use a car or bus to get to Praia Adraga.

Take a full day by car, bus, or taxi to see the sights in Queluz and Mafra.

Enjoy a fine goumet meal at Cozinha Velha.

Day 6 - Overnight in **Óbidos**.

Recommend you stay at the Pousada do Castelo or the Casa de S. Tiago do Castelo.

If you would like to go to a beach, use a car or bus to Praia de Santa Cruz.

Take a full day by foot to see the sights in Óbidos.

Enjoy a fine goumet meal at the Pousada do Castelo.

Day 7 - Overnight in **Rio Maior**.

Recommend you stay at the Quinta da Corticada.

Take a half day to wander around the city center and Roman excavations.

Take a half day to wander around Marinhas do Sal and Alcobertas.

Day 8 - Overnight in **Rio Maior**.

Relax at the quinta and enjoy a day of horseback riding and hiking.

Take a half day to visit the nearby Natural Park and its Neolithic sights.

Day 9 - Overnight in **Buccaco**.
Recommend you stay at the Palace Hotel do Bussaco.
Take a half day by foot to see the sights in the Buccaco forest.
Enjoy great wine from the Palace of Buccaco's caves.
Enjoy a fine goumet meal at the Palace of Buccaco.

Day 10 - Overnight in **Buccaco**.
Take a full day by car to see the sights in Coimbra.
Enjoy a fine meal at Pompeu.

Day 11 - Overnight in **Porto**.
Recommend you stay at the Hotel Infante Sagres.
Take a full day by foot, metro, bus tour, or private sedan to see the sights in Porto.
Enjoy great vintage Port wine at the Solar do Vinho do Porto.

Day 12 - No Overnight.
Last minute shopping before departing from Porto.

FLY IBERIA TO PORTUGAL!

4. LAND & PEOPLE

LAND

The mainland of Portugal lies in the western Iberian peninsula of southwestern Europe and covers some 91,500 square kilometers (about 34,350 square miles). The Atlantic Ocean has carved over 845 kilometers (524 miles) of dramatic coastline forming the country's southern and western beach-laden borders, while Spain surrounds Portugal to the north and east. Inland, the country is covered with remarkable mountains, vast plains, tranquil river valleys, lakes abundant with fish, unpolluted rivers, and all but forgotten hamlets.

The country's territory also includes two island chains: the Azores Archipelago and the Islands of Maderia. The Azores are about 1,402 kilometers (869 miles) west of the mainland in the Atlantic Ocean, and the Islands of Maderia some 824 kilometers (511 miles) southwest of the mainland also in the Atlantic.

The government has divided Portugal into 6 regional areas: Costa Verde, Montanhas, Costa de Prata, Planícies, Costa de Lisboa, and the Algarve. Within these six regional areas are 11 separate provinces: Minho, Trás-os-Montes, Douro, Beira Alta, Beira Baixa, Beira Litoral, Estremadura, Ribatejo, Alto Alentejo, Baixa Alentejo, and the Algarve, each with its own unique geography, traditions, cuisine, wines, religious practices, and climatic conditions.

Lisboa, the capital city of Portugal, is also the largest metropolitan area in the country with over 975,000 residents. Originally settled by the Phoenicians in the second millennium before Christ, this intriguing city rests on the banks of the Tejo River and is only a 15 minute ride away from the Atlantic Ocean and its fine sandy beaches. Although much of the city was destroyed by the great earthquake of 1755, the Marquês de Pombal rebuilt the modern downtown core of Lisbon, which continues to expand outwards into what were formerly suburban wastelands.

Nowadays, there are thousands of fine boutiques, museums, cultural institutions, restaurants, and diversions to be enjoyed in Lisbon's modern and historic districts. In 1998, a large section of the river front will be host to the world's fair, **Expo '98**.

The industrialized city of **Porto** is the second largest metropolis in Portugal with a population that exceeds 350,000. Located along the northern bank of the Douro River, the city is one of the country's major centers of business. Besides having many Gothic and Baroque monuments, just below the city rests the suburb of Vila Nova de Guia that is best known for the production of its famous red and white fortified **Port Wines**. There are several caves open to the public where the Port can be tasted for free.

MINHO
● BRAGA

TRAS-OS-MONTES

● VILA REAL

DOURO
● OPORTO

BIERA ALTA
● VISEU

ATLANTIC OCEAN

● COIMBRA
BIERA LITORAL

BIERA BAIXA
● CASTELO BRANCO

RIBATEJO
● SANTAREM

EXTREMADURA

ALTO ALENTEJO

LISBON

● EVORA

● BEJA

BAIXA ALENTEJO

N

ALGARVE
● FARO

CULTURAL PROVINCES

Many visitors are also drawn here for high quality men's and women's clothing, leather goods, jewelry, and antiques. The **Costa de Lisboa** region contains portions of southern **Estremadura** and northwestern **Baixa Alentejo**, as well as a sliver of southwestern **Ribatejo** province. The vast majority of tourists to this area come to enjoy miles of wind-swept sandy beaches that line the coast. There are a few upscale resort towns such as **Cascais** and **Estoril** that are worth a visit. Those more interested in monumental architecture and remarkable palaces will enjoy **Sintra**.

North of Lisbon is the peaceful region of **Costa de Prata**. The provinces of **Beira Litoral**, the northern section of **Estremadura**, and a small piece of western **Beira Alta** are located in Costa de Prata. Although it boasts some magnificent beaches, most of the region consists of forests and countryside. Among the highlights here are the remarkable medieval walled city of **Óbidos**, the beautiful university city of **Coimbra**, the forest and palace of **Buçaco**, the religious pilgrimage sight at **Fátima**, and of course the canal lined town of **Aviero**.

The region known as the **Costa Verde** rests at the extreme northwest section of Portugal and contains both **Douro** and **Minho** provinces as well as a small part of northwestern **Trás-os-Montes**. Many mountains, fertile valleys, and rivers surround the cities and towns here. Besides producing much of Portugal's wine, there are several worthwhile destinations including the wealthy Roman era village of **Ponte de Lima**, the regal and royal city of **Guimarães**, and several small towns on the Douro River that have not changed much in centuries.

The **Montanhas** is the most mountainous region in all of Portugal and is rarely visited by tourists. This area includes large chunks of the **Trás-os-Montes**, **Beira Baixa**, and **Beira Alta** provinces, and is dominated by rugged snow-capped mountains, dense pine forests, and huge boulder spiked valleys. Besides producing the finest cheeses and meats in the country, this region is also home to the mystical **Festas dos Rapazes** rituals during which young men dress up in bizarre masks and colorful costumes.

The **Planícies** is the nation's largest region and is mainly comprised of vast plains. Consisting of the **Alto Alentejo** province, as well as most of **Ribatejo** and **Baixa Alentejo** provinces, the majority of this highly agricultural region is covered with cork, eucalyptus, and olive trees, and is also dotted with prehistoric megaliths, cave drawings, and opulent cathedrals. Traditionally dressed peasants can often be spotted riding oxen and donkeys down the small rural highways in this area. The most important sectors are the walled university city of **Évora**, the royal town of **Estremoz**, the major horse and bull breeding areas of **Golegã** and **Santarém**, as well several small towns that are close to the Spanish border.

The **Algarve** is Portugal's southernmost region and is lined with fine stretches of Atlantic Ocean coastline. While the northern reaches of this area are surrounded by a series of mountain ranges, it is clearly the beaches that have made it into the single most popular region for tourists. Although the vast majority of the Algarve's coastline has unfortunately been developed with hundreds of hotels, there are still a few scattered areas of pristine nature left in areas near **Tavira**, **Estoi**, and just north of **Sagres**.

Even so, most foreign visitors spend their days on crowded sandy beaches, and their nights hopping between the many pubs and loud discos in such famous international resort areas as **Albufeira**, **Armação de Pera**, **Faro**, **Praia da Rocha**, and **Vilamoura**.

PEOPLE

Most of the 10 million people living in Portugal have bloodlines from a mixture of Visigothic, Arab, Roman, and other assorted European civilizations. The look of the Portuguese people varies greatly depending on how far north or south you travel.

Most of the people living here share a strong commitment to family, and a good balance of hard work and even harder play. Lunches are frequently enjoyed at home with loved ones. They can take several hours and usually include locally produced wine. In southern Portugal, do not be surprised if you find the downtown areas of cities and whole towns deserted in the mid-afternoon. Most Portuguese are somewhat shy and humble by nature, are never in a rush, and tend to be quite late for appointments and meetings.

As you travel through small villages in the heart of rural districts and regions, you will notice that most of the older inhabitants still wear vaguely traditional clothing or even ride around town atop a donkey. There are even a few scattered fishing villages along the coast where the fishermen still hand knit their nets and practice their trade in much the same way as their ancestors. Unfortunately, the children of these traditional people are almost all leaving the little hamlets for a modern education and lifestyle in the cities.

Young Portuguese have been influenced by the constant bombardment of US and northern European media and foreign tourists, which has started to affect their perspective on life and the pursuit of both happiness and material items. Even in cities that are supposed to have economic problems, there are often long lines at trendy boutiques, restaurants, and major discos. Credit cards are in the wallets of most urban dwellers, and the idea of buying now and paying later has certainly caught on in a big way, much to the liking of major banks who have hiked up interest rates to well above 30% annually.

Some things that have managed to remain the same: pride, sense of history, and regional cultural identity. There is not one Portugal, but rather several smaller Portugals, each with it's very own customs, seasonal festivals, cuisine, wines, and way of life.

Language

There is only one official language, Portuguese. It is a romance language similar to Spanish. And although most locals can understand Spanish, centuries of political infighting makes them less than happy to admit it. If you do not speak Portuguese, you are much better off speaking English (or in some cases French) rather than Spanish since well over 20% of the population is reasonably fluent in our mother tongue.

Religion

Almost 92% of the people consider themselves to be Roman Catholic. With well over 8,450 churches, this is still considered a fairly religious nation, although mandatory Christian lessons in public schools have been done away with. The remaining small percentage of citizens are mainly Protestants, Muslims, and Jews. Religious freedom is now protected in the constitution.

While not long ago it was unacceptable to even enter a church with shorts or aT-shirt, things have changed greatly since the mid-1970's. Today families are smaller (unlike the old days when a family with seven children was commonplace), and divorce is more common and acceptable. The nation is undergoing a dramatic liberalization in attitudes about religion.

5. A SHORT HISTORY

Little is known about the prehistoric Mediterranean Paleolithic residents who lived in what is now Portugal as far back as 8,000 years ago. These seemingly tribal people have left little evidence of their existence besides a few scattered burial caves and dolmens. Sometime around 3500 BC the Neolithic Iberians began to settle into the fertile valleys of northern Portugal and were later merged together with invading Celtics who had arrived in northern Portugal by about the 7th century BC.

This skilled Celt-Iberian herding civilization built and lived mainly in fortified hilltop villages (known as **Citânias**) of which several ruins can still be seen throughout the **Montanhas** region where they flourished during the Iron Age. The descendants of these Celt-Iberians came to be known as the Lusitanians and has left us several strange granite pigs - Berrões - and phallus shaped fertility symbols - menhirs, monoliths, megaliths, and cave drawings which are scattered throughout the **Planícies**, **Costa Verde**, and **Montanhas** regions. It was about this time the Phoenicians created trading posts on the coast near Lisbon, while the Carthaginians traded on the **Algarve**.

After the Second Punic War in the 2nd century BC, the Romans began their annexation of the Iberian peninsula. The local Lusitanian chief Viriatus opposed the advance of the Romans, and was assassinated in 139 BC after many years of defending his territory. The Roman empire now controlled much of the region, and their regional capital became **Lisbon**. The Romans built cities, temples, roads, aqueducts, and cultivated several new crops such as grapes, olives, and almonds on the plains. Swabian farmers settled in what is now **Costa Verde** and **Montanhas**.

In the early 5th century AD, after increasing violence and social upheaval, the Romans requested the help of the Visigoths to thwart the advance of barbarian tribes and mayhem on the Iberian peninsula. The Visigoths settled in several parts of what is now Spain and Portugal and helped to restore order. When the Roman empire started to decline, the Swabians and Visigoths merged into one culture and accepted Christianity, and the land was under their control.

In 711, the Arab **Moors** began their conquest of Spain and Portugal. It was from their capital in the Algarve that the Moorish people dominated most of Portugal for over 4 centuries. Most of the residents in the south were forced to practice Islam.

ONWARD, CHRISTIAN SOLDIERS

In the late 10th century, the new country of **Portucale** emerged in the Christian-dominated northern reaches of what is now Portugal. This new land was ruled by a crusader called Henry of Burgundy. Christian forces begin their movement south to defeat the Moors. Afonso Henriques (son of Henry of Burgundy) named himself **King Dom Afonso** of Portucale in 1139. He promised to free his new country from Moorish rule and reconquered Lisbon in 1147 with the help of thousands of European crusaders.

In the early 13th century, a parliamentary system - *cortes* - was established and it administered centralized governmental authority. In 1249, King Dom Afonso III captured the city of Faro in the Algarve, and the Moors were expelled from Portugal forever. In 1290, King Dom Dinis founded the first university in Lisbon, Portugal (the University was moved to Coimbra in 1308), and established Portuguese (a Costa Verde dialect of Spanish) as the country's official language, replacing Latin.

In 1385, King Dom João I defeated the Castilians' advancing troops at Aljubarrota and removed their constant threat to occupy Portugal. Peace reigned in Portugal for over two centuries. Now the Portuguese could spend their time and resources on the exploration of the sea and undiscovered territories. In 1386, the **Treaty of Windsor** forged a long standing Anglo-Portuguese alliance and was sealed with the marriage of King Dom João I to Phillipa of Lancaster (sister of the soon to be King Henry IV of England).

In the early 15th century, the son of King Dom João I, **Prince Henry the Navigator**, set up a school of navigation in the town of Sagres in the Algarve to foster what would become Portugal's massive 15th century expansion. Their desire was to put together in one building the cartographers, cosmographers, and navigators who together would formulate a sea passage from Portugal to India via the southern cape of Africa (the Cape of Good Hope). This was the first school in the world to teach and research principles of navigation for transoceanic voyages.

The school at Sagres was responsible for many successful voyages: to Cape Bajador in 1434; the rounding of the Cape of Good Hope by **Bartolomieu Dias** in 1487; the discovery of a sea route to India in 1498 by **Vasco da Gama**; Pedro Cabral's voyage to Brazil in 1500; and **Magellan's** circumnavigation of the world in 1522. With these discoveries, Portugal became the richest kingdom in Europe for several years. In 1494, after realizing that the Castilian backed discovery of the Americas by Christopher Columbus would also make Spain a world power, the Portuguese negotiated the Treaty of Tordesillas. This treaty divided the world in to 2 sections, giving the East to Portugal and the West to Spain.

In 1492, the **Spanish Inquisition** forced thousands of Jews to flee Spain and many resettled in Portugal. In 1496, King Dom Manuel was forced to accept the all expelled Jews in Portugal as a condition of his marriage to the Castilian Princess Isabel. Then the Inquisition came to Portugal. Although a number of Jews converted to Catholicism, many fled once again. Some Jews remained and practiced their religion secretly in the more remote provinces of northern Portugal. Since many Jews worked in the banking sector in Portugal, the banks lost their ability to manage the kingdom's fortune, invested unwisely, and Portugal's wealth began to diminish.

King Dom Sebastião was killed in 1578 when the Portuguese troops were defeated trying to annex Morocco. This in turn led to the beginning of Spanish rule by King Philip II after the Spanish invasion of Portugal in 1580. In 1640, a rebellion within Portugal allowed the Duke of Bragança to seize power and crown himself the new Portuguese King Dom João IV. War continued until Spain recognized Portugal's sovereignty in 1688. In 1703, Portugal signed the Methuen Treaty which created a defensive agreement with both the English and the Dutch. This helped to further assure Portugal's protection from any Spanish incursion. As the mid-18th century unfolded, gold and gems were found in Brazil: a new source of wealth for Portugal.

A DEVASTING EARTHQUAKE

On November 1, 1755, a major **earthquake** all but destroyed Lisbon. Major fires and tidal waves added to the tremendous devastation and loss of life. Immediately, King José I ordered his head minister, Marquês de Pombal, to rebuild Lisbon and later Vila Real de Santo António. His forceful tactics and stern attitude made him a feared and powerful man, but he managed to quickly bring Lisbon into the next century and forever changed its appearance, which has many elements of the appropriately named Pombaline style (after the Marquês de Pombal).

In 1807, the Napoleonic War reached Portugal. French troops under the direction of Gen. Junot captured Lisbon. The royal family was rescued by British forces, and sailed to Brazil to begin their 14 year exile. British troops commanded by General Wellington landed in Portugal in 1808. Wellington's troops were victorious during the bloody battle of Buçaco. France failed to conquer Portugal and the English General Beresford remained in charge of the Portuguese army.

King Dom João VI returned to Portugal from exile in Brazil in 1821 to face an army backed coup d'état in Porto. The coup leaders created a new parliament and imposed new restrictions on the power and wealth of the former feudal lords and religious hierarchy. Brazil gained its independence during this period of Portugal's civil war. King Dom João VI died in 1826 and the throne passed to King Dom Miguel.

With the assistance of the British, King Dom João VI's brother, Dom Pedro, soon returned from Brazil to capture the throne in his name. Dom Pedro became king in 1834, and sent King Dom Miguel into exile. In 1908, King Dom Carlos and his son were assassinated in Lisbon. For the next two years, King Dom Carlos' other son, Dom Manuel II, sat on the throne. In 1910, the monarchy ended when Republicans took power and the King was sent into exile.

REPUBLICS, COUPS, & DEMOCRACY

The **Proclamation of the Republic** was signed by the Republicans on October 5, 1910. This was the end of the Portuguese monarchy forever. Popular discontent developed when the Republic was unable to provide a stablized economy and social order. Portugal's limited participation in World War I led to additional internal pressures.

In 1928, a new Minister of Finance, Dr. António de Oliveira Salazar, was appointed. Massive budgetary changes allowed Dr. Salazar to reverse the country's deficit and balance the budget. In 1932, Dr. Salazar became Prime Minister, and continued to improve the economic, political, and social conditions while imposing strong arm tactics to suppress his enemies. His leadership soon took on dictatorial aspects. In his **Nova Estado** (new state) constitution he seized more power, abolished other political parties, and enforced censorship. Salazar became critically ill in 1968 and passed power to his successor, **Marcelo Caetano**. Dr. Salazar died in 1970. War with former colonies in Africa drained the government's financial resources.

On April 25, 1974, another coup, this time by the **Movimento das Forças Armadas** (Movement of the Armed Forces), toppled the Caetano government. All African colonies were given their independence. Over 650,000 Portuguese citizens lost everything they owned in Africa (many industries were nationalized and huge tracts of land were seized) and became refugees in their homeland.

But the country soon began to make its way back to democracy. Currently a new constitution is in place which allows free speech, freedom of the press, multiple political parties, and equal voting rights to all of Portugal's citizens. In 1986, Portugal became a member of the European Economic Community (EEC). In 1996, the Portuguese people voted in the Socialist Party, replacing the government of Mário Soares, who had been president since 1986. Jorge Sampaio is the new President and Antonio Guterres is the new Prime Minister. This naturally led to many ministerial and other high level personnel changes.

Lisbon was recently selected to host **Expo '98** (the 1998 World Exposition), and several prestigious international sporting and trade events will also be held in this country over the next couple of years.

6. PLANNING YOUR TRIP

BEFORE YOU GO

WHEN TO GO

For great sightseeing weather and relatively low cost travel, your best bet is to go during the months of March, April, May, June, September, and October. The spring and fall offer the visitor generally pleasant warm weather, an abundance of available accommodations, and airfare at low season rates. Rain fall is low during these months with the possible exception of the northern regions of the country.

If you are interested in visiting beaches to swim in warm ocean waters and to sunbathe under the heat of the sun, you are better off going during the June through August summer season. During the summer, all of Portugal is burning hot and overcrowded with vacationing tourists from all over the globe. Since most Europeans receive a full month of paid vacation and typically take their vacations in August, the airlines and hotels have no problem with increasing their rates by over 100%. Although I have enjoyed the summers in Portugal, they are certainly not inexpensive.

The winter season, November through February, is the time to stick to southern Portugal or to just visit the major cities. Rain, snow, and wind are not uncommon to most regions of Portugal, with the exception of the Algarve, this time of the year. The roads in the northern regions are often closed to traffic, and most of the central zone is rather cold at night. However, the Algarve is drenched with sunshine during the winter, but the climate is warm, not hot.

WHAT TO PACK

What you pack should be based on the season that you will be in Portugal. Since summers can be quite hot, I suggest lots of thin cotton clothing. In the spring and fall, it would be wise to pack for mostly warm days and chilly nights, with the possibility of rain at any time. In the winter you should be prepared for anything from rain and snow to unexpected heat waves.

In all seasons I suggest that you pack a money belt, an umbrella, bathing suit, sweater, comfortable walking shoes, sneakers, a waterproof windbreaker, extra glasses or contact lenses, necessary medications with copies of prescriptions, personal hygiene items, sunglasses, an empty nylon bag for gifts and shopping, an electric converter, sunscreen, camera with extra film and batteries, a waterproof key holder for swimming, copies of your passport, travel insurance documents, a list of travelers check numbers, good maps, this book, and the phone number of your travel provider in case of emergencies.

Most visitors will not need suits, ties, expensive dresses, and formal clothing. Only a handful of 5 star gourmet restaurants and snobby nightclubs enforce a strict dress code. Any hotel will be pleased to welcome guests that are neatly attired. Even the most important churches no longer insist on visitors wearing long pants or long sleeve shirts.

AVERAGE TEMPERATURES			
	Lisbon	*Porto*	*Faro*
January	*53F/12C*	*48F/9C*	*54F/12C*
February	*54F/12C*	*51F/11C*	*56F/14C*
March	*57F/14C*	*53F/12C*	*58F/15C*
April	*60F/16C*	*57F/14C*	*62F/16C*
May	*63F/17C*	*59F/15C*	*65F/18C*
June	*67F/20C*	*63F/17C*	*72F/22C*
July	*69F/21C*	*67F/19C*	*76F/24C*
August	*72F/22C*	*69F/21C*	*77F/25C*
September	*70F/21C*	*65F/18C*	*73F/23C*
October	*67F/19C*	*61F/16C*	*66F/12C*
November	*59F/12C*	*54F/12C*	*61F/16C*
December	*54F/12C*	*49F/9C*	*55F/13C*

BOOKING YOUR VACATION

With the help of this guide book, you should have most of the information and suggestions necessary to begin planning your trip. The next step is to book and pay for your exciting vacation. Airlines require that you pay in advance, and you usually get a better fare by booking at least fourteen days in advance. I strongly recommend that you consider prepaying a rental car and some if not all of your accommodations and pay for it on a credit card, if possible. It is much easier to dispute charges if you paid for them by credit card and through a domestic agency.

If you are traveling to Portugal between June and September, available hotel rooms are slim and a prepaid room should cover you from any availability or overbooking problems. The accommodations I highly recommend in this guide tend to sell out quickly, particularly on weekends and during holidays. In the low season, I suggest that you book at least the first and last few nights in advance, and then try to find a few places on your own.

Travel Agents

Travel agents are consultants who usually get paid on a commission basis. If a client desires a standard package tour, no additional fee should be charged as the agent's commission of between 8% and 12% is deducted from the package's list price. For custom vacations (known in the industry as an **F.I.T.**), travel agents may charge as much as $150 in advance to cover the extra hours and long distance calls required for customized trips. Each revision, even those made well in advance of your departure or cancellation can result in stiff penalties or may be non-refundable.

Travel agents have access to computer databases that search out the least expensive regularly scheduled airfares offered by international airlines, and also can look up information on over 8,500 hotels throughout the world. Travel agents also have access to large books like the Hotel and Travel Index or the Official Hotel Guide which gives basic information on tens of thousands of hotels.

Unfortunately, many of the best deals on airfare, and most of the remarkable accommodations in Portugal do not appear in a travel agent's computer or hotel book. Your best bet is to either find an agent who has been to Portugal or even better, one that specializes in the country, or do most of your own research before booking your trip.

Tour Operators

Tour operators are the wholesale sources for well over 75% of the packages and 35% of the F.I.T. custom vacations sold in North America. A good tour operator will specialize in just one or a few countries, and have a staff of experts who have been to almost every hotel and inn located in the countries they represent. Unfortunately, many tour operators do not sell directly to the public and prefer to deal with agencies.

I have included a list of a few fine tour operators who are quite willing to sell directly to the public. Because the staff of most tour operators do not get paid a commission, their suggestions tend to be honest evaluations based on first hand experiences.

Unlike travel agencies, these companies will often charge a more reasonable penalty for each revision or cancellation made in advance. The only drawback with booking through tour operators is that many of them do not have the time to discuss your travel plans at length. I have called many tour operators and travel agencies to research this guide book. Only the most honest, experienced, and informative tour operators are listed below in order of their helpfulness and accuracy.

AN EXCELLENT FULL SERVICE TOUR OPERATOR

*After making more than 85 phone calls to three dozen tour operators that are supposed to be experts on Portugal, the one company that was the most honest, accurate, and informative every time I called was **Marketing Ahead** in New York City. This office is the only fully authorized representative for the 42+ government owned pousadas, and also has the right connections to guarantee a pre-paid reservation in well over 250 different hotels, inns, quintas, farm houses, seaside resorts, spas, and awesome palaces throughout Portugal and Spain.*

*My suggestion is to first call one of I.C.E.P.'s North American-based Tourist Commission offices, read this book, and do a few weeks of initial research. After you have a good idea of your basic itinerary, call **Marketing Ahead** toll free from anywhere in North America, Tel. 800/223-1356, and ask their reservations department for current rates at the hotels I have suggested or that they suggest as alternatives.*

Instead of making dozens of expensive phone calls and faxes to Portugal to reserve and prepay a room, let these folks do it for you, and perhaps save you more money by getting you special rates at selected hotels. The same office can also get you low prices on rental cars, hotel packages, city tours, private guides, motor coach tours, and special group and incentive arrangements.

ALTA TOURS, *Tel. 800/338 4191.*

This is a great San Francisco based tour operator with two employees that exclusively handle F.I.T. customized vacations for Portugal and Spain. Eugene and Joanne can arrange hotels and unique inns in just about every price range, car rental, airfare, and excursions to fit just about anyone's budget. Their recommendations are based on first hand experiences, and I have had many letters from satisfied clients wanting me to suggest them to you. Serves all of North America.

PERRYGOLF, *Tel. 800/344-5257.*

An excellent golf program tour operator that offers a full range of one-week or longer golf vacations in the Costa de Lisboa and Algarve regions' finest resorts and courses. They can provide airfare, accommodations, and golf. You'll receive excellent service from a staff of dedicated golf enthusiasts, some of which have been to Portugal. Serves all of North America.

PETRABAX TOURS, *Tel. 800/367-6611.*

Back when I was still active in the travel industry, I would send many of my most serious referral clients to this great tour operator. Based in Los Angeles, with additional offices in New York, Petrabax offers a full range of pre-packaged fly/drives, customized F.I.T. vacations, and excellent, yet affordable, escorted motor coach trips through all regions of Portugal and Spain. Serves all of North America.

ABREU TOURS, *Tel. 800/223-1580.*

Abreu Tours is a large full service package tour operator that offers airplane tickets, bus tours, hotel reservations, car rentals, long stay vacations, pousadas, and a selection of semi-customized fly/drive packages that concentrate mostly on major Portuguese resort destinations. Most of the staff has been to Portugal, and the service is pretty good if you don't ask too many questions. Serves all of North America.

PORTUGUESE TOURS, *Tel. 800/526-4047.*

This is a good full service tour operator that will occasionally allow direct bookings. They offer airfare, hotels, pousadas (minimum of 3 nights), resorts, fly/drive packages, long stay vacations, golf packages, and more. The staff has been to Portugal, and the service is pretty good. Serves all of North America.

T.A.P.-DISCOVERY VACATIONS, *Tel. 800/247-8686*

A large full service package tour operator managed in conjunction with TAP airlines, they offer airplane tickets, bus tours, hotel reservations, car rentals, long stay vacations, pousadas, and a selection of semi-customized fly/drive packages that concentrate mostly on major Portuguese resort destinations. Most of the staff has been to Portugal, and the service good if you can ever get more than a just a constant busy signal on the line. Serves the US.

DELTA DREAM VACATIONS, *Tel. 800/872-7786.*

A full service tour operator managed by Delta airlines, they offer airfare, hotels, cars, and other services for Lisbon and the Costa de Lisboa area only. They also have the ability to sell vouchers for hotels in some other regions. A small percentage of the staff has been to Portugal, and the service is pretty good for such a big company. Serves all of North America.

AMERICAN EXPRESS VACATIONS, *Tel. 800/241-1700.*

This is a full service tour operator that offers airfare, hotels, cars, and other services for the Lisbon area only. Most of the staff has unfortunately not been to Portugal, and the service is efficient but not particularly informative. However, this is a good choice for business people going on short trips to Lisbon. Serves all of North America.

FLYING TO PORTUGAL

TAP AIR PORTUGAL
• **TAP Airlines US**, *Tel. 800/221-7370*
• **TAP Airlines Lisbon**, *Tel. (01) 386-1020*

The national carrier of Portugal is called **TAP**, and it recently cut back on its once large selection of flights from North America. It only offers daily non-stop flights from New York or Newark to Lisbon and (at press time) announced that it intends to schedule at least one weekly non-stop flight between Newark and Faro during the high season.

TAP has an agreement with Delta Airlines for connecting flights from throughout the US to the New York area for a reasonable fee. For the past few years it has been possible to purchase round trip tickets on TAP for as little as $579 during the very limited winter specials, about $659 during the low season, and about $899 during the high season.

CONTINENTAL AIRLINES
• **Continental Airlines US**, *Tel. 800/525-0280*
• **Continental Airlines Canada**, *Tel. 800/525-8020*

To meet the growing demand for additional service to Portugal, Continental Airlines started new daily service between Newark, New Jersey and Lisbon, Portugal. This new service not only has great low prices, but if you sign up, you'll receive One Pass frequent flier points for your trip. Continental also has a variety of special add on fares for their own flights within North America and Europe. Their level of service is extremely good, and the planes are almost always on time.

DELTA AIRLINES
• **Delta Airlines US**, *Tel. 800/241-4141*
• **Delta Airlines Canada**, *Tel. 800/221-1212*

Delta Airlines has signed a code sharing aggrement with TAP to connect Delta's domestic flights to TAP's international non-stop flights from New York and Newark to Lisbon. This new service benefits travelers due to the price competition on this route and allows Delta frequent fliers to collect points for the entire trip. Delta offers a large selection of add on fares for their own flights within North America and Europe. Service on Delta is rather good, and the planes are usually on time. The food is reasonable, but I still suggest that you consider ordering a special meal (vegetarian, low fat, low salt, fish only, etc.) as these are better.

THE EASIEST WAY TO FLY TO PORTUGAL

· *Iberia Airlines US, Tel. 800/772-4642*
· *Iberia Airlines Canada, Tel. 800/423-7421*

In my experience, the best way to get to Portugal from Canada and the US is to take advantage of the wide variety of connecting flights to both Lisbon and Porto via Madrid that are scheduled several times weekly from Montreal, and daily from New York, Los Angeles, and Miami on Iberia Airlines, the renowned international carrier of Spain. Affordable add-on fares are also available from domestic Canadian and American carriers, allowing for easy connections to the above gateways.

The lowest currently published round trip prices (known in the travel industry as promotional apex fares) to Lisbon via Madrid start at around $568 plus taxes from New York, $658 plus taxes from Miami, $808 plus taxes from Los Angeles, and $778 CD plus taxes from Montreal. Generally when traveling with an adult, children under 12 years old qualify for a 25% discount, while infants not occupying a seat are entitled to a 90% discount. Special student and senior citizen fares are also available. All these fares are subject to advance purchase requirements, specific dates of travel, and cancellation/revision penalties. Additional Iberia Airlines services include special boarding for the physically challenged, a wide variety of special meals, and more.

More affluent passengers should give strong consideration to flying in either the extremely comfortable Business Class or luxurious Gran Clase (First Class). While tickets for these more spacious seats are more expensive, the benefits include special VIP airport lounges with open bars and fax machines, special priority check-in and baggage services, complimentary limousine transfers, hotel discounts, a practical overnight amenity kit and much more. Round trip promotional prices and special companion fares for both Business Class and Gran Clase are also available, so check with Iberia Airlines for more details.

All of the delicious in-flight meals are prepared by the talented chefs at Iberswiss. Gran Clase and Business Class passengers are offered meals featuring dishes such as sirloin steak in pepper sauce, poached filet of sole, and rack or lamb, all accompanied by vintage wines. First run movies are presented on each transcontinental flight, and the cheerful staff will make sure to offer you beverages, meals, coffee/tea, extra pillows, and blankets for your comfort. On-board duty free shopping is considered the best in the industry and offers some of the lowest prices available.

If you join the Iberia Plus frequent flyer program, you can earn valuable points towards free airline tickets on all member carriers of the Iberia group, free car rentals, hotel accommodations and much more.

TRANS WORLD AIRLINES – TWA
• **TWA US,** *Tel. 800/892-4141*
• **TWA Canada,** *Tel. 800/448-2665*

TWA offers at least two non-stop flights to Lisbon a week from the New York area. Prices usually match rates on TAP and Delta. TWA offers a large selection of add on fares for their own flights within North America and Europe, as well as prices with other major European carriers. If you want to travel by plane to another city in Portugal, TWA usually cannot match the rates that TAP offers because they do not operate flights within Portugal.

Service on TWA is reasonably good, and the planes are generally on time. The food is reasonable, but consider ordering a special meal (vegetarian, low fat, low salt, fish only, etc.) as these are usually better. TWA has a generous frequent flyer program.

Flights with Connections to Portugal
Several international airlines offers service to Lisbon, Faro, and Porto from several North American cities. These flights take longer than the above mentioned airlines because they require a change of planes in Europe before continuing on to Portugal. The fares are often the same price as non-stop choices, but sometimes a free stop over in the city where you change planes is allowed.

The following is a partial listing of airlines with service to Portugal via another European gateway:
• **Air France** (via Paris)
Air France in the US, *Tel. 800/237-2747*
Air France in Canada, *Tel. 800/667-2747*
• **Alitalia Airlines** (via Rome)
Alitalia Airlines in the US, *Tel. 800/221-4745*
Alitalia Airlines in Canada, *Tel. 800/361-8336*
• **British Airways** (via London)
British Air in the US, *Tel. 800/247-9297*
British Air in Canada, *Tel. 800/247-9297*
• **Iberia Airlines** (via Madrid)
Iberia Airlines in the US, *Tel. 800/772-4642*
Iberia Airlines in Canada, *Tel. 800/423-4642*
• **KLM Airlines** (via Amsterdam)
KLM Airlines in the US, *Tel. 800/374-7747*
KLM Airlines in Canada, *Tel. 800/361-5073*
• **Lufthansa Airlines** (via Frankfurt)
Lufthansa Airlines in the US, *Tel. 800/645-3880*
Lufthansa Airlines in Canada, *Tel. 800/645-3880*

• **Sabena Airlines** (via Brussels)
Sabena Airlines in the US, *Tel. 800/955-2000*
Sabena Airlines in Canada, *Tel. 800/955-2000*
• **Swiss Air** (via Zurich)
Swiss Air in the US, *Tel. 800/221-4750*
Swiss Air in Canada, *Tel. 800/267-9477*

Charter Flights

In the high season (July-September), several charter operators offer flights to Portugal from New York, Boston, Toronto, and other North American gateways. Be extra careful whenever booking a charter flight since they are not bound by the same regulations as regular scheduled carriers.

It is not uncommon for these flights to be delayed for hours or days and you'll be stuck at the airport. Charter flight tickets are normally non-changeable/non-refundable and are often not covered by travel insurance. For more details, call your travel agent.

Here are three charter companies with good reputations:
• **Council Charter** (US), *Tel. 800/800-8222*
• **Air Transat Charters** (Canada), *Tel. 800/523-0537*
• **Sata Express** (Canada), *Tel. 416/588-8216*

Discount Ticket Consolidators

There are many discount ticket brokers who offer last minute and special advance purchase round trip fares for airlines who have not sold enough seats on specific flights. While some of these companies are in the habit of ripping off clients, several large companies have been doing a fairly good job of supplying the traveling public with good deals on very restrictive tickets. First ask your travel agent for their recommendations, or call the local consumer protection agency or Better Business Bureau about any complaints on the consolidator you are considering.

We strongly recommend that you either purchase your tickets from a travel agent or specialty tour operator, or use a major credit card if you purchase this type of ticket directly from the consolidator. This way you'll be better protected should problems arise.

These are a few consolidators with good reputations:
• **Travac** (US), *Tel. 212/563-3303*
• **Air Travel Discounts** (US), *Tel. 212/922-1326*
• **Unitravel** (US), *Tel. 800/325-2222*
• **World Travel** (US), *Tel. 800/886-4988*
• **Travel Cuts** (US), *Tel. 416/979-2406*
• **New Frontiers** (US), *Tel. 514/526-8444*

Courier Flights

Agencies exist that book passengers on flights to Europe and use their luggage allotment to transport documents to European clients. The courier gives up his or her right to the luggage allotment and is only allowed to bring carry-on luggage. Upon arrival, a representative from the courier company takes possession of the documents.

These flights can run as low as $199 round-trip and usually are valid for only one week. This is not the best way to travel because you never know what is really in those suitcases, and you are completely responsible for their contents. Another major disadvantage is that you may be booked on a standby, or a next available day basis. Travel agencies do not reserve these types of tickets, so check the travel section of your local newspaper.

Some reasonably good courier agencies include:
• **D.T.I.** (US), *Tel. 212/362-3636*
• **Now Voyager** (US), *Tel. 212/431-1616*

CUSTOMS REGULATIONS

Upon Arrival

Customs and immigration officials are relaxed in Portugal. I have rarely seen anyone subjected to a luggage search. The following is excerpted from the official Portuguese customs regulations. Please check with the Portuguese consulate if you need further details.

North Americans arriving into Portugal are allowed to bring an unlimited amount of cash for payment of tourist or travel expenses. Adults are each allowed to import into Portugal the following amounts of these products: 200 cigarettes or 100 cigarillos or 50 cigars; 50 grams of perfume; one liter of liquor; and two liters of wine.

All North American visitors are allowed to bring in the following items for personal use and must leave with them upon departure: personal jewelry, cameras and video cameras, a reasonable quantity of film and accessories, binoculars, sports equipment such as tents and camping gear, fishing gear, guns (check with airline for restrictions), non-motorized bicycles, tennis rackets, windsurfing boards, delta wings, musical instruments, sound recording equipment, radios and televisions, video recorders, typewriters, calculators, and personal computers.

Upon Departure

Upon exiting Portugal, a limit of 100,000$00 escudos and a limit of the equivalent of 1,000,000$00 escudos in foreign currency may be exported without documentation. Additional amounts will require proof of the importation of such quantities.

Upon Your Return to North America

All US citizens can return to America with up to $400 US worth of goods duty free if you left the USA for over 48 hours and haven't made another international trip within the last 30 days. Each family member is eligible, and the amounts may be pooled together. Normally a 10% duty is assessed on goods that exceed the $400 limit, but are below $1,400 in total value. Above $1,400, the duty varies depending on the merchandise being imported.

Each adult may also bring in up to one liter of wine or alcohol and either 100 cigars (except from Cuba) or 200 cigarettes. There is no duty on antiquities or works of art that are over 100 years old. Bring all receipts with the merchandise to customs to avoid any problems.

All Canadian citizens can return to Canada with up to $300 CDN of goods once each year if you leave Canada for over seven days, or up to $100 CDN several times each year if you leave Canada for over 48 hours. Each family member is eligible for the same limit. Normally a combination of federal and provincial taxes are assessed on goods that exceed the $300 CDN value, depending on the specific items involved.

Each adult can also bring in 1.14 liters of alcohol or 8.5 liters (24 12-ounce cans or bottles) of beer. For those at least 16 years old, up to 50 cigars, 200 cigarettes, and 400 grams of tobacco is permitted. Receipts will help you avoid problems.

PASSPORTS & VISAS

All US and Canadian citizens are required to have a valid passport to enter Portugal. Visitors who intend to spend over 60 days in Portugal must register with the police to receive an extension before the end of the first 60 day period. Visas are not needed for US and Canadian tourists.

Portuguese Embassies

- In the US: *2125 Kalorama Rd, N.W., Washington, D.C. 20008, Tel. 202/328-8610*
- In Canada: *645 Island Park Drive, Ottawa, Ontario K1Y OB8, Tel. 613/729-0883*

PORTUGUESE TOURIST OFFICES

In North America

As you begin to plan your vacation to Portugal, you might want to contact the Portuguese **Tourism Commission** in your country (formerly known as the Portuguese National Tourist Office). The Instituto Comercío Externo de Portugal (ICEP) runs the Tourism Commission. They can send a you maps, tourist information in English, artistically designed regional summaries, phrase books, and sometimes a few glossy brochures from well connected major tour operators (although these companies are not necessarily the best). The material sent to you will be more relevant if you are specific about what you want.

The receptionists at these offices are usually very informative Portuguese citizens who do their best to keep up with the tidal wave of daily inquiries. Tourist Commissions tend to be understaffed, so be patient. A personal visit to the ICEP Tourism Commission office can mean more focused attention and more relevant material. Below is a list of Tourism Commissions in North America:

• In the US: **ICEP Tourism Commission**, *590 Fifth Ave, 4th Floor, New York City, N.Y. 10036, Tel. 212/354-4403*
• In Canada: **ICEP Tourism Commission**, *60 Bloor St. West - Suite 1005, Toronto, Ontario, Canada M4W 3B8, Tel. 416/921-7376*

STUDENT IDENTITY CARDS

For full time students under the age of 26 who can document their status as a current student, there is a great card I strongly recommend. The **International Student Identity Card** (ISIC) is valid for one year and should be obtained in North America before you depart for about $15. It allows its holder discounts on international flights, museums, public transportation, and other services. Included with the cost of this card is special emergency medical insurance that can cover $3,000 in medical bills as well as $100 a day in hospital bills for up to two months.

To obtain a card, contact one of the following offices:
• **Council Travel**, *New York, Tel. 212/661-1450*
• **Travel Cuts**, *Toronto, Tel. 416/979-2406*

TRAVEL EMERGENCIES & MEDICAL INSURANCE

One key issue on any trip abroad is what to do in case of an emergency, particularly a medical emergency. You should seriously consider whether you want to take out a health insurance policy before you depart. Be sure to ask your own health insurance company whether your policy is valid while you are overseas and specifically ask about conditions and limitations.

One of the most comprehensive types of travel health insurance is "Primary Coverage." In an emergency, most of these policies provide 24 hour toll free help desks, lists of approved specialists, airlift to a hospital with the proper facilities for your condition, and non-medical assistance such as refunds on additional expenses and unused prepaid hotel rooms. Every policy is different, so you should be sure to examine any policy closely before purchase.

TRIP CANCELLATION & INTERRUPTION INSURANCE

Policies are also available that will cover vacation refunds if a family member gets ill and you must cancel your trip, if the airline you were supposed to be flying goes out of business, if you must depart early from your trip due to sickness or death in the family, if the airline fails to deliver your baggage on time, if your luggage is stolen from your car, if your stay is extended do to injury, etc.

One element normally not covered are airplane schedule changes, missed connections, and flight cancellations. Please check with your travel agent or tour operator for further details.

Three good travel insurance companies are:
• **Mutual of Omaha (Tele-Trip)**, *Tel. 800/228-9792 in the US; Tel. 402/351-8000 in Canada*
• **Travel Guard**, *Tel. 715/345-0505 in the US and Canada*
• **Access America**, *Tel. 800/284-8300 in the US and Canada*

GETTING AROUND PORTUGAL

BY AIR

There are several large commuter and tourist airports within Portugal. Most of the air traffic tends to be among Lisbon, Faro, Porto, and the autonomous coastal islands of Madeira and the Azores. Flights are very expensive if booked within Portugal. I have paid over 28,000$00 for a last minute one-way ticket from Lisbon to Faro.

If you intend to fly into one Portuguese airport and fly out of another, it is best to include this segment on your international ticket. Several companies offer inter regional flights on a daily basis, but not all are on jets. Please contact your specialty tour operator or travel agent for prices, reservations, and ticketing.

TAP-Air Portugal provides service between Lisbon and Faro, service between Lisbon and Madeira, service between Lisbon and Porto, service between Lisbon and the Azores, service between Madeira and Porto Santo. There are additional routes.

SATA-Air Azores provides service between most of the islands in the Azores.

Portugalia provides service between Lisbon, Porto, and Faro.

BY BUS

Portuguese buses offer a good alternative to driving in Portugal, but is generally more expensive than the train for the same route. I suggest you stick with the train system unless there is only bus service to the place you want to go.

The majority of the inter-regional and inter-city buses are now run by a series of new, privately operated transportation groups, many of which were created recently, just after the privitization of the once powerful government own Rodoviaria National (RN) bus service.

Most major cities have bus stations and are covered by regularly scheduled express (**Expressos**) bus service. Local and regional busses (**Carreiras**) get you to smaller towns where there may be just a bus stop instead of a bus station. These buses are usually slow since they make many more stops than an express bus. During weekends and holidays, many routes may not operate so make sure to stop by the bus station to confirm schedules.

Additional service to various regions of Portugal are provided by dozens of large and small sized private bus companies including Stagecoach, Empresa Mafrense, Solexpresso, Cabanelas, and Avic. These companies sell their tickets through local travel agents and at most bus stations. Many of these buses offer videos or music throughout the journey. If you are traveling south of Lisbon, you may have to take a ferry from the Praça do Comercío's (Terreiro do Paço) ferry landing to reach the bus station in Cacilhas.

Several bus companies offer air conditioned deluxe express bus service in both directions between Lisbon and the Algarve (about 2950$00 each way). Most of the private companies' buses depart from the kiosks just behind the Marquês de Pombal statue in Eduardo VII park in central Lisbon. Lisbon's main bus terminal is located just a few blocks away on Ave. Casal Ribeiro, 18.

Remember: schedules are constantly changing. You can pick schedules up directly from the Turísmo (tourist offices) and at various bus terminals in most major cities. Remember that many bus depots and stops do not publish their phone numbers, and you may have to call a travel agency or a major bus station for information. In each regional chapter of this book I include bus station locations and phone numbers.

Major Bus Routes in Portugal

Contact any major city bus station ticket office or local Turismo for current schedules, exact prices, and reservations. Some routes are added or omitted on specific buses and specific days of the week. Transfers to other buses, trains, or ferries may be necessary to complete some routes. The following are normal buses and may not be as deluxe or expensive as some of the express services to the same destinations.

Lisbon to:
- **Agueda**: Several times daily in both directions (may require a change of bus in Coimbra); 4 hour trip; 1,900$00.
- **Albufeira**: Several times daily in both directions; 3 hour 45 minute trip; 2,100$00.
- **Alcobaca**: Several times daily in both directions; 2 hour trip; 1,300$00.
- **Beja**: Several times daily in both directions; 3 hour 20 minute trip; 1,600$00.
- **Braga**: Several times daily in both directions; 5 hour 45 minute trip; 2,400$00.
- **Caldas da Rainha**: Several times daily in both directions; 1 hour 30 minute trip; 1,300$00.
- **Chaves**: Several times daily in both directions; 8 hour trip; 2,800$00.
- **Coimbra**: Several times daily in both directions; 3 hour trip; 1,900$00.
- **Elvas**: Several times daily in both directions; 4 hour 25 minute trip; 1,750$00.
- **Évora**: Several times daily in both directions; 2 hour 50 minute trip; 1,650$00.
- **Faro**: Several times daily in both directions; 4 hour 45 minute trip; 2,400$00.
- **Fátima**: Several times daily in both directions; 1 hour 45 minute trip; 1,600$00.
- **Guarda**: Several times daily in both directions; 6 hour 10 minute trip; 1,950$00.
- **Guimarães**: Once daily (except Saturday) in both directions (may require a change of bus in Vila Nova Famalicão); 6 hour trip; 2,250$00.
- **Leira**: Several times daily in both directions; 1 hour 45 minute trip; 1,600$00.
- **Nazaré**: Several times daily in both directions; 2 hour 5 minute trip; 1,450$00.
- **Peniche**: Several times daily in both directions; 1 hour 45 minute trip; 1,200$00.
- **Porto**: Several times daily in both directions; 4 hour 10 minute trip; 2,100$00.
- **Redondo**: Several times daily in both directions (may require a change of bus in Évora); 3 hour 25 minute trip; 1,650$00.
- **Santarém**: Several times daily in both directions;1 hour 20 minute trip; 1,200$00.
- **Santiago do Cacém**: Several times daily in both directions; 2 hour 30 minute trip; 1,400$00.
- **Tomar**: Several times daily in both directions; 2 hour 20 minute trip; 1,550$00.

• **Torres Vedras**: Several times daily in both directions; 1 hour trip; 950$00.
• **Vila Nova Milfontes**: Several times daily in both directions; 4 hour trip; 1,550$00.
• **Viseu**: Several times daily in both directions; 4 hour trip; 1,900$00.

BY CAR

Despite the fact that driver's seat is on the left side (as it is in North America), driving in Portugal is not an easy task. If you are arriving in Lisbon, the hectic rotary exit from the airport is just the tip of the iceberg. It is best to pre-plan your driving route by using a good map and a highlighter. Ask the rental car company or hotel staff to give you detailed directions to your first location, you won't regret it.

The Portuguese often drive like maniacs. Expect cars to pass on blind curves, pull multiple lane changes at high speeds, and generally disregard any form of manners on the road. If you drive very carefully, and stay in the appropriate lane for your desired velocity, you should be just fine. Be especially careful when driving into the northern reaches of Portugal. Many roads in small towns and the countryside do not have lights or reflectors. Official speed limits (unless otherwise posted) are 60 km/hr in towns and villages, 90 km/hr on normal roads, and 120 km/hr on highways. But do not despair, I have driven over 25,000 km in Portugal, and have never had an accident.

Gas is extremely expensive in Portugal. Until very recently, the government had a monopoly on all gas stations, and still controls the pricing. At press time, gas costs approximately 165$00 per liter (about $4.30 per gallon). Since all of the rental cars are rather small in Europe, fuel efficiency tends to be high. Also, many privatedly owned cars in Portugal run on leaded (chumbo) gas, while the vast majority of the newer rental cars use unleaded (sem chumbo) gas. Be careful not to use the wrong type of fuel. Normal service station hours are from 8am until 7pm Monday – Friday, and from 9am – 1pm on Saturday. Some small town stations still close on Sundays. Over the last few years, hundreds of 24 hour, seven day a week super-stations have popped up throughout Portugal.

Most roads in Portugal are named using the prefix **Estrada Nacional**, a national route. I have abbreviated national routes with the letter **N**, which is followed by a dash and the road number. For example, you will find that Estrada Nacional 10 will appear in this book as N-10. Note that some maps and older road signs might post the road as EN 10.

With the exception of about fifteen high speed roads, including the major A-1 highway running from Lisbon to Porto (which can cost as much as 3,000$00 in tolls), road and bridge tolls are rare and when they do exist, are quite reasonable. It is a good idea to have a lot of 100$00 coins and 1,000$00 bills handy in case you run into an unexpected toll. The high tech traffic engineers in Portugal have designed a computerized automatic toll paying system called the **Via Verde** for commuters. Do not use these specially marked lanes (generally located on the far left) as your car may be stopped by the police for non-payment of a toll. There are only a handful of police radar systems in all of Portugal and speeding tickets are extremely rare.

While crime is not a major issue for tourists in Portugal, a rental car is easy prey anywhere in the world. Please remember not to leave anything in your car when it is parked, and if possible it is advisable to lock your gas cap. Since exposed hatchback cars have increased risks, cover the hatch or avoid renting these vehicles (usually the less expensive categories).

Many companies (especially Europcar) maintain a very rapid car replacement service in the event that you have a breakdown or an accident in Portugal. It is important to know where the branch offices of your rental car company are located, and their emergency phone numbers. The official representative in Portugal for members of AAA and CAA auto clubs is the **Automóvel Clube de Portugal** (ACP) and, if necessary, they can be reached at *Rua Rosa Araujo, 24, Lisbon*. You can call them for the locations of additional branch offices and towing facilities, *Tel. (01) 574-732.*

In the event of an accident, contact the police if possible. If you are unable to get the police to come to the scene of the accident, write down the license plate number of the other car(s) involved, and license and insurance information of the other parties to the accident. Immediately go to the closest police station, file an accident report and have them give you a copy of an accident report or the report number. Call your car rental company as soon as you obtain this documentation.

Car Rentals

All major international airlines arrive in the capital city of Lisbon, the Algarve city of Faro, or the northern commercial city of Porto. In all three locations, there are an abundance of well known car rental companies that operate both airport kiosks and downtown offices. Avis, Budget, National, Europcar, and several other local and international companies maintain airport hours from early morning until the last flight is scheduled to arrive. If your flight is extremely late, you may have to camp out at the airport until the next morning to rent your car.

All that is required to rent a car is a major credit card, passport, and a valid US or Canadian drivers license. International drivers licenses are not required for North Americans driving in Portugal.

If you intend to use a rental car in Portugal, you can save up to 45% of the normal rate if you book and pay in advance from North America. If you decide to rent a car once you have arrived in Portugal, rentals can be arranged from any Portuguese travel agency or car rental company office.

Call your credit card company before you leave for Europe to determine if any insurance is covered if you rent your car with your credit card. Most forms of insurance (collision damage waiver, liability, personal accident injury insurance, property theft insurance) will be offered when you pick up the car and can add well over $25 per day to your bill.

With advance booking and prepayment from the US or Canada, prices range from below $225 per week for a small two door manual car (Fiat Uno or similar) to well over $395 per week for an automatic or 4-door sporty car. Specialty rentals such as a Mercedes Benz or Mazeratti are available at rather hefty prices from local Lisbon based companies like Facil Car. Also, keep in mind that the Lisbon airport has just added a new tax of about 1,800$00 to all airport rental car pick ups.

If you so desire, you can pick up a rental car in one major city in Portugal and drop it off in another (usually no drop off charges are added). If you want to drop off your car outside of Portugal, large drop off charges, sometimes well over $300, will apply. Keep in mind that taking a rental car from Portugal into Spain is only allowed if you inform the rental company that you are doing so in advance, and if they present you with special international insurance papers.

MAJOR CAR RENTAL COMPANIES IN NORTH AMERICA	
AutoEurope in the US	*Tel. 800/223-5555*
AutoEurope in Canada	*Tel. 800/223-5555*
Avis in the US	*Tel. 800/331-1084*
Avis in Canada	*Tel. 800/879-2847*
Budget in the US	*Tel. 800/527-0770*
Budget in Canada	*Tel. 800/268-8900*
Hertz in the US	*Tel. 800/654-1101*
Hertz in Canada	*Tel. 800/263-0600*

Discounted Car Rentals in Portugal

If you book your car rental through **Auto Europe**, *Tel. 800/223-5555 in both the US and Canada,* before you depart from North America, you could save up to 40%. This excellent company offers incredible discounts on all categories of rental cars throughout the world, and can save you money on airline tickets and hotel reservations. As one of the travel industry's main suppliers of rental cars for package and customized tours, they have contracts with Budget, Avis, and Europe Car. The last time I went to Portugal, Auto Europe saved me $93.25 per week on my car rental and I ended up with a much better car at no additional charge.

Their friendly and knowledgeable staff will beat any written quote on the market, and can provide repeat client discounts, AAA and CAA discounts, long stay rates, low season super specials, and great deals on optional insurance against collision damage, theft, and even property loss. Their fully refundable car rental vouchers can be instantly faxed to you or your travel agent, and reservations usually only require a small prepaid deposit by credit card or check.

Call all the others first, and then ring up Auto Europe; it's the best way to get a great car and receive better service at truly unbeatable prices!

Parking Your Car

Most major cities and beach resort areas have replaced all the old fashioned coin operated parking meters with new computerized ticket dispensing machines. In most (but not all) cases, if you park your car in the downtown section of a city or near a famous beach, you will pay for the privilege. Normal cosmopolitan street parking spots require that you pay somewhere between 60$00 and 150$00 per hour, Monday through Saturday, during regular business hours. Just look for the electronic ticket vending machine. There is usually at least one on every block and the multilingual instructions are easy to follow.

If you forget to put money in the meter, or take up a reserved or illegal space, you may be subject to huge fines and could be booted or towed to a municipal garage. Private and municipal parking garages (be careful because not all are open 24 hours a day) can be found by following the blue sign with a white "P" in the center. These can cost upwards of 250$00 or more per hour, depending on the exact time and location. In small villages or remote areas, parking is generally free of charge.

BY TRAIN

The government owns and operates a rail company called **Caminhos de Ferro Portugueses** or CP. Although occasionally prone to work stoppages (strikes), the fares are usually inexpensive when compared with the equivalent bus fare. There are currently five different categories of trains.

The **Rapido** or **Alfa** express trains stop less frequently and are an excellent way to travel long distances between larger cities. The **Intercidade** or **IC** trains are usually the second fastest train between major population bases, but stop more than the express trains. The **Inter-regional** or **IR** trains are somewhat slow and stop often. There are also several regional commuter trains known as either **Suburbano** or **Regional** trains that are slower trains with many stops between smaller cities and villages.

Some trains require advance reservations such as the first class express or Alfa trains. Some trains have special facilities such as sleeping compartments and automobile compartments that must be booked in advance and include supplemental charges. Many trains offer first class seats and the all to often crowded second class seats.

Most of the trains in Portugal offer reasonably good food and beverages in their dining cars. If you are traveling south of Lisbon, you may have to take a ferry from the Praça do Comercio's (Terreiro do Paço) ferry landing to reach the train station on Barreiro. To purchase train tickets you can contact **Rail Europe** before departing North America, or go to a CP station or a travel agency once you are in Portugal. All major train stations in Portugal are open by 9am.

TAKE A SCENIC TRAIN RIDE!

For those of you interested in scenic train rides, there are a few remaining scenic narrow gauge railways and river front lines left in northern Portugal. Some of these railroads include antique steam engines and railroad cars that date back to the late 1800s. Although the government is in the process of phasing out these lines, you may still find a few that run occasionally. This is a wonderful experience if you have the time. The schedules and routes of the trains have been known to change so a visit to any Turismo, travel agency, or CP station or office will be necessary for more detailed information. I have included listings of some of these lines in the regional chapters, and below in the train route section.

Several types of tourist train passes are available directly from CP offices and stations with proper identification. These Portugal only unlimited first–class train passes, **Bilhetes Turisticos**, are available for seven days (about 19,000$00), 14 days (about 29,000$00), and 21 days (about 39,000$00) and must be purchased within Portugal.

Various discounts are offered. If you are over the age of 65, you may receive a discount of 30% off any normal fare with a passport. If you are over 65 years old and purchase a special senior citizen card, **Cartão Dourado**, from a major train station, you may be entitled to up to 50% off normal fares during off peak hours. Children under the age of 4 can travel for free as long as they can sit on an adult's lap. Children between the ages of 4 and 12 years old may receive up to a 50% discount on their fare. Families with children are also eligible to purchase a special family card, **Cartão de Familia**, that reduces the price of their tickets when traveling together. Young adults between the ages of 12 and 26 years of age are permitted to purchase a special youth card, **Cartão Jovem**, that allows for discounts of up to 50% on long journeys during limited time periods.

Official CP Rail schedules are available from the CP stations in major cities and are called **Guia Horario Official** (about 400$00). If you intend to use the train system in Portugal, you should get one of these schedules. Make sure to inquire about the **Suplemento** (supplemental section), which updates the Guia Horario Official. Another good source is the **Thomas Cook** train timetables that can be found in travel book shops in major cities throughout the world.

Trains don't always run on time, so plan your connections with enough time to catch the next train. Since the train schedules change quite often, you may want to spend a few minutes planning your trip with up to date information. If you have trouble contacting any of the CP stations, any major travel agency in Portugal will usually assist you.

Keep in mind that train stations may be several kilometers from town centers, and transportation may or may not be provided to the heart of town. In the regional chapters of this book, I include many train station locations and phone numbers.

Eurail Passes

Eurail passes are accepted on the CP train system, although some services require a supplemental charge. *Passes must be purchased before your departure from North America.* There are now over a dozen types of youth and adult Eurail passes that allow travel for a specific amount of time through 17 different countries in Europe or within one specific country. You can purchase Eurail passes from a specialty tour operator, travel agency, or directly from the prompt and reliable staff of **Rail Europe** in both the US and Canada.

When using a rail pass, you usually can upgrade your journey by reserving seats, couchettes, and sleeping cars for a supplemental charge. In Portugal, you can request these upgrages directly with CP at one of their train stations, or before you leave, you can make reservations with Rail Europe in the US or Canada. You can choose from among the following passes:

The **Eurail Portugal–only pass** is a **first–class** train pass valid for people of all ages. The pass is valid from the first day you use it in Portugal. It allows for unlimited travel in Portugal for a maximum number of predetermined days within a given time period:

• 4 days of travel within a 15 day period: $129
• 7 days of travel within a 21 day period: $185
• Accompanied children aged 4-11 can receive a 50% discount.

Eurail Youthpass is a **second–class** train pass that is valid for people under 26 years of age. This pass is valid from the first day you use it in Europe. It allows for unlimited train travel in 17 European countries (as well as certain bus and ferry routes) for a maximum number of predetermined days:
• 15 day pass: $418
• 1 month pass: $598
• 2 month pass: $798

Eurail Pass is a **first–class** train pass that is valid for people of all ages. This pass is valid from the first day you use it in Europe. It allows for unlimited train travel in 17 European countries (as well as certain bus and ferry routes) for a maximum number of predetermined days:
• 15 day pass: $522
• 21 day pass: $678
• 1 month pass: $838
• 2 month pass: $1148
• 3 month pass: $1468
• Accompanied children aged 4-11 can receive a 50% discount.

Eurail Saver Pass is a special **first–class** train pass for people of all ages traveling on the exact same schedule in 17 European countries (as well as certain bus and ferry routes). It is valid for unlimited travel during a predetermined length of time. Between the months of October through March this pass requires a minimum of two people traveling together, between the months of April and September this pass requires a minimum of three people traveling together:
• 15 day saver pass: $452
• 21 day saver pass: $578
• 1 month saver pass: $712
• Accompanied children aged 4-11 can receive a 50% discount.

Eurail Youth Flexipass is a **second–class** train pass that is valid for people under 26 years of age. It is valid from the first day you use it in Europe. It allows for unlimited train travel in 17 European countries (as well as certain bus and ferry routes) for a maximum number of predetermined days within a given time period:
• 10 days of travel within a 2 month period: $438
• 15 days of travel within a 2 month period: $588

Eurail Flexipass is a **first–class** train pass that is valid for people of all ages. It is valid from the first day you use it in Europe. It allows for unlimited train travel in 17 European countries (as well as certain bus and ferry routes) for a maximum number of predetermined days within a given time period:
• 10 days of travel within a 2 month period: $616
• 15 days of travel within a 2 month period: $812
• Accompanied children aged 4-11 can receive a 50% discount.

Rail Europe is the best source in North America for Eurail passes, European train tickets, confirmed rail reservations, and special fares on trains in Portugal and throughout Europe. They have also recently added special train/rental car combination packages, and a wholesale hotel booking division for your travel agent.

The staff is prompt, professional, and well trained. They can answer all European rail questions, and they are happy to work directly with the public and with travel professionals. Advance purchase tickets are sent by regular mail or express mail for a small surcharge.

Europass is a **first class** train pass that is valid for people of all ages. It is valid from the first day you use it in Europe. It allows for unlimited train travel in specific groupings of between three and five pre-selected European countries (as well as certain bus and ferry routes) for a maximum number of predetermined days within a given time period. Additional countries may be added to create a customized Europass valid for up to nine pre-selected European countries, but the price increases depending on the number of countries you choose. Be sure to call Rail Europe for more information on this complicated pass and for the exact country groupings they offer.

If you travel with a second passenger on the exact same schedule, you can each save about 25%. Prices range from $316 for one person traveling to three pre-selected countries on any five days within a 60 day period, and go up to $736 for one person traveling to five pre-selected countries on any 15 days within two months.

Europass Youth is a **second class** train pass that is valid for people up to age 25. It is valid from the first day you use it in Europe. It allows for unlimited train travel in specific groupings of between three and five pre-selected European countries (as well as certain bus and ferry routes) for a maximum number of predetermined days within a given time period. Additional countries may be added to create a customized Europass Youth valid for up to nine pre-selected European countries in total, but the price increases depending on the number of countries you choose. Be sure to call Rail Europe for more information on this complicated pass and for the exact country groupings they offer.

Prices range from $210 for one young adult traveling to three pre-selected countries on any 5 days within a 60 day period, and go up to $500 for one young adult traveling to five pre-selected countries on any 15 days within two months.

Rail Europe offices in North America can be reached at:
- **Rail Europe in the US,** *Tel. 800/438-7245*
- **Rail Europe in Canada,** *Tel. 800/361-7245*

Major Train Routes

The following train routes are used by a variety of trains with numbers that do not correspond to the route numbers below. Stops are added and deleted on certain trains and on specific days of the week.

Transfers to other trains, buses, or ferries are often necessary to complete some portions of these routes. Contact any CP office for updated schedules and reservations.

Route 100: Several times daily in both directions; **Lisbon** – Vila Franca de Xira – Santarém – Encontrocamento –Coimbra – Curia – Aveiro – Estarreja – Ovar – Espinho – Vila Nova de Guia – Porto – **Braga**.

Route 100A: Several times daily in both directions; **Lisbon** – Santarém – Entrocamento – Fátima – Seica-Ourem – Pombal – Alfarelos – Coimbra – Pampilhosa – Mealhada – Curia – Aveiro – Ovar – Esmoriz – Espinho – Granja – Valadares – Vila Nova de Guia – **Porto**.

Route 102: Several times daily in both directions. **Lisbon** – Vila Franca de Xira – Azambuja – Santana-Cartaxo – Santarém – Entrocamento – Lamarosa – **Tomar**.

Route 110: Several times daily in both directions; **Lisbon** – Santarém – Coimbra – Buçaco-Luso – Nelas (connections to Viseu) – Mangualde – Gouveia – Celorico de Beira – Guarda – Castelo Mendo – **Vilar Formoso**.

Route 120: Several times daily in both directions; **Lisbon** – Vila Franca de Xira – Santarém – Entroncomento – Almourol – Abrantes – Torre das Vargens (connections to Portalegre – Elvas – Badajoz, Spain) – Castelo de Vide – Marvão – **Valencia de Alcântara**.

Route 130: Several times daily in both directions; **Lisbon** – Vila Franca de Xira – Santarém – Entroncamento (connections to Porto) – Almoural – Abrantes – Castelo Branco – Alpedrinha – Penamacor – Fundão – Covilha – Belmonte-Manteigas – Sabugal – **Guarda**.

Route 140: Several times daily in both directions; **Lisbon** – Queluz-Belas – Mafra – Torres Vedras – Bombarral – Óbidos – Caldas da Rainha – São Martinho de Porto – Marinha Grande – Leira – **Figueira da Foz**.

Route 141: Several times daily in both directions; **Lisbon** – Queluz-Belas – **Sintra**.

Route 142 (Lisbon Coastal Train): Several times daily in both directions; **Cais de Sodre** – Santos – Alcântara – Belem – Paços de Arcos – Oeiras – Carcavelos – Parade – São Pedro de Estoril – São João de Estoril – Estoril – Monte Estoril – **Cascais.**

Route 200: Several times daily in both directions; **Porto** – Ermesinde – Nine (connections to Braga) – Barcelos – Viana do Castelo – Afife – Praia Ancora – Caminha – Vila Nova de Cerveira – **Valenca.**

Route 201: Several times daily in both directions; **Porto** – Ermesinde – Famalição – Nine – **Braga.**

Route 203: Several times daily in both directions; **Porto** – Pedras Rubras – Vila do Conde – Povoa de Varzim – **Famalição.**

Route 205: Several times daily in both directions; **Porto** – Maia – Lousado – Santo Tirso – Vizela – **Guimaraes.**

Route 210: Several times daily in both directions; **Porto** – Penafiel – Livração – Regua – Tua – **Pocihno.**

Route 211 (ask for tickets on the famed scenic **Tâmega** line): Several times daily in both directions; **Porto** – Livração – Vila Caiz – **Amarante.**

Route 212 (ask for tickets on the famed scenic **Corgo** line): Several times daily in both directions; **Porto** – Regua - Alvacoes – Povoção – Carrazedo – **Vila Real.**

Route 213 (ask for tickets on the famed scenic **Tua** line): Several times daily in both directions; **Porto** – Tua – Vilarinho – Mirandela – Macedo de Cavaleiros – **Bragança.**

Route 300: Several times daily in both directions; **Barreiro** (ferry Connection from Lisbon to Barreiro) – Casa Branca (connections to Tojal – Monte das Flores – Évora) – Alvito – Beja – **Tunes** (connections to Algoz – Silves – Estombar-Lagoa – Portimão – Lagos) (and connections to Albufeira – Loule – Almancil – Faro – Olaho – Luz – Tavira – Cacela – Castro Marim – Vila Real de Santo António).

Route 302: Several times daily in both directions; **Barreiro** (ferry connection from Lisbon to Barreiro) – Pinhal Novo – Casa Branca – Monte das Flores – **Évora** (bus connections to Montoito – Reguengos).

Route 303: Several times daily in both directions; **Barreiro** (ferry connection from Lisbon to Barreiro) – Pinhal Novo – Casa Branca – Monte das Flores – **Évora** (bus connections to Azarja – Estremoz – Borba – Vila Viçosa).

Route 306: Several times daily in both directions; **Lisbon** – Entroncamento – Abrantes – **Portalegre** (bus connections to – Cabeco de Vide – Sousel – Estremoz).

Route 307: Several times daily in both directions; **Barreiro** (ferry connections from Lisbon to Barreiro) – **Beja** (bus connections to Baleizão – Serpa-Brinches – Pias – Moura).

TRAIN ROUTES

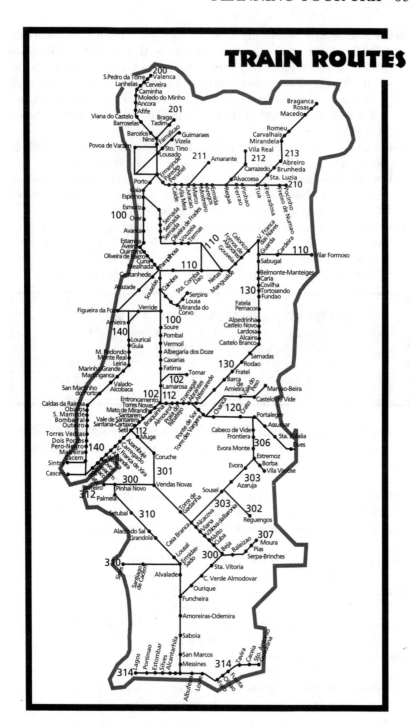

Route 310: Several times daily in both directions; **Barreiro** (ferry connection from Lisbon to Barreiro) – Setúbal – Alcacer do Sal – Grandôla – Ermidas-Sado (connection to Santiago do Cacém – Sines) – Santa Clara-Saboia – **Tunes** (connection to Algoz – Silves – Estombar-Lagoa – Portimão – Lagos) (and connection to Albufeira – Loulã – Almancil – Faro – Olhão – Luz – Tavira – Castro Marim – Vila Real de Santo António).

Route 311: Ferry service from Lisbon to Barreiro several times daily in both directions; **Terreiro de Paço** (Lisbon) — **Barreiro**.

Route 312: Several times daily in both directions; **Barreiro** (ferry connection from Lisbon to Barreiro) – Pinhal Novo – Palmela – **Setúbal** (ferry connection from Setúbal to the Sado beaches).

Route 314: Several times daily in both directions; **Lagos** – Meia Praia – Alvor – Portimão – Estombar-Lagoa – Silves – Tunes – Albufeira – Loule – Almansil – Faro – Olhão – Livramento – Luz – Tavira – Cacela – Castro Marim – Monte Gordo – **Vila Real de Santo António**.

MAIN CP RAIL INFORMATION OFFICES

• *Aveiro,* Tel. *(034) 381-632 or (034) 244-85*
• *Coimbra,* Tel. *(039) 272-63*
• *Lisbon,* Tel. *(01) 888-5101 or (01) 876-025 or (01) 877-509*
• *Porto,* Tel. *(02) 201-9517 or (02) 564-141 or (02) 565-670*

Train Prices & Travel Times from Lisbon to Major Cities

Train, bus, and ferry connections may be necessary for some routes:

• **Albufeira** (via the **Inter-cidade** train), 3 hour 5 min. trip
   2850$00 1st class   1850$00 2nd class
• **Albufeira** (via the **Inter-regional** train), 4 hour 50 min. trip
   2600$00 1st class   1550$00 2nd class
• **Aveiro** (via the **Inter-regional** train), 3 hour 20 min. trip
   2700$00 1st class   1750$00 2nd class
• **Beja** (via the **Inter-regional** train), 3 hour 10 min. trip
   1900$00 1st class   1230$00 2nd class
• **Cascais** (via the **Suburbano** train), 30 min. trip
   250$00 1st class No 2nd class on train
• **Coimbra** (via the **Inter-regional** train), 2 hour 30 min. trip
   2250$00 1st class   1400$00 2nd class
• **Estoril** (via the **Suburbano** train), 25 min. trip
   250$00 1st class No 2nd class on train
• **Évora** (via the **Inter-regional** train), 2 hour 50 min. trip
   1950$00 1st class   1425$00 2nd class

- **Faro** (via the **Rapido Inter-cidade** train), 4 hour trip
  3150$00 1st class   1950$00 2nd class
- **Fátima** (via the **Regional** train), 4 hour 50 min. trip
  1700$00 1st class   1150$00 2nd class
- **Guimaraes** (via the **Inter-regional** and **Regional** trains), 7 hour 20 min.
  trip   3850$00 1st class   2150$00 2nd class
- **Luso - Buçaco** (via the **Inter-regional** train), 3 hour 30 min. trip
  2700$00 1st class   1750$00 2nd class
- **Porto** (via the **Alfa** train), 3 hour trip
  5200$00 1st class   3300$00 2nd class
- **Porto** (via the **Inter-regional** train), 4 hour 25 min. trip 3300$00 1st
  class   1975$00 2nd class
- **Setúbal** (via the **Inter-regional** train), 1 hour 25 min., trip
  925$00 1st class   600$00 2nd class
- **Sintra** (via the **Suburbano** train) , 50 min. trip
  250$00 1st class No 2nd class on train
- **Tomar** (via the **Regional** train), 2 hour 25 min. trip
  1800$00 1st class   900$00 2nd class
- **Viana do Castelo** (via the **Inter-regional** and **Regional** trains), 7 hour 40
  min. trip   3950$00 1st class   2300$00 2nd class
- **Viseu** (via the **Inter-regional** train), 5 hour 5 min. trip
  3100$00 1st class   2250$00 2nd class

ACCOMMODATIONS

There are over 475 different government-rated places to spend the night in Portugal. The ratings range from 1 to 5 stars, but the system isn't always as accurate as you would expect. I include reviews, in the destination chapters, of over 200 properties throughout Portugal that I have visited.

Whenever possible I include each hotel's published **rack rates** (the price they charge full paying customers) for both high and low seasons (usually includes all taxes and service charges). Special, and usually lower, off-season, corporate, weekend, package, and long stay rates may be available if you ask before you pre-pay, or if it is a last minute reservation, before you check-in. All prices in the destination chapters are in escudos.

The price guideline (for all types of accommodations) that I use is based on the average rate for two people staying in a double room for one night and almost always includes taxes and service charges.

In most (but not all) cases, I divide each destination's hotel reviews into the following price categories:

• **Cheap**	1,750$00	to	6,500$00
• **Inexpensive**	6,500$00	to	10,000$00
• **Moderate**	10,000$00	to	20,500$00
• **Expensive**	20,500$00	to	30,000$00
• **Very Expensive**	30,000$00	to	50,000$00

Portugal offers a number of different kinds of accommodations, some that may not be familar to you. Here is an overview of the various types of accommodations you will find all over the country.

Albergarias are typically properties that are ranked just below a hotel in quality and the facilities offered. Many albergarias are rather nice and offer most of the facilities of a smaller hotel. Almost all albergarias are rated with **4 stars** and will usually offer private bathrooms, restaurant, bar, air conditioning, heating, mini-bars, in-room phones, TV, safe deposit boxes, multilingual staff, heating, parking, and sometimes even a pool. Bookings for these properties can be made from a specialty tour operator, travel agent, or directly with the albergaria.

Estalagens are nice medium to high quality inns that are usually rated with either **4 or 5 stars**. Normally, you will find private bathrooms, heating, a restaurant, lounge, breakfast room, TV, parking, safe deposit boxes, and a front desk staff at each estalagem. Bookings for these properties can be made from a specialty tour operator, travel agent, or directly with the estalagem.

Hotels in Portugal run the full gamut of quality and accommodation levels and are available in several types of classifications. Hotel properties throughout the country can be housed in everything from multi-story modern buildings to centuries old convents and palaces. Any property that uses the word hotel in its name is rated by a series of stars. If a hotel offers **1 or 2 stars**, chances are that it will have private bathrooms and facilities such as a restaurant, bar, and heating. Properties with **3 stars** or more will often be loaded with additional facilities including parking, cable TV, pool, in room phones, mini-bars, and a breakfast room. Most **4 and 5 star** hotels may have gourmet restaurants, snack bars, lounges, air conditioning, health clubs, sports facilities, marble bathrooms, room service, multilingual staff, a concierge desk, and bellboys.

Aparthotels are usually full service **2 to 4 star** hotels that offer rooms with kitchens and either one or two bedrooms for family-style use. Bookings for these properties can be made from a specialty tour operator (see Chapter 6, *Planning Your Trip*), a hotel representation company (see below), a good travel agent, or by faxing the hotel directly.

GLOSSARY OF HOTEL TERMS

Low Season	*Usually from October through March, excluding holidays.*
High Season	*Usually from April through September.*
Rack Rate	*The full retail price of a room, special rates may be available.*
Corporate Rate	*Available to almost anyone who presents a business card*
Weekend Rate	*Limited number of discounted priced rooms on weekends.*
Double Room	*A room designed and priced for 2 people staying together.*
Apartment	*A unit with cooking facilities.*
EP	*European Plan, no meals included in the price.*
CP	*Continental Plan, a small breakfast included in the price.*
BP	*Breakfast Plan, a full breakfast included in the price.*
MAP	*Modified American Plan, breakfast and dinner included*
AI	*All Inclusive Plan, all meals included in the price.*

Pensoes are the lowest rated accommodations in Portugal. These basic and simple inns are rated from **1 to 4 stars** and have minimal facilities. Most (but not all) pensoes offer rooms without private bath, but almost every pensão listed in this book has at least a few rooms with their own bathrooms (but are more expensive). Some of these inns have breakfast rooms and attached restaurants. Since these inns often do not pay commissions to travel agents and tour operators, you can only book most of them by calling the pensão directly.

Pousadas are a series of about 30 properties that are part of a government owned company known as Enatur. Originally designed as inexpensive inns that hosted Portuguese travelers, these inns have become a favorite of foreign visitors. As a result of their popularity, they are now much more expensive. They are often housed in castles, former mansions of civil engineers, or well located traditional homes that have been converted into fashionable hotels with many amenities including private bathrooms. Each pousada is unique, and the quality of service varies quite substantially from one to another.

Bookings for these properties can be made from a specialty tour operator, travel agent, directly with each pousada, or by calling **Marketing Ahead** in New York, *Tel. 800/223-1356*. Be advised that prepayment will be requested at the time of booking, and that penalties can apply for no shows and cancellations. Many of the pousadas are sold out well in advance, and it can take several days to receive a confirmation.

Quartos Privativos are essentially rooms for rent in private houses with shared bathrooms. These accommodations are not officially recognized by the government, and are usually part of the underground economy. I do not include these units because they come and go each season and there is no quality control. The most common way to find a private room is to either inquire at a Turísmo office, or go to a local train station and look for signs or the hawkers who earn a 15% commission for each tourist they successfully bring in.

Quintas are typically private estates that offer guests a chance to stay in traditional manor homes and farm houses. Using funds provided by EEC economic development programs, many estate owners have found a low cost way to improve their properties, albeit for tourism purposes. Quintas range from wonderfully ornate former palaces to wine producing mansions and rustic mountain lodges. It is common for the host family to greet each client personally and sometimes even offer a glass of wine.

These properties can provide a memorable cultural experience for visitors as they often provide deluxe antique filled rooms with private bathrooms in unforgettable settings. Some quintas offer apartments and guest rooms with fireplaces, four poster beds, scenic patios, and occasionally even kitchens. Other quintas can be rented as complete private houses and estates for families, for groups, and for business meetings. Many of these properties have special features such as horseback riding, bicycles, jeeps, romantic gardens, TV rooms, priceless artwork, farm fresh meals, and in-house wineries. Be advised that a few of these quintas have shared bathrooms in their least expensive rooms.

Most of the 150+ quintas in Portugal are classified by the Portuguese government into 3 types of **Turísmo no Espaço Rural** (Tourism in the Countryside): Turísmo de Habitação, Turísmo Rural, and AgroTurísmo. **Turísmo de Habitação (TH)** properties are usually historic manor houses that are of the highest architectural value and comfort level.

The vast majority of quintas I recommend fall into this category. **Turísmo Rural (TR)** properties are mostly nice mansions with gardens and old homes with comfortable accommodations in rural areas near towns. **AgroTurísmo (AT)** properties are usually basic inns on working farms that offer guests a chance to help with the daily farm work, but is never mandatory. Bookings for all types of quintas can be made from North America by contacting a expert specialty tour operator. It is also possible to call the quintas directly, but not all of the managers speak English. The last resort could be contacting a Portuguese company such as **Turihab** in Ponte de Lima, *Tel. (351 058) 942-749.*

Keep in mind that full prepayment will be requested at the time of booking, and that penalties will be applied for revisions, cancellations, or no shows. Many quintas are sold out well in advance during the summer months, so book ahead.

Residencials are basic inns, usually in or near towns. These inns are rated from **1 to 4 stars** and do not have as many facilities or services as an estalagem. In many residencials, you will find rooms with private baths, a breakfast room, a restaurant, and sometimes a TV. Since these inns often do not pay commissions to travel agents and tour operators, you can only book most of them by calling the residencial directly.

RECOMMENDED HOTEL REPRESENTATIVES

The Small Hotel Company, Tel. 800/552-6844

The Australian based Small Hotel Company represents some of the finest resorts and hotels in the world, and now has an office in California. They can help you book some of the country's finest and most charming hotels in the higher price ranges. A great source for special rates on selected superb hotels.

Leading Hotels of the World, Tel. 800/223-6800

With a wonderful selection of medium and larger sized famous 4 and 5 star hotels throughout the world, their name says it all! They represent six of the highest quality luxury properties in major cities and coastal resort areas in Portugal. All of these remarkable hotels offer a vast array of services and conference facilities, and provide a great setting for deluxe and business travelers.

Utell International, Tel. 800/448-8355

This highly respected industry powerhouse offers instantaneous pricing, information, and reservations at well over 6,500 2 - 5 star hotels worldwide, including 110 in Portugal at every imaginable price range. Their hard working reservation agents just need to know what price range you are looking for, and their advanced computer system selects several options for you.

Hotéis de Charme, Tel. (351 01) 346-7168

This Lisbon based office represents the interests of about 10 of Portugal's finest deluxe hotels including several that I recommend in Chapter 10, Best Places to Stay. They can help to arrange reservations, send you a great new color booklet on their member properties, and point you in the right direction if you're looking for luxurious accommodations in unique small and medium sized hotels with the best possible quality.

Villas and **Apartamentos** are usually multiple bedroom houses or condominiums with all the comforts of home. Since these are usually privately owned and not rated by the government, you should contact a specialist to insure that you get what you pay for. These villas and apartments range in quality from basic bungalows with two bedrooms, a bathroom, and a kitchen to two bedroom sea-view condos to 12 bedroom castles with dramatic sea-views and private pools.

Usually, you must rent these properties for a minimum of a week, but in low season a three night stay is possible. If you are looking for a long term rental, you will should have no problem finding one from either a good tour operator in North America, or if necessary from an English speaking realtor once you arrive in Portugal. If you need long term housing in the Lisbon area, you should know the vacancy rate in this area is about 1%. To book a villa or apartment in advance from North America, you might start by giving a call to highly reliable villa representation companies like **Villas International** in San Francisco, *Tel. 800/221-2260*, and **Vacances Provencales** in Toronto, *Tel. 800/263-7152*.

You may also want to pick up a copy of the United Kingdom based **Private Villas Magazine** if you're lucky enough to find a copy at a newsstand in a major North American city. This 150 page monthly lists all sorts of properties with pricing details, large color photos, and phone or fax contacts of their London based agents. Be advised that reservations for villas and apartments must be prepaid in full in advance, and penalties will apply for cancellations, revisions, and no shows.

Youth Hostels (*Pousadas de Juvenude*), managed by the **Movijovem** Hostel Association, provide a highly economical alternative to budget hotels for adults and youths alike. Each hostel is different, so expect anything from bunk bedded modern buildings with shared bathrooms, to more spacious private bungalows and nice rooms with private bathrooms in old converted houses. Many of these hostels provide both separate dormitory style accommodations for each sex, as well as private double rooms for couples and family-sized units.

The hostels tend to be located in major resort and population zones and are usually open from 9:00am until 12:00pm and from 6pm until 12 midnight. Many hostels have curfews that are strictly enforced, and lots of rules including an eight day maximum stay. The current price range is from about 1,100$00 to 3,400$00 per person, per night depending on the season and type of room requested. Many hostels offer inexpensive meals for a small surcharge.

All guests must hold a valid hostel membership card that is available for about $25 per year from any International Federation of Youth Hostels (IFYH) office. These cards also enable their holders to receive discounts on rooms, as well as on restaurants and sports rental equipment. Special cards may be available for people under 17 and families at differing prices.

To book reservations, it is best to contact the official member of the IFYH in the country you live. Some hostels request 10 day advance booking made via an IFYH branch office, but if space is available you can just walk in and stay. A new computer system called the International Booking Network can often be used to reserve rooms and print out confirmations for prepaid bookings in many hostels throughout the world for a mere $2.50, plus the price of the accommodation. Most Portuguese hostels are open year round, but it is not uncommon for several of them to be sold out well in advance for the summer season, so book early.

Hostel Information & Reservations

• **American Youth Hostel Federation**, *Washington DC, Tel. 202/783-6161*
• **Council Travel**, *New York, Tel. 212/661-1450*
• **Canadian Hostelling Association**, *Ontario, Tel. 613/237-7884*
• **Travel Cuts**, *Toronto, Tel. 416/979-2406*

HOSTELS IN PORTUGAL

Alcoutim, Algarve, Tel. (081) 460-04
Praia de Areia Branca, Costa de Prata, Tel. (061) 422-127
Braga, Costa Verde, Tel. (063) 616-163
Catalazete, Costa de Lisboa, Tel. (01) 443-0638
Coimbra, Costa de Prata, Tel. (039) 229-55
Fão-Esposende, Costa Verde, Tel. & Fax (053) 891-790
Lagos, Algarve, Tel. (082) 761-970
Leira, Costa de Prata, Tel. (044) 318-68
Lisbon, Lisboa, Tel. (01) 353-2696
Mira, Costa de Prata, Tel. & Fax (031) 471-275
Ovar, Costa de Prata, Tel. & Fax (056) 591-832
Penhas da Saude, Montanhas, Tel. (075) 253-75
Portimão, Algarve, Tel. (82) 857-04
Porto, Costa Verde, Tel. (02) 606-5535
São Martinho de Porto, Costa de Prata, Tel. (062) 999-506
Sintra, Costa de Lisboa, Tel. (01) 924-1210
Vila Nova de Cerveira, Costa Verde, Tel. (051) 796-113
Vila Real de S. António, Algarve, Tel. (081) 445-65
Vilarinho das Furnas, Costa Verde, Tel. (053) 351-339

For more information, contact: **Movijovem Portuguese Hostel Association**, *Rua Duque D'Avila, 137, Lisboa. Tel. (01) 355-9081, Fax (01) 352-1466.*

Camping

There are over 150 official public and private campgrounds throughout the country. If you follow normal precautions and don't leave anything valuable in your tent or caravan you will have a wonderful time. One of the most important issues besides security is where to stay. Most of the campgrounds and caravan sights are fairly attractive and located in areas that are close to tourism spots, city centers, beach resorts, and beautiful parks.

Besides the typical almost-hot showers and sanitary facilities, you often find bungalows, mini-markets, snack bars, tennis courts, rental boats, laundry machines, telephones, on site parking, and swimming pools.

Many sights are open year round and you can expect to pay between 200$00 and 400$00 per night for a two person tent site, 300$00 to 600$00 for a four person tent site, and 600$00 to 1100$00 for a caravan site. Parking, showers, meals, sports facilities, and electrical hook ups may be additional. It would also be a good idea to get an International Camping Card from a local camping supply shop or from the **National Campers Association**, *Tel. 716/668-6242.*

If you intend to avoid the official campsites and try to stay on private land you may end up with buckshot in your rear end. If you attempt to illegally camp anywhere in the Algarve, you may very well be arrested. To put it simply, the campgrounds are so numerous and cheap that there is almost no reasonable excuse to avoid them. If you happen to find a wonderful secluded rural spot that is not within 1 km of a beach, city, or water source you can always cross your fingers and chances are you will be all right.

Before departing for Portugal, you should make sure that you have all the camping supplies you will need. Don't forget to bring extra waterproofed tent flies and strong bug repellent as they will most certainly come in handy. If you need to buy camping supplies in Portugal, you can expect to pay double or triple what they cost at home.

If you want specific information on every campsite in Portugal, a copy of the current *Roteiro Campista* guide is helpful and costs about 600$00 from a bookstore in Portugal. Turísmo offices offer either a listing of regional campsites or a copy of *Guia Official de Parques de Campismo.* You can always ask any ICEP Tourist Office if they can send you information before you depart.

The following towns offer camping:

Albufeira, Alcobaca, Alezur, Alpiarca, Alvito, Alvor, Arganil, Azeitão, Beja, braga, Braganca, Caldas da Rainha, Caminha, Caparica, Castelo de Bode, Castelo Branco, Celorico de Beira, Chaves, Coimbra, Costa Nova, Elvas, Ericeira, Espinho, Évora, Faro, Figueira da Foz, Fundão, Geres, Golega, Gouveia, Guarda, Guimaraes, Guincho, Ilhavo, Lagoa de Albufeira, Lagoa de Melides, Lagoa de Santo Andre, Lagos, Lamego, Lisbon, Lourinha, Lousa, Melgaco, Mira, Miranda do Douro, Mirandela, Monção, Monte Gordo, Nazaré, Oeiras, Olhão, Ovar, Penacova, Peniche, Portalegre, Portimão, Porto, Porto Covo, Porto de Mos, Praia de Areia Branca, Praia de Gale, Praia Grande, Praia da Luz, Praia da Mira, Praia de Ponte Gordo, Praia de Salema, Praia de Santa Cruz, Quarteira, Sagres, São Pedro de Moel, São Pedro do Sul, Serpa, Sesimbra, Setúbal, Sines, Tavira, Tomar, Vagos, Viana do Castelo, Vila do Conde, Vila Flor, Vila Nova de Gaia, Vila Praia de Ancora, Vila Real, Viseu, Zambujeira.

7. BASIC INFORMATION

BANKS & CURRENCY

The units of Portuguese currency are called the **escudo** and the **centavo**, and one escudo equals 100 centavos. Currency in Portugal comes in coins and multicolored bank notes that range from 1$00 to 10,000$00.

In Portugal, the "$" sign is placed between the escudo and the centavo just as a decimal point is used in our part of the world. For example, prices are listed in the following way: 2,000$50 (2,000 escudos and 50 centavos). Sometimes the centavo value is dropped and the same amount may be shown as 2,000$.

EXCHANGE RATES
$1 US is roughly 153 escudos
$1 CDN is roughly 147 escudos

Converting your cash and travelers checks into Portuguese escudos is quite simple, and can be done in several ways. Converting foreign currency at international airports is recommended for small amounts only since you will not get the best exchange rate there. If you're arriving and need cash for airport tips and taxis, or if you are arriving on a holiday or weekend, you can make your exchange at Lisbon's **Portela** international airport exchange booth (always open).

Rates at the many banks in every city are usually the best. Almost all banks require a valid passport for identification and banks usually charge a commission of 1,000$00 - 1,750$00 per foreign cash transaction and as much as 2,750$00 for a foreign travelers check transaction for any amount. Look for the cambio or exchange counter, not a teller. A few banks in very busy areas (especially Cascais) prefer not to exchange your money and pretend they don't offer this service. Banks are usually open from 8:30 am - 3 pm, Monday - Friday. Computerized ATM machines and

24 hour automated cash machines are available in many tourist zones. American Express offices in Lisbon and Porto exchange their travelers checks free of charge.

Private exchange bureaus also exist in the major shopping areas of Cascais and the Algarve, although the rate is not always good. Hotels also will exchange cash and travelers checks for guests, but, again, the rates are usually not as good as a bank.

There is no black market in Portugal.

Credit Cards

Credit cards have become a necessary part of most European trips. These days, it is usually necessary to present a credit card for an imprint to cover phone calls, minibar usage, and any service fees charged to your room. Also, many rental car companies will not let you rent from them without a credit card deposit.

Most 3 and 4 star hotels will accept Visa, MasterCard, and Eurocard but will not accept American Express or Diners Club because of the high usage fees they are charged. This situation also exists in many stores and restaurants throughout Portugal. When using your Visa or Mastercard abroad, the rate of exchange is seldom as good as the official bank rates for cash and travelers checks in Europe.

It is a good idea to have a combination of cash, travelers checks and either Visa or MasterCard. Another advantage to bringing your credit card(s) is that if you need a cash advance, this may be possible with a special PIN number (depending on your card).

Travelers Checks

Most places accept travelers checks. One suggestion is to keep the denominations fairly small to ensure that cashiers will have enough Portuguese money for proper change.

While Thomas Cook and Visa travelers checks are usually not a problem, American Express travelers checks are more widely recognized and accepted. Another advantage to American Express if you have lost or stolen checks is their refund center in England. **American Express** is available 24 hours a day and can be reached toll free from anywhere in Portugal by dialing *Tel. (0505) 449-080*. You might also try calling American Express collect at *Tel. 919/333-3211* for a US travelers check refund and replacement office.

BUSINESS HOURS

Most retail stores are open from 9am until 1pm and then from 3pm until 7pm Monday through Friday, and 9am until 1pm on Saturday. There are some shopping centers in major cities that are open until midnight. Banks are open from 8:30am until 2:45pm Monday through Friday.

Government offices are generally open from 9am until 5pm (although many take lunch between 1pm and 3pm).

CRIME

After dozens of trips to Portugal, I have not once had the slightest problem with theft, nor have I ever heard of any theft besides missing gasoline from unlocked gas tanks.

When you drive around, cover any visible items in the trunk or hatch area. If possible, you should avoid rental cars with an open uncovered hatchback. Do not leave luggage, cameras, or any type of valuable item within sight and grasp. Be extra careful around gypsies and in bus and train stations. If you have any special items, leave them in the safety deposit box at your hotel's front desk.

Be careful about walking around deserted city neighborhoods at night. In case you run into the one in a million chance of a theft, visit the nearest police station or if you must, call the nationwide emergency hotline, *Tel. 115*.

In Lisbon, the chances of theft are much higher, but still relatively slim. There is a **special tourist police unit** on *Rua Capela, 13, Tel. (01) 346-6141*. To make an insurance claim, assuming you have coverage on either your homeowner's or a special policy, you must have a police report.

ELECTRICITY

Portuguese outlets are designed for 220 Volts AC and 50 Hertz and the plugs are two round pins (the thinner variety of the two types used in Europe). If you bring electrical appliances or components, you should bring a transformer and a plug converter with the appropriate wattage.

Many appliances such as hair dryers, razors, and personal computers have switchable transformer built in, and may only require an adapter for the plug. Check your owner's manual carefully.

EMBASSIES

• **American Embassy**, *Avenida das Forças Armadas, Lisboa, Tel. (01) 726-6600*
• **Canadian Embassy**, *Avenida Liberdade, 144, Lisboa, Tel. (01) 347-4892*

FADO

Fado is a unique and traditional form of music that expresses the typically Portuguese attitude of how bad luck and tragedy are always just around the corner again. With the help of guitar players, a female singer

(Fadista) belts out a beautiful, yet sad, story of fate. Fado originated in 19th century Lisbon and is performed in small restaurants known as *adega típicas* and *casas de Fado* in Lisbon, Coimbra, and several resort areas. Most adega tipicas offer traditional dinners and may also have cover charges.

HEALTH & MEDICAL CONCERNS

Portugal currently requires no inoculations or special immunizations for visitors from the US and Canada. In fact, there haven't been any outbreaks of major infectious diseases in many years. The best thing to do in case you worry about these things is to contact the State Department in your country and ask if there are any current travel advisories for Portugal. I am sure you will find none.

If you are currently taking medication, you should bring a copy of your prescription (with the generic name for the drug) along with your medicine. If necessary, a local pharmacy (*farmácia*) can refill it. To find a 24 hour drug store or emergency room just call directory assistance, *Tel. 118*, or look in a local newspaper.

Hospitals are available in major population areas and can be found by calling directory assistance, *Tel. 118*, or in case of an emergency by calling *Tel. 115* for an ambulance. For a free list of English speaking doctors in Portugal, contact **IAMAT** in North America at *Tel. 716/754-4883*.

The **British Hospital**, *Rua Saraiva Carvalho, 49, Lisbon, Tel. (01) 606-020*, is perhaps the best hospital, if you find you need one. I also include a few major medical centers in the destinations chapters.

HOLIDAYS & FESTIVALS
Official Holidays

The government of Portugal occasionally moves holidays around to form long weekends. Many additional regional holidays exist that are not included in this list as they vary with each province. On holidays, expect many museums, castles, restaurants, banks, government offices, and most private companies to be closed.

If a holiday falls on a Friday or Monday, you can expect many places to close for the entire holiday weekend. Trains and buses tend to run on limited schedules during these time periods.

Here are the official holidays:

January – *New Year's Day* (1st); **April** – *Carnival, Good Friday, Liberation Day* (25th); **May** – *May Day* (1st); **June** – *Corpus Christi Day, Camões Day* (10th); **August** – *Assumption Day* (15th); **October** – *Republic Day* (5th); **November** – *All Saints' Day* (1st); **December** – *Independence Day* (1st), *Feast of Immaculate Conception Day* (8th), *Christmas Eve* (24th), *Christmas* (25th).

Festivals

Every region of Portugal hosts several festivals, fairs, religious processions (romarias) and special celebrations each year. The following list contains some of the most important religious, cultural, historical, and agricultural festivities.

To receive information on the exact dates of a specific event, contact either one of the Portuguese National Tourist Offices, or the Turismo office in the region you are visiting. Several more fairs and festivals are listed in each regional chapter.

February

Carnival in Ovar, Sines, Loulé, Nazaré, Funchal, and many other cities. This Mardi Gras type of event in late February is one of the liveliest festivals of the year. Each city has a variety of events, which usually includes a parade of masked or costumed participants, carnival floats, and flower battles.

March/April

Holy Week in Braga, Ovar, and Pavoa de Varzim. Many different types of ritual processions with the Ecce Homme.

May

Festival of the Crosses in Monsanto. First Sunday in May – girls parade through the streets and up to the ruined castle to throw flowers to commemorate the siege of Monsanto.

Festival of the Crosses in Barcelos. A major regional event in the first week of May including concerts, flower covered streets, craft fairs, fireworks, and the Procession of the Holy Cross.

Rosé Festival in Vila Franca do Lima. A very unusual parade in which a woman wears a massive 80 pound tray of arraigned flowers (representing a regional coat of arms) on her head during the procession.

Pilgramage to Fátima in Fátima. Over 250,000 Christians from around the globe converge on Fátima to honor the anniversary of first apparition of the Virgin Mary by three young shepherds on May 13, 1917.

Leiria Festival in Leiria. A folk art and traditional dancing festival each Sunday in May.

Queima Das Fitas in Coimbra. Each year in mid may, when the school year is finished, the University students of Coimbra burn their graduation gowns and collage ribbons and drink for at least one week. There are concerts and river front parties throughout the city.

June

Feast of Saint Gonçalo in Amarante. During the first weekend of June, Amarante pays tribute to the Saint of Marriage with celebrations and gift exchanges for those in love.

National Agricultural Fair in Santarém. The most famous event in Portuguese agriculture takes place for a week and a half starting on the first Friday of the month. Santarém, home to many producers of livestock, hosts a week long celebration which includes bullfights, livestock competitions, and other cultural events. This festival is much like a state fair.

All Saints Festival in Lisbon, Porto, and many other cities. Celebrations with massive parades and unusual ritual processions take place in many areas. The St. Anthony festival in Lisbon (June 12 and/or 13) is carried out in the heart of the city with marching bands singing and dancing down the Avenida Liberdade, and small groups of revelers wander through the Alfama. In Porto, the St. John festival (June 24) is full of singing, dancing, and bonfires throughout the night. Many other cities and towns join in the festivities with smaller celebrations.

Festival of São Pedro in Montijo. Festivals and processions around June 24 are capped off by a release of bulls into the streets.

International Lusitano Horse Show in Lisbon. This world class event features exhibitions and competitions of pure bred Lusitanian horses. The exact dates change each year.

July

Colete Encarnado Festival in Vila Franca de Xira. This festival in the first half of July honors the area's cattlemen who parade through the streets. Additional festivities include fairs, folk dancing, bullfights, and the releasing of bulls into the streets.

Feiro Do Artisanto in Estoril. Estoril hosts a nightly market with an array of local handicrafts as well as a sampling of traditional folklore and cuisine at its fairgrounds. Open 6pm until midnight daily in July and August.

Tabuleiros Festival in Tomar. In every odd numbered year for the first two weeks of July, a harvest festival is celebrated, including, on the first Sunday only, a strange march of hundreds of supposed virgins wearing huge hats decorated with flowers and other agricultural products.

August

Saint Walter Festival in Guimarães. A centuries old festival with fairs, bullfights, torch lit processions, and the Marcha Gualteriana, a satirical parade with marching bands and strangely costumed participants.

Our Lady of Safe Journey Festival in Peniche. This important festival takes place on the first Sunday in August. Boats from the local fishing fleet carry religious statues in the hopes of another safe year at sea.

Our Lady of Agony Festival in Viana do Castelo. This is a highly unusual festival held the third weekend of August with side shows, magic, fireworks, folklore, a bull run, and a final parade in regional costume, in which Our Lady is carried over a huge tapestry of flowers.

Festival of Santa Barbra in Miranda do Douro. On the 3rd Sunday in August, the young men of this isolated border town celebrate by dressing in costumes to perform the stick dance, the pauliteiros.

September

Grape Harvest Festival in Palmela. The harvest of wine grapes is celebrated with a benediction of the grapes, wine tastings, parades, fireworks, folklore, and a bull run. Exact dates change each year.

Folk Music and Dance Festival in Praia da Rocha. A week long event sometime during September that combines traditional folk singing, folklore, and dancing events throughout the Algarve.

The New Fairs in Ponte de Lima. A huge regional market and festival on the second and third weekend in September when thousands of people gather to watch dances, concerts, markets, firework displays, and processions.

Our Lady of Good Voyages Festival in Moita. The annual blessing of the fishing boats.

October

The Final Pilgrimage To Fátima in Fátima. This major event honors the final appearance of the Virgin Mary in Fátima on October 13, 1917.

National Gastronomy Festival in Santarém. This 10 day event at the end of October celebrates the fine regional cuisines of Portugal. Scheduled events usually include cooking contests, lectures by famous chefs, exhibitions, sampling of traditional dishes from various restaurants, and authentic folklore and music.

November

Saint Martins Festival and National Horse Show in Golegã. A major fair, during the first two weeks of November, is combined with equestrian competitions and parades.

December

Festival of the Rapazes throughout the Montanhas. Starting on December 26, local unmarried boys dress up in multicolored costumes and menacing masks while they run around town terrorizing neighbors.

INSURANCE COVERAGE

Since you are not a Portuguese citizen, health care will not be provided for free. Americans with private insurance may be covered under their policies, but that may only help you after months of detailed paper work. Canadians may find that their provincial health insurance covers or reimburses certain procedures, but don't count on it. See the Travel Emergency and Medical Insurance section of the *Planning Your Trip* chapter for additional information.

NEWSPAPERS & MAGAZINES

There are a vast assortment of Portuguese language dailies and weeklies for sale at newsstands, hotel lobbies, and local tobacco shops (tabacaria). Of these, I usually read the informative *Diário de Notícias, Diario Economico* and *Público* papers from Lisbon. Excellent weeklies include the serious *Expresso,* and the arts and entertainment laden *Blitz* and *Se7e,* great sources for things to do in Lisbon. Most hotels and tourist offices will give you a copy of the free monthly *Cultural Agenda.*

Among the only English language weeklies are the *Portugal Post* and the *Anglo-Portuguese News (ANP)*. They are on sale at most tourist resorts and in large cities. If you search around the Costa de Lisboa or the Algarve, you can also find current copies of the *International Herald Tribune, The European,* and *USA Today.* If you don't mind reading old news, backdated issues of the *New York Times, Wall Street Journal,* and the *London Times* sometimes collect dust in hotel-based tobacco shops and a few newsstands in the financial districts of Lisbon and Porto.

Special European editions of English-language magazines such as *Time* and *Newsweek* are also available at leading hotels.

NIGHTLIFE

Each city and town in Portugal has a vast assortment of evening entertainment. Many establishments offer fine theater, symphony concerts, jazz bands, rock shows, and even opera. There are also establishments that are not unlike the bars, discos, and nightclubs you are already accustomed to. I include several local nightlife spots in each regional and major city chapter, but you should always try to find a resident or hotel worker to fill you in on the latest in places.

Bars tend not to get busy until at least 11:00pm, and discos are most enjoyable between 1:00am - 7:00am. Many clubs and discos give you a drink card when you pay the cover charge. The card is stamped when you order a beverage and you pay your bill before you depart. If you lose the card, it could cost you a minimum of 15,000$00.

PASSPORTS - LOST OR STOLEN

Just in case you happen to misplace your passport contact your embassy. Embassy personnel can also provide other services your tax dollars pay for, including travel advisory information on other nations you may want to visit while overseas, lists of local English speaking medical specialists, and other valuable information. However, they do not help with travel arrangements.

PHYSICALLY-CHALLENGED TRAVELERS

Traveling in Portugal for the physically-challenged person can be a bit complicated. Getting to the country is the easy part of your journey, as most airlines offer special seating assignments, wheelchair storage, and boarding assistance to anyone who requests it in advance. Upon arrival in Lisbon, additional airport services are offered free of charge by the airlines. Now that you have arrived in Lisbon, things get a little more difficult.

Although well marked, reserved handicapped parking spaces can be found at the airport and in some cities, none of the major rental car companies offer specially adapted vehicles. With advance notification, the **Association of Rental Car Companies** (ARAC), *Rua António Candido, 8, Lisbon, Tel. (01) 356-3737,* might be able to assist in finding vehicles with hand controls or other specially adapted vehicles.

New regulations from the European Economic Community (EEC) are finally starting to have a positive effect on the availability of special services and facilities, especially in the larger cities of Lisbon, Coimbra, and Porto. The best resource for information is the office of the **Secretariado Nacional de Reabilitacão,** *Ave. Conde de Valbom, 63, Lisbon, Tel. (01) 793-6517.* A special booklet entitled *Guia de Turismo para Pessoas com Deficiencias* provides detailed lists (in Portuguese only) of hotels with minimal obstacles for wheelchairs, customized buses with ramps, taxi companies that are pleased to assist people with special needs, and service station bathrooms that are wheelchair accessible.

Wheelchair accessible bathrooms, entrance ramps, and well designed elevators with braille and chime features are becoming more common in the larger 4 and 5 star hotels in resort areas and business centers. Whenever possible, I include a notation in the hotel reviews where special facilities are offered. Regional Turismo offices may be able to direct visitors to transportation services, accommodations, and restaurants that are properly equipped.

There are also new daily dial-a-ride door-to-door bus services in some cities that must be arranged at least two days in advance. A special card might be required from the bus operators. For dial-a-ride details, call *Tel.*

(01) 758-5657 in Lisbon, *Tel. (039) 441-441* in Coimbra, and *Tel. (02) 606-6646* in Porto. For groups who need to charter a special accessible bus for private use, contact the **Companhia Carris-Sector de Alugueres**, *Rua 1 de Maio, 101, Lisbon, Tel. (01) 363-9226.*

The following organizations offer special trips and access details:
- **Society for The Advancement of Travel for the Handicapped**, *New York City, NY, Tel. 212/447-7284.* A members-only service with basic information about travel needs for the physically challenged. Yearly membership is $45.00 for adults and $25.00 for students.
- **Moss Rehab Travel Information Services**, *Philadelphia, PA, Tel. 215/456-9600.* A free information and referral service with valuable hints and suggestions on companies that offer travel services for the physically challenged.
- **Flying Wheels Travel**, *Owatonna, MN, Tel. 800/535-6790.* A great full service travel agency and group tour operator that can provide helpful information and reservations for the physically challenged. Services include all forms of special transportation and accommodation reservations, and guided group tours.
- **Wheeling Around the Algarve**, *Almancil, Algarve, Portugal, Tel. (351 089) 399-844, Fax (351 089) 397-448.* This is a specialized tour operator and travel agency that can help book all sorts of trips for physically challenged people who wish to vacation in the Algarve. You can also send a fax to the director, Mr. David Player, for specific details and information.

POST OFFICES & MAIL

Throughout the country there is a vast network of post offices (correios) that are open from about 9am until 12:30pm and 2:30pm until 6pm Monday through Friday. In major cities, it is possible to find a few main post offices open during lunch and on Saturday mornings.

Letters sent via air mail (por avião) from Portugal to North America cost about 130$00 and can take up to two weeks to arrive. Mail within Portugal usually costs about 80$00 and finds its way to the addressee in about five days. Most post offices sell stamps (selos) and can help with normal postal needs.

You can send and receive mail as well as make phone calls at several of the main branches. If you wish to have a main post office hold mail for you, general delivery can be arranged after a visit to a post office to register your name. Incoming letters must be marked "Posta Restante-Lista do Correios" and must be sent to the station where you are registered. Letters can be picked up at the post office for a 70$00 fee per letter.

You can also receive mail and telegrams via an **American Express** office if you contact them in North America, *Tel. 800/221-7282*, before you depart. Client letter services are free to American Express cardholders, vacation clients, and travelers check holders, and can be obtained by others for a small fee.

RADIO

Radio in Portugal is a wonderful source of free entertainment and most hotel rooms and rental cars have radios. There are hundreds of stations broadcasting every type of music and talk show imaginable. One of the funniest things about hearing the radio here is that after several sets of unfamiliar local music, you will then be pelted with tasteless old American songs like *Yummy, Yummy, Yummy, I've Got Love in My Tummy* or some all but forgotten disco era tune.

Stations in large cities and resort areas like Lisbon, Albufeira, Coimbra, and Porto sometimes offer great rock, blues, and jazz shows. If you want to listen to English language radio, carefully search the dial for the US Armed Forces Radio.

There are also special tourist programs in English that are broadcast in the morning on some stations in the Algarve and the Lisbon area. If you are lucky enough to have a short-wave set (almost no North Americans do) you can also get the Voice of America and BBC World Service from most of Portugal.

I purchased an inexpensive shortwave radio receiver to bring with me overseas. For under $200 you can purchase a great compact portable shortwave radio receiver, such as the top rated Grundig Yacht Boy 400. This radio allows you to pick up a multitude of English (and other language) broadcasts. It's also a great way to be informed, in advance of your vacation or business trip, about special cultural events, weather conditions, festivals, important news, and other helpful tips. Once you have arrived in Europe, you will find it easy to keep in touch with the current events back home in Canada or the US.

Among the most enjoyable news, information, and entertainment programs on shortwave bands are those that are broadcast multiple times daily by Radio Canada International, the Voice of America, Swiss Radio International, and the superb Radio Netherlands. For specific frequency locations for these and many other networks, ask your local book shop to order you a copy of *Passport to World Band Radio*, published annually by International Broadcasting Services Ltd. in Penns Park, PA (ISBN # 0-914941-37-2). You can also send a quick fax or letter to Marbian Productions International, *P.O. Box 1051, Pointe Claire, Quebec, Canada H9S 4H9, fax 514/697-2615*. This organization's president, Mr. Ian Mc Farland, a former shortwave radio program producer & host, will be glad to send current programming and frequency schedules for a variety of shortwave stations, including the above mentioned networks, directly to your home or office for free.

SHOPPING

Shopping in Portugal is a pleasure. Each region produces items ranging from hand painted ceramics to fine, tailored designer clothing. In each regional chapter, I let you know which unique products are made there. Many products exported to North America marked "made in Italy" are really made in Portugal.

Fine shoes, shirts, sweaters, dresses, handbags, belts, suits, linens, ceramics, tiles, embroidery, vintage wines, jewelry, and all sorts of additional items can be purchased at a fraction of their export price. Larger sized clothes and footwear may not be available (such as shoes over size ten and a half). Most jewelry is made with 19 karat gold (ouro) or sterling silver (prata), but many filigree items are only gold plated.

Most stores are open from 9am until 7pm on weekdays (many close for lunch from 1pm until 3pm), and on Saturdays from 9am until 1pm. I include a selection of my favorite shops and boutiques in several cities in destination chapters.

When Portugal joined the EEC, a program of tax refunds on selected export items began. The **Tax Free for Tourists** program means that as a tourist, you can be reimbursed for the tax you pay on most purchases. One thousand, six hundred shops in Portugal display the black and blue Tax Free sticker on their door.

When you make a purchase of over 10,000$00, ask for a Tax Free voucher. An unsigned check will be made out to you (you must have your passport with you) and you cash the check at the airport upon departure. The value of the check depends on the percentage of tax charged on the item purchased and the cost of the item. Clothes are usually taxed at 12%, while some luxury items such as gold are taxed at almost 30%. At the airport, cashiers are open seven days a week. If you have any problem locating a cashier, ask at an information booth before you reach your gate. For more details, pick up a Tax Free brochure at the airport or call *Tel. (01) 418-8703* in Lisbon.

Antiques

For those of you interested in antiques (antiguidades), the best places to find good values are at the outdoor markets. Most major cities have a few select antique shops as well. Bargaining is not uncommon, particularly if the proprietor wants to make a sale.

Among the best antique values are old paintings, estate jewelry, rare books, old lamps, ancient door knockers, and wonderful wooden picture frames. Furniture is also a good bargain, but the shipping, insurance, and customs hassles can be discouraging. I note some good places to find antiques in several cities in the destination chapters.

Be aware that less reputable shops may display reproductions of antique objects without revealing the true age of the item.

REGIONAL HANDICRAFTS

Most towns and villages in Portugal offer unique regional crafts (artigos regionais). These crafts are easily found in shops, markets, craft fairs, and artisan's (artesanatos) kiosks in each area. Several Turismo offices have copies of a pamphlet called Feiras de Artesanato that lists all regional craft fairs for the year. If you happen to be in Lisbon, you can pick up one of these pamphlets at the Associação Industrial Portuguesa (AIP), Praça das Industrias, Tel. (01) 362-0100.

The most sought-after regional crafts include these fine products:

Alcobaça (Costa de Prata) – Hand and machine painted tiles
Arraiolos (Planícies) – Fine handmade carpets
Barcelos (Costa Verde) – Unusual clay figurines
Caldas da Rainha (Costa de Prata) – Ceramics, murals, and azulejos
Castelo Branco (Montanhas) – Hand embroidered bedspreads
Chaves (Montanhas) – Black pottery
Coimbra (Costa de Prata) – Ceramic crocks
Gondomar (Costa Verde) – Gold and silver filigree jewelry
Illhavo (Costa de Prata) – Vista Alegre porcelain
Lamego (Montanhas) – Hand woven baskets
Mafra (Costa de Lisboa) – Miniatures
Marinha Grande (Costa de Prata) – Fine crystal
Nazaré (Costa de Prata) – Hand knit sweaters
Portalegre (Planícies) – Tapestries
Peniche (Costa de Prata) – Handmade lace
Redondo (Planícies) – Hand painted glazed ceramics
São Pedro do Corval (Planícies) – Hand painted earthenware
Tavira (Algarve) – Handmade saddles
Viana do Castelo (Costa Verde) – Handmade lace
Vila do Conde (Costa Verde) – Bobben lace

EUROPEAN SIZE CONVERSIONS

These sizes are an approximate conversion and may not be accurate in certain cases. Please ask for a free measurement and try on items before you purchase them.

Men's Shoes

North America	8	9	10	11	12	13
Europe	40	42	43	44	46	47

Women's Shoes

North America	4	5	6	7	8	9
Europe	34	35	36	37	38	39

Men's Suits

North America	36	38	40	42	44	46
Europe	46	48	50	52	54	56

Women's Dresses

North America	6	8	10	12	14	16
Europe	32	34	40	42	44	46

Men's Shirts

North America	14	15	16	17	18
Europe	36	38	41	43	45

Outdoor Markets & Fairs

Every region in Portugal offers a variety of outdoor markets. The wide assortment of goods for sale include local cheeses, meats, live poultry, ceramics, crafts, leather jackets, shoes, clothing, tapestries, furniture, antiques, and an assortment of imported items and trinkets.

Be very careful about purchasing goods such as shoes or other leather goods as they may be synthetic (even if the label says otherwise). Bargaining is somewhat acceptable, especially if you are purchasing in quantity. Local markets are excellent excursions and are a lot of fun.

Many markets exist and can be found by simply stopping by the local Turismo office or asking the front desk of any hotel. Here are the main markets by town and city:

Águeda: A rather small yet charming market takes place downtown each Saturday. You can find great bargains on shoes, shirts, and belts.

Albufeira: A market takes place here on the first and third Tuesday of each month.

Almancil: Each first and fourth Sunday, a large and entertaining market comes to Almancil.

Almeirim: On the first Sunday of each month, this quiet town hosts a wonderful artisan and produce market in the center of town. Look for the fine locally grown melons.

Almoçageme: This small village just west of Sintra offers a cute country market on the third Sunday of each month. Local pottery can be bought at good prices.

Alpedrinha: This mountain view town hosts a nice market on the first Sunday of each month.

Amares: This northern town hosts a weekly market with good handicrafts every Wednesday.

Aveiro: A monthly market known as the Feira dos 28 takes place on the 28th day of most months in this town.

Azeitão: This old market happens only on the 4th Sunday of each month. Look for the hand painted decorative pottery in the shape of small houses and villages. Another country market takes place on the first Sunday of each month. Specialties include fresh produce and cheeses.

Barcelos: This charming market runs each Thursday and provides locals and visitors with every imaginable product. Look for wonderful colorful wood and ceramic items.

Benafim: A small local market takes place here on the first Saturday of each month.

Boca do Inferno: A small crafts market (open daily) can be found just off the Boca do Inferno. Prices at this market are way too high and the quality is low.

Braga: This northern city hosts a market known for cheap shoes and shirts on Tuesdays.

Carcavelo: This market opens each Thursday and offers a wide array of household goods, clothing, and seemingly useless items. A daily fish auction takes place at about 4pm at the fish market near the beach.

Celorico de Beira: On the Friday of each fortnight, there's a huge cheese market known for the quality and freshness of its remarkable Queijo de Serra cheeses.

Cascais: The Cascais market, behind the town center on Rua Mercado, is open on every Wednesday and Saturday. This market is a good source for sweaters and shoes.

Coimbra: On weekdays, the old section of the city hosts a small but interesting market. While produce and cheeses are sold in the covered market, gypsies can be seen selling lambs wool sweaters and unusual tablecloths on the road above the market.

Elvas: The town hosts a great weekly regional market near the aqueduct on each Monday.

Espinho: A very good weekly market comes into the heart of town every Monday.

Estoi: On the second Sunday of every month a local market with lots of atmosphere comes to this historic community. Look for fine leather goods and linens.

Estremoz: On Saturdays, a very good market rolls into town. Furniture, traditional tapestries, unusual foods, woolens, and crafts are all available at reasonable prices.

Évora: On the second Thursday of each month a huge regional market takes place in the Rossio São Brás just outside the town's walls. Keep your eye out for the wonderful tapestries and shepherd's capes which are found only here.

Figueiro da Foz: An amusing market and fair called the Ferreira a Nova takes place on the 3rd day of each month.

Grandôla: A large market takes place here on the second Monday of each month.

Guarda: The town host a daily market in the southeastern corner of town. Each Wednesday there is also a market on the city's fairgrounds.

Guimarães: Each Friday the town has a local market where you can find nice filigree.

Lagos: Each Saturday morning a local produce market takes place near the bus station.

A regional market takes place here on the first Sunday of every month.

Lisboa: The Feira da Ladra (Thief's Market), every Tuesday and Saturday, is an excellent source for antiques and flea market type products.

Lourinhã: A cattle market takes place on the first Sunday of each month except in September.

Loulé: This huge market is one of the best in Portugal. Lasting until midnight on every Saturday, the Loulé market offers more variety than can be imagined. A must for any visitor to the Algarve. This is the place to bargain with vendors.

Melgaço: An outstanding traditional weekly market comes to this border town each Friday.

Moncarapacho: A large market on the first Sunday of each month is hosted in this old Algarve town. My favorite bargains include boots, shoes, and tapestries.

Olhão: A daily (except Sunday) morning seafood and produce market takes place near the river. This is the best market for fresh shellfish in the Algarve.

Pinhal Novo: A local market takes place here on the second Sunday of each month.

Ponte de Barca: A regional produce and general merchandise market is open each Wednesday.

Ponte de Lima: On alternating Mondays, a local market and cattle auction takes place on both sides of the river.

Portimão: A large outdoor market runs here the first Monday of the month.

Porto: This major city offers several daily markets such as the Bolhão market as well as the special Sunday morning bird fair, flower market, and stamp market. A daily artisan fair is held in Praça da Batalha.

Quarteira: Every Wednesday a handicrafts and produce market takes place off the main street of Rua Vasco da Gama.

São Brás de Alportel: Every Saturday a very nice regional market is held here.

São Pedro de Sintra: This market is located on the main road from Lisboa to Sintra. Running on the second and forth Sunday of each month, this market is huge. Good buys on folk art, antiques, ceramics, and locally made cheeses are easy to find.

São João das Lampas: This village, located about 28 kilometers north of Sintra, hosts a market on the first Sunday of each month.

Sines: A large market comes to town on the fourth Monday of each month.

Sobral de Monte Agraco: Each month, on the first Monday, a small market takes place. Look for the fine clay figures and unusual metalwork.

Terras de Bouro: This small village in the Serra do Gerês offers a charming traditional market on the second Monday of each month.

Valença do Minho: On Wednesdays there is a regional produce and crafts market here.

Viana do Castelo: Friday is market day in this beautiful town. Look for handmade embroidery.

Viseu: Viseu hosts a daily produce market in the heart of town.

Each Thursday the town also hosts a larger regional crafts and produce market in the northern sector of the city near the river.

TELEPHONES, FAXES & TELEGRAMS

The **telephone** system in Portugal still has its problems, but it has finally started to develop into a sophisticated communications network with advanced technological abilities. Although many Portuguese public telephones may prove to be consistently out of order, and the multilingual instructions printed on some phones are only moderately helpful, with a bit of persistence you can easily reach your family and business associates

TELEPHONE CODES

• *To reach the US and Canada from Portugal: dial 001, area code, phone number.*

• *To reach Portugal from the US and Canada: dial 011 351, area code, phone number. If the Portuguese area code shows a zero as a first digit, drop the zero.*

• *To call between 2 Portuguese cities within the same area code: drop the area code and just dail phone number.*

• *To call between 2 Portuguese cities in different area codes: dial area code with the zero and then the phone number.*

throughout the world for a reasonable price. The cheapest times to call overseas from Portugal is between 12:01am and 7:59am when the fees are discounted up to 31% below normal full rates.

The standard corner public phone booth accepts 20$00 and 50$00 coins that are inserted into a horizontal slot in the upper right hand corner of the phone before dialing. A typical call within one region or city from a pay phone costs about 20$00 and does not require additional coins until after the first few minutes of calling time. Calling outside a region can cost between 18$00 and 72$00 per minute, depending on the time of day and distance. Calling North America from a pay phone usually costs between 138$00 and 214$00 per minute. Unfortunately, most of the coin-operated public phones seem to always be broken.

Over the past several years, Portugal Telecom has installed thousands of special pay phones that accept only pre-paid calling cards for both domestic and international calls. These specially marked phones are found all over the country. These phones utilize one of two different types of plastic cards that can be purchased from any post office (correio), Portugal Telecom business office, or most newsstands. While these special computerized pay phones in the cities of Lisbon and Porto accept only the **Telecom Card**, almost every other city and village in Portugal has a slightly different system that exclusively accepts the **Crediphone** card.

I strongly suggest buying one of each type of calling card while traveling around Portugal as these phones are easier to use and are much less likely to be broken than their coin-operated rivals. Both types of calling cards have a predetermined amount of calling units (impulsos) that are each worth about 17$50 each, and allow for multiple use of the same card. The cards tick away like a taxi meter in the LCD display at the top of the phone. The starting price for either type of calling card is 850$00 for 50 units. These phones deduct about 8 units per minute in a call to North America.

If you intend to use a US or Canadian telephone company calling card instead, be sure to call your long distance phone company before you depart for Europe and get their access numbers and dialing out procedures for use in Portugal.

Another suggestion is to place calls from any **Portugal Telecom** storefront business office, or any city or village post office. Both of these establishments generally offer at least a few phones that allow you to call anywhere in the world, and pay at the cashier when your call is over. These pay-after-use calls tend to cost about 15% more than a normal pay phone, and in some cases a major credit card may be used for payment (be sure to ask in advance).

Hotels can also place both local and international calls (even if you are not a guest). You will be billed at a much higher rate than at a pay phone, but the assistance with the process often proves worthwhile. Keep in mind, however, that calling collect, or with a North American based telephone company calling card, from your hotel room may include a hefty connection fee.

Cellular telephones are quite popular in Portugal, but your North American cell phones will not function on Europe's totally different **GSM** cellular operating system! If you're like me, and like to have some means of communicating while on the road, your best option is to rent a GSM cell phone. I have even been able to connect to the Internet, and send most of my faxes, via these phones. While major rental car companies offer European cell phone rentals, I have not had much luck with their services.

The best company to contact for GSM cell phone rentals is **Global Cellular Rental**, *New York, Tel. 800/699-6861* (with additional offices in London and Paris). This great new company can deliver a phone on time to your hotel in just about any city in Europe with a few days advance notice. Another advantage is that they can provide you with an exact phone number before you depart North America so people back home will know exactly how to reach you abroad. Their rates are around $15 per day, $99 per week, or $249 per month for the rental. Additionally, a minimum usage fee of $80 will be charged to your credit card. When you're finished, the phone can be picked up at your hotel for a small charge, but a new plan may go into effect that will allow you to drop it in a Federal Express envelope and ship it back to New York upon your arrival in the US. The per minute incoming and outgoing charges vary depending on the hours and locations the service will be used, but a quick toll free call or fax to their offices can get you all the information you need.

Most hotels also provide a convenient way to send **faxes** (expect to pay a hefty surcharge) or receive faxes. This service can save you a lot of money since you can send a large amount of information at high speeds.

Reasonably priced public fax facilities can be found at almost all Portugal Telecom business offices and post offices.

Many big city post offices also offer **telegram** services at moderate rates. You can also check with the local Portugal Telecom business office for further details.

GOOD NUMBERS TO KNOW
• Local Information, Tel. 118
• International Operator Assistance, Tel. 098
• US Country Code, 001
• Canada Country Code, 001
• United Kingdom Country Code, 0044
• AT&T US Direct Access Number, Tel. 05-017-1288
• MCI CALL US Access Number, Tel. 05-017-1234

TELEVISION

Portugal has two government owned TV stations, managed by the RTP broadcasting company, as well as couple of private networks, including SIC. These stations transmit their signal to most parts of the country, and offer a combination of locally produced game shows, Brazilian talk shows, news programs, and poorly subtitled or dubbed international movies. The prospect of seeing a Woody Allen movie in Portuguese may seem unbearable, but I find it rather amusing.

Most of the better hotels offer a selection of satellite TV programs from Germany, France, and Italy, and in some cases you will find CNN International and the NBC super channel. Additionally, one of these stations usually is the SKY or BBC news networks from England. The only word of caution, particularly if you have children with you, is that the German and Spanish networks have a tendency to show soft-core porno flicks on weekend evenings.

TIME

Portugal is on par with Greenwich Mean Time (GMT). However, Portugal currently follows the same daylight savings time system as the US and Canada, and from April through October is at GMT + 1 hour.

Portugal is five hours ahead of the Eastern Standard Time (New York, Boston, Montreal, Toronto) in North America, six hours ahead of Central Standard Time, seven hours ahead of Mountain Standard Time, and eight hours ahead of Pacific Standard Time.

TIPS

Tips are acceptable and appreciated, and are sometimes automatically included in your bill. Many Portuguese do not tip for some services that are commonplace in North America. If someone gives you back a tip, do not take it as an insult. In most cases, feel free to use your judgment based on the quality of services rendered.

TIPPING CHART

Taxi Driver	*10% of the meter's rate.*
Hotel Porter	*150$00 per bag.*
Hotel Concierge	*500$00 per favor.*
Room Service	*250$00 per meal.*
Hotel Doorman	*200$00 per taxi.*
Bartender	*100$00 per round.*
Waiter	*10% to 15% of the bill.*
Ushers	*150$00 per event.*
Private Guides	*1,700$00 per person per day.*
Private Drivers	*1,600$00 per person per day.*
Tour Guides	*1,800/$00 per person per day.*
Tour Bus Drivers	*1,000$00 per person per day.*

TOURIST INFORMATION OFFICES

Once you've arrived, there are many places to pick up tourist information in several languages. Major cities, tourist destinations, and rural town halls (cãmara municipal) operate small tourist offices to assist visitors to their region. These tourist information offices are usually marked with a sign which says **Turismo.**

These offices are open during typical business hours, and may be closed on weekends. Turismos are normally staffed by just one or two local residents who can communicate in multiple languages. Turismos are managed by the local government and most of the employees are extremely friendly and helpful.

I suggest that when you arrive in a city or town you pop into the local Turismo and find out if they can offer any maps, suggestions, or assistance. They will often advise you of totally off the beaten path attractions and unique accommodations that only a local resident would know about. I include addresses and phone numbers of many Turismos in the destination chapters.

8. SPORTS & RECREATION

There are many sports and recreational activities to enjoy in Portugal. Check the destination chapters for activities available in a particular place and information regarding suppliers, venues, and outfitters.

BICYCLES

During the last several years, bicycling has become more and more popular in Portugal. It is now possible to plan long or short cycling excursions in each region of the county. Many hotels, quintas, and local bike shops offer bicycle rentals for those who are interested in a few hours or a few days of two wheeled fun. Use reflectors, flags, and lights when cycling in Portugal — your safety may depend on them. Cars often will not give a bicyclist the right of way. I have included a some places that rent bicycles, but for further information contact a local Turismo office.

For those of you who intend to travel extensively by bicycle, you should consider the following: most airlines will permit the transportation of bikes, but can charge you for extra baggage; trains in Portugal also permit the transportation of bikes with a small additional fee; buses will often not allow bikes on board due to limited luggage capacity; and most spare parts are quite expensive in Portugal, so bring them with you.

BULLFIGHTS

One of the most exciting spectator sports in the country is the **tourada** – a Portuguese bullfight. These events have been enjoyed in Portugal since the 14th century, and are a great source of regional pride.

Unlike the brutal Spanish form of the sport, in Portugal the bulls are not killed at the end of a fight. Here the sport is more like a test of wills rather than a grisly slaughter of a helpless animal.

Many cities and towns all over Portugal hold weekly or monthly bullfighting events in specially designed bullrings, Praça de Touros. The season runs from April through October and tickets typically range from 700$00 to 5000$00 per seat, depending on the seat's location.

Before the start of the evening's events, there is often a prayer service for the men involved in the fight, followed by a small indoor parade of ornately costumed and highly trained horses with costumed mounted warriors. When you are first escorted to your seat, it is customary to give a small tip of around 75$00 per person to the usher. As you sit back and enjoy the fight, vendors will walk through the audience selling snacks and drinks.

After a trumpet blast, the participants of the night's events enter the ring to salute both the officials and audience before the action begins. When the ring is cleared, a bull is released from the ringside bullpen. A gate soon opens and a well trained horse and it's ornately dressed mounted fighter, the cavaleiro, begin to taunt the bull into action. The object of this sport is for the fighter to charge towards the bull in order to plant a series of spears into the bull's body.

After a couple of rounds (about six spears) the cavaleiro departs the ring and the bull is restrained and returned to the pen for the night. To subdue the bull, a strangely dressed team of about eight seemingly suicidal men, forcados, line up to torment the bull into charging at them head on in a uniquely Portuguese test of courage known as a pega.

The lead forcado will attempt to jump on the bull's head and try to avoid being injured while the other seven men grab the bull and remove it from the ring. This is the most dangerous aspect of the bullfight, and many forcados have been seriously injured during their relentless attempts to control the animal. The fight will soon continue with more bulls, cavaleiros, and pegas and an intermission before the night is over.

CAR RACING

Professional car racing is a major attraction in Portugal. I have been to a few grand prix races here and they are serious events. The most widely attended racing event in the country is the **Rallye de Portugal do Vinho de Porto** held each March. This week long event brings professional racers to locations throughout the country and is watched by perhaps millions of Portuguese. People take their vacation to coincide with the rally and follow it from location to location.

The more famous event in the racing circuit is the world renowned **Grande Premio de Portugal** formula one grand prix held each September in the **Estoril Autodromo** near Sintra. If you decide to spend the big bucks (10,000$00 or more) for a pass to this weekend event, be aware that the track layout makes it difficult for spectators to know what is going on. If you must see this formula one race, get the specially marked paddock club gold passes from the ticket offices in Estoril (30,000$00 or more) or you might want to bring a portable TV with you to the stands so you can see what's going on. Ear plugs are definitely a necessity, and traffic is at a standstill anywhere near Sintra, Cascais, and Estoril during the race weekend.

Every hotel room is booked anywhere within 50 km of either of these races.

FISHING

The rivers, lakes, reservoirs, and coast of Portugal contain a vast array of fine fish. No license is required for ocean fishing, but if you intend to fish inland you may need a special permit from either a local town hall or a park ranger. Each season presents opportunities to catch a different assortment of wonderful fresh and salt water fish.

The most common targets for ocean fishing include grouper, bass, bream, swordfish, shark, bluefish, tuna, mackerel, rays, and dolphin fish. For those of you more interested in river and lake fishing, you can expect to find trout, salmon, bass, shad, and barbel. Many companies offer excursions by boat into the most famous fishing areas of Portugal.

I include a list of fishing clubs and outfitters in each regional chapter, but you should also check with a Turismo office for more information and the local rules.

GOLF

Golf is a tremendously popular pastime in Portugal for visiting British, German, and North American visitors. Due to the excellent year round climate, many courses have sprung up throughout the country, and several more are in the planning and construction stages. Many courses were designed by the world's leading professionals such as Robert Trent Jones and Frank Pennink.

Although golf in Portugal is not particularly inexpensive, the unique conditions and dramatic views make this an unbeatable location for world class facilities. Most clubs offer a full range of services including access to opulent clubhouses. A brief description of the 28 major courses is listed below. Remember to reserve your tee times as far in advance as possible, especially from April-October. The **Portuguese Federation of Golf**, Federacão Portuguesa de Golfe, can provide you with specific course maps and green fees; they can be reached at *Tel. (01) 674 658.*

Most golf courses (even private clubs) allow non-members to use their facilities. The Algarve and Costa de Lisboa regions are studded with a vast array of choices for all levels of skill, and there are other courses in most regions of the country with perhaps the exception of the Montanhas.

Just because everything else in Portugal seems like a bargain, don't expect golf to be cheap. I spent over 11,000$00 for a round of golf on a nice course last year. Electric carts, equipment rental, locker rooms, lessons, and caddies are usually available at additional cost. Many hotels offer discounts and preferred tee times to their guests, so ask at their front desk for details.

The destination chapters include golf courses located in each region, and I also include a handy chart of all major golf courses below and on the following page. Note: those courses with multiple loops are rated for the longest segment.

Major Golf Courses in Portugal

The Algarve
- **Quinta do Lago**, *Almancil, Tel. (089) 394-782*, 4 x 9 Holes, 3263 Meters, Par 36
- **Pinheiros Altos**, *Almancil, Tel. (089) 394-340*, 18 holes, 6049 Meters, Par 72
- **Pine Cliffs**, *Almancil, Tel. (089) 501-787*, 9 Holes, 2324 Meters, Par 33
- **San Lorenzo**, *Almancil, Tel. (089) 396-534*, 18 Holes, 6238 Meters, Par 72
- **Alto Golf**, *Alvor, Tel. (082) 416-913*, 18 Holes, 6125 Meters, Par 72
- **Vale de Milho Golf**, *Carvoeiro, Tel. (082) 358-502*, 9 Holes, 970 Meters, Par 27
- **Carvoeiro Golf**, *Lagoa, Tel. (082) 526-10*, 18 Holes, 5919 Meters, Par 72
- **Vale de Pinto**, *Lagoa, Tel. (082) 526-10*, 18 Holes, 5861 Meters, Par 71
- **Palmares**, *Lagos, Tel. (082) 762-953*, 18 Holes, 5961 Meters, Par 71
- **Vale do Lobo**, *Tel. Loulé, Tel. (089) 394-444*, 3 x 9 Holes, 3334 Meters, Par 36
- **Penina Golf**, *Portimão, Tel. (082) 415-415*, 9/18 Holes, 6439 Meters, Par 73
- **Vilamoura 1**, *Vilamoura, Tel. (089) 313-652*, 18 Holes, 6331 Meters, Par 73
- **Vilamoura 2**, *Vilamoura, Tel. (089)313-652*, 18 Holes, 6256 Meters, Par 71
- **Vilamoura 3**, *(Vilamoura, Tel. (089) 313-652*, 3 x 9 Holes, 3180 Meters, Par 36
- **Club do Golfe Vila Sol**, *Vilamoura, Tel. (089) 302-144*, 18 Holes, 6183 Meters, Par 72
- **Parque da Floresta**, *Vila do Bispo, Tel. (082) 653-33*, 18 Holes, 5888 Meters, Par 72

Costa de Lisboa
- **Clube de Campo**, *Aroeira, Tel. (01) 226-1802*, 18 Holes, 6040 Meters, Par 72

• **Lisbon Sports Club**, *Belas, Tel. (01) 431-2482*, 18 Holes, 5278 Meters, Par 69
• **Quinta da Marinha**, *Cascais, Tel. (01) 486-9881*, 18 Holes, 6014 Meters, Par 71
• **Tróia Golf Club**, *Setúbal, Tel. (065) 441-12*, 18 Holes, 6337 Meters, Par 72
• **Golf Estoril Sol**, *Sintra, Tel. (01) 923-2461*, 2 x 9 Holes, 3609 Meters, Par 62
• **Penha Longa**, *Sintra, Tel. (01) 924-0320*, 18 Holes, 6228 Meters, Par 72
• **Quinta da Beloroura**, *Sintra, Tel. (01) 924-0046*, 18 Holes, 5877 Meters, Par 72
• **Palácio Estoril Golf**, *Sintra, Tel. (01) 468-0176*, 18 Holes, 5267 Meters, Par 68
• **Guia Estoril**, *Sintra, Tel. (01) 486-9881*, 2 x 9 Holes, 2350 Meters, Par 34

Costa da Prata
• **Vimeiro Golf Club**, *Vimeiro, Tel. (061) 984-157*, 2 x 9 Holes, 2431 Meters, Par 34

Costa Verde
• **Miramar Golf**, *Valadares, Tel. (02) 762-2067*, 9 Holes, 5146 Meters, Par 34
• **Oporto Golf**, *Espinho, Tel. (02) 722-008*, 18 Holes, 5668 Holes, Par 71
• **Estela Golf**, *Estela, Tel. (052) 685-567*, 2 x 9 Holes, 3090 Meters, Par 72

Montanhas
• **Vidago Golf Club**, *Vidago, Tel. (076) 971-06*, 9 Holes, 2449 Meters, Par 33

HORSEBACK RIDING

With a long equestrian tradition, Portugal offers a wide variety of horseback and carriage riding facilities. Many quintas, hotels, resorts, herdades, and riding centers offer hourly riding on wonderful Lusitanian horses for as little as 1200$00 an hour.

Each region contains several different places to ride, but the Planícies region may be the most dramatic area for scenic rides. I list a selection of my favorite riding establishments in the destination chapters of this book. If you need further details, contact your hotel's front desk or a local Turismo office. There are no horserace tracks in Portugal.

HUNTING

It is possible to hunt in Portugal, but you must obtain a hunting license. To receive a license, every foreigner must present a passport and a gun license from their country of origin to the **Instituto Florestal**, *Ave João Crisostomo, 26, Lisbon*. Getting a license can be a bit of a hassle, but if you love to hunt, Portugal will not disappoint you.

If you come to Portugal with firearms, you must leave a 30,000$00 deposit for each gun at customs when you arrive. If you are not bringing in arms, finding equipment is not always an easy task.

The most common game and bird hunting areas are deep within the Planícies and Montanhas regions. In these areas, there are several hunting clubs and herdades that offer organized hunting adventures at reasonable prices. Expect to find sanctioned hunting areas for quail, rabbit, partridge, pheasant, duck, and wild boar. I have noted a few of hunting organizations in this book, but your best bet is to visit the main Turismo office at Palácio Foz in Lisbon for a more complete list.

You'll be impressed with the hunting outfits Portuguese sportsmen wear. Between the hand-sewn Machado boots and antique engraved rifles commonly used, a visiting hunter can easily feel underdressed and even intimidated.

OFF-ROAD VEHICLES

You can rent jeeps by the hour or day from several large car rental companies in major tourist zones. You should check whether your insurance will cover you in case of an accident before you depart for Portugal.

There are a number of outfitters in the Costa de Lisboa, Algarve and Planícies regions that offer guided excursions into remote areas. One of the best jeep safari companies is **Frescuras** in *Sintra, Tel. (01) 726-2183*. My favorite source for jeep excursions is the **Quinta Horta da Moura** in Monsaraz. I include several companies and properties that offer these services in the destination chapters.

SKIING

I don't know anybody who comes to Portugal during the winter especially to ski, but for those of you who need to know, this is the story. In the **Serra da Estrêla** mountains of the Montanhas region there is a ski area at Torre. This slope will certainly not impress all but the most inexperienced downhill skier. Cross-country skiing is a better option with several trails through the parks and villages of the same region. Contact a Turismo office for more details.

SOCCER

Like the rest of Europe, soccer (futebol) is a major national pastime in Portugal. September through May is soccer season and there are many serious soccer league matches throughout the country (especially in Lisbon and Porto) that draw upwards of 80,000 spectators at any given game. Tickets range from 550$00 to 3500$00, and games are often completely sold out well in advance.

The games that feature the leading teams (Benfica, Sporting Clube de Portugal, Belém, Porto) often create huge all night traffic jams because spectators tend to use the highways as giant parking lots. If you are interested in seeing a match, check with the stadium box office to see if any seats are available. Be extremely careful not to cheer too loudly for the visiting team, as fans can get a bit rough with their adversaries. Soccer matches are generally accompanied by a series of events not unlike our pro football half time and pre-game festivities.

SWIMMING

Portugal has countless fine beaches, lagoons, rivers, and lakes where you can enjoy a fine swim. Please keep in mind that most swimming areas do not have full time lifeguards, so it is important to take the proper precautions. When swimming in the ocean, there may be strong under-tows and cross-currents. A blue flag lets you know the area has passed current EEC safe water requirements for purity.

Another option for swimming is the hundreds of municipal swimming pools in major towns. These public pools are normally open during the warmer months and often provide lifeguards, showers, changing rooms, lockers, and pool side lounge chairs. Some public pools may charge a small admittance fee. Check with a local Turismo office for hours and locations of public pools and municipal beaches. I include reviews of my favorite beach areas throughout this book.

TENNIS

You can find both private and municipal tennis courts and centers in most major tourist resorts. As with golf, there is a higher concentration of these types of facilities in both the Algarve and Costa de Lisboa regions. Many hotels also offer a few courts for the exclusive use of their guests, but sometimes they can be persuaded to welcome others. If you are looking for lessons or court time, you can inquire at either the front desk of your hotel or at a local Turismo office. I include several tennis centers in the destination chapters.

WATER SPORTS

With hundreds of miles of superb coastline, Portugal offers many opportunities to swim, sail, wind surf, water-ski, jetski, surf, dive, and snorkel. Since there are so many different areas to enjoy water sports, I include some of the best facilities in each destination chapter.

For the most part, you can expect to find world class windsurfing in the Costa de Lisboa and Algarve, excellent jet skiing and water-skiing on the rivers and lakes of the Costa Verde and Montanhas, fine surfing, sailing, diving, and snorkeling all over the Algarve, and countless spots for either salt or fresh water swimming and sailing in all regions of the country. Check with the local Turismo office for details on additional sights and equipment rentals.

9. FOOD & WINE

FOOD

Each region of Portugal offers a huge selection of unique traditional food. While wandering through the country, it is possible to enjoy sumptuous dishes in small local restaurants and adegas at reasonable prices. Part of any experience in a foreign country must include sampling the food, and in the case of Portugal, drinking its spectacular wines. You won't be disappointed in what Portugal has to offer.

The following is a list of the most commonly prepared soups, appetizers, main courses, and desserts from around Portugal. Many of these items have become so popular that they can be found throughout the country. Additional dishes and cooking styles are described in the dictionary chapter of this book.

Açorda - A bread and garlic stew with seafood, found in coastal areas.
Alheiras - Hearty veal and bread sausages, found in the Montanhas.
Arroz de Marisco - A tomato based rice and seafood stew found everywhere.
Arroz Doce - Thick and creamy rice pudding, found everywhere.
Atum Grelhado - Huge grilled fresh tuna steaks, found in the Algarve.
Bacalhau - Dried cod fish served in various ways, found everywhere.
Bife à Portuguesa - A grilled steak often cooked with Port wine, found everywhere.
Bola de Sardinhas - Rolls filled with sardines, found in the Costa Verde.
Cabreiro - Slightly sharp goat's milk cheese, found in the Planícies.
Caldeirada - A salty mixed fish and vegetable stew, found in coastal areas.
Caldeirada a Pescador - A spicy stew with a mix of fish, found in the Costa de Prata.
Caldo Verde - A green cabbage, potato, and sausage soup, found everywhere.
Cataplana - A covered brass pan with fish and vegetables, found in the Algarve.
Churrasco - Sticky barbecued chicken, found everywhere.

Chouriço - Smoked spicy pork sausages, found everywhere.

Cozido à Portuguesa - Mixed meat boiled with vegetables, found everywhere.

Espetadas - Grilled kebobs of either fish or meat with vegetables, found everywhere

Frango Piri-Piri - Barbecued chicken with a mild hot sauce, found everywhere.

Frango na Pucara - Stewed chicken with garlic and vegetables, found everywhere.

Leitão Assado - Roast suckling pig, found mainly in the Costa de Prata.

Mexilhões de Escabeche - Mussels in vinegar sauce, found in the Costa de Prata.

Pão de lo - Light and airy sponge cakes, found everywhere.

Pão de Rala - A pumpkin and almond paste dessert, found in the Planícies.

Pastéis de Camarões - Delicious shrimp filled fried dumplings, found everywhere.

Pastéis de Nata - Rich little custard tarts with cinnamon top, found everywhere.

Porco a Alentejana - Pork cooked with clams and peppers, found in the Planícies.

Presunto - A full flavored smoked ham, found in the Montanhas.

Queijo da Serra - Sheep's milk cheese that is incredible, found in the Montanhas.

Sapateira Gratinada - Oven baked stuffed spider crabs, found in the Costa Verde.

Sardinhas Assado - Sardines grilled over charcoal, found mainly in the Algarve.

Sopa de Legumes - A thin chicken based vegetable soup, found everywhere.

Sopa de Marisco - A filling soup made with shellfish, found everywhere.

Sopa Dourada - A soup of bread, egg yolks, and sugar, found in the Costa Verde.

Torta da Noz - Sweet little baked almond tarts, found everywhere.

Restaurants

There are many good eating establishments, in all price ranges, throughout Portugal. In each regional chapter, I recommend several restaurants, but I strongly suggest that you try to find a few gems of your own. It is easy to find great restaurants, serving either regional or international cuisine, by asking at your hotel's front desk or even at a store, or by asking fellow travelers if they happened to eat at a great place, for example.

Many restaurants accept Visa and Mastercard and put the card's logo on the front door; American Express is often not accepted. Many restaurants are rated with a crossed fork symbol on a plaque near the front door with 1 to 4 stars. I have not found this official rating system to be particularly accurate, so ask for recommendations and trust your own instincts.

A full American style breakfast in a restaurant with eggs, bacon, toast, and coffee usually costs about 375$00 per person. A typical Portuguese three course lunch special ranges from 650$00 to 1950$00 per person, depending on the main dish you select and how fancy a restaurant you select. A Portuguese five course dinner with wine can cost from 1800$00 to well over 4500$00 per person depending again on what you choose and where you eat.

Hotels may charge higher prices (especially 5 star hotels), while little hole in the wall eating establishments usually charge a fraction of the cost of hotel restaurants. If you want to reduce your expenses, you should have no problem in most of Portugal. Also remember that many hotels include either a continental breakfast (little more than juice, rolls, and coffee) or a buffet American breakfast with all the trimmings in the room price.

RESTAURANT PRICE SCALE

The restaurants reviewed in this book are divided into four price categories. These categories reflect the average cost of a full meal, per person, without wine.

Inexpensive:	*500$00 to 1,500$00*
Moderate:	*1,500$00 to 2,750$00*
Expensive:	*2,750$00 to 3,500$00*
Very Expensive	*3,500$00 and up*

Meals are generally served from 7am to 10am for breakfast (pequeno almoço), from 12pm to 3pm for lunch (almoço), and from 7:30pm to 10pm for dinner (jantar). During breakfast, most Portuguese tend to have bread, cheese, and coffee. Many hotels and restaurants in big cities and resort areas offer full American style breakfasts with familiar items such as scrambled eggs and bacon. Lunch is a major meal here, and many people take well over an hour to consume the multiple courses typical in a lunch and wash it down with a fair quantity of wine. Dinner is a late event that consists of several courses and more wine.

Restaurants come in many types, each with a different ambiance. Many cities will have full service restaurants (restaurantes) with a large selection of either regional or international cuisine. For a little more local atmosphere, you may want to visit a quintessential local restaurant called a restaurante típico. There are also some wonderful bars that serve great food (cervejarias) at moderate prices. For a fine dinner with live Fado music you should visit a Fado house (adega típica). Many cities offer a wide range of simple taverns (tascas) where only a few inexpensive selected dishes will be offered. Most seaside towns have fine seafood restaurants (marisqueiras) that have large tanks of live shellfish.

In the countryside of northern Portugal you can find places that specialize in roasted meats (churrascarias). You can also find snacks and sandwiches (sandes) in pastry shops (pastelarias), cafes (cafes), and assorted fast food joints. When it's time for desserts (sobremesas) you can head for the nearest local bakery (confeitaria) or tea house (sala de chá). If you need help translating a menu, look in the dictionary chapter in this book.

In most restaurants you can find selections that are a la carte (a lista), daily specials (lista do dia), multiple course specials of the day (prato do dia), scaled down three or four course tourist menus (ementa turistica), and half size portions of selected items (meia dose). Several restaurants offer their shellfish items by the kilogram (2.2 pounds), usually half of a kilogram (meia kilo) is enough. Also, most restaurants will bill your table a small cover charge (couvert) if you indulge in the assortment of bread, cheese, olives, and smoked meats that are presented to you before your meal arrives.

When you get the bill (a conta), you may have a 16% charge added for IVA. This is a government tax, and is not a service charge or gratuity. I recommend giving a 10% tip for good service and a 15% tip for extraordinary service, to be left in cash on the table. If you put a tip on your credit card, I can assure you the waiter will never get it.

DRINK
Beer
There are some great Portuguese beers, cerveja, including Super Bock, Europa, and the most common of all, Sagres. Beer usually costs about 95$00 per bottle or can, with a refundable deposit, at a store and costs between 80$00 and 400$00 per glass at a bar or restaurant. Other major European brands such as Kronenburg, Heineken, Bass, and Becks are usually available by the bottle at upscale clubs and bars for a premium.

Coffee
Coffee or café can be ordered as either an espresso, bica, coffee with warm milk, café com leite, or a rich café au lait style mixture known as galão. Decaffeinated instant coffee is available in most larger cities and is called by its brand name, *Nescafe.*

Juice

If you ask for a juice, sumo, just remember that in the large cities and resort hotels you may end up with a sugar dowsed drink that tastes like tang. If you want to receive fresh juice, ask for a natural juice, sumo natural, and the waiter will usually understand what you want.

Water

Water from taps in any foreign country can have its risks, so I recommend drinking bottled water. In Portugal, there are many brands of spring and mineral waters including my favorite, Luso. These waters cost about 130$00 per liter in a store and as much as 350$00 in a restaurant.

Most mineral water can be ordered with bubbles, agua com gas, or without bubbles, agua sem gas, and is always at its best when served cold, fresca. There is also an assortment of carbonated soft drinks like Coca Cola, Sumol (a citrus flavored soda), and Fanta Laranja (orange soda). They cost about 110$00 per can or bottle in stores, and 180$00 in most restaurants.

WINE

With an average annual production of over 100,000,000 cases of wine, Portugal ranks among the world's largest producers. The history of its wine production can be traced back to the Phoenicians who established the first vineyards in what is now Portugal. The nation's economy now depends heavily on the production of wine, and each year huge revenues are derived from the exportation of well over 17,000,000 cases of wine all over the world.

There are many different types of wine available: white wine (vinho branco), red wine (vinho tinto), Rosé wine (Rosé), sparkling wine (espumante), Port wine (porto), and dessert wine (mosatel). At present, there are over 125 different varieties of wines. Wine is grown in almost every corner of the country. Local residents of small villages and rural hamlets commonly make their own table wine, often for their own consumption.

The government of Portugal, in connection with the **Instituto da Vinha e do Vinho** (IVV), established nine production zones: the Vinho Verde, Douro, Dão, Bairrada, Colares, Carcavelos, Bucelas, Moscatel de Setúbal, and Algarve. These Demarcated Regions (Regioes Demarcadas) have been painstakingly analyzed and have been determined to be the finest sectors in the country for high quality wine production. They are strictly controlled as to their exact boundaries, types of wine allowed for production, maximum yields, production methods, and length of aging. All bottles of wine produced for resale in Portugal must carry an official stamp of origin, which lets the consumer know the wine has been approved for sale.

For a vineyard or producer to bottle wine in these designated regions, the wine is subjected to a series of tests and tastings by experts. Once the wine is approved for sale, it receives a special paper stamp over the cork or on the back of the bottle with the producer's code and a serial number.

While the demarcated regions tend to produce the most famous wines in the country, several other parts of Portugal produce wines that are also quite good and rather affordable. Almost anywhere you travel, it is possible to find local wineries that make tasty red, white, Rosé, fortified, and sparkling wines.

The most common place to find a large assortment of wine is at a supermarket (hypermercado). A good place to find vintage wines is at a wine shop (loja de vinho, garrafeira) where the proprietors will often open a bottle and give you a free sample. You can enjoy wine tastings and tours at one of the cellars (adegas) of the many wineries that are open to the public. Another way to find wine in Portugal is to look out for a sign in front of a farm or rural house that says "vende sé vinho," which means wine for sale. These small, unofficial producers often enjoy meeting and selling foreigners hearty and inexpensive homemade table wines.

Vinho Verde Demarcated Region

This huge zone is located in the countryside of the Costa Verde region in the northwest corner of Portugal. The refreshing wine of this area is misleadingly called Vinho Verde (green wine), but is actually red and white. You can find good Vinho Verde in Portugal for as little as 400$00 per bottle. The grapes are picked and immediately fermented in large vats before being bottled.

The white (branco) wine from this zone looks mildly yellow in color. It is light, refreshing, a bit fruity, and just slightly sparkling with an alcohol content between 8% and 11.5%. Most of these blended wines do not age well and should be consumed immediately. Only the fine white wines made from pure Alvarinho grapes have a longer shelf life. White Vinho Verde is often served chilled, and goes well with seafood.

The red (tinto) wine from this zone appears almost purple in color. It is also a bit fruity, but tends to exhibit a slightly acidic flavor as well. Red Vinho Verde wine goes rather well with hearty meat dishes and may be served chilled or at room temperature.

Vinho Verde Labels: *Paço d' Anha, Quinta da Franqueira, Palácio da Brejoeira, Quinta de Aderiz, Paço do Cardido, Casa da Tapada, Casa de Sezim, Quinta do Outeiro de Baixa, Adega Cooperativa de Ponte de Barca, Casa do Valle.*

Douro Demarcated Region

This zone is located along the terraced banks of the Douro River and its surrounding countryside in the Montanhas region of north central Portugal. About 60% of the grapes cultivated here are used in the production of hearty red and white Douro table wines while the remaining 40% are used for the famous fortified Port wine. You can find good Douro wine in Portuguese shops for as little as 500$00 a bottle, while the Port wine ranges from 1,200$00 to over 5,500$00 a bottle.

The white (branco) table wine from this zone appears straw colored. It is a dry, smooth, and hearty wine with an alcohol content of at least 11%, and is meant to be enjoyed cold. White Douro wine goes well with seafood.

The red (tinto) wine from this zone is a ruby red color. Red Douro wine has a fruity rich flavor with an alcohol content of at least 11%, and is served at room temperature. Red Douro wine goes with meat, fowl, and hearty stews.

The blended white wine is aged for a minimum of nine months and the red wine for a minimum for 18 months before bottling, and can be consumed immediately or a few years after production.

Best Vintages: 1960, 1980, 1966, 1964, 1965, 1975, 1981, 1984

Douro Labels: *Vinha das Madrucas, Casa dos Varais, Sogrape, Borges & Irmão, Quinta do Cotto, Casa Ferreira, Quinta do Confradeiro, Barca Velha, Ramos Pinto.*

Ports of Douro

The Port wine produced exclusively in this zone is made from a selection of over 20 grape varieties. After each September's harvest, the crushed grapes are stored in a vat. To facilitate a higher sugar content, an addition of wine brandy equaling 20% of the wine's volume is added. This also ceases the fermentation process and assures an alcohol content of 19% to 22%. After transport to Vila Nova de Gaia, the wine remains in vats or wooden casks for at least two years before it is ready to be either carefully blended with other Ports, or is separated for special use if harvested in a great year.

There are several types of Port wine. The young Port wine may be blended with other harvest's wines and aged in a cask for three to five years to produce the sweet red Ruby Port. This dessert wine is served at room temperature. Further aging of Ruby Port in barrels results in the lighter colored and less sweet Tawny Port. Tawny Port is served at room temperature as either an aperitif or a dessert wine. In the event that white grapes are used in the same way, the resulting semi-dry, dry, or extra dry wine is White Port and is served chilled as an aperitif. These types of Port are not dated, and are immediately ready for consumption.

Some producers of fine Tawny Port are allowed to label bottles as Ports With an Indication of Age. On the label of these bottles you will find the date of bottling and either a 10, 20, 30, or Over 40: this is an indication of the average age of the contents. Other specially marked Ports are those from a single harvest during an especially good year and aged in casks for over seven years. These bottles are known as Port with the Date of Harvest; the label will show the year of harvest and date of bottling. These wines can be consumed immediately, or several years after purchase.

The most prized type of Port is the single harvest wine produced during the most outstanding years. Called **Vintage Port**, it is aged for two to three years in casks and aged further in the bottle. It is labeled as L.B.V. with the vintage year and and date of bottling, and requires at least 10 years in the bottle before consumption. The final type of specially marked Port wine is the Late Bottled Vintage Port, which remains in a wooden cask from four to six years before bottling. L.B.V. Port requires at least 10 years in the bottle before consumption.

Best Vintages: 1908, 1912, 1927, 1945, 1955, 1963, 1966, 1978, 1904, 1917, 1906, 1920, 1924, 1927, 1928, 1934, 1935, 1937, 1947, 1948, 1950, 1955, 1957, 1960, 1963, 1966, 1970, 1975, 1977, 1978, 1980, 1982, 1983, 1985, 1987, 1988, 1989, 1991

Douro Port Labels: *Fonseca, Casa Ferreira, Taylor, Burmeister, Niepoort, Ramos Pinto, Quinta do Infatado, Quinta da Romaneira, Montez Champalimaud.*

Dão Demarcated Region

Located along the banks of the Dão River and its surrounding hilly countryside in the Montanhas region of northern Portugal, this demarcated region produces fine red and white wines. You can find good Dão wines in Portugal for as little as 300$00 per bottle.

The white (branco) wine from this zone appear citrus colored. It is a dry and smooth wine with an alcohol content of at least 11%. It is meant to be enjoyed cold and goes well with fish and seafood.

The red (tinto) wine from this zone is a ruby red color. The majority of red Dão wine develops a velvety rich flavor with an alcohol content of at least 11%. Meant to be enjoyed at room temperature, red Dão wine goes well with meat, fowl, hearty stews, and cheese.

The blended white wine is aged in casks for a minimum of six months and the blended red wine for 18 months before bottling, and can be consumed immediately or several years after production.

Best Vintages: 1970, 1980, 1983, 1985, 1961, 1964, 1967, 1969, 1971, 1974, 1975, 1987, 1991

Dão Labels: *Vinicola do Vale do Dão, Portas dos Cavaleiros, Duque de Viseu, Quinta do Roques, Grão Vasco, Caves Messias, Quinta da Alameda, Quinta dos Carvalhais.*

Bairrada Demarcated Region

Located amidst the tranquil countryside of the Costa de Prata region in northern Portugal (just above Coimbra), this demarcated region produces remarkable red wine as well as a small quantity of white, Rosé, and sparkling wines. You can find superb Bairrada wine in Portuguese wine shops and supermarkets for as little as 700$00 per bottle.

The white (branco) wine from this zone has a yellow color. It is a dry, fruity, and smooth wine with an alcohol content of at least 11%. It is served chilled and goes well with fish, pasta, salads, and light meals.

The red (tinto) wine from this zone has a garnet color. This wine develops a deeply rich full flavor with an alcohol content of at least 11%. It's best served at room temperature and goes well with meat and strong cheeses, or can be enjoyed alone.

Both the white and red wines are initially aged and fermented in casks before bottling, but the red must be at least 18 months old before going to market. They both can be consumed in a couple of years or many years after production. The red wine gets much better with age.

The Rosé wine is produced in limited quantities. This wine is made from a blend of red grapes and must be lightly fermented in an uncrushed form. It is further processed and quickly bottled. This wine is ready for consumption immediately after bottling and has a minimal alcohol content level of 11%. This wine can be dry, semi sweet, or sweet, and can sometimes have a slight sparkling quality. It's generally served chilled, and is used either as an aperitif, or offered with salads and hors d'oeuvres. Rosé labels from this region to look for include: Quinta do Carvalhinho, Nobilis, and João Pato.

Sparkling (espumante) wine is also produced in limited quantities. It is made from either red or white grape blends that are either fermented in large vats and transferred into bottles for immediate consumption, or are subjected to fermentation directly in the bottle. This wine can be sweet, medium sweet, medium dry, dry, or extra dry. The specially aged bottles are marked to let the consumer know how long the wine was aged before degorgement and recorking. These classifications include Reserva (1 to 2 years), Extra Reserva (2 to 3 years), or Velha Reserva (more than 3 years). Espumante labels from this region to look for include: Caves Messias, João Pato, Sogrape, Caves Alianca, Caves Borlido, Caves de Solar de São Domingos.

Best Vintages: 1960, 1962, 1970, 1975, 1980, 1983, 1963, 1966, 1972, 1974, 1978, 1985

Bairrada Labels: *Bucaco Tinto, Quinta de Pedralvites, Casa de Saima, Quinta do Valdoeiro, Quinta do Carvalhinho, Buçaco Branco, Encostas de Mouos, Luís Pato, Quinta da Rigodeira, Frei João, Adega Cooperativa de Vilarinho do Bairro, Caves Valdarcos, Caves São João, Adega Cooperativa de*

Souselas, Caves Messias, Quinta do Poco do Lobo, António Cardoso, Caves Alianca.

Colares Demarcated Region

This zone is located on the windswept hills of the Costa de Lisboa region near Sintra. These sand topped, clay based vineyards have been producing fine wine for over 600 years, and were not affected by the Pholloxera epidemic that wiped out most of Europe's grape varieties in 1865. This zone produces small quantities of high quality, strong red and white wines.

The white (branco) wine from this zone is citrus in color. This is a strong and slightly fruity, semi dry wine with an alcohol content of at least 10%. It is meant to be enjoyed quite cold and goes well with fish, cheese, and seafood.

The red (tinto) wine from this zone has a velvety quality and appears reddish brown in color. This robust dry wine reaches a minimal alcohol content of 10%, and is meant to be enjoyed at room temperature. Red Colares wine goes rather well with meat, or can be enjoyed alone.

The white wine is aged for 6 months and the red wine for 18 months before bottling and can be consumed several years after production. The red wine gets much better with age.

Best Vintages: 1964, 1966, 1966, 1975, 1983, 1984, 1960, 1967, 1968, 1969, 1971, 1973, 1979, 1980, 1981, 1982, 1985, 1987

Colares Labels: *Caves Visconde de Salreu, Real Vinicola, Tavares & Rodrigues, Adega Regional de Colares, Viuva José Gomes da Silva.*

Carcavelos Demarcated Region

This tiny zone is located near the seaside in the Costa de Lisboa region near Estoril. The few remaining vineyards still produce a fine topaz colored and somewhat nutty flavored fortified white wine known as Carcavelos. It is aged in a wooden cask for at least four years.

To boost the sugar content, a small amount of Moscatel de Setúbal is usually added. It ceases the fermentation process and has an alcohol level of about 19%. This wine is quite rare, and comes in either sweet or medium dry varieties. It is ready for immediate consumption as an aperitif. If you can find a bottle, expect to pay at least 4,000$00.

Some Carcavelos Labels: *Quinta da Bela Vista, Quinta do Barão, Quinta dos Pesos.*

Bucelas Demarcated Region

This small zone is located in the Trancão River Valley of the Costa de Lisboa region. This area's vineyards produce a fine sharp dry white wine known as Bucelas. It is fermented in open vats and later transferred to age in wood casks for at least 10 months before bottling.

This fine wine has a minimal alcohol content of 10.5% and is ready for immediate consumption. If you can find a bottle, expect to pay at least 1,400$00.

Best Vintages: 1966, 1971, 1974, 1976, 1979, 1980, 1983, 1985, 1987
Bucelas Labels: *Caves Velhas, Quinta da Romeira, Prova Regia.*

Moscatel de Setúbal Demarcated Region

This small zone is located between the Tejo and Sado Rivers in the southern portion of the Costa de Lisboa region around Setúbal. The local vineyards produce a rather sweet fortified dessert wine. It is made by adding a small amount of brandy to the must and later adding cut grapes to the mixture. This mixture is then aged for a year in casks before being strained and further aged before bottling. The longer the wine ages, the darker it becomes.

The regular honey colored five year old Muscatel is available throughout Portugal at prices starting at 1,100$00. The darker colored 20-year old Muscatel Roxo is rather rare and expensive but offers much deeper flavor. These wines have a minimum alcohol content of 16.5% and are ready for immediate consumption.

Some Muscatel Labels: *João Pires, José Maria da Fonseca, Herdade de Rio Frio.*

Algarve Demarcated Region

This large zone is located in several parts of the **Algarve** region including the areas near Lagoa, Lagos, Portimão, and Tavira. The refreshing wines of this area are produced in both red and white varieties. Since the region is blessed with lots of sun, the grapes tend to have a higher sugar content which leads to a higher alcohol content. Good wines from this region can be found in stores for as little as 400$00 per bottle.

The white (*Branco*) wine from this zone is usually dry and fruity with a pale straw coloring and a minimum alcohol content of 11.5%. This wine is served chilled with fish or as an aperitif.

The red (*Tinto*) wine from this zone is full flavored and fruity with a deep red coloring and a minimum alcohol content of 12%. It is served at room temperature and goes well with meat dishes.

The white wine is fermented in vats and aged for six months and the red wine for eight months before being bottled.

Adega Cooperativa da Lagoa is a very good label.

Other Good Wine Producing Areas

These areas all produce fine wines and spirits in every conceivable variety. If you are near any of these zones, you should try to sample their local wines:

Varosa, Chaves, Valpacos, Planalto Mirandes, Lafões, Encostas da Nave, Castelo Rodrigo, Pinhel, Cova da Beira, Encostas de Aire, Tomar, Alcobaça, Obidos, Santarém, Chamusca, Portalegre, Cartaxo, Alenquer, Coruche, Borba, Redondo, Reguengos, Vidigueira, Torres, Arruda, Palmela, Setúbal, Arrábida.

ONE OF THE VERY BEST WINERIES!

There is a fantastic wine that is not part of the extended demarcated regions. Under the direction of the famed Barons de Rothschild, a hand picked team of expert French wine makers including Arnaud Warnery and Joachim Roque (both trained at Chateau Lafite) have been producing simply outstanding red and white wines under the **Quinta do Carmo** *label since 1992. The winery is located near the Planicies' royal city of Estremoz on the property of an opulent 18th century quinta. Once the residence of a Portuguese king's mistress, it is now used as a vacation home by the wealthy Bastos family (who are partners with the Rothschilds in this wine venture).*

Using a combination of Alicante Bouchet, Trincadeira, Perequita, and Aragonez grape varieties that are matured in cement vats and oak barrels, the Quinta do Carmo red wines are unquestionably among the most delicious and full bodied Portuguese bottles available at any price. The whites are equally impressive and are made using a mixture of Rabo de Ovelba, Fernao Pires, Roupeiro, and Perrum grapes.

Keep your eyes out for these wines on fine restaurant's wine lists and at better wine shops in Portugal. These wines should cost between 2,400$00 and 5,000$00 each. I think they are the best in the country and are well worth twice the price!

COMMONLY USED WINE & SPIRIT NOTATIONS

Acido – Acidic
Adega – Wine Cellar
Adamado – Sweet
Aguardente – Firewater Brandy
Alcool – Alcohol
Bagaceira – Grape Marc Brandy
Branco – White
Brandimeil – Honey Brandy
Bruto – Extra Dry
Castas – Grapes
Caves – Wine Cave or Cellar
Cerveja – Beer
Colheita – Vintage
Demarcada – Demarcated
Doce – Sweet
Engarrafado – Bottled
Espumante – Sparkling Wine
Garrafa – Bottle
Garrafeira – Cellar Aged Vintage
  Reserves

Ginja, Ginginha – Cherry Brandy
L.B.V. – Late Bottled Vintage Port
  Wine
Maduro – Table Wine
Medronha – Berry Brandy
Meio – Medium
Produzido – Produced
Quinta – Estate
Região – Region
Reserva – Reserve Wine
Rosé – Rosé Wine
Seco – Dry
Selo de Origem – Seal of Origin
Tinto – Red
Vinha – Vineyard
Vinho – Wine
Vinho da Casa – House Wine
Vinho de Mesa – Table Wine
Vinicola – Wine Production
Velha – Old

10. BEST PLACES TO STAY

After visiting more than 300 hotels, estalagens, albergarias, pensoes, pousadas, quintas, villas, condos, and resorts throughout Portugal, these are the places I will not forget. I base my selection on a combination of factors including overall beauty, location, quality of service, value, cuisine, special features, attitude of the staff, and my own sense of what a hotel should offer. Of course, there are plenty of other fine hotels throughout the country, but these are the places I highly recommend.

The hotels are in the order that I would recommend them to a friend. Not all of these fine properties are expensive, but most tend to be in the middle to upper end of the price range.

1. PALACE HOTEL DO BUSSACO, *3050-Mealhada, Buçaco. Tel. (031) 930-101, Fax (031) 930-509. US and Canada bookings with The Small Hotel Co., Tel. 800/552-6844. Low season rack rates from 20,000$00, double room, BP; high season rack rates from 29,000$00, double room, BP. All major credit cards accepted.*

Super-deluxe hotel in a magnificent, converted royal palace.

Without a doubt, this is one of the most impressive hotels in all of Europe. Originally built as a royal hunting lodge for King Dom Carlos, this wonderful palace provides the perfect getaway for those seeking a romantic escape. The palace's exterior has incredible hand carved stonework and beautiful azulejos panels. The interior of this air conditioned hotel is more amazing than the exterior and boasts massive sitting rooms, opulent lounges filled with countless antiques, fine European works of art, a stunning central stairway, and patios overlooking both the adjacent forest and formal box gardens.

Each of the 66 completely unique, spacious rooms and suites contain antique and hand-crafted hardwood furnishings, beautiful designer fabrics, direct dial telephones, remote control satellite television, giant

KEY

1 Palace Hotel do Bussaco
2 Hotel Convento de Sao Paulo
3 Vila Vita Parc
4 Quinta de Corticada
5 Pousada Flor da Rosa
6 Monte do Casal
7 Sheraton Algarve
8 Hotel Lisboa Plaza
9 Hotel Infante Segres
10 Vilalara
11 Posada dos Loios
12 Palacio Estoril
13 Metropole Lisboa
14 Horta da Moura
15 Cabeco dos Tres Moinhos
16 Casa Fajera

BEST PLACES TO STAY

marble lined private bathrooms stocked with high quality hair and skin care products, extremely comfortable beds, executive style desks, and superb views. Adjacent to the hotel is a spectacular 17th century Carmelite monastery, a pond with swans, sumptuous box gardens, and several unforgettable walking trails through over 250 acres of pristine forest.

The gourmet cuisine, served in a dining room with frescos, is among the finest in Portugal. You may wish to dress up for dinner, but it is not mandatory. To accompany an unforgettable meal at the palace, I recommend a bottle of the Buçaco Reserva wine (Bairrada region) made in limited quantities in the palace's famous underground winery. For the bravest of guests, I suggest tasting the palace's legendary Águardente (Fire Water), the best I have ever tasted.

The service at this hotel is extraordinary, with a highly professional staff that is eager to please each guest. I have seen the manager, Sr. Castro Ribeiro, roll up his sleeves and help carry baggage and serve dinners during the busiest nights. The unique ambiance is warm and friendly and a couple of nights stay at this one-of-a-kind hotel is a must for all visitors to Portugal. Reservations should be made well in advance during the high season.

2. HOTEL CONVENTO DE SÃO PAULO, *Aldeia da Serra, Redondo. Tel. (066) 999-100, Fax (066) 999-104. US and Canada bookings with Alta Tours, Tel. 800/338-4191. Low season rack rates from 18,000$00, double room, BP; high season rack rates from 28,500$00, double room, BP. All Major Credit Cards Accepted.*
Deluxe hotel converted from a magnificent medieval convent.

Situated on the edge of a tranquil mountain range dotted with cork trees amidst over 1,400 acres of fine countryside some 20 minutes northeast of Évora, I can't imagine a better place to rest up and explore the historic walled villages of the Planicies region. This super deluxe 4 star hotel (it really deserves 5 stars) is housed in a wonderfully restored and converted 14th century convent with some 50,000 original azulejos (tiles) and fine medieval frescoes. Each inch of the convent reveals yet another piece of dramatic art.

The Convento de São Paulo's 21 luxurious rooms (converted from medieval monks' cells) are air conditioned and feature deluxe marble private bathrooms, a superb collection of antique and custom crafted hardwood and cast iron furnishings, fireplaces, remote control satellite television with free nightly movie screenings, in-room music systems, direct dial telephones, fresh cut flowers, and picturesque views of the mountains and valley below.

There are several lounges filled with card tables and plush sofas, a fantastic inner cloister courtyard, well maintained box gardens, fabulous fireside sitting rooms that double as fine art galleries, and a billiard room. A recently completed outdoor swimming pool and garden lined sun deck provide a wonderful retreat, while a walk up one of the many adjacent hillside trails is perfect for those wishing to explore the estate's grounds. Horseback riding is also available.

Breakfast in bed is a special event and includes homemade breads, fruits, and fresh squeezed juices from the convent's own lush gardens, while their complimentary full buffet breakfast includes eggs and sausage. The convent also has a spacious dining room that serves well prepared regional cuisine.

The service is extremely warm and typical of the region due to the hotel staff who are charming and sensitive local residents. The convent's policy is to hire and train people from the area as a way to benefit both the hotel and the surrounding community. The convent's management team, Sr. José Almeida and Sra. Maria Regina Moreira, are among the most delightful and hard working hotel managers I have ever met, and their experiences working at the Ritz during its heyday is revealed in the quality of service found here.

The ambiance is completely relaxed, and many guests can even be found wearing jeans during much of their stay.

3. VILA VITA PARC, *Armação de Pêra 8365, Alporchinos. Tel. (082) 315-310, Fax (082) 315-333. US & Canada bookings with Leading Hotels of the World, Tel. 800/223-6800. Low season rack rates from 26,000$00, double room, BP; high season rack rates from 56,400$00, double room, BP. All major credit cards accepted.*

Super deluxe seaside luxury resort and spa complex.

Vila Vita Parc is the most luxurious hotel in the Algarve. Situated on eighteen hectares of breathtaking landscaped gardens and seaside lawns dotted with palm trees and birds of paradise, this outstanding 5 star property is a magnificent example of Moorish influenced Algarvian architecture. The hotel has three separate sections that are each more stunning than the next: a five floor main building with sea-views; a 29 room residence wing; and 30 awesome duplex villas with family suites that are the most lavishly decorated and spacious rooms, junior suites, and memorable one and two bedroom suites found anywhere in Europe.

All accommodations come complete with one or more marble and hand painted tile private bathrooms with dual basins, individually controlled air conditioning and heating systems, handsome bleached pine furnishings, terra cotta floors embellished with either tapestries or azulejos murals, original oil paintings of Algarve scenery, 30 channel remote control color satellite televisions, direct dial telephones, a fully stocked mini-bar, hair dryer, retractable make-up mirrors, mini-safe, giant closets, and magnificent private terraces that look over massive gardens and pristine lakes full of swans and exotic flowers or a direct view of the seaside.

The hotel is a remarkable oasis of tranquillity and boasts an impressive array of world class services and facilities including a complimentary full American buffet breakfast served daily, several restaurants serving everything from light snacks to delicious formal gourmet meals, lounges with live music, five massive fresh water heated indoor or outdoor swimming pools fed by cascading water falls, a fully equipped health club with state of the art computerized exercise equipment as well as modern sauna and steam rooms, five outdoor tennis courts, an indoor racquetball court, a full service Vital Center spa center with a full range of optional natural health and beauty treatments, a unisex beauty salon, business meeting and elegant reception rooms, boutiques, a nine hole, par 3 pitch and put golf course, mini-golf, mountain bicycles, hundreds of extremely comfortable lounge chairs with sun umbrellas, 24 hour room service, snack and natural juice bars, cobble stone walking paths, plenty of free secure parking, a daily schedule of exciting activities, and of course a fantastic secluded white sand cove beach. During the high season there are also optional supervised children's programs each day, a water sports center featuring everything from para-sailing to water-skiing, dozens of interesting optional excursions including yacht cruises and jeep safaris, live entertainment nightly, a discotheque, special buffet dinners with exotic themes, organized walking tours of the cliffs that straddle the ocean, water aerobics classes, and more.

The clientele is upscale and arrive in search of sun and sand from Germany, the United Kingdom, and North America. The hotel's excellent Portuguese manager, Sr. Luís de Camoes, has a professional multilingual staff that know how to pamper every guest. Make sure to ask about their surprisingly affordable low season golf or tennis packages, doctor supervised spa treatment packages that include tailor-made specialty menus (low salt, low calorie, high protein, etc.).

Vila Vita Parc is, in my opinion, the most beautiful, relaxing, and romantic full service oceanfront resort hotel in all of Portugal, and I highly recommend it for those who can afford to stay here at least a few days and really spoil themselves.

4. QUINTA DA CORTICADA, *2040-Rio Maior, Outeiro da Corticada. Tel. (043) 478-182, Fax (043) 478-772. US and Canada bookings with Alta Tours, Tel. 800/338 4191. Low season rack rates from 15,000$00, double room, EP; high season rack rates from 16,000$00, double room, EP. Most major credit cards accepted.*

Luxury full service bed & breakfast on a private estate.

This quinta is a fantastic new manor house constructed in traditional style. It is located about 10 minutes from Rio Maior on several acres of exquisite rural countryside in the Costa de Prata region. This stately property consists of a lovely pastel colored mansion surrounded by breathtaking gardens, a calm lake full of swans and fish, a working rural farm, tennis courts, a great outdoor swimming pool and sun deck, an esplanade, lavish gardens, a barbecue area, and a private dining hall and business meeting center.

In the tradition of only the finest quintas, this inn keeps a full time staff of professional managers, cooks, and housekeepers. The staff are extremely nice, and the owners, the Nobre family, have spared no expense in converting their private farm into a wonderful and romantic hideaway. The ambiance here is casual with a touch of class.

The charming main house itself is filled with rare iconography, marble and parquet flooring, beautiful antiques, tapestries, a billiard room, oil paintings, cozy lounges, a large breakfast room, an honor bar, and large eight deluxe air conditioned rooms and suites with private bathrooms.

The area of Outeiro da Corticada is full of traditionally dressed local residents who can often be seen driving to work in horse drawn wagons. To get here, ask the staff to arrange private transfers from anywhere in Portugal, or rent a car or take a taxi from the train station in Santarém or the bus station in Rio Maior (about 15 minutes away).

Your efforts to get this far off the tourist path will be well rewarded the minute you arrive. The quinta offers delicious homemade meals if requested and confirmed in advance, nearby complimentary horse riding and optional lessons, and is commonly used as a retreat and meeting center for small corporate groups.

Quinta da Corticada is a fine example of how welcoming and well managed a Portuguese bed and breakfast can really be. A stay in a quinta like this will bring you close to seeing the soul of Portugal.

5. POUSADA FLÔR DA ROSA, *Flôr da Rosa, Crato. Tel. (045) 997-210, Fax (045) 997-212. US & Canada bookings with Marketing Ahead, Tel. 800/223-1356. Low season rack rates from 23,000$00, double room, BP; high season rack rates from 28,000$00, double room, BP. All major credit cards accepted.*

Deluxe government owned hotel in a converted monastery.

The wonderful pousada at Flôr da Rosa has been the subject of controversy since plans were announced a few years ago to restore and convert this ruined Gothic 14th century monastery (with 16th century Manueline additions) into a deluxe hotel. Now that the pousada has opened its doors to the public, its unique mixture of medieval architectural elements and ultra modern interior design features delights guests from around the world. For those of you interested in the preservation, restoration, and conversion of important historical landmarks, every part of this fine pousada is guaranteed to grab your attention.

Situated on acres of tranquil farmlands in the north central section of the Planicies region, Flôr da Rosa is near the city of Portalegre. This pousada represents a new approach to the creation of full service hotels: establishing them in rural areas never before on the itineraries of foreign travelers. This unusual and rather deluxe property features some 24 individually designed air conditioned rooms in a new wing attached to the monastery. All rooms have either king or double bed, sophisticated Memphis style designer furnishings, ultra-modern halogen lighting fixtures, rich hand carved wooden ceilings and floors, giant marble lined dual basin private bathrooms, remote control satellite televisions, mini-bar, mini-safe, direct dial telephones, executive style desks, large closets, and in many cases there are also large patios overlooking the adjacent countryside.

The public rooms include a fine regional restaurant, a quiet bar and reading room full of plush designer sofas, amazing restored cloisters, a relaxing outdoor swimming pool and sun deck, and even a small historical museum on the monastery and dozens of nearby prehistoric dolmens and megaliths.

The service is polite and friendly, with a staff of hard working area residents that seem to enjoy meeting people from other cultures and countries. The guests dress in a casual yet elegant manner, and tend to spend their time just relaxing and listening to the sounds of passing goats and sheep led to pasture by traditionally dressed shepherds. I really enjoyed my stay at this unusual pousada, and I think you will as well.

6. MONTE DO CASAL, *Cerro do Lobo, (Estói), Faro. Tel. (089) 951-03, Fax (89) 913-41. Low season rack rates from 12,480$00, double room, BP; high season rack rates from 24,240$00, double room, BP. Most major credit cards accepted.*

Deluxe country house surrounded by hillside gardens.

Located atop a picturesque hillside laced with flowering tropical plants some 11 kilometers north of Faro, this former 18th century farmhouse has been imaginatively converted into a wonderful deluxe inn and gourmet restaurant. Under the direction of owner/manager/chef Bill Hawkins (who has spent over a dozen years working in the finest hotels in London, Geneva, and Bermuda), Monte do Casal has become one of the best, and most welcoming, full service small luxury hotels in all of the Algarve. This unique English style country-house hotel provides its guests with simply outstanding accommodations, unsurpassed international cuisine, and a level of friendly personalized service that is hard to find anywhere else.

There are 13 beautifully furnished spacious rooms and suites that all feature large private bathrooms, powerful air conditioning and heating systems, direct dial telephones, comfortable furnishings, locally produced lithographs, and in most cases unforgettable private sun-drenched terraces (where your complimentary breakfast is served daily) that look past the adjacent hills and out onto the Atlantic.

Among the property's many excellent facilities are a fantastic international gourmet restaurant serving both lunch and dinner in either a romantic old coach house or peaceful garden-side terrace, an opulent bar complete with traditional Algarvian bamboo roofing, a large heated outdoor swimming pool and sun deck, a professionally surfaced outdoor tennis court, cozy sofas in fireside sitting rooms stocked with good English novels, and easy access by car to several of the country's best 18 hole championship golf courses and countless miles of pristine secluded sandy beaches.

Monte do Casal is a perfect base from which to explore the southern coast of Portugal and take day- trips to the nearby Spanish cities such as Sevilla. From here you can also visit almost any beach, sporting establishment, casino, traditional village, attraction, or major city in the Algarve. Popular with more mature English and European travelers, this exceedingly charming little property is among my favorite places to stay in the south of Europe, and I am sure that you will be happy to make it your home away from home.

7. SHERATON ALGARVE, *Praia da Falésia, Albufeira. Tel. (089) 501-999,Fax (089) 501-950. US & Canada bookings with Sheraton Luxury Collection, Tel. 800/325-3535. Low season rack rates from 27,000$00, double room, BP; high season rack rates from 45,500$00, double room, BP. All major credit cards accepted.*

Luxury full service golf resort hotel and beach club.

Located a stone's throw away from a series of dramatic cliffs resting above the pristine Praia da Falésia beach and just an eight minute drive from downtown Albufeira, this is another great place to stay in the Algarve. The Sheraton is a three level modern Árabesque styled hotel that is beautifully embellished with rare multicolored marbles, peaceful inner courtyards surrounded by Moorish styled arches and hand painted azulejos, cascading fountains, lush semi-tropical gardens, regal tapestries, tranquil reading rooms, and fine paintings by regional artists.

There are a total of 215 spacious ocean or garden-view rooms and suites that all feature deluxe marble bathrooms stocked with high quality hair and skin care products, powerful air conditioning systems, elegant custom designed hardwood furnishings, hand painted tile murals, remote control satellite television, executive desks, terra cotta tile floors, mini-bar, walk-in closets, direct dial digital telephones, mini-safe, and huge private terraces.

Thousands of guests come back year after year to enjoy an extensive array of services and facilities including a challenging 9 hole par 33 oceanside golf course complete with a pro shop and golf academy, huge indoor and outdoor fresh water swimming pools, three professionally surfaced night-lit tennis courts, a fully equipped health club with both a sauna and a jacuzzi, optional massage and spa treatments, a state of the art business center with computer access, car rental and excursion desks, several boutiques, unisex beauty salon, wine shop, well stocked newsstand and tobacconist, 24 hour room service, guest relations and concierge desks, a high season children's activities program, and several business meeting rooms.

The property's own sun-drenched beach can be reached via a four minute decent along a cliff-side footpath, and is home to a private beach club that offers optional water sports and snacks. The resort also has a superb and somewhat elegant a la carte gourmet restaurant, a casual dining room specializing in buffets and international cuisine, several snack bars and cafés, and a cocktail bar.

Every one of the 300 hard working employees here are extremely polite, friendly, and helpful, and they all work together as a team to make sure you become a repeat client. The Sheraton Algarve is the perfect place to stay for romantic couples of all ages, families, and even executives that want to experience a fine hotel with some of the highest levels of service and quality that the Algarve has to offer.

8. HOTEL LISBOA PLAZA, *Travessa do Salitre, 7, Lisbon. Tel. (01) 346-3922, Fax (01) 397-1630. US & Canada bookings with Marketing Ahead, Tel. 800-223-1356. Low season rack rates from 19,500$00, double room, BP; high season rack rates from 28,000$00, double room, BP. All major credit cards accepted.*

Charming full service medium sized hotel in central Lisbon.

This delightful family owned and operated 4 star hotel is one of the most welcoming places to stay in all of Lisbon. The Hotel Lisboa Plaza is situated one a quiet side street just a handful of steps away from downtown's famous Avenida da Liberdade. With one of the highest repeat client rates in the country, this superb property is equally popular among Portuguese, European, and North American visitors due to the simple fact that it is amazingly well managed and staffed by people that really seem to love working in the hotel business.

There are some 106 charming rooms and suites that have individually controlled air conditioning and heating systems, deluxe private bathrooms with marble tiles, remote control satellite television, direct dial telephones, antique etchings of Portugal in the old days, mini-bars, executive style desks, hair dryers, am-fm clock radios, custom designed hardwood furnishings, lavish fabrics and carpeting, large closets with mini-safes, and truly sound-proof windows with views over the city streets or nearby botanical gardens. There are also many connecting rooms, family sized units, and super deluxe suites that are impressively designed for the comfort of both vacationers and business travelers.

Among the full array of special services are one of the city's best traditional Portuguese cuisine restaurants serving excellent buffet lunches and dinners, complimentary full American breakfast (or continental breakfast in bed, if preferred) served daily, 24 hour room service, complete valet and concierge services, express laundry and dry cleaning, five state of the art business meeting rooms, a great turn of the century bar and cocktail lounge, spacious sitting rooms, dedicated non-smoking accommodations, and even optional secretarial and baby-sitting services upon request.

The best feature of the hotel is its unparalleled multilingual staff that are without a doubt the most professional and welcoming of any hotel in Lisbon. If you are looking for the perfect balance of a central location, beautiful rooms, fine cuisine, a full range of facilities, and outstanding service, this is certainly a great place to call home while in town.

9. HOTEL INFANTE DE SAGRES, *Praça Dona Filipa de Lancastre, 62, 4000, Porto. Tel. (02) 200-8101, Fax (02) 314-937. Year round rack rates from 29,000$00, double room, BP. All major credit cards accepted.*
Deluxe grand hotel in the heart of Porto.

In the city of Porto, an enchanting mansion has been converted into a 5 star deluxe hotel. Hotel Infante de Sagres regularly hosts heads of state and corporate chairmen who are in town on official business. As you pass through its elaborate entrance, the hotel's opulent interior is immediately apparent. The hotel boasts several fine public rooms and salons filled with art. There is also a curious courtyard patio and a unique spiral staircase just off the main lobby. The hotel's 80 large air conditioned and sound-proofed guest rooms and suites have period furnishings and huge bathrooms. The location is superb: to see the sights, all you have to do is walk one block and you will be on Ave. dos Aliados.

The service here is top notch with a staff to guest ratio of almost one to one. The staff are quite professional and are multilingual. The front desk is quite willing to give you advice and directions even if you are not a guest. The ambiance of the hotel is exclusive, serious, and formal, and most guests are wealthy businessmen. However, I have always been comfortable walking around the hotel with nice but casual clothes.

The hotel has an amazing main restaurant called the Dona Filipa. It has white glove service and some of the most elaborate silverware and china I have ever seen in Portugal. The extensive menu and wine list can be a bit overwhelming at first, but all you have to do is ask the head waiter for suggestions. In the warmer months, the patio is used as a less formal outdoor location to enjoy the same gourmet cuisine and wines that are served in the restaurant. A good choice for travelers who demand the finest in everything.

10. VILALARA HOTEL AND SPA, *Armação de Pêra. Tel. (082) 314-910, Fax (082) 314-956. US & Canada bookings with Lumina Tours, Tel. 514/858-1586. Low season rack rates from 25,000$00, double room, BP; high season rack rates from 48,000$00, double room, BP. All major credit cards accepted.*
Luxury oceanside hotel and thalasso therapy spa complex.

Vilalara is a superb 5 star hotel and spa situated just steps away from one of Portugal's most picturesque and private sandy coves. This remarkable hotel offers its international clientele a relaxing stay and some of Europe's most advanced sea water spa treatments.

There are 89 stunning junior suites housed in several traditional Iberian style low rise wings. Each of these spacious units come complete with giant dual basin marble bathrooms loaded with fine imported hair and skin care products, powerful air conditioning systems, remote control satellite televisions, in-room radios, tropical rattan furnishings, mini-bar, direct dial telephone, mini-safe, huge closets, hand painted tile decorations, exceedingly comfortable king or double beds, and fine covered balconies that usually overlook the ocean or swimming pools. Vilalara also offers over a dozen gigantic and deluxe one, two, and three bedroom apartments that include fully stocked kitchens, ensuite bathrooms, opulent living rooms, and hotel services.

The entire complex is surrounded by over 110,000 square yards of lavishly manicured gardens and lawns. In the center of the property is a unique state of the art Thalosso therapy spa staffed by European spa experts and currently ranked among the best in all of Europe. Many guests choose to reserve special programs aimed at helping reduce weight, cellulite, stress, or smoking problems with natural sea-water products. You will also be treated to soothing massages and aquatic work-outs.

Additionally, there are six of the most beautiful outdoor fresh and salt water swimming pools imaginable, several patios overlooking the ocean and the flowering gardens, six professionally surfaced tennis courts, a fully equipped exercise room, a complete children's activities program in the summer, room service, a superb beach with water sports, complimentary sauna and steam baths, a billiard room, walking trails, and more.

The cuisine here is excellent and is served with style in three different restaurants including an informal breakfast room and patio with the best buffet anywhere in the Algarve, a special dietetic restaurant where complete dinners add up to less than 1,000 calories, and a more elegant and formal main gourmet dining room with a huge al la carte menu of Portuguese specialties accompanied by live piano music.

Enjoy a cool drink at one of the bars,or sit at one of the oceanview tables on the sun deck and sip the afternoon away. There are also snack bars, game rooms, lounges, meeting rooms, and a particularly good room service menu. The front desk can provide recommendations as well as access to several nearby world class golf courses, local sport fishing outfitters, equestrian centers, sail boats, and all sorts of other activities.

The service here is professional and manager Wilfried Royer has worked hard to train his friendly team of Portuguese staff who make you want to stay here forever. With its prime location, delightful accommodations, peaceful ambiance, and excellent world class facilities, Vilalara is a wonderful place to relax and enjoy the best of the Algarve.

11. POUSADA DOS LÓIOS, *Largo do Conde de Vila Flor, 7000-Évora. Tel. (066) 240-51, Fax (066) 272-48. US & Canada bookings with Marketing Ahead, Tel. 800/223-1356. Low season rack rates from 23,000$00, double room, BP; high season rack rates from 28,000$00, double room, BP. All major credit cards accepted.*

Deluxe government owned hotel in a converted convent.

This large converted 15th century cloister is situated in the the most historic sector of central Évora in the Planícies region. The former convent's red roof and whitewashed facade give little clue to the unbelievable beauty that awaits each visitor. Inside this impressive pousada are marvelous remnants of the original chapter house, glass enclosed vaulted cloisters, fine public lounges, detailed stone carvings, ancient fountains, imposing arches, massive columns, and a huge grand hall.

The setting of this remarkable deluxe inn could not possibly be more enchanting. Directly in front of the pousada's main entrance you will see a famous Roman temple, and just steps away there are countless fine museums, cathedrals, palaces, mansions, and shops.

Many of the 30 guest rooms (and two suites), all with private bathrooms, were built from the remains of the convent's original monastic cells and are furnished with Arraiolos carpets and fine period pieces.

The ambiance here is rather laid back, as most guests tend to spend their days in Évora. At night things get formal and sophisticated, and proper attire at dinner is suggested. Their wonderful regional restaurant is in the most romantic part of the inn, and the cuisine is surprisingly good. Make sure that you ask in advance for a table since people who are not staying at the inn have been known to fill up the dining room.

There are many diversions available at the pousada including a swimming pool and esplanade. I have spent countless hours wandering around this place, and I am impressed every time I've stayed here.

12. HOTEL PALÁCIO ESTORIL, *Parque do Estoril, Es   Tel. (01) 468-0400, Fax (01) 468-4867. US & Canada Bookings with Leading Hotels of the World, Tel. 800/223-6800. Low season rack rates from 30,000$00, double room, BP; high season rack rates from 37,000$00, double room, BP. All major credit cards accepted.*

Deluxe old world luxury hotel, golf, and tennis resort.

There is no better hotel in Estoril than this lavish 5 star property just a two minute walk from the beach. The Palácio has been famous for several decades as having the finest rooms, service, and gourmet cuisine in the entire Costa de Lisboa.

There are 162 beautifully decorated air conditioned rooms and suites with deluxe marble bathrooms stocked with fine hair and skin care products, remote control satellite television, direct dial telephone, mini-bar, hair dryers, nice art deco furnishings, and terraces, in many cases. The property also offers its fortunate guests amazingly delicious meals at the opulent Four Seasons grill, a complimentary full American buffet breakfast, a nearby 18 hole championship golf course, private tennis center with 18 professionally surfaced courts, a huge outdoor swimming pool, several luxurious sitting rooms and lounges, a turn of the century style bar, a fully equipped health club with sauna, acres of private gardens, fine boutiques, meeting and reception rooms for businesses, a full time concierge, car rental and excursion desks, plenty of free outdoor and valet parking, baby-sitting and secretarial services, and easy access to the adjacent Estoril Casino complex.

The Hotel Palácio has a unique refined ambiance that draws a truly international clientele of vacationers and businessmen that demand the best quality from the hotels they choose.

13. HOTEL METROPOLE LISBOA, *Rossio, 30, Lisbon. Tel. (01) 346-9164, Fax (01) 346-9166. US and Canada bookings with The Small Hotel Co., Tel. 800/552-6844. Low season rack rates from 15,500$00, double room, BP; high season rack rates from 19,800$00, double room, BP. All Major Credit Cards Accepted.*

Small charming boutique hotel in the center of Lisbon.

The gem of Lisbon's hotels during the 1920's, the stunningly beautiful Hotel Metropole recently re-opened after a massive reconstruction and modernization project that took several years to complete. The De Almeida family has done a fantastic job in restoring the opulent art deco design of this extremely friendly hotel. Hotel Metropole is located in the heart of the Rossio, Lisbon's most famous and central square.

Now one of my favorite places to stay in this exciting city, this 3 star (it really deserves 4 stars) property features 36 lavishly appointed rooms all with individual air conditioning and heating systems, deluxe marble private bathrooms with hair dryers, original art deco handmade wood furnishings, direct dial telephone, mini-safe, remote control satellite television, opulent custom designed fabrics and carpeting, a selection of art and lithographs from the early part of this century, and large sound-proof windows or balconies that look out to either Rossio square or some of Lisbon's interesting side streets.

The Hotel Metropole is just steps away many of the city's best boutiques and famous historical sights and attractions. You are conveniently near municipal bus and metro stations, and taxis are plentiful. While there is no parking garage at the hotel, parking is available in one of several nearby garages. The staff here are friendly professionals from all over Portugal who help make your stay enjoyable. All prices include a delicious freshly prepared buffet breakfast.

14. QUINTA HORTA DA MOURA, *Reguengos de Monsaraz-7200. Tel. (066) 550-100, Fax (066) 550-108. Low season rack rates from 15,000$00, double room, BP; high season rack rates from 16,500$00, double room, BP. All major credit cards accepted.*
Rural county inn below an awesome walled city.

Horta da Moura is a fabulous new quinta on 40 acres of prime farm land just below the ancient and mysterious walled city of Monsaraz in the Planícies region. This deluxe and artistically designed estate offers a truly stress free environment for its guests. The inn's traditionally styled white and blue structures are surrounded by herds of sheep, fruit trees, prehistoric megaliths, Roman wells, vineyards, tennis courts, an equestrian center and riding academy, winery, patios, and a delightful swimming pool with a sun terrace.

Inside this architectural masterpiece you'll find comfortable lounges, a fine game room with a great billiard table, a bar, and wine cellars. The accommodations consist of 26 air conditioned rooms, junior suites, and a separate little self contained house, all with air conditioning, heating, satellite television, huge private bathrooms, and mini-bar. Most of the units also contain working fireplaces, patios, living rooms, local artwork, and handicrafts.

The service here is quite good, and the manager greets each guest personally. Horta da Moura's ambiance is casual and down to earth, and guests are made to feel as though they are staying in a friend's home.

The inn also offers a fine regional restaurant with special dishes created from a variety of produce and cheese from their own farm. The large wine list includes local wines from their huge cellar and winery. You may never be offered these wines anywhere else. The inn can provide wonderful excursions including jeep safaris, horseback and carriage rides, river trips on the nearby Guadiana River, and tours to local sights.

15. CABEÇO DOS TRÊS MOINHOS, *EN-1, Alto da Serra, Rio Maior-2040. Tel. (043) 991-165, Fax (043) 991-363. Midweek rack rates from 6,000$00, double room, EP; weekend rack rates from 7,000$00, double room, EP. Cash only - No credit cards accepted.*
Old windmills converted into an unusual romantic inn.

This tiny mountain-top hideaway is one of the most unusual inns I have ever seen. There are a series of three standing 18th century windmills that have been converted, amazingly, to one and two bedroom duplex apartments. Owned and operated by the hard working Coito family, the inn offers its guests the chance to stay in beautifully round apartments that feature private bathrooms, ground floor living rooms with wood burning stoves and television, direct dial telephone, antique style furnishings, an assortment of locally produced handmade quilts, mini-refrigerators, exposed beam ceilings, original 18th century stone walls, chapel ceilings, small windows looking out to the valleys and mountains, and more charm than you can imagine.

The inn also offers horseback riding, great hiking trails through the adjacent lush hillsides full of wild rabbits and wild spice plants, an open air grill, plenty of privacy, and a friendly innkeeper. This is a wonderful place to get away from it all with someone special.

16. CASA FAJARA, *Sítio do Rio, Carrapateira. Tel. (082) 971-19, Fax (082) 971-86. Low season rack rates from 6,500$00, double room, EP; high season rack rates from 10,000$00, double room, EP. Cash and travelers checks only - No credit cards accepted.*

Rural Bed & Breakfast surrounded by a nature reserve.

Located in the heart of the federally protected Parque Natural da Costa Vincentina nature reserve near Sagres, the Casa Fajara is one of the only small, charming rural inns in the Algarve. This exceptional, peaceful and affordable country bed and breakfast, managed by Henrique Ferra, was converted from a typical farmhouse and continues to be one of Portugal's best kept secrets. There are nine medium sized double rooms containing complete private bathrooms, a comfortable bed, direct dial telephone, individually controlled heating systems, large private terraces overlooking 600 hectares of lush rural valley, and exposed beam ceilings in some cases.

The inn features a huge professionally equipped kitchen for the guests to use, a nearby regional restaurant serving delicious steaks and fresh seafood, a well maintained outdoor swimming pool and sun deck, a television lounge with fireplace, a game room and library with a massive snooker table, private stables that offer rides on Luso-Arabian horses to awesome cliffs and the coastline, a tennis court, countless hiking trials through unspoiled landscape, guided day trips to superb fishing spots for catching sea bream, and jeep safaris. Casa Fajara's locations is perfect for car and bicycle rides to several secluded white sand beaches.

The whole idea here is for the guests to feel at home and to meet fellow travelers from both Portugal and the rest of Europe. During the evenings you can either prepare your own dinners or walk down the road to their excellent and affordably priced Sítio do Rio regional restaurant. During the day most guests either relax by the pool, take a four minute walk down to the amazingly beautiful Praia da Bordeira beach in the Parque Natural da Costa Vincentina, or drive a few minutes away to explore several traditional fishing villages lined with old whitewashed houses. Casa Fajara is a remarkable undiscovered gem for those that desire a laid back ambiance and a unique glimpse into the last undeveloped corner of the Algarve.

11. LISBON

Lisbon – *Lisboa* – the capital of Portugal, is among the friendliest of European cities. Located about 18 km from the Atlantic Ocean, this bustling city is home to more than 1.3 million residents. This is Portugal's center of politics, finance, commerce, economic power, arts and entertainment.

The pace of downtown Lisbon is rather hurried and often confusing to first time visitors. Each business day starts with a seemingly endless stream of autos and commuters pounding the pavement near the rail, ferry, and bus stations. The center of town is filled with people of all classes searching for a quick, strong coffee before work. Many people are well educated and speak a fair amount of English. The huge banks that dominate the city's skyline are proof that there is serious business and economic growth taking place in this city.

While the busy downtown commercial areas near the **Baixa** seem to run at full speed for most of the day, the older and more traditional districts, such as the **Alfama**, **Bairro Alto**, **Chiado**, **Belém**, **Alcântara**, and **Lapa**, have a more laid back and natural rhythm. Vendors stand outside their establishments and chat with their customers and those just passing by. In the markets, fishmongers can be heard extolling the virtues of the day's catch. Manual laborers still hand-cut and set square cubes of black and white rock into the many steep and winding ancient streets. Children walk to school clutching the bottom of their grandmothers' dresses. And yes, the old village way of life can still be found in some parts of Lisbon.

In just a few days, you can experience this blend of old and new by visiting impressive art collections, eating inexpensive regional cuisine, exploring neighborhoods and walking past hundreds of impressive old homes, shopping for bargain priced fine European goods, and enjoying a late night out. Lisbon is a relatively safe, inexpensive, and welcoming city to explore.

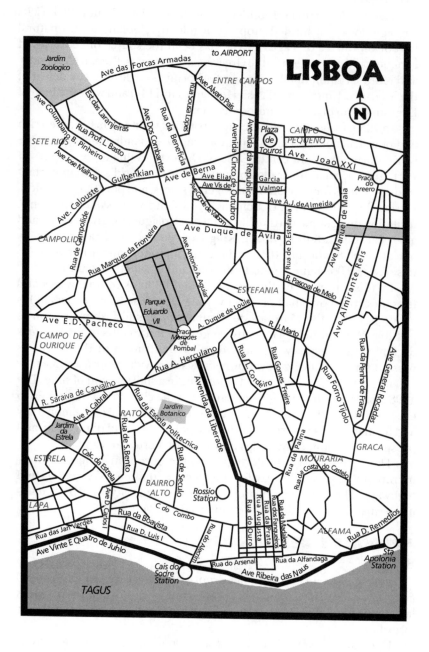

HISTORY

Lisbon was originally founded by the Phoenicians about 1200 B.C. Its strategic location, nestled atop seven hills overlooking a safe natural harbor on the **Tejo** (**Tagus**) River, has been the source of centuries of conquest and occupation by the Greeks, Carthaginians, Romans, Visigoths, and Moors. Lisbon finally came under Portugal's rule after the defeat of the Moors by King Dom Afonso Henriques in 1147, and with the help of English, German, and Flemish crusaders.

In 1255, Lisbon became the capital of what would soon become a rich and powerful nation. The Portuguese empire expanded throughout the world during the 15th century Age of Discoveries due to the success of Portuguese navigators. Lisbon became one of the world's most important trading centers for precious metals, gems, spices, and porcelain products. During the 16th century, Lisbon was thrown into a series of tragic events, including devastating earthquakes, the black plague, the Inquisition, and a 60-year annexation by Spain. **King Dom João IV** of Bragança finally defeated the Spanish in 1640 and created an independent Portugal. To this day, the Portuguese tend to distrust and dislike the Spanish.

In 1755, a major earthquake, followed by massive tidal waves and fires, destroyed over half of the city. King Dom José I gave orders to his Prime Minister, the **Marquês de Pombal**, to rebuild Lisbon as soon as possible. With the help of inventive engineers and architects, the Marquês de Pombal successfully redesigned and rebuilt much of the city to its present form, featuring downtown streets and wide central avenues.

Life returned to normal in Lisbon within a short period of time. The 1908 assassination of King Dom Carlos I in the city's Praça do Comércio eventually led to the revolution that marked the downfall of the monarchy and formation of a new republic. Lisbon grew in size and population, and prospered economically, and is now a major European capital.

The 1986 inclusion of Portugal into the European Economic Community (EEC) paved the way for the recent addition of skyscrapers and highways. The new construction makes Lisbon a city with both ultramodern and ancient elements existing side by side.

ARRIVALS & DEPARTURES

By Air

Portugal's main international airport, **Aeroporto de Lisboa**, *Tel. (01) 802-060 or (01) 848-110,* is usually referred to as **Portela** owing to its location in the suburb of Portela some 8 km (5 miles) north of the heart of Lisbon.

Upon arrival, you will be bused from your plane to the new arrivals wing and an immigration check point. You'll be asked to present your passport, after which you follow the signs to the baggage claim area, grab a free luggage cart if you need one, load up, and clear customs.

After passing through customs, you enter a small lounge that has a 24-hour currency exchange kiosk, a few tourist information booths, and several limo drivers and private guides holding up signs for their clients. Just past the arrivals lounge is the entrance to the main terminal wing where you will see all the major car rental kiosks, another tourist information booth, and the main taxi stand.

If you're supposed to meet someone here and can't locate them, the airport information booth will page them over the public address system.

Almost everybody at the airport speaks English and is happy to assist you. The airport also has a cafeteria, snack shop, café, bar, and some small gift shops. There are also duty-free stores for departing passengers only.

From the Airport to the City

A **taxi** ride should cost about 1850$00 for up to four passengers, plus 300$00 for luggage, to any downtown location unless traffic is intolerably bad. Taxis are found at most hours just in front of the arrivals terminal. Make sure you have enough Portuguese currency to cover your ride.

A great **express bus**, # 91 (sometimes referred to as the Aero-bus), runs from the front of the airport's arrival area and stops at major city plazas throughout central Lisbon on the way to Rossio and Praça do Comercío squares (downtown). Buses run in each direction every 20 minutes between 7:00am and around 8:00pm. Tickets can be bought on the bus, cost 430$00 per person each way, and include free use of the Lisbon bus and tram system on the same day. A special 3-day round-trip airport transport pass, including three days of unlimited bus and tram rides, can be purchased on the bus for 1000$00 per person.

Carris public transit authority buses such as lines #5, #8, #22, #44, #45, and #83 depart across the street from the airport's Shell gas station (turn left after exiting the arrivals terminal and follow the road for 150 yards), continues to many stops in downtown Lisbon, and costs only 150$00 per person. These buses do not usually let travelers with lots of luggage board. If you have several pieces of luggage, I suggest taking the faster and more comfortable express bus mentioned above.

By Bus

Bus service is provided by a recently privatized bus company. You purchase bus tickets at the main bus station and you can get their current schedule at the same time.

For more information call or visit the following:
• **Main Bus Station**, *Avenida Casal Ribeiro, 18, Tel. (01) 577-715*
• **Main Bus Office**, *Ave. Columbano B. Pinheiro, 86, Tel. (01) 726-7123*

By Car

Rental cars can be picked up or dropped off at either at the airport or at a downtown location. Last minute bookings are subject to heavy surcharges. If you are travelling to Portugal from another European country, make sure you have insurance for Portugal. And of course, if you are departing Portugal by a rental car, make sure you have insurance coverage for every country you'll visit.

- **Avis Rent a Car**, *Ave. Praia da Victoria, 12, Tel. (01) 356-1176*
- **Hertz Rent a Car**, *Ave. 5 de Outubro, 10, Tel. (01) 579-027*
- **Europcar Rent a Car**, *Ave. António A. de Aguiar, 24, Tel. (01) 353-5119*

By Ferry

Ferry service across the Tejo River to Barreiro, Montijo, Seixal, Cacilhas, Trafaria, and other points is provided by either **CP** or **Transtejo**, a private company. Ferries depart from numerous docks along the Tejo River.

For more information call or visit the following:

- **CP Ferry Information**, *Terreiro de Paço, Tel. (01) 877-179*
- **Transtejo Ferry Information**, *Lisbon, Tel. (01) 879-035*

By Train

CP rail offers extensive train service into and out of Lisbon from most points in Portugal. For tickets and schedules please stop by any travel agency or contact CP Rail. Several southern train routes require ferry connections. Ferries to the city of **Barreiro** (just across the river) can be boarded at the **Terreiro de Paço** fluvial station.

For more information call or visit the following:

- **CP Rail Head Office**, *Rua de Vitor Cordon, 45, Tel. (01) 346-3181*
- **Santa Apolónia Train Station**, *Ave. Infante D. Henrique, Tel. (01) 876-025*. This is the main international and inter-city station.
- **Cais de Sodré Train Station**, *Cais de Sodré, Tel. (01) 347-0181*. Trains to Estoril, Cascais, mass transit tickets and passes are sold in the main building.
- **Rossio Train Station**, *Rossio, Tel. (01) 346-5022*. Trains to Sintra and other areas depart from this station.

ORIENTATION

Lisbon is located in central Portugal, on the northern bank of the Tejo River and about 20 km (12 miles) from the Altantic Ocean. The sun-drenched southernmost reaches of Portugal are about a three hour drive away, while the mountainous northern reaches require a six hour drive.

Downtown Lisbon is divided into higher and lower levels, while the rest of the city is relatively flat. Elevators, known as Elevadores, will transport you from one level to the next. There are several small neighborhoods, or barrios, that make up the higher part of town. In many cases, these quaint neighborhoods date back to either Moorish, Roman or medieval times. As you wander around Lisbon, remember that the Tejo River and the giant Ponte 25 de Abril suspension bridge are usually visible to the south: this will help you figure out which direction you are moving in should you get turned around.

During the intensive reconstruction of the city after the 1755 earthquake, several major downtown streets were turned into wide avenues, such as Avenida da Liberdade, that run primarily north and south. In turn, these avenues run into traffic circles that can be murder to navigate. Many of the streets do not run on a grid, so a map is really a necessity. While this can make the city confusing to get around, it is part of the history and charm of the city.

GETTING AROUND TOWN

Public transportation is inexpensive (usually 70$00 or 150$00 per ride) and efficient. Mass transit is well organized, and with the exception of a few pick-pockets, extremely safe at all hours. Hours of operation for the Metro, Carris, and Elevadors are usually from 6:30am until 1am daily, and for the Electricos from 6:30am until midnight daily.

I suggest you figure out how much you intend to travel by mass transit and then purchase one of the several discount passes sold at major stations. There are discounted unlimited use one day passes for 430$00 and three day passes for 1000$00 (per person) that are valid on all Carris operated systems (not the metro). The Carris transportation authority produces a map of their mass transit routes called the **Planta dos Transportes Publicos da Carris** that the main Turísmo office in the Palácio Foz at the Praça dos Restauradores will give you for free.

A special unlimited use tourist pass, valid on all city center mass transportation systems including metro, bus, funicular, and trolley lines, is available to foreigners only (you must bring a valid passport) and can be bought a most major transport terminals, including the Cais de Sodre station, for 1550$00 for four days and 2190$00 for seven days.

Some private companies sell maps of Lisbon that include public transportation routes and are available from newsstands throughout the city.

By Bus

Dozens of buses, autocarros, are operated by the Carris public transportation authority and are a good way of getting around in central

Lisbon. Tickets for inner-city buses cost 150$00 each way and can be purchased on the bus.

By Car

Rental cars can be picked up either at the airport or at a downtown location. Last minute bookings are subject to heavy surcharges.
For more information call or visit the following:
• **Avis Rent a Car**, *Ave. Praia da Victoria, 12, Tel. (01) 356-1176*
• **Hertz Rent a Car**, *Ave. 5 de Outubro, 10, Tel. (01) 579-027*
• **Europcar Rent a Car**, *Ave. António A. de Aguiar, 24, Tel. (01) 353-5119*

By Elevador

There are four funicular systems called Elevadores, also operated by Carris, that connect the higher elevation districts of Lisbon such as the Barrio Alto and Barrio do Castelo with the lower lying central districts around the Rossio. Tickets on these funiculars cost the same as bus tickets.

By Ferry

You can also cross the Tejo River by ferry (fluvial) at Lisbon's river front and several communities across the river such as **Barreiro** and **Cacilhas**; check at the Terrio de Paço ferry station (Terminal Fluvial) across from Praça do Comercio for specific details.

By Metro

Metro (Metropolitano de Lisboa) stations are marked with a large "M" above the entrance. Currently, there are only two connecting Metro lines (you may need to transfer from one metro line to another to get to some destinations), with a total of 25 stops at or near most areas of interest. By the year 2001, there should be several more lines and dozens of additional stations.

Tickets and metro maps are available at ticket booths in the Metro stations, and you can also buy tickets from vending machines. Metro tickets are 70$00 each or you can purchase a book of 10 tickets for 550$00. There are also unlimited use passes: 200$00 for a one day pass, 600$00 for a seven day pass, and 2,000$00 for a 30 day pass.

Make sure you put the ticket into the self-service ticket validation box before descending to the subway platform. Smoking is tolerated in metro stations but not in subway cars.

By Taxi

Taxis are inexpensive but are known for overcharging foreigners. Watch out for baggage overcharges, the maximum is 300$00 per ride, and the illegal use of night rates during the day. The normal "T-1" weekday meter rate is used from 6:00am until 10:00pm and starts at 250$00 for the first 400 meters and adds an additional 10$00 for every 175 meters traveled within the city limits, or 52$00 per kilometer if going outside of Lisbon proper.

The special "T-2" meter rate is used all day on weekends, holidays, and weekday evenings from 10:00pm until 6:00am and starts at 250$00 for the first 250 meters and adds an additional 10$00 for every 130 meters traveled within the city limits, and 52$00 per kilometer if going outside of Lisbon proper. Taxis may also be hired for sightseeing at the rate of 1,540$00 an hour.

SAVE MONEY SEEING THE SIGHTS

The Lisbon City Council's Tourism Department offers visitors the **Lisboa Card,** *which entitles the card holder to unlimited use of almost every local bus, metro, funicular, and tram line, as well as entrance to 27 municipal museums, palaces, and important national monuments. It also entitles the card holder to discounts of 5% – 65% on entrance fees to many other popular services, shops, attractions, river cruises, cultural performances, aero-bus airport express bus, and sight-seeing trips.*

Included in the price of the card is a handy 54 page booklet describing all participating venues and establishments. For adults, cards costs 1500$00 for 24 hours, 2,500$00 for 48 hours, and 3,250$00 for 72 hours. The Lisboa Card is about 65% less for children up to 11 years old. These cards can be purchased at the Lisboa Card's main office. It's open daily from 9:00am until 5:00pm and is located just two blocks up from the Rossio on the Rua Jardim do Regedor, 51. Cards can also be purchased at Jeronimos Monastery and the National Museum of Ancient Art.

A vacant taxi should have its "taxi" light, on top of the car, illuminated. You flag them down in much the same way you would in any North American city, or you can go to one of many taxi lines and wait your turn. Recently, a law was passed that requires all taxis to post their price regulations in several languages including English. Good luck trying to read this sign while being bounced around.

If you have any further questions about transportation within Lisbon, visit one of the several Turismo offices located throughout the city, ask your hotel's concierge for help, or call one of these numbers:

• **Metro Information**, *Ave. Fonte de Melo, 28, Tel. (01) 575-974*
• **Bus, Tram, Elevador Information**, *Rua 1 de Maio, 103, Tel. (01) 363-2021*
• **Lisboa Card Information**, *Rua Jardim do Regedor, 50, Tel. (01) 343-3673*

By Train

For those of you who are staying in or visiting **Cascais** and **Estoril**, a fast and comfortable electric train runs frequently between these points and the Cais de Sodré train station in Lisbon. Tickets cost about 175$00 each way and provide an excellent alternative to getting stuck in terrible commuter traffic.

By Trolley

The electric trolley system called Electricos, also operated by Carris, is a very effective means of local rapid transit. The trolley stops are marked with a sign reading *paragem*. Tickets for the electricos cost the same as bus tickets.

WHERE TO STAY

Very Expensive

HOTEL DA LAPA, *Rua do Pau da Bandeira, 4. Tel. (01) 395-0005, Fax (01) 395-0665. USA and Canada bookings with Leading Hotels of the World, Tel. 800/223-6800. Year round rack rates from 46,000$00, double room, EP. All major credit cards accepted.*

The chic Hotel da Lapa has now become one of Portugal's most expensive and exclusive hotels. There are 87 beautifully designed air conditioned rooms and suites located about a 10 minute drive from the center of the city in the embassy row district of the Lapa neighborhood. This hotel has become a second home to heads of state and the most demanding members of the international jet set. Facilities include a bar, a good restaurant, a great pool, sauna, boutiques, and valet garage. They are usually sold-out well in advance, so call ahead if you wish to reserve a room at any time of the year.

RITZ INTER-CONTINENTAL LISBOA, *Rua Rodrigo da Fonseca, 88. Tel. (01) 383-2020, Fax (01) 383-1783. US and Canada bookings with Inter-Continental Hotels, Tel. 800/327-0200. Year round rack rates from 38,000$00, double room, EP. All major credit cards accepted.*

Located across from the tranquil Eduardo VII park, this super-deluxe 5 star business class hotel has had a great reputation for service and quality since it first opened a few decades ago. A modern high rise of some 15,000 tons of marble and precious stone, the Ritz has 270 lavish rooms and suites that are all air conditioned and contain deluxe private bathrooms, mini-bar, direct dial telephone, remote control satellite television, nice furnishings, and great views in many cases. The more luxurious rooms and suites also have fax modems, executive desks, and other special amenities. Facilities include several restaurants, a famous bar, a health club, business meeting and convention rooms, a snack bar, underground parking, a terrace, concierge, several boutiques, a newsstand, currency conversion desk, 24 hour room service, a talented staff, and a regal ambiance.

HOTEL TIVOLI LISBOA, *Avenida da Liberdade, 185. Tel. (01) 353-0181, Fax (01) 357-9461. US and Canada bookings with Utell, Tel. 800/448-8355. Year round rack rates from 39,250$00, double room, BP. All major credit cards accepted.*

A favoured address among top executives, the Tivoli offers 330 modern air conditioned rooms with satellite television, direct dial phone, comfortable furnishings, large windows, mini-bar, and more. It is situated in a pleasant central location. The hotel's facilities include two restaurants, a nice bar, business meeting rooms, a swimming pool, barber shop, and parking.

Expensive

SHERATON LISBOA HOTEL & TOWERS, *Rua Latino Coelho, 1. Tel. (01) 357-5757, Fax (01) 354-7164. US & Canada bookings with Sheraton, Tel. 800/325-3535. Year round rack rates from 35,000$00, double room, BP. All major credit cards accepted.*

This deluxe, executive class 5 star hotel just a few blocks from the Avenida da Liberdade and the Parque Eduardo VII park is among Lisbon's most prestigious addresses for visiting businessmen. This modern tower offers some 384 newly renovated and redecorated rooms and suites all featuring private marble bathrooms, individually controlled air conditioning systems, remote control satellite televisions with optional pay per view movies, direct dial telephones, executive desks, hair-dryers, mini-bar, mini-safe, king or twin beds, wall to wall carpeting, large windows looking over the downtown quarters, and lots of space.

For those looking for special amenities such as a private lounge and butler service, the hotel's top four floors are dedicated to special Executive Club accommodations that include optional fax machine and computer modem ports, speaker phones, additional workspace, plush bathrobes, a complimentary wet bar, a private breakfast room, daily newspapers, and even a 4:00pm check-out time.

Among the extensive facilities at the hotel are two good restaurants serving international cuisine, 24 hour room service, a daytime concierge, car rental and excursion desks, giant business meeting and reception rooms, a panoramic top floor bar with live music on most nights, several boutiques, an outdoor swimming pool, optional use of a work out room, a business center featuring computers and Internet access, full porter service, a taxi stand, electronic message retrieval, express check-out, secure underground parking, an adjacent shopping center, and special privileges for Sheraton Club International members.

HOTEL ALTIS, *Rua Castilho, 11. Tel. (01) 314-2496, Fax (01) 353-4496. US and Canada bookings with Golden Tulip, Tel. 800/344-1212. Low season round rack rates from 26,000$00, double room, BP; high season rack rates from 32,000$00, double room, BP. All major credit cards accepted.*

This modern and surprisingly comfortable 5 star hotel is one of the best equipped and managed properties in the city. Located halfway between the Rossio and the Praça Marquês de Pombal in central Lisbon, the Altis has 303 large air conditioned rooms and suites that feature deluxe private bathrooms, remote control satellite television, nice furnishings, am-fm clock radio, hair dryers, direct dial telephone, and mini-bar. Facilities include two good restaurants, 24 hour room service, a lounge, child care services, indoor heated swimming pool, boutiques, private parking, business meeting rooms, express laundry and dry cleaning, a health club, and a good staff. Highly Recommended.

HOTEL ALFA LISBOA, *Ave. Columbano B. Pinheiro, Tel. (01) 726-2121. Year round rack rates from 27,500$00, double room, BP. All major credit cards accepted.*

A huge 5 star hotel, this is a great choice for those in Lisbon on business. The 440 air conditioned rooms are well designed and the service is excellent. Facilities include bar, restaurants, pool, sauna, health club, TV, shops, mini-bars, and parking.

YORK HOUSE, *Rua Janelas Verdes, 32. Tel. (01) 396-2435, Fax (01) 397-2793. US and Canada bookings with The Small Hotel Co., Tel. 800/552-6844. Low season rack rates from 20,900$00, double room, BP; high season rack rates from 30,000$00, double room, BP. Most major credit cards accepted.*

The York House is a famous small luxury inn and restaurant located in a peaceful converted 16th century convent near the Tejo River. There are 37 antique filled rooms and suites all with private bathrooms, a new central air conditioning system, direct dial telephones, cable television, huge closets, and plenty of charm. The hotel also boasts a wonderfully peaceful inner courtyard and garden, a full service gourmet restaurant with an exotic menu, an opulent wood paneled bar, and a good staff. I have been told that some scenes from the movie *The Russia House* were filmed here. The hotel tends to be sold-out often so make your reservations in advance and ask for a courtyard-view room. Highly Recommended.

PARK ATLANTIC HOTEL, *Rua Castilho, 149. Tel. (01) 690-900, Fax (01) 383-3231. Year round rack rates from 33,500$00, double room, EP. All major credit cards accepted.*

Formerly known as the Meridian Lisboa, this large 330 room executive hotel and conference center is located just across from the Eduardo

VII park in the business center of the city. The hotel offers some nicely designed rooms and suites, all have private marble bathrooms with scales, air conditioning, direct dial telephone, mini-bar, satellite television with pay per view movies, mini-safes, hair dryers, radios, and great park views in with many rooms. There are also special non-smoking floors, rooms for those who are physically challenged, boutiques, restaurants, room service, an underground garage, laundry service, business meeting rooms and conference facilities, a sauna, currency exchange desk, and a business center with secretarial services.

HOTEL SOFITEL, *Avenida da Liberdade, 123. Tel. (01) 342-9202, Fax (01) 342-9222. US and Canada bookings with Resinter, Tel. 800/221-4542. Low season rack rates from 29,000$00, double room, EP; high season rack rates from 35,000$00, double room, EP. All major credit cards accepted.*

This brand new French owned 4 star hotel is situated directly on the most prestigious section of downtown Lisbon's largest avenue. There are some 170 air conditioned rooms and suites with private bathrooms, satellite television, mini-bar, direct dial phones, and large windows. There is also a good restaurant, business meeting rooms, a private garage, a piano bar, and secretarial services.

Moderate

HOTEL METROPOLE LISBOA, *Rossio, 30. Tel. (01) 346-9164, Fax (01) 346-9166. US and Canada bookings with The Small Hotel Co., Tel. 800-552-6844. Low season rack rates from 15,500$00, double room, BP; high season rack rates from 19,800$00, double room, BP. All Major Credit Cards Accepted.*

This superb, newly re-opened art deco boutique hotel has great views of the Rossio. There are 36 beautiful rooms with private bathrooms, satellite television, art deco furnishings, direct dial telephone, air conditioning, designer fabrics, custom wall-to-wall carpeting, and nice city views. Facilities include bar, lounge, breakfast room, and a great location. This hotel is a great value.

Selected as one of my *Best Places to Stay* (see Chapter 10 for more details).

HOTEL LISBOA PLAZA, *Travessa do Salitre, 7. Tel. (01) 346-3922, Fax (01) 397-1630. US & Canada bookings with Marketing Ahead, Tel. 800-223-1356. Low season rack rates from 19,500$00, double room, BP; high season rack rates from 24,300$00, double room, BP. All major credit cards accepted.*

The Hotel Lisboa Plaza is situated on a quiet side street steps away from the famous Avenida da Liberdade. There are 106 beautifully designed rooms and suites that feature air conditioning, deluxe private marble bathrooms, satellite television, direct dial phones, antique artwork, mini-bar, executive style desks, hair dryers, am-fm clock radios, elegant hardwood furnishings, mini-safes, and sound-proof windows with great city or botanical garden views, complimentary breakfast served in the restaurant or in your room, valet and concierge services, express laundry and dry cleaning, business meeting rooms, a tranquil bar and cocktail lounge, and non-smoking rooms. The staff is multilingual and among the best and friendliest in Lisbon.

Selected as one of my *Best Places to Stay* (see Chapter 10 for more details).

AS JANELAS VERDES, *Rua das Janelas Verdes, 47. Tel. (01) 396-8143, Fax (01) 396-8144. US and Canada bookings with Utell, Tel. 800-448-8355. Low season rack rates from 18,500$00, double room, BP; high season rack rates from 26,000$00, double room, BP. Most major credit cards accepted.*

This peaceful inn was built inside the fantastically converted 18th century mansion of Eça de Queirós, a famed Portuguese writer. Situated just above the Tejo River and just down the block from the fabulous National Museum of Ancient Art, this romantic 4 star property is like staying in the opulent residence of a rich friend!

There are 17 uniquely designed air conditioned rooms complete with deluxe marble and tile bathrooms, remote control satellite television, period furnishings, direct dial telephone, and natural sunlight pouring in from large picture windows that in some cases overlook the waterfront. Facilities here include a relaxing ivy covered inner patio, a delightful piano bar and lounge where complimentary breakfasts are served (unless you prefer your breakfast in bed), adjacent indoor private parking, and an inn-keeper who will make you feel right at home from the moment you arrive.

HOTEL ORION EDEN, *Praça dos Restauradores, 18. Tel. (01) 321-6600, Fax (01) 321-6666. Low season rack rates from 19,900$00, studio, EP; high season rack rates from 30,800$00, one bedroom apartment, EP. Most major credit cards accepted.*

This brand new nine floor French owned aparthotel in the heart of downtown Lisbon is a good value for the money. There are a total of 134 studio and one bedroom apartments equipped with fully stocked kitchens with dishwashers, air conditioning, private bathrooms, dining rooms, remote control satellite television, direct dial telephone, and either sofa beds or separate bedrooms with twin beds. There is also weekly maid service, a swimming pool, a laundromat, optional daily breakfast, and business equipment. Good for visiting executives and longer stay clients. Special rates apply for bookings of at least one week.

HOTEL DOM RODRIGO, *Rua Rodrigo da Fonseca, 44. Tel. (01) 386-3800. US and Canada bookings with Utell, Tel. 800/448-8355. Year round rack rates from 19,500$00, studio apartment, EP; year round rack rates from 24,000$00, one bedroom apartment, EP. All major credit cards accepted.*

A special apartment hotel owned by the Tivoli company with 39 nice studio apartments and huge one and two bedroom suites in the heart of town. Facilities include bar, kitchens, TV, pool, and parking.

HOTEL MARQUES DE SA, *Avenida Miguel Bombarda, 120. Tel. (01) 793-6794, Fax (01) 793-6986. Year round rack rates from 14,000$00, double room, BP. Most major credit cards accepted.*

Sparkling new, this hotel is just three blocks away from the Calouste Gulbenkian museum in the north end of Lisbon. The modern and fully equipped 10 floor hotel features several dozen spotless air conditioned double rooms with nice marble embellished private bathrooms, remote control satellite television, mini-safe, direct dial telephone, modern comfortable pine furnishings, designer fabrics, and huge terraces in many rooms. The hotel also has nearby parking and a restaurant. This a good choice for those who prefer to avoid the crowded and noisy central districts.

REAL PARQUE HOTEL, *Ave. Luís Bivar, 67. Tel. (01) 357-0101, Fax (01) 357-0750. Year round rack rates from 22,500$00, double room, BP. Most major credit cards accepted.*

The Real Parque is a new 4 star hotel with excellent service, staff, and facilities near the Mârquês do Pombal area. All 147 rooms and six suites are air conditioned and have private bathrooms, mini-safes, mini-bars, remote control satellite television, sound-proofed windows, and hair dryers. This hotel is one of the better bargains in Lisbon. Facilities include bar, café, restaurants, newsstand, room service, rooms for the physically challenged, business meeting rooms, laundry, and a garage.

HOTEL TIVOLI JARDIM, *Rua Júlio Caesar Machado. Tel. (01) 539-971. US and Canada bookings with Utell, Tel. 800/448-8355. Year round rack rates from 27,000$00, double room, EP. All major credit cards accepted.*

A famous 4 star property in the center of downtown Lisbon, this 119 room hotel is known for great service and good value. Facilities include bar, restaurant, air conditioning, pool, tennis, TV, and parking.

HOTEL LISBOA, *Rua Barata Salgueiro, 5. Tel. (01) 355-4131, Fax (01) 355-4139. US and Canada bookings with Utell, Tel. 800/448-8355. Mid week rack rates from 17,500$00, double room, BP; weekend special rates from 15,000$00, double room, BP. All major credit cards accepted.*

The Hotel Lisboa is a nice centrally located business style hotel with 55 large, modern, and well equipped rooms that all have private bathrooms, air conditioning, satellite television, mini-bar, direct dial telephones, radio, and sound-proof windows. A good place to stay if you need to be near the Avenida da Liberdade. Facilities include piano bar, a breakfast room, free indoor parking, and a piano bar.

HOTEL BRITANIA, *Rua Rodrigues Sampaio, 17. Tel. (01) 315-5016, Fax (01) 315-5021. US and Canada bookings with Marketing Ahead, Tel. 800/*

223-1356. *Low season rack rates from 19,800$00, double room, BP; high season rack rates from 23,500$00, double room, BP. Most major credit cards accepted.* This small old world hotel was originally designed in the 1940's by noted architect Cassiano Branco. It is located just off the Avenida da Liberdade in the center of Lisbon's downtown sector and has just completed a major renovation project that is sure to make it one of the best 3 star hotels in town. There are 30 gigantic classically styled rooms that all feature air conditioning, private bathrooms, direct dial telephones, remote control satellite television, mini-bar, sound-proof windows, and nice period furnishings.

HOLIDAY INN CROWNE PLAZA, *Ave. Antonio Jose de Almeida, 28. Tel. (01) 793-5222, Fax (01) 793-6672. Year round rack rates from 28,500$00, double room, BP. Most major credit cards accepted.*

This huge, modern hotel is best for those who need to be near the airport on their first or last night in Lisbon. There are 169 air conditioned rooms and suites with private bathrooms, am-fm clock radio, direct dial telephone, remote control cable television, mini-bar, and hair dryer. The service and rooms are good and the facilities include a bar, restaurant, sauna, health club, shops, and parking.

HOTEL BARCELONA, *Rua Laura Alves, 10. Tel. (01) 795-4273, Fax (01) 795-4281. Year round rack rates from 19,750$00, double room, BP. Most major credit cards accepted.*

The Barcelona is a new and modern highrise hotel near the Caloste Gulbenkian museum. All of the 125 large and comfortable air conditioned rooms have private bathrooms, remote control cable telelvision, nice modern furnishings, direct dial telelphones, mini-bar, and most also have great patios or private balconies. Facilities include bar, breakfast room, business meeting rooms, a garage, and a ground floor restaurant.

HOTEL MUNDIAL, *Rua Dom Duarte, 4. Tel. (01) 886-3101, Fax (01) 887-9129. Year round rack rates from 21,000$00, double room, BP. Most major credit cards accepted.*

A large full service 4 star hotel behind the Rossio, Hotel Mundial has 147 renovated air conditioned rooms (many with great views) with private bathrooms, direct dial telephones, remote control cable television, mini-bar, and comfortable furnishings. Facilities in this friendly hotel include bar, restaurants, parking, and extremely helpful staff.

HOTEL EDUARDO VII, *Ave. Fontes Pereira de Melo, 5. Tel. (01) 353-0141, Fax (01) 353-3879. Year round rack rates from 18,500$00, double room, BP. Most major credit cards accepted.*

Located near the heart of town, this is a pretty good but basic older 3 star hotel. The 130 comfortable rooms have air conditioning, private bathrooms, cable television, and acceptable furnishings. There is also a famous panoramic roof top restaurant, a bar, a tour desk, and parking.

Inexpensive

HOTEL ALIF LISBOA, *Campo Pequeno, 5. Tel. (01) 795-2464, Fax (01) 795-4116. Year round rack rates from 14,750$00, double room, BP. All major credit cards accepted.*

The Alif is a new and beautiful hotel with a great view of Lisbon's famed bullring. All of the 115 rooms have private marble bathrooms, remote control satellite television, air conditioning, direct dial telephones, mini-bars, and most have large windows looking over the city center. Its ninth floor glass enclosed breakfast room provides one of the best views imaginable. Facilities include bar, roof top breakfast room, and a garage.

HOTEL A.S. LISBOA, *Ave. Almirante Reis, 188. Tel. (01) 847-3025, Fax (01)847-3034. Year round rack rates from 16,000$00, double room, EP. Most major credit cards accepted.*

This is a small and cozy 75 room modern hotel located fairly close to both downtown and the airport. All units are air conditioned and contain private bathrooms, remote control cable television, direct dial telephone, mini-bar, mini-safe, and hair dryers. Facilities include bar, breakfast room, and nearby parking. This is a good budget choice.

HOTEL BORGES, *Rua Garret, 108. Tel. (01) 346-1951. Year round rack rates from 11,750$00, double room, EP. Most major credit cards accepted.*

Hotel Borges is a clean and comfortable hotel with 100 basic rooms, all with private bathroom, at bargain prices. Facilities include bar, restaurant, phones, and that's about all. Good luck finding any nearby parking. The hotel, however, is next to the famous A Brasileira café in the charming Chaido section.

CASA DE SÃO MAMEDE, *Rua da Escola Politecnica, 15. Tel. (01) 396-3166. Year round rack rates from 13,500$00, double room, BP. Most major credit cards accepted.*

A nice and comfortable converted house with 28 rooms, with and without private bathroom, near Eduardo VII park. Parking on site.

Cheap

PENSÃO RESIDENCIAL GEREZ, *Calçada do Gracia, 6. Tel. (01) 889-2039. Year round rack rates from 6,000$00, double room, CP. Some credit cards accepted.*

Located just a one minute walk from the Rossio, this simple family run budget inn has several nice and comfortable units with shared, and, in some cases, private bathrooms.

PENSÃO LONDRES, *Rua Dom Pedro V, 53. Tel. (01) 346-2203. Year round rack rates from 7,000$00, double room, CP. Cash only - No credit cards accepted.*

This is another of the few very cheap properties in Lisbon with a bit of class. Located in an old building in the Bairro Alto section, this basic and simple establishment offers nice comfortable rooms for budget minded tourists with or without private bathrooms.

PENSÃO DUBLIN, *Rua de Santa María, 45. Tel. (01) 355-5489. Year round rack rates from 6,750$0, double room, CP. Cash only - No credit cards accepted.*

A clean and basic inn, this hotel has 34 rooms with and without private bathrooms. Located a few blocks from Ave. de Liberdade, this establishment offers reasonably nice rooms with minimal facilities at bargain prices.

WHERE TO EAT
Expensive

CASA DO LEÃO, *Castelo de São Jorge. Tel. (01) 875-962. Dress code is smart casual. All major credit cards accepted.*

This is my favorite gourmet dining establishment in the entire city of Lisbon! Situated within the walls of the 12th century Castelo de São Jorge on a hill just above downtown Lisbon, this restaurant is the perfect place to enjoy a superb meal. Patrons can choose to dine under the vaulted ceilings and among the hand painted tile murals of the elaborately decorated main dining room or to relax in the al fresco terrace area, both with stunning views of the city center and Tejo River.

The menu includes a vast array of specialties that are all worth trying. Entrees range from incredible seafood dishes such as shrimp with asparagus in saffron creme sauce and cataplana of rice and mixed seafood to poultry dishes made of delectable chicken sautéed in white wine, to a heartier chateaubriand or lamb cutlets with cheese and spinach. If you can't decide which entree to try, do not hesitate to ask Fernando, the restaurant's excellent maitre d', for his suggestions. The extensive wine list includes over two dozen affordable selections and the desserts will take your breath away. You can expect to spend between 4,500$00 and 7,500$00 per person for a meal that you will never forget.

Casa do Leão is open daily for lunch and dinner until around 10:00pm. Make sure to call ahead for reservations.

ALCANTARA MAR CAFE, *Rua María Luísa Holstein, 15. Tel. (01) 363-7176. Dress code is smart casual. Most major credit cards accepted.*

This lively and architecturally unique restaurant is located in a converted warehouse in the Alcantara area. Its slightly nouveau Portuguese cuisine is pleasantly served to a casual but elegant clientele, and the average meal price is 4250$00 per person. After midnight, the adjoining bar (with an unusual design and artwork) and disco attract hundreds of Lisbon's most serious revelers.

BACCHUS, *Largo da Trindade, 9. Tel. (01) 322-828. Dress code is smart casual. Most major credit cards accepted.*

Bacchus has a wonderful wood paneled wine bar and restaurant on two floors. The chef creates extraordinary meals and the restaurant offers a good selection of wine from its extensive wine collection. The slightly formal atmosphere is comfortable and the service is excellent. A dinner here costs around 4,950$00 per person. Make sure you call in advance for reservations, particularly on weekends.

AVIS, *Rua Serpa Pinto, 12. Tel. (01) 342-8391. Dress code is semi-formal. All major credit cards accepted.*

This is one of the city's most deluxe and beautiful old world establishments in the Baixa area. The well dressed clientele choose between French, Portuguese, and other internationally inspired dishes. Not only is the food delicious, but the chef does a great job in its presentation. The service is prompt, but is a bit too intrusive. Expect to spend at least 6,750$00 per person, plus wine, for lunch or dinner.

TAVARES RICO, *Rua da Misericórdia, 35. Tel. (01) 795-0134. Dress code is formal. Most major credit cards accepted.*

This opulent restaurant is decorated with tons of gilded woodwork and antique furnishings. It's known for serving fine continental cuisine to well dressed business clientele and Lisbon's elite, but I was not all that impressed with my last meal. And it also cost me about 6,950$00 a person.

Moderate

CERVEJARIA DA TRINDADE, *Rua Nova da Trindade, 20. Tel. (01) 342-3506. No dress code. Most major credit cards accepted.*

This is one of my favorite places to eat in Lisbon. The Cervejaria is a unique and delicious restaurant in the Bairro Alto area. It is built inside an ancient church encrusted with beautiful antique tile murals. The relaxed ambiance is only surpassed by the fine seafood and meat specialties (try their incredible stuffed crab). Open until about 2:00am on most nights, you can expect to pay around 1,950$00 for a wonderful three course meal. One of the truly superb dining attractions in Lisbon.

CAFE CREME, *Avenida Conde de Valbom, 53. Tel. (01) 796-4360. Dress Code is smart casual. All major credit cards accepted.*

With its prime location just a two minute walk from the Calouste Gulbenkian Foundation museum, this old world brasserie and piano bar is a great choice for lunch or dinner, particularly after seeing some of the world's finest art collections. The menu features internationally inspired specialties such as tropical salads, burger plates, seafood dishes (acorda with shrimp, grilled swordfish in lemon butter, salmon with spinach), and pastas (fettuccini Alfredo, green lasagna), meat entrees (grilled chicken breasts, beef steaks, steak in pepper sauce), and pizzas. After a satisfying meal, save room for great desserts and coffees laced with imported liqueurs. The average bill here is about 2,350$00 a person, but their wonderful lunch specials are usually priced around 1,200$00 a person. **MASSIMA CULPA**, *Rua da Atalaia 35. Tel. (01) 342-0121. Dress code is smart casual. Most major credit cards accepted.*

Recently opened, this modern Italian restaurant in the Barrio Alto is packed by 9:30pm with locals that know a good thing when they see it. The dining room has about 24 small tables and is decorated in soft pastel colors. The restaurant's menu includes mixed salads, Parma ham, salmon and ricotta cheese salad, antipasto, risotto with four cheeses, spaghetti with shrimp and garlic, ravioli in marinara sauce, pasta carbonara, grilled filet of beef, and tiramisu. Expect to spend around 2,950$00 per person for an authentic Italian dinner.

QUINTA D'AVENIDA *in the Hotel Lisboa Plaza, Travessa do Salitre, 7. Tel. (01) 346-3922. Dress code is smart casual. All major credit cards accepted.*

This is about the only hotel restaurant in Lisbon that is favored by local business people and residents. The Quinta D'Avenida has a relaxed, medium sized dining room that serves delicious traditional Portuguese cuisine cooked to perfection. Besides offering a giant daily buffet lunch and dinner featuring over three dozen assorted salads, meats, fish, vegetables, cheeses, and pastries, they also present a wonderful buffet brunch on weekends. If you prefer, an al la carte menu can be requested.

A la carte items include huge portions of onion and cheese soup, mushrooms sautéed in garlic, smoked salmon, seafood au gratin, rice with shrimp, cod fish roasted in garlic, grilled chicken, beef steak in mushroom cream sauce, filet of sole meuniere, and assorted omelets. Expect to spend around 3,800$00 per person for a great meal.

PATIO ALFACINHA, *Rua do Guarda Loias, 44. Tel. (01) 642-171. Dress code is smart casual. Most major credit cards accepted.*

An excellent restaurant, it features typical Portuguese cuisine and occasionally great Fado. Located in Ajuda, this famous establishment may require reservations. A meal here will cost around 4,900$00 a person.

LABOR E ARTE, *Travessa da Espera, 29. Tel. (01) 347-1846. No dress code. Cash only - No credit cards accepted.*

A small bar and restaurant that serves up wonderful Italian inspired cuisine including several types of exotic salads, assorted pizzas, three different types of lasagna, and some serious desserts. A meal here will set you back around 1,950$00 per person including wine.

GREMIO, *Rua do Gremio Lusitana, 18. Tel. (01) 346-8868. Dress code is smart casual. Most major credit cards accepted.*

A good fusion restaurant in the center of the Barrio Alto, Gremio is well worth the search. The candle-lit interior is decorated with nice art and the mood is complimented with classic jazz music. Their menu includes gazpacho, dates with bacon, shrimp in garlic, steak in Roquefort cheese sauce, stuffed pork chops with prawns and apples, scallops with mushrooms, cod fish in Port wine, seafood salad, and over a dozen daily specials. A meal here will set you back around 2,300$00 a person.

O BARIGAS, *Travessa de Queimada, 31. Tel. (01) 347-1220. No dress code. Most major credit cards accepted.*

If you are looking for a good moderately priced Mediterranean restaurant in the Barrio Alto, check out this cozy establishment with its unusually good open kitchen. Among their specialties are fried calamari, cream of fish soup, grilled swordfish, veal primavera, octopus risotto, trout stuffed with ham and shrimp, steak with mushroom sauce, mixed grill, pork chops, and a four course tourist menu. A dinner here will cost around 2,550$00 per person.

PAP'ACORDA, *Rua da Atalaia, 57. Tel. (01) 346-4811. Dress code is smart casual. Most major credit cards accepted.*

A nicely designed and popular regional restaurant inside an old converted bakery, this restaurant is conveniently located in the heart of the Bairro Alto. You'll find great food and good ambiance. Expect to spend over 4,000$00 a person to dine here.

COTAS DAS ARMAS, *Beco São Miguel, 7. Tel. (01) 868-682. Dress code is smart casual. Most major credit cards accepted.*

This is a small traditional restaurant in the Alfama area. This two level restaurant has the look of a converted stable. The hearty dishes are served by friendly staff who speak several languages. The owner is on hand to personally greet you. The average meal price is around 3,750$00 a head.

Inexpensive

RESTAURANTE ALFAIA, *Travessa da Queimada, 18. Tel. (01) 346-1232. No dress code. Cash only - No credit cards accepted.*

This is a popular, simple, and charming local restaurant in the heart of the Bairro Alto. The owners continue to serve up delicious inexpensive traditional Portuguese food to primarily a packed crowd of university students. The menu features tomato soup, fish soup, grilled calamari, fried eel with rice, broiled grouper, grilled cod fish, fried pork, roast beef with potatoes, blood sausage, tuna salads, beef steak, and many daily specials. Get there before the line starts at about 9:00pm and expect to spend less than 1,650$00 a person.

RESTAURANTE JAGUAR, *Avenida Conde de Valbom, 87. Tel. (01) 757-2695. No dress code. Most major credit cards accepted.*

Located around the corner from the Calouste Gulbenkian museum, this simple and rather narrow little lunch restaurant is a real treat. Packed with hungry office workers from the adjacent Berna district, Jaguar serves up giant portions of Portuguese favorites. On my last visit to this laid back and crowded establishment, I stood in line for 25 minutes for an empty table (well worth the wait). The menu changes daily and includes delicious huge salads, plates of grilled pork cutlets in a secret sauce, fresh broiled local grouper, grilled sea bass, roast pork loin, codfish with potato, and about a dozen other filing meals that all cost under 1,150$00. Nothing fancy, but the food will speak for itself!

HUA LI TOU, *Rua da Misericórdia, 93. Tel. (01) 346-9478. Dress code is casual. Most major credit cards accepted.*

I hate to admit it, but after three weeks of eating grilled fish, even I needed a break from Portuguese food. This small and friendly Chinese restaurant in the center of Bairro Alto serves surprisingly good food. Excellent noodle and rice dishes are prepared and served by Chinese exchange students who are studying in Lisbon. My last lunch here cost 2,950$00.

CAFETERIA O ARCO, *Rua dos Sapateiros, 161. Tel. (01) 346-4230. No dress code. Most major credit cards accepted.*

After a long day of shopping around the Rossio, make sure to check out this beautiful little restaurant. Popular with local office workers at lunch time, the O Arco has an intimate pastel colored and tiled interior with a couple of dozen tables. The affordable menu features such items as braised cod fish, grilled squid, oven baked fish with vegetables, veal steak, and pork chops. A full lunch in this great little place costs about 1050$00 a person plus drinks.

PALMERINHA, *Rua da Conceição, 32. Tel. (01) 887-9155. No dress code. Cash only - No credit cards accepted.*

Situated just a couple of blocks from the Placa do Comercío, this small and informal working class restaurant has about a dozen paper covered tables that are full during lunch on weekdays. They specialize in typical Portuguese cuisine including cod fish, grilled swordfish, filet of white fish, rice with lamb, entrecote, clams in white sauce, and rice pudding. A huge lunch will cost about 1,150$00 and is all homemade.

Cheap

YIN YANG, *Rua dos Correeiros, 14. Tel. Unlisted. No dress code. Cash only - No credit cards accepted.*

For vegetarians and those on macrobiotic diets, this simple second floor restaurant halfway between the Rossio and the Praça do Comercío is well worth the effort to find. The simple caféteria interior has a long line of hungry office workers on most weekday afternoons, and they only have to wait a few minutes to choose between over a dozen daily specials including tofu stew, veggie egg rolls, pizzas, rice dishes, and other Asian inspired items. A lunch here will set you back around 875$00 a person.

TELEPIZZA, *Rua Braancamp, 7. Tel. (01) 315-9309. No dress code. Cash only – No credit cards accepted.*

Whether you're in the mood for a quick bite in their small dining room or prefer to have them deliver a hot snack to your hotel, this fast food restaurant near the Praça Marquês de Pombal serves some of the best pizza in town. The price is just 800$00 for individual pizzas, 1,200$00 for medium pizzas, or 1,850$00 for family size pizzas, and 160$00 for each topping: peppers, tuna, shrimp, anchovies, olives, onion, mushrooms, pepperoni, capers, bacon, pineapple, or extra cheese.

This is a great choice for a meal when you just don't feel like leaving the hotel but don't want to pay hotel restaurant prices. They have several other central locations in town.

TACO BAR, *Travessa Água de Flor, 20. Tel. (01) 343-1863. No dress code. Cash only - No credit cards accepted.*

This tiny nine seat bar and Mexican restaurant in the heart of the Barrio Alto is open most nights until at least 3:00am and offers a limited, but delicious, menu of south-of-the-border favorites like vegetarian, chicken, or beef tacos for about 450$00 each. They also have good prices on Mexican beer and tequila.

SUBWAY, *Placa de Figueira and several other locations. Tel. Unlisted. No dress code. Cash only - No credit cards accepted.*

That's right, now there are over a dozen Subway sandwich shops scattered around the Lisbon area. For those of you who may not know, this is an American franchise deli. Subway is becoming popular with the Portuguese, and feature the same sandwiches made to order that you are used to back home as well as several slightly modified varieties. You can eat-in or take-out their six inch (350$00 each) or 12 inch subs. They also have salads, breakfast specials, drinks, desserts, and other healthier alternatives to fat saturated burgers and fries served in most fast food joints.

SEEING THE SIGHTS

Wondering around on your own is the best way to see Lisbon. Make sure to bring this guide book and a good map of the city with you. Although crime is almost unheard of, I still suggest wearing a money belt or hideaway wallet.

Do not use a car to see the sights if you have one. The traffic and parking in Lisbon is among the worst of any European capital. The best way to see Lisbon is to leave your car in a parking lot, and travel by a combination of foot, taxi, metro, bus, funicular and trolley. Walking on the patterned stone sidewalks is a delight, and the reasonable size of the city allows you to see all of downtown by foot.

CITY TOURS

*During the high season, the **Carris** public transportation authority offers visitors two special City Tours two to six times a day between May and the end of September. They usually begin around 11:00am from the Praça do Comercío, take about 90 minutes, and are given by either a multilingual guide or narrated tape recording. If you want to do some extended sightseeing, you are also allowed to get on and off the bus or tram as you please.*

*The **Circuito Colinas** (Hill Tour) is on an antique electric tram and visits the sights along the higher elevations of Lisbon. The trip costs 2,800$00 per person and is popular. The second tour, **Circuito Tejo** (Tagus River View Tour), is on an open top bus and runs along the sights adjacent to the river. This excursion costs 2,000$00 a person and is great on warm sunny days.*

Tickets for either trip can be purchased directly from the bus or tram driver. For more information, visit any Turísmo office or call Carris, Tel. (01) 363-9345.

DOWNTOWN
Baixa

The **Baixa** district is in the lower elevation section of downtown Lisbon. It starts at the **Tejo River** (Tagus) and heads upward to Avenida da Liberdade. Before the destruction of much of Baixa in the 1755 earthquake, most of the area was built on stilts to avoid flood waters from the river. After the earthquake, the reconstruction of Lisbon by the Marquês de Pombal left the streets of Baixa in a grid pattern, with wide open avenues and pedestrian only streets lined with sidewalk cafés and boutiques.

Immediately in front of the river is the famed **Praça do Comercío** (Commerce Square). It is locally known as the **Terreiro do Paço** (the Palace's Marketplace) because 17th century merchants sold rare spices in the square next the Royal Palace before the palace was destroyed by the 1755 earthquake. These days, the square consists of an assortment of pink colored 18th century government office buildings that surround a large bronze statue of King Dom José I on a horse.

It was in this very square, right near the parking lot, that in 1908, King Dom Carlos I and his son Prince Luís Filipe were assassinated. On the northernmost border of the square is the vast **Arco Monumental da Rua Augusta**. The gateway leads to the banks, shops, and restaurants in the lower part of the downtown. Directly across the arch, on the southern side of the square, is a large marble staircase that leads down to the banks of the Tejo River. You get a very nice view from the staircase. Also in this general area you will find the **Terreiro do Paço** ferry terminal with service to the opposite side of the Tejo River and the towns of Barreiro, Montijo, Seixal, and Cacilhas.

If you pass under the Arco Monumental in Praça do Comercío you will walk through the pedestrian only Rua Augusta and into the northern section of the Baixa. This small 24 square block area contains several 19th century stone streets that have descriptive names like Rua da Ouro (Street of Gold) and Rua da Prata (Street of Silver). To this day, this area still contains beautiful shops that sell the items they are named after like fine silver filigree and hand-crafted gold jewelry. I found some of the best values on fine European shoes, suits, and lamb's wool sweaters in the large assortment of shops in this area.

Located at the northern end of these streets is the wonderful public square known simply as the **Rossio** (also called the Praça de Dom Pedro IV) with both a fountain and a statue of King Pedro IV in the center. Cafes line the Rossio and the commuter crowds flock here for café (expresso) and pasteis (pastries with meat, fish or sweat fillings). A stop for rich galão (café-au-lait) at Cafe Suica or Cafe Nicola in the Rossio is a great way to experience the local ambiance. The beautiful **Teatro Nacional D. María II** (National Theater) rests at the northern end of the Rossio. Across the avenue from the theater is the ornate facade of the Rossio train station: don't miss it.

Just above the Rossio is the beginning of Avenida da Liberdade (Liberty Avenue) that leads up through town and into the **Praça dos Restauradores** (Square of the Restorers). This delightful square is named for the men who led the revolt against Spanish annexation in 1640. The square is dominated by the red facade of the **Palácio Foz**. The Italian designed structure now houses the offices of the Secretary of State for Tourism and his staff. This is the building to go if you need a good **Turísmo** office for advice and maps. It is open every day of the week from 9:00am - 8:00pm.

If you walk east for one block from the lower section of Avenida da Liberdade, you will run into Rua das Portas de Santa Antão (runs parallel with Avenida da Liberdade). This street is filled with a vast selection of seafood restaurants and small shops. Although the world-famous Restaurante Gambrinus is the most deluxe place to eat here, there are many other fine restaurants all over.

As you wander a few blocks further north, Rua Portas de Santa Antão becomes Rua Alves Correira, a street with many good antique stores.

Chiado

The **Chiado** district is a wonderful world of its own. The most interesting way to get to this part of town is to take the fabulously strange elevator called the **Elevador de Santa Justa** from its base on the western edge of the Baixa at Rua da Ouro. You will be dropped off near the **Largo de Carmo**.

This small and exclusive district consists of a handful of streets that run westward towards the restaurant and boutique lined Rua da Misericórdia, the western border. Traditionally Lisbon's most elegant shopping district, much of the Chiado was destroyed by a major fire in 1988. Fortunately the area is currently being restored to its original beauty. It still contains some very upscale stores that sell jewelry, leather goods, designer clothing, and excellent porcelain.

Among the finest sights in the Chiado is the Gothic church, **Convento do Carmo**, *located on Rua do Carmo* near the exit of the Elevador Santa Justa. Constructed in the 15th century, the convent lost its roof during the earthquake of 1755. Nowadays the structure is home to the **Museu Arqueologico do Carmo** (Archaeological Museum) and is filled with prehistoric, Roman, Visigothic, Arab, and medieval artifacts. You really should visit this museum (closed on Sundays).

Bairro Alto

The **Bairro Alto** section of Lisbon is located on the upper elevations of downtown Lisbon just west of the Baixa. This area contains some of the best boutiques, antique stores, and rare book shops in Lisbon.

One of the most relaxing places in Bairro Alto is the excellent A Brasileira café, *Rua Garrett #120*. This café has a history of literary patrons, and provides the best place in Lisbon to people watch and enjoy a good café and pastry. A short way down the street is a peaceful little park called the **Praça Luís de Camoes**. Luís de Camoes was a great Portuguese writer who frequented this area.

From the Praça Luís de Camoes, walk up the Rua da Misericórdia and make a left (west) turn on the Travessa da Espera. You are now in the small enclave of stone roads that make up the heart of the Bairro Alto. After strolling through the streets, Rua da Rosa, Rua da Barroca, and Rua Diario Noticias, you should head east on the Travessa da Queimada to rejoin the Rua da Misericórdia. A few blocks north (up) on Rua Misericórdia the street name will change to Rua de Sâo Pedro de Alcantara. Continue north and you will come to **Miradouro de Sâo Pedro de Alcantara** park. There is an unforgettable lookout point where you have a panoramic view of Lisbon.

An afternoon visit to the **Solar do Vinho do Porto**, *Rua Sâo Pedro de Alcantara #45* (just across from the park), will give you the opportunity to taste, by the glass, many vintage Port wines at very reasonable prices. It is open until 10:00pm and closed on Sundays. For those of you who prefer dry white wines, try a glass of Porto Branco, a dry white variety all but unknown to North Americans.

A few blocks further up, Rua de São Pedro de Alcantara bends towards the west and merges into Rua Dom Pedro V, where you will find antique shop after antique shop. The wonderful stately homes and shops of the **Praça Príncipe Real** square is located here. Once again the street changes its name, this time to Rua Escola Politecnica, and brings you to the remarkable **Jardim Botanico** (Botanical Gardens).

During the evening, thousands of young revelers disappear into the maze of narrow alleys in the center of the Bairro Alto to frequent the vast assortment of small clubs, bars, **Fado** (typical Portuguese folk music) houses, and restaurants. Many local families and students enjoy dinner in adega tipicas (restaurants where traditional Fado music is played live) that are found throughout the Bairro Alto. Dinner here is a late event, usually starting after 8pm, while the Fado music and nightclubs usually start up around 11pm. If you have some time to kill before dinner, I suggest a drink at the wonderfully ornate **Pavilhão Chines** bar, *Rua Dom Pedro # 89.* An unusual collection of Art Deco objects clutter the walls.

You can either take a taxi back to your hotel, or if it's before midnight, you can take the **Elevador da Glória** tram from just south of the Alcantara lookout and park to the Palácio Foz on Avenida da Liberdade and then walk back into the Rossio before getting a bus, metro, or taxi.

Cais de Sodre & Bica

Directly south of the Chiado and Bairro Alto districts, at the end of Rua do Alecrim on the banks of the Tejo River, are the markets in and around the **Cais de Sodre** area. Known primarily as an entrance point into Lisbon for many of the city's workers, this district contains a fluvial station with ferries that cross from here to the southern banks of the Tejo and an adjacent train station for the packed electric commuter trains to and from the suburban cities of Cascais and Estoril. On most weekdays, Cais de Sodre is filled with huge numbers of commuters in the morning and afternoon.

This noisy, hectic little neighborhood is home to a few markets that are stocked every day (except Sunday) with a vast assortment of fresh fish and vegetables. The fish market is next to the station, and is open all day. The early morning wholesale fruit and vegetable market, a few blocks further west along the river front, is busiest around 5am. Also worth a quick stop is the **Ribeira** meat and produce market, housed in an old domed building just across from the station and just east of the busy bus and trolley stops at **Praça Duque da Terceira** square.

The streets just above the Ribeira market and the adjacent **Praça Dom Luís I** square make up the **Bica** district. Filled with small old buildings that house some of the market suppliers, this small area is also worth strolling through.

Bairro do Castelo

Atop one of Lisbon's seven famous hills is the remarkable **Bairro do Castelo** district. The district is just a handfull of blocks east of the Baixa and has wonderful historic sights and ancient enclosed neighborhoods. The most famous and obvious of these attractions is the 5th century **Castelo de São Jorge** (St. George's Castle) which is open daily until sunset and is free. Visable from almost anywhere in town, this stunning castle was originally built by the Visigoths and has passed through the hands of several different cultures. During the Moorish occupation, Lisbon was completely surrounded by a defensive wall known as the **Cerca Moura**, and later a palace known as the **Alcazar** was built inside the castle walls.

After Lisbon was conquered by King Dom Afonso in 1147, the former Moorish Alcazar palace was replaced with the **Palácio Real de Alcacova** and became home to the Portuguese royal family for a few centuries. Although the castle was seriously damaged by the 1755 earthquake, it was restored in the 1938.

Unfortunately, most of the Alcacova palace lies in ruins, but there is a small museum you can visit. The gardens of the castle (open daily until sunset) are still filled with magnificent cannons, towers, fortified walls, plazas, pools, and a dramatic panoramic walkway called the **Caminho de Ronda** that looks out over the entire city. Within the walls of the castle complex you can stroll along the old enclosed **Santa Cruz** quarter. You will find ancient homes and lanes, and a simply awesome restaurant called **Casa do Leão** that is among the city's finest.

The slightly confusing Rua da Costa do Castelo circles most of the castle and can be taken to reach several other quarters including the old **Mouraria** (Moorish quarter). The Mouraria can be found by walking a block or so north of the castle, and is centered around the streets and lanes which run off of Rua da Mouraria. Although there are not many sights, a good walk around this area is a nice adventure. After visiting the Mouraria, you can head back down to the Rua da Costa do Castelo and follow it as winds its way around to the castle's east side.

This street soon leads to the Largo Rodrigues de Freitas, which then feeds into Rua São Tome. If you walk south towards the river on Rua São Tome, you will pass the an original Arabic gateway in the tavern-laden **Largo das Portas do Sol**. Just off the south end of the Largo is the wonderful **Fundação Ricardo do Espirito Santo e Silva** foundation that is housed in a converted 17th century palace. The foundation is home to the fantastic **Museu de Artes Decorativas** (Museum of Decorative Arts). This large museum has vast collections of antique furnishings, paintings, Arraiolos carpets, ceramics, and rare silver. From the museum, take Rua do Limoeiro down a block or so before reaching the Igreja da Santa Luzia and its spectacular lookout point from **Miradouro da Santa Luzia**. After a brief rest and some picture taking, you are ready to continue down the Rua do Limoeiro to **Sé Cathedral**, and the heart of the neighboring **Alfama** district.

Alfama

Nestled below the imposing Castelo de São Jorge, the **Alfama** district is perhaps the most famous part of Lisbon. The maze-like stone streets have been here since the Moors occupied this area in the 8th century, and the Alfama retains much of its ancient ambiance since it was largely spared from the 1755 earthquake. A long and leisurely walk through the Alfama is the only way to see it and getting completely lost in the maze is inevitable. I suggest that you wander around and keep your eyes open for some of the sights and streets I describe.

Streams of laundry are suspended between delightful old white-washed houses, many with elegant, faded tile facades, as young children play soccer on the streets. Among the many impressive sights in the Alfama is the **Sé Cathedral**, *Rua Augusto Rosa*. This prominent cathedral dates back to the 12th century and was built on the sight of Lisbon's main mosque as an insult to the newly defeated Moors. Among the most unique and compelling streets in the Alfama is the **Beco do Carneiro** (Alley of Sheep) with its extremely narrow passages that typify life in this district in the old days.

The Rua da Judiaria (Street of Jewish quarter) is another interesting area in what was once the Jewish quarter and dates back to the 16th century. The tile covered houses off the **Patio das Flores** plaza are worthwhile sights. Another interesting stop is the 16th century **Igreja de São Vicente de Fora** church, *Rua São Vicente*, in the eastern section of the Alfama. The church houses the tombs of several Portuguese kings in its eerie, tiled cloisters (open daily).

A great flea market takes place on Tuesday mornings and all day on Saturday right near the Igreja de São Vicente de Fora in the **Campo de Santa Clara** square. This unique market is called the **Feira da Ladra** (thief's market) and is a great place to find excellent antiques at great prices (don't be afraid to bargain) mixed in with lots of junk. At a recent visit to this market I purchased two wonderful and authentic 19th century brass cupid picture frames for less than 5,000$00 each.

After a long day of wandering around the Alfama and undoubtedly getting lost several times in the process, you'll want to walk to the southern edge of this district near the river. Just off the many markets along Rua de São Pedro you can wander around the **Largo do Chafariz de Dentro** square where the locals spend their spare time gossiping. You will also find a vast array of good and inexpensive restaurants and bars throughout this area. If you happen to be in Lisbon in mid-June, don't miss the amazing St. Anthony festival that makes this part of town really come to life.

CENTRAL LISBON

The central Lisbon district starts along the northern edge of the Avenida da Liberdade, Lisbon's main drag. Here you will see a fine example of the wide open boulevards created by the Marquês de Pombal after the great earthquake of 1755. Many of Portugal's largest companies have their headquarters on this avenue, including the TAP reservations center at the top of the street.

At the end of Avenida da Liberdade is the busiest and most irritating major intersection in Lisbon, the **Praça Marquês de Pombal**. This giant rotunda and its statue are a monument to the 18th century restorer of Lisbon and is located immediately in front of the 65 acre **Parque Eduardo VII**. The park's name commemorates a visit by the former British King and contains ponds, paths, statues, and an outdoor terrace. A wonderful panoramic view of Lisbon and the river can be seen from a vantage point atop the high point in the Eduardo VII park. A short walk away is the beautiful **Estufa Fria** (cold greenhouses) where an assortment of exotic flowers and plants are displayed beside lakes and waterfalls (open daily).

If you are in the mood for some serious shopping, from the southern edge of the Eduardo VII park, follow the Ave. Joaquim António de Aguiar west, past the the Ritz hotel for several blocks, until you reach the huge ultra-modern **Amoreiras** shopping center and office complex.

Lapa

The **Lapa** district is home to some of the most elaborate residences, although some smaller rustic houses still exist, and embassies in Lisbon. Situated high above the Tejo River about a kilometer or so west of the Bairro Alto, Lapa has become one of the most desirable districts to live.

Lisbon's most deluxe accommodations can be found at the snobby **Hotel da Lapa**, *Rua do Pau da Bandeira*, which has become the home away from home for the many diplomats and world leaders. The entire neighborhood is dotted with several ornate embassies and regal mansions that are on the verge of collapse.

Lapa is a great place to wander through, from the small alleys to gazing at massive villas with their dramatic river views. The **Museu**

Nacional de Arte Antiga (National Museum of Antique Art), *Jardim 9 de Abril* off Rua das Janelas Verdes, is a must-see for anyone interested in Portuguese and international art from the 11th century to the present. There are four floors full of religious icons, oil paintings, gold and silver works, statues, and jewelry (closed Mondays).

The intimate **York House** and **As Janelas Verdes** hotels are both located on the same street as the museum.

Belem

The **Belem** district is a mainly residential area about five km west of Praça do Comercío. The best way to get here is to take a taxi or the #15 tram from the Praça do Comercío. It is from this district's river front park that several of Portugal's greatest voyages were launched.

On the banks of the river rests the **Torre de Belem** tower, a 16th century fortress designed to protect Lisbon's harbor (closed Mondays). If you looking for a place to rest, the adjoining palm tree gardens are lovely. Another obvious river front attraction is the **Monument of the Discoveries**, completed in 1960 to commemorate the 500th anniversary of the death of Prince Henry the Navigator.

As you move inland from the marina, the first structure you will see is the **Centro Cultural de Belem** (Belem Cultural Center). Inside you will find art exhibitions and an international conference center. The next vast structure is the **Mosterio dos Jeronimos** (closed Mondays). The monastery dates back to about 1502 when it was commissioned by King Dom Manuel to commemorate the return of Vasco de Gama. Designed by the famous architect Diogo Boitac, this structure has been called the masterpiece of all Manueline architecture, and was unfortunately damaged by the 1755 earthquake. The vaulted double cloister must be visited to experience the true beauty of this impressive architectural achievement. Inside the structure are the tombs of both Vasco de Gama and Luís de Camoes.

The monastery and the adjacent **Praça do Imperio** are home to several different museums including these three fine choices: the **Museu de Arquelogico** (Archaeology Museum) that contains a collection of paleolithic and Roman artifacts (closed Mondays); the **Museu da Marinha** (Navy Museum) that contains boats, model boats, seaplanes, a cartography room, and a vast collection of navigational implements (closed Mondays); and the **Gulbenkian Planetarium**, offering delightful simulated sky gazing sessions on weekends.

Also worth a visit is the nearby **Museu Nacional de Coches** (National Coach Museum) where fine examples of 16th-19th century coaches, as well as several royal portraits are on display (closed Mondays). No visit to Belem would be complete without standing in line at the popular **Fabrica**

dos Pasteis de Belem (Belem Pastry Factory), *Rua de Belem 86*, where hundreds of people wait each day and night to buy fresh from the oven custard pastries (also try their wonderful coconut macaroons).

Ajuda

A short walk north of Belem on the **Calçada da Ajuda** brings you into the **Ajuda** district. The first sight is the immense 19th century **Palácio da Ajuda** palace, which contains a museum of antique furnishings, books, and silver (closed on Wednesdays and holidays). Very close to the palace is the 9.5 acre **Jardim Botanico de Ajuda**. Portugal's oldest botanical garden, founded in 1768, has many exotic species of flowers and plants (closed on Mondays).

Alcantara

If you prefer a long walk after visiting Ajuda, follow the river and head east towards the omnipresent **Ponte 25 de Abril**, a copy of San Francisco's famed Golden Gate Bridge. In about 10 minutes, you will pass the many bars and clubs of the **Alcantara** district. At night, many of Lisbon's most popular clubs have huge lines of revelers waiting to be admitted inside. Like other major cities in the world, you have to know the right people to get in the door of some of these clubs.

Additional restaurants and nightspots are located in the back streets of Alcantara, close to the bridge. If you have the chance, stop in at the rather unusual **Alcantara-Mar Cafe**: their legendary B-52 drinks are made with absinthe (absinto), a strong bitter green herb liqueur that taste like licorice.

NORTHERN LISBON

This expanding area near the international airport contains several interesting sights. From the Marquês de Pombal rotunda at the end Avenida da Liberdade, turn right (northwest) and follow Ave. Fontes Pereira de Melo until reach the next rotunda, the **Praça Douque de Saldanha**. Look around at the fine buildings that make up this square and rotunda. Next, follow the only big street, Avenida da República, as it winds its way up several blocks towards the **Praça de Touros** (bullring) in the **Campo Pequeno** area. The bullring is a beautiful structure that seats over 8,000 spectators. Seasonal evening bullfights generally take place on Thursdays and Sundays from April-October. In Portugal, the bull is never killed.

Head a few blocks eastward from the bullring on Ave. João XXI until you reach Ave. da Roma. This delightful street has a large assortment of fine boutiques and designer shops that sell high end goods. If you continue a few blocks south on Ave. de Roma, you will find additional boutiques at **Praça de Londres.**

A few blocks north of Campo Pequeno is the Campo Grande area that contains several attractions including the huge **Biblioteca National** (National Library). The library has a fine **Museu de Musica** (Musical Instrument Museum) with a collection of 16th-20th century instruments (open by appointment only). Also in the same general area you will find the **Museu da Cidade** (Museum of the City) that is housed in the 18th century **Palácio Pimenta** and contains historical information and iconography about Lisbon (closed on Mondays). Campo Grande also has lovely gardens and a large indoor shopping center, **Calaidoscopo.**

Traveling west of Campo Pequeno on Ave. de Berna you will find the **Praça Espanha** (Spanish Square) and the incredible **Museu Calouste Gulbenkian** (Calouste Gulbenkian Foundation Museum), *Avenida de Berna, 45,* open Tuesday, Thursday, and Sunday from 10:00am - 5:00pm, and Wednesday and Saturday from 2:00pm - 7:30pm, admission: 500$00 per person. The museum and the adjacent Modern Art Center is surrounded by a wonderful park and a sculpture garden with a performance area. There is also a reasonably priced caféteria on the grounds.

The museum is a slender low-rise modern building. In the first galleries of the museum, there are unparalleled pieces of **Egyptian art** displayed in chronological order including a 5,000 year old alabaster bowl from the tomb of Reqaqnah, an exquisitely carved obsidian head of Amenemhat III, an ivory cosmetics spoon, a funerary figure of Lady Henut Tauy, a bronze cat coffin, and a fine silver death mask. From here, you enter another series of rooms that contain the **Classic art** collection of Graeco-Roman pieces. Among the highlights of this section are a mid-5th century BC ceramic vase from Attica, a selection of remarkably well preserved gold and silver coins from the 6th century BC (the collection includes over one thousand coins), Roman glassware from Syria and Palestine, and Greek sculpture including the marble head of a woman from the 2nd century, beautifully carved jewelry, ointment and funerary vases, and several jewel encrusted gold medallions including several that bear the image of Alexander the Great and are presumed to be gold medals from the first Olympics.

In the same part of the museum, there is a good selection of **Mesopotamian** objects such as a limestone bas-relief from the 9th century BC Palace of Nimrud and a limestone cylinder seal. From this area, you move to **Armenian art** exhibits including several hand painted bibles and gospels from the 17th century.

Another series of large salons contain unique examples of **Islamic art** from the Middle East including a 16th century Persian silk carpet from the tomb of Iman Riza, 17th century "Polish Carpets" and "Portuguese

CALOUSTE GULBENKIAN:
ART & ANTIQUITIES COLLECTOR

Born in Istanbul in 1869, Calouste Sarkis Gulbenkian was the son of a wealthy Armenian merchant. Soon after graduating as an engineer from London's famed King's College, Gulbenkian became one of the leading oil barons in the Persian Gulf. The millions he made from the sale of Middle Eastern crude oil to Europe transformed this casual collector of precious works of art into a serious connoisseur. In 1930, the Gulbenkian collection became known throughout the world due to the first major exhibition of his European paintings (primitive through impressionist) at the National Gallery in London.

At about this time, post-revolutionary Russia began to sell off the masterpieces in the Hermitage Gallery (once owned by Catherine the Great) and Gulbenkian bought many of these priceless pieces. Additionally, with the help of friends he made in the fine arts trade, he collected thousands of paintings by Van der Weyden, Carpaccio, Frans Hals, Rubens, Van Dyck, Rembrandt, Gainsborough, Renoir, Manet, Monet, and Houdon, as well as thousands of well preserved Egyptian sculpture, French furnishings, Oriental ceramics and tapestries, rare books, ancient coins, and jewelry by Lalique (many of which were custom designed for French actress Sarah Bernhardt).

After the end of World War II, Gulbenkian arrived in Portugal. Eventually, he moved into a Lisbon hotel where he died in 1955. Upon his death, an educational foundation bearing his name began the construction of the Calouste Gulbenkian Foundation Musuem to share his first rate collection of western and Oriental art and jewelry with the public.

Carpets" that were actually made in Iran, velvet textiles from Tabriz, silk brocades from Turkey, 12th century glazed ceramic tiles from Kashan, Kubashi ceramic pieces from the 17th century, stunning 14th century glassware from Syria, and hand painted copies of the Koran made during the reign of Shah Abbas. The **Far East art** collection begins with Chinese porcelain dating as far back as the Yuan period. The pieces of most interest are the 15th century Ming dynasty glazed plates, 17th century K'ang-hsi enamels, 18th century carved jade, and 19th century Japanese prints and lacquers.

The next galleries feature **Western art**. This area of the museum is the largest and contains a vast assortment of rare pieces from all over Europe. The exhibit starts with several ivory triptychs from France's Gothic cathedrals, old parchment manuscripts from all over Europe, a beautiful

13th century English book of the Apocalypse, and other rare items. It continues with 14th through 17th century paintings by masters including Van der Weydenm, Jean avn Eyck, Cima da Conegliano, Moretto, Rubens, Rembrandt, Van Dyck, Frans Hals, Ruysdael, and others. There are also a set of sculptures by Jean de Liege, Tylmann Riemenschneider, Antoine Coysevox, Lemoyne, Falconet, Pigalle, Claude Micel, and Jean-Antoine Houdon. A selection of 18th century French paintings by Antoine Watteau, Jean-Honore Fragonard, Francois Boucher, Largilliere, Nattier, Quentin de la Tour, and Lepicie follow.

Several more rooms are filled with unbelievably beautiful 15th through 17th century textiles, gold and silver settings, church vestments, sculptures, ceramics, decorative pieces, functioning antique clocks, and the most incredible selection of opulent furnishings from all over Europe. The next few galleries show off Gulbenkian's 18th and 19th century English paintings by artists such as Gainsborough, Romney, Hoppner, and Turner. The Italian paintings of the 18th century now come into view with many superb examples by Venetian born artist Francisco Guardi. From here the works move on to 19th century France with examples of work by Roxeau, Daubigny, Millet, Corot, Lepine, Fantin-Latour, Manet, Renoir, and Monet.

Last are the glass display cases filled with over 150 imaginative Art Nouveau period objects created in the Paris studios of **Rene Lalique** between 1895 and 1937. Many of these powerfully suggestive objects are figures of women, dragons, or insects with their extremities forming intricate motifs. Among the most famous pieces in this one of a kind collection of Lalique objects are the jewels designed for French actress Sarah Bernhardt.

Continuing westward past the Praça Espanha on Avenida Calouste Gulbenkian you will find yourself at the **Aqueducto das Águas Livres**, an 11 mile long aqueduct that was constructed in 1728 to supply drinking water to Lisbon. A series of glazed ceramic murals can be seen on the way to the aqueduct. The huge **Parque Florestal de Monsanto** (Monsanto Floral Park) surrounds most of this area and includes beautiful zodiac patterned box gardens at the **Palácio dos Marqueses de Fronteira**. This 17th century Italian Renaissance palace contains several remarkable paintings, azulejos and delft tile panels, a wonderful terrace, and fantastically furnished grand rooms (closed on Sundays).

Near the palace, you can also pop into the **Jardim Zoologico** if you want to look at some caged wildlife. The oddest sight in this beautiful park is the presence of a huge campsite that is filled to capacity in the summer.

EXPO '98 COMES TO LISBON

From May through September 1998, Lisbon will host **Expo '98,** *the final World's Fair and Exposition of this millennium. Located near the Tejo River in an area not far from downtown, this major international event has been four years in the planning and an estimated 8.5 million visitors are expected. For admission fees, schedules of events, and additional information, contact the ICEP (Portuguese tourist) office in your country; see Chapter 6, Planning Your Trip, for these phone numbers.*

The theme for the World's Fair will be **"The Oceans – A Heritage for the Future."** *Much of the focus will be on events since Vasco de Gama departed Lisbon in 1498 on his way to find a new route to India and on what the future will hold for the development and conservation of the world's oceans.*

The exhibition grounds will cover over 50 hectares and will feature several new structures that will contain displays and exhibits from hundreds of different nations, organizations, and multinational corporations. Highlights include the brand new **Pavilhão de Água** *(Water Pavilion) and* **Pavilhão dos Oceanos** *(Ocean Pavilion).*

The city will be crowded during this special event and I strongly advise you to book your hotels and rental cars for Lisbon at least six months in advance.

NIGHTLIFE & ENTERTAINMENT
Fado

Fado is traditional Portuguese music mostly about bad luck and tragedy, which originated in 19th century Lisbon. With the help of one or more guitar players, typically a female singer (Fadista) belts out a beautiful yet sad story of twisted fate. Fado is performed in small restaurants known as adega tipicas and casas de Fado in the Alfama, Mouraria, Lapa, and especially the Bairro Alto districts. Usually the singing starts at 10:00pm or so, so don't get there too early. Most adega tipicas and casas de Fado offer traditional Portuguese dinners, and while the music is usually included in the meal prices, some require an additional cover charge of up to 2,500$00 per person (especially when dinner is not ordered).

Here is a list of some good Fado houses in Lisbon:

ARCADAS DO FAIA, *Rua da Barroca, 54. Tel. (01) 342-1923. Dress code is casual but neat. Most major credit cards accepted.*

This traditional and intimate white stucco and exposed beam Fado house and restaurant in the heart of the Bairro Alto district is perhaps the best in Lisbon. The menu features over two dozen delicious Portuguese fish, seafood, meat, chicken, and lamb dishes. They change seasonally and cost an average of 3,350$00 each. Along with dinner, there are continuous Fado shows with a talented singer and a couple of guitar players. Performances are daily except Sunday from about 9:45pm until 2:00am. The service is warm and friendly, and the family that runs the venue are charming. Ask to speak with Pedro Ramos, the owner's son, if you have any questions or just want to say hello: he speaks English perfectly.

A SERVERA, *Rua das Gaveas, 51. Tel. (01) 342-8314. Dress code is smart casual. Most major credit cards accepted.*

This is a famous Fado house named after an infamous Fadista. This Bairro Alto hot spot offers fun Fado and good meals.

O FORCADO, *Rua da Rosa, 219. Tel. (01) 346-8579. Dress code is smart casual. Most major credit cards accepted.*

Well known for several decades now, this Barrio Alto Fado house presents talented fadistas almost every night of the week until well past midnight. The food here is pretty good, and the cover charge is ususally under 2,000$00 a person.

SENHOR VINHO, *Rua Do Meio a Lapa, 18. Tel. (01) 397-2681. Dress code is smart casual. Most major credit cards accepted.*

A larger Fado restaurant in the Lapa area, it draws a mixed crowd of tourists and Portuguese. The food is pretty good and the Fado is compelling. Closed on Sunday.

CLUBE DE FADO, *Rua de São João de Praça, 92. Tel. (01) 885-2704. Dress code is smart casual. Cash only - No credit cards accepted.*

This is a geat place for enthusiasts of Fado that is within walking distance of the famous Sé Cathedral in the old part of the city. It's open until well past 1:00am on most nights.

PARREIRINHA, *Beco do Espirito Santo, 1. Tel. (01) 386-8209. Dress code is smart casual. Cash only - No credit cards accepted.*

This is a smaller, more intimate Fado house in the Alfama that serves large meals with good Fado.

CANTO DO CAMOES, *Travessa da Espera, 38. Tel. (01) 346-5464. Dress code is smart casual. Cash only - No credit cards accepted.*

The Fado here is a bit more powerful than most places, and has a wonderful seafood restaurant that matches the Fado.

ADEGA MACHADO, *Rua do Norte, 91. Tel. (01) 360-095. Dress code is smart casual. Most major credit cards accepted.*

Adega Machado is a larger, well known establishment where both the Fado and the meals are priced a bit high.

Bars & Clubs

For those of you who love the nightlife, Lisbon will not disappoint. As with many European countries, people dine later than in the US and

Canada, finishing about 10:30pm. The bar and club scene, therefore, isn't into full swing until 11:00pm or later.

One of the most popular hot spots is the **Bairro Alto** section. Over 35 small clubs and bars can be found, along with quirky little gallery/ restaurants, on every stone block in the area. Clubs sometimes have unmarked entrances, and if you find the doors locked, you'll need to ring a bell for admission. Tourists are usually not discriminated against, and you should have little problem entering any bar or club. Cover charges are rare in the Barrio, but a few discos and live music clubs such as the wonderful Cafe Luso or Fragil may charge you.

Sometime around 9:00pm or so, **Docas de Santos**, a newly developed area of former shipping warehouses, springs into life. Located in the western edge of Lisbon alongside a harbor full of yachts and just under the Ponte 25 de Abril, this brand new district has about 16 bars, eight restaurants, and several boutiques that stay open until at least 2:00am. The crowd here is a mix of casually dressed and friendly students and locals between the ages of 17 and 35. It's busy on the weekends and everyone is clearly out to have a good time.

After midnight or so, the action switches to the bars and discos on or just off the **Avenida 24 Julho** near the Ponte 25 de Abril. There is a combination of fun taverns, rock bars, packed dance clubs, and a few discos that select their patrons from the usually large line outside their establishment (they prefer beautiful women and famous Portuguese clientele). By 1:00am, over a thousand people are in the streets immediately outside the full clubs.

For the past few years, the **Alcantara** section has become home to a number of large converted warehouses that are now discos. Many of the "in" people who frequent Lisbon's nightlife scene prefer this area. By about 4am, most of these clubs close, and the action shifts to private parties or "outlaw" after hours clubs.

Any taxi driver or good hotel concierge will know the location of any of these places. Cover charges at most major dance clubs run about 1,500$00. Many larger clubs will hand you a drink card upon entry and each drink you order will be stamped on the card. When you exit, you will be asked for your card so that your bill can be totaled. Do not lose your drink card or else you will be asked to pay a hefty surcharge!

Alright, now you know the neighborhoods – here are the bars and clubs I recommend:

PAVILHÃO CHINES, *Rua Dom Pedro V, 89.*

If you are looking for a remarkable old world bar to relax in and have a cool drink, try this establishment on the edge of the Bairro Alto. This romantic bar is filled with glass cases displaying massive collections of antiques, art nouveau, and art deco items including rare candelabras, statuettes, hand painted ceramics, toy soldiers, model trains, and more. There are two awesome bars with inlaid wood and brass details, about 56 small booths and tables, and three pool tables. Drinks are a little expensive at 500$00 for a beer and around 1,000$00 for a cocktail, but there is no cover charge and the museum-like ambiance is interesting.

Make sure to look at the wonderful bar and table menus complete with sexy art deco illustrations (a great gift for 3,500$00 a copy). Open nightly from 6:00pm until 2:00am, this place is a must see, but be sure to get there before 11pm.

GARTEJO, *Rua J. Oliveira Miguens.*

A huge multi-level club, concert hall, and bar in the Alcantara section, this fashionable night spot is designed and owned by a well known architect. They also have great live music on some nights. Any taxi driver should know how to get you here.

THE HOT CLUB, *Praça da Alegria, 38.*

This small jazz bar behind Ave. da Liberdade features the finest live jazz in Lisbon. The Hot Club charges very reasonable cover charges (usually around 1,000$00 a person) and drink prices. There are weekly jam sessions and a friendly local crowd, and almost no tourists. Open Tuesday through Satuday from 10:00pm until 2:00am.

ALCANTARA-MAR, *Rua da Cozinha Economica.*

This huge industrial club in the Alcantara area draws a younger crowd who dance all night. Some side rooms contain oversized sofas and candle lit tables. Try a B-52.

RECORD, *Rua da Atalaia.*

This huge bar in the former Barrio Alto offices of a major Lisbon newspaper is the perfect place to start your evening. The beer costs only 200$00, and the music is a great blend of Rock, Blues, Fado, and more. The crowd wears jeans, is totally relaxed, usually between 25 and 35 years old, and sit at long wooden tables to chat with one another. This is my favorite place to hang out in this district, even on quiet nights.

SALSA LATINO, *Docas de Santos.*

If you want to dance to Latin salsa and tango music, head straight for this huge converted warehouse in the new Docas de Santos district. The crowd ranges from 18 to 40 years of age and really know how to dance. On weekends, there is a cover charge of up to 1,500$00 per person (includes one drink) and a line that starts at 10:30pm.

NOVA, *Rua Rosa, 261.*

A smaller more relaxed bar, the Nova has a high percentage of Nordic clientele. It's a good place to party all night in the Barrio Alto.

CASA DE LOUCOS, *Rua da Barroca, 30.*

This small candle-lit bar plays great classic rock and roll music such as the Rolling Stones and Jimi Hendrix. It caters to mainly couples and laid back singles. My only problem with this intimate place is that the drink prices are about double what they should be.

CAFE LUSO, *Travessa da Queimada, 10.*
Cafe Luso is an excellent small bar and occasional live music club. Probably the most relaxing place to hang out in the Barrio Alto.

FRAGIL, *Rua da Atalia.*
An extremely exclusive and trendy medium-sized club and bar, it caters to models, film stars, famous artists, and rock and rolls musicians who frequent the Barrio Alto. Make sure to arrive here before midnight or you may never get past the doorman.

SANTO AMARO CAFE, *Docas de Santo Amaro.*
A great modern bar and café, it's located in the new Docas de Santos section of town just near the bridge. They play cool jazz and rock music to a casual crowd of mostly single 25 to 30 year olds. There's no cover charge, and ice cold beer is only 300$00 a glass.

KAPITAL, *Ave. 24 de Julho.*
One of the hot-spots in the Santos area, Kapital has doormen who make people wait hours to get in. Once inside this multi-level glamour palace, you pay big bucks for drinks.

ESTADIOU, *Rua São Pedro de Alcantara.*
A dimly lit bohemian hang out for local artists and students, this is the place to drink coffee and feel like you're in East Berlin.

KREMLIN, *Escadinhas da Praia, 5.*
A cavernous disco in the Santos area just around the corner from Ave. 24 de Julho, the young crowd dances to hip hop and rock mixes.

PLATEAU, *Escadinhas da Praia, 7.*
Located immediately next to the Kremlin in Santos, this noisy and impolite dance club has an aggressive beat. If they know you're a tourist, you'll get in quicker.

ANOS SESSENTA, *Largo do Terreirinho, 21.*
Open only on weekend evenings, this cozy Alfama venue has good rock bands from Portugal and beyond. It's a great place to check out good local talent for a small cover charge.

ELEFANTE BRANCO, *Rua Luciano Cordeiro, 83.*
Did I say bar? This place is really Lisbon's most famous brothel. There is a minimum of about 5,000$00 a person, roughly equal to just a couple of drinks and the bill can go sky high from there, depending on what services you request. Be careful about going to a place like this (use a condom). This place is extremely popular with visiting executives.

SPORTS & RECREATION
Horseback Riding
•**Sociedade Hipica**, *Campo Grande, Tel. (01) 774-881*

Sailing
• **Clube Naval**, *Doca de Belem, Tel. (01) 363-0061*
• **Paço de Arcos Sailing**, *Paço de Arcos, Tel. (01) 443-2238*

Swimming
• **Aqua Park**, *Ave. Descobertas, Tel. (01) 617-000*

Tennis
• **Monsanto Parque Tennis**, *Parque Florestal, Tel. (01) 648-067*

SHOPPING

Lisbon is a great place to shop, and bargains can be found. I recommend a number of stores in various districts below. I have purchased great products at good prices at these places.

Baixa streets, such as Rua do Ouro, Rua dos Sapateiros, and Rua Augusta, offer visitors a vast array of shops that have reasonably priced clothing, leather goods, jewelry, and designer goods. The best place to look for good deals on antiques, old books, tiles (*azulejos*), and fine furnishings is along the Rua Dom Pedro V and Rua do Alecrim in the Bairro Alto as well as on Rua Alves Correira near the central Avenida da Liberdade area. For those of you interested in fine hand woven **Arraiolos carpets**, your best bet is in the Chiado.

For the finest European designer clothing, look around the Avenida da Roma off the Praça de Londres square.

For those of you who are more interested in finding real bargains in **outdoor markets**, there are several to choose from. The most interesting markets in Lisbon include the Feira da Ladra flea market at Campo Santa Clara in the Alfama (Tuesdays mornings and Saturday), the clothing markets at Praça de Chile (closed Sundays) and at the Aeroporto Rotunda near the airport (Sundays). Additional shopping can be found at the large mall style shopping complexes, listed below.

Don't forget to ask about the Tax Free refund vouchers that are discussed under shopping in Chapter 7, *Basic Information*.

Baixa

Malhas Achega, *Rua dos Fanqueiros, 30.*

A modern and bright store, they always seem to have a clearance sale on classic lamb's wool sweaters for about 4,000$00. I have seen these sweaters in New York for $95.

Sofia Lavores, *Rua Augusta, 179.*

A great little shop that sells fine hand embroidered tablecloths and fabrics starting at about 10,000$00.

Esquina da Roupa, *Rua de S. Nicolau, 44.*
This small and crammed shop has several racks of men's and women's pants, shirts, and jackets at very low prices. Last trip, I purchased pure wool pants (they all say "Made in Italy") for 3,800$00 each.
Moda Viva, *Rua dos Fraqueiros, 259.*
A busy clothing boutique, they offer last seasons best fashions at bargain basement prices. I bought pure wool, hand tailored suits for 21,000$00.
Barbosa, Esteves, *Rua da Prata, 295.*
Specializing in gold and silver jewelry, this pleasant shop contains several inexpensive gift items. A sterling silver key chain costs only 2,200$00.
Sapataria Lisbononse, *Rua Augusta, 202.*
A well stocked shoe store, their prices start at 6,900$00 for a pair of shoes.

Bairro Alto
Casa Saboia, *Rua Garrett, 66.*
This is a good designer shop that sells fine European menswear at good prices.
Fabrica Sant'ana, *Rua do Alecrim, 95.*
A workshop, factory outlet, and store that sells reproductions of classic Portuguese tiles (azulejos). They will custom manufacture tiles from your design.
Antiquario Dom Pedro V, *Rua Dom Pedro V.*
One of the better antique shops along this street, they offer a large assortment of European furnishings and accessories at good prices.

Chiado
Casa Quintão, *Rua Ivens, 34.*
A great store, they have a wonderful collection of fine Arraiolos carpets. Unfortunately, they have hefty prices, but they are certainly worth looking.
Vista Alegre, *Largo do Chiado, 18.*
This is an elegent shop where you will find the finest porcelain made in Portugal. Their creations start at about 5,000$00 for a place setting, and they are extraordinary.
Interio, *Rua Garrett, 49.*
This store is a good source for accessories used in interior decorating. Great stuff!

Shopping Centers

The following malls are air conditioned and open seven days a week from 9am - midnight.

Centro Comercío das Amoreiras, *Ave. Eng. Duarte Pacheco.*

This mall is currently the largest mall in Portugal with over 360 shops and indoor parking.

Centro Comercío Alvalade, *Praça de Alvalade.*

This medium sized center has about 80 shops.

Centro Comercío Imaviz, *Ave. Fontes Pereira de Melo* (next to the Sheraton).

An upscale shopping center, it has reasonable prices and about 60 shops.

Centro Comercío Fonte Nova, *Estrada de Benfica.*

A large center on the outskirts of town, it has over 100 shops.

PRACTICAL INFORMATION FOR LISBON

Currency Exchange

All banks in Lisbon have currency exchange counters (cambios) that are open from 8:30am until 3pm (some take a lunch break).

Embassies

• **US Embassy,** *Avenida das Forcas Armadas, Tel. (01)726-6600*
• **Canadian Embassy,** *Avenida da Liberdade, 144, Tel. (01) 347-4892*
• **UK Embassy,** *Rua S. Domingos a Lapa, 37, Tel. (01) 396-1191*

Emergency & Useful Phone Numbers

• **ACP** (emergency road service), *Tel. (01) 942-5095*
• **Ambulance service,** *Tel. (01) 617-777*
• **British Hospital,** *Tel. (01) 602-020 day, (01) 603-785 night*
• **Emergency services** (S.O.S.), *Tel. 115*
• **Fire Department,** *Tel. (01) 342-2222*
• **Police,** *Tel. (01) 346-6141*
• **Tourist Police,** *Tel. (01) 346-6141*
• **Directory Assistance,** *Tel. 118*
• **Airport** (Portela), *Tel. (01) 802-060*
• **Delta Airlines** in Lisbon, *Tel. (01) 353-7610*
• **Portugalia Airlines,** *Tel. (01) 848-6693*
• **TAP at Lisbon Airport,** *Tel. (01) 386-0480*
• **TAP Reservations,** *Tel. (01) 386-1020*
• **Taxi,** *Tel. (01) 793-2756*

Museums, Palaces, & Monuments

Unless otherwise indicated, the venues below are closed on Mondays and most holidays. Children under 12 years of age can usually receive discounts of up to 65%. Many museums, historical sites and monuments are free on Sunday afternoons after 2:00pm.

Call the specific museum, palace, or monument listed below for further information:

• **Museu Arqueologico do Carmo** (Archaeological Museum of Carmo), *Rua do Carmo, Largo do Carmo. Tel. (01) 346-0473. Open 10:00am - 1:00pm and 2:00pm - 5:00pm, October-April, 10:00am - 5:00pm May-September. Admission: 250$00 per person.* Contains prehistoric through medieval era art, rare medieval coins, ancient epigraphy, sculptures, tiles, and ceramics.

• **Museu Calouste Gulbenkian** (Calouste Gulbenkian Museum), *Avenida de Berna, 45. Tel. (01) 793-5131. Open 2:00pm - 7:30pm Wednesday and Saturday, 10:00am - 5pm, Tuesday, Thursday, Friday, and Sunday. Admission: 500$00 per person, 20% discount with Lisboa Card.* Contains a millionaire's private collection of ancient through 19th century paintings, fabrics, pottery, glass, brass, sculptures, jewelry, furniture, porcelain, ivory, books, and decorative arts.

• **Castelo de São Jorge** (Saint George's Castle), *Rua da Costa do Castelo. Open every day 8:00am to at least Sunset. Admission: No fee.* Contains the Alcacova royal palace ruins and museum (the museum is currently not open), as well as several towers and defensive walls that can be seen from a panoramic walking path that also has fine views of most of Lisbon. There is also a superb gourmet restaurant called Casa do Leão in the castle ruins.

• **Museu da Cidade** (City Museum), *Campo Grande, 245. Tel. (01) 757-1725. Open 10:00am - 1:00pm and 2:00pm - 6:00pm year round. Admission: 320$00 per person, free with Lisboa Card.* Located in the 18th century Palácio Pimenta, this museum contains documents and relics regarding the evolution of Lisbon from prehistoric days until the revolution of 1910. Also includes an 18th century Ensemble Epoque.

• **Museu de Artes Decorativas Portuguesas** (Decorative Arts Museum of the Espirito Santo Silva Foundation), *Largo das Portas do Sol, 2. Tel. (01) 886-2183. Open 10:00am - 1:00pm and 2:00pm - 5:00pm year round. Admission: 500$00 per person, 20% discount with Lisboa Card.* Contains collection of antique Portuguese and European fine furniture, ceramics, Arraiolos carpets, textiles, silver, and 15th - 19th century Portuguese paintings.

• **Centro de Arte Moderna de Dr. J. Azeredo Perdigão** (Dr. Perdigão Modern Art Center at the Gulbenkian Foundation), *Rua Dr. Nicolau Bettencourt. Tel. (01) 795-5131. Open 10:00am - 5:00pm. Admission:*

500$00 per person. Contains modern paintings, sculpture, and engravings from around the world.

• **Museu Nacional de Arte Antiga** (National Museum of Ancient Art), *Rua das Janelas Verdes, 9. Tel. (01) 396-4151. Open 10:00am - 1:00pm and 2:30pm - 6:00pm year round. Admission: 500$00 per person, free with Lisboa Card.* Contains 14th through 19th century local and European sculpture, jewelry, silverware, ceramics, as well as Oriental and African art, textiles, designs, furniture, porcelain, engravings and 16th century filigree.

• **Museu Nacional de Arqueologia de Dr. Leite Vasconcelos** (National Museum of Archaeology), *Praça do Imperio. Tel. (01) 362-0000. Open 10:00am - 1:00pm and 2:30pm - 6:00pm year round. Admission: 350$00 per person, free with Lisboa Card.* Contains Portuguese archaeological findings from the Paleolithic period onward. Includes ancient jewelry, coins, sculpture, mosaics, and a vast library on the subject.

• **Museu do Teosouro da Sé** (Lisbon Cathedral's Treasury Museum), *Largo da Sé. Tel. (01) 886-6752. Open from 10:00am - 5:00pm, closed on Sundays and religious holidays. Admission: 400$00 per person.* Includes the countless treasures of the Cathedral such as gold and silver religious loate, paintings, jewelry, and costumes.

• **Museu do Chiado** (Chiado District Museum), *Rua Serpa Pinto, 4. Tel. (01) 343-2148. Open 10:00am - 6:00pm. Admission: 400$00 per person, free with Lisboa Card.* Contains 19th and 20th century painting and sculpture.

• **Museu Nacional dos Coches** (National Museum of Coaches), *Praça Afonso de Albuquerque. Tel. (01) 363-8022. Open 10:00am - 5:30pm year round. Admission: 450$00 per person, free with Lisboa Card.* Contains a collection of royal coaches from as far back as the 17th century. Also includes bullfighting costumes and a royal portrait gallery.

• **Museu Nacional do Traje** (National Museum of Costumes), *Largo Júlio de Castilho, Parque do Monteiro-Mor. Tel. (01) 759-0318. Open 10:00am - 1:00pm and 2:30pm - 5:30pm year round. Admission: 400$00 per person, free with Lisboa Card.* Contains Coptic fabrics from as far back as the 4th century, clothing from the 17th century onward, antique toys, and textile weaving and printing documents.

• **Palácio Nacional da Ajuda** (National Palace of Ajuda), *Largo da Ajuda. Tel. (01) 363-7095. Open 10am - 5:00pm year round, closed Wednesdays and holidays. Admission: 400$00 per person, free with Lisboa Card.* This royal palace from the 19th century is loaded with fine collections of paintings, sculptures, and amazing decorative arts.

• **Palácio dos Marqueses de Fronteira** (Palace of the Marques of Fronteira), *Largo São Domingos de Benfica, 1, Tel. (01) 778-2023. Open for a one hour tour at 11:00am and 12:00 noon in low season, or every half hour 10:30am*

- *12:00 noon during the high season, closed Sundays and holidays. Admission: 1,300$00 per person.* This is a 17th century palace with outstanding gardens.

• **Museu do Marioneta** (Marionette Museum), *Largo Rodrigues de Freitas, 19A. Open 11:00am - 1:00pm and 3:00pm - 6:00pm year round. Admission: 350$00 per person.* Contains a collection of marionettes dating from the 19th century.

• **Museu da Musica** (Musical Instrument Museum), *Rua Maestro de João Freiras Branco. Tel. (01) 778-8074. Open with advance arrangement only, call for details.* Contains a collection of over 130 antique instruments.

• **Museu Rafeal Bordalo Pinheiro** (Rafeal Bordalo Pinheiro Museum), *Campo Grande, 382. Tel. (01) 759-0816. Open 10:00am - 1:00pm and 2:00pm - 6:00pm. Admission: 250$00 per person, free with Lisboa Card.* This museum is dedicated to the Portuguese artist R.B. Pinheiro and contains many fine examples of his engravings, paintings, ceramics, and drawings.

• **Museu de Arte Sacra** (Museum of Sacred Art), *Largo Trindade Coelho. Tel. (01) 346-0361. Open 10:00am - 5:00pm. Admission: 150$00 per person.* This museum has many rare examples of Portuguese and European art that was saved from the interiors of now demolished churches.

• **Museu Nacional do Azulejo** (National Museum of Tiles), *Convento on Rua da Madre de Deus. Tel. (01) 814-7747. Open 10:00am - 12:30pm and 2:00pm - 6:00pm year round. Admission: 350$00 per person, free with Lisboa Card.* Contains a collection of Portuguese and foreign tiles from as far back as the 15th century. Also includes a collection of 17th and 18th century paintings.

• **Mostereiro dos Jeronimos** (Monastery of St. Jeronimos), *Praça do Imperio, Tel. (01) 362-0034. Open 10:00am - 1:00pm and 2:30pm - 5:00pm October - May, 10:00am - 6:30pm June - September. Admission: 400$00 per person, free with Lisboa Card.* A Manueline style 16th century monastery with exceptional cloisters.

• **Torre de Belem** (Tower of Belem), *Praça do Imperio. Tel. (01) 362-0034. Open 10:00am - 6:30pm June - September, 10:00am - 1:00pm and 2:30pm - 5:00pm October - May. Admission: 400$00 per person, free with Lisboa Card.* A 16th century defensive structure on the Tejo River.

Post Office
• **Central Post Office**, *Praça do Comercio, Tel. (01) 346-3231*

Tour Guides & Tour Operators
Private guides can be arranged by the half or full day through your travel agent or tour operator, or as a last resort by contacting the Sindicato

National de Actividade Turística, *Tel. (01) 346-7170.* The typical price for a licensed private guide starts at about 17,500$00 plus expenses per day. Perhaps the best alternative to the high cost of a private guide is a bus tour. You can choose between half and full day tours that usually include admission to a variety of museums and places of interest. The tours are conducted by licensed multilingual local guides and utilize large deluxe air conditioned busses. They can be reserved in advance through your travel agent, tour operator, hotel concierge, the bus company directly, or by showing up at tour company kiosks in front of Eduardo VII park. Advance reservations may include a complimentary transfer from your hotel in Lisbon, Estoril, and Cascais. Call the bus company directly for details.

Citirama, *Avenida Praia da Vitória, 12. Tel. (01) 355-8567,* offers the following tours:

• **Three Hour Lisbon City Tour**, departs daily at 9:30am and 2:30pm, 4,900$00 per person. Includes Marquês de Pombal area, a ride across the Tagus River bridge, panoramic view from top of Eduardo VII park, admission and tour of Coach Museum (except on Monday when closed), visit to Jeronimos monastery, visit to Tower of Belem and the Monument of Discoveries, a wine tasting and walk around St. George's castle, a short walk in the Alfama, and a drive past the Rossio.

• **Four Hour Lisbon by Night Tour**, departs Monday, Wednesday, and Friday at 8:00pm, 11,900$00 per person. Includes Marquês de Pombal area, Ave. da Liberdade, Rossio, Monument of the Discoveries, Tower of Belem, Jeronimos monastery, Ponte 25 Abril, Alcantara, and dinner with two drinks at a Fado restaurant with folkloric show.

• **Ten Hour Lisbon and Estoril Coastal Area Tour**, departs daily at 9:30am, 12,900$00 per person. Includes St. George's castle, walking tour in the Alfama, Coach Museum visit, Jeronimos monastery visit, Tower of Belem, Monument of the Discoveries, free time for lunch at Marquês de Pombal, afternoon visit to the Basilica de Mafra, Palácio de Pena in Sintra (except when closed on Monday), a brief stop at Palácio de Queluz (except when closed on Tuesday), a visit to Cabo da Rocha, Guincho, Boca do Inferno, Cascais, and Estoril.

Greyline Tours, *Ave. Praia da Vitória, 12. Tel. (01) 352-2594,* offers the following tours:

• **Eight Hour Lisbon and Costa Azul Tour**, departs Monday - Friday between April - October at 9:30am, departs Tuesday and Thursday between November - March at 9:30am, 11,900$00 per person. Includes downtown Lisbon, Jeronimos monastery, Coach museum, Tower of Belem, Monument of the Discoveries, St. Jorges castle, a

typical local lunch, visits to the coastal areas of Sesimbra, Setúbal, Palmela, and a wine tasting in Azeitão.
• **Eight Hour Óbidos and Surroundings Tour**, departs daily at 8:30am. 13,900$00 per person. Includes Óbidos, the monastery at Alcobaca, a tour and a typical lunch in Nazaré, a stop at the Monastery in Batalha, and a visit to the famous religious center of Fátima.

Tourist Information Offices

Open seven days a week, they provide maps, brochures, reservations, and suggestions in English. They also sell gift items and books at good prices.
• **Main Turismo Office**, *Palácio Foz, Praça dos Restauradores (just off Avenida da Liberdade)*, *Tel. (01) 346-3643*
• **Airport Tourist Office**, *Tel. (01) 848-5974*

Travel Agencies

If you are in need of hotel reservations, plane tickets, sight-seeing tours, guides, train tickets, or rental cars you can contact one of the following agencies:
• **Quasar**, *Rua Artilharia Um, 39. Tel. (01) 691-919*. This is the best travel agency in Portugal. Most of the staff speak perfect English and can book any imaginable hotel, quinta, pousada, car rental, guided tour, and airline ticket.
• **Abreu**, *Ave. da Liberdade, 160. Tel. (01) 347-6441*. A large travel agency with offices throughout Portugal, they can book all types of travel arrangements but specialize in packages.
• **Top**, *Ave. Duque de Loulé, 108. Tel. (01) 315-5885*. The official American Express agent in Lisbon, this office has full ticketing facilities.

12. COSTA DE LISBOA

The **Costa de Lisboa** – Coast of Lisbon – consists of the southern portions of **Estremadura** and **Ribatejo** provinces and the cities, villages, and ocean resort areas that surround Lisbon. The Costa de Lisboa is a perfect place to explore many historical villages, mountaintop castles, authentic fishing towns, sporting centers, long sandy beaches with dramatic windswept cliffs, and of course the impressive capital city of Lisbon. As the region extends into the interior of the country, many beautiful valleys, hills, and rivers are also in evidence. The short distances between major attractions in this region make it easy to take day trips from a central location.

Among the most impressive sights in this region are the fine beaches at **Guincho**, **Estoril**, **Praia Adraga**, **Caparica**, and **Tróia**, the fine castles and palaces of the beautiful and mysterious town of **Sintra** and nearby **Queluz**, the dramatic cliffs at **Cabo da Roca**, the traditional fishing village of **Sesimbra**, the fine golf courses throughout the **Estoril** area, the bullfighting village of **Vila Franca de Xira**, and the jet-set resort town of **Cascais**.

ARRIVALS & DEPARTURES

The main airport servicing this region is Portela International Airport just outside of downtown Lisbon.

From the airport, the easiest way to get to various destinations in this region is to either rent a car, pre-arrange transfer to your hotel from your travel agent, or take a somewhat expensive taxi ride.

Those looking for a more affordable way to reach the resorts and major towns within the Costa de Lisboa can take the airport's great Aerobus (a shuttle bus) into downtown Lisbon and transfer to frequent bus, rail, and ferry services that take you to over 47 different Costa de Lisboa destinations. The Turismo office in the airport's international arrivals area can give you current schedules and price information.

ORIENTATION

The Costa de Lisboa is situated along the western edge of south central Portugal and borders the Atlantic Ocean. This tiny yet heavily populated region surrounds the capital city of Lisbon, goes north up the coast about 21 kilometers (13 miles) to the town of Ericeira, and heads southward along the coast for approximately 84 kilometers (53 miles) before ending at Sines.

GETTING AROUND THE REGION

By Car

Driving in this region is a fairly easy task. The vast majority of roads in the Costa de Lisboa are in excellent condition and many of the region's super-fast highways have tolls of up to 400$00 per car for even the shortest of drives. Since this area also includes the Lisbon suburbs, rush hour is 7:30am until 10:00am and 4:45pm until 7:30pm. Traffic conditions are horrific, and North Americans who do not live in large urban areas may be stunned at how slow the traffic can move.

Street parking is a rarity in major resort areas and cities in this part of the country, so expect to pay at least 175$00 an hour for municipal or private garages.

By Bus, Train, & Ferry

Mass transportation is available in the Costa de Lisboa, and almost all systems use Lisbon as a connecting point. The most common link to the extremely popular resort areas of Cascais, Carcovelos, and Estoril is the comfortable and inexpensive **electric commuter train**. It runs along the seaside every 15 minutes to and from Lisbon's Cais de Sodre train station. Those going to the large suburban cities of Sintra, Sesimbra, Setúbal, Mafra, Queluz, and Caparica will find no problem with rail connections via Lisbon's Rossio train station.

Places such as Palmela, Azeitão, Vila Nova de Milfontes, Cabo da Roca, and most other cities and villages in this region are serviced by a growing number of **private bus companies** that operate out of centrally located depots or covered bus stops in the heart of almost every town including Lisbon.

In the unlikely event that you wish to access one of the residential suburbs along the southern coast of the Tejo River such as Barreiro, Montijo, Seixal, and Cacilhas, you will need to use the **ferry** from Lisbon's water-front Terreiro do Paço ferry terminal.

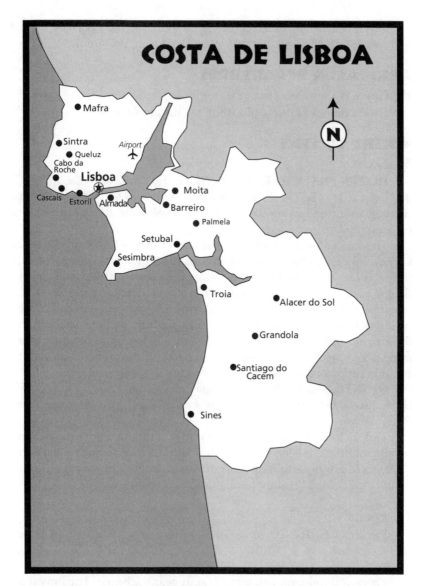

OEIRAS, CARCAVELOS, & NEARBY COASTAL BEACHES

Oeiras is a beautiful historic village and a few kilometers southwest of town you will find the Costa de Lisboa's longest stretch of windswept sandy beach in the affordably priced summer resort area of **Carcavelos** (also known as **Parede**). This area attracts a mixture of local and foreign vacationers that stay for at least a few weeks at a time.

Other beaches further west along the coast, at **São Pedro de Estoril** and **São João de Estoril**, get very crowded during the summer.

ARRIVALS & DEPARTURES
By Car
Oeiras lies 15 km west of Lisbon off Route N-6 west.

WHERE TO STAY
Moderate
HOTEL PRAIA MAR, *Rua do Gurue, 16, Carcavelos. Tel. (01) 457-3131, Fax (01) 457-3130. Low season rack rates from 13,000$00, double room, BP; high season rack rates from 18,000$00, double room, BP. All major credit cards accepted.*
The Praia Mar is a modern 4 star hotel facing a fine sandy beach at Carcavelos. This nine floor property has 158 medium sized air conditioned rooms that either face the ocean or the town's streets, and all have deluxe private bathrooms, comfortable wooden furnishings, direct dial telephone, remote control satellite television, hair dryers, and either large windows or private balconies. Additional facilities include a superb top floor panoramic gourmet restaurant, a nice bar, a large outdoor swimming pool, sun deck, a TV lounge, free parking, and an excellent staff of multilingual professionals. I highly recommend this hotel.

QUINTA DAS ENCOSTAS, *Largo Vasco d'Orey, Parede, Tel. (01) 457-0056, Fax (01) 458-2647. Year round rack rates from 16,500$00, double room, BP. Cash only - No credit cards accepted.*
This is a beautiful 18th century manor house and former wine producing estate. It is located only a few minutes away from the beach and offers six fine antique filled guest rooms with private bathrooms. Facilities include gardens, TV room, pool, library, and parking.

Inexpensive
PENSÃO NARISCO, *Praia de Carcavelos, Tel. (01) 457-0157. Year round rack rates from 10,500$00, double room, EP. Cash only - No credit cards accepted.*
This is a simple, yet comfortable, inn near the beach. The inn offers 15 good rooms with private bathrooms. Facilities include bar, restaurant, TV, and nearby parking.

WHERE TO EAT
Moderate
ROSA DOS VENTAS, *Hotel Praia Mar, Rua do Gurue, Carcavelos. Tel. (01) 457-3131. Dress code is smart casual. All major credit cards accepted.*

I was impressed by the superb cuisine, service, and panoramic view of this surprisingly affordable gourmet restaurant on the top floor of the Hotel Praia Mar. The interior dining room is decorated with frescoes and has an elegant yet comfortable ambiance. The wait staff are all experts at helping you choose the right dishes.

Their extensive menu features such delicious items as cheese soufflé, prawn cocktails, mixed salads, smoked salmon, mushrooms in creamy wine sauce on toast, cured ham, smoked local swordfish, French onion soup, seafood stew, grilled tiger prawns, steamed clams, skewers of angler fish and shrimp, filet of sole with anchovy sauce, poached salmon, braised rump steak, veal cutlets with Roquefort cheese, broiled chicken with bacon, lamb chops with mint, chateaubriand, roast duckling with cherries, pork medallions cooked in clams, beef steak, and a great array of tasty desserts.

Make sure to order a bottle of Buçaco wine, and expect dinner to cost around 4,200$00 a person.

DOM PEPE, *Ave. Marginal-Parede. Tel. (01) 247-0636. Dress code is smart casual. Most major credit cards accepted.*

Dom Pepe is a wonderful and sophisticated regional restaurant on the Estrada Marginal. They serve superb shellfish, grilled meat and fish specialties in an upscale setting. Expect to pay 4,500$00 per person, and up for dinner.

A CHOUPANA, *Estrada Marginal-São João de Estoril. Tel. (01) 468-3099. Dress code is smart casual. Most major credit cards accepted.*

This is a very good fish and steak restaurant on Estrada Marginal with good service, and one of the best views in the entire area. Closed on Mondays. Dinner here will set you back 4,350$00 a person and up plus wine.

SEEING THE SIGHTS

In **Oeiras** you can view the former 18th century **Palácio do Marques**, once home to the Marquês de Pombal. Now part of the Gulbenkian Foundation, this lovely pink palace is generally closed to the public but nobody stopped me from entering its tranquil gardens.

There is little else to see in town other than the fine 17th century church, **Igreja Matriz**, and a few oceanfront fortresses from the 16th-18th century just south of the town.

If you happen to be in **Carcavelos** on a Thursday, check out its weekly **mercado** (market) in the town center. You'll find local produce and cheap leather goods.

SPORTS & RECREATION
Tennis
• **Oeiras Tennis Club**, *Oeiras*, *(01) 443-6699*

ESTORIL

This exclusive resort town is primarily known for its palm lined avenues, beaches, a casino, and the villas of exiled European royalty. Estoril has become a second home for the rich and famous. Recently, Estoril and neighboring Monte Estoril have become a bit crammed with hotels and condo complexes that seem to pop up overnight.

ARRIVALS & DEPARTURES
By Bus
• **Main Bus Office**, *Ave. Marginal, Tel. (01) 468-2293*

By Car
Estoril is about 26 km west (down river) of Lisbon on Route N-6.

By Train
• **CP Rail**, *Ave. Marginal, Tel. (01) 468-0113*

GETTING AROUND TOWN
By Car
Traffic is a major problem in this area, and it is best to avoid the roads during morning and evening rush hours.
• **Avis Rent a Car**, *Estrada Marginal, Tel. (01) 468-5728*

By Taxi
• **Estoril Taxi**, *Tel. (01) 468-0067*

WHERE TO STAY
Very Expensive
HOTEL PALÁCIO ESTORIL, *Parque do Estoril. Tel. (01) 468-0400, Fax (01) 468-4867. US & Canada Bookings with Leading Hotels of the World, Tel. 800/223-6800. Low season rack rates from 30,000$00, double room, BP; high season rack rates from 37,000$00, double room, BP. All major credit cards accepted.*

This elegant 5 star old world property is just a two minute walk from the beach. The Palácio Estoril has 162 deluxe air conditioned rooms and suites with marble bathrooms, remote control satellite television, direct dial telephone, mini-bar, hair dryers, nice art deco furnishings, and terraces in many cases.

The hotel also is home to the incredible Four Seasons grill, a complimentary full American buffet breakfast, a nearby 18 hole championship golf course, 18 tennis courts, a wonderful outdoor swimming pool and sun deck, lavish sitting rooms and lounges, a health club with sauna, private gardens, fine boutiques, business meeting and reception rooms, car rental and excursion desks, plenty of free outdoor and valet parking, baby-sitting and secretarial services, and easy access to the adjacent Estoril Casino complex. Selected as one of my *Best Places to Stay* (see Chapter 10 for more details).

Expensive

HOTEL DA INGLATERRA, *Rua do Porto, 1. Tel. (01) 468-4461, Fax (01) 469-2108. US and Canada bookings with Best Western, Tel. 800/528-1234. Year round rack rates from 22,750$00, double room, CP. Most major credit cards accepted.*

A restored mansion in the hills above central Estoril, this hotel has 52 rooms with private bathrooms, cable television, air conditioning, and direct dial telephones, and recently underwent extensive renovations to once again become one of Estoril's best. Facilities include bar, restaurant, swimming pool, sun deck, and free parking.

LENOX COUNTRY CLUB, *Rua Alvaro Pedro de Sousa, 5. Tel. (01) 468-0424, Fax (01) 467-0859. Year round rack rates from 24,500$00, double room, CP. Most major credit cards accepted.*

The Lenox is a welcoming and well respected medium sized hotel located a few blocks from the ocean. Each of the 34 rooms contains private bathrooms, air conditioning, direct dial phones, and cable television. The rooms have been uniquely designed for the comfort of guests. Some of the better rooms and suites have nice patios. Facilities include bar, restaurant, pool, sun deck, and parking.

HOTEL ESTORIL PRAIA, *Estrada Marginal. Tel. (01) 468-1811, Fax (01) 468-1815. Year round rack rates from 23,000$00, double room, CP. Most major credit cards accepted.*

The Praia is a nice comfortable 4 star hotel located downtown. You will find friendly service, and 91 air conditioned rooms with private bathrooms and televisions. This hotel also has some good amenities and minimal facilities including bar, pool, barber, disco, direct dial phones, and parking.

HOTEL CLUBE MIMOSA, *Ave. do Lago. Tel. (01) 467-0037, Fax (01) 467-0374. Year round rack rates from 27,500$00 per apartment per night, E.P. Most major credit cards accepted.*

This nice modern 59 unit apartment-hotel complex is situated very close to downtown Estoril. This hotel is a good selection for those who prefer to cook their own meals. There are studios, one and two bedroom apartments, and penthouses to choose from. All rooms have kitchens, satellite television, telephone, and radio. Facilities include bar, snack bar, restaurant, health club, pool, sauna, boutiques, mini-market, and parking.

Moderate

CASAL DE SÃO ROQUE, *Ave Marginal. Tel. (01) 468-0217. Year round rack rates from 19,750$00, double room, CP. Most major credit cards accepted.*

This small, but comfortable oceanview inn near the heart of Estoril offers four nice guest rooms with and without private bathrooms. The facilities are minimal, but there's lots of atmosphere.

HOTEL LIDO, *Rua do Alentejo, 12. Tel. (01) 468-4123, Fax (01) 468-3665. Year round rack rates from 17,250$00, double room, EP. Most major credit cards accepted.*

Hotel Lido is a pretty good hotel about five minutes away from the beach. All 62 rooms have air conditioning, private bathrooms, television, and in many cases there are also nice balconies. It offers several facilities including a bar, snack bar, restaurant, swimming pool, sun deck, sauna, shops, children's activities, billiards, ping pong, and lots of free parking.

Inexpensive

RESIDENCIAL SMART, *Rua José Viana, 3. Tel. (01) 468-2164. Year round rack rates from 9,750$00, double room, EP. Cash only - No credit cards accepted.*

One of the better budget properties in the area, it has 13 clean guest rooms with private bathrooms. Facilities include bar, garden, TV room, and parking.

WHERE TO EAT

Expensive

FOUR SEASONS GRILL, *Hotel Palácio Estoril, Parque do Estoril. Tel. (01) 468-0400. Dress code is jacket and tie. All major credit cards accepted.*

This superb gourmet restaurant keeps getting better year after year. The art deco and candle-lit duplex interior is richly decorated with handcrafted hardwood furnishings, antique chandeliers, and beautiful works of art. The Four Seasons has a wonderfully relaxed and intimate setting for its lucky patrons.

Diners are well dressed and enjoy a vast selection of outstanding specialties such as mixed salads, consommé with Port wine, smoked serrano ham, stuffed crepes with three cheeses, Vichyssoise, clams in coriander sauce, Beluga caviar, Tamariz fish soup, shrimp salad, venison with chestnuts, roast duck with orange sauce, tortelini with Roquefort cheese, salmon baked with shrimp sauce, steak in pepper sauce, spaghetti Bolognese, grilled lobster and prawns, chicken Diablo, flamed shrimps in Pernod, peach Melba, mango Benedictine, and crepes flamed at your table.

Expect to spend at least 4,500$00 per person for a delightful three course meal, and call in advance for reservations.

FURUSATI TAMARIZ, *Praia do Tamariz. Tel. (01) 468-4430. Dress code is jacket and tie. All major credit cards accepted.*

This is a beautiful and authentic Japanese restaurant located at waters edge in a converted mansion. They offer a selection of the highest quality sushi, sashimi, tempura, and hibachi grilled Kobe steak and fresh seafood specialties. Expect to spend around 5,500$00 and up, per person, for dinner.

Moderate

THE ENGLISH BAR, *Ave. Marginal. Tel. (01) 468-0413. Dress code is casual. Most major credit cards accepted.*

The old English wood and leather interior will make you feel at home in this well established, simple restaurant. Fresh seafood is always available at somewhat reasonable prices. A meal here will cost you around 2,250$00 a head.

A MARE, *Ave. Marginal. Tel. (01) 468-5570. Dress Code is casual. Most major credit cards accepted.*

This is a small, informal restaurant and pub with nice views off the Ave. Marginal in Monte Estoril. They specialize in low priced international cuisine with friendly service. Expect to spend around 2,900$00 a person for a full dinner.

SEEING THE SIGHTS

In the center of the city is a large public garden with an international **casino** set in the middle. Although rather small by North American standards, the casino attracts many tourists to its nightly dinner shows featuring topless dancers and orchestrated Hollywood-type music. To enter any of the gaming rooms you must show your passport, dress fairly well, and pay a small entrance fee. The public garden is relaxed and is fun to stroll through. When you're done strolling, there are several outdoor cafés around the garden for a respite.

During the warmer months many of the area's young people relax on the sand and the outdoor tables in front of the **Praia do Estoril** and **Praia do Tamariz** beaches. A rather attractive oceanview esplanade runs all the way to Cascais.

Some of the most impressive sights in town are the immense stately houses tucked away on quiet side streets and water view cul-de-sacs. Ferraris and Porsches can be seen disappearing behind the gated driveways of well guarded villas of foreign dignitaries.

Huge events such as the summertime **concert series**, and the yearly evening **crafts festival** (Feira do Artesanto) brings thousands of new visitors to the Estoril area in July and August. A massive **Formula 1 Grand Prix** in September attracts sell-out crowds of over 90,000 spectators to the Estoril Autodromo.

NIGHTLIFE & ENTERTAINMENT

The nightlife in Estoril centers around a series of pubs and dance clubs around the center of town, the Monte Estoril area, and the oceanfront. Many people tend to start off at bars along Ave. Saboia that runs through both Estoril and Monte Estoril like **Bauhaus** and **Mr. Busby's**.

Others stay around downtown Estoril and go to the cafés and small clubs that line the **Parque do Estoril**. After 1am, the crowds gravitate to the hip hop dance clubs like the wonderful **Ruinha** and less attractive **Louvre** on Ave. Fausto Figueiredo. The real late night people tend to dance the night away in São João de Estoril at the oceanfront **Forte Velho** on Ave. Marginal. Estoril's older crowd tends to enjoy themselves at the **Casino de Estoril** or at the nearby **Frolic Club**.

SPORTS & RECREATION

The Estoril area offers its visitors an abundant amount of sporting activities. There are several golf academies in the area, as well as tennis, sailing, sea fishing, water-skiing, and horseback riding.

Golf
• **Estoril Golf Club**, Estoril, Tel. (01) 468-0176

Tennis
• **Estoril Tennis Club**, Estoril, Tel. (01) 466-2770

CASCAIS

This former fishing village has become home to a younger, jet set crowd and has evolved from obscurity to become the favored suburb of Lisbon's upper class. Known by some as the Portuguese Riviera, many European expatriates live in the area and have created a huge English speaking community. Although the mosaic lined lanes through much of the city are now filled with designer boutiques, Cascais has managed to maintain an elegant old world charm.

ARRIVALS & DEPARTURES
By Air
The major airport nearest to Cascais is Portela International Airport in Lisbon. From the airport, the easiest way to get to Cascais is to either rent a car, pre-arrange a transfer from your travel agent, or take a taxi for around 4,250$00. A less expensive method is to take Portela airport's rapid Aero-bus (a shuttle bus) as close as you can to the Cais de Sodre electric train station near the Tejo River in downtown Lisbon. From the station you can hop aboard one of the frequent electric trains to Cascais' train station just off the beach for about 175$00 a person.

By Car
From Lisbon, follow Avenida 24 de Julho westward through Estoril. Cascais is only 5 km from Estoril on Route N-6 west. The road follows the river, and be careful because the road changes its name several times.
When you arrive, your first obstacle is finding parking. I suggest you head directly into the heart of the city and look for either metered parking or head for the municipal parking lots at the end of Ave. Marginal.

By Train
If you arrive by train into the Cascais station, all you do is walk out of the station and you will be on the major street in town, Ave. Marginal, and only a few blocks from the ocean.

ORIENTATION
Cascais sits along the beaches of the Atlantic Ocean 17 kilometers (11 miles) west of downtown Lisbon. The most obvious point of reference is the ocean, from which you will never be more than a five minute walk away.

GETTING AROUND TOWN
By Bus
Municipal buses are easy to both find and utilize, but are not really necessary since the distances you will cover in town are short.

By Car

Finding street parking in Cascais is just about impossible these days, but there are several private and municipal parking lots that can be used for around 225$00 per hour or 2,150$00 per day.

Park your car in one of these lots and get around town by foot since the traffic in town can be terrible. Cascais has terrible rush hour traffic from 7:00am - 9:00am and again from 4:45pm - 7:30pm each weekday.

If you want to rent a car, try:
• **Europcar Rent a Car in Cascais**, *Ave. Marginal, (01) 486-4419*

By Foot

This is the best way to get around Cascais: everything is within walking distance and you don't have to deal with traffic or parking.

By Taxi

Taxis are easy to find, but are not necessary to use while in town since the distances you will cover are short.

WHERE TO STAY

Very Expensive

HOTEL ALBATROZ, *Rua Frederico Arouca. Tel. (01) 483-2821, Fax (01) 484-4827. Year round rack rates from 30,750$00, double room, BP. Most major credit cards accepted.*

The Hotel Albatroz is certainly the finest hotel in Cascais. This mansion is perched on top of a sea cliff with dramatic views from several rooms and the dining room. Service is top quality, and the food is superb. It's a smaller hotel, with just 40 rooms. Facilities include bar, restaurant, room service, pool, air conditioning, cable TV, and garage.

ESTALAGEM SENHORA DA GUIA, *Estrada do Guincho. Tel. (01) 486-9239, Fax (01) 486-9227. Year round rack rates from 24,500$00, double room, BP. Most major credit cards accepted.*

A beautiful medium sized country inn, it has the ambiance and charm of a rich friend's summer home. The 43 rooms and suites are uniquely decorated with beautiful furnishings and, in some cases, fine antiques. Rooms also have air conditioning, private bathrooms, cable television, mini-bar, mini-safe, direct dial telephone, and some have oceanview terraces. Facilities include bar, restaurant, business meeting center, nearby golf course, huge gardens, swimming pool, and parking.

HOTEL ESTORIL SOL, *Parque Palmela. Tel. (01) 483-2832, Fax (01) 483-2280. Year round rack rates from 26,500$00, double room, CP. All major credit cards accepted.*

This is a huge and uninspiring deluxe 5 star ocean view hotel with 404 modern air conditioned rooms. All rooms have private bathrooms, satellite television, direct dial telephones, and mini-bars. Although the hotel offers friendly service, its location is a bit far from the center of town. Facilities include bar, restaurants, shops, swimming pool, sauna, health club, business meeting rooms, lounges, and free outdoor parking.

Expensive

VILLAGE CASCAIS, *Rua Frei N. de Oliveira. Tel. (01) 483-7044, Fax (01) 483-7319. US and Canada bookings with Utell, Tel. 800/448-8355. Year round rack rates from 23,750$00, per apartment, per night, EP. Most major credit cards accepted.*

The Village is a modern, six floor, oceanview, apartment-hotel with 233 very comfortable rooms that all have air conditioning, private bathrooms, kitchenettes, direct dial telephones, mini-bar, and in-room music systems. This hotel is situated directly across from the ocean and a famous lighthouse. This is a great place to stay. Facilities include a bar, restaurant, pool, sun deck, great ocean or garden views, and free parking.

QUINTA DA MARINHA, *Estrada do Guincho. Tel. (01) 486-9881, Fax (01) 486-9032. Year round rack rates from 23,250$00, per apartment, per night, EP. Most major credit cards accepted.*

This complex of fully equipped deluxe townhouse apartments and semi-private villas rests on a fine 18 hole golf course. A perfect spot for a family vacation if you love golf and tennis. Facilities include bar, restaurant, pool, golf course, tennis, TV, sun deck, and parking.

HOTEL BAIA, *Estrada Marginal. Tel. (01) 483-1033, Fax (01) 483-11095. Year round rack rates from 19,500$00, double room, BP. Most major credit cards accepted.*

The Baia is a large yet simple beach front 3 star hotel in the heart of old Cascais. Most of the rooms have air conditioning, ocean views, and a balcony. It's a good place to save some money. Facilities include bar, restaurants, snack bar, pool, air conditioning, TV, and parking.

CASA PERGOLA, *Avenida Valbom, 13. Tel. (01) 484-0040. Year round rack rates from 13,000$00, double room, CP. Most major credit cards accepted.*

A seasonal bed and breakfast inn located two blocks from the ocean, the rooms are very comfortable although there is no air conditioning. Open April through October. Almost no facilities.

ESTALAGEM DO FAROL, *Estrada Boca do Inferno. Tel. (01) 483-0173. Year round rack rates from 19,500$00, double room, CP. Most major credit cards accepted.*

A cute oceanside country inn near the Farol lighthouse, Estalagem do Farol has 11 good rooms with private bathrooms. Facilities include bar, restaurant, pool, tennis, and parking.

Inexpensive

APARTMENTOS FÉRIASOL, *throughout the town of Cascais. Tel. (01) 486-8232. Year round rack rates from 14,500$00, per studio, per night, CP. Most major credit cards accepted.*

You can rent a studio or one to three bedroom apartments or villas through this company. There is an English speaking staff to help you pick your place.

APARTHOTEL EQUADOR, *Alto da Pampilheira. Tel. (01) 484-0524, Fax (484-0703. Year round rack rates from 11,500$00, per apartment, per night, CP. Most major credit cards accepted.*

This is perhaps the least expensive, reasonably comfortable, hotel in Cascais. The location is far from downtown, but free shuttle service is included. All 117 studios and apartments have air conditioning, kitchenettes, private bathrooms, and simple furnishings. Facilities include bar, restaurant, shops, pool, sun deck, beach bus, and parking.

RESIDENCIAL PALMA, *Avenida Valbom, 15. Tel. (01) 483-7797. Year round rack rates from 10,500$00, double room, CP. Most major credit cards accepted.*

This is a nice family run bed and breakfast just a four minute walk from the beach on a nice side street in the heart of town. You can get a simple, yet charming double room with continental breakfast.

SOLAR DOM CARLOS, *Rua Latino Coelho, 8. Tel. (01) 486-5154. Year round rack rates from 11,250$00, double room, BP. Cash only - No credit cards accepted.*

This converted 16th century mansion has 17 comfortable guest rooms with private bathrooms. Facilities include bar, TV room, breakfast room, and nearby parking.

WHERE TO EAT

Expensive

JOÃO PADEIRO, *Rua Visconde da Luz, 12. Tel. (01) 483-0232. Dress code is jacket preffered. All major credit cards accepted.*

This famous seafood restaurant, in the heart of town, creates delicious lobster and sole specialties. Although a bit expensive, the dining rooms are full on most nights. Expect to spend at least 4,950$00 a person.

BALUARTE, *Ave. Dom Carlos. Tel. (01) 286-547. Dress code is jacket preferred. All major credit cards accepted.*

This is a formal and exclusive seafood restaurant. It has a great ocean view from its promenade near the beach. Dinner is at least 4,150$00 a person plus wine.

HOTEL ALBATROZ, *Rua Frederico Arouca. Tel. (01) 483-2821. Dress code is a semi-formal. All major credit cards accepted.*

This famous hotel's formal dining room serves expensive, but delicious and elegantly prepared international fish, meat, and poultry dishes. The hotel/restaurant is on a superb vantage point above the ocean waves. Reservations are a must. Dinner can set you back as much as 5,950$00 a person plus wine.

Moderate

VISCONDE DA LUZ, *Jardim Visconde da Luz. Tel. (01) 486-6848. Dress code is casual. Most major credit cards accepted.*

Hidden behind a small park in downtown Cascais, this small and tranquil restaurant serves fine Portuguese food. My last meal cost me around 3,350$00.

LUCULLUS, *Rua Palmeira, 6. Tel. (01) 284-4709. Dress code is casual. Most major credit cards accepted.*

Located in the heart of Cascais, Lucullus is a great pizzeria and Italian restaurant with a wonderful hidden outdoor patio section. They serve the best pizza in town at reasonable prices, and full meals start about 2,100$00 a person.

TRAM VELHO, *Alameda Duquesa de Palmela. Tel. (01) 486-7355. No dress code. Cash only - No credit cards accepted.*

This late night snack shop is housed in an old train car next door to the electric train station that takes people from Cascais to Lisbon. You can get good sized and well prepared light meals including cheeseburgers, roasted pork sandwiches, salads, grilled cheese sandwiches, fried shrimp, grilled beefsteak, sausages with french fries, and plenty of mixed drinks. A great place to go after midnight when everyone in town that is still awake (and not too drunk) heads here for a quick bite before hitting the discos. Meals start at under 1,200$00 a person.

DUKE OF WELLINGTON, *Rua Direita. Tel. (01) 483-0394. Dress code is casual. Most major credit cards accepted.*

If you're looking for a change from Portuguese food, this English pub is the place to go. You should find some familiar entrees on the large daily menu. Their good food and great beer will set you back around 1,250$00 a person.

SEEING THE SIGHTS

Your first stop in Cascais should be the **Praia da Ribeira** town beach. It is lined by palm trees, colorful fishing boats, and a romantic mosaic walkway. This area is a great place to stroll along and to see the fine, regal mansions along the waterfront. If you walk to the eastern edge of the beach you will find a nice pier that jets outward into the ocean. This pier and the buildings at its base are the last remaining vestiges of Cascais' fishing industry. If you walk to this area at about 4:30pm on most days you can witness the fish auction at the fish **mercado** (market building) near the pier.

There are some beautiful azulejo (tile) decorated mansions up the steps, at the base of the pier, that lead on to the Rua Fernandez Tomás. From this street you intersect with Rua da Saudade. Turn sharply to your right to find the **Largo da Praia da Rainha** plaza and its lovely little **Praia da Rainha** beach area. If you wander up this edge of town you will soon find the luxurious **Hotel Albatroz**, which is built right on the side of a cliff. Even if you are not staying here, you must take a peek inside.

After a good look around the main beach areas of town, you are now ready to stroll back up the Ave. Marginal and this time turn right (east) onto Rua Frederico Arouca. This pedestrian only street is the heart of the old town, and is where you will find some of Europe's most famous designer shops. The street is also full of restaurants, cafés, and the fabulous **Panisol** bakery. They make the best coffee and pastries in town, so you might want to consider stopping for a break. This street is well worth visiting, but don't expect to find any bargains here.

After you walk down the entire street, you should return towards the Ave. Marginal, and cross it to reach the **Largo Luís Camoes** square. You will find several bars and restaurants with outdoor tables in the square. At night, the square is a great place to have a strong beer and to be cooled by a constant gentle wind. If you happen to be in town on Wednesday, I suggest you visit the regional **mercado** (market). To get there, follow Ave. Marginal up to Ave. 25 de Abril and take the first right (east) turn onto the Rua do Mercado.

To reach several additional cultural and historic sights on the west side of town, walk back down to the west end of the beach. Follow the water as it turns sharply onto the dramatic, mansion-lined Ave. Dom Carlos. Keep your eye out for the first street that goes inland at the start of this turn and follow the Rua Marques Leal Pancada as it winds its way inland to the **Largo da Assunção**. This plaza is home to a whitewashed 18th century baroque church known as the **Igreja de Nossa senhora da Assunção**. Inside the church you will find beautiful azulejos as well as several remarkable paintings by famed artists Josefa D'Óbidos and José Malhoa. Across from the church you can pop inside the famed **Ceramicarte**. The shop sells high quality ceramics, tapestries, and azulejos.

If your in the mood for a little culture, from the Largo da Assunção follow the Rua da República west for a block and turn right (north) into the lovely **Jardim da Parada** gardens. Inside the gardens you can visit the **Museu do Mar** (closed Saturdays, Sundays, and Mondays). There is a collections of unusual profane and religious artifacts related to the ocean and sailors. From here you, might want to consider getting your car because theother sights further west of town are a bit far away. However, you can walk it if you don't mind a two hour walk by the ocean.

Return to the Ave. Dom Carlos and continue westward as it turns yet again and merges into the **Estrada da Boca do Inferno**. The edge of town is dominated by the **Forte Militar Cidadela** fortress that once served as a royal residence but now houses army training facilities. As you continue on the coastal road you will soon wind up in front of the tranquil **Parque do Maréchal Cermona**, a municipal park, that contains the remarkable **Museu-Biblioteca dos Condes de Castro Guimaraes** (Museum-Library of the Counts of Castro Guimaraes). This impressive castle contains a vast collection of rare books, furniture, gold, and ceramics (closed Mondays). Almost directly across from the museum is a great little oceanfront esplanade known as the Esplanada de Santa Maria. From here, there is a great panoramic view and a cute snack bar built right on a cliff. Inexpensive, fresh, grilled fish is served.

Further down the same road is the lighthouse, **Farol da Guia**, the huge **Coconuts** nightclub (with its impressive ocean front terraces), and an assortment of hotels and inns that are next to decaying and vacated ocean front palaces. If you continue up the Estrada da Boca do Inferno for two kilomerers or so, you will arrive at the famed **Boca do Inferno** (Jaws of Hell) where the ocean's waves crash down into an abyss. Tourist shops, cafés, snack bars, and small crafts mercado (market) are located next to the entrance to Boca do Inferno, but the prices are rather high.

On Sunday nights, bullfights take place at the **Praça de Touros** (bullring) in the northwestern corner of town. There is a large complex of movie theaters, fast food joints, and fancy European boutiques called **Cascaishopping** about 10 minutes north on Route N-9 towards Sintra. In the summer, several concerts and festivals are held throughout the area.

NIGHTLIFE & ENTERTAINMENT

The nightlife in Cascais starts fairly early, when the after beach crowd crams into the bars and pubs throughout the downtown streets that intersect the pedestrian only **Rua Federico Arouca**. There are also a series of English pubs, like the famous **John Bull**, that surround the **Largo Luís Camoes** plaza.

The best place to be after 11pm is, without doubt, the massive **Coconuts** disco and outdoor bar. It's next to the lighthouse a few kilometers up the coastal road towards Guincho.

SPORTS & RECREATION
Bicycles
• **Tip Tours** (bicycle rentals), *Cascais, Tel. (01) 486-5150*

Boating & Fishing
• **Yacht and Fishing Club**, *Cascais, Tel. (01) 486-8712*

Golf
• **Quinta da Marinha Golf Club**, *Cascais, Tel. (01) 486-0881*

Horseback Riding
• **Areia Horse Center**, *Cascais, Tel. (01) 289-284*
• **Quinta da Marinha Horse Riding**, *Cascais, Tel. (01) 486-9084*

GUINCHO

Famed for hosting the **International Windsurfing Championship**, the beach at Guincho seems much like a giant sand dune and is one of my favorites in all of Portugal. Beach chairs and umbrellas are available for rent at the beach clubs. Several oceanview restaurants in this area serve delicious seafood.

ARRIVALS & DEPARTURES
By Car
Guincho is about 9 km west of Cascais. Follow the Estrada da Boca do Inferno, it turns into Route N-247 north, until you reach Guincho.

WHERE TO STAY
Very Expensive
HOTEL DO GUINCHO, *Praia do Guincho. Tel. (01) 487-0492, Fax (01) 487-0431. Low season rack rates from 25,000$00, double room, CP; high season rates from 29,000$00, double room, CP. All major credit cards accepted.*

This is a beautifully converted 17th century fortress that rests on the edge a rocky cliff above Guincho's fine sandy beach. This inspiring hotel is a favorite spot for young honeymoon couples looking for a romantic getaway. You enter the pastel colored fortress through a massive doorway that leads past a cute inner courtyard and straight into the hotel. Inside the hotel you will find beautifully designed lounges, antique tapestries, suits of armor, ocean view picture windows, and mysterious alcoves, cellars, and staircases. Many of the 36 air conditioned rooms offer fine views of the ocean, columned terraces, fireplaces, canopy beds, cathedral ceilings with embedded coats of arms, tile floors, and large bathrooms.

The international cuisine at the restaurant is extremely good, and fortunately the service is first rate. I once asked the wine steward for suggestions, and he went on for over an hour explaining the history and production methods of each regional wine. If you have dinner here you should consider having their fantastic Crepes Suzette. The ambiance is relaxed and casual; dinner guests are not required to wear a jacket or tie. Service is fair at best, but with a little persistence you can occasionally receive assistance from the front desk. I like this hotel a lot and recommend it, but don't expect 5 star service.

Moderate

ESTALAGEM DO MUCHAXO, *Praia do Guincho. Tel. (01) 487-0221, Fax (01) 487-0444. Year round rack rates from 15,500$00, double room, EP. Cash only - No credit cards accepted.*

This 60 room, windswept inn offers reasonably comfortable accommodations, but unfortunately they also have several rooms I thought were in desperate need of repair. I suggest you see a few rooms first and then select the best one. Facilities include bar, restaurant, health club, saltwater swimming pool, sauna, and parking.

WHERE TO EAT

Very Expensive

HOTEL DO GUINCHO, *Praia do Guincho. Tel. (01) 487-0492. Dress code is jacket and tie requested. All major credit cards accepted.*

Although the hotel is a nice place to stay if you don't mind the staff's bad attitude, the restaurant is another story altogether. Sitting high up on a oceanside bluff, the opulent candle-lit dining room is a bastion of gourmet cuisine. Their extensive menu usually includes shrimp cocktails, hot and cold asparagus, fish bisque, French onion soup, locally caught filet of sole, skewered shrimp with ham, beef with pepper sauce, spinach with fresh cream, grilled sea bass, pork Alentejo style, veal cutlets, fresh local lobster, chateaubriand for two, crepes Suzette, and many more delicious items served with class.

Dinner should set you back about 4,500$00 a person plus wine. Reservations are necessary on weekend nights.

Moderate

RESTAURANTE FAROLEIRO, *Estrada do Guincho. Tel. (01) 487-0225. No dress code. Most major credit cads accepted.*

Faroleiro is my selection for the best affordable seafood in the area. Located just across from the ocean, the friendly service and great food make this place irresistible. The house specialty, acorda de lagosta, is a casserole with lobster in a pudding of bread and garlic, but they also offer over two dozen different fresh local fish specialties and many steak, veal, and pork items as well. I paid about 1,900$00 a person for an excellent meal.

PORTO DE SANTA MARIA, *Estrada do Guincho. Tel. (01) 487-0240. Dress code is casual but elegant. Most major credit cards accepted.*

This modern ocean view Portuguese restaurant offers great grilled sea bass, sole, steak, and mixed grill dishes at around 1,450$00 each. The waiters are prompt and multilingual. Closed on Mondays.

SEEING THE SIGHTS

A fortress high above the beach is now home to the architectural marvel known as **Hotel do Guincho**. It has wonderful vaulted ceilings and an expensive gourmet dining room with live piano serenades and great wines. Otherwise, people are here to enjoy the beach and salt air.

CABO DA ROCA & AZOIA

After a wonderfully scenic drive or bus ride, you will pass through the **Serra de Sintra** mountains, sheep pastures, and several abandoned windmills on the way to a small village called **Azoia**. The village offers a glimpse of what life was like in the old days, but offers no specific attractions other than a nice little hotel and a few handmade craft shops. If you follow the signs from Azoia, you will travel on a somewhat scary mountain top road for a little over 4 km to reach the rocky cliff known as **Cabo da Roca**.

ARRIVALS & DEPARTURES

By Bus

From Cascais or Sintra, it is a half hour, 300$00, bus ride to Azoia.

By Car

Azoia is a 14 km ride north on route N-247 from Guincho.

WHERE TO STAY

Moderate

ALDEIA DE ROCA, *Estrada Azoia-Colares, Azoia. Tel. (01) 928-0001, Fax (01) 928-0163. Low season rack rates from 11,500$00, double room CP; high season rack rates from 14,000$00, double room, CP. Most major credit cards accepted.*

The cute and tranquil Aldeia da Roca hotel complex is just a few minutes walk from the heart of Azoia. The property is centered around delightful gardens and features 14 beautifully decorated partial ocean view attached rooms with air conditioners, nice private bathrooms, exposed wood beam ceilings, mini-safe, mini-bar, direct dial telephone, satellite color television, wood parquet floors, white stucco walls, hair dryer, nice pine furnishings, plenty of space, and lots of sunlight. The hotel also has a good regional restaurant, an outdoor swimming pool, a tennis court, bicycle rentals, covered parking, business meeting rooms, laundry and baby-sitting service, and more.

SEEING THE SIGHTS

Follow the signs from Azoia on a somewhat scary mountain top road for a little over four km to reach the rocky cliff known as **Cabo da Roca**. This cape is Europe's westernmost point and was once thought of as the end of the world. The cape itself is scoured by severe winds, and has a barren look. A lighthouse is located on the tip of the cape. Beautiful calligraphy and wax stamped "diplomas" can be purchased (550$00 for white paper, 850$00 for parchment) at the Turísmo building, open daily until 7:00pm, to document your personal exploration of this point.

COLARES & NEARBY COASTAL BEACHES

This camellia covered village dates back to Roman times. These days, an abundance of 300 year old houses and beautiful flowers surround the village square. For several centuries Colares has grown and produced a very special red wine from the oldest native grape variety in Europe. Many wine lovers (including me) consider these wines to be among the finest in Portugal.

ARRIVALS & DEPARTURES

By Car

The quaint town of Colares is seven km on Route N-247 north of Cabo da Roca.

WHERE TO STAY

Moderate

HOTEL MIRAMONTE, *Praia das Macas. Tel. (01) 929-1230, Fax (01) 929-1480. Year round rack rates from 17,500$00, double room, CP. Most major credit cards accepted.*

This is a nice, modern 2 star hotel near the ocean with 90 air conditioned rooms with private bathrooms and simple furnishings. The hotel has several facilities including a very nice pool. This is a good choice for this area. Facilities include bar, restaurant, pool, sun deck, and parking.

HOTEL DA PISCINA, *Praia Grande. Tel. (01) 929-2145, Fax (01) 929-2420. Year round rack rates from 14,500$00, double room, CP. Most major credit cards accepted.*

This reasonable 2 star hotel overlooks a rather large pool with comfortable rooms near the beach. Facilities include bar, restaurant, pool, sun deck, TV, and parking.

CASA POR DO SOL, *N-247-Colares. Tel. (01) 931-4337. Year round rack rates from 16,250$00 per apartment, per night, EP. Cash only - No credit cards accepted.*

Por do Sol is a cute rustic house that has a 2 bedroom apartment with kitchen, bathroom, and patio just off route N-247 near the tiny village of Ulgueira. Good luck finding it!

PENSÃO DO CONDE, *Quinta do Conde. Tel. (01) 929-1652. Year round rack rates from 13,700$00, double room, EP. Cash only - No credit cards accepted.*

A remote and rustic manor house, it has 11 rooms and a few cabanas. The quinta is very comfortable and has excellent views. Facilities include bar, TV room, heating, and parking. Closed in low season.

WHERE TO EAT
Inexpensive
RESTAURANTE NAUTILUS, *Rua Goncalves Zarco, Praia das Macas. Tel. (01) 929-1816. No dress code. Cash only - No credit cards accepted.*

While there are many different restaurants to choose from in this area near the ocean, this is by far the best and most authentic one. Located just a one minute walk from the fabulous sandy cove beach at Praia das Macas, the small dining room has only eight tables. However, they serve absolutely delicious homemade meals at reasonable prices.

The extensive menu here includes shrimp cocktails, melon with ham, vegetable soup, cream of shrimp soup, grilled grouper, shrimp with curried rice, poached octopus, deep fried hake with rice, assorted pizzas, sirloin steak, marinated pork with clams, grilled chicken, mixed salads, and a superb and inexpensive house wine. Dinner will only set you back about 1,850$00 including wine. Highly Recommended!

SEEING THE SIGHTS
From Colares, it is an easy 10 to 15 minute drive to reach the dramatic coastal beaches and surfer hangouts at **Praia Adraga**, **Praia Grande**, **Praia Pequena**, **Praia das Macas**, and the lovely picturesque cliff village of **Azenhas do Mar**. A visit to these wonderful beaches is a must during the summer.

SPORTS & RECREATION
Tennis
•**Buzio Tennis Center**, *Praia da Maçãs, Tel. (01) 929-2172*

SINTRA

Sintra is one of my favorite towns in Europe. Surrounded by the Serra de Sintra mountains, this wonderful area really must be seen by all visitors to Portugal. Rich with artistic and royal history, Sintra is an elegant town with many castles. During the Romantic period of the 18th and 19th centuries, several famous writers, artists, and poets came here to work and play including William Beckford, William Burnett, Gil Vicente, Luís de Camoes, Lord Byron, and Robert Southey. Many European royal families built their summer residences in this area, often attempting to outdo their neighbors by constructing an even more glamorous mansion.

ARRIVALS & DEPARTURES

By Air

The main airport serving Sintra is Lisbon's Portela International Airport. From the airport, the easiest way to get to Sintra is to either rent a car, pre-arrange a transfer from your travel agent, or take a taxi for around 5,750$00.

A more affordable way to reach Sintra is to take Portela airport's Aero-bus (a shuttle bus) to downtown Lisbon and get off at the Rossio square stop in downtown Lisbon and take the train from there.

By Bus

It is a 20 minute bus ride into town from the nearby cities of Cascais or Mafra and costs around 550$00 a person.
• **Main Bus Office**, *Largo D. Manuel I, Tel. (01) 923-0662*

By Car

From Lisbon, take the IC-19 toll motorway west. Take Route N-9 north from Cascais for 27 km. You can also take Route N-9 south from Mafra or the scenic and coastal Route N-247 north from Guincho or Cabo da Roca. Exit at Sintra's "Centro" exit.

By Tour

Many visitors prefer to arrange a guided half day excursion to Sintra. It costs around 7,500$00 a person and includes all entrance fees and round-trip door to door transfers from your hotel in Lisbon, Cascais, or Estoril.

By Train

Trains from Lisbon's Rossio train station are frequent and take about 25 minutes to reach the Sintra rail station. Tickets are less than 675$00 a

person. The train station is a 15 minute walk west of the center of Sintra.
• **CP Rail Station – Sintra**, *Largo D. Manuel I, Tel. (01) 923-2605*

ORIENTATION

The main sections of Sintra are along a series of hills and valleys 24 kilometers (15 miles) west-northwest of Lisbon. The "Vila Velha," or old town, consists of a dozen or so compact lanes and streets. But many of the most important royal palaces, mansions, and formal gardens are located several kilometers away on secluded estates set along the rugged cliffs of the Serra de Sintra mountains.

GETTING AROUND TOWN

By Bus

Local bus services unfortunately do not stop anywhere near the palaces, castles, and gardens of upper Sintra.

By Car

Finding parking in the center of Sintra is not a problem, unless you arrive on a busy day. There is a free parking lot just off Largo Rainha D. Amelia square in downtown Sintra. There are also a series of well marked country roads that head towards the other main palaces and castle-estates from this square, and each of these attractions has free parking lots as well.
• **Hertz Rent a Car in Sintra**, *Quinta da Penha Longa, Tel. (01) 924-9011*

By Taxi

If you don't have a car, taxis are essential if you to see the sights. Normally you can expect to pay around 1,450$00 each way for a ride to any one of the palaces, castles, or gardens. I suggest that you try and negotiate a flat rate of around 1,750$00 an hour: you can see most, if not all, the major sites in around four hours.
• **Sintra Taxi**, *Tel. (01) 923-0067*

WHERE TO STAY

Very Expensive

HOTEL PALÁCIO DE SETEAIS, *Rua Barbosa du Bocage, 10. Tel. (01) 923-3200, Fax (01) 923-4277. US & Canada Bookings with Utell, Tel. 800/ 448-8355. Low season rack rates from 28,000$00, double room, BP; high season rack rates from 47,000$00, double room, BP. All major credit cards accepted.*

A converted nobleman's palace in the historic and enchanted town of Sintra, this magnificent 5 star hotel is among the most respected deluxe properties in the country. The hotel has hosted heads of state, movie stars, royal family members, executives from multinational corporations, and many of the world's most famous people. Its fantastic 18th century facade is breathtaking, and the opulence and tranquillity that awaits you inside is even more impressive. There are several dozen unique, antique-filled rooms and suites. The newer wing, that was added to the original structure, has several rooms that are less impressive than the rooms in the older and more opulent section of the hotel. The ambiance of the hotel is formal and conservative.

The common areas of the palace contain many antiques, statues, fine tapestries, exotic drawing rooms, grand stairways, chandeliers, opulent lounges, and one the world's most beautiful antique pianos. Outside the hotel, you will find romantic box gardens, a large outdoor pool and sun deck, tennis courts, a horse riding center, huge lawns, and great views of the castles and village of Sintra. You will need to use a car or a taxi to get from this property to any of the major sights in the area.

Young people may find themselves in the minority here, as most guests are older rich Europeans. Service is often too snobby and uptight for my tastes, but many of the older wealthy European clients here seem to like it that way! They are demanding and usually keep pretty much to themselves.

CAESAR PARK PENHA LONGA GOLF CLUB & RESORT, *Estrada da Lagoa Azul, Sintra. Tel. (01) 924-9011, Fax (01) 924-9007. US & Canada bookings with Leading Hotels of the World, Tel. 800/223-6800. Low season rack rates from 35,000$00, double room, BP; high season rack rates from 39,000$00, double room, BP. All major credit cards accepted.*

Situated on the outskirts of Sintra, just a 20 minute drive from Lisbon, this is a popular Japanese owned 5 star resort and conference center. The property features 174 beautifully decorated rooms and suites that feature remote control air conditioning, luxurious dual basin private bathrooms with hair dryers, custom designed hardwood furnishings, executive style desks, direct dial telephone, mini-bar, satellite color television, double or twin beds, large closets, in-room music, mini-safe, and in many cases private terraces with awesome views over 600 acres of strikingly manicured grounds.

The hotel also offers an 18 hole par 72 and a 9 hole par 35 golf course with special rates for guests, a country club with tennis courts and various other sports, complimentary use of a modern work-out room and health club with sauna and Turkish bath, baby-sitting services, optional massage and beauty treatments, boutiques, and specially designed business meeting rooms and conference facilities that can seat well over 300 executives. There is also a gourmet Japanese restaurant, an international cuisine dining room with terrace, a less formal restaurant at the golf course, several bars and sitting rooms that often feature live piano music, free round-trip shuttle service to Lisbon's Portela international airport, plenty of garage and above ground parking spaces, full time concierge desk that can book rental cars and excursions, currency conversion, express check out, and a great 24 hour room service menu.

Expensive

QUINTA DE SÃO THIAGO, *Estrada de Monserrate. Tel. (01) 923-2923. Year round rack rates from 24,500$00, double room, CP. Most major credit cards accepted.*

An expensive and deluxe convent house, their 10 beautiful rooms with private bath are usually rented to an older and somewhat exclusive clientele. They are often sold out in the summer. Facilities include bar, tennis, TV room, gardens, and parking.

QUINTA DA CAPELA, *Estrada de Monserrate. Tel. (01) 929-0170. Year round rack rates from 20,500$00, double room, CP. Most major credit cards accepted.*

A 16th century estate and Manor house, its 10 deluxe guest rooms with private bathrooms and antiques are lovely. Facilities include bar, pool, trails, heating, library, gardens, dining room, health club, sauna, TV room, and parking.

TIVOLI SINTRA, *Praça da República. Tel. (01) 923-3505, Fax (01) 923-1572. US and Canada bookings with Utell, Tel. 800/448-8355. Year round rack rates from 23,500$00, double room, EP. All major credit cards accepted.*

This modern hotel is located in the heart of the old town. While its facade is nothing special, the 75 air conditioned rooms are very comfortable and have private bathrooms, remote control satellite television, mini-bar, direct dial phones, and great views of Sintra in many cases. The service here is excellent and facilities include a bar, restaurant, business meeting rooms, a tour desk, and free outdoor parking.

Moderate

QUINTA DAS SEQUOIAS, *Estrada de Monserrate. Tel. (01) 924-3821, Fax (01) 923-0342. Year round rack rates from 19,750$00, double room, CP. Most major credit cards accepted.*

This wonderful old estate and five room manor house, once known as Casa da Tapada was converted into a great bed and breakfast. The owner, a delightful retired doctor, enjoys talking with her guests. Facilities include bar, billiards, TV room, dining room, library, parking, and a new swimming pool should be completed by now. Highly Recommended.

VILLA DAS ROSAS, *Rua António Cunha, 4. Tel. (01) 923-4216. Year round rack rates from 17,750$00, double room, CP. Cash only - No credit cards accepted.*

This antique house is now a small and charming inn. The couple who own and manage the property are always eager to be of assistance to every guest making it a nice place to stay. Facilities include a lounge, antiques, dinning room, TV room, garden, and parking.

Inexpensive

RESIDENCIAL SINTRA, *Travessa dos Avelares, 12. Tel. (01) 923-0738. Year round rack rates from 9,550$00, double room, EP. Most major credit cards accepted.*

This nice old house in the São Pedro de Sintra area has nine nice rooms with private bathrooms. Facilities include bar, pool, garden, breakfast room, and parking.

RESIDENCIAL RAPOSA, *Rua Dr. Alfredo Costa, 3. Tel. (01) 923-0465. Year round rack rates from 9,750$00, double room, EP. Cash only - No credit cards accepted.*

This eight room inn contains simple yet comfortable rooms. It's a good choice for those of you who are on a tight budget. Almost no facilities, but still a decent place to stay.

WHERE TO EAT

Expensive

CANTINHO DE SÃO PEDRO, *Praça D. Fernando, 18. Tel. (01) 923-0267. Dress code is jacket preferred. All major credit cards accepted.*

A combination of French and Portuguese specialties are served in an elegant yet rustic setting at the Cantinho de São Pedro. This may be the finest food in all of Sintra, but a meal here can cost upwards of 4,850$00 a person plus wine. Closed on Mondays.

JARDIM PRIMAVERA, *Caesar Park Penha Resort, Estrada da Lagoa Azul. Tel. (01) 924-9011. Dress code is jacket preferred. All major credit cards accepted.*

Situated inside the main building of a famous golf and conference resort, this delightful restaurant offers its own unique blend of Mediterranean cuisine and international specialties. Among the many delicious items on the menu are sardines in tomato sorbet, fresh salmon tartar, shrimp cocktails with watermelon, escargot with wild mushrooms, salad Nicose, gazpacho, vegetable lasagna, risotto with asparagus, spaghetti in shrimp sauce, penne with broccoli, grilled sea bass, bream baked in salt, bouillabaisse, fish crepes, duck breast with figs, stuffed leg of rabbit, veal in tarragon sauce, lamb saddle cooked in a puff pastry, and many others. Dinner here will cost around 5.650$00 a person plus wine.

SOLAR DE SÃO PEDRO, *Largo de Feira, 12. Tel. (01) 923-1860. Dress code is smart casual. All major credit cards accepted.*

Another French-Portuguese restaurant near the outdoor market, they serve very good food, but the service is not wonderful, especially during market day. Closed Wednesdays. My last lunch here set me back about 3,750$00.

Inexpensive
RESTURANTE REGIONAL DE SINTRA, *Travessa do Municipio. Tel. (01) 923-4444. Dress code is casual. Most major credit cards accepted.*
A good regional restaurant, it serves local meat and seafood specialties including great soups and desserts. The prices are quite reasonable and you can leave without spending more than 2,200$00 a person.

TULHAS, *Rua Gil Vicente, 4. Tel. (01) 923-2378. No dress code. Most major credit cards accepted.*
A very good and unpretentious restaurant and bar, this is a great place to relax and be casual. Fish is the specialty of the house and a full meal here starts at around 1,500$00 a person.

SEEING THE SIGHTS
The **Vila Velha** (old town) is comprised of several ancient houses, many of which contain bars, cafés, and souvenir shops. An abundance of public and private golf, tennis, and equestrian clubs are located throughout Sintra and the surrounding area. On the second and fourth Sunday of each month, a wonderful large outdoor regional **mercado** (market) takes place in **São Pedro de Sintra** (located about three km from the old town). Make sure to look for the wonderful local ceramics and fresh cheeses sold at the market.

There are several castles and fine museums in Sintra. You should start in the heart of the Vila Velha at **Largo Rainha D. Amelia** which is dominated by the **Palácio Nacional de Sintra** (also known as the Paço Real). This former home to Portuguese royalty, including King Dom João I and King Dom Manuel I, can be easily recognized by the two large cone shaped chimneys that extend upward from the kitchens. The interior is laced with beautiful old Mudejar azulejos, frescoes, and royal coats of arms. There are guided tours of several of the palace's rooms every half hour or so. Also located in the heart of the old city are the **Museu Ferreira de Castro**, *Rua Consiglieri Pedroso*, an art museum, (closed Mondays) and the **Museu de Sintra**, *Praça da República, 23*, a municipal museum of art and archaeology (closed on Mondays).

The **Estrada de Pena** winds its way through the densely wooded hills of the Serra de Sintra mountains, above the south zone of the Vila Velha, to spectacular castles. The reasonably well preserved 8th century **Castelo dos Mouros** (Castle of the Moors) can be reached by taking the well marked path for about three km from the road. The views over the region from this castle are extraordinary. A bit further up the Estrada da Pena is the outrageously designed **Palácio da Pena**. This remarkable castle was built by the Prussian engineer Baron Ludwig von Eschwege for the Prince of Bavaria who later became Portugal's King Ferdinand II. Its multicolored facade includes several turrets, ornate windows, and a large dome.

The palace (the entrance fee is 500$00 a person and it is closed on Mondays) was constructed in 1840 on the ruins of a 16th century Hieronymite monastery. Although there are generally no guided tours, you can park your car or take a taxi to the gateway and walk up a steep road for about 15 minutes to reach the palace.

Inside, there are multilingual descriptions of the period furnishings in each of over a dozen royal chambers and ornate rooms. Make sure to take a good look at the 16th century Manueline cloister which is about all that remains from the sight's original monastery. In the cloister you can see a fine azulejos covered altar by Nicolas Chanterene. The palace is surrounded by the romantic 500 acre **Parque de Pena** with a wonderful assortment of exotic trees and beautiful plants, lakes, fountains, and birds. A well marked footpath near the statue of Baron Von Eschwege leads up the stone **Cruz Alta** (high cross), offering stunning panoramic views of the region.

There are lovely gardens and breathtaking mansions located on the road towards Colares known as the Rua Barbosa du Bocage. This road merges with the **Estrada de Monserrate** and runs through the hills above the old city. Make sure you peek through the gates of the amazing palaces and villas on both sides of this narrow road. Some of these properties are abandoned or not open to the public, but a good zoom lens can help you look inside the gates. A fine example of perfectly manicured box gardens can be seen at the 18th century **Palácio de Seteais**. The name loosely translates to the palace of seven sighs, but the real story is that after the owner received the bill for building this palace, he muttered something profane seven times. Formerly the residence of a Dutch Consul, this grand property has been converted into a deluxe hotel where visitors are sometimes scared away by the less than polite front desk employees, but you should ignore them and look around anyway.

A bit further along the same road you will pass the gardens of the 18th century **Quinta de Monserrate** manor house that was once inhabited by William Beckford and later by Sir Francis Cook. These magnificently designed gardens are quite impressive (the mansion itself is not open to the public) and cost about 300$00 per person to enter. Additionally, several fine, antique-laden inns such as Quinta das Sequoias, Quinta da Capela, and Quinta de São Thiago are just off of this wonderful road and worth seeing.

SPORTS & RECREATION
Golf
• **Estoril Sol Golf**, *Sintra, Tel. (01) 293-2461*
• **Penha Longa Golf**, *Sintra, Tel. (01) 924-9022*

Horseback Riding
• **Bazano Horse Center**, *Sintra, Tel. (01) 929-1324*
• **Palácio Seteais Horse Center**, *Sintra, Tel. (01) 923-3200*
• **Sintra Equestrian Center**, *Sintra, Tel. (01) 923-3778*

Tennis
• **Liberdade Park Tennis**, *Sintra, Tel. (01) 924-1139*

QUELUZ
This is a modern city, full of high rise apartment buildings and not of much interest except for the beautiful 18th century Palácio de Queluz.

ARRIVALS & DEPARTURES
By Car
The large suburban city of Queluz is located about 11 km southeast of Sintra just off Route IC-19 east.

WHERE TO STAY
Expensive
POUSADA D. MARIA I, *Palácio Nacional de Queluz. Tel. (01) 435-6158, Fax (01) 435-6189. US & Canada bookings with Marketing Ahead, Tel. 800/223-1356. Low season rack rates from 23,000$00, double room, BP; high season rack rates from 28,000$00, double room, BP. All major credit cards accepted.*

Located in a fantastically ornate, pink-colored wing of the Palácio de Queluz that contains the clock tower, this is one of the most memorable and deluxe new pousadas in the country. Recently opened after the government spent millions of dollars and many years restoring and converting this 18th century national landmark, the Pousada D. Maria I offers visitors the chance to spend the night in a one-of-a-kind luxury hotel. The charming and tranquil ambiance is surrounded by centuries of history.

The pousada has 25 deluxe sun-drenched rooms and a huge suite featuring lavish marble private bathrooms stocked with high quality hair and skin care products, custom designed hardwood furnishings, remote control satellite television, direct dial television, hand stenciled ceiling borders, exceedingly comfortable beds, mini-bar, mini-safe, beautiful pieces of art, hand woven tapestries, and large picture windows looking out over the palace grounds.

Facilities here include one of Portugal's finest and most elegant gourmet restaurants, a unique duplex theater and conference room, luxurious sitting rooms and lounges, occasional live music concerts, a relaxed breakfast room serving a hearty full buffet breakfast daily, plenty of free parking, a great staff of talented multilingual professionals, and much more. Very Highly Recommended.

WHERE TO EAT
Very Expensive
COZINHA VELHA, *Palácio Nacional de Queluz. Tel. (01) 435-0232. Dress code is semi-formal. All major credit cards accepted.*

Located in the former open kitchen of the royal palace of King Dom Pedro III, this famous and elegant formal restaurant is one of Portugal's most important culinary landmarks. Both of the restaurant's regal main dining rooms are embellished by fine oil paintings, priceless antiques, soft pastel colored walls, exposed wooden beam ceilings, custom designed carpets, rare chandeliers, and the finest Christolfe silver and crystal settings. Guests are served by a team of professional white gloved waiters who keep their eyes on every table so as to appear whenever anything is needed.

The extensive menu of delicious old world specialties includes smoked swordfish, fried prawns in garlic, green salads with chicken and nuts, lobster and shrimp salad, breast of duck surrounded by mango and watercress, fish bisque, French onion soup, black grouper medallions, poached filet of sole, grilled tiger prawns, entrecote with a three pepper sauce, grilled veal cutlets, fried kid with turnip sprouts, roasted chicken, sirloin steak with smoked ham, sautéed pork with clams, crepes with champagne, tropical fruit salad, and homemade cakes and ice cream. A typical dinner will cost around 6,250$00 per person including a half bottle of good house wine. Reservations are strongly advised during the weekends and summer nights. Highly Recommended.

SEEING THE SIGHTS
The beautiful 18th century **Palácio de Queluz** at the edge of town is certainly worth the trip. This rococo style royal summer palace and garden was inspired by Versailles and is painted in a deep pink color. Built from plans by architect Mateus Vicente de Oliveira for King Dom Pedro III in 1747, the palace was later enlarged by French born architect Jean Baptiste Robillion when Queen Maria I took the throne in 1786. The

palace's remarkable interior includes beautiful crystal chandeliers, gilded woodwork, fine 18th century azulejos, and superb collections of oil paintings. There are also several acres of surrounding landscaped hedge and flower gardens (created in the style of Le Notre in France) that contain several ponds, statues, and Baroque fountains. Visiting heads of state are often entertained here with the palace staff dressed in period costume. Tours are offered everyday except Tuesday.

While at the palace, I suggest a fine gourmet lunch or dinner at the wonderful **Cozinha Velha** formal restaurant.

MAFRA

In 1711, the still childless King Dom João V swore he would build a monastery if an heir to his throne was born. After the long awaited birth of his first child six years later, the king commissioned German engineer Friedrich Ludwig to create a structure to house 13 Franciscan monks. The large tract of land selected by Mr. Ludwig became the town of Mafra.

ARRIVALS & DEPARTURES
By Car
Mafra lies 22 km from Sintra on Route N-9 north.

WHERE TO STAY
Moderate
HOTEL CASTELÃO, Ave. 25 de Abril. Tel. (061) 812-050. Year round rack rates from 9,750$00, double room, EP. Cash only - No credit cards accepted.

A simple 2 star hotel, this hotel is located near the Turísmo in the heart of Mafra. The rooms are clean and comfortable, but not very memorable. Facilities include bar, restaurant, air conditioning, direct dial phones, mini-bars, TV, and parking.

SEEING THE SIGHTS
Construction of King Dom João V's promised monastery began in 1717. German engineer Friedrich Ludwig and the Italian trained German artist Johann Ludwig brought in master tradesmen in from Italy to oversee the estimated 50,000 peasant workers who toiled for many years. Upon its completion in 1735, the monastery had grown significantly in size (over 10 acres) in order to accommodate over 400 monks and trainees, as well as a royal palace, limestone basilica, 37,000 volume baroque library, and over 4,500 doors and windows.

The world's largest collection of church bells are housed in the monastery's ornate bell towers. On Sunday mornings, carillon concerts are performed. A famed school of sculpture flourished here in the 18th century attracting students and teachers such as Joaquim Machado de Castro, Alessandro Guisti, and Giovanni António. The monastery is closed on Tuesdays.

ERICEIRA

The former fishing town of Ericeira consists of sandy beaches, a few fishing areas, and huge condo developments. The town is based around the main square, Praça da República. From here, it is a short walk down Rua Dr. Eduardo Burnay to the beach. Although this area has a reputation for being a relaxing summer resort, I don't find much charm left here.

ARRIVALS & DEPARTURES
By Car

Ericeira is 11 km northwest of Mafra on Route N-116 west.

WHERE TO STAY
Moderate

HOTEL DE TURÍSMO DA ERICEIRA, *Rua Porto Revez. Tel. (061) 864-608. Year round rack rates from 18,750$00, double room, BP. Most major credit cards accepted.*

A large ocean front hotel, it has over 150 rooms with private bathrooms. The view from many of the rooms' large balconies are very impressive. Facilities include multiple swimming pools and tennis courts.

HOTEL PEDRO O PESCADOR, *Rua Dr. E. Burnay, 22. Tel. (061) 864-032, Fax (01) 623-21. Year round rack rates from 13,500$00, double room, EP. Most major credit cards accepted.*

A nice 2 star hotel on the way to the beach, it has about 25 good air conditioned guest rooms with private bathrooms. Facilities include bar, restaurant, radio, and parking.

ESTALAGEM DOM FERNANDO, *N-247-Ericeira. Tel. (061) 855-204, Fax (01) 855-264. Year round rack rates from 11,500$00, double room, EP. Cash only - No credit cards accepted.*

A well located bed and breakfast, it has 12 nice rooms with private bathrooms. This is a good place to stay: the staff is pleasant and the many facilities include a bar, restaurant, TV room, kitchens, and parking.

HOTEL MORAIS, *Rua Dr. Miguel Bombarda. Tel. (061) 864-200, Fax (01) 864-308. Year round rack rates from 13,750$00, double room, CP. Most major credit cards accepted.*

This 2 star hotel has 40 comfortable and spacious rooms. The service here is very friendly and prompt. You'll find this a good place to relax and enjoy the ocean breeze. Facilities include bar, restaurant, pool, sun deck, billiards, TV, mini-bars, and parking.

SEEING THE SIGHTS

There isn't much to see in Ericeira. Its most redeeming quality is the reasonable prices charged for ocean view accommodations and meals. If you're in the area anyway, visit the local beaches such as the town's rocky **Praia do Sul** and the pretty **Praia do São Sebastião**, about six km up the coast. **Praça da República** square is lined with cafés and restaurants.

VILA FRANCA DE XIRA

The northernmost city on the Lisbon coast is Vila Franca de Xira. This bustling industrial city rests on the Tejo River at the border with Ribatejo district. The city is historically linked to breeding bulls for the country's bullfights and Vila Franca de Xira remains a renowned host for bullfights in its huge Praça de Touros de Palha Branca bullring.

ARRIVALS & DEPARTURES

By Car

Vila Franca de Xira is 32 km northeast of Lisbon on the A1 highway.

WHERE TO STAY

Expensive

HOTEL LEZIEIA PARQUE, *EN-10. Tel. (063) 266-70, Fax (063) 269-90. Year round rack rates from 17,250$00, double room, EP. Most major credit cards accepted.*

This modern 3 star low rise hotel is located just outside of town off the highway. There are 71 air conditioned rooms, all with private bathroom, satellite television, radio, mini-bar, and functional modern furnishings. The hotel also has a restaurant, room service, a bar, and free outdoor parking.

Moderate

QUINTA DO ALTO, *Monte Alto. Tel. (063) 268-51, Fax (063) 260-27. Year round rack rates from 13,500$00, double room, BP. Cash only - No credit cards accepted.*

A great inn just outside of town, it offers 10 guest rooms with private bathroom. Facilities include bar, restaurant, pool, sauna, tennis, bicycles, billiards, library, walking paths, gardens, horse back riding, ping pong, TV, and parking.

SEEING THE SIGHTS

If you are in Vila Franca de Xira during bullfighting season, I recommend you get tickets for a bullfight. If not, a visit to the **Praça de Touros de Palha Branca** bullring (closed on Monday) should be included in your stay. Every July, during the **Colete Encarnardo** (Red Waistcoat) festival, visitors from all over Europe come here to participate in the running of the bulls and the colorful parade through the city's center.

The city offers several sights including a fishermen's quarter (**Avieiros**) *off Rua Luís de Camoes*, the regal **Praça Câmara Municipal** (town hall square) with an adjacent 16th century pillory, the 17th century **Igreja da Misericórdia** church with an azulejos and gilt wood interior, and several nearby charming old stone streets such as Rua Miguel Bombarda and Rua Direita.

The town also has a few interesting museums including the **Museu Municipal** museum (closed Mondays), *Rua Serpa Pinto*, an ethnographic museum near the bullring, and a gallery featuring the work of local artists.

SPORTS & RECREATION

Horseback Riding

• **Quinta do Alto Horse Center**, *Vila Franca de Xira, Tel. (063) 268-50*

CAPARICA

Caparica and the surrounding area, the **Costa da Caparica**, have become a favored vacation spot for residents of Lisbon. The large beaches are surrounded by condo and apartment complexes, and has turned into a mecca for sun worshippers.

ARRIVALS & DEPARTURES

By Car

From Lisbon, follow the A-2 highway south across the bridge and connect to Route IC-20 west for 5 km.

WHERE TO STAY

Expensive

HOTEL COSTA DA CAPARICA, *Monte da Caparica. Tel. (01) 291-0310, Fax (01) 290-6404. Year round rack rates from 21,500$00, double room, EP. All major credit cards accepted.*

Located near the beautiful beaches of Caparica, this brand new 4 star high rise hotel has 357 nice rooms and suites with air conditioning, satellite television, mini-safe, mini-bar, direct dial telephone, private terraces, and special rooms for the physically challenged. Facilities include a huge swimming pool, a restaurant, two bars, nearby golf and tennis, business meeting rooms, and free parking. Highly Recommended.

Moderate
QUINTA DE VALE MOURELOS, *Via Rapida da Caparica, Sobreda. Tel. (01) 295-4871, Fax (01) 294-2566. Year round rack rates from 16,750$00, double room, EP. Cash only - No credit cards accepted.*

This is certainly my favorite place to stay in the Caparica area. This cute 18th century manor house is located in a tranquil residential area not too far from the beach. It has been lovingly converted into a deluxe five room bed and breakfast inn full of antiques and fine furnishings. The rooms overlook a nice outdoor swimming pool, and the owners are a nice Portuguese couple. Highly Recommended.

HOTEL PRAIA DO SOL, *Rua dos Pescadores, 12. Tel. (01) 290-1913, Fax (01) 290-2541. Year round rack rates from 13,500$00, double room, EP. Most major credit cards accepted.*

This medium sized 54 room hotel barely overlooks the ocean. The rooms are somewhat bare but reasonably nice for this area, and the service is good. Facilities include bar and parking.

APARTAMENTOS CAPARICO OCEANO, *Rua Mestre Manuel, 26. Tel. (01) 290-5732. Year round rack rates from 15,500$00 per apartment, per night, EP. Most major credit cards accepted.*

This large 124 unit apartment complex has limited hotel services. The rooms are fairly comfortable and include kitchens. Facilities include a bar, pool, TV room, and parking.

PATIO ALENTAJANA, *Rua Professor S. de Sousa. Tel. (01) 290-0044. Year round rack rates from 11,500$00, double room, EP. Cash only - No credit cards accepted.*

Located not far from the beach, this cute Belgian-owned inn has several comfortable rooms with private bathrooms. They also have a good restaurant.

WHERE TO EAT
Moderate
MANIE'S, *Ave. General H. Delgado, 7. Tel. (01) 290-3398. No dress code. Most major credit cards accepted.*

Huge portions of well prepared arroz de marisco (seafood and rice) and other specials are served in this cute seafood restaurant with a rustic interior of hanging pots and pans. Meals cost about 1,350$00 each.

RESTAURANTE CAPOTE, *Rua dos Pescadores, 9. Tel. (01) 290-1274. No dress code. Most major credit cards accepted.*

This casual seafood restaurant offers reasonably priced, freshly caught, fish including several local specialties such as tamboril (a very good but ugly fish). Expect to pay around 1,850$00 a person for a filling meal.

SEEING THE SIGHTS

The main drag of town, Rua dos Pescadores, is full of inns and good restaurants. Over 20 km of almost unspoiled beaches attract different crowds: Caparica caters to families, while the more southern beaches attract singles, nudists, and gays. The fishing village origins have all but vanished in the wake of tourist development. Further out, near **Monte da Caparica**, the development starts to become less congested, and you can find some nice quiet spots on both the coastline and the interior areas.

SPORTS & RECREATION
Horseback Riding
• **Caparica Equestrian Center**, *Caparica, (01) 295-5581*

PALMELA

Palmela is situated on the border of the Serra do Lurro mountains. The town itself is made up of several medieval stone lanes and whitewash houses. Above town is an impressive pousada converted from the ruins of a Moorish castle, with some elements that date back to the Roman period.

ARRIVALS & DEPARTURES
By Car
Palmela is about 31 km southeast of Lisbon just off the A2 highway south.

WHERE TO STAY
Expensive
POUSADA PALMELA, *Castelo de Palmela. Tel. (01) 235-1226, Fax (01) 233-0440. US & Canada bookings with Marketing Ahead, Tel. 800/223-1356. Low season rack rates from 23,000$00, double room, BP; high season rates from 28,000$00, double room, BP. All major credit cards accepted.*

This beautiful deluxe hotel and restaurant sits on a windswept mountaintop above the charming town of Palmela. The property started as a fortified 12th century Moorish castle that was transformed into a monastery before being all but destroyed by the great earthquake of 1755. Imaginatively rebuilt into a fine government owned hotel and regional restaurant, the Pousada Palmela is certainly the best place to stay and eat in the entire area.

There are 28 exceedingly comfortable rooms (many offer nice views over the sea and nearby hillside) that feature air conditioning, private marble bathrooms, remote control satellite television, nice custom designed furnishings, direct dial telephone, mini-bar, and lots of ambiance. Additional facilities at the pousada include a nice bar, a cloister with a wonderful terrace, several tranquil sitting rooms, plenty of free parking, and direct access to the adjacent historic church and museum of archaeology. The staff are really nice locals that know how to make visitors feel at home (make sure to say hello to Fernanda at the front desk).

PALÁCIO DE RIO FRIO, *Rio Frio. Tel. (01) 230-340. Year round rack rates from 17,500$00, double room, EP. Cash only - No credit cards accepted.*

This magnificent azulejos decorated palace is about 21 km northeast of Palmela. The palace is surrounded by trees and offers four nice rooms with private bathrooms. Facilities include pool, horses, TV, and parking. You'll find this place worth the extra drive.

Moderate

RESTHOTEL PALMELA, *N-252, Carrascas. Tel. (01) 387-6500. Year round rack rates from 10,500$00, double room, EP. Most major credit cards accepted.*

Located just outside of town, this motel-style inn offers 60 nice rooms at reasonable rates. It's perfect for those who require hotel accommodations at motel prices. Facilities include bar, restaurant, air conditioning, TV, direct dial phones, and parking.

WHERE TO EAT

POUSADA PALMELA, *Castelo de Palmela. Tel. (01) 235-1226. Dress code is casual but neat. All major credit cards accepted.*

This deluxe inn is a really good gourmet restaurant that is among my favorite places to eat in the region. The menu includes French onion soup, fish soup, smoked salmon mousse, asparagus with shrimp in garlic sauce, watercress and endive salad, clams with coriander, crab crepes with leeks, spaghetti with garlic and shrimp, roasted cod fish with sweet red peppers, rice with octopus, sirloin steak with capers, kid with turnip, duck breasts in orange sauce, rack of lamb, breaded pork chops, chicken stew in Muscatel wine, filet of sole in black beer sauce, and a fantastic selection of wines and desserts. Expect to pay around 4,250$00 per person for a great three course meal.

SEEING THE SIGHTS

By the 15th century, the **Convento de Santiago** and the **Igreja de Santa Maria do Castelo** were both built inside the castle's fortified walls, and now a new Turísmo office, an interesting little museum of archaeology (closed on Mondays), and several boutiques selling handicrafts and local wine have been added. While in town, you can also view lovely 18th century azulejos (tiles) inside the **Igreja Matriz de São Pedro**, a parish church, its pillory, the awesome throne room of the **Paços do Concelho** town hall, and walk along old lanes to the gargoyle embellished old town fountain.

Be sure to also try some of the fine **Moscatel** dessert wines produced locally by small wineries such as **Vinhos Terrabela**. The wineries are more than happy to sell directly to the public and even give free tours. Also worthy of note are the prehistoric **Quinto do Anjo** caves 2 km from town on the road to Azeitão.

AZEITÃO

Vila Nogueira de Azeitão is a wonderful little wine producing town.

ARRIVALS & DEPARTURES

This town is about 12 km away from Palmela on Route N-379 west.

WHERE TO STAY

Moderate

QUINTA DAS TORRES, *N-10-Azeitão. Tel. (01) 208-0001. Year round rack rates from 16,750$00, double room, BP. Most major credit cards accepted.*

This tranquil 15th century manor house offers superb rooms and fine dining. This is a very special place. There are also suites and small villas for rent. Facilities include bar, great restaurant, swimming pool, gardens, trails, and parking. Highly Recommended.

QUINTA DE SANTO AMARO, *Aldeia da Piedade. Tel. (01) 218-9230, Fax (01) 218-9390. Year round rack rates from 18,250$00, double room, BP. Cash only - No credit cards accepted.*

Five minutes south of Azeitão, you'll find this lovely wine producing estate and 18th century manor house. It has eight rooms with private bathrooms. There is a swimming pool, tennis, antiques, an old azulejos covered chapel, gardens, TV room, nearby horse riding, and parking. Highly Recommended.

QUINTA DA PIEDADE, *Aldeia da Piedade. Tel. (01) 208-0381, Fax (01) 218-9381. Year round rack rates from 17,500$00, double room, BP. Cash only - No credit cards accepted.*

This relaxing family run country inn is about five minutes south of Azeitão and offers four rooms with private bathrooms. The inn has a pool, mountain view patio, lounge, TV room, gardens, reading room with fireplace, nearby horse riding, and parking.

WHERE TO EAT
Moderate
QUINTA DAS TORRES, *N-10, Azeitão, Tel. (01) 208-0001. Dress code is smart casual. Most major credit cards accepted.*

A wonderful inn with an even better restaurant, they serve remarkably good international cuisine including fresh meats and vegetables from the area. Expect to spend around 2,950$00 per person for a great dinner. Highly Recommended.

SEEING THE SIGHTS
One of the most enjoyable stops in town is the **Jose María de Fonseca** wine cellar. Visitors can take a tour through the winery and taste several fine Setùbal sweet white Moscatel wines. Among the best buys in the retail shop are the ancient returned voyage port wines that were brought back to Portugal after years of crossing the ocean. A vast collection of antique wine awards and certificates of merit are displayed among beautiful azulejos. There is also a fine garden for your enjoyment. Across from the winery is the 16th century **Tavora Palace**, once home to the disgraced and later executed Duke of Aveiro. Several small streets with beautiful old houses can be found just behind the palace.

A few kilometers away is **Vila Fresca de Azeitão**. In this famous wine producing town, several regal villas and palaces are hidden behind ancient walls and hedges. The **Quinta de Bacalhoa** contains Portugal's oldest azulejos and produces an incredible wine from California grape varieties. Although the property is not open to the public, it can be rented as a deluxe family retreat along with its excellent chef and staff.

A 16th century manor house called **Quinta das Torres** is also located in the area and rents 11 beautiful rooms that overlook impressive gardens and vineyards. The huge wine producing firm of **J.P. Vinhos**, producers of Lancers and João Pires brand wines (as well as several expensive brand names blended by Australian master vintner Peter Bright), is also located in this town.

SESIMBRA
This dramatic fishing beach and resort area is on the shore below the cliffs of the Serra da Arrabida mountains. Every day, many fishermen line the beach and the narrow downtown streets behind the 17th century

Santiago fortress while they hand sew fishing lines and prepare for another day on the open sea. Sesimbra is one of Portugal's last remaining large traditional fishing towns, and must be explored by foot to be fully appreciated.

At night the area's ocean view cafes and restaurants are brimming with both locals and tourists who come to enjoy some of the finest inexpensive seafood in Portugal. If you look out towards the ocean you can still see many row boats net fishing, just as their ancestors did.

ARRIVALS & DEPARTURES
By Car
From Azeitão, take Route N-370 west for about 14 km.

GETTING AROUND TOWN
By Foot
Sesimbra is best explored on foot.

WHERE TO STAY
Expensive
HOTEL DO MAR, *Rua General. H. Delgado, 10. Tel. (01) 223-3326, Fax (01) 223-3888. Year round rack rates from 22,500$00, double room, BP. All major credit cards accepted.*

An excellent 4 star oceanview hotel with nice rooms perched above the ocean on a cliff. There are 166 air conditioned rooms with private bathrooms, satellite television, direct dial telephones, terraces, mini-safe, and comfortable modern furnishings. Facilities include bar, restaurant, indoor and outdoor pools, sun deck, tennis, business meeting rooms, and free parking.

VILLAS DE SESIMBRA, *Altinho de São João. Tel. (01) 228-0005, Fax (01) 223-1355. Year round rack rates from 20,000$00 per apartment, per night, EP. All major credit cards accepted.*

This large 4 story apartment-hotel is on the edge of town overlooking the ocean. There are 207 medium sized holiday apartments that feature fully equipped kitchenettes, private bathrooms, air conditioners, direct dial telephones, video systems, radios, and terraces. Facilities include bars, restaurants, two outdoor pools, sun deck, tennis, health club, sauna, squash, mini-market, business meeting rooms, and free parking

Moderate
ESTALAGEM DOS ZIMBROS, *N-379-Azoia. Tel. (01) 268-4954, Fax (01) 268-4956. Year round rack rates from 10,500$00, double room, EP. Most major credit cards accepted.*

This is a nice 4 star inn near the tip of the peninsula at Cabo Espischel. It has 35 nice rooms with private bathrooms and televisions. There is also a bar, restaurant, pool, billiards, and nearby parking.

CASA NOSSA SENHORA, *Argeis-Sesimbra. Tel. (01) 797-1984, Fax (01) 223-0637. Year round rack rates from 14,500$00, double room, CP. Most major credit cards accepted.*

A small bed and breakfast inn owned by a religious Christian woman. The rooms are quite comfortable, although not all have a private bathroom. Very relaxing views.

HOTEL ESPADARTE, *Ave. 25 de Abril, 11. Tel. (01) 223-3189. Year round rack rates from 11,750$00, double room, EP. Most major credit cards accepted.*

This is a basic and somewhat bleak 3 star hotel facing the ocean. Several rooms have private bathrooms, but not all. Some rooms are less than acceptable, so look at a few before you commit to this hotel.

APARTMENTOS VARANDAS DA FALESIA, *Ave. Ponte d'Argeis. Tel. (01) 223-3769. Year round rack rates from 14,000$00, double room, EP. Most major credit cards accepted.*

You'll find these tourist apartments, with kitchens, are reasonably nice and well located outside of the downtown area. A good choice for families who don't mind limited facilities.

Inexpensive

PENSÃO NAUTICO, *Bairro Infante Dom Henrique, 3. Tel. (01) 223-3233. Year round rack rates from 11,750$00, double room, EP. Cash only - No credit cards accepted.*

A well located 3 star inn, Pensão Nautico has a dozen good rooms with private bathrooms. Facilities include bar, telephones, safe deposit boxes, garden, and TV room.

CONSIDER RENTING A CONDO

A large number of new condo units can be rented by the night or week at reasonable rates. Check with the Turismo office, Largo da Marinha, Tel. (01) 223-5743, for details.

WHERE TO EAT
Moderate

ESCONDIDINHO, *Rua Industriais. Tel. (01) 223-3480. No dress code. Most major credit cards accepted.*

Located on the back streets of downtown Sesimbra, this wonderful little seafood restaurant offers some of the best reasonably priced fresh fish lunches and dinners in town. Expect to spend around 1,450$00 a person for a great meal.

PEDRA ALTA, *Largo Bombaldes. Tel. (01) 223-1791. No dress code. Most major credit cards accepted.*

Pedra Alta is a good, informal seafood restaurant that serves huge portions of freshly caught seafood and local meat specialties. Great home style service and ambiance with an average dinner bill of 1,675$00 a person.

SEEING THE SIGHTS

The narrow downtown streets are the foreground to the 17th century **Santiago** fortress. A harbor area, known as the **Porte de Abrigo**, is located on the western edge of town. It's home to a more modernized fishing fleet and hosts an interesting daily fish auction. Just behind the harbor entrance is a well preserved 17th century fortress. A Moorish **castelo** (castle) is located about 2 km away, high above of the western flank of the old town and has a great panoramic view of the area.

SPORTS & RECREATION

Boating
• **Sesimbra Yacht Club**, *Sesimbra, Tel. (01) 223-3451*

Fishing
• **Ernesto Carapinha Fishing**, *Sesimbra, Tel. (01) 223-0260*

Horseback Riding
• **Quinta do Rio Horse Center**, *Sesimbra, Tel. (01) 208-1043*

Water Sports
• **Hotel do Mar Water Sports**, *Sesimbra, Tel. (01) 223-3666*

EXCURSIONS & DAY TRIPS

If you're interested in a nice excursion, take a bus or car ride over to the haunting and almost desolate area known as **Cabo Espichel**. It's about 12 km west of Sesimbra at the southwestern tip of the peninsula. This cape has been a well known pilgrimage area for over seven centuries and contains the simple 18th century **Santuario de Nossa Senhora do Cabo** church. The church was built to commemorate the glowing image of the Virgin Mary that helped direct a local fisherman to safety after almost being lost at sea. The cliffs and lighthouse at this cape offer superb views over the ocean and beaches below.

If you follow the northern coastline you can also visit several fine beaches such as **Praia do Meco**, located on the southern end of the long **Lagoa de Albufeira** lagoon.

SETÚBAL

This large city sits near the banks of the Sado estuary. Setúbal is one of Portugal's largest ports, and is still an important fishing harbor. The city's new industrial zone has several large factories and is becoming increasingly polluted.

ARRIVALS & DEPARTURES

By Bus
• **Main Bus Office**, Ave. 5 de Outubro, Tel. (065) 525-051

By Car
Setùbal lies about 10 km south of Palmela on the A2 highway.

By Train
• **CP Rail**, Ave. da Portela, Tel. (065) 571-458

WHERE TO STAY

Expensive
POUSADA DE SÃO FILIPE, Castelo de São Filipe. Tel. (065) 523-844, Fax (065) 532-538. US & Canada bookings with Marketing Ahead, Tel. 800/223-1356. Low season rack rates from 23,000$00, double room, BP; high season rates from 28,000$00, double room, BP. All major credit cards accepted.

This is the best place to stay in the area if money is no object and you reserve a room far enough in advance. The castle-like structure has 14 comfortable rooms with private bathrooms, air conditioning, and great views. Facilities include bar, restaurant, and parking.

Moderate
QUINTA DO PATRICIO, Encosta de São Filipe. Tel. (065) 338-17, Fax (065) 338-17. Year round rack rates from 16,500$00, double room, BP. Cash only - No credit cards accepted.

This beautiful manor house has five double rooms and an apartment in a converted windmill. The quinta is well decorated and the service is very friendly. Facilities include bar, dinning room, pool, sun deck, gardens, and parking.

Inexpensive

HOTEL IBIS, *EN-10, Vale de Rosa. Tel. (065) 772-200, Fax (065) 772-447. Year round rack rates from 12,000$00, double room, EP. Most major cards accepted.*

Located outside of downtown, this typical chain motel has 102 medium sized rooms that are well furnished and have air conditioning, televisions, and direct dial telephones. It's not very memorable, but a good place to sleep. Facilities include bar, restaurant, and parking.

ALBERGARIA LAITAU, *Ave. General de Sousa, 89. Tel. (065) 370-31. Year round rack rates from 10,250$00, double room, EP. Cash only - No credit cards accepted.*

This nice little inn has 41 respectable rooms with telephones and mini-bars. Facilities include bar, restaurant, air conditioning, TV, and parking.

PENSÃO BOCAGE, *Rua de São Cristovão, 14. Tel. (065) 215-99, Fax (065) 218-09. Year round rack rates from 13,750$00, double room, CP. Cash only - No credit cards accepted.*

This medium sized bed and breakfast inn and annex has a total of 38 rooms with air conditioning and private bathrooms. Service is very good, and the nice rooms make this a good budget choice.

WHERE TO EAT
Moderate

CACTUS, *Rua Vasco da Gama, Tel. (065) 346-87. No dress code. Most major credit cards accepted.*

Cactus is a nice steak and seafood restaurant with great service and very good food. There is also a fairly popular bar scene here in the evenings. A typical bill will run around 2,050$00 a person plus wine.

GALANTINO, *Rua Occidental do Mercado, 8, Tel. (065) 319-24. No dress code. Cash only - No credit cards accepted.*

This packed local seafood restaurant serves the freshest fish in Setùbal. Its great atmosphere in a casual setting appeals to everybody. Dinner will set you back around 1,350$00 a head.

SEEING THE SIGHTS

The old section of town is bordered by the **Praça Almirante Reis** and the **Largo Defensores da República**. In this ancient part of town you can wander along several stone alleys full of beautifully preserved old houses and other vestiges of the way things used to be. Just off the **Miguel Bombarda** plaza is the 15th century marble **Igreja de Jesus** with its interesting early Manueline design and remarkable vaulted Gothic interior designed by Diogo Boitac. A municipal museum, the **Museu da**

Cidade, is housed in the church's Gothic cloister, and contains several collections of antique azulejos (tiles) and oil paintings. Nearby, *on Rua de Dr. Paulo Borba*, is the 18th century azulejos-covered **Igreja de São Julião**. A Spanish built **castelo** (castle) and chapel is located just above the city. This 16th century structure has been converted into the deluxe **Pousada de São Filipe** and has an excellent panoramic view of the area. The pousada is currently under extensive renovation but had 14 beautiful rooms and a very good restaurant that served regional specialties.

Recently, a large shopping center opened on the main road from Setúbal to Lisbon. Open from 9am until midnight, the mall contains some very large stores and boutiques with constant clearance sales.

SPORTS & RECREATION
Boating
• **Setúbal Yacht Club**, *Setúbal, Tel. (085) 523-915*

Tennis
• **Setúbal Tennis Club**, *Setúbal, Tel. (085) 270-38*

TRÓIA

Tróia is a long and sandy peninsula separated from the mainland by a bay and a river. Although the sand dune beaches are quite clean, major tourism development has created a city-like atmosphere with towering modern buildings.

ARRIVALS & DEPARTURES
By Car
Tróia is four km south of Setúbal. You will need to take a 19 minute ferry ride from Setúbal's Doca do Comercio dock. The ferry cost 250$00 per person, and your car will cost an additional 500$00.

WHERE TO STAY
Moderate
COMPLEXO TURISTICO, *Ponta do Adoxe. Tel. (065) 442-24, Fax (065) 441-62. Year round rack rates from 18,750$00, double room, EP. Most major credit cards accepted.*

The number given is the central reservations number for the 450 room high rise complexes that dominate most of Tróia. All the properties are air conditioned apartments and condos in the Rosa Mar, the Tulipa Mar, and Magnolia Mar.

SEEING THE SIGHTS

The only historic element in Tróia are the Roman ruins at **Cetobriga**. However, these are not the best Roman ruins and I think you'll find your interest limited.

SPORTS & RECREATION

Golf

• **Tróia Golf**, *Tróia, Tel. (065) 441-12*

Tennis

• **Torralta Tennis**, *Tróia, Tel. (065) 442-21*

ALCÁCER DO SAL

The lovely town of Alcácer do Sal was first inhabited during the Iron Age. This area was of primary importance to the Romans who created a major road system that ran through this town. At one time the village was a Moorish stronghold and was used as a market town with access to the nearby Sado River estuary.

ARRIVALS & DEPARTURES

By Car

Drive southeast about 51 km from Setubal on Route IP-1 south (also called Route E-01).

WHERE TO STAY

Moderate

HERDADE DA BARROSINHA, *N-5-Barroshina. Tel. (065) 623-63. Year round rack rates from 14,250$00, double room, BP. Cash only - No credit cards accepted.*

Located about 5 km outside of town in the village of Barroshina, this is a clean and comfortable inn with 11 good double rooms and a restaurant.

SEEING THE SIGHTS

The ruins of a Moorish **castelo** (castle), dating to the time this town was a Moorish stronghold, remain, but is now home to several stork nests.

Three beautiful churches are worth visiting in Alcácer do Sal. The oldest church is the 12th century **Igreja de Santa María** up by the castle. Its chapel has beautiful azulejos. The 15th century **Convento de Santo Antonio** is located below the castle and contains some rather impressive

Renaissance artwork. Another church, **Igreja do Espirito Santo**, *Largo Pedro Nunes*, has become home to the **Museu Pedro Nunes** municipal museum of Archaeology (closed Saturdays and Sundays). This area is famed for handicrafts including ceramics and hand woven baskets. They can easily be found in local shops. You may find that a stroll along the town's river esplanade is a relaxing way to end your visit.

SPORTS & RECREATION
Hunting
• **Herdade de Porches**, *Alcácer do Sal, Tel. (066) 622-42*

SANTIAGO DO CACÉM

Located in the Serra de Grandôla mountains, the historic town of Santiago do Cacém contains the restored defensive walls of a Moorish castelo (castle) that now protect a cemetery. Several regal mansions still grace the zig-zagging stone lanes in the old town. Windmills can be seen dotting the landscape.

ARRIVALS & DEPARTURES
By Car
Santiago do Cacém can be reached from Alcácer do Sal by taking Route N-120 south (also called Route IP-1 and Route E-01) for 21 km, connect to Route IP-8 south for 33 km, and bear right (east) onto Route N-261 for another four km or so.

WHERE TO STAY
Moderate
POUSADA DE SÃO TIAGO, *Estrada Nacional. Tel. (069) 224-59. US & Canada bookings with Marketing Ahead, Tel. 800/223-1356. Low season rack rates from 12,000$00, double room, CP, high season rates from 16,500$00, double room, CP. All major credit cards accepted.*

A simple yet comfortable government run inn, it is located on the outskirts of town. The pousada features seven air conditioned rooms with televisions, a swimming pool, and a good regional restaurant.

QUINTA DA ORTIGA, *Santiago do Cacém. Tel. (069) 228-71. US & Canada bookings with Marketing Ahead, Tel. 800/223-1356. Low season rack rates from 12,000$00, double room, CP; high season rates from 16,500$00, double room, CP. All major credit cards accepted.*

This nice country home on a peaceful farming estate has been converted into a 12 room quinta with private bathrooms, a bar, a restaurant, a pool, nearby water sports facilities, TV, horses, gardens, and parking. It is located just a few minutes out of town.

QUINTA DA CERCA VELHA, *Cercal do Alentejo. Tel. (069) 944-04. Year round rack rates from 11,500$00, double room, BP. Cash only - No credit cards accepted.*

A small inn with two nice rooms and a pool, it's located in the small hamlet of Cercal about 28 km south of Santiago do Cacém off Route N-120 south.

ALBERGARIA DOM NUNO, *Ave. Dom Nuno Alveres Pereira, 92. Tel. (069) 233-25. Year round rack rates from 11,250$00, double room, EP. Most major credit cards accepted.*

A bland but well equipped 4 star inn, its 77 air conditioned rooms all have private bathrooms. Facilities include bar, restaurant, TV room, safe deposit boxes, and parking.

Inexpensive

PENSÃO GABRIEL, *Rua Prof. Egas Moniz, 24. Tel. (069) 233-45. Year round rack rates from 9,250$00, double room, EP. Cash Only - No credit cards accepted.*

A nice 3 star inn near the heart of town, it offers a couple of dozen comfortable rooms with private bathrooms, breakfast room, TV room, and nearby parking.

SEEING THE SIGHTS

On top of a hill in the center of town are the restored defensive walls of a Moorish **castelo** (castle) that now protect a cemetery.

The **Museu Municipal** on **Praça do Municipo** is located in a 19th century former prison (closed on Fridays, Saturdays, and Mondays) that was used by the infamous leader Salazar to house his undesirables. Today it exhibits several decorated cells and various local artifacts.

The most interesting sight are the Roman ruins known as **Mirobriga** that can be reached by following the Rua de Lisboa for about a km and turn right at the posted access road. These excavated ruins (closed on Sundays and Mondays) of a temple, baths, and market area provide a glimpse into the Roman era. Some experts have suggested that this area was first settled by the Celts.

SPORTS & RECREATION
Horseback Riding
• **Quinta da Ortiga Horse Center**, *Santiago do Cacém, Tel. (069) 228-71*

EXCURSIONS & DAY TRIPS

My favorite reason for visiting Santiago do Cacém is its proximity to several breathtaking cafe and pub filled lagoon beaches such as **Lagoa de**

Santo André and **Lagoa de Melides** approximately 20 km northwest of town. There are also beautiful cave beaches at **Porto Covo** about 28 km southwest of Santiago do Cacém, and a little further south are more wonderful coastal beaches like those across from the almost deserted island of **Ilha do Pessegueiro**. The only way to reach the island is to pay an area fisherman to take you there (and back).

Hotels in these areas are terrible, so staying in Santiago do Cacém and taking day trips to the ocean is your best bet.

VILA NOVA DE MILFONTES

The town's position on both the ocean and the Mira River has made this town a favored summer resort for northern Europeans and Portuguese families alike. Vila Nova de Milfontes is a charming beach front community and when its windswept sand dune beaches become saturated with sun worshippers in the high season, and accommodations become extremely scarce.

ARRIVALS & DEPARTURES

By Car

From Santiago do Cacém, take Route N-120 south for 29 km and just before the village of Cercal turn right onto Route N-390 south for another 15 km.

WHERE TO STAY

Expensive

CASTELO MILFONTES, *V.N. Milfontes. Tel. (083) 961-08. Year round rack rates from 21,250$00, double room, CP. Cash only - No credit cards accepted.*

The owners of this deluxe castle are unusually picky and only allow selected guests to stay in one of their seven ocean view and antique filled rooms. Meals are often mandatory.

Moderate

QUINTA DO MOINHO DE VENTO, *V.N. Milfontes. Tel. (083) 963-83, Fax (083) 995-34. Year round rack rates from 15,500$00, double room, EP. Cash only - No credit cards accepted.*

A welcoming country inn near town, it has seven comfortable rooms and apartments with private bathrooms. Facilities include restaurant, pool, sauna, tennis, mini-bars, and parking. The owners are extremely nice and speak English.

Inexpensive

CASA DOS ARCOS, *V.N. Milfontes. Tel. (083) 962-64. Year round rack rates from 9,750$00, double room, EP. Cash only - No credit cards accepted.*

This is a clean and comfortable modern inn and all rooms have private bath.

SEEING THE SIGHTS

The town boasts a beautiful 16th century castle, **Castelo Milfontes**, that has been converted into a deluxe inn. Owned by a woman who prefers to screen her guests, she has been known to tell people the inn is full when in fact it is not. At the very least, try to get her to let you inside to see its unusual interior.

The town seems to always be in a good mood, and in low season you can still enjoy the the beaches and the water, without paying too much for the privilege. From here, you can also visit the dramatic beach areas of **Almograve** and **Zambujeira do Mar**.

PRACTICAL INFORMATION FOR THE COSTA DE LISBOA

Casinos

• **Estoril Casino**, *Parque do Estoril, Estoril, Tel. (01) 468-4521*

Currency Exchange

Most of the banks on the Lisbon Coast will exchange foreign currency and travelers checks without hesitation. On my past few visits to Cascais, I was stunned to learn that several banks claim to not offer this service. If a bank refuses to help you exchange money, ask to speak with the manager.

Private exchange booths and hotel front desks usually offer a poor exchange rate. Remember that banking hours are from 8am - 3pm Monday through Friday.

Emergency & Useful Phone Numbers

• **Emergency Services** (S.O.S.), *Tel. 115*
• **District Hospital- Cascais**, *Tel. (01) 484-4071*
• **Sintra Health Center**, *Rua Visconde de Monsarrete, Tel. (01) 923-3400*
• **Automobile Club of Portugal** *(Lisbon), Tel. (01) 942-5095*
• **Director Assistance**, *Tel. 118*
• **Lisbon's Portela Airport**, *Tel. (01) 802-060*
• **TAP at Lisbon Airport**, *Tel. (01) 386-0480*

Museums, Palaces, & Monuments

• **Archaeological and Ethnographic Museum**, *Ave. Luisa Todi, 162, Setúbal, Tel. (065) 393-65*. Contains collections of archaeological and ethnographic items and findings from the paleolithic through Roman eras. Open 9:30am until 12:30pm and 2pm until 5:30pm, Tuesday through Saturday. Open 9:30am until 12:30pm on Sundays. Closed Monday and holidays.

• **Ethnographic Museum of Vila Franca de Xira**, *Praça de Touros de Palha Blanco, Vila Franca de Xira, Tel. (063) 230-57*. Contains collections of paintings and sculptures from the region. Open 10am until 12:30pm and 2pm until 6pm, Tuesday through Sunday. Closed on Mondays and holidays.

• **Municipal Museum and Sea Museum of Sesimbra**, *Largo Luís de Camões, Sesimbra, Tel. (01) 223-3885*. Contains collections of archaeological findings, and information about fishing. Open 10am until 12:30pm and 2pm until 5:30pm, Tuesday through Friday. Closed on Weekends and Mondays

• **Municipal Museum of Vila Franca de Xira**, *Rua Serpa Pinto, 65, Vila Franca de Xira, Tel. (063) 220-31*. Contains collections of archaeological findings, sculpture, paintings, and medals. Open 9:30am until 12:30pm and 2pm until 5:30pm, Tuesday through Sunday. Closed on Mondays and holidays.

• **Museum-Library of the Counts of Castro Guimarães**, *Palácio dos Condes de Castro Guimarães, Ave. Rei Humberto de Ialia, Cascais, Tel. (01) 284-0861*. Contains collections of 18th century books, oil paintings, antique furniture, jewelry, ceramics, silver, gold, archaeological artifacts, and rare documents and manuscripts. Open 10am until 5pm, Monday through Friday. Open 10am until 1pm, Saturdays. Closed Sundays and holidays.

• **National Palace**, *Sintra, Tel. (01) 923-4118*. Open 10am until 1pm and 2pm until 5pm, Thursday through Tuesday. Closed on Wednesdays.

• **National Palace of Mafra**, *Casa do Adro-Rio Fria-Mafra, Tel. (061) 523-32*. Open 10am until 1pm and 2pm until 5pm, Wednesday through Monday. Closed on Tuesdays and holidays.

• **National Palace of Queluz**, *Queluz, Tel. (01) 435-0039*. Open 10am until 1pm and 2pm until 5pm, Wednesday through Monday. Closed Tuesdays and holidays.

• **Pena Palace**, *Sintra, Tel. (01) 923-0227*. Open 10am until 5pm, Monday through Friday. Open 10am until 1pm and 2pm until 5pm on weekends. Closed Mondays and holidays.

• **Municipal Museum of Santiago do Cacém**, *Town Hall, Praça do Municipio, Santiago do Cacém, Tel. (069) 224-11*. Contains a collection of local artifacts and crafts. Open 10am until 12pm and 2pm until 5:30pm,

Sunday through Thursday. Closed on Fridays, Saturdays, and holidays.

- **Regional Museum of Sintra**, *Praça da República, 23, Sintra, Tel. (01) 923-4121.* Contains collections of archaeological and ethnographic artifacts and documents. Open 9:30am until 12pm and 2pm until 6pm, Tuesday through Friday. Open 2pm until 6pm on weekends. Closed on Mondays.
- **Setúbal Museum (Museu da Cidade)**, *Igreja de Jesus-Largo de Jesus, Setúbal, Tel. (065) 524-772.* Contains collections of 16th century European oil paintings, jewelry, azulejos, ceramics, rare coins, sacred art, and historic archives. Open 9am until 12pm and 2pm until 5pm, Tuesday through Sunday. Closed on Mondays and holidays.
- **Toy Museum**, *Largo Latino Coelho, 9, Sintra, Tel. (01) 923-5079.* Contains a collection of toys from as far back as the 16th century. Open 10am until 12:30pm and 2pm until 6pm, Tuesday through Sunday. Closed on Mondays and holidays.

Tourist Offices *(Turismos)*

- **Cabo da Roca Tourist Office**, *Cabo da Roca, Tel. (01) 928-0081*
- **Cascais Tourist Office**, *Rua Visconde da Luz, 14, Tel. (01) 486-8204*
- **Colares Tourist Office**, *Alamada C.L. de Lima, Tel. (01) 929-2638*
- **Ericeira Tourist Office**, *Rua Dr. E. Burnay, 33, Tel. (061) 631-22*
- **Estoril Tourist Office**, *Arcadas do Parque, Tel. (01) 468-0113*
- **Mafra Tourist Office**, *Ave. 25 de Abril, Tel. (061) 812-023*
- **Sesimbra Tourist Office**, *Câmara Municipal, Tel. (01) 223-1926*
- **Setúbal Tourist Office**, *Travessa Frei Gaspar, Tel. (065) 524-284*
- **Sintra Tourist Office**, *Praça da República, 3, Tel. (01) 923-1157*
- **Queluz Tourist Office**, *Palácio Nacional, Tel. (01) 436-4315*

Travel Agencies

- **Feriasol Viagens**, *Ave. Gonçalo V. Cabral, 194-#7C, Tel. (01) 486-8232.* This small and personalized Cascais-based agency specializes in booking unusual accommodations throughout Portugal. The helpful staff speak perfect English, French, and German. Perhaps the best agency for adventurous travelers.
- **Abreu**, *Ave. 25 de Abril, 79, Tel. (01) 483-5282.* The Cascais branch office of the huge Abreu organization. Come here for all types of transportation or large hotel bookings.
- **Wagon-Lits**, *Galerias do Parque, Tel. (01) 268-0264.* This Estoril branch office of a major company can reserve tickets for bus tours, airplanes, trains, rental cars, resort hotels and some other services.

13. COSTA DE PRATA

The relatively peaceful region known as the Costa de Prata (The Silver Coast) has some magnificent beaches, but is mostly forests and countryside. Many small roads wind their way through centuries old villages and cities, each with their own special charm.

Among the many worthwhile visits in this area are the walled medieval village of **Óbidos**, the fishing port of **Peniche**, the enchanted forest and **Palace of Buçaco**, the canal city of **Aveiro**, the seaside resort city of **Nazaré**, the turn-of-the-century spa town of **Curia**, the ceramic producing towns of **Alcobaça** and **Caldas de Rainha**, the bed and breakfast-filled countryside around **Tomar**, the historic university city of **Coimbra**, the market of **Águeda**, many fine wineries, and, for the truly adventurous, the **Berlenga Islands**.

The towns and sights in this chapter are arranged from south to north.

ARRIVALS & DEPARTURES

By Air

The Costa de Prata is accessible from either the Portela International Airport just outside of downtown Lisbon or from the smaller Dr. Francisco Sá Carneiro International Airport about 15 kilometers outside of Porto.

From either airport, the easiest way to get to the destinations in this region is to either rent a car or pre-arrange transfer to your hotel through your travel agent. A taxi ride to any point in this region from either airport will be expensive.

By Bus

Those with minimal luggage who are looking for an affordable way to reach the resorts and cities in the Costa de Prata can take a bus from either airport to downtown Lisbon or Porto, and transfer to bus or rail services to reach over 98 Costa de Prata destinations.

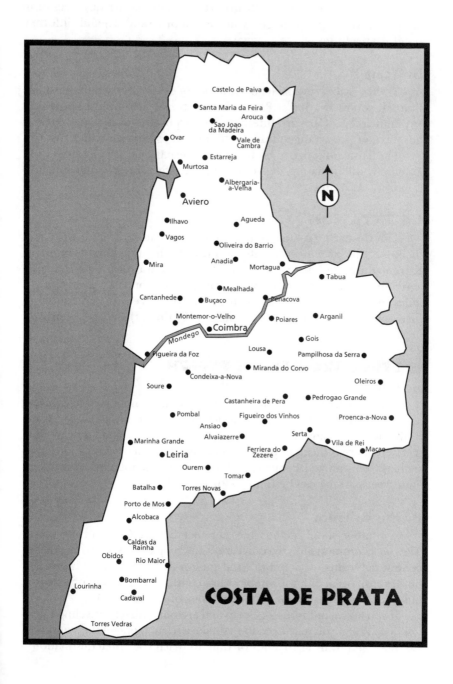

The Turismo office in both airport international arrivals areas or in either city will be happy to give you current price and schedule information for area buses.

By Train

Train service is available to a number of destinations in the Costa de Prata. If you're arriving at Portela International Airport in Lisbon or at Dr. Francisco Sá Carneiro International Airport in Porto, you can take a bus, taxi, or pre-arranged transfer to the train station in either city.

The Turismo office in both airport international arrivals areas or in either city will be happy to give you current price and schedule information for area trains.

ORIENTATION

The Costa de Prata is located in western and central Portugal and includes the provinces of **Beira Litoral**, the northern section of **Estremadura**, and a small piece of western **Beira Alta**. This is a large agricultural and industrial region that begins about 21 kilometers (13 miles) north of Lisbon, near the town of Torres Vedras, and continues further north for about 186 kilometers (115 miles) until just north of Ovar.

GETTING AROUND THE REGION

By Car

Since much of this region is covered by well maintained toll highways and non-toll roads, driving is not difficult during the day. However, many of the non-toll roads are poorly lit at night and have many slow moving trucks that are difficult to pass. Other than a few major cities and resorts such as Coimbra and Peniche, rush hour traffic is not a major problem and street parking can be found with some effort.

By Bus & Train

A number of rail and bus lines connect through Coimbra and Porto. The most common links to resort areas and major cities in this region are **commuter trains** to Coimbra's rail station A. Several other trains and **busses** stop off at either Coimbra's less central B rail station or a nearby bus depot, both just a few kilometers west of rail station A.

If you arrive in Lisbon or Porto and are immediately traveling to the Costa de Prata, you may need to first take a train to one of the stations in Coimbra and transfer to a bus or train to reach your final destination.

TORRES VEDRAS

The town charter dates back to the 12th century when King Dom Afonso Henriques captured the area from the Moors. The ruins of a medieval castle is perched above the highest point in town.

In 1809, a secret system of defensive trenches and forts was designed by Britain's General Wellington to defend Lisbon from the invading Napoleonic army. This strategic defensive system, know as the **Linhas Torres Vedras**, led to the retreat of Napoleonic troops, and a fine example of this system can still be seen at Forte de São Vicente. An ancient mile and a half long aqueduct also runs through the city. On the outskirts of town are functioning windmills.

ARRIVALS & DEPARTURES

By Car

From Lisbon, take the A-8 highway north for about 30 km and take Route N-8 north for another 29 km.

WHERE TO STAY

Moderate

HOTEL DAS TERMAS, *Cucos. Tel. (061) 231-27, Fax (061) 321-901. Seasonal rack rates from 13,250$00, double room, EP. Most major credit cards accepted.*

A grand old pink mansion not far from the city, it contains a health spa (open May 1 - September 30), a relaxing garden, a good restaurant and about 21 rooms with private bathroom and TV.

Inexpensive

HOTEL IMPERIO JARDIM, *Praça 25 de Abril. Tel. (061) 314-232, Fax (061) 321-901. Year round rack rates from 7,500$00, double room, EP. Most major credit cards accepted.*

A modern 2 star business hotel, it's located in the heart of town. The hotel offers 47 rooms with small twin beds, TV, direct dial telephones, and private bathrooms. Facilities include bar, sidewalk cafe, snack bar, restaurant, barber, and free parking.

APARTHOTEL SÃO JOÃO, *Rua Dr. Afonso Costas. Tel. (061) 240. Year round rack rates from 9,500$00, per apartment, per night, EP. Most major credit cards accepted.*

This is a nice, modern apartment complex in the heart of town. The hotel has 37 comfortable one bedroom apartments with kitchens, a bar, disco, tennis, and parking.

RESIDENCIAL DOS ARCOS, *Praça Rua Norte, 1. Tel. (061) 312-489, Fax (061) 238-70. Year round rack rates from 7,000$00, double room, CP. Cash only - No credit cards accepted.*

This simple and modest inn has 28 single and double rooms with private bathrooms, direct dial phone, and heating. It is located in the historic Bairro Arenes section.

HOTEL SANTA CRUZ, *Praia de Santa Cruz. Tel. (061) 937-148, Fax (061) 932-585. Year round rack rates from 9,000$00, double room, EP. Most major credit cards accepted.*

A 2 star hotel with 32 comfortable double rooms with private bathroom and television. It's located near the beach. Facilities include bar, restaurant, disco, and parking. Perhaps the most modern place to stay in Santa Cruz.

WHERE TO EAT

RESTAURANTE BARRETO PRETO, *Rua Praia de Andrada. Tel. (061) 220-63. No dress code. Cash only - No credit cards accepted.*

This good and reasonably priced local restaurant is conveniently located near the train station. It serves fine meat dishes in a casual setting with friendly service. My last dinner here cost me just 1,400$00.

SEEING THE SIGHTS

The small **Museu Municipal** is located in part of the 17th century azulejos-filled **Convento Graça**, *Rua Serpa Pinto*, near the central Praça 25 de Abril square. This museum contains examples of 17th century coins, weapons, and crowns. Also in the town center is a Gothic fountain from 1331 called the **Chafariz dos Canos**, and several interesting churches including the 12th-century Romanesque **Igreja de Santa Maria do Castelo** and the Manueline **Igreja de São Pedro**.

About 13 km from Torres Vedras off Route N-9 west, there are wonderful wide beaches at the village of **Santa Cruz** that are well worth the side trip. During the warm season you can rent chairs and cabana sized tents at Santa Cruz's **Praia Norte** (North Beach). Also in the area is a famous health spa, **Termas do Vale dos Cucos** (closed October-April), located about three km east in the town of Cucos. It's known for its healing, thermal springs.

Before leaving the area, try one of the special reserve wines produced by the **Adega Cooperativa de Torres Vedras**.

SPORTS & RECREATION
Horseback Riding
• **Picadeiro Paio Correia Horse Center**, *Torres Vedras, Tel. (061) 981-218*

VIMEIRO & NEARBY COASTAL BEACHES

The little town of **Vimeiro** is known for its thermal waters, historical battles, and its proximity to several great beaches. Vimeiro is home to the historical (Romans used to come here) springs known as **Termas do Vimeiro**. It was here, in 1808, that the British forces under Wellington's command dominated the invading Napoleonic troops and sent them on their way back to France.

Most vacationers visit Vimeiro for the excellent spa-hotel that has several curative and sports based programs including thermal baths, massage, golf, and horseback riding.

ARRIVALS & DEPARTURES
By Car

Vimeiro is 12 km northwest of Torres Vedras off of Route N-8-2 north.

WHERE TO STAY
Moderate

HOTEL DAS TERMAS, *Rua Joaquim Belchor. Tel. (061) 984-496, Fax (061) 984-152. Year round rack rates from 14,000$00, double room, EP. Most major credit cards accepted.*

A comfortable 2 star hotel, it's known for its spa and sports programs. There are 88 double rooms with private bathroom and television. In addition to the spa, the hotel has a bar, a restaurant, a nice swimming pool, golf, and tennis. Open only in high season.

HOTEL GOLF MAR, *Praia do Porto Novo. Tel. (061) 984-157, Fax (061) 984-621. Year round rack rates from 16,250$00, double room, CP. Most major credit cards accepted.*

This is a huge 300 room, 3 star hotel complex, with balconies overlooking the sea. The full service hotel has two pools, a nearby golf course, tennis, ping-pong, restaurants, and a nice beach area.

Inexpensive

RESIDENCIAL RAINHA SANTA, *Quinta da Piedade-Vimeiro. Tel. (061) 984-234. Year round rack rates from 10,000$00, double room, EP. Cash only - No credit cards accepted.*

This nice, inexpensive inn with 18 good rooms with private bath is located in a nice part of town. Closed from mid October - January 1. It's a good budget choice.

PENSÃO PROMAR, *Praia do Porto Novo. Tel. (061) 984-220. Year round rack rates from 8,000$00, double room, EP. Cash only - No credit cards accepted.*

A clean and comfortable 2 star inn, it has 29 rooms with private bathrooms just across from the ocean. Facilities include restaurant, TV room, and nearby parking.

SEEING THE SIGHTS

You come to Vimeiro to go to the beach or to go to the spa. I had an extremely relaxing visit to the spa. From Vimeiro, there is easy access to some of the finest sandy beaches in Portugal. If you head just seven km or so to the west (towards the ocean), you'll reach the relatively quiet beach towns of **Porto Novo** and **Santa Rita**. In this coastal area you can find nice beaches, large swimming pools, tennis, golf, lots of water sports, excellent local fish restaurants, and good nightlife. People here really know how to party!

SPORTS & RECREATION

Golf

• **Vimeiro Golf Club**, *Vidago, Tel. (076) 971-06*

LOURINHÃ

Founded in 1160 after many years of Arab occupation, this small city has several ancient buildings, beautiful churches, and a slightly confusing maze of stone streets that create a medieval atmosphere.

ARRIVALS & DEPARTURES

By Car

Lourinhã is 19 km northwest of Torres Vedras on Route N-8-2 north.

WHERE TO STAY

QUINTA DA MOITA LONGA, *Toxofal de Cima. Tel. (061) 422-385, Fax (061) 422-385. Year round rack rates from 15,750$00, double room, CP. Cash only - No credit cards accepted.*

This beautiful, traditional manor house has a large pool, gardens, and three lovely rooms, plus one fully equipped apartment all with private bathroom, TV, and heating. The complete house can also be rented by the week with advance booking. It's conveniently located and is just a five minute drive away from the city. Highly Recommended.

QUINTA DA SANTA CATARINA, *Rua Visconde de Palma de Almeida. Tel. (061) 422-313, Fax (061) 422-313. Year round rack rates from 15,500$00, double room, CP. Cash only - No credit cards accepted.*

This is a nice family owned and managed 16th century manor house located on the outskirts of Lourinhã and just a three km drive to the beach. The inn has five deluxe rooms with private bathrooms, and a swimming pool, tennis, breakfast room, a piano room, and a garden. Highly Recommended.

ESTALAGEM BELA VISTA, *Rua Dom Sancho I. Tel. (061) 414-161, Fax (061) 414-138. Year round rack rates from 14,000$00, double room, CP. Most major credit cards accepted.*

The Bela Vista is a peaceful, comfortable and very secure inn with 29 rooms. The many hotel facilities include pool, tennis, gardens, restaurant, bar, TV room, and free parking

ESTALAGEM AREIA BRANCA, *Praia da Areia Branca. Tel. (061) 412-491, Fax (061) 413-143. Year round rack rates from 14,500$00, double room, CP. Most major credit cards accepted.*

A good 4 star inn on a cliff above the ocean, this inn has 29 comfortable rooms, several with private bathrooms, television, and great views. Facilities include a swimming pool, bar, billiard, a nice beach, and a restaurant.

APARTAMENTOS SÃO JOÃO, *Praia da Areia Branca. Tel. (061) 422-491, Fax (061) 413-020. Year round rack rates from 13,750$00, per apartment, per night, EP. Most major credit cards accepted.*

A good place for couples and families who desire reasonable accommodations with kitchen. Lots of facilities including pools and a great location.

SEEING THE SIGHTS

While strolling through the old part of the city, stop in at the Gothic 14th century **Igreja de Nossa Senhora do Castelo**, a parish church.

Of all the area's fine beaches, I suggest a visit to the almost undiscovered beaches, cliffs, and good shellfish restaurants at **Porto das Barcas**. The beaches at **Praia da Areia Branca** and **Porto Dinheiro** have become a little developed and but maintain a small resort town ambiance. You must try some of the local fish chowders (caldeiras) served in the small ocean front restaurants and cafés.

CADAVAL

The tranquil village of **Cadaval** rests in the valley at the foot of the beautiful **Serra de Montejunto** mountains. Wine is the main product in this area, but local artisans can still be found producing wicker and ceramic pieces by hand.

ARRIVALS & DEPARTURES
By Car

Cadaval is about 29 km from Lourinhã on Route N-361 east.

WHERE TO STAY
Moderate
QUINTA DA NOGUEIRA, *Portela-Bombarral. Tel. (062) 624. Year round rack rates from 14,050$00, double room, CP. Most major credit cards accepted.*

A nice rustic estate that operates as a bed and breakfast inn. There are only four rooms and a two bedroom apartment with private bathrooms. This quinta is located off Route N-361.

Inexpensive
RESIDENCIAL LOURENCO, *Rua H, 10,Cadaval. Tel. (062) 664-76. Year round rack rates from 8,750$00, double room, EP. Cash only - No credit cards accepted.*

Located in the center of town, this budget hotel has 22 cheap and reasonably comfortable rooms with private bathroom. This is a good budget choice for those who require few facilities.

SEEING THE SIGHTS
Many visitors to this picturesque village come for the many religious festivals, including the annual festival of **Our Lady of Snow** held on August 5 at the beautiful **Igreja de Nosa Senhora de Neves**.

In the general area of Cadaval are several interesting sights, including the Neolithic cave dwellings 9 km southeast in **Pragança** and the beautiful gardens at the **Palácio de Gorjões** about 10 km northwest in pretty town of **Bombarral**. Also worth a dare are hang-gliding excursions from the top of the **Serra de Montejunto**.

PENICHE & THE BERLENGA ISLANDS
The seaside city of **Peniche** juts out to the sea on a rocky peninsula that was once a separate island. Peniche has become an important fishing harbor and processing center.

ARRIVALS & DEPARTURES
By Car
Peniche is 19 km northwest of Lourinhã just past the end of Route N-247 north.

WHERE TO STAY
Moderate
HOTEL PRAIA NORTE, *Ave. Monsenhor Bastos. Tel. (062) 781-166, Fax (062) 984-152. Year round rack rates from 17,000$00, double room, BP. All major credit cards accepted.*

A large modern ocean view resort hotel, it has 92 comfortable rooms with private bathrooms and televisions. This full service property also has swimming pools, restaurants, a bar, and several other facilities.

A COUTADA, *Quinta das Tripas, Atouguia da Baleia. Tel. (062) 759-733, Fax (062) 759-733. Year round rack rates from 14,000$00, double room, EP. Cash only - No credit cards accepted.*

A beautiful old private farming estate, it was recently converted into a rural hotel near the ocean. They rent out 35 rooms with private bath. Facilities include bar, swimming pool, horses, and parking.

Inexpensive

FORTE DE S. J. BAPTISTA, *Berlenga Grande Island. Tel. (062) 789-571. Year round rack rates from 4,000$00, double room, EP. Cash only - No credit cards accepted.*

You can book a basic and barely furnished room at this amazing fortress on a tranquil island by calling the Turismo office, *Rua Alexandre Herculano, Tel. (062) 789-571.* You must arrange your own transportation via seasonal ferry or fishing boat service. It's quite rustic, but well worth the experience. Highly Recommended for adventurous travelers.

RESIDENCIAL FELITA, *Largo Prof. F. Friere, 12. Tel. (062) 721-190. Year round rack rates from 7,700$00, double room, EP. Cash only - No credit cards accepted.*

A small inn with eight reasonably comfortable rooms.

WHERE TO EAT

Moderate

RESTAURANTE NAU DOS CORVOS, *Cabo Carvoeiro, Peniche. Tel. (062) 724-10. No dress code. Most major credit cards accepted.*

This is an excellent ocean view seafood restaurant with a wonderful menu of reasonably priced grilled fish specialties. If you can, get a table near the windows. Expect to pay around 2,150$00 a person plus wine.

Inexpensive

RESTAURANTE ANCORA, *Ave. do Mar, 78, Peniche. Tel. (062) 714-56. No dress code. Cash only - No credit cards accepted.*

One of several fine inexpensive and casual fish restaurants, Restaurante Ancora is located near the ocean on Avenida do Mar. Try anything grilled, especially the sardines when available.

SEEING THE SIGHTS

Peniche has a large harbor with a promenade called **Largo da Ribeira**. Each afternoon, the fishing fleet returns with an impressive catch of sardines and other fish. Next to the harbor is a 16th century **Fortaleza** (fortress) that was used as a maximum security prison and is now a local museum (closed on Mondays) displaying crafts and former prison cells. In town, there is a 16th century church known as the **Igreja de Nossa Senhora da Ajuda**. The local artisans of Peniche produce fine lace work that can be found in the better shops around the waterfront.

At the tip of the peninsula is **Cabo Carvoeiro** cape where you can visit the **Forte da Luzo** (a fortress), a windmill, and paths that take you to strange rock formations in the ocean, such as the stone called the **Nau dos Corvos** (Stone of the Crows), as well as an area with a great panoramic view. If you drive just a bit further on the winding, northbound coastal road, you can visit the colored tile church called **Igreja de Nossa Senhora dos Remédios** in the small village of **Remédios**.

About five km east of Peniche is the small town of **Atouguia da Baleia**. This town has a medieval castle and several nice churches including the 13th century **Igreja de São Leonardo** that has a beautiful nativity scene. A few kilometers further east is the 14th century royal palace of King Dom Pedro I and a beautiful windmill in the peaceful hamlet of **Serra de El-Rei**.

Several nice beaches grace the Peniche area including the town's own **Praia de Peniche**. Unfortunately, it's getting a bit dirty. The southern coast beaches, **Praia de Consolação** and **Praia São Bernadino**, are much nicer and are only a few more kilometers away. The beach just north of Peniche at **Praia do Baleal** is also quite nice but the undertow is strong.

Each year, on the first Sunday in August, Peniche hosts the festival of **Nossa Senhora de Boa Viagem** (Our Lady of Safe Voyages). The boats of the fishing fleet carry religious statues that are blessed by the local parish priest. Great firework display and dancing following the celebration.

A series of almost deserted granite islands known as the **Ilhas Berlengas** are located 11 km out to sea. Only the largest of the islands, **Berlenga Grande**, is accessible to visitors. During the summer, a ferry runs to and from Peniche two or three times a day (if the weather is good) and costs about 1,100$00 round trip. You can also catch a ride in a fisherman's boat if you don't mind being knee deep in sardines for an hour or so. The island is inhabited by a few families who make their living fishing and thousands of wild seabirds. The island can be visited on a day trip, and if you are in the mood for something unique you can overnight there as well.

On the island, which is an official National Bird Reserve, there is an ancient fortress, a lighthouse, and several ocean caves including the memorable **Blue Grotto**. If you wish to explore the ocean caves and tunnels around the island you can take a boat tour from the island's pier for about 400$00. Berlenga is for the truly adventurous.

The fortress, **Forte de São João Baptista**, was built on the island in the 17th century and has been converted into a hostel of sorts, with minimal facilities and a cooperative kitchen. A small camping area has also been set up for those with tents. On my first visit to the fort at Berlenga Grande many years ago, my oceanfront room had no windows. As a result, my face was hit with ocean spray every few minutes. Bring warm blankets since there is no heating system at the fort. Some of the fishermen's wives sell fantastic homemade fish cakes for 95$00 each and a local supply store and restaurant also sells basic provisions and reasonably good food.

SPORTS & RECREATION
Horseback Riding
• **Quinta das Tripas Horse Center**, *Atouguia da Baleia, Tel. (062) 757-33*

Tennis
• **Peniche Tennis Club**, *Baluarte-Peniche, Tel. (062) 789-500*
• **Tenisplash Tennis Club**, *Peniche, Tel. (062) 759-667*

ÓBIDOS

Although hundreds of international tourist are bussed into this tiny town daily, it has somehow managed to retain much of its medieval ambiance. The original castle was built in this strategic location by Celts about 308 B.C., and was later transformed by the Romans, the Visigoths, and then the Moors. Óbidos was captured by King Dom Afonso Henriques in 1148 and was granted its official charter in 1195. In the early 13th century, the town was given to Queen Urraca as a gift from her husband King Afonso II. In 1282, Queen Isabel and King Dinis spent their honeymoon here. By the 16th century, a royal palace was constructed on the sight of the old Moorish castle.

For several centuries the town remained the property of the Portuguese royal family and was included as part of all royal dowries. In 1755, the earthquake that destroyed Lisbon also made ruins of the castle. A massive reconstruction project completed between 1910 and 1950 restored the old walls, and converted the palace into the most famous pousada in Portugal, Pousada do Castelo.

ARRIVALS & DEPARTURES
By Bus
• **Obidos Main Bus Depot**, *Porta da Vilha bus stop, no office*

By Car
Follow Route N-114 east from Peniche for about 20 km and connect

to Route N-8 north for another kilometer or so. Turn onto the access road that leads to Óbidos.

By Train
• **Obidos CP Rail Train Station**, *at the foot of the town, Tel. (062) 959-186*

WHERE TO STAY
Expensive
POUSADA DO CASTELO, *Paço Real. Tel. (062) 959-146, Fax (062) 959-148. US & Canada bookings with Marketing Ahead, Tel. 800/223-1356. Low season rack rates from 23,000$00, double room, BP, high season rates from 28,000$00, double room, BP. All major credit cards accepted.*

This fairy tale, 16th century, restored royal castle is the most requested (and most often sold-out) pousada in Portugal. Its dominating stone block battlements, towers, and walls encircle and loom over the quaint village of Óbidos. The nine rooms and suites have private bathrooms. Some of the rooms have old iron candlesticks (now converted for electricity), solid stone block walls, period furnishings, picture windows, and large wooden canopy beds.

The public spaces in the pousada have wonderful artwork and beautiful furnishings. Large central lounges and inner courtyards are great places to relax and wonder what life must have been like for the former royal inhabitants of this delightful structure.

The pousada also has a regal dining room that features hearty regional cuisine and Portuguese wines. The ambiance at the pousada is relaxed and casual, but during dinner it's best to dress nicely. I strongly suggest that you try to get a reservation here, and be persistent because you never know when there might be a cancellation. Highly Recommended.

Moderate
CASA DE S. TIAGO DO CASTELO, *Largo de São Tiago. Tel. (062) 959-587, Fax (062) 959-587. Low season rack rates from 12,500$00, double room, CP, high season rates from 15,000$00, double room, CP. Most major credit cards accepted.*

This is a superb and welcoming quinta that is perhaps the best place to stay in town! There are seven uniquely designed rooms (each with a different color scheme) with remote control television, direct dial phones, an amazing array of designer fabrics and antique furnishings, tiled private bathrooms, and windows with remarkable views of the best parts of town.

The inn also features a billiard room, a video room, a game room, a library stocked with books in several languages, a beautiful outdoor terrace with a grill area, a great bar and lounge, several sitting rooms, and more charm than I could possibly describe. The staff is delightful. Highly Recommended.

ABERGARIA JOSEFA D'ÓBIDOS, *Rua D. João de Ornelas. Tel. (062) 959-228, Fax (062) 959-533. Low season rack rates from 8,000$00, double room, CP; high season rates from 11,000$00, double room, CP. Most major credit cards accepted.*

Don't be fooled by the antique exterior, this inn, just outside the old city walls, offers 37 modern air conditioned rooms with great beds. Facilities include bar, restaurant, student disco, TV, and parking.

ALBERGARIA RAINHA SANTA ISABEL, *Rua Direita. Tel. (062) 959-323, Fax (062) 959-115. Low season rack rates from 9,000$00, double room, CP; high season rates from 10,500$00, double room, CP. Most major credit cards accepted.*

This is a decent inn located on the main street in the heart of Óbidos. The 20 air conditioned rooms are fairly nice yet simple, but several need a bit of renovation. Facilities include bar, breakfast room, and TV.

CASA DO POCO, *Travessa da Rua Nova. Tel. (062) 959-358. Year round rack rates from 15,500$00, double room, EP. Cash only - No credit cards accepted.*

A traditional little townhouse in the heart of old Óbidos, they have four twin rooms with private bathrooms. Look for the Moorish well in the patio.

CASAL DO PINHÃO, *Barrio Senhora da Luz. Tel. (062) 959-078. Year round rack rates from 13,750$00, double room, EP. Cash only - No credit cards accepted.*

This is a cute country estate about three km northeast of town that has six nice guest rooms with private bathrooms. Facilities include a lounge with a fireplace and a dining room.

Inexpensive

CASA DE RELOGIO, *Rua da Graca. Tel. (062) 959-282. Year round rack rates from 12,750$00, double room, EP. Cash only - No credit cards accepted.*

A wonderful authentic village house, it has six double rooms with private bathrooms in the heart of the walled city. It is comfortable, but few facilities are offered.

CASA DE CARLOS PARADA, *Bairro da Raposeira. Tel. (062) 959-744. Year round rack rates from 11,500$00, double room, EP. Cash only - No credit cards accepted.*

This house is located a few kilometers outside of town and rents three clean and reasonable guest rooms. This is a good choice for budget minded travelers.

WHERE TO EAT
Expensive
POUSADA DO CASTELO, *Paço Real. Tel. (062) 959-146. Dress code is semi-formal. All major credit cards accepted.*

Without a doubt, this is the best place in town for fine cuisine in a romantic storybook setting. The menu changes frequently but features such delicacies as fish soup, cabbage soup, nice salads, stuffed veal, grilled bass, braised kid, stewed pork loin, and cod fish. Expect to spend between 3,250$00 and 4,950$ per person for lunch or dinner, not including wine. Reservations are a must.

Moderate
O LIDADOR, *Rua Direita. Tel. (062) 959-213. No dress code. Most major credit cards accepted.*

While it calls itself a snack bar, this cute little restaurant on the main street of Óbidos is also a great place for a casual lunch at affordable prices. They have two indoor dining rooms with a capacity of about 50 people as well as an outdoor patio on Rua Direita with seating for about 26. The menu changes daily, but on my last visit it featured several dishes all between 350$00 and 1,250$00 including gazpacho, pizza, shrimp acorda, roasted chicken, huge salads, steak, omelets, burgers, grilled chicken, grilled ham & cheese sandwiches, and more. This is a nice place to go after walking all around the old city.

RESTAURANTE ALCAIDE, *Rua Direita. Tel. (062) 959-220. No dress code. Cash only - No credit cards accepted.*

This little bar and restaurant has a lot of atmosphere and is located in the heart of town. It primarily serves fine grilled meats and seafood dishes. The main dining area is upstairs from a noisy bar. My last lunch here cost about 1,250$00 a person.

RESTAURANTE DAS MURALHAS, *Rua Dom João d'Ornelas. Tel. (062) 959-816. No dress code. Most major credit cards accepted.*

A great regional restaurant, they serve fine local cuisine at moderate prices in a relaxed and comfortable setting. The friendly staff speak a bit of English. Expect to spend less than 1,800$00 a person for a huge meal.

SEEING THE SIGHTS
Just before ascending the hilltop into the medieval walled village of Óbidos, there are the remnants of a three kilometer long aqueduct that was built on the orders of Queen Catherine in 1573. When you proceed up the hill, you will enter Óbidos through a narrow, 18th century azulejos (tile) covered **Porta da Vila**. This town gate is dedicated to Our Lady of Piety and is still the main entrance tunnel into Óbidos. Be extremely

careful if you are driving through this narrow, twisting gateway. Because it is so narrow, many cars have been damaged over the years (including my own).

You will be bombarded by beauty in every direction and walking through town is quite an adventure. On the left side of the Rua Direita, the main boutique-lined street that now comes into view, is one of several entrances to the village's defensive walls. You will walk up a staircase and onto a walkway that is the top of the defensive walls. After walking around the walls and taking some photographs, I suggest you head back down to the Rua Direita to explore the side streets and attractions of this tiny town. The small houses are beautifully maintained and usually display large clay pots filled with flowers. Each door knocker, window sill, archway, stone lane, terra cotta roof, and whitewashed ancient house is worthy of a photograph. Every step taken through Óbidos leads you to yet another architectural jewel.

As you continue along the Rua Direita you will first pass by dozens of overpriced boutiques and a few acceptable restaurants. A couple of blocks down the street on the left hand side is the exceptionally friendly and helpful Turísmo office that is open daily year round. They will be able to answer all your questions and they give out free maps of the area. Another block and a half further along on the left side of the street, descend down a staircase and you will be the main square, **Praça de Santa María**. Besides the post office and several stunning mansions, this is also the sight of the azulejos-filled 14th century **Igreja de Santa María**. An important 17th century female artist named Josefa d'Ayala, now called Josefa D'Óbidos, is responsible for the beautiful panels in this church.

The town square also is home to a fine Manueline 15th century **Pelourinho** (whipping post) that bears the royal seal of Queen Leonor. Behind the Igreja de Santa María is the **Museu da Cidade** (municipal museum). The museum has an interesting collection of Josefa D'Óbidos works, archaeological finds, and weapons from the Napoleonic battles (closed Mondays).

A couple of blocks down from the Praça de Santa María is another small square that includes the 13th century Gothic **Capela de São Martinho** (chapel), the 16th century **Igreja de São Pedro** (church) with its fine golden altar, and the nearby 15th century baroque **Igreja da Misericórdia** (Almshouse church) filled with hand painted tiles.

Be sure to try a glass of the locally brewed *Ginja*, an incredibly sweet cherry liqueur.

Also worth a visit while in Óbidos is the Óbidos Lagoon (**Lagoa de Óbidos**) where you can rent wind-surfing and fishing equipment, and the beaches of **Praia do Cortico** and **Praia d'el Rei** at the mouth of the lagoon.

SPORTS & RECREATION
Boating
· **Neptuno Boating Club**, *Obidos, Tel. (062) 950-271*

RIO MAIOR
While most tourists never make it to this municipality, the friendly city of Rio Maior and the small agricultural villages that surround it are worth visiting. Rio Maior is a great place to stay while you take day trips to various villages described below in *Day Trips & Excursion*. Downtown Rio Maior is somewhat modernized but it has several historical sights and interesting shops.

WHERE TO STAY
Moderate
QUINTA DA CORTICADA, *Outerio da Corticada. Tel. (043) 478-182, Fax (043) 478-772. Low season rack rates from 15,000$00, double room, EP, high season rack rates from 16,000$00, double room, EP. Most major credit cards accepted.*

This peaceful and welcoming deluxe bed and breakfast inn is among my favorite places to stay in Portugal. It's about a 10 minute drive from Rio Maior. Built a few years ago in the traditional style of the region, the property sits among dozens of acres of remarkably landscaped gardens including ponds with swans, blossoming fruit trees, and a variety of wild birds. The quinta was built by a successful Portuguese industrialist who wanted to create the perfect getaway for comfort minded vacationers and stressed out executives.

All of the eight giant rooms and suites come fully equipped with deluxe private bathrooms, a breathtaking selection of rare antique furnishings, and large picture windows overlooking a seemingly endless landscape of trees, plants, and colorful crops. About the only sound you will hear from your room are those made by the crowing roosters in the adjacent farm. This farm provides fresh fruit and other produce for the inn.

The quinta also features a wonderful outdoor swimming pool and sun deck, a tranquil breakfast room, optional made to order lunches and/or dinners of delicious regional cuisine, nearby complimentary horse back riding, comfortable sitting rooms filled with priceless antiques and oil paintings, a lounge, a private meeting room/dinner hall, plenty of free parking, and a staff of charming local residents.

Selected as one of my *Best Places to Stay* (see Chapter 10 for more details).

QUINTA DA FERRARIA, *Ribeira de São João. Tel. (043) 950-01, Fax (043) 956-96. Low season rack rates from 11,200$00, double room, CP; high season rack rates from 13,500$00, double room, CP. Most major credit cards accepted.*

Situated on a huge farm estate roughly halfway between Santarém and Rio Maior, this relaxing "rural hotel" is a great place to stay while exploring the Ribatejo region. The quinta is comprised of several converted farm houses and a few new annexes that have been designed to accommodate travelers and small corporate gatherings. The property boasts 12 spacious air conditioned rooms and two fully equipped two bedroom apartments. The rustic apartments have kitchenettes, private bathrooms, comfortable beds, direct dial telephones, and great views of the adjacent farm lands.

The quinta also offers optional homemade lunches and dinners, complimentary horse back riding at their stables, a huge outdoor swimming pool and sun deck, mountain bikes, a private museum of rural traditions, hiking trails, antique oil presses and a functioning 19th century water wheel, state of the art business conference facilities and reception rooms, a snooker room, plenty of geese and wild birds to watch, nearby 18 hole golf course, and countless acres of land with herds of domesticated farm animals. Perfect for couples, families, and executives that want to sit back and relax. Highly Recommended.

Inexpensive

CABEÇO DOS TRÊS MOINHOS, *EN-1, Alto da Serra, Rio Maior. Tel. (043) 991-165, Fax (043) 991-363. Midweek rack rates from 6,000$00, double room, EP; weekend rack rates from 7,000$00, double room, EP. Cash only - No credit cards accepted.*

This tiny mountain-top hideaway is an unusual inn. There are three antique windmills that have been convereted into rustic one or two bedroom duplex apartments. All the apartments have private bathrooms, living rooms with wood burning stoves, televisions, direct dial telephones, antique style furnishings, handmade quilts, mini-refrigerators, exposed beam ceilings, antiques, original 18th century stone walls, chapel ceilings, small windows with great views, and plenty of charm.

The inn also offers horseback riding with advance notice, great hiking trails through the adjacent lush hillside, an open air grill area, plenty of privacy, and a friendly innkeeper.

Selected as one of my *Best Places to Stay* (see Chapter 10 for more details).

CASA DO FORAL, *Rua da Boavista, 10. Tel. (043) 992-610, Fax (043) 992-611. Year round rack rates from 8,000$00, double room, CP. Cash only - No credit cards accepted.*

This quaint manor house is located a few blocks from the heart of downtown Rio Maior, but has the ambiance and surroundings of a small country inn. There are five rooms and one suite with limestone and marble private bathrooms, terra cotta floors, twin or double beds, cable television, heating systems, large windows looking into the gardens, and a small loft for additional children's beds. The suite has a small kitchen with a microwave oven and mini-refrigerator.

The property features tranquil gardens, halls filled with many fine antiques, a small outdoor swimming pool, a billiard room, a breakfast room, and a private meeting room.

WHERE TO EAT

Moderate

PATIO DO NICOLAU, *Estrada para Marinhas de Sal. Tel. (043) 991-372. Dress code is casual but neat. Cash only - No credit cards accepted.*

This extremely cozy and welcoming local restaurant about 1.5 kilometers away from the center of Rio Maior is a must for all visitors to this region. Located in a beautiful converted farmhouse near the salt pans, Patio do Nicolau is an oasis of superb regional cuisine. There is no set menu here, and during lunch and dinner only the freshest fish, pork, sausage, chicken, rabbit, and veal dishes will be offered to you along with a mind blowing array of appetizers that I have found in few other restaurants in Portugal. The exposed beam interior of the restaurant has several whitewashed dining rooms lined with wine bottles and local handicrafts, and the extremely friendly owner will stop by your table and ask how everything was.

Expect to pay under 2,500$00 per person for a meal you will never forget. Packed on weekends, so get here early. Highly Recommended.

RESTAURANTE ADEGA CANTINHO DA SERRA, *EN-1, Alto da Serra, Rio Maior. Tel. (043) 991-367. No dress code. Cash only - No credit cards accepted.*

The Cantinho da Serra is unforgettable dining establishment that offers a huge array of homemade regional specialties. You will be served dozens of small plates full of unusual items such as beans in garlic, roasted pork, fish eggs, calamari, prawns, fried green eggs, and fresh corn bread to munch on until your main course arrives. The menu includes about three dozen different well prepared meat, seafood, and poultry dishes cooked in a variety of spices and sauces. The dessert is also fantastic and features a variety of local fruits that have been marinated in red, white, and Port wines.

The average lunch or dinner costs around 2,400$00 per person. Cantinho da Serra is closed on Mondays. Highly Recommended.

SEEING THE SIGHTS

Next to the city's main cemetery, a team of archaeologists from around the world, under the direction of Dr. José Beleza Moreira and Dr. Carlos Pereira, has almost completed the excavation of circular mosaics from a **Roman era villa**. A fine Roman marble statue found at this sight has been moved into the entrance hall of the modern **Paços do Concelho de Rio Maior** (municipal offices and city hall) off the Praça da República. By the time you read this book, a brand new **museum of archaeology** should be open on *Rua Serpa Pinto, 88*. The museum is in a restored 15th - 18th century manor house next to the city's beautifully decorated medieval baroque parish church. It will contain artifacts from this excavation and many other artifacts found in the region.

The Paços do Concelho de Rio Maior has a ground floor Turísmo office, a great source of information and maps about the region. The center of the city also has a nice tree lined park, several good bars, and a few cafés. If you happen to be here in early September, you can witness Rio Maior's famed annual onion festival.

SPORTS & RECREATION

Horseback Riding

· **Quinta da Cortiçãda Horse Riding**, *Rio Maior, Tel. (043) 479-182*

Tennis

· **Rio Maior Tennis Club**, *Jardim Municipal, Tel. (043) 921-04*

EXCURSIONS & DAY TRIPS

Even more interesting may be a relaxing day trip to a set of small and memorable villages just a short drive outside of town. These days, livestock, agricultural, and the organic production of rock salt from the area's many saline ponds are the main sources of this large municipality's income. Start by heading down a series of tranquil country roads through beautiful valleys that produce grapes, tomatoes, onions, and apples. You will pass through small villages lined with traditional white and yellow bordered farm houses and traditionally dressed local farmers driving mule drawn wagons (although many farmers have recently purchased their very first tractor).

I suggest following the signs from Rio Maior to the suburb of **Marinhas de Sal** (three km north of Rio Maior) where man has been collecting salt since upper-paleolithic times. The salt pans that straddle the left side of the road in this area are locally known as the Salinas and were built a couple of hundred years ago. These small man-made ponds were designed to hold the salt water that passed through an underground rock salt deposit. The liquid's sodium chloride is about 700% above normal sea water levels. After sitting under the heat of the sun for a few days during the warmest months of the year, the water evaporates and leaves huge amounts of pure salt. The salt is harvested by area residents between March and September. A series of traditional log cabins have been constructed along the salt pans to store the salt, and several have been converted into craft boutiques and restaurants. The shops and restaurants are packed on weekends.

From Marinhas de Sal bear left on an unnamed road that runs alongside the salt pans. At the intersection of the next main road, turn left onto Route EN-1 and proceed through the little village of **Alto da Serra**. After 1.5 km or so, on the right hand side of the road you will see a series of windmills (some of which have been converted into homes and rural inns) sitting high up on the hills. Three of these windmills are part of an unusual bed and breakfast inn called **Cabeço Dos Três Moinhos**. Each one of these 18th century windmills is a wonderful duplex room with private bathroom and fireplace. The road up to this inn is rather steep and made of rock, so be extremely careful if you are staying at or visiting this unique property (the gate may also be locked if the inn is not expecting guests).

Go back to Marinhas de Sal and follow the signs to **Alcobertas** (11 km north of Marinhas de Sal). This unnamed road skirts the southern border of the magnificent **Serra de Aires e Candeeiros**. There are a couple of horseback riding lodges that specializes in pleasant trips through the nearby valleys and a couple of rustic former forest ranger's houses that can be rented (check with the tourist office on the first floor of the Paços do Concelho de Rio Maior for details).

Once you're in the village of Alcobertas, you'll see a small white sign on the right side of the road for **Silos Ou Potes Mouros**. Take this exit, and continue ahead for 200 yards or so until you reach a fork in the road. Bear left and you will reach several Moorish underground grain silos. They have been excavated and are still in good condition.

Return to the main road and drive through the village. Keep your eyes open for a white sign and a turn off on the right side for the **Igreja Paroquial e Dolmen Anta**. After turning off, you have to drive about 35 yards and the church will be on the left side of the road. The parish church is dedicated to St. Mary Magdalena and was first constructed in the 16th century under orders from the Archbishop of Lisbon. The church has been rebuilt several times since it was first constructed. Once inside the church, walk through the tiled archway to enter a 5,000 year old Neolithic dolmen. The dolmen was eventually converted into an unusual side chapel and is now used for Christian worship.

Continue along the same road and follow the signs (expect to get lost at least once around here) to **Alcanede**, about 11 km east of Alcobertas. As you drive through this town you will notice a large stone block castle resting on a hill above the left side of the road. Follow the signs leading uphill towards the castle, park your car, and walk around the exterior of this giant 18th century fortress. Unfortunately the gates leading inside the castle are almost always locked, so a glimpse from the outside may be as close as you get.

From the castle, follow Route N-362 past the town of Tremês (about 9 km southeast of Alcanede) and turn right on a small country lane with signs to **Outeiro da Corticada** (about 6 km southwest of Tremês). The luxurious **Quinta da Corticada** estate and its superb bed and breakfast inn is a great place to stay if you want a change from Rio Maior. From Outeiro da Corticada, continue along the same small country lane for around 2 km. Bear left down another small lane with signs to **São João da Ribeira**. Turn left onto Route N-114 and after about 1 km turn left at the sign to **Torre Mourisco**. Some 100 meters along this road you will find a small plaza, **Largo Padre Francisco Saramago**, with beautiful azulejo murals decorating a fountain with benches. The murals depict a local legend about the Arabs who once lived in this area, who left two urns buried near here: one containing gold and the other containing a lethal form of bacteria.

Park your car near the fountain and walk to the front door of the stunning 18th century **Igreja de São João da Baptista**. A parish church has stood on this spot, believed to have also been the sight of a Moorish mosque, since the 13th century. It had to be completely rebuilt after it was wrecked by the great earthquake of 1755. Inside the church you will find a side chapel with a pair of wonderful 300 year old statues (including one that depicts Mary breast feeding Jesus) and, by the main altar, you can see rare Hispano-Arab tiles that were brought here from Seville during the 16th century. The adjacent fortress-like tower is believed by several experts to be the remains of an Arab mosque. The church is open on most days during normal business hours and is free.

On the other side of the plaza is the **Museu Rural e Etnografico** (Rural Museum of Ethnography). The museum exhibits antique wine presses, agricultural instruments, farming equipment, ceramics, glassware, local costumes, and replicas of a farmhouse bedroom and kitchen including personal effects used in the old days. The museum is open Tuesday through Sunday from 2:00pm until 6:00pm.

Hop back into your car and head back to Route N-114. Turn left for about 7 km until you find a sign on the left to **Azambujeira**. Make a left turn at the sign and once you reach the main square, **Largo Alsino Torodão**. You can park your car in front of the old pillory. This was once an important and rich town. The pillory is in front of an amazing 18th century church, **Igreja Matriz**. This house of worship is filled with a collection of beautiful azulejo murals depicting biblical stories. You can return to Rio Maior by making a right turn onto Route N-114.

CALDAS DA RAINHA

The royal history of Caldas da Rainha dates back to 1484 when Queen Leonor took her first bath in the town's healing waters. The town got its name, "baths of the Queen," from this auspicious event. Besides the spa, Caldas da Rainha is known for its production of porcelain and ceramic wares. These wares can be found in shops around the town's central Praça da República square. There is also a daily fruit and vegetable mercado (market) in this square.

ARRIVALS & DEPARTURES

By Bus
• **Caldas da Rainha Main Bus Depot**, *Rua C. S. Brito, Tel. (062) 220-67*

By Car
Caldas da Rainha is about 6 km from Obidos on Route N-8 north.

By Train
• **Caldas da Rainha CP Rail Station**, *Ave. Indepencia Nacional, Tel. (062) 236-93*

WHERE TO STAY

Moderate
CASA DOS PLATANOS, *Rua Rafael B. Pinheiro, 24. Tel. (062) 841-810, Fax (062) 843-417. Year round rack rates from 14,850$00, double room, CP. Cash only - No credit cards accepted.*

A whitewashed 18th century house near the park, it has eight nice rooms with private bathrooms. Facilities include fireplace lounge, dining room, and parking.

QUINTA DA FOZ DO ARELHO, *Largo do Arraial, Foz do Arelho. Tel. (062) 979-369. Year round rack rates from 15,250$00, double room, BP. Cash only - No credit cards accepted.*

A pretty and historic 16th century manor house, the quinta is located 7 km west of town near the beach. There are five beautifully decorated rooms with private bathrooms. Facilities include bar, fireside lounge, dining room, horses, gardens, TV room, chapel, gardens, and parking. Highly Recommended.

QUINTA DOS BUGALHOS, *Matoeira. Tel. (062) 930-517. Year round rack rates from 14,000$00, double room, BP. Cash only - No credit cards accepted.*

A charming farm house, it is located a few kilometers southeast of town in a peaceful location. The house rents six rooms and a couple of two bedroom apartments with private bathrooms, pool access, and nice views.

CALDAS INTERNACIONAL HOTEL, *Rua Dr. F. Rego, 45. Tel. (062) 832-307, Fax (062) 844-482. Year round rack rates from 16,750$00, double room, EP. All major credit cards accepted.*

This large, 83 room hotel is centrally located. It has many facilities including bar, restaurant, pool, sun deck, air conditioning, TV, and parking. The rooms are a bit bland but comfortable and you'll find the front desk staff a little unfriendly at times.

Inexpensive

HOTEL MALHOÃ, *Rua Antonio Sergio, 31. Tel. (062) 842-180, Fax (062) 842-621. Year round rack rates from 9,900$00, double room, EP. Most major credit cards accepted.*

This simple 3 star hotel is located in the center of the city. It has 113 air conditioned rooms with television, mini-bar, and private bathroom. Facilities include a bar, restaurant, swimming pool, sauna, and nearby parking.

PENSÃO ESTRAMADURA, *Rua Dr. J. Barbosa, 23. Tel. (062) 823-313. Year round rack rates from 8,000$00, double room, EP. Cash only - No credit cards accepted.*

A clean and comfortable 2 star inn, it has 22 rooms with and without private bathrooms. There are no real facilities, but it's close to everything you might want.

WHERE TO EAT

Moderate

ADEGA DO BORLÃO, *Rua Eng. C. de Abreu. Tel. (062) 842-690. Dress code is smart casual. Most major credit cards accepted.*

This wonderful little restaurant is located on a quiet side-street. They serve unusual local game and beef dishes at reasonable prices from an open kitchen. A great meal here will set you back around 2,450$00 a person plus wine.

PATEO DA RAINHA, *Rua de Camoes, 39. Tel. (062) 246-72. No dress code. Cash only - No credit cards accepted.*

This warm and friendly restaurant serves well prepared Portuguese food and fondues. Try the arroz com tamboril (rice with dogfish), it's great! The average bill here is about 2,050$00 a person for dinner.

RESTAURANTE ZE DO BARRETE, *Travessa Cova da Onca, 18. Tel. (062) 832-787. Dress code is smart casual. Cash only - No credit cards accepted.* This great local restaurant serves fine roasted meats that are prepared to order. There seems to be more locals than tourists in this restaurant. I recommend you call for a table. Expect to spend at least 2,400$00 a person.

SEEING THE SIGHTS

Across the town's central square, Praça da República, is the famous spa at the **Hospital Termal Rainha Dona Leonor**. The spa specializes in treatments using heavy mineral infused waters of local thermal springs.

Adjacent to the spa is the wonderful 15th century church, **Igreja de Nossa Senhora do Populo**. It has fine azulejos and a Josefa D'Obidos painting.

Just behind the hospital is **Parque Dom Carlos I**, a municipal park. This wonderful park has a nice lake with boats for rent and tennis facilities. My favorite reason for walking around the park is the fine artistic museums located in the park: the **Museu de José Malhoa**, a museum of contemporary art (closed on Monday); the remarkable house that is the **Museu de Ceramica**, a ceramics museum (closed on Monday), and the adjacent **Altier Museu António Duarte**, a sculpture museum (open daily).

Another fine museum, **Museu-Casa de São Rafael**, *Rua Rafael Bordalo Pinheiro*, has ceramics made by São Rafael, a local ceramics master whose name still graces a large ceramics plant in town.

After leaving the park, walk back to **Praça da República**, the main square, and follow the Rua Diário de Notícias for a block further to the lovely 18th century **Chafariz das 5 Bicas** fountain. Now make your way to the bottom of the square and take the Rua Herois de Grande Guerra east for about four blocks until you arrive at the **Praça 25 de Abril** plaza. There are several ornate buildings here including a fine church, **Igreja de Nossa Senhora da Conceição**, with a vaulted azulejos interior. A bullring is also nearby.

NIGHTLIFE & ENTERTAINMENT

This city has a lively night scene that tends to be most active near the ocean in an area called **Foz de Arelho** just northwest of town. The major attractions are the **Foz Praia**, **Big Apple**, **Green Hill**, and **Dreamers**.

SPORTS & RECREATION

Horseback Riding

• **Caldas de Rainha Horse Center**, *Quinta da Rainha, Tel. (062) 358-51*

ALCOBAÇA

In 1153, the first king of Portugal, Dom Afonso Henriques, decided to build the wonderful Gothic church and monastery, Mosteiro de Alcobaça. It is located in the center of what is now the city of Alcobaça. The town itself offers few attractions other than the many tile stores across from the church.

ARRIVALS & DEPARTURES

By Car

From Caldas da Rainha, Alcobaça can be reached by taking Route IC-1 north for about 22 km.

WHERE TO STAY

Moderate

CASA DA PADEIRA, *N-8-Aljubarrota. Tel. (062) 508-272, Fax (062) 508-272. Year round rack rates from 13,000$00, double room, CP. Cash only - No credit cards accepted.*

A great bed and breakfast inn, it has 10 great rooms and apartments with private bathrooms. It's located about 6 km northeast of Alcobaca in Aljubarrota. The house has a pool, billiards, breakfast room, and parking.

HOTEL SANTA MARIA, *Rua Dr. Francisco Zagalo. Tel. (062) 597-395, Fax (062) 596-715. Year round rack rates from 11,500$00, double room, EP. Cash only - No credit cards accepted.*

This is a small 2 star hotel in town. The 31 rooms are comfortable and have TV, phones, private bathrooms, and some rooms have church views. This is the only decent hotel in town.

HOTEL TERMAL DA PIEDADE, *Piedade. Tel. (062) 420-65, Fax (062) 596-971. Year round rack rates from 13,900$00, double room, EP. Most major credit cards accepted.*

A decent 3 star hotel, it's located in the spa area. There are 63 basic rooms with private bathrooms. Facilities include bar, restaurant, TV, and parking. Closed in winter.

Inexpensive

RESIDENCIAL MOSTERIO, *Ave. João de Dues, 1. Tel. (062) 421-83. Year round rack rates from 8,250$00, double room, EP. Cash only - No credit cards accepted.*

This good, basic 3 star inn is centrally located. Its 12 rooms come with or without private bathrooms. Facilities include restaurant and TV room.

PENSÃO CARVALHO, *São Martinho de Pedro. Tel. (062) 989-605. Year round rack rates from 7,750$00, double room, EP. Cash only - No credit cards accepted.*

A clean and comfortable 3 star inn, it's lcoated near the beach. There are several rooms with and without private bathroom. Facilities include restaurant, and TV room.

WHERE TO EAT
Moderate
RESTAURANTE CAFE TRINDADE, *Praça Dom A. Henriques, 22. Tel. (062) 423-97. No dress code. Most major credit cards accepted.*

A good regional meat and seafood restaurant and cafe where you eat outdoor during the warmer months. My dinner cost me 2,100$00.

RESTAURANTE A CURVA, *N-8-Ponte Jardim. Tel. (062) 431-33. No dress code. Cash only - No credit cards accepted.*

This is a nice and simple little restaurant with good basic food. It's located near the wine museum. Expect to spend around 1,975$00 a person plus wine.

SEEING THE SIGHTS
Mosteiro de Alcobaça is Portugal's largest church and took 25 years to build. The understated abbey has huge open spaces and sparse ornamentation. Inside you will find the tombs of King Dom Pedro and his forbidden, and later assassinated, wife, Queen Dona Inês de Castro. The church also has several fine **claustros** (cloisters) that are open to the public and contain fine statues of early Portuguese kings, and a massive kitchen.

High above town you can visit the ruins of an ancient **castelo** (castle).

If you're interested in wine, I recommend going to the **Wine Museum** (Institute da Vinha e Vinho), *Tel. (062) 422-22.* The museum's exhibit explains several methods for making wine and has a collection of wines from around Portugal. The musuem is open 9am - 12pm and 2pm - 5pm Monday through Friday and is closed on Saturdays, Sundays, and holidays.

SPORTS & RECREATION
Tennis
• **Alcobaça Tennis Club**, *Tel. (062) 596-745*

SHOPPING
Across the street from Mosteiro de Alcobaça are serveral shops that sell Portuguese tile. I have found several large azulejos murals at good prices after some creative negotiation.

EXCURSIONS & DAY TRIPS

A couple of kilometers northwest is the spa town of **Piedade**, known mostly for rheumatic and digestive relief.

It is an easy 11 km drive south and then east to the wonderful ocean view cafes and sun-drenched shallow beaches of **São Martinho do Porto**.

NAZARÉ

The formerly quaint fishing village of Nazaré has grown into a major ocean front tourist resort located at the foothills of the Serra da Pederneira mountains. The city has lost most of the traditional fishing methods that used to lure visitors here. The town's wide sand beach has lost much of its appeal since the oxen-dragged fishing boats were replaced by motorized craft. Occasionally you can find some fishermen, or their widows (dressed in black skirts), sifting through the sand on the beach.

ARRIVALS & DEPARTURES
By Bus
• **Nazaré Main Bus Depot**, *Ave. Vieira Guimares, no phone*

By Car
Nazaré is about 11 km northwest of Alcobaça on Route N-8-4 west.
• **Avis Rent a Car in Nazaré**, *Hotel Mare, Tel. (062) 519-28*

WHERE TO STAY
Moderate
HOTEL MARE, *Rua Mouzinho de Albuquerque. Tel. (062) 561-226. Year round rack rates from 13,800$00, double room, EP. Most major credit cards accepted.*

This is a modern hotel with 52 air conditioned rooms that have private bathrooms, mini-bars, and satellite televisions. There are lots of facilities including a snack bar, restaurant, bar, billiard, baby-sitting services, and nearby parking.

HOTEL PRAIA, *Ave. Vieira Guimaraes, 39. Tel. (062) 561-375, Fax (062) 561-436. Year round rack rates from 14,250$00, double room, EP. Most major credit cards accepted.*

A simple 3 star hotel, it has 40 good rooms with television, mini-bar, and private bathroom. Facilities include bar, restaurant, shops, billiards, and parking

HOTEL DA NAZARE, *Largo Afonso Zuquete. Tel. (062) 561-311. Year round rack rates from 15,000$00, double room, CP. Most major credit cards accepted.*

This modern 3 star hotel has 52 comfortable rooms (some with views) near the beach. Facilities include bar, restaurant, disco, mini-bars, TV, and some air conditioning.

Inexpensive

PENSÃO MADEIRA, *Praça Sousa Oliveira, 71. Tel. (062) 551. Year round rack rates from 8,500$00, double room, EP. Cash only - No credit cards accepted.*

This small and slightly cramped inn offers decent rooms in the heart of town.

WHERE TO EAT

Moderate

ARTE XAVEGA, *Calçada do Sitio. Tel. (062) 552-136. Dress code is smart casual. Most major credit cards accepted.*

This is a great international restaurant for the connoisseur. It is classy retreat on the edge of town with wonderful food and ambiance. Expect a fine dinner to set you back around 3,100$00 a person.

O CASALINHO, *Praça Sousa Oliveira. Tel. (062) 551-328. No dress code. Cash only - No credit cards accepted.*

O Casalinho is a great, underrated, seafood restaurant in the heart of town. They serve large portions of grilled local fish and seafood. Try whatever they suggest and bring at least 1,450$00 a head for a meal.

RESTAURANTE RIBAMAR, *Rua Gomes Freire, 9. Tel. (062) 551-158. Dress code is smart casual. Most major credit cards accepted.*

One of the better reasonably priced local seafood restaurants, they specialize in grilled fish dinners served with fries and salad. Try the gigantic caldeirada (fish stew). My last lunch here set me back around 1,400$00.

SEEING THE SIGHTS

During the high season, every imaginable square inch of the beach is packed with tents and beach towels. And unfortunately, the city recently installed a public address system that blasts out terrible music all day. If you're looking for a beach around Nazaré with fewer people, try **North Beach** (Praia Norte) just a few minutes away, or the southern beaches at **Praia Nova**.

Above town is the peaceful **Sitio** cliff, which can be reached during the high season by a funicular. The panoramic ocean view from this cliff and the **Fortaleza de São Miguel** (fortress) are wonderful. **Bullfights** are held on Saturdays, and it's always packed.

SHOPPING

Although Nazaré is famed for fine lace work, I have never found a good deal here.

BATALHA

Batalha is a bustling town of hard working residents and several dozen tourist shops scattered on a handful of cobblestone lanes and plazas. Known primarily for its astonishing 14th century monastery, thousands of tourists arrive here daily on large guided bus tours from all over Europe.

Because tourists usually overnight in nearby Fátima and take day trips to Batalha, I strongly recommend that you do the exact opposite and stay in this much more charming community and take a day trip to the less enchanting Fátima. The accommodations at both the Pousada Mestre Afonso Domingues and the Quinta do Fidalgo (both with stunning views of the monastery) are a better value than anything available for even twice the money in Fátima.

ARRIVALS & DEPARTURES

By Car

Batalha is about 20 km northeast of Alcobaca on Route N-8 north and about 123 km north of Lisboa off A-1 highway.

WHERE TO STAY

Moderate

QUINTA DO FIDALGO, *Ave. D. Nuno Alveres Pereira, Batalha. Tel. (044) 961-14, Fax (044) 767-401. Low season rack rates from 10,000$00, double room, CP; high season rates from 12,000$00, double room, CP. Cash & travelers checks only - No credit cards accepted.*

Situated just across the road from the monastery, this 300 year old manor house has been owned and managed by the same family for most of its history. The Portuguese King and Prince even spent the night here way back in 1744.

There are five fantastically decorated rooms that all have deluxe bathrooms with handmade tiles, ornate antique hardwood furnishings, wooden ceilings, and private patios and four poster beds in some cases. All of the rooms are equally charming, and the price includes a breakfast in bed or in the dining room. There is also a nice garden, a charming private chapel, a bar stocked with vintage wines and aguardente fermented on the quinta's own farm, and a great lounge filled with rare art and other curiosities. The exceptionally friendly Oliveina Simoes family welcome you in a style fit for a king. Highly Recommended.

POUSADA MESTRE AFONSO DOMINGUES, *Largo M.A. Domingues, Tel. (044) 962-60, Fax (044) 962-47. US & Canada bookings with Marketing Ahead, Tel. 800/223-1356. Low season rack rates from 12,000$00, double room, CP; high season rates from 16,500$00, double room, CP. All major credit cards accepted.*

This welcoming government owned and operated high quality inn is just a stone's throw away from the famous monastery. It has some of the most memorable views of Manueline and Gothic architecture in the entire country.

There are 19 rather large and nicely appointed rooms and two superb suites that have deluxe granite lined private bathrooms, comfortable modern hardwood furnishings, mini-bars, wall to wall carpeting, satellite color televisions, direct dial telephone, hair dryers, white stucco walls, huge closets, local artwork, and plenty of natural sunlight.

Facilities include a great regional restaurant that serves three delicious meals a day (including a buffet continental breakfast that is included in all room rates), plenty of free secure outdoor parking, access to a nearby bus station, tranquil private guest lounges full of interesting books about Portugal, and lots of charm.

The pousada is staffed by some of the nicest and most polite multilingual area residents. They go well out of their way to answer all your questions and to point you in the right direction. This place is a great deal for the money, and a good place to meet fellow travelers from around the globe.

Inexpensive

RESIDENCIAL BATALHA, *Largo da Igreja, Batalha. Tel. (044) 767-500, Fax (044) 767-467. Year round rack rates from 8,000$00, double room, CP. Most major credit cards accepted.*

This simple 3 star inn is located a two minute walk away from the monastery on a main road in central Batalha. There are 22 medium sized rooms that feature private bathrooms, air conditioning, direct dial telephone, satellite television, and comfortable furnishings. Facilities here include a restaurant, a bar, an indoor garage, and a nice terrace with good views of the town.

COMPLEXO TURÍSTICO MOTEL SÃO JORGE, *EN- 1, Batalha. Tel. (044) 962-10, Fax (044) 963-13. Year round rack rates from 7,500$00, double room, EP. Most major credit cards accepted.*

This large motel complex just off N-1 a couple of kilometers south of Batalha is a fairly nice place to stay in this price range. There are 58 simple but nice and modern rooms with private bathrooms, satellite television, direct dial telephone, and comfortable furnishings. There is also a nice pool, free parking, tennis, a restaurant, meeting rooms, and a snack shop.

WHERE TO EAT
Moderate
POUSADA MESTRE AFONSO DOMINGUES, *Largo M.A. Domingues, Tel. (044) 962-60. Open daily for lunch and dinner. No dress code. All major credit cards accepted.*

This pousada's excellent kitchen prepares delightful regional and national favorites such as fish soup, chick pea and vegetable soup, baked hake, fresh salads, local pork and steak dishes, and a great shrimp in cream sauce that is a real treat. Lunch and dinner specials start at under 1,850$00, per person, plus wine. This is the best place in town for a delicious meal, and there is no dress code. Highly Recommended.

Inexpensive
RESTAURANTE A CAVE, *Largo Papa Paulo VI, Tel. (044) 966-88. Open daily for lunch and dinner. No dress code. Most major credit cards accepted.*

Located just around the corner from the post office and Pousada Mestre Afonso Domingues, this simple restaurant is a good place to enjoy an inexpensive home cooked Portuguese meal. Besides offering a three course 1,650$00 tourist menu, they also have al la carte dishes such as grilled swordfish, grilled salmon, filet of sole, all sorts of cod fish items, beefsteak, pork chops, salads, assorted soups, rice with seafood, omelets, tiger shrimp, entrecote, tournedos of beef, and good inexpensive house wine. This restaurant is extremely popular with locals during lunch hours.

SEEING THE SIGHTS
The center of Batalha is dominated by the giant **Mosteiro de Batalha**, a masterpiece of Gothic and Manueline architecture. The crenellated monastery is an architectural mixture of both Gothic and Manueline styles, and is supported by a series of massive flying buttresses, etched arches, and wide pillars. Construction of the monastery started in 1386 shortly after Portuguese King Dom João I led his troops in an overwhelming victory over the Spanish at the neighboring town of Aljubarrota in August 1385.

The original architect was Afonso Domingues (1386 to 1402), who used his extensive knowledge of High Gothic design to create much of the main body of the monastery including the Igreja de Santa María da Vitória and its elaborate Dom João I cloister. From 1402 until 1448, the project was taken over by Portuguese born Martim Vasques and a Catalan architect named Huguet who proceeded to redirect the construction to feature flamboyant Gothic elements that can be found in the church's main facade, Founder's Chapel, and the Unfinished Chapels. Between 1448 and 1477, Fernão de Évora added several linear Gothic touches to the building, while from 1477 to 1515 the remaining (an some of the most important) design elements were added by Mateus Fernandes and João Rodrigues in their newly created Manueline style.

You enter the monastery through a highly decorated portal featuring stone carvings of the 12 apostles. Proceed into **Igreja de Santa María da Vitória** (Saint Mary of the Victory Church). The understated 14th century Gothic stone block church rests below two rows of towering columns and stained glass murals. Embedded into the floor about 20 feet inside the middle of the church is the tomb of Batalha's Manueline architect Mateus Fernandez I.

From here, a series of well marked multilingual plaques (a commendable recent addition) point out the route towards the monastery's other main attractions. Just off to the right side of the church, near the aforementioned tomb, is a doorway leading into the awesome **Capela do Fundador** (Founder's Chapel). This side chapel was a later addition to the monastery's original plans and was built in the mid 15th century by Huguet to serve as a pantheon for King Dom João I and Queen Dona Filipa de Lencastre. Their crypt can be found in the center of the room surrounded by an octagonal grouping of columns. Additional royal family members from this period, including Prince Henry the Navigator, can be found in crypts along the chapel's walls.

When you re-enter the main part of the church, continue back towards the left side of the choir, and on the left side you will find an entrance that leads to the **Museu Mosteiro Santa María Vitória**. This museum has formal gardens that are surrounded by the magnificently embellished filigree-like **Claustro da Dom João**. This cloister is among the world's first examples of Manueline architecture, a style that originated in this monastery and was later used in the design of many famous structures all over the Iberian peninsula.

A short walk along the cloister will take you to room on the right side that is known as the **Sala do Capitulo** (Chapter House). This room houses the **Chama da Patria** (Eternal Flame of the Nation) and is guarded by armed soldiers in respect for the tomb of the unknown soldiers. The flame burns pure Portuguese olive oil and donations placed in the adjacent wooden box are used to purchase the oil (and are greatly appreciated). The same room also features a 16th century Flemish influenced stained glass window and bold Gothic vaulting.

Entrance to the **Adega dos Frades** (Monk's Cellar) is around the corner past the cloister. This is now used as an exhibition space but was once used as a monk's dormitory. Once you have passed a fantastic fountain and turned another corner you will pass two more doorways. The doorway on the left leads to the somber **refeitorio** (refectory). The refectory is used as a small gift shop and as an exhibition space for the plaques and commemorative items that were given to the monastery from visiting religious groups and dignitaries. The doorway next to the refectory leads down a small corridor past several rooms full of original architectural fragments currently under restoration, and then intersects with the **Claustro de Dom Afonso V**. This smaller cloister is an extension of the monastery that was added in the 15th century.

While the rooms just off the cloister have always served non-religious purposes, these days they are closed to the general public and house the workshops of the **Escola Nacional de Artes e Oficios Tradicionais da Batalha** (National School of Traditional Arts). The ongoing restoration work at the monastery takes place in these workshops.

You can exit the monestary at this point. Follow the signs and make a right hand turn (along the side of the building) to an unmarked portal. This is the entrance to the remarkable **Capelas Imperfeitas** (Unfinished Chapels). Added to the monastery in the 1530's, these unique chapels were ordered by King Dom Duarte who rests with his wife in a crypt here. Due to a lack of funds, and the attention given to additional projects of this era, a roof was never added to this section.

The monastery is open daily except for holidays from 9:00am until at least 5:30pm, and admission is free to the church and founders chapel. It costs 400$00 for adult and 200$00 for youths under 24 for the museum, including the cloisters.

NIGHTLIFE & ENTERTAINMENT

CIRCUMSTANCIA BAR, *Estrada de Fátima, Batalha. Tel. (044) 987-77.*

This modern bar is just a few minutes walk from the monastery and is Batalha's best place to party. Besides having three pool tables (800$00 an hour), Circumstancia has low drink prices, a good selection of imported and domestic liqueurs, no cover or minimum charges, a great audio-video system that plays rock music, and the nicest bartenders in town. Busiest from 10:00pm until closing, this is where most of the casually dressed local students and residents under 30 tend to hang out. After the bar closes, they move on to the mega-discos in Leiria that stay open much later. Open daily from 1:00pm until the doors shut at 2:00am.

SHOPPING

If you are interested in purchasing hand painted ceramic products and china, I suggest you take the five minute ride to the neighboring village of Jardoeira to shop at the **Loja Fapor** factory outlet. You can get great mugs, plates, bowls, and dishes for 400$00 and 1,200$00. Fapor's loja (shop) is currently open Monday through Saturday from 10:00am until 5:15pm, and accepts cash only.

EXCURSIONS & DAY TRIPS

About 8 km south of town on Route N-362 south is the castle-dominated town of **Porto de Mós**. The 13th century **castelo** (castle) and its strange tower ramparts are not open to the public, but they are still worth a quick look.

Below the town, you will find the Serra dos Candeeiros and Serra de Aire mountain ranges. These ranges form the boundaries of the lovely **Parque Natural das Serras de Aire e Candeeiros** regional park. The park offers many tranquil villages and rivers that seem to have been lost in time. There are also a series of underground caves in the eastern sector of the park such as the eerie stalagmite and stalactite laden **Grutas de Mira de Aire**, **Grutas de Alvados**, and the **Grutas de Santo António** (all open daily) near the town of **Mira de Aire**.

FÁTIMA

The world-famous apparitions of the Virgin Mary were first witnessed by three shepherds on May 13, 1917 during a walk through a nearby field called Cova de Iria. After the sightings reoccurred on the 13th day of the next six months, the apparition of the Virgin told the shepherds three secrets. The first two secrets were later revealed to predict World War II and the spread of both Communism and atheism. The third secret remains locked in a drawer in the Pope's chamber in the Vatican and has never been revealed. After several years of debate between religious scholars, the Bishop finally declared the visions authentic.

In Fátima today, you will find Christian pilgrims from around the world trying to escape the grips of the shark-like souvenir peddlers and pick pocketers.

ARRIVALS & DEPARTURES

By Bus
• **Fátima Main Bus Depot**, *Ave. Correia da Silva, Tel. (049) 531-651*

By Car
Fátima is about 17 km southeast of Batalha on Route N-356 east.

WHERE TO STAY
Expensive
HOTEL DE FÁTIMA, *Rua João Paulo II. Tel. (049) 533-351, Fax (049) 532-691. Year round rack rates from 20,250$00, double room, BP. Most major credit cards accepted.*

The Hotel de Fátima is a large modern hotel near the sanctuary. There are 126 well designed and comforably furnished rooms and suites that all have private bathrooms, air conditioning, direct dial telephones, cable television, radio, and mini-bar. Facilities include a bar, restaurant, business meeting rooms, and parking.

Moderate

HOTEL ALECRIM, *Rua Fransisco Marto. Tel. (049) 531-376, Fax (049532-817. Year round rack rates from 8,500$00, double room, EP. Most major credit cards accepted.*

This centrally located 2 star hotel has 54 air conditioned rooms with private bathroom, a bar, restaurant, TV room, and parking.

ESTALAGEM DOM GONCALO, *Rua Jacinto Marto,100. Tel. (049) 533-062, Fax (049) 532-088. Year round rack rates from 12,500$00, double room, CP. Most major credit cards accepted.*

A nice inn located close to the heart of Fátima, it has 41 air conditioned rooms with cable television, private bathrooms, direct dial telephone, and mini-bar. There is also a bar, restaurant, conference rooms, and parking.

HOTEL CINQUETENARIO, *Rua Fransisco Marto, 175. Tel. (049) 533-465, Fax (049) 532-992. Year round rack rates from 11,000$00, double room, EP. Most major credit cards accepted.*

A nice 3 star hotel, it has 132 comfortable rooms with private bath and television that are just steps away from the sanctuary. Facilities include bar, restaurant, air conditioning, and parking.

Inexpensive

CASA BEATO NUNO, *Ave. Beano Nuno, 51. Tel. (049) 531-522. Year round rack rates from 6,250$00, double room, EP. Cash only - No credit cards accepted.*

This large boarding house has 132 simple rooms with private bath and telephone. It's a good budget hotel managed by Carmelite fathers.

WHERE TO EAT

Moderate

RESTAURANTE O ZE GRANDE, *Rua Jacinto Marto, 32. Tel. (049) 531-367. No dress code. Cash only - No credit cards accepted.*

Restaurante O Ze Grande is a simple and basic regional restaurant located in the heart of town. It serves reasonably priced meat and fish dishes that start at just 1,100$00 each. The polite staff speak some English.

SEEING THE SIGHTS

The city has many commemorative shrines, chapels, and a large **basilica** that houses the tombs of two of the shepherds who originally saw the vision of the Virgin Mary. The area adjacent to the basilica is where pilgrims gather during the 12th and 13th day of each month. On the anniversary of the first and last sightings (May 13 and October 13) the town swells with up to 1,300,000 faithful visitors who stand on the sanctuary grounds for masses, candlelight processions, and the passage of the statue of Virgin Mary through the crowd.

Near Fátima, in the small village of **Aljustrel**, are the cottages of the of the three shepherds and the **Chapel of Apparitions**.

The best way to deal with visiting Fátima during the middle of any month is to overnight out of town (perhaps Tomar or Batalha), and get in and out of town as early as possible. I don't go near Fátima during the pilgrimage since it tends to be a zoo.

TOMAR

Tomar is located at the base of a hill on the banks of the **Rio Nabão** and is a wonderful place to visit. Unlike other convent and monastery dominated towns like Fátima and Batalha, Tomar has a life of its own. The city is divided by the river, has a castle on the hill overlooking town, and has an old stone bridge and waterwheel.

ARRIVALS & DEPARTURES

By Bus
• **Tomar Main Bus Depot**, *Ave Combatentes, Tel. (049) 312-738*

By Car
From Fátima, take Route N-356 north for 6 km and connect to Route N-113 east for another 26 km.

By Train
• **Tomar CP Rail Station**, *Ave. Combatentes, Tel. (049) 312-815*

WHERE TO STAY

Moderate
QUINTA DA ALCAIDARIA MOR, *Vila Nova de Ourem. Tel. (049) 422-31. Year round rack rates from 16,000$00, double room, CP. Cash only - No credit cards accepted.*

A beautiful 17th century manor house and estate, it's managed by a wonderful older man whose family has owned this property for generations. There are seven beautiful double rooms and two apartments with private bathrooms. Facilities include a nice swimming pool, TV room, library, gardens, a working farm, and a host who is glad to offer advice on day trips. Highly Recommended.

HOTEL DOS TEMPLARIOS, *Largo Candido dos Reis. Tel. (049) 321-730, Fax (049) 322-191. Year round rack rates from 17,250$00, double room, EP. Most major credit cards accepted.*

Located in the heart of town, this large modern air conditioned hotel has good service and 176 nice rooms with private bathrooms, satellite television, radio, mini-bar, and river-view balconies. Facilities include swimming pool, tennis, health club, squash court, business meeting rooms, a restaurant, and a bar.

QUINTA DO VALLE, *Santa Cita. Tel. (049) 381-165, Fax (049) 381-165. Year round rack rates from 13,850$00, per apartment, per night, CP. Cash only - No credit cards accepted.*

This deluxe manor house is located 7 km south of Tomar in Santa Cita. There are seven nice apartments, horses, and a nice swimming pool.

QUINTA DA ANUNCIADA VELHA, *Tomar. Tel. (049) 345-218, Fax (049) 321-362. Year round rack rates from 15,000$00, double room, CP. Cash only - No credit cards accepted.*

This beautiful 300 year old manor house offers four double rooms and a two bedroom apartment with private bathroom. Facilities include a bar, swimming pool, hiking trails, gardens, TV room, and parking.

POUSADA DE SÃO PEDRO, *São Pedro de Tomar. Tel. (049) 381-175. US & Canada bookings with Marketing Ahead, Tel. 800/223-1356. Low season rack rates from 12,000$00, double room, CP; high season rates from 16,500$00, double room, CP. All major credit cards accepted.*

This government owned small lake-view inn is located 11 km southeast of Tomar. This was the home of engineers who built the Zezere dam. There are 15 simply decorated rooms with television and private bathrooms, and lots of water sports are available.

ESTALAGEM ILHA DO LOMBA, *Ilha do Lomba. Tel. (049) 371-108, Fax (049) 371-403. Year round rack rates from 15,500$00, double room, CP. Most major credit cards accepted.*

A nice, simple inn, that's located on a peaceful island in the Zezere River about 14 km east of Tomar. This relaxing retreat can be reached by ferry (you can call the hotel for a schedule). There are 17 rustic rooms with private bathrooms. Facilities include bar, restaurant, pool, TV room, tennis, hiking trails, garden, and water sports.

Inexpensive

RESIDENCIAL SINAGOGA, *Rua Gil Avo, 31. Tel. (049) 316-783. Year round rack rates from 9,150$00, double room, EP. Most major credit cards accepted.*

A modern and centrally located 3 star inn, it has 24 nice rooms with private bathrooms. Facilities include a bar, air conditioning, elevators, radio, TV, and nearby parking.

RESIDENCIAL UNIÃO, *Rua Serpa Pinto, 94. Tel. (049) 312-831. Year round rack rates from 7,000$00, double room, EP. Cash only - No credit cards accepted.*

This is a clean, comfortable, and well located 3 star inn. It has over 20 good rooms with private bathrooms. Facilities include bar, restaurant, TV room, and nearby parking.

WHERE TO EAT

Moderate

A BELA VISTA, *Travessa Fonte Choupo, 3. Tel. (049) 312-870. Dress code is smart casual. Cash only - No crdit cards accepted.*

This unusual little restaurant offers reasonably priced regional cuisine and strong local wines in a friendly casual environment. My last dinner here set me back about 1,950$00 a person.

RESTAURANTE NUNO ALVARES, *Ave. Dr. Nuno Pereira, 3. Tel. (049) 312-873. No dress code. Cash only - No credit cards accepted.*

A modest regional restaurant that prepares some splendid roasted meats and grilled fish dinners at extremely affordable prices. A good choice for those that want to spend less than 1,750$00 a person for dinner.

SEEING THE SIGHTS

Almost all of the best sights in Tomar lie on the western bank of Nabão River.

The old part of town has flower-lined stone streets and mosaic paved plazas that are a delight to wander around. I recommend that you park your car somewhere off the central **Praça da República** square. From the square you can see and visit a 16th century church, **Igreja de São João Baptista**, with wonderful Gregório Lopes panels. Two blocks south on Rua Dr. Joaquim Jacinto is the 15th century **Abraham Zacuto Sinogoga**, a Jewish temple in the heart of the old **Judiaria** (Jewish quarter).

A few blocks further south turn right (west) on Ave. Dr. Candido Madureira and pass the Turismo office in **Praça Infante Dom Henrique** to reach **Parque Sete Montes**, a beautiful park where I usually stop for a quick rest. Every two years (1996, 1998, 2000, etc.) on the first Sunday of July, a wonderful festival called the **Festa dos Tabuleiros** is held in Tomar and culminates in a strange and beautiful procession. During the event, hundreds of young women dress in white and wear giant hats made of bread and flowers while they walk through town. The festival also includes a fair, folklore stories, fireworks displays, and the generous donation of food and wine to less fortunate families in the area.

Imposing itself over the western side of town is the huge **Castelo dos Templarios** (Castle of the Templars), which protects the **Convento de**

Cristo (Convent of Christ). Its construction began in 1162 and took over 150 years to finish. This fortified convent was the home and operations center of the Knights of Templar. Upon entering the church, take note of the ornate carvings on the doorway, designed by the Spaniard João de Castilho.

The cloisters inside the fortified walls were built around an octagonal arch that surrounds the 12th century **Charola** (Templars' Rotunda) where you'll find the high altar. Two opposing passages lead from the 16th century Manueline nave inside the Charola to several claustros (cloisters) including the bare and simple Renaissance main cloister. While you are in the cloisters, you should see the famous Manueline chapter house window. Known throughout the world, this ornate sculptured window contains several sea and ship motifs topped by the royal crest of King Dom Manuel I. It is considered the finest example of the Manueline style.

SPORTS & RECREATION
Boating
•**Zêzere Boating Club**, *Sertã, Tel. (074) 997-45*

Tennis
•**Tomar Tennis**, *Park Desportivo, Tel. (049) 322-604*

EXCURSIONS & DAY TRIPS
The area surrounding Tomar is filled with picturesque traditional farming communities and river front resort areas that are full of country inns. The wonderful town of **Vila Nova de Ourém** is about 21 km northwest of Tomar on Route N-113 west. Here you can stay in a number of fine country inns and visit the beautiful 15th century **Igreja Matriz** and view the royal 15th century Gothic **castelo** (castle).

About 10 km east of Tomar, you can access the dammed-up **Zêzere River** valley where you can swim, fish, trek, rent boats, and stay at a number of good B&B inns that line the river and the **Castelo de Bode** dam. In the middle of the river is a remote and tranquil island called **Ilha de Lomba**, which can be reached via ferry service. If you are looking for serenity, nature, and rustic accommodations in a natural setting, this is the place. For ferry schedule details, contact the Turismo office in Tomar.

Further north, the Zêzere becomes even more beautiful. The area around **Dornes** also has some interesting sights including a 12th century tower. The city of **Torres Novas** can also be visited by taking IC-3 south for 18 km from Tomar. The city offers a beautiful 14th century castle. From Torres Novas, a splendid trip can be made to **Constância** and on to the dream-like castle on the island of **Almourol** (see the Planícies chapter).

LEIRIA & NEARBY COASTAL BEACHES

Leiria is a nice town with good places to stay, a few historical sights, and some nice beaches nearby where you can relax and soak up the sun.

ARRIVALS & DEPARTURES

By Bus
• **Leiria Main Bus Depot,** *Jardim Municipal, Tel. (044) 220-49*

By Car
Leiria is located approximately 46 km northwest of Tomar off Route N-113 west on the banks of the Liz River.

By Train
• **Leiria CP Rail Station**, *3 km northeast of town, Tel. (044) 882-027*

WHERE TO STAY

Moderate
HOTEL EUROSOL, *Rua D. Jose A. da Silva. Tel. (044) 811-205, Fax (044) 811-205. Year round rack rates from 13,750$00, double room, CP. Most major credit cards accepted.*

The Eurosol is a modern high-rise hotel on the banks of the Liz River. It has 135 air conditioned rooms, all with private bathrooms, direct dial telephones, and cable television. Facilities include bar, restaurant, swimming pool, sauna, health club, barber, disco, garden, shops, and free parking.

ALBERGARIA DO TERREIRO, *Largo Candido Dos Reis, 17. Tel. (044) 813-580, Fax (01) 351-90. Year round rack rates from 12,000$00, double room, EP. Most major credit cards accepted.*

I enjoyed my stay at this charming 4 star bed and breakfast inn located inside a 19th century building in the heart of the old quarter. There are 31 beautifully designed rooms featuring private bathrooms, air conditioning, television, direct dial telephone, and radio. The inn also has a piano bar, meeting rooms, and plenty of charm. Highly Recommended.

HOTEL SÃO LUIS, *Rua Henrique Sommer. Tel. (044) 813-197, Fax (044) 813-897. Year round rack rates from 14,250$00, double room, CP. Most major credit cards accepted.*

This friendly seven floor city center hotel has 2 stars and 47 medium sized rooms. All rooms have air conditioners, private bathrooms, direct dial telephones, satellite television, and nice simple furnishings.

HOTEL DOM JOÃO III, *Ave. Dom João III. Tel. (044) 812-500, Fax (044 812-235. US and Canada bookings with Best Western, Tel. 800/528-1234.*

Year round rack rates from 14,000$00, double room, EP. Most major credit cards accepted.

This is a well located, modern 3 star business hotel. The 64 rooms all have air conditioning, private bathrooms, direct dial telephones, mini-bars, and cable television. Facilities include bar, restaurant, and free parking.

HOTEL MAR E SOL, *São Pedro de Muel. Tel. (044) 599-182. Year round rack rates from 14,250$00, double room, EP. Most major credit cards accepted.*

This comfortable resort hotel is located near the beach. Its 42 air conditioned rooms have private bathrooms, TV, minibars, and telephones. Facilities include bar, restaurant, and parking.

HOTEL SÃO PEDRO, *São Pedro de Muel. Tel. (044) 599-120. Year round rack rates from 14,250$00, double room, EP. Most major credit cards accepted.*

This is a good 3 star hotel near the beach that offers 53 nice rooms with private bathrooms. Facilities include bar, restaurant, air conditioning, TV, mini-bars, and parking.

Inexpensive

PENSÃO LEIRIENSE, *Rua A. de Albuquerque, 6. Tel. (044) 320-61. Year round rack rates from 7,600$00, double room, EP. Cash only - No credit cards accepted.*

A nice and clean 3 star inn, it's located in the heart of the old town. Its 16 good rooms all have private bathrooms. Facilities include bar and TV room.

SEEING THE SIGHTS

Above the town on a hill is an ancient Moorish **castelo** (castle) that has a beautiful loggia, a former royal **Palácio** (palace), and the Gothic 15th century church, **Igreja de Nossa Senhora da Pena**.

The town has a nice old section that starts below the castle near the 16th century **Sé** cathedral and continues across Rua Barão de Viamonte where the old Jewish quarter once was. From here you can walk down towards the center of the old town to **Praça Rodrigues Lobo** square, where you'll find plenty of cafés and restaurants. Near the square you will find several regal old homes and overhanging arches on Rua Afonso Albuquerque and Rua Dom Diniz.

SPORTS & RECREATION
Fishing

• **Amadores Fishing Club**, *Marinha Grande, Tel. (044) 504-516*

Tennis
• **Leiria Tennis School**, *Leiria, Tel. (044) 315-06*

EXCURSIONS & DAY TRIPSS

About 9 km out of town are the glass workshops and stores of nearby **Marinha Grande**. Some of the finest decorated glassware in Portugal is made here.

There are also a few beautiful beaches that are bordered by forests just west and northwest of Marinha Grande, including **São Pedro de Muel**, **Praia Velha**, **Pedras Negras**, and **Praia de Vieira**.

FIGUEIRA DA FOZ

Huge industrial harbors surround the city and have polluted the waters a little, but many families still spend their summer vacations here. The city faces a series of wide sandy beaches bordered by a busy road.

ARRIVALS & DEPARTURES

By Bus
• **Figueira da Foz Main Bus Depot**, *Rua J. da Silva Fonseca, Tel. (033) 230-95*

By Car
Figueira da Foz is about 55 km from Leiria on Route N-109 north.
• **Hertz Rent a Car**, *Rua M. D. Sousa, 103, Tel. (033) 251-80*

By Train
• **Figueira da Foz CP Rail Station**, *Largo de Estação, Tel. (033) 243-56*

WHERE TO STAY

Expensive
GRANDE HOTEL DA FIGUEIRA, *Ave. 25 de Abril. Tel. (033) 221-46, Fax (033) 224-20. Year round rack rates from 20,500$00, double room, EP. All major credit cards accepted.*

The Grande Hotel is a large 4 star hotel on the city's main avenue, with views of the beach. There are 102 comfortable air conditioned rooms with private bathrooms, mini-bar, remote control satellite television, and in some cases balconies that look out over the ocean. Facilities include a bar, good restaurant, complimentary use of an adjacent health club with outdoor swimming pool, business meeting rooms, and nearby parking.

Moderate

HOTEL INTERNACIONAL, *Rua da Liberdade, 20. Tel. (033) 266-02, Fax (033) 224-20. Year round rack rates from 13,500$00, double room, CP. Most major credit cards accepted.*

The Internacional is a newly renovated mid-sized hotel located next to the casino and about a three minute walk to the beach. The hotel has 50 air conditioned rooms with mini-bars, direct dial phones and television. Facilities include a bar, restaurant, TV room, complimentary use of an adjacent health club with outdoor swimming pool, and nearby parking.

CLUBE VALE DE LEÃO, *Vais-Buarcos. Tel. (033) 330-57, Fax (033) 325-71. Year round rack rates from 14,250$00, per apartment, per night, EP. Most major credit cards accepted.*

This club is actually a smaller apartment complex located in the mountains overlooking Buarcos and the ocean. They offer 25 studio, one and two bedroom apartments with kitchens, private bathrooms, and TV. Facilities include bar, restaurant, pool, squash, sauna, and parking.

CASA DA AZENHA VELHA, *Caceira de Cima. Tel. (033) 250-41. Year round rack rates from 13,600$00, double room, CP. Cash only - No credit cards accepted.*

Located 4 km west of town, this farming estate has six double rooms with private bathrooms and nice rural views. There are horses, a swimming pool, a breakfast room, billiards, tennis, hiking trails, a bar, a TV room, gardens, and plenty of local charm. Highly Recommeded.

APARTHOTEL ATLANTICO, *Ave. 25 de Abril. Tel. (033) 283-06, Fax (033) 224-20. Year round rack rates from 13,750$00, per apartment, per night, EP. Most major credit cards accepted.*

The Atlantico is a large modern tower across from the beach with 70 nice comfortable one and two bedroom units with kitchenettes, cable television, private bathrooms, direct dial telephone, and heating systems. The building also contains a small shopping center, and guests have access to a nearby swimming pool and health club.

HOTEL TAMARGUEIRA, *Marginal Oceanico-Buarcos. Tel. (033) 325-14, Fax (033) 210-67. Year round rack rates from 12,850$00, double room, CP. Most major credit cards accepted.*

This is a full service 3 star hotel with 88 air conditioned rooms on a great beach. The rooms are not all that impressive but do have private bathrooms, mini-bar, direct dial telephone, and television. The hotel has a bar, restaurant, and parking.

Inexpensive

RESIDENCIAL CENTRAL, *Rua Bernardes Lopes, 36. Tel. (033) 223-08. Year round rack rates from 7,500$00, double room, EP. Cash only - No credit cards accepted.*

This is a good 3 star inn near the casino. It has 15 large rooms with and without private bathrooms. The facilities are minimal, but the inn is near everything in town.

RESIDENCIAL MODERNA, *Praça 8 de Maio, 61. Tel. (033) 227-01. Year round rack rates from 6,800$00, double room, EP. Cash only - No credit cards accepted.*

This is your basic no frills inn with small, but clean rooms in the heart of Figueira da Foz.

WHERE TO EAT

Moderate

SEREIA DO MAR, *Ave. do Brasil, Buarcos. Tel. (033) 261-90. Dress code is casual. Most major credit cards accepted.*

This excellent seafood restaurant in Buarcos offers several house specials, all worth ordering including their famous espetadas (fish kabob). They cost around 1,150$00 per order.

ESCONDIDINHO, *Rua Dr. F. Diniz, 60. Tel. (033) 224-94. No dress code. Cash only - No credit cards accepted.*

A remarkably good, exotic restaurant that serves fine fish and meat dishes with an unusual flavor from Goa in India. Be careful, some items are spicy. A great value with good service.

SEEING THE SIGHTS

Walk around **Largo Luís de Camões** and the artistic townhouses across from the ancient pillory. Walk through town to the lovely fountains in **Praça 8 de Maio**. From the old town center casually stroll down the old streets and pay special attention to the villas and mansions that can be found practically everywhere. Several nice parks are located throughout the city including my favorite café and swimming pool in **Parque Santa Catarina**.

An 18th century ocean front museum, **Casa do Paço**, *Largo Professor Victor Guerra*, has several rooms covered in Dutch tiles rescued from a local shipwreck (closed weekdays). The **Palácio Sotto Mayor**, *Rua Joaquim Sotto Mayor,* is open to the public and has some beautiful period paintings (closed weekdays).

Another museum, **Museu Municipal do Santos Rocha**, *Rua Caloste Gulbenkian*, has interesting photographs and ceramic. The 17th century fortress, **Fortaleza da Santa Catarina**, and its chapel can be visited at the eastern end of the main beach area.

Figueira da Foz has a fairly large **casino**, *Ave. Bernado Lopes*, with a beautiful 19th century gaming room and a dinner theater, Le Belle Epoque, with revue shows.

NIGHTLIFE & ENTERTAINMENT

The nightlife in this resort area starts about 9pm when the younger set hops towards the **Beach Club**, *Esplanada Silva Guimarães*, the **Perfumaria Pub**, *Rua Dr. Calado*, or the **Branco e Negro** bistro, *Rua da Fonte*.

The late night action takes place over at the **Amnistia Disco**, *Rua de Coimbra*, as well as in **Silver Dreams**, *Rua Maestro David de Sousa*, **Solário** in Buaracos, and **Flashen** at the Praia de Quiaios. The older folks tend to enjoy themselves at the **Casino** complex that includes a disco and a piano bar.

SPORTS & RECREATION

There are beach front **tennis courts**, a **yacht club**, **bicycle** and **windsurfing** rental shops, **fishing** excursions, a **bullring**, and of course several large beaches and pools that rent chairs and umbrellas in the summer.

The cleanest beaches are located just north of town at the former pirate heaven and onetime fishing village of **Buarcos**. A little further up the road from Buarcos you should stop at the **Cabo Mondego** lighthouse for a panoramic view.

Bicycle
• **Afga Travel** (bicycle & moped rentals), *Figueira da Foz, Tel. (033) 277-77*

Fishing
• **Amadores Fishing Club**, *Figueira da Foz, Tel. (033) 294-34*

Squash
• **Vale do Leão Squash Club**, *Buarcos, Tel. (033) 230-57*

Tennis
• **Figueira da Foz Tennis Club**, *Ave. 25 de Abril, Tel. (033) 222-87*

EXCURSIONS & DAY TRIPSS

About 16 km from Figueira da Foz off Route N-111 east is the village of **Montemor-o-Velho**. On a hill above town is an impressive ancient fortress constructed first by the Romans, and later rebuilt to help defend nearby Coimbra after the expulsion of the Moors. The double perimeter walls contain several towers and surround **Igreja de Santa Maria de Alcácova**. This church has unusual twisted arch and columns. The view from the castle's ramparts is beautiful.

CONDEIXA & CONIMBRIGA

The most important attraction near the small village of Condeixa is the ruins of the Roman city of Conimbriga.

ARRIVALS & DEPARTURES

Condeixa is about 17 km southeast of Montemor-o-Velha off N-1 highway.

WHERE TO STAY

Moderate

POUSADA DE SANTA CRISTINA, *Rua Francisco Lemos. Tel. (039) 941-286, Fax (039) 943-097. US & Canada bookings with Marketing Ahead, Tel. 800/223-1356. Low season rack rates from 12,000$00, double room, CP, high season rates from 19,000$00, double room, CP. All major credit cards accepted.*

Just a few minutes drive from the Roman ruins at Conimbriga, this sparkling new pousada has recently risen from the ruins of a 17th century mansion owned by the powerful Sotto Mayor family of bankers and industrialists. This deluxe and tranquil pousada is filled with a stunning collection of priceless antiques and offers 45 gigantic air conditioned rooms, each with granite and marble private bathrooms stocked with high quality hair and skin care products, remote control satellite TV, direct dial telephones, mini-bar, mini-safe, stylish hardwood furnishings, designer floral fabrics and lithographs, large closets, wall to wall carpeting, and either a small verandah or a larger terrace overlooking lush lawns.

The wonderful Pousada de Santa Cristina has many facilities and services including a superb restaurant featuring regional lunch and dinner specialties, a spacious lounge area and reading room, private luncheon and business meeting rooms, secure outdoor parking, a nice outdoor swimming pool, a pool-side bar and sun deck, seasonal chamber music concerts, a well maintained tennis court, direct bus service to and from downtown Coimbra, and a talented multilingual staff that is sure to make you feel at home.

The pousada is perfect a base from which to take day trips to Conimbriga, Coimbra, Figueira da Foz, and even Porto. Highly Recommended.

WHERE TO EAT

Expensive

POUSADA DE SANTA CRISTINA, *Rua Francisco Lemos. Tel. (039) 941-286. Open daily for lunch and dinner. Dress code is casual elegant. All major credit cards accepted.*

The pousada's excellent dining room has a uniquely relaxing ambiance in which to enjoy some of the region's best gourmet cuisine. Although the menu changes daily, among the most commonly offered dishes are fish soup, asparagus au gratin, amazing jumbo shrimp grilled on a spit freshly cut from the garden's laurel tree, succulent stuffed filet of sole, braised kid, swordfish with coriander and onions, tender roasted hen with pepper sauce, medallions of lamb au gratin, veal with buttered onions, and many others. Expect to spend about 7,250$00, per couple, plus drinks, for an unforgettable meal served in impeccable style. The the service is truly first rate. Highly Recommended.

SEEING THE SIGHTS

Conimbriga is about 1 km southeast of Condeixa along Route N-342. It was originally settled during the Iron Age when it was built as a Celtic hamlet. Then sometime before the 1st century, the Romans founded a city on this spot, alongside the **Estrada Romana**, a major Roman military and trade road between Braga and Lisboa. Despite the eventual addition of defensive walls in the 4th century, the city was unfortunately all but totally destroyed by Swabian warriors in the 5th century.

The ruins are now protected as part of the **Museu Monographico de Conimbriga** complex, most famous for its stunning exhibition of beautifully preserved Roman mosaic floors made with tiny gray and pink pebbles. When you purchase your ticket, I recommend you get a copy of the optional 125$00 "Guia para Visita das Ruinas," an explanatory brochure and map in English. The first rooms have permanent exhibits of locally found artifacts such as coins, weapons, ceramics, and agricultural implements.

From here you can exit the museum and continue along a path that leads a few hundred yards away to the excavation site. This area was inhabited from the 1st to the 4th centuries and then abandoned when the defensive walls were added. Among the highlights (many have explanations on multilingual plaques) are the walls, mosaic floors, column fragments, basements, and foundations of shops, public buildings, and regal residences such as the **Casa da Cruz Suastica** (House of the Swastica), **Casa dos Esqueletos** (House of the Skeletons), and the **Termas de Leste** (Eastern Public Baths).

The path also leads past a segment of the defensive walls and into the section of Conimbriga that was added after the 4th century. The most famous excavations here include a magnificent **Basilica** (cathedral), the **Centro Monumental** (Town Square and Center), and the massive **Casa do Cantaber** (House of Cantaber), which contains a secondary peristyle, remnants of an ancient warm air ventilation system, private baths, plumbing system, and indoor hot and cold water baths.

If you follow the path back through an opening in the defensive wall, you will come to the ruins of the awesome 2nd century **Casa de Repuxos** (House of the Fountains). This house has a central peristyle, landscaped pool, fine mosaics, and ornamental gardens all under a modern steel protective awning. The Roman ruins and museum are open Tuesday through Sunday from 9:00am until at least 5:00pm (may be closed at lunch) and costs 350$00, per person.

COIMBRA

The enchanting old university city of Coimbra is a wonderful place to explore, especially if you are in the mood for lots of walking. In every corner of town there is a youthful element that seems to blend in well with the medieval character of the city. The city is full of ancient history, but functions at full 20th century speed.

While the site of present day Coimbra has been inhabited since prehistoric times, this former Roman village greatly grew in both population and importance just after the Swabians conquered the nearby city of Conimbriga. When Dom Afonso Henriques I moved the royal court from Guimarães, he chose the Christian stronghold of Coimbra as nation's next capital. Coimbra continued to prosper as Portugal's capitol until King Dom Afonso III moved the royal court to Lisbon in the mid 13th century. In 1537, Coimbra's royal palace became home to Portugal's oldest university, which was first established in Lisbon over 200 years earlier. To this day, the city has maintained strong links to its traditions and history. Many students can still be seen walking around town dressed in traditional black robes with colored ribbons that indicate the college they belong to.

ARRIVALS & DEPARTURES
By Air
Coimbra is situated roughly halfway between Porto and Lisbon, so you can fly into either Lisbon's Portela airport or Porto's Dr. Francisco Sá Carneiro airport.

By Bus
Most buses in Portugal stop off at Coimbra's main bus depot which is located on the river about 2 km west of Largo da Portagem plaza.
• **Coimbra Main Bus Depot**, *Ave. F. de Magalhaes, Tel. (039) 270-81*

By Car
Coimbra is about 16 km northeast of Condeixa off Route N-1 north on the banks of the Mondego River.

From Lisbon, take either the expensive A-1 motorway, or the no-toll N-1 highway and get off at the exit for the city's "Centro" (downtown).

Parking is difficult, but there are several public lots along the river at Ave. Marginal and Ave. Emidio Navarro. To rent a car, go to:

• **Europcar Rent a Car**, *Rua da Sota, 2, Tel. (039) 270-11*

By Train

There are frequently scheduled local and express trains from both downtown Lisbon and Porto that arrive into either Coimbra's new downtown riverside Estação A rail station or the older Estação B rail station another 3 kilometers west of downtown. A taxi will charge around 700$00 to get you from Estação B rail station to downtown.

• **Coimbra CP Rail Station A**, *Largo das Amenias, Tel. (039) 272-63*
• **Coimbra CP Rail Station B**, *3 km north of town, Tel. (039) 246-32*

ORIENTATION

Coimbra is a medium size town on a bluff rising up from the Mondego River. It is about 118 kilometers (73 miles) south-southeast from Porto and about 196 kilometers (121 miles) north-northeast of Lisbon.

The bustling old city center is covered with hundreds of narrow stone lanes and alleys that begin at the river and proceed uphill towards the city's famous 13th century university — the highest point in Coimbra. If you start your exploration of the city from the Largo da Portagem plaza near the river as I suggest, the university buildings can be used as fixed beacons to help guide you through town.

GETTING AROUND TOWN

By Bus

Although public buses connect just about every point in Coimbra, there is normally no need to use them since you can walk to most places around town. Bus system maps can be found at the main Turismo office just off the Largo da Portagem, and tickets cost about 135$00 per person.

By Car

Since finding parking in Coimbra is almost impossible, navigating around the narrow downtown streets is rather difficult, and traffic jams here are a common occurrence, I do not suggest using your car to explore this city.

In the event that you have rented a car, I recommend you park it at your hotel's garage and leave it there until you are ready to exit the city. There are a number of hotel and private parking garages that cost about 1,850$00 a day or so.

Coimbra has a serious rush hour from 7:45am - 9:15am and again from 4:45pm - 7:15pm on weekdays.

By Taxi

Taxis are an effective and inexpensive way to get around Coimbra. The average ride anywhere within the downtown area should cost no more than 675$00 and all the drivers know how to best avoid traffic jams.

You can usually identify a vacant taxi if the "Taxi" light on top of the cab is illuminated. You flag them down in much the same way you would at home, or you can go to one of many taxi lines and wait your turn. Since downtown Coimbra is rather compact, you may never actually need to use a taxi unless your feet get too tired from walking uphill all day.

WHERE TO STAY

Expensive

QUINTA DAS LAGRIMAS, *Santa Clara District, Coimbra. Tel. (039) 441-615, Fax (039) 441-695. Low season rack rates from 16,000$00, double room, EP; high season rates from 17,500$00, double room, EP. Most major credit cards accepted.*

This magnificent 18th and 19th century mansion has recently been converted into a deluxe 5 star hotel catering to international visitors and the Portuguese jet-set, including kings, presidents, famous artists, notorious writers, poets, and generals. Located across the river from downtown Coimbra, it sits amidst beautiful gardens overlooking the city. There are 29 stunningly decorated rooms and suites, with marble bathrooms, satellite color TV, mini-bars, mini-safes, beautiful hand crafted furnishings, and terraces looking onto to either serene gardens or the city.

The property features the city's finest gourmet restaurant, a wonderful bar and billiard room, a private botanical garden full of rare trees and plants (including two sequoias planted by the Duke of Wellington after his successful battles against Napoleonic forces), a great outdoor swimming pool, an historic chapel, several business meeting rooms, lavish sitting rooms, impressive collections of antique and modern art, a fine library full of rare volumes, plenty of free parking, and a highly trained staff of professionals. Highly Recommended.

Moderate

HOTEL ASTÓRIA, *Ave. Emidio Navarro, 21. Tel. (039) 220-55, Fax (039) 220-57. Low season rack rates from 12,000$00, double room, BP; high season rates from 15,000$00, double room, BP. All major credit cards accepted.*

This well located art deco grand hotel is one of my favorite places to stay in downtown Coimbra. There are 64 large and well appointed guest rooms, all with private bathrooms, air conditioning, direct dial telephone, cable television, hardwood furnishings, and in many cases a great view over the Mondego River or the city. The staff are extremely helpful, and the facilities include a good restaurant, a nice bar and lounge, and nearby parking. Highly Recommended.

HOTEL TIVOLI COIMBRA, *Rua João Machado. Tel. (039) 269-34, Fax (039) 268-27. US and Canada bookings with Utell, Tel. 800/448-8355. Year round rack rates from 18,000$00, double room, EP. All major credit cards accepted.*

This is a modern business hotel in the commercial district of town. The 110 air conditioned rooms and suites are rather large and have deluxe private bathrooms, remote control satellite television, direct dial phones, mini-bars, and more. The hotel has a bar, restaurant, pool, sauna, health club, and parking.

HOTEL DOM LUÍS, *N-1, Santa Clara. Tel. (039) 442-510. Year round rack rates from 17,500$00, double room, EP. Most major credit cards accepted.*

This new tower 3 star hotel, across the bridge from Coimbra, has good city views and 100 big air conditioned rooms with cable TV.

Inexpensive

RESIDENCIAL PARQUE, *Ave. Emidio Navarro, 42. Tel. (039) 292-02. Year round rack rates from 11,500$00, double room, EP. Cash only - No credit cards accepted.*

A nice and simple inn, it has 29 clean and comfortable rooms with private bathrooms. This is a good budget choice.

PENSÃO MODENA, *Rua Adelino Veiga, 9. Tel. (039) 254-13. Year round rack rates from 10,500$00, double room, EP. Cash only - No credit cards accepted.*

A fairly nice 3 star inn near the Praça de Comercío, it offers 30 small but comfortable rooms with private bathrooms. Facilities include TV room and phones.

HOTEL MONDEGO, *Largo das Ameias, 4. Tel. (039) 290-87. Year round rack rates from 10,500$00, double room, EP. Cash only - No credit cards accepted.*

This is a rather simple 1 star hotel in the commercial district with almost acceptable small rooms, with and without private bathroom.

WHERE TO EAT
Expensive
ARCADAS DA CAPELA, *Quinta Das Lagrimas, Santa Clara District, Coimbra. Tel. (039) 441-615. Dress code is semi-formal. Most major credit cards accepted.*

This is certainly one of the finest gourmet restaurants in northern Portugal. Located across the river from Coimbra on the ground floor of a quinta, Arcadas da Capela is a true gem. The lavishly decorated main dining room is set in cool pastel tones and overlooks a dramatic garden.

After being seated for lunch or dinner, you will be given a superb menu featuring exceptionally well prepared and presented specialties such as crepes filled with shrimp, vegetable creme soup, seafood soup, tagliatelle Carbonara, tiger shrimp grilled with garlic butter, oven roasted pork, steamed clams, grouper filets in rice, and over two dozen other great steak, veal, and seafood dishes. The service is the best I have ever seen in Portugal, and both the wine list and dessert cart will make your mouth water. Expect to pay around 3,750$00 per person for a meal you will never forget. Be sure to call in advance for reservations. Highly Recommended.

Moderate

TROVADOR, *Largo da Sé Velha, Tel. (039) 254-75. Dress code is semi-formal. Most major credit cards accepted.*

An almost fancy restaurant right near the old cathedral, you'll find great service, excellent meat dishes, a casual atmosphere, and Fado on weekends. Closed Mondays. Expect to spend around 2,450$00 a person.

Inexpensive

ZE MANUEL, *Beco do Forno, 12. Tel. (039) 237-90. No dress code. Cash only - No credit cards accepted.*

This packed and well known Coimbra hot-spot is adorned with rustic furniture and walls full of old poems. The cuisine here are amazing, and the portions are huge considering they average around 1,300$00 each.

ADEGA PAÇO DO CONDE, *Rua Paço do Conde, 1. Tel. (039) 256-05. No dress code. Cash only - No credit cards accepted.*

This is a simple barbecue restaurant that caters to mostly students. A meal costs less than 1,000$00.

SEEING THE SIGHTS

The **Largo da Portagem** is the best place to start your excursion to the heart of Coimbra. This delta-shaped public plaza, directly across from the **Ponte de Santa Clara** (bridge), marks the beginning of the **Baixa** (lower) section of town. The Largo da Portagem funnels down onto the Rua Ferreira Borges, which has several cafés full of students and local blue collar workers loudly gossiping every morning.

After a stop for a good coffee, continue up Rua Ferreira Borges, and if you're interested, shop at the many boutiques along this road. When you're ready to continue, walk a few hundred yards, and turn left where you can descend a set of stairs towards the **Praça do Comércio**. This square is the crossroads of downtown. Besides the fine shops, bakeries, and cafés that line the plaza, you can't help but notice the dramatic **Igreja da São Tiago** off to the far right side. This 13th century church is usually covered with pigeons, but you can still see its arched spiral columned doorway and bold facade.

Almost all of the streets that commence at the Praça do Comércio have small shops that sell everything from high quality shoes and fabrics to horse meat. An occasional Mormon from Utah can be found stalking the plaza looking for the day's convert.

After a good look around Praça do Comércio, head back down the Rua Ferreira Borges for a block or so until you reach the 12th century **Porta Almedina** gate with an adjacent medieval tower. If you walk through the gate you will find yourself on Rua Quebra Costas. This road leads to several stairs and the **Largo de Sé Velha** square. The 12th century Romanesque **Sé Velha** (old cathedral), dating back to the time when Coimbra was the new capital of Portugal, is here. The fortress-like design of Sé Velha was created by the Frenchman Robert of Auverne. Although the facade is not particularly unusual, the interior has a beautiful Gothic altar designed by the Flemish artists Gand and Y'pres, several Jean de Rouen carvings from the early 16th century, and a 13th century cloister.

A few blocks away from Sé Velha, up Rua de Borges Carneiro, you will find the **Museu Nacional Machado de Castro** inside the former archbishop's ornate palace (closed on Mondays). The museum contains many ancient artworks including statues, sculptures, gold, silver, pottery, altar pieces, and paintings from as far back as the 12th century. The museum also exhibits prehistoric artifacts, Roman ruins, and a magnificent courtyard with a two level loggia and terrace. Just outside of the museum is the 12th century church, **Igreja de São Salvador**, as well as the 17th century **Sé Nova** (New Cathedral), both worth a short tour.

From the Sé Nova walk south for a block to reach **Velha Universidade** (old university) via the 17th century **Porta Ferrea** (The Iron Gate). This arch opens onto a three sided courtyard called the **Patio das Escolas** (student's patio). It contains several regal buildings, an 18th century clock tower, the former royal palace, and a large statue of King Dom Pedro III.

From here, use the stairs to get to the **Sala dos Capelos**, which contains paintings of former kings. A chapel known as the **Capela de São Miguel** is entered through a regal Manueline doorway encrusted with royal symbols. Don't miss its wonderful azulejos, frescoes, and ancient pipe organ. Just off to the left is an 18th century library known as the **Biblioteca Joanina**. It has three huge rooms with gilded shelves loaded with leather and gold bound antique volumes, fine antique furniture, and

Baroque trimmings everywhere. I have never seen a library like this anywhere else in the world. From behind the university you can access the **Jardim Botánico**: don't miss the aqueduct, **Aqueducto de São Sebastian**.

From the botanical gardens, you can walk along the Mondego River until you are once again at the Largo da Portagem plaza. Continue up Rua Ferreia Borges and again pass through the **Almedina** gate. This time, turn left (north) on Rua de Sobre Ripas until you reach the **Palácio de Sub Ripas** (palace). The beautiful tower was once part of the city's wall fortifications but was subsequently converted into a private mansion and remains closed to the public.

You can however enter the **Torre de Anto** tower further up Rua de Sobre Ripas. It is now an artist's cooperative and store (closed most Saturdays and Sundays). Double back through the Almedina gate and turn right (north) up Rua Rua Ferreira Borges (turns into Rua Visconde Visconde da Luz).

Several hundred yards up Rua Visconde da Luz you will run into the **Praça 8 de Maio**. I suggest a brief rest and relaxation stop in **Café Santa Cruz** (closed on Sunday), a converted chapel. From the café's outside tables you can stare at the 12th century **Mosteiro de Santa Cruz**, perhaps the most dramatic church in all of Coimbra. The monastery was almost completely rebuilt in the 16th century, and the facade has been severely eroded by pollution. Inside this massive structure you can marvel at a beautiful Manueline ceiling, 16th and 17th century master paintings, fantastically carved choir chairs, haunting royal tombs, an azulejos-lined nave, and a remarkable Renaissance pulpit.

At the back of the church is the pretty **Jardim de Manga**, with gardens and a fountain. Just a block or so behind the gardens are the town's covered daily **mercado** (market) and gypsy fair.

NIGHTLIFE & ENTERTAINMENT

Since the majority of the nightlife is centered around the students, most of the better cafés and bars are near the university, the Sé Velha, and the Praça da República.

AQUI HA RATO, *Largo da Sé Velha, 20. Tel. (039) 248-04.*

This three level dance club and bar, in the heart of the old part of town, is certainly the best place to spend a few hours. The name actually translates to "There's a Rat Here." It's open nightly from 10:00pm until around 6:00am. The music is a mix of European and American rock and house tunes, and the clients are mostly university students and locals that dress in jeans and button down shirts. The minimum charge is 250$00, which also happens to be the price of a beer. This place is packed on weekend after 11:30pm.

PIANO NEGRO, *Rua Borges Carneiro, 19. Tel. (039) 274-65.*

For a mellow time, check out this great combination café, miniature concert venue, and art gallery. It's owned by a Frenchman with a good sense of humor. Located near the Sé Velha, this dark and cozy bar plays lots of blues music and has some of the best drink prices in town.

SCOTCH, *N-1, Santa Clara, Tel. (039) 441-236.*

Without a doubt, this highly popular disco, just across the river from downtown Coimbra, is the best place to party late at night. Open from 11:00pm until 6:00am, Thursday through Saturday nights, this huge disco has a great dance floor, a Scottish pub, a concert venue, and can hold over 750 people. Clients tend to be casually dressed 17 - 30 year old singles. There is a cover charge if you get there by 3:00am and the minimum is about 500$00 per person. Expect to hear the thumping sounds of European house and hip-hop music until the cows come home.

SPORTS & RECREATION
Fishing
• **Coimbra AAC Fishing Club**, *Tel. (039) 280-72*

Horseback Riding
• **Coimbra Hipico Horse Center**, *Mata do Choupal, Tel. (039) 376-95*

Tennis
• **Coimbra Tennis Club**, *University Stadium, Tel. (039) 441-384*

EXCURSIONS & DAY TRIPS

Across the Ponte de Santa Clara bridge, in **Santa Clara**, are a few sight worth visiting. Just off the Ave. João das Regras you will find the ruins of the Gothic 14th century **Convento de Santa Clara a Velha**. The tombs of Inês de Castro (the murdered wife of King Dom Pedro) and Queen St. Isabel were once located here, but had to be moved after several floods began to destroy this old convent.

A few blocks behind this convent stands the newer 17th century **Convento de Santa Clara a Nova**, which contains both the original stone tomb of Queen St. Isabel and the 17th century silver tomb she was moved into, as well as a variety of fine paintings and gilted woodwork. The small and uninteresting **Museu Militar** (military museum) is located in this convent (open daily).

In the same vicinity as these convents is the **Portugal dos Pequenitos** (children's park). It contains scale models of various Portuguese buildings and other minature structures.

The other remaining sight on this side of the river is the eerie **Quinta das Lagrimas** manor house and park off Rua António Goncalves. This private estate is where Dona Inês de Castro, the forbidden wife of then Prince Pedro, was assassinated under orders of his father, King Afonso IV. Although the quinta is not in great shape, you can still see much of it from the roadside. Entrance is strictly forbidden.

BUÇACO, LUSO, & MEALHADA

Buçaco (also spelled Bussaco or Buccaco) is one of the most picturesque areas in all of Portugal. This is due to a magical forest, Mata do Buçaco, and a monestary built by Carmelite monks in the 17th century.

ARRIVALS & DEPARTURES
By Car
From Coimbra, take Route IC-2 or the A-1 highway north for about 19 km to the Mealhada exit, and follow Route N-234 east for another 7 km through Luso, where you will find signs to Buçaco.

WHERE TO STAY
Expensive
PALACE HOTEL DO BUSSACO, *Mata do Buçaco. Tel. (031) 930-101, Fax (031) 930-509. US and Canada bookings with The Small Hotel Co., Tel. 800/552-6844. Low season rack rates from 20,000$00, double room, BP; high season rack rates from 29,000$00, double room, BP. All major credit cards accepted.*

Originally built as a royal hunting lodge for the last Portuguese king, this wonderful palace is beautifully decorated with incredible hand carved stonework and beautiful azulejos panels. This superb property features massive sitting rooms, opulent lounges filled with countless antiques, fine European works of art, a stunning central stairway, and patios overlooking both the forest and formal box gardens.

All 66 deluxe air conditioned rooms and suites have antique and hand-crafted hardwood furnishings, beautiful designer fabrics, direct dial telephones, remote control satellite television, giant private marble bathrooms, extremely comfortable beds, executive desks, and superb views.

There is also a fantastic gourmet restaurant, an old monastery, formal box gardens, lounges, hiking trails, tennis, and an equally fantastic winery. The ambiance here is warm and friendly, with a highly professional staff that is eager to please each guest. A couple of nights stay at this one of a kind hotel is a must for all visitors to Portugal, and reservations should be made well in advance during the high season.

Selected as one of my *Best Places to Stay* (see Chapter 10 for more details).

Moderate

VILLA DUPARCHY, *Mealhada. Tel. (031) 939-120, Fax (031) 930-307. Year round rack rates from 14,750$00, double room, CP. Cash only - No credit cards accepted.*

This tranquil, antique-filled 19th century manor house and estate is located on the road to Luso. It has six great rooms with private bathrooms. Facilities include dining room, lounges with fireplaces, pool, gardens, TV room, and fine furnishings.

VILA AURORA, *Luso. Tel. (031) 930-150, Fax (031) 930-193. Year round rack rates from 15,950$00, double room, CP. Cash only - No credit cards accepted.*

This dramatic castle-like antique manor house and its annex offer six nicely decorated rooms with private bathrooms. The main house is opulent and has a dining room, lounges, and fine works of art.

GRANDE HOTEL DAS TERMAS DE LUSO, *Rua dos Banhos, Luso. Tel. (031) 930-450, Fax (031) 930-350. Year round rack rates from 14,500$00, double room, EP. Most major credit cards accepted.*

This large 173 room hotel is located next to a quiet, central park in Luso. The spa and Fonte de São João spring are located steps away. All units are air conditioned and have reasonably nice furnishings, television, direct dial telephone, and private bathroom. There are lots of facilities including bar, restaurant, pool, tennis, squash, billiards, disco, and parking.

HOTEL EDEN, *Rua Emidio Navarro, Luso. Tel. (031) 930-191, Fax (031) 930-192. Year round rack rates from 13,250$00, double room, EP. Most major credit cards accepted.*

This full service hotel has 56 good rooms with telelvison and private bathroom. Facilities include bar, restaurant, mini-bars, TV, and parking. Very close to the spa.

Inexpensive

PENSÃO ALEGRE, *Rua Emidio Navarro, Luso. Tel. (031) 939-251. Year round rack rates from 7,500$00, double room, EP. Cash only - No credit cards accepted.*

This budget 3 star inn has large, comfortable rooms with private bathrooms.

WHERE TO EAT

Expensive

PALACE HOTEL DO BUSSACO, *Palacio Bucaco. Tel. (031) 930-101. Dress code is jackets preffered. All major credit cards accepted.*

Some of the best meals in Portugal are served in this frescoed dining room full of stained glass windows and hand-cut terra cotta sculptures. The extensive menu changes every night and feature a variety of fine items including prawn cocktails, melon with aged ham, made to order salads, seafood bisque, consommé, filet of sole, baked wild boar, roast suckling pig, grilled tuna steak, sirloin steak, cod fish with wine sauce, chicken Kiev, stuffed lamb chops, grilled jumbo shrimp, and seasonal specials.

You may want to dress up for dinner, but it is not mandatory. To accompany an unforgettable meal at the palace, I strongly suggest a bottle of superb red or white Buçaco Reserva wine (Bairrada region) made in limited quantities in the palace's own underground winery. For the bravest of guests, taste the palace's legendary Águardente (Fire Water): it's the best I've ever tasted. Service at this restaurant is extraordinary. The wines and desserts are unbelievably good. Dinner here will set you back around 5,500$00 a person. Highly Recommended.

Moderate

PEDRO DOS LEITOS, *N-1-Mealhada. Tel. (031) 220-62. No dress code. Cash only - No credit cards accepted.*

This large and well known churrascaria (roasted suckling pig) restaurant serves great food. The large dining room is usually full and the service is good. My last meal here cost only 1,400$00 a person.

SEEING THE SIGHTS

The **Mata do Buçaco** forest, covering 248 acres, was originally inhabited by Benedictine monks over 1,200 years ago. Upon the arrival of the Carmelite monks in the 17th century, a monastery was constructed and the forest was surrounded by a stone wall about a yard high with several gated entrances. Women were forbidden from entering. As these barefooted monks wandered through their forest they constructed simple hermitages throughout the forest so they could survive in complete isolation for long periods of time. Eleven hermitages can still be seen.

The Carmelites were obsessed with the preservation of this area, and planted hundreds of exotic species of trees from all over the world including Australian Bunya-buyna pine, Tasmanian eucalyptus, Californian sequoias, Moroccan cedars, and many other species. In order to protect Europe's most unique forest, Pope Urban VIII signed an edict in 1643 that would excommunicate any person harming a tree in Buçaco.

Things were relatively quiet at Buçaco until September 1810 when Napoleonic troops under Massena challenged Wellington's English and Portuguese forces in what would be remembered as the Battle of Buçaco. French troops attacked up a foggy hill and were repeatedly repelled back down. Wellington was victorious and left Buçaco to regroup his troops behind the secret Torres Vedras lines. Repulsion of the invading French forces led to final victory.

After the dismantling of all religious orders in 1834, the Carmelites were evicted from Buçaco, and the property was taken by the state. The preservation still continues, and the forest is one of my favorite places to visit in Europe. The Department of Waters and Forests has administered the land and has since planted many more varieties of plants.

In the 18th century, conversion of the monastery grounds into a royal hunting lodge began. The lodge was designed in 1888 by Italian architect Luigi Manini in a neo-Manueline style. Now known simply as **Palácio Buçaco**, its fantastic facade is adjacent to the remaining parts of the monastery including a mosaic chapel and some monastic cells. Beautiful azulejos cover both the interior walls and exterior perimeters. The public spaces are filled with fine antique furniture, beautiful paintings, terra cotta trimmings, ornate patios, and many amusing artifacts of an age long gone. The huge, red carpeted, main staircase is surrounded by historical azulejos, a large stained glass window, and a suit of armor that guides you up to what are now the deluxe guest rooms.

The project was completed in 1907, but the royal family never officially used the palace before King Dom Manuel II abdicated the throne and the royal family was banished from power. In 1910, the palace became a deluxe hotel with its own excellent winery and one of the most elegant restaurants in the world. In my opinion, this is the best hotel in Portugal.

The grounds at Buçaco are well maintained and include beautiful gardens that surround a large pond with swans. There are several trails that wind through the forest and provide a wonderful afternoon of trekking past streams, waterfalls, and historical monuments.

You can wander through the forest on well-marked paths and visit some of the hermitages, the **Fonte Fria** spring with 144 stone stairs, 17th century chapels along the **Via Sacra** (Sacred Way), Rua dos Fetos (Fern Alley), several original gates such as the **Portas de Coimbra**, and a beautiful view of the whole region from the **Cruz Alta** cross. Outside the wall there is an Obelisk monument to the Battle of Buçaco as well as the **Museu Militar** (military museum) that is closed Mondays.

Just below the forest is the pretty spa town of **Luso** and its famous curative thermal springs. Visitors from around the world come to bathe in the warm mineral rich, slightly radioactive, waters that are piped into the town's spa. To compliment its well known healing facilities, the town of Luso boasts tennis courts, swimming pools, walking trails, and boating. Luso also bottles a less potent mineral water that, in my opinion, is the best tasting water in Portugal.

A bit further east from Luso is the traditional town of **Mealhada**. On Route N-1, you'll find the region's finest churrascaria (roasted suckling pig) restaurants. Ask the concierge at your hotel to make reservations for you at **Pompeu**, a special restaurant and former stage coach in the village of **Malaposta**.

CURIA

This once grand, old world, spa town know as Curia attracted the upper class of Europe's social elite. Nowadays, it still evokes the feeling of a resort town, but many of the old houses are falling to bits.

ARRIVALS & DEPARTURES
By Car

Curia can be reached from Luso by taking Route N-234 west for 7 km and connecting to Route IC-2 north for another 8 km or so.

WHERE TO STAY
Moderate

PALACE HOTEL DA CURIA, *Curia. Tel. (031) 515-157, Fax (031) 515-531. Year round rack rates from 15,750$00, double room, BP. Most major credit cards accepted.*

This turn of the century 4 star hotel is located next to the Curia springs. The hotel offers 114 rooms with period furnishings, direct dial telephones, satellite television, and private bathrooms. Hotel facilities include a remarkable bar, gourmet restaurant, tennis, pool, billiards, gardens, spa access, and free parking. Highly Recommneded.

GRAND HOTEL DA CURIA, *Curia. Tel. (031) 515-720, Fax (031) 515-317. Year round rack rates from 17,000$00, double room, EP. Most major credit cards accepted.*

A beautiful large hotel, it has 86 nicely decorated rooms with televison, nice furnishings, television, mini-bar, direct dial telephone, and private bathroom. The property boasts a fully supervised spa with indoor pool and sauna, a bar, a good restaurant, library, lounge, free parking, and great room service.

SEEING THE SIGHTS

People come to Curia for the thermal baths. The hotels are still noteworthy, including the **Grand Hotel de Curia** and its advanced, medically supervised spa programs, and the **Palace Hotel** which has maintained many original turn of the century aspects.

ÁGUEDA

Águeda is a great little town, originally settled by the Celtics, on the Águeda River, and is rarely visited by tourists.

ARRIVALS & DEPARTURES

By Car

Situated halfway between Coimbra and Porto, Águeda can be reached by taking Route IC-2 north from Coimbra for about 47 km.

WHERE TO STAY

Moderate

POUSADA DE SANTO ANTONIO, *Serem. Tel. (034) 523-192. US & Canada bookings with Marketing Ahead, Tel. 800/223-1356. Low season rack rates from 12,000$00, double room, CP; high season rates from 16,500$00, double room, CP. All major credit cards accepted.*

A small government owned inn a few kilometers outside of Agueda with 13 nice rooms that have television and private bathrooms. Facilities include bar, restaurant, swimming pool, and parking.

SEEING THE SIGHTS

The downtown area is charming. The shops in the enchanting commercial district have unusual raised tile facades. The weekly Saturday market is off *Ave. 25 de Abril* and is one of the best in the region.

An interesting house and museum, the **Foundation of Dionisio Pinheirho**, *Praça Dr. António Breda,* contains great examples of 19th century oil paintings and furnishings. An ancient 16th century renaissanc chapel, **Capela do Sacramento**, has fine azulejos and an altar.

The town is located very close to excellent wineries such as the **Caves São João** (5 km away) and provides an excellent base from which to explore Coimbra, Aveiro, Porto, and nice coastal beaches.

The historic **Quinta da Borralha** was one of Portugal's finest quintas and had been converted into the Hotel Palácio Águeda. At press time, it was closed due to bankruptcy. If you're in the area, I recommend checking to see whether it's back in business.

AVEIRO & NEARBY COASTAL BEACHES

I first visited Aveiro over a decade ago, and I wouldn't even think of a trip to Portugal without a stop here. The town is known primarily for its canals and the salt pans that pile up on the edge of town. Several brightly painted fishing boats (they are actually used to collect seaweed) are moored to the sides of the canals that run through the center of town.

ARRIVALS & DEPARTURES
By Bus
•**Aveiro Main Bus Depot**, *Ave. Dr. L. Peixinho, Tel. (062) 217-55*

By Car
Aveiro is located about 27 km northwest of Águeda on Route N-230 west in the heart of the Ria de Aveiro estuary.

By Train
•**Aveiro CP Rail Station**, *Ave Dr. L. Piexinho, Tel. (062) 244-85*

GETTING AROUND TOWN
By Foot
Aveiro is a wonderful city to explore by foot because the town is small and the main streets are covered with mosaics of sea creatures.

WHERE TO STAY
Moderate
HOTEL PALOMA BLANCA, *Rua Luis Gomes de Carvalho, 23. Tel. (034) 381-992, Fax (034) 381-844. Year round rack rates from 14,500$00, double room, CP. Most major credit cards accepted.*

The Paloma Blanca is a great, traditional hotel converted from a beautiful old house in the center of the city. There are 50 nicely furnished rooms with air conditioning, private bathrooms, satellite television, and nice artwork. Facilities include bar, TV, gardens, and garage parking. Highly Recommended.

HOTEL ARCADA, *Rua Viana do Castelo, 4. Tel. (034) 230-01, Fax (034) 218-86. Year round rack rates from 15,250$00, double room, CP. Most major credit cards accepted.*

This is a delightful 2 star hotel with 49 comfortable rooms overlooking the canals in the center of town. All rooms have private bathroom, satellite television, and central heating. A good value for this location, the Arcada offers pleasant service. Highly Recommended.

HOTEL IMPERIAL, *Rua Dr. N. Leitão. Tel. (034) 221-41, Fax (034) 241-48. Year round rack rates from 14,000$00, double room, EP. Most major credit cards accepted.*

Hotel Imperial is a large 3 star hotel just a block or so from the city's famous monastery. The 107 rooms have private bathrooms, television, good views and soft beds. Facilities include a bar, restaurant, and nearby parking.

POUSADA DA RIA, *Bico do Muranzel, Murtosa. Tel. (034) 483-32. US & Canada bookings with Marketing Ahead, Tel. 800/223-1356. Low season rack rates from 12,000$00, double room, CP; high season rates from 16,500$00, double room, CP. All major credit cards accepted.*

This is a modern motel-like pousada right on the Ria estuary north of Aveiro in the town of Murtosa. It has over a dozen room with private bathrooms and color television. Facilities include water-view bar, restaurant, water sports, and parking.

HOTEL QUINTA DA LOGOÃ, *Mira. Tel. (031) 458-688, Fax (031) 458-688. Year round rack rates from 12,400$00, double room, EP. Most major credit cards accepted.*

This hotel and apartment complex is located close to the beaches. It has 25 one and two bedroom villa units with kitchens, and 140 or so nice rooms, all with private bathroom, direct dial telephones, and television. Facilities include bar, restaurant, disco, pool, tennis, water sports, and ample parking.

Inexpensive

PENSÃO SANTA JOÃNA, *Ave. Dr. L. Peixinho, 27. Tel. (034) 286-04. Year round rack rates from 7,250$00, double room, EP. Cash only - No credit cards accepted.*

This modern and clean inn is close to the train station. It has 16 good rooms with private bathrooms. Probably the best, inexpensive place to stay in Aveiro.

WHERE TO EAT

Moderate

TAVERNA DOM CARLOS, *Rua Dr. N. Leitão, 46. Tel. (034) 220-61. Dress code is jacket preferred. Most major credit cards accepted.*

Taverna Dom Carlos is a traditional restaurant in a nice old mansion in the center of town. Specialties include fresh roasted meats and grilled seafood. Expect very good service and an average bill of about 2,790$00 a person plus wine.

Inexpensive

PIZZARTE, *Rua Eng. Von Hafe, 27. Tel. (034) 271-03. No dress code. Cash only - No credit cards accepted.*

Surprisingly good pizzas are served in this ultra-modern restaurant and bar. Lots of students come here because a pizza for one is under 1,000$00.

SEEING THE SIGHTS

To fully appreciate Aveiro, you should start you excursion from the centrally located **Praça Humberto Delgado**. From this spot you can see the canals and the historic houses that line Rua João Mendonca (including the Turismo office of the **Rota da Luz** subregion). I would be leary of any hotel recommendations you receive from this Turismo office since I have been told that the staff receives kickbacks from the hotels they recommend.

The bustling fish market, *Rua Marnotos,* is located in this part of town, as well as several old streets with traditional houses, a nice park called **Largo do Rossio**, the solemn chapel of **São Goncalinho**, and several boutiques. When you're ready, wander back to the **Praça Humberto Delgado** and cross the bridge over the canal. If you look to you left you will see a tile mural of seaweed collectors at work.

On this side of the canal you should visit the 15th century Baroque convent, **Mosterio de Jesus**, *Rua de Santa Joana Princesa*. Portugal's Princess Joana once lived here and now lies in a marble tomb here. In the 18th century, the interior of the convent's church was redesigned by António Gomes and José Correia to include beautiful frescoes and azulejos murals showing scenes from the life of Joana, gilded woodwork, and a fantastic altar. The convent is now a museum, **Museu de Aveiro**, and contains various paintings, porcelains from the nearby **Vista Alegre** factory, statues, coaches, rare books, religious articles, and an unforgettable portrait of Joana from the 15th century (closed on Mondays).

I also recommend that you take one of the Ria ferries or boat tours that run on the Aveiro canals during the summer.

South of Aveiro are some of the most peaceful coastal towns and beaches in Portugal. The fishing town of **Costa Nova** is known for its striped houses and an amusing weekend fish market. You'll find cheap seafood meals in any one of several outdoor restaurants and cafes. The town also has a stand that sells "American Cookies" that are actually very good crepes with a waffled exterior and a chocolate interior.

If you continue south on the coastal road you'll reach **Vagueira** and a wide sand dune beach at **Praia de Vagueira**. This town has traditional oxen pulled fish nets. Try a piece of local sardine filled bread at a small stand named **Casa Rocha** on the road towards the beach. Also in the area are traditional fishing villages at **Praia de Mira**, 21 km south of Aveiro. You can watch the fishermen and oxen at work here in the summer months. The fishermen are surrounded by a series of interesting houses on stilts. There is seasonal ferry service from Aveiro to **São Jacinto**, a port town with a nice beach about 7 km north. Singles like this area and come to mingle in the bars and cafes.

The finest factory for high quality porcelain in Portugal is in **Vista Alegre**. To get there, head south from Aveiro for about 7 km until you reach the signs for Vista Alegre (just south of Ílhavo). They have a porcelain museum and they will ship their products all over the world (closed on Saturday and Sunday).

SPORTS & RECREATION
Horseback Riding
• **Aviero Equestrian Center**, *Vilarinho, Tel. (034) 912-108*

OVAR

This market city is near the northern edge of the Ria de Aveiro waterway. There are several nice homes and buildings covered with azulejos.

ARRIVALS & DEPARTURES
By Car
Ovar is about 29 km from Aveiro off Route N-109 north.

WHERE TO STAY
Moderate
HOTEL MEIA-LUA, *Rua das Luzes. Tel. (056) 575-031, Fax (056) 575-232. Year round rack rates from 14,450$00, double room, CP. Most major credit cards accepted.*

The Meia-Lua is a modern, low rise, 4 star hotel in a great location. It offers 54 nice and large rooms with air conditioning, private bathrooms, mini-bars, and television. Facilities include a bar, swimming pool, solarium, business meeting rooms, and gargage parking.

ALBERGARIA SÃO CRISTOVÃO, *Rua Aquilino Ribeiro, 1. Tel. (056) 575-105, Fax (056) 575-107. Year round rack rates from 13,500$00, double room, EP. Most major credit cards accepted.*

A great 4 star inn, it has 56 nice air conditioned rooms with private bathrooms and TV. There is also a bar, a restaurant, and free parking.

SEEING THE SIGHTS
The town has an interesting musuem, the **Museu Regional e Etnografica de Ovar**, *Rua Helidoro Salgado, 11*, which is full of local costumes, paintings, ceramics, and other exhibits (closed on Fridays). I also recommend that you visit a beautiful 17th century church, **Igreja Matriz**. Close to town are wonderful pine-bordered beaches at **Furadouro**. Be sure to try the local Pão de lo sponge cakes sold in the local cafes and bakeries.

SPORTS & RECREATION
· **Ovarense Sports Association**, *Ovar, Tel. (056) 512-36*

PRACTICAL INFORMATION FOR THE COSTA DE PRATA

Casinos
· **Casino de Figueira da Foz**, *Rua Bernardo Lopes, Tel. (033) 220-41*

Currency Exchange
Most of the banks in the Costa de Prata area will exchange foreign currency and travelers checks without hesitation. Banking hours are from 8am - 3pm, Monday through Friday. Private exchange booths, shops, restaurants, and hotels will exchange your money, but usually at a lower rate.

In the more touristy areas and big towns you may be able to find 24 hour ATM machines and currency exchange machines.

Emergency & Useful Phone Numbers
· **Emergency Assistance** (S.O.S.), *Tel. 115*
· **Águeda Hospital**, *Rua C. José Coutinho, Tel. (034) 622-075*
· **Caldas da Rainha Hospital**, *Parque Rainha D. Leonor, Tel. (062) 832-133*
· **Coimbra University Hospital**, *Praça Pr. Mota Pinto, Tel. (039) 722-116*
· **Leira Hospital**, *Largo D. M. Aguiar, Tel. (044) 321-33*
· **Tomar District Hospital**, *Ave. Dr. C. Mandueira, Tel. (049) 313-074*
· **Directory Assistance**, *Tel. 118*
· **Automobile Club of Portugal**, *Porto, Tel. (02) 830-1127*
· **Automobile Club of Portugal**, *Lisbon, Tel. (01) 942-5095*
· **Lisbon's Portela Airport**, *Tel. (01) 802-060*
· **TAP Reservations in Lisbon**, *Tel. (01) 386-1020*

Museums, Palaces, & Monuments
· **Wine Museum**, *Institute da Vinha e Vinho, Alcobaça, Tel. (062) 422-22.* Contains examples of different methods for wine making and a collection of wines from around Portugal. Open 9am until 12pm and 2pm until 5pm Monday through Friday. Closed on Saturdays, Sundays, and holidays.
· **House Museum of the Pinheiro Foundation**, *Praça Dr. António Breda, Águeda, Tel. (034) 623-720.* Contains a collection of 19th century porcelain, ceramics, ivory, tapestries, silverware, furniture, and fine

oil paintings. Open 3pm until 6pm Tuesday, Thursday, Saturday, and Sunday. Closed Mondays, Wednesdays, Fridays, and holidays.

• **Aveiro Museum** (Museu de Cidade), *Igreja de Jesus-Rua de Santa Joana Princesa, Aveiro, Tel. (034) 232-97.* Contains a collection of antique paintings, clothing, ceramics, sculpture, and jewelry. Open 10am until 12:30pm and 2pm until 5pm Tuesday through Sunday. Closed on Mondays and holidays.

• **Military Museum of Buçaco**, *Buçaco, Tel. (031) 939-310.* Contains collections of weapons and artifacts from the Battle of Buccaco. Open 10am until 5pm Tuesday through Sunday. Closed Mondays and holidays.

• **House Museum São Rafael**, *Rua Rafael Bordalo Pinheiro, Caldas da Rainha, Tel. (062) 231-57.* Contains a collection of ceramics and equipment that once belonged to Pinheiro. Open 9am until 12:30pm and 2:30pm until 5:30pm Monday through Friday. Closed Saturdays, Sundays, and holidays.

• **José Malhoa Museum**, *Parque Rainha Leonor, Caldas da Rainha, Tel. (062) 831-984.* Contains a collection of paintings from José Malhoa and several other Portuguese artists. The museum also contains several sculptures. Open 10am until 12:30pm and 2pm until 5pm Tuesday through Sunday. Closed on Mondays and holidays.

• **Joanina Library**, *Velha Universidade de Coimbra, Coimbra.* This library is an 18th century library with three huge rooms filled with leather and gold bound antique volumes, fine antique furniture, and Baroque trimmings everywhere. Open 9:30am until 12:30pm and 2pm until 5pm Monday through Saturday. Closed on Sundays and holidays.

• **Barreto Museum**, *Rua da Infantry, 23, Coimbra, Tel. (039) 224-68.* Contains collections of antique furniture, azulejos, rare books, paintings, and china. Open 3 pm until 5 pm, Tuesday through Friday. Open 10 am until 12 pm and 3 pm until 5 pm on Saturday and Sunday. Closed Mondays and holidays.

• **de Castro National Museum**, *Largo Dr. José Rodrigues, Coimbra, Tel. (039) 237-27.* Contains collections of 16th century oil paintings, Renaissance sculptures, ceramics, azulejos, baroque sculptures, tapestries, and oriental art. Open 9:30am until 12:30pm and 2pm until 5:30pm, Tuesday through Sunday. Closed on Mondays and holidays.

• **Mosteiro de Santa Cruz**, *Praça 8 de Maio, Coimbra, Tel. (039) 229-41.* Open 9am until 12pm and 2pm until 6pm daily.

• **National Museum of Science**, *Rua dos, 23, Coimbra, Tel. (039) 249-22.* Contains collections of models from Leonardo da Vinci inventions to equipment from Madame Curie experiments, and other exhibits in various buildings of the museum. Open 9am until 12:30pm and 2pm until 5:30pm Monday through Friday. Open 2pm until 6:30pm on

Saturday. Closed Sundays and holidays.

- **Sacred Art Museum of Coimbra University**, *Capela da Universidade, Coimbra, Tel. (039) 354-48.* Contains collections of ecclesiastical items and religious books. Open 9:30am 12:30pm and 2pm until 5pm. Closed during Christmas.
- **Sé Velha**, *Largo de Sé Velha, Coimbra, (039) 252-73.* Open 9:30am until 12:30pm and 2pm until 5:30pm daily.
- **Monographic Museum of Conimbriga**, *Condeixa-a-Nova, Tel. (039) 941-1177.* The archaeological excavations of the Roman village Conimbriga is on display and the museum also displays collections of Roman coins, artwork, and artifacts from the site. Open 10am until 5pm Tuesday through Sunday. Closed on Mondays.
- **Fátima Museum**, *Rua Jacinto Marta-Edificão João Paulo II, Fátima, Tel. (049) 532-858.* Contains statues and a multimedia show on the Fátima miracle. Open 9am until 6pm daily.
- **Wax Museum of Fátima**, *Rua Jacinto Marto, Fátima, Tel. (049) 532-102.* Contains wax figures based on the apparitions in Fátima. Open 10am until 5pm daily
- **Dr. Santos Rocha Museum**, *Ave. Calouste Gulbenkian, Figueira da Foz, Tel. (033) 245-09.* Contains collections of Roman stamps, antique furniture, and archaeological items. Open 9am until 12:30pm and 2pm until 5:30pm, Tuesday through Sunday. Closed on Mondays and holidays.
- **Vista Alegre Ceramic Museum**, *Vista Alegre Factory, Ílhavo, Tel. (034) 322-365.* Contains a collection of rare Vista Alegre porcelain including some Royal pieces. Open 9am until 12:30pm and 2pm until 4:30pm, Tuesday through Sunday. Closed on Mondays and holidays.
- **Leira Museum** (Museu de Cidade), *Castelo de Leiria, Leiria, Tel. (044) 813-982.* Contains a collection of paintings, sculptures, porcelain, tapestries, rugs, coins, furniture, medals, and glassware dating back over 5 centuries. Open 10am until 12:30pm and 2pm until 5pm, Tuesday through Sunday. Closed on Mondays and holidays.
- **Archaeological Museum of Nazaré**, *Rua D. Fuas Roupinho, Sito da Nazaré, Nazaré, Tel. (062) 551-687.* Contains collections of archaeological artifacts, fishing implements, paintings, sculptures, and ceramics. Open 10am until 12pm and 2pm until 5pm, Tuesday through Sunday. Closed on Mondays and holidays.
- **Óbidos Museum** (Museu da Cidade), *Praça Santa Maria, Óbidos, Tel. (062) 959-263.* Contains a collection of Josefa D'Obidos works, oil paintings, weapons from local battles, furniture, sacred art, and some artifacts. Open 9am until 1pm and 2pm until 6pm daily.
- **Ovar Museum** (Museu Etnografica), *Rua Heliodoro Salgado, 11, Ovar, Tel. (056) 572-822.* Contains antique paintings, ceramics, and local cos-

tumes. Open 10am until 12pm and 2pm until 6pm daily. Closed on Fridays and holidays.
- **Peniche Museum** (Museu da Cidade), *Campo da República, Peniche, Tel. (062) 781-848*. Contains collections of handicrafts, paintings, sea shells, azulejos, and other artifacts. Open 10am until 12pm and 2pm until 6pm, Tuesday through Monday. Closed Mondays and holidays.
- **Portugal dos Pequenitos Children's Park** (Jardim do Portugal dos Pequenitos), *Santa Clara-Coimbra, Tel. (039) 441-215*. A garden theme park with a display of miniature buildings and castles from all over Portugal and its colonies. The museum contains miniature furnishings and toys. Open 9:30am until 12:30pm and 2pm until 5pm each day.
- **Aquiles de Mota Match Box Museum**, *Convento de São Fransisco, Tomar, Tel. (049) 322-601*. Contains a huge collection of match books and boxes. Open 2pm until 5pm, Sunday through Friday. Closed on Saturdays and holidays.
- **Convent of Christ of Tomar**, *Tomar, Tel. (049) 313-481*. Open 9:30am until 12:30pm and 2pm until 5pm, Monday through Friday. Closed on Saturdays, Sundays, and holidays.
- **Abraham Zacuto Synagogue and Museum**, *Rua da Judiaria, 73, Tomar, Tel. (049) 322-601*. Open 9am until 12:30pm and 2:30pm until 6pm daily.
- **Torres Vedras Museum**, *Rua Serpa Pinto, 7, Torres Vedras*. Contains collections of 16th century paintings, stamps, azulejos, and artifacts. Open 10am until 12pm and 2pm until 5pm, Tuesday through Sunday. Closed on Mondays and holidays.

Tourism Offices *(Turismos)*
- **Águeda Tourism Office**, *Rua 5 de Outubro, Tel. (034) 601-42*
- **Alcobaça Tourism Office**, *Praça 25 de Abril, Tel. (062) 423-77*
- **Aveiro Tourism Office**, *Rua João Mendonca, 8, Tel. (062) 236-80*
- **Batalha Tourism Office**, *Largo Paulo VI, Tel. (044) 961-80*
- **Caldas da Rainha Tourism Office**, *Rua E. D. Pacheco, Tel. (062) 831-003*
- **Coimbra Tourism Office**, *Largo da Portagem, Tel. (039) 238-86*
- **Costa Nova Tourism Office**, *Praia Costa Nova, Tel. (034) 369-560*
- **Fátima Tourism Office**, *Ave. Correia da Silva, Tel. (049) 531-139*
- **Figueira da Foz Tourism Office**, *Ave. 25 de Abril, Tel. (033) 226-10*
- **Leiria Tourism Office**, *Jardim Luís de Camões, Tel. (044) 237-73*
- **Nazaré Tourism Office**, *Ave. Viera Guimares, Tel. (062) 561-154*
- **Obidos Tourism Office**, *Rua Direita, Tel. (062) 959-231*
- **Peniche Tourism Office**, *Rua Alexandre Herculano, Tel. (062) 789-571*
- **Rio Maior Tourism Office**, *Praça da República, Tel. (061) 941-154*
- **Torres Vedras Tourism Office**, *Rua 9 de Abril, Tel. (061) 314-094*

Travel Agencies

- **Afga Travel**, *Rua Miguel Bombarda, 79, Figueiro da Foz, Tel. (033) 27-777.* A full service travel agency in the heart of Figueiro da Foz (also rents bicycles).
- **Viajens Melia**, *Rua da Sofia, 33, Coimbra, Tel. (039) 205-71.* This travel agency offers all types of reservations and tickets.
- **RN Tours**, *Rua Coronel Sampaio Rio, 3, Leira, Tel. (044) 324-13.* This is the Leira branch office of a large government owned full service travel company.

14. PORTO

The massive city of **Porto** (also called **Oporto**) is located at the mouth of the **Douro River**. With a population of over 470,000 people, Porto is the second largest city in Portugal. At first sight, the city may not seem particularly pretty, but as you explore Porto, its inner beauty will become apparent. Constantly under construction, this major cosmopolitan area is typically noisy, somewhat polluted, and always difficult to drive around (avoid rush hour completely, or better yet arrive in town on Saturday).

HISTORY

Porto's history can be traced back to well before it was known as the Lusitanian village of Portus. During Roman times, the city was an important trading zone on the Douro River. It was connected to its sister city across the Douro River, **Cale** (now called Vila Nova de Gaia), by ferries.

By the 8th century, the area was occupied by both the Swabians and the Moors, but local Christian forces managed to take back control of the area. Soon the city became know by a combination of its two original names (Portus and Cale), Portucale. As the Christian dominated territory grew in size, the entire region under their control became known as Portucale. In 1139, when Afonso Henriques declared himself king of this new nation, Portucale then became the country's official name. Over time, the named changed slightly to the current spelling of Portugal. In the late 14th century, Porto became a major European trading harbor.

It was in this city that Prince Henry the Navigator was born, raised, and began his love of the sea. Henry the Navigator captured Cuerta and Morocco, and the the Age of Discoveries began.

In 1703, the English and Portuguese signed the **Treaty of Metheun**, which lowered taxes on several products including Portuguese wines that were beginning to find a small market in the United Kingdom. Later in the 17th century, a trade dispute stopped the flow of French wines into England, and the British turned to Portugal as its major supplier of wine.

While seeking larger quantities of wine, British merchants set up shipping companies and syndicates that, despite the efforts of the Marquês de Pombal, still control much of the international distribution of Port wine.

In 1809, the Napoleonic troops led by Soult captured Porto but were subsequently routed by Wellington's British troops. The English occupation of Porto lasted 11 years before a popular uprising removed them from power. Several anti-monarchical revolts may have been the catalyst for the eventual abdication of King Dom Manuel II and the proclamation of the republic in Lisbon in 1910.

ARRIVALS & DEPARTURES

By Air

The main airport servicing this region is the Dr. Francisco Sá Carneiro International Airport. It's just a 10 minute ride from downtown Porto. From the airport, the easiest way to get to the city is to take a taxi that should cost no more than 1,275$00 to any downtown location.

Those with minimal luggage looking to save a few dollars can hop on public bus # 56 for about 150$00 a person. The bus goes to the more or less central Praça de Lisboa square from which you can either walk or take a taxi to your final destination.

By Bus

Dozens of buses come to Porto from other Portuguese and European destinations daily, and pull into one of several different bus depots scattered around town. The most frequently used bus stations are located at the Praça D. F. de Lancastre, Rua Alexandre Hurculano, or Rua das Carmelitas in downtown Porto.

• **North Bus Depot**, *Praça D. F. de Lancastre, Tel. (02) 200-3152*
• **South Bus Depot**, *Rua Alexandre Hurculano, Tel. (02) 200-6954*
• **Internorte Bus Depot**, *Praça Galiza, 96, Tel. (02) 693-220*
• **Caima Bus Depot**, *Rua das Carmelitas, 32, Tel. (02) 318-668*
• **Cabanelas Bus Depot**, *Rua da Alegria, Tel. (02) 200-2870*

By Car

The best way to reach Porto by car is to take either the expensive A-1 motorway, or the no-toll, N-1 highway, and get off at the exit for the city's "Centro" (downtown).

• **Avis Rent a Car Porto**, *Rua Guedes Azevedo, 125, Tel. (02) 315-947*
• **Hertz Rent a Car Porto**, *Rua Santa Catarina, 899, Tel. (02) 312-387*
• **Europcar Rent a Car**, *Rua Santa Catarina, 1158, Tel. (02) 318-398*

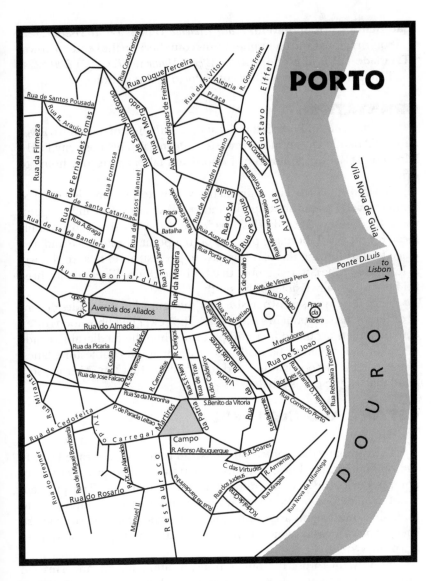

By Train

Although the city has three rail stations, most of the trains that arrive in Porto from Lisbon and other large European cities pull into the Estação de Campanhã Rail Station about 3.5 kilometers (2 miles) east of the city center. Regional and commuter trains stop at the São Bento Rail Station off the Praça Almeida Garret in the middle of the city.

• **Campanha CP Rail Station**, *Rua da Estação, Tel. (02) 564-141*. Most long distance and international trains come to this large station.

• **São Bento CP Rail Station**, *Praça Almeida Garret, Tel. (02) 200-2722.*
Some regional and commuter trains come here, in the center of town.
• **Trindade CP Rail Station**, *Rua. Alferes Malheiro, Tel. (02) 200-5224.*
Trains from northern cities enter Porto at this station.

ORIENTATION

The huge city of Porto is located at the confluence of the Douro River and the Atlantic Ocean in northwestern Portugal. This busy city is 314 kilometers (195 miles) north of Lisbon, and takes about four hours to drive.

Downtown Porto has a distinctively hilly terrain and is centered around several major urban parks and grand squares. I strongly suggest using the famous Avenida dos Aliados and the massive and centrally located Praça da Liberdade plaza as both a point of reference and as a place to start touring the city. It is easy to get lost, and I'm sure you will at least a few times, so remember that both the Douro River and its three bridges are usually visible to the south.

Since the city has grown in size over the centuries, it includes dozens of different districts built in various eras. The newer neighborhoods often contain streets arranged in a grid pattern, while the medieval riverside neighborhoods tend to be made up of winding old cobblestone lanes. These neighborhoods can be hard to locate for first time visitors, so a good map of the city is needed.

GETTING AROUND TOWN
By Bus

The company that controls the bus and tram system is called STCP. Although public bus lines, along with the tram, connect just about every point in Porto, the system is rather difficult to figure out. This problem is not at all helped by the fact that route maps are simply impossible to find. Since most sights are within walking distance, and taxi rides are so cheap, you can easily avoid the bus if you rather not spend the time to learn the system.

If you want to use the public transportation system, any Turismo office can help you with route information before you head off into transportation hell.

When you enter a bus, tell the driver your destination and he will tell you the cost. The average downtown ride is about 175$00. Discount bus fare booklets can be bought at some newsstands, or at kiosks located next to major bus stops. You can purchase books of 20 fares for about 1,500$00, four day tourist passes for about 1,575$00 per person, or seven day passes for about 2,150$00.

By Car

Since parking is almost impossible, navigating around town is rather difficult, and downtown traffic jams are just as bad as in Lisbon, I suggest that you do not bring a car to Porto. If you've rented a car, I suggest parking it at the airport (ask the company you rented from if they will let use their airport parking lot for free) until you leave the city. There are a number of private parking garages in Porto, but they are expensive (around 2,750$00 a day), and car theft has been increasing lately.

By Taxi

Taxis are definitely the preferred method for getting around Porto. Prices for taxis are reasonable, and the drivers are unusually honest. Normal weekday meter rates are used from 6:00am - 10:00pm and start off at 225$00 for the first 350 meters and an additional 15$00 for each 200 meters traveled within the city. A special meter rate is used all day on weekends, holidays, and weekday evenings from 10:00pm - 6:00am and starts off at 275$00 for the first 300 meters and an additional 15$00 for each 150 meters traveled within the city. Taxis may also be hired for sightseeing at the rate of 1,750$00 per hour. A surcharge of 300$00 per ride is allowed for baggage placed in the taxi's trunk or on the roof.

A taxi is usually vacant when the "Taxi" light on top of the cab is illuminated. You can flag them in much the same way you would in any North American city, or you can go to one of many taxi lines and wait your turn. Recently, a law passed that requires all taxis to post price regulations in several languages, including English.

• **Porto Taxi**, *Praça da Liberdade, Tel. (02) 676-093*

By Tram

The company that controls the tram and bus system is called STCP. Although tram lines, along with the buses, connect just about every point in Porto, the system is rather difficult to figure out. This problem is not at all helped by the fact that route maps are simply impossible to find. Since most sights are within walking distance, and taxi rides are so cheap, you can easily avoid the tram if you rather not spend the time to learn the system.

If you want to use the public transportation system, any Turismo office can help you with route information before you head off into transportation hell.

When you enter a train, tell the driver your destination and he will tell you the cost. The average downtown ride is about 175$00.

WHERE TO STAY
Expensive

HOTEL INFANTE DE SAGRES, *Praça D. Filipa de Lancastre, 62. Tel. (02) 200-8101, Fax (02) 314-937. Year round rack rates from 29,000$00, double room, EP. All major credit cards accepted.*

The fantastic Infante de Sagres is the finest deluxe hotel in downtown Porto. This extravagantly decorated formal hotel was first built in 1951 by a local industrialist and has since become a favorite among visiting heads of state, executives, super-models, and rock stars.

All 74 air conditioned rooms and suites are uniquely decorated and offer luxurious private bathrooms, remote control satellite television, double glazed sound-proof windows, mini-bar, direct dial telephone, and lavish traditional Portuguese furnishings. The hotel also has a superb gourmet restaurant, a great formal bar, a private inner courtyard, priceless art and antiques, amazing public lounges, business meeting rooms, an extremely professional staff, an unbeatable location in the center the city, and an unusually quiet and reserved ambiance. Selected as one of my *Best Places to Stay* (see Chapter 10 for more details).

HOTEL SHERATON PORTO, *Ave. Boavista, 1269. Tel. (02) 606-8822, Fax (02) 609-1467. US and Canda bookings with ITT-Sheraton, Tel. 800/325-3535. Year round rack rates from 23,750$00, double room, BP. All major credit cards accepted.*

The Sheraton is an excellent 19 floor American business hotel in the heart of downtown Porto. The hotel offers its guests 251 large rooms and suites, all with air conditioning, deluxe private bathrooms, remote control satellite television, mini-bar, direct dial telephones with computer modem and fax ports, am-fm radio, sound-proofed windows, and nice modern furnishings. There are also dedicated executive and non-smoking floors with rooms that may have private elevator access, mini-safes, special valet services, cordless phones, executive desks, and extra amenities.

The Sheraton also has two restaurants, a piano bar, a fully equipped health club, a heated indoor swimming pool, squash courts, a sauna and Turkish bath, advanced business meeting and conference rooms, newsstand, boutiques, and garage parking. Highly recommended for visiting business people.

IPANEMA PARK HOTEL, *Rua de Serralves, 124. Tel. (02) 610-4174, Fax (02) 610-2809. Year round rack rates from 20,500$00, double room, BP. All major credit cards accepted.*

The Ipanema Park is a welcoming 5 star, modern, high-rise hotel in front of the river in a quiet part of downtown Porto. The hotel has 281 spacious air conditioned rooms and suites with private bathrooms, remote control satellite television, mini-bar, direct dial telephones, am-fm radio, sound-proofed windows, and nice modern furnishings. There are also business meeting rooms, a great restaurant, access to a health club with an indoor swimming pool, a newsstand, and plenty of parking.

Moderate

GRANDE HOTEL DA BATALHA, *Praça de Batalha, 116. Tel. (02) 200-0571, Fax (02) 200-2468. US and Canada bookings with Best Western, Tel. 800/528-1234. Year round rack rates from 19,750$00, double room, BP. Most major credit cards accepted.*

After a massive renovation project, this lovely 4 star executive class hotel near the city's rail station has certainly become one of the best hotels in its price category. There are 149 nice rooms and suites, all with air conditioning, remote control satellite television, mini-bar, direct dial telephones, mini-safes, am-fm radio, sound-proofed windows, and impressive furnishings. The hotel also has specially equipped rooms for the physically challenged as well as non-smokers and female executives.

Facilities include a good regional restaurant, a nice bar, business meeting and conference rooms, parking, and a great staff. Highly recommended for both vacationers and business people.

GRANDE HOTEL DO PORTO, *Rua de Santa Catarina, 197. Tel. (02) 200-8176, Fax (02) 311-061. Year round rack rates from 16,250$00, double room, CP. All major credit cards accepted.*

This old world, 3 star hotel in the heart of Porto's best and most exciting shopping streets is a good choice for those who love wandering around. While it is a bit rough on the edges, the hotel has a really friendly staff and plenty of charm. There are about 100 medium sized air conditioned rooms that have satellite television, mini-bar, direct dial telephones, and simple furnishings. Facilities include bar, restaurant, and nearby parking.

HOTEL DO IMPERIO, *Rua da Batalha, 127. Tel. (02) 200-6861, Fax (02) 200-6009. Year round rack rates from 14,500$00, double room, EP. Most major credit cards accepted.*

This is a relatively good and basic 3 star tourist class hotel near the heart of town. It has 100 nice and big rooms with private bathrooms. Facilities include a bar, restaurant, and parking.

HOTEL BOA VISTA, *Esplanada do Castelo. Tel. (02) 617-3818, Fax (02) 208-3882. Year round rack rates from 14,000$00, double room, CP. Most major credit cards accepted.*

This old, river view mansion is located in the Foz district. It offers 39 large, comfortable air conditioned rooms with private bathrooms, television, and direct dial telephones. There is also a great restaurant with a panoramic view, a bar, a swimming pool, a gym, a sauna, and friendly service.

PENSÃO REX, *Praça da República, 117. Tel. (02) 208-3882. Year round rack rates from 13,250$00, double room, EP. Cash only - No credit cards accepted.*
This unusual converted mansion in the city center offers minimal services, a great location, and 21 or so unique rooms with private bathrooms.

Inexpensive

HOTEL PENINSULAR, *Rua Sa da Bandeira, 21. Tel. (02) 200-3012. Year round rack rates from 9,750$00, double room, EP. Cash only - No credit cards accepted.*
This fairly good 2 star hotel near the São Bento rail station has 59 comfortable rooms with private bathrooms, mini-bars, and TV.

PENSÃO PÃO DE AÇUCAR, *Rua do Almada, 262. Tel. (02) 200-2425. Year round rack rates from 8,550$00, double room, EP. Cash only - No credit cards accepted.*
A nice 3 star art deco inn, it has over 40 good rooms with private bathrooms in a central part of town. This is a good budget choice if rooms are available.

PENSÃO UNIVERSAL, *Ave. dos Aliados, 38. Tel. (02) 200-6758. Year round rack rates from 5, 750$00, double room, EP. Cash only - No credit cards accepted.*
This inexpensive budget hotel has some great views and is in a central location. It's a bit noisy and far from deluxe, but at these prices what do you expect!

WHERE TO EAT

Expensive

PORTUCALE, *Rua da Alegria, 598. Tel. (02) 570-717. Dress code is semi-formal. Most major credit cards accepted.*
An excellent, formal restaurant with great food, excellent service, an impressive wine list, and the best views of Porto imaginable. You must call for a reservation and expect to spend at least 3,950$00 a person plus wine.

DONA FILIPA RESTAURANTE, *Hotel Infante Sagres, Praça D. Filipa de Lancastre. Tel. (02) 200-8101. Dress code is semi-formal. All major credit cards accepted.*
This beautiful and formal restaurant is located in the Infante de Sagres Hotel. It serves some of the finest cuisine in the city. Specialties change daily and are a fusion of both Portuguese and French cuisine. My last dinner here was superb and cost just under 5,250$00.

Moderate

CASA FILHA MAE PRETA, *Cais da Ribeira, 39. Tel. (02) 315-515. No dress code. Most major credit cards accepted.*

This is a good, local seafood restaurant that serves excellent fried fillets. The location is just off the river in the old part of town. The service is friendly, and a filling seafood meal will only cost around 1,900$00 a person.

O BECO PUB AND RESTAURANTE, *Rua Padre L. Cabral, 974. Tel. (02) 618-5601. Dress code is smart casual. Most major credit cards accepted.*

O Beco is a charming old converted house in the Foz area with several rustic dining rooms and a terraced patio. The traditional cuisine and the service is good. The average bill is about 1,975$00 a head plus drinks.

Inexpensive

TAVERNA DE BEBOBOS, *Cais da Ribeira, 21. Tel. (02) 313-565. No dress code. Cash only - No credit cards accepted.*

This dimly lit antique tavern is full of charm and good fish meals. Located in the old part of town along the river, it is perhaps the restaurant with the most atmosphere. A great dinner here should cost no more than 1,300$00 plus wine.

CHEZ LAPIN, *Rua dos Canatreiros, 40. Tel. (02) 310-291. No dress code. Cash only - No credit cards accepted.*

One of the more popular Ribeira establishments serving good food in a nautical environment. The tiny restaurant is rustically decorated. A good value considering most dishes are less than 1,250$00 each.

CONFEITARIA DE BOLHÃO, *Rua Formosa, 339. Tel. (02) 200-9291. No dress code. Cash only - No credit cards accepted.*

This wonderful bakery has a downstairs restaurant with a rustic and traditional ambiance. Lunch costs around 975$00 a person and is a real delight.

SEEING THE SIGHTS

Begin exploring the city of Porto in the heart of the city. I recommend an early start at the narrow park in the middle of Avenida dos Aliados. On this avenue, you can find parking meters and nearby parking lots (marked with a big P). If you're staying in town for the night, leave your car at the hotel's parking lot and take a taxi or a bus to this point. From the Avenida dos Aliados you will see the bell tower topped **City Hall** (Câmara Municipal). It's worth a short visit, but is closed on weekends.

You may want to head into the Turismo office just to the left (west) of City Hall on *Rua Clube dos Feniados, 25, open 9am daily, Sundays 10am.*

At the Turismo, you can get a copy of a map of Porto, list of current events, and a tourist guide.

As you look down the avenue you will see several 19th century buildings that lead to the **Praça da Liberdade**. Facing the front of city hall, you should turn right (east) onto Rua Formosa and walk a block or so to the lively market called the **Bolhão**. This marketplace (closed Saturday afternoon and Sunday) sells mostly seafood, meats, and produce, but there are some small boutiques with fine jewelry as well. If you wish, you can find excellent breads, olives, cold Vinho Verde wine, and fresh cheeses for a great picnic a bit later.

Nearby the Bolhão market is the wonderful **Confeitaria de Bolhão** bakery, *Rua Formosa, 339*, where you can find strong coffee and great pastries. A couple of blocks further west is the famed **merchant street** of Rua de Santa Catarina with a fascinating assortment of fine shops. This street has the best shopping for high quality men's and women's clothing, leather goods, jewelry, and antiques. I buy all of my European made ties and scarves on this street at about half of what they cost at home.

After a nice stroll around Rua de Santa Catarina, head back to the city hall area. If you're interested in buying local vintage wines (or are just curious), stop in at **Casa Januario**, *Rua do Bonjardim, 352*. From Avenida dos Aliados, head towards the statues in **Praça da Liberdade**. From the square you can walk one block south to **Estação de São Bento** train station. The interior of the train station is beautifully covered in azulejos. After looking at the train station, cross the street and walk through the **Praça Almeida Garret** to Rua das Flores. On Rua das Flores you will find yourself in front of the 16th century **Misericórdia** church. While in the church, go to the offices next door to see the beautiful Renaissance painting of the royal family with Jesus.

From the train station, cross the Largo de São Domingos and head south onto the Rua Ferreira Borges to the **Mercado Ferreira Borges**. The enclosed kiosk stalls are packed on the 2nd and 4th Saturday morning of each month for the **Vandoma** fair.

At the end of the street is the **Praça do Infante Dom Henrique**. The Gothic 14th century church, **Igreja de São Fransisco**, and its unforgettable vaulted baroque interior, is located here. Adjacent to the church you will find **Palácio da Bolsa**, now home of the **Porto Stock Exchange**. This 19th century structure has a few grand rooms that can be visited, including the richly decorated Arabian hall.

For most people, it's time to take a break. Head south to Rua Nova da Afândega until you reach the riverfront area known as the **Ribeira**. The stone streets and maze-like alleys of the Ribeira haven't changed much in centuries. Look inside the **Center of Traditional Arts and Crafts**, *Rua da Reboleira, 37*. Arts and crafts are for sale at reasonable prices.

On the way to the river front, take a seat on the benches near the rotating cube statue in **Praça da Ribeira**. It's a nice rest and you can amuse yourself by watching children chasing stray cats against the backdrop of old colored ceramic facades. From here, it's just steps away to both the esplanade and the lower level of the **Cais da Ribeira**. There are several stalls in front of the river that sell assorted tourist items if you're looking for souvenirs. Make sure to wander around the ancient streets of Rua Lada and Rua de Cima do Muro just behind the Cais de Ribeira.

The Ribeira has several great inexpensive fish restaurants that serve the largest portions you could imagine. If you brought a picnic lunch, you can carefully cross the upper level of the **Ponte Dom Luís** bridge and have lunch on one of the benches along the river. You will have a panoramic view of the Douro River and old Porto.

From the Ribeira, you can see the bridges that lead to the Port wine caves in **Vila Nova de Guia** including the iron bridge, **Ponte Maria Pia**, designed by Eiffel. After lunch I suggest a stop or two in the **Port wine caves**. Several world famous Port Wine producers such as Sandeman, Calem, and Taylor offer free tours and wine tasting (see Vila Nova de Gaia section).

After you've had a good lunch, a couple of glasses of assorted Port wines, and a good rest, you will be ready to cross the bridge back to Porto. When you come off the bridge, head up Ave. de Vimera Peres to the **Sé Cathedral**. This 12th century fortress and church was modified considerably in the 17th and 18th centuries by Manuel Teixeira, Manuel Guedes, and Nicolau Nasoni. Its interior boasts a Gothic cloister and several baroque elements while its main entrance includes both a pink Romanesque window and a baroque entrance.

Just around the corner from the church you will find the **Museu Guerra Junqueiro**. The museum exhibits rare 15th and 16th century tapestries, pottery, furniture, gold and silver. This building was designed by the Italian architect, Nicolau Nasoni.

If you're interested in a good view of the town, head back to the base of **Praça da Liberdade**, turn left (west) onto Rua dos Clérigos. You will come to a church and tower, **Torre de Clérigos**. This highly unusual Baroque and rococo church was also designed Nasoni in the mid-17th century. The church itself is renowned for its highly detailed carved granite facade. The 249 foot tower (closed on Wednesdays) was built during the same period, and has a long stairway. From the stairway you have a superb panoramic view of the city and the surrounding area.

For those of you who are interested in wine tasting and want a special treat, take a taxi over to the **Solar do Vinho do Porto** (closed on Sundays). Located in the river front mansion known as **Quinta da Macieirinha**, *Rua de Entre Quintas, 220,* this beautiful exposed beam and granite bar is a great place to relax after a long day of sightseeing. Most of the staff are too shy to speak English, but the wine menu is easy to understand. You can sample over 105 vintage Ports by the glass in a truly remarkable atmosphere. The Quinta was once the residence of King Carlos Alberto of Sardinia, and is home to the **Romantic Museum** exhibiting his unusual household items.

From here you can take a taxi to the western part of town known as the **Foz** district, around the **Praça de Zarco Goncalves**. Besides the **Foz de Douro** beaches, there is the **Castelo de Queijo** (Castle of Cheese). Stroll down Ave. de Montevideu towards the beautiful **Esplanada de 28 de Maio**, which overlooks the rocky riverfront. From the river front, you can walk several blocks inland and admire some huge mansions as you can walk to the beautiful gardens at **Jardim do Passeio Alegre** and the old **Forte de São João de Foz**.

If you walk a few more blocks toward the bridges you will come to the historic **Farol de São Miguel** lighthouse.

NIGHTLIFE & ENTERTAINMENT

As you might expect from any large city, Porto has a fair amount of evening activities. The many students in town tend to go to the small and crowded bars and clubs a block or so behind the Cais da Ribeira like **Postigo do Carvão**. Several other clubs are located across the river in **Vila Nova de Guia** just off Largo Miguel Bombarda.

The section of town known as the **Foz** is home to several larger clubs and pubs such as **Bonaparte** and **Twins**. Ask your hotel's concierge or a local student to tell you about the latest "in" place.

SHOPPING

Porto is full of shopping possibilities. The streets just east of Avenida dos Aliados contain lots of great stores. Rua de Santa Catarina is perhaps the most centralized shopping street in Porto.

You can find excellent gold and silver work in some of the fine stores listed below. Since the fine filigree of Portugal comes from nearby **Gondomar**, you can get great deals on these items in Porto's shops. I also have found unique calfskin wallets with unusual linings for as little as 3,200$00.

I suggest a lot of comparison shopping before you make a final decision on any large ticket item. Don't forget to inquire about the **Tax Free** refund voucher discussed under Shopping, Chapter 7, *Basic Information*. There are a few shopping centers that are open until midnight, but bargains take a lot of work to find.

These are just a few of my favorite shops in Porto that offer great products at good prices:

Dom Manuel Joias, *Store 53-Centro Brasília*. The best values in fine gold and precious stone jewelry. Have a look at the women's 19 karat gold rings with diamonds and emeralds for under 50,000$00 after the tax rebate. The very helpful English speaking staff will cut deals.

Vista Alegre, *Rua Candido dos Reis, 18*. If you like fine porcelain, this is the best place in town. The original Vista Alegre pieces are among the finest in Europe. They make great special gifts, but are not cheap.

Joias Rolando, *Praça Mouzinho Albuqurque, 83*. A great place to find filigree silver and gold pieces including sterling silver filigree perfume bottles for 3,400$00 each. No pressure tactics here.

Amazenes Marquês Soares, *Rua de Santa Catarina, 21*. Lots of men's and women's wear and accessories at great prices.

Shopping Centers

Some stores are open on Sundays as well, especially in the Brasília and Dallas shopping centers. These centers are usually open from 10am until midnight, Monday through Saturday:

- **Brasília**, *Praça Mouzinho Albuqurque*
- **Dallas**, *Ave. Boavista, 1616*
- **Clérigos**, *Rua dos Clérigos*
- **Foz**, *Ave. Brazil*
- **Aviz**, *Ave. Boavista*

PRACTICAL INFORMATION FOR PORTO

Emergency & Useful Phone Numbers

- **Emergency Assistance** (S.O.S.), *Tel. 115*
- **Porto Police**, *Tel. (02) 200-6821*
- **Porto Fire Dept.**, *Tel. (02) 484-121*
- **São João Hospital**, *Alamada Prof. H. Monteiro, Tel. (02) 487-151*
- **Santo António Hospital**, *Largo Prof. Abel Salazar, (02) 200-7354*
- **A.C.P. in Porto** (Emergency road services), *(02) 830-1127*
- **Directory Assistance**, *Tel. 118*
- **Pedros Rubras Airport** (15 km out of town), *Tel. (02) 948-2141*
- **T.A.P.Airlines Porto**, *Praça Mouz. Albuqurque, 105, Tel. (02) 600-5555*
- **T.W.A. Airlines Porto**, *Rua Julio Dinis, 585, Tel. (02) 600-0873*
- **US Embassy in Porto**, *Rua Julio Dinis, 826, Tel. (02) 690-008*
- **Main Post Office**, *Praça Gen. H. Delgado, Tel. (02) 208-0251*

Directory of Museums & Monuments

• **Eng. António de Almeida Museum**, *Rua Tenente Valadim, 231, Tel. (02) 667-481*. Contains collections of ancient coins, 17th and 18th century Portuguese and French furniture, 17th century paintings, antique porcelain from China, Persian tapestries. Open 2:30pm until 5:30pm. Closed on Sundays and holidays.

• **Botany Institute, and Botanical Garden of Dr. Gonçalo Sampaio**, *Rua de Campo Alegre, 1191, Tel. (02) 698-134*. Contains a museum, library, laboratory, and huge botanical garden. Open 9am until 12am, Monday through Saturday by appointment only. Closed on Sundays and holidays.

• **Câmara Municipal (City Hall)**, *Praça Gen. Humberto Delgado, Tel. (02) 200-9871*. Open 8:30am until 12pm and 2pm until 5pm, Monday through Friday. Closed Saturdays, Sundays, and holidays.

• **António Carneiro House & Museum**, *Rua de António Carneiro, 363, Tel. (02) 579-668*. Contains collections of António Carneiro paintings and drawings. Open 10am until 12pm and 2pm until 5:30pm, Tuesday through Friday. Open 2pm until 6pm on Saturday. Closed on Sundays, Mondays, and holidays.

• **Ethnological Museum of Porto**, *Palácio de São João Novo, Tel. (02) 200-2010*. Contains collections of ethnological and archeological objects from the region including wine making equipment, costumes, handicrafts, and litho instruments. Open 10am until 12pm and 2pm until 5pm. Closed on Sundays, Mondays, and holidays.

• **Casa do Infante**, *Rua da Afândega, Tel. (02) 316-025*. The restored birthplace of Prince Henry the Navigator. Open sporadically with special temporary exhibits.

• **Guerra Junqueiro House & Museum**, *Rua D. Hugo, 12, Tel. (02) 213-644*. Contains collections of art collected by this famous poet including ceramics, jewelry, paintings, furniture, textiles, pottery, and carvings. Open 10am until 12pm and 2pm until 5pm, Tuesday through Saturday. Closed on Sundays, Mondays, and holidays.

• **Military Museum of Porto**, *Rua do Heroismo, 329, Tel. (02) 565-514*. Contains collections of military equipment from the past up until World War I. Open 2pm until 5pm, Wednesdays through Monday. Closed on Tuesdays and holidays.

• **Modern Art Museum**, *Rua de Serralves, 977, Tel. (02) 680-057*. Contains collections of paintings, sculpture, jewelry, and photography. Open 2pm until 8pm, Tuesday through Sunday. Closed on Mondays and holidays.

• **Palácio da Bolsa**, *Rua Ferreira Borges, Tel. (02) 200-4497*. Contains several gilded halls and a collection of fine jewelry. Open 9am until

12pm and 2pm until 5:30pm, Monday through Friday. Closed on Saturdays and Sundays.

- **Romantic Museum**, *Rua Entre-Quintas, 220*. Contains a collections of 19th century furniture and unusual household items. Open 10am until 12pm and 2pm until 5pm, Tuesday through Saturday. Closed on Sundays, Mondays, and holidays.
- **Sé Cathedral**, *Terreiro da Sé, Tel. (02) 314-837*. Open 9am until 12pm and 3pm until 6pm daily.
- **Museum Soares dos Reis**, *Rua de Dom Manuel II, Tel. (02) 200-7110*. Contains collections of António Soares dos Reis sculptures, international paintings from the 16th-19th century, ceramics, gold, silver, furniture, and ceramics. Open 10am until 12pm and 2pm until 5pm. Closed on Sundays, Mondays, and Holidays
- **Torre dos Clérigos**, *Rua dos Clérigos, Tel. (02) 200-1729*. Contains a 225 step staircase that leads to a panoramic view of Porto. Open 10am until 12pm and 2pm until 5pm, Thursday to Tuesday. Closed on Wednesdays and holidays.

Tourist Information & Tour Options

If you have any tourist questions, contact the **Porto Tourist Office**, *Rua Clube dos Feniano, 25, Tel. (02) 312-470*.

An assortment of half, full, and multiple day guided motorcoach and barge tours are offered by several leading companies and offer a good first look at Porto. Reservations should be booked directly with the tour operator, by contacting your travel agent, or by visiting a local Portuguese agency in the city you are visiting. The following is a selection of tours I've enjoyed. Two good tours in particular are:

RN Tours, *Tel. (02) 382-303, about 4800/$00 per person*, offers the following tour:

- **Four hour Porto Panoramico Tour**: Includes visits to the Cais da Ribeira, Foz beach front, Crystal Palace, Palácio da Bolsa, Sé cathedral, and Vila Nova de Guia with a wine cave visit. Departs at 9:30am every day.

Endouro Cruise Lines, *Tel. (02) 324-236, about 1900$00 per person*, offers the following tour:

- **One hour Four Bridges Tour**: The ferry departs from Cais da Ribeira and you travel on the Douro River and see great panoramic views of old Porto and Vila Nova de Guia. Departs several times daily.

There's also the **12 hour Marvelous Douro Tour**, *about 18,000$00 per person*. The vessel departs from Cais da Ribeira. Breakfast is served on the way to Régua, you tour the Crestuma dam, taste Portugues wine, have lunch on board, tour the Carrapatelo area, disembark in Peso da Régua and take a first class train back to Porto. Departs several times each month.

Endouro offers several overnight Douro barge cruises that are quite good and include a river view cabin and all meals. Contact Endouro for more information.

Travel Agencies

- **Star Travel**, *Ave. dos Aliases, 210, Tel. (02) 200-3637.* A large travel company with nice staff who can be helpful with all types of bookings.
- **Mapa Mundo**, *Rua Sá de Bandeira, 784, Tel. (02) 310-129.* A well established tour operator and travel agency with full service capabilities.
- **ACP-Porto**, *Rua da Santa Catarina, 848, Tel. (02) 200-2499.* A large full service agency with special rates for better hotels, cars, and city tours.

15. THE COSTA VERDE

The **Costa Verde**, or Green Coast, is in the northwestern section of Portugal and has **Douro** and **Minho** provinces, the cities of Porto and Braga, and a tiny slice of northwestern **Trás-os-Montes** within its borders. Many mountains, valleys, and rivers surround the Costa Verde's major population areas. The land in this region is fertile, and much of Portugal's wine production occurs here. Within the last several years, a major increase in industry has resulted in an increase in the population.

Many of Portugal's oldest and most established families originated in the Costa Verde and maintain magnificent estates and quintas (manor houses), many of which are know bed and breakfast inns. Steam engine narrow gauge railroads still occasionally run near the banks of the wide **Duoro River** and the adjacent valley. It is on the banks of this river that the famous Port wine vineyards are cultivated, crushed, aged, and later transported to Porto for worldwide export.

Among the many interesting places to visit are the rich and regal cities of **Ponte de Lima** and **Viana do Castelo**, the former capital city of **Guimarães**, the quaint and tranquil village of **Amarante**, the bizarre and mystical church of **Bom Jesus** near **Braga**, the historic market town of **Barcelos**, the northern fortified border towns of **Monção** and **Melgaço**, the unforgettable **Peneda-Gerês Parque Nacional**, the wonderful city of **Porto** (Chapter 14, *Porto*), and of course **Vila Nova de Gaia**, to taste a Port wine at a caves.

ARRIVALS & DEPARTURES
By Air

Most visitors to this part of Portugal fly into the Dr. Francisco Sá Carneiro International Airport some 15 kilometers outside of Porto.

From this airport, the best way to get to various destinations in this region is to either rent a car or pre-arrange a transfer from your travel agent. A taxi ride to most points in this region from the airport will be rather expensive.

Those with minimal luggage looking for a less expensive way to reach the resorts, historic villages, and major cities of the Costa Verde can take public bus # 56 from the airport to downtown Porto and transfer to one of several bus and rail routes that proceed to over 58 different Costa Verde destinations.

The Turismo office in the airport's international arrivals area will be glad to give you current schedules and price information on most regional buses and trains.

ORIENTATION

This small region, full of Roman era villages and sprawling industrialized cities, runs along the coast just below the city of Porto and continues upward for about 113 kilometers (70 miles) until it reaches the Minho River, Portugal's border with Spain.

GETTING AROUND THE REGION

By Bus

There are a number of private bus companies with routes throughout the Costa Verde. As with the trains, Porto is the main connecting point for the region.

By Car

Driving around the Costa Verde is easy during the day. The biggest problem you'll have, particularly in the rural areas, is a series of poorly lit, winding country roads full of slow moving trucks that are too dangerous to pass.

Other than in the cities of Porto and Braga, rush hour is not much of an issue and street parking is easy to locate.

By Train

There is a good network of regional rail lines that service the Costa Verde, and most tend to use Porto as a main connecting point. The most common links to the resort areas and major cities in this region are the commuter trains that go in and out of Porto's centrally located Estação de São Bento Rail Station.

ESPINHO

Over the past several decades, Espinho has become the summer getaway for a large numbers of tourists from Portugal and northern Europe. The long strip of white sandy beaches that stretches over the western edge of town are completely packed in the warmer months.

Besides being home to Portugal's oldest golf course, Espinho has several attractions including a large municipal swimming pool, several tennis facilities, a **casino** (bring your passport), and some fairly nice cobblestone lanes with benches.

Espinho offers very little charm, but that hasn't stopped the hordes of Dutch and German tourists from filling almost all its hotels during July and August.

ARRIVALS & DEPARTURES

By Car
Espinho is about 19 km south of Porto off the A-1 highway.

By Train
• **Espinho CP Rail station**, *Ave. 8, (02) 720-087*

ORIENTATION
The city is laid out on a grid of parallel odd numbered streets that run from east to west and intersect north to south even numbered streets.

WHERE TO STAY

Expensive
HOTEL SOLVERDE, *N-109, Praia da Granja. Tel. (02) 726-111.*

This nice 5 star ocean front hotel is just a few kilometers north of crowded Espinho on Praia da Granja. Facilities include three pools, tennis, squash, golf, restaurants, and a disco.

HOTEL PRAIAGOLFE, *Rua 6, Espinho. Tel. (02) 720-630.*

This large modern 4 star hotel is located near the ocean. The hotel offers nice rooms (many with ocean views), a large health club, pool, sauna, restaurant, disco and golf discounts.

Moderate
HOTEL APARTAMENTO SOLVERDE, *Rua 21, Espinho. Tel. (02) 722-819.*

This beach front property has 83 apartments (many with ocean views) with kitchens. Although facilities are fairly limited, this is a good choice for families.

Inexpensive
VILA MARIA, *Rua 62, Espinho. Tel. (02) 720-353.*

This red 19th century mansion rents five comfortable rooms with private bathrooms. The house is in a garden setting just five blocks from the beach.

WHERE TO EAT

Expensive
BAIA MAR, *Rua 4, #565, Tel. (02) 725-415.*

Baia Mar is a large well known restaurant with views right near the casino. The menu is a bit pricey, but the meals are impressive. Try the excellent fresh seafood.

Moderate

PIPOLIM, *Rua 19, #768, Tel. (02) 725-305.*

This tile covered narrow restaurant serves excellent fish and meat dishes that are prepared with great care. Try their incredible cod fish.

LAREIRA RESTAURANTE, *Rua 62, #592, Tel. (02) 727-980.*

Small and traditional, this restaurant has good daily seafood specials, live Fado music on weekends, excellent house wine, and a friendly staff.

SEEING THE SIGHTS

The busy outdoor **mercado** (market), *Rua 16,* is right in the center of town and open every Monday. There are seasonal bullfights at the **Praça de Touros**, *Rua 41,* in the southern sector of the city.

The best beaches in the area can be found at **Praia da Granja**, *about 4 km north of Espinho,* and at **Praia de Esmoriz**, *6 km south of town.* Make sure that the blue flag for clean water is up on any beach you want to swim at because the area is notorious for pollution.

SPORTS & RECREATION

Golf

Espinho has the oldest golf course in Portugal.

• **Porto Golf Club**, *Espinho, Tel. (02) 722-008*

EXCURSIONS & DAY TRIPS

When you've had your fill of beaches and want some cultural diversion, I suggest a nice day trip to the historic **castelo** (castle) at the old Roman town of **Santa Maria da Feira**. From Espinho, follow route N-109-4 south for about 19 km or so to reach this amazing town. When you arrive, you can't miss the dramatic 11th century Gothic **Castelo da Feira** that looms above.

A wonderful walkway takes you around the castle grounds and to several towers, a great panoramic view of the region, and the massive **Torre de Menagem** keep. In the keep, there's a remarkable grand hall that was rebuilt in the 15th century.

VILA NOVA DE GAIA

The suburban industrial city of Vila Nova de Gaia is on the southern bank of the **Douro River**, just across from Porto. Known primarily for its world famous Port wine **caves** and lodges (warehouses), this city has played an important role in the production and distribution of Port wines since the 17th century.

ARRIVALS & DEPARTURES
By Train
• **Vila Nova de Gaia CP Rail station**, *Rua de Estação, Tel. (02) 304-961*

WHERE TO STAY
Expensive
GAIAHOTEL, *Ave. da República, 2038. Tel. (02) 396-051.*

An ultramodern 4 star hotel, the Gaiahotel has 92 deluxe rooms in the center of the city. Facilities include a fancy health club, restaurant, minibars, shopping center, and a garage.

HOTEL CASA BRANCA PRAIA, *Rua da Belgica-Afurada. Tel. (02) 781-3691.*

This modern 4 star, 56 room, resort hotel is near the beach at Praia de Lavadores, 5 km south of Vila Nova de Gaia. Facilities include health club, pool, tennis, restaurant.

Moderate
QUINTA SÃO SALVADOR, *Oliveira do Douro. Tel. (02) 309-222.*

This beautiful manor house is located just out of town and has seven beautiful guest rooms with private bathrooms, minibars, and cable TV. Horseback riding facilities are available for guests.

HOTEL IBIS, *Lugar de Chas-Afurada. Tel. (02) 781-4242.*

Hotel Ibis is a French owned, 2 star, chain motel with comfortable and well equipped modern rooms and an indoor pool. Located just outside of town in the Afurada district.

Inexpensive
RESIDENCIAL ORLA MARATIMA, *Praia da Madelena, Tel. (02) 711-6080.*

This is a restaurant that offers a few simple and comfortable rooms with private bath. Besides good rooms, the dinners are reasonable and hearty.

WHERE TO EAT
Moderate
RESTAURANTE CARPA, *Ave. da República, 1731. Tel. (02) 397-129.*

Located in the center of downtown, this simple restaurant serves good seafood and meat dishes. Specialties include fresh shrimp and grilled meats.

Inexpensive
RESIDENCIAL ORLA MARATIMA, *Praia da Madelena, Tel. (02) 711-6080.*
This restaurant serves reasonable and hearty dinners.

SEEING THE SIGHTS
There are several river front warehouses that offer 20 minute guided tours, in your language of choice, of their Port wine casks and bottling facilities (closed Sundays). After the tour, you will be invited to taste a few small glasses of complimentary red and white Port wines. If you want, you can spend an entire afternoon tasting wines from one cave to the next. You can purchase vintage bottles directly from the caves at reasonable prices. Make sure to taste at least one dry white Port wine.

Besides the wine trade, there are only a few other attractions in **Vila Nova de Gaia**. There is a 16th century beautiful church, the **Convento da Serra do Pillar**, on a hill above the city. Its location offers a great panoramic view over Porto, but I have never seen the church open to the public.

For art lovers, there is the **Museu de Teixeira Lopes**, *Rua Teixeira Lopes, 32* (closed Mondays). The collection consists mainly of sculptures by both the museum's namesake and Diogo de Macedo.

There are a few reasonably attractive beach areas just south of town at **Madalena, Valadares,** and **Praia de Lavadores**. You can find inexpensive meals at the restaurants near these beaches.

NIGHTLIFE & ENTERTAINMENT
There are several small bars and clubs just behind the river front wine caves as well as on Largo Miguel Bombarda. These bars and clubs are full in the evening with hundreds of people.

SPORTS & RECREATION
Golf
• **Miramar Golf Club**, Valadares, *Tel.* (02) 762-2067

Horseback Riding
• **Quinta São Salvador**, *Oliveira do Douro, Tel. (02) 309-222*

DOURO RIVER TOWNS
Most tourists never get to the small towns and wine producing villages that line the banks of the Douro River. This is one of the most tranquil and beautiful areas you can imagine.

In the old days, many small wooden vessels would sail up and down the river to bring fresh Port wines to Vila Nova de Gaia for further fermentation and eventual bottling. Now the river has been dammed up, resulting in several man made lakes and beaches.

ARRIVALS & DEPARTURES

By Car

The advantage of a car is that you can take your time and stop where you like. In *Seeing the Sights*, I suggest where you should drive and towns for you to stop in.

By Train

There is a great train line that runs from Porto's São Bento station east to **Livração**, then south up the Douro River's northern bank to **Peso da Régua** and points further east. The three hour ride to Peso da Régua is quite interesting as it passes through wine country. There are also seasonal connections from Livração to Amarante by historic narrow gauge railroads. The future of these narrow guage railroads is somewhat in doubt.

Contact the **São Bento CP Rail station** in Porto at *Tel. (02) 200-2722* for further details, or visit any Turismo in the north.

By Boat

Endouro cruise lines offers excursions up river from Porto to Peso de Régua. These ferry cruises are a relaxing alternative to the car and train routes, but do not allow for much in the way of local wine tasting and water sport activities. Endouro can be reached in Porto by calling *Tel. (02) 324-236* or *Tel. (02) 208-4161*.

WHERE TO STAY

Moderate

QUINTA DA LOMBA, *N-222, Lomba. Tel. (055) 663-36. Their main number is Tel. (02) 482-714.*

This fantastic 18th century manor house on the south bank of the Douro River is owned by a charming English speaking retired doctor. Facilities include tennis, jet skis, water-skiing, pool, sauna, grill area, and six luxury rooms and apartments. The staff are local peasant women.

CASA DAS TORRES DE OLIVEIRA, *Oliveira. Tel. (054) 237-43.*

This wine producing estate and 18th century regal manor house is about 9 km northeast of Mesão Frio. It has four rooms with private bathrooms. Facilities include bar, dining room, pool, bicycles, gardens, TV room, and parking.

CASA DO LARANJAL, *N-108, Porto Manso. Tel. (055) 551-232.*

This olive oil producing estate is located on the north bank of the Douro River near Penha Longa. It has five rooms with semi-private bathrooms. Facilities include lounge, gardens, winery, boats, fishing, TV room, ping pong, and parking.

QUINTA DO PAÇO, *N-600, Vila Marim. Tel. (054) 699-346.*

This historic 18th century manor house is 4 km north of Mesão Frio. They have four rooms with private bathrooms for rent. Facilities include bar, gardens, pool, billiards, and TV room.

CASA DOS VARAIS, *N-2, Lamego. Tel. (054) 232-51.*

This relaxing 18th century manor house and wine growing estate offers three rooms with private bathrooms. It's located near town and has views of the southern bank of the Douro River.

CASA DE SÃO PEDRO, *N-108, Santa Marinha. Tel. (054) 981-14.*

Five rooms with private bathrooms are available in this 17th century stone house near the river. Facilities include lounge, dining room, gardens, TV room, and parking.

HOTEL PANORAMA, *Mesão Frio. Tel. (054) 992-36.*

This nice, modern, 31 room hotel is in the heart of town and has a bar, restaurant, and parking.

ESTALAGEM SANTIAGO, *Aboinha-Gondomar. Tel. (02) 984-0034.*

This reasonable 4 star inn has 14 guest rooms in the village of Aboinha. Facilities include a good restaurant, bar, TV room, disco, parking, and direct dial phones.

CASA DEFRONTE, *N-108, Entre Os Rios. Tel. (055) 634-84.*

Casa Defronte is a granite manor house, near the Crestuma-Lever dam, that rents one large three bedroom apartment and a comfortable two bedroom apartment.

WHERE TO EAT
Moderate

PORTA DO RIO, *Marginal-Gondomar. Tel. (02) 964-3032.*

This unassuming river front restaurant off Ave. Clube Cacadores in Gondomar offers great views, good service, and reasonably priced fresh fish and seafood.

SEEING THE SIGHTS

From Porto, take Route N-209 east through **Gondomar**. Continue for about 7 km until you reach the Douro River and the memorable Route 108. This road continues up the Duoro River to the lovely countryside near **Mesão Frio** and onward to **Peso da Régua** (see Chapter 16, *Montanhas*). You can take this beautiful route up the river and cross one of several dams to the almost forgotten southern bank and Route N-222. This road winds its way back to the Port wine vineyards of **Lamego** and back into Porto through Vila Nova de Guia.

On the southern bank of the Douro, some 20 minutes southeast Porto, is the lovely town of **Lomba**. This sleepy peasant town is home to traditional folks who are not used to seeing many tourists. You will also find several dams and reservoirs including the **Barragem de Crestuma** and you can water-ski and sail in this part of the river. Just in front of the river at Lomba is a fantastic manor house, **Quinta da Lomba**, where you can rent opulent rooms and grand apartments.

As you pass the dams on the river, you will see many people enjoying water sports like windsurfing, jet skiing, water-skiing, sailing, and swimming. The small villages contain original stone houses and many of the local residents use mules and oxen as transportation. I strongly recommend the Lomba area for those who wish to visit Porto, but prefer to be a bit away from the noise, pollution, traffic, and over-priced accommodations in the city.

AMARANTE

The peaceful town of Amarante is divided by the Tâmega River and has an 18th century granite bridge, the Ponte de São Gonçalo. Surrounded by the Serra do Marão mountains, every view from Amarante is impressive. This river front is one of my favorite picnic sights in the region.

ARRIVALS & DEPARTURES
By Car
Amarante is about 67 km northeast of Porto on Route IP-4 east.

By Train
• **Amarante CP Rail station**, *Rua Candido dos Reis, Tel. (055) 422-608*

WHERE TO STAY
Moderate
POUSADA DE SÃO GONÇALO, *Curva do Lancete-Ansiaes. Tel. (055) 461-113.*

Situated about 17 km east of town, this pousada offers 15 rustic rooms with dramatic views of the Serra de Marão mountains and is a peaceful place to stay.

CASA DE PASCOAES, *São João de Gatão. Tel. 055) 422-595.*

This fine historic manor house is located along the Tâmega River off Route N-210 about 3 km north of Amarante. It has four guest rooms decorated with antiques, and all rooms come with private bathrooms. Facilities include dining room, lounge, library, museum, billiards, TV, and parking.

HOTEL NAVARRAS, *Rua António Carneiro. Tel. (055) 424-036.*

A modern 3 star hotel in the heart of town, Hotel Navarras has 63 good sized air conditioned rooms, a restaurant, bar, roof top pool, garage, cable TV, and direct dial phones.

Inexpensive

HOTEL SILVA, *Rua Candido do Reis, 53. Tel. (055) 423-110.*

The scenic patio that comes with each comfortable room makes this small 1 star hotel in the center of town a decent place to stay. The hotel offers very few facilities besides a great outdoor breakfast area.

WHERE TO EAT

Expensive

RESTAURANTE ZÉ DA CALÇÃDA, *Rua 31 de Janeiro, 83. Tel. (055) 422-023.*

This good, local restaurant specializes in meat and fish dishes from the region. The restaurant's fireplace, terrace, and down home ambiance are wonderful.

Moderate

RESTAURANTE SÃO GONÇALO, *Largo de São Gonçalo. Tel. (055) 422-707.*

This is a pretty good, but somewhat overpriced, regional restaurant and snack bar that serves everything from sandwiches to full dinners mostly to tourists. It's located next to a church.

SEEING THE SIGHTS

Amarante is a great place to wander through and shop, especially during the weekly Wednesday morning **mercado** (market) right near the Ponte de São Gonçalo. This granite bridge was built in the 18th century.

Several 16th and 17th century terraced houses line one side of the river, while the other side has the **Convento de São Gonçalo**. In the interior of this 16th century monastery, you will find fine gilding, an amazing 17th century organ, Renaissance cloisters, a loggia filled with statues, and the tomb of St. Gonçalo who lived in Amarante during the 13th century. Many singles touch the tomb of Saint Gonçalo, the match-maker, in the hopes of being blessed with a spouse. Each year on the first Saturday in June, Amarante hosts the colorful **Romaria São Gonçalo** festival in honor of this popular saint of love and marriage.

From the foot of the Ponte de São Gonçalo, you can walk to the quaint **Praça da República** square. The side streets off the square are filled with local merchants and old plazas. You can also cross the bridge to Rua 31 de Janeiro, which runs along the river, and have lunch or coffee in one of the many cafes.

Amarante is lucky to be home to a great little museum, **Museu de Amadeo de Sousa Cardosa** (closed on Mondays). This unique collection is located next to the town hall in the Convento de São Gonçalo complex. There are paintings by cubist artist Amadeo de Sousa-Cardoso, and the artists António Carneiro, Eduardo Viana, and Resende. Fine sculptures as well as archeological finds from the area are also exhibited in the museum.

The baroque 18th-century church, **Igreja de São Pedro**, *Rua 5 de Outubro,* has unusual azulejos and a beautifully carved wooden ceiling.

CELORICO DE BASTO

The peaceful wine producing town of Celorico de Basto is located in the Serra do Marão mountain range. It is the perfect base from which to hike, fish, or just enjoy the countryside while sampling fine local Vinho Verde, a slightly sparkling fruity white wine, and staying in historic country inns and manor houses.

ARRIVALS & DEPARTURES
By Car
Celorico de Basto is 27 km northeast of Amarante on Route N-210 north, just off the Tâmega River.

WHERE TO STAY
Moderate
CASA DO CAMPO, *N-210, Celorico de Basto. Tel. (055) 361-231.*

A dramatic 18th century manor house 4 km north of town that offers eight incredible rooms with private bathroom. Facilities include bar, dining room, pool, and gardens.

Inexpensive
QUINTA DE VILA POUCA, *N-210, Codecoso. Tel. (055) 321-766.*

A rustic 18th century house 7 km south of town offering four guest rooms with private bathrooms for hikers and tourists. Facilities include bar, bicycles, and TV room.

MATOSINHOS

Although Matosinhos is quite developed with modern structures, there are small pockets near the ocean that remain tranquil and appealing. More Portuguese than foreign tourists come to the resorts here. I usually stay in Matosinhos when I want to visit Porto during the summer, and also want budget accommodations just a few minutes away.

ARRIVALS & DEPARTURES
By Car
Matosinhos is just north of Porto on the coast.

WHERE TO STAY
Moderate
HOTEL PORTO MAR, *Rua Brito Capelo, 167. Tel. (02) 938-2104.*

This simple 2 star hotel has 32 well furnished, comfortable rooms in the center of town. The hotel offers its guests a bar, restaurant, private bathrooms, TV, and good service.

ESTALAGEM DA VIA NORTE, *Via Norte, Leça do Balio. Tel. (02) 948-0294.*

A full service 12 room inn, it has lots of facilities including bar, restaurant, room service, laundry services, air conditioning, TV, parking, and a friendly, helpful staff.

Inexpensive
PENSÃO CENTRAL, *Rua Brito Capelo, 599. Tel. (02) 937-2590.*

This establishment is centrally located and modest. Most of the basic rooms have private bathrooms. The hotel offers only breakfast.

WHERE TO EAT
Expensive
OS LVISADAS, *Rua Tomas Ribeiro, 257. Tel. (02) 937-8242.*

Os Lvisadas is a beautiful and intimate restaurant with a romantic atmosphere and exceptional service. The chefs serve top quality, fine cuisine to a well dressed clientele.

Moderate
LAGOSTA REAL, *Rua Lo Ferreira, 239. Tel. (02) 937-1363.*

This traditional lobster and fish house has a busy downtown location next to city hall. I suggest an order of the house specialty, Sortido de Marisco.

O GAVETO, *Rua Roberto Ivens, 826. Tel. (02) 937-8796.*

This excellent seafood house specializes in whatever just arrived from the docks. The service here is wonderful, and the huge portions are enough for two to share.

SEEING THE SIGHTS

Most people come to Matosinhos for the ocean or to use one of three large swimming pools. The harbor is one of the largest fishing ports in the country, and hosts a daily auction of fish that is quite a scene.

The aggressively fortified 13th century Gothic church, **Mosterio de Leça do Balio**, is located just outside of town.

SPORTS & RECREATION

• **Naval Club of Leça**, *Leixoes-Matsosinhos, Tel. (02) 995-1700*
• **Oporto Sports Club**, *Matsosinhos, Tel. (02) 995-2225*

VILA DO CONDE

In the past, Vila do Conde was a famous wood boat building center, but the demand for such vessels has decreased. Although the town has a nice beach, it has not yet been over-developed.

I much prefer the small town atmosphere in Vila do Conde to the larger seaside resorts of Espinho and Póvoa de Varzim because the town has maintained some authentic medieval flavor. The rich tradition and royal heritage of this town can still be seen in the wonderful old part of town where you can find an assortment of 16th century houses, unusual religious buildings, and museums.

ARRIVALS & DEPARTURES

By Car

Vila do Conde is about 28 km north of Porto on Route N-13 at the mouth of the Ave River.

WHERE TO STAY

Moderate

ESTALAGEM DO BRASÃO, *Ave. Dr. José Canavarro. Tel. (052) 642-016.*

This converted mansion is now a full service 4 star inn with good rooms, a bar, restaurant, disco, air conditioning, private bathrooms, and TV. A good place.

SOPETE SANT'ANA, *Azurara. Tel. (052) 641-767.*

This is a waterfront apartment-hotel complex across the river from town. The 35 pleasant one, two, and three bedroom apartments have access to a pool, restaurant, and hotel services. This is an especially affordable property for families or couples traveling together.

QUINTA DAS ALFAIAS, *Fajozes. Tel. (052) 662-146.*

A nice 19th century house, Quinta das Alfaias is about 5 km east of town in the village of Fajozes. The quinta has five large guest rooms with semi-private bathrooms, bar, pool, and gardens.

Inexpensive

RESIDENCIAL PRINCESA DO AVE, *Ave. Dr. A.S. Pereira, 261. Tel. (052) 642-482.*

This basic and comfortable inn has minimal services and facilities and is located above a restaurant.

WHERE TO EAT

Moderate

RESTAURANTE PRAIA MAR, *Ave. Infante Dom Henrique, 58. Tel. (052) 685-723.*

This simple seafood and beef restaurant has a large menu with good prices.

MAR A VISTA, *Praia do Mindelo. Tel. (052) 671-197.*

The menu changes often, but there are always seafood specialties at this large restaurant. There are huge picture windows with great views of the ocean. The service is great.

SEEING THE SIGHTS

I suggest a quick visit to the Turismo office, *Rua 25 de Abril*, to pick up a free local map of the area's sights.

The Gothic 16th century church, **Igreja Matriz**, in the town's center has a beautiful Manueline portico, a 17th century bell tower, beautiful paintings by artists such as Francisco Machado, and handmade azulejos from the 18th century. Part of the church houses the **Museu de Arte Sacra**, which has a fine collection of gold and silver ecclesiastical artifacts. Nearby on the north bank of the river is the massive 14th century **Convento de Santa Clara**, containing the heavily ornamented stone tombs of King Dom Afonso Sanches and several of his relatives. Connected to the church is an 18th century aqueduct with over 900 arches. Also worth a visit is the 16th century city hall building that has an impressive gilded tribune. Near the docks you can view the ruined 16th century polygonal fortress, **Castelo de São João Baptista**.

Also of interest is the **Museu José Régio**, *Rua José Régio, 138,* a museum in a house that exhibits the private art collection of José Régio, a well known local poet.

This religious community is known for several big festivals. The **Festa do Corpus Christi** is held every fourth year in June (the next one is in the year 2000). Carpets of beautiful flowers are placed on the streets and a silver and precious stone monstrance makes its way down the procession.

SHOPPING

Vila do Conde is famous for the production of fine bobbin lace. This unique lace has been produced here for over five centuries by young local girls. If you wish to see how the bobbin lace is made, stop by the school, **Escola de Rendas**, *Rua do Lidador*.

There is also an interesting **Centro Artisanato** handicrafts center, *Rua 5 de Outubro,* that sells local bobbin lace, heavy hand knitted sweaters, wood carvings, and some leather items.

Vila do Conde hosts a nice weekly **mercado** (market) and fair every Friday in the center of town, as well as a daily produce market. For a fortnight beginning the last week of July, the town hosts an impressive regional handicrafts fair.

PÓVOA DE VARZIM

This resort town is now a large tourist mecca for vacationing northern Portuguese families. It is quite developed with high-rise condos, apartment buildings, and hotels facing the ocean.

ARRIVALS & DEPARTURES

By Car

Póvoa de Varzim is about 4 km up the coast from Vila do Conde on Route N-13 north.

By Train

• **Póvoa de Varzim CP Rail station**, *Rua Almirantes Reis, Tel. (052) 624-698*

WHERE TO STAY

Expensive

HOTEL VERMAR, *Rua Alto Martin Vaz. Tel. (52) 615-566.*

Hotel Vermar is an ocean front 4 star resort hotel with 208 air conditioned rooms (some deluxe rooms have patios), two pools, bar, restaurant, health club, tennis, and a nearby golf course.

GRANDE HOTEL DA PAVOA, *Largo Passeio Alegre. Tel. (52) 615-464.*

This 3 star hotel is in the heart of town, near the casino. It has 96 air conditioned rooms (some with ocean views), café , restaurant, bar, TV, and nearby golf course and tennis.

Moderate
ESTALAGEM SANTO ANDRÉ, *Praia da Agucadouro. Tel. (52) 615-766.*

Located on a quiet beach just outside of town, this very good ocean front inn has 49 ocean view rooms, a bar, restaurant, TV, squash, and a nearby golf course.

HOTEL TORRE MAR, *Lugar da Fonte Nova. Tel. (52) 613-677.*

A charming 31 room hotel in a residential section of town, the Hotel Torre Mar has excellent service, nice rooms, private bathrooms, heating, minibar, TV, parking, and laundry services.

Inexpensive
RESIDENCIAL GETT, *Ave. Mouzinho Albuquerque, 54. Tel. (52) 683-206.*

A basic inn, there are 20 simple rooms with private bathroom, TV, and telephones.

WHERE TO EAT
Moderate
O CHEF, *Ave. dos Banhos, 318. Tel. (052) 684-126.*

This nice and friendly seafood restaurant is right near the beach. The large menu offers huge portions of well prepared regional food and the best steaks in town.

BELO HORIZANTE, *Rua Tenete Valadim, 63. Tel. (052) 624-787.*

This unassuming restaurant specializes in fresh seafood at good prices.

SEEING THE SIGHTS
In the summer months, the beach is lined with rows of cabana tents full of screaming children and sun weary parents. Besides the beaches and water sports, many visitors come here to gamble or to see the tacky revue of half-naked women in the city's pink **casino** (bring your passport).

The fishing industry still maintains its presence here, although the traditional methods of fishing are no longer profitable. The entertaining weekday fish auction still takes place near the docks, and it is work a look if you need a break from the beach. The nearby town of **Rates** contains a well preserved 13th century Romanesque church, **Igreja de São Pedro**.

SPORTS & RECREATION
Golf
• **Naval Club Povonese**, *Póvoa de Varzim, Tel. (052) 624-617*
• **Estela Golf Club**, *Póvoa de Varzim, Tel. (052) 685-567*

SHOPPING

Traditional handicrafts are produced in the area including hand embroidered sweaters, lace, weaving, and silver filigree.

GUIMARÃES

This medieval city was the first official capital of Portugal and is the hometown of Portugal's first king, Dom Afonso Henriques. The 10th century castle that he was born and raised in still stands. This was also the birthplace of Gil Vicente, the 15th century writer and creator of Portugal's national theater.

The city has managed to maintain much of its tradition and original ambiance. Many old houses are built directly into the original walls of the city. To this day, Guimarães produces fine linens and fabrics that can be purchased in several shops throughout the city.

ARRIVALS & DEPARTURES

By Bus

• **Guimarães Main Bus Depot**, *Ave. Conde de Margaride, Tel. (053) 411-222*

By Car

Guimarães is located about 37 km northeast of Póvoa de Varzim on Route N-206 east.

One of the few municipal parking lots is two blocks west of the Turismo office, *Alameda da Resistencia Fascismo, 83,* near the corner of the Largo da República do Brasil.

By Train

• **Guimarães CP Rail station**, *Ave. D. João IV, Tel. (053) 412-351*

WHERE TO STAY

Expensive

POUSADA S MARINHA DA COSTA, *Lugar da Costa. Tel. (053) 514-453.*

This vast pousada is a converted 12th century Augustine cloister a few kilometers out of town at Pena. The 51 rooms were monastic cells and tend to be small, but the atmosphere is quite unusual and worth the squeeze. Facilities include bar, restaurant, minibars, TV, and parking.

POUSADA DE N.S. DA OLIVEIRA, *Rua Santa Maria. Tel. (053) 514-204.*

This charming pousada has the best location in town. The 16 guest rooms are quite comfortable, the service is good, and the food is a real treat. Facilities include bar, restaurant, direct dial phones, and parking. A nice place to stay.

Moderate

CASA DE POMBAIS, *Ave. de Londres. Tel. (053) 412-917.*

This great 18th century manor house on the east side of town has only two guest rooms with private bathrooms. Call, you may get lucky and they'll have space.

HOTEL DE GUIMARÃES, *Rua Eduardo de Almeida. Tel. (053) 516-234.*

This modern 4 star hotel has 70 air conditioned, large rooms. Facilities include indoor pool, health club, squash, sauna, garage, a bar, and a large restaurant.

CASA CONDE DE PAÇO VIEIRA, *Paço Vieira-Mesão Frio. Tel. (053) 532-881.*

This beautiful 19th century manor house has a 17th century chapel. They rent out four pretty rooms with private bathrooms. The property is about 4 km east of town off Route N-101. Facilities include bar, dining room, library, TV, and parking.

CASA DE SEZIM, *Santo Amaro. Tel. (053) 523-196.*

This old manor house 5 km outside of Guimarães looks just like the Palácio Seteais. The property is owned by two former diplomats who produce fine Vinho Verde and rent six rooms. Ask to see the painting of New York when it was still owned by Indians.

Facilities include bar, dining room, gardens, horse back riding, winery, and parking.

Inexpensive

HOTEL DO TOURAL, *Largo do Toural. Tel. (053) 411-250.*

This is your basic cheap 1 star city hotel with decent rooms and private bathrooms.

SEEING THE SIGHTS

The Turismo office, *Alameda da Resistencia Fascismo, 83,* is located at the southern tip of this oval shaped city and is a good place pick up a free map. Just two blocks west of the Turismo office is the **Largo da República do Brasil**, and a good place to begin walking around. From the Largo, you can wander into the old city via the passage at the end of the town's wall. Once you have passed through the wall, walk straight up the short winding street and you will soon find yourself at the **Largo do Oliveira** plaza.

Inside the **Largo do Oliveira** is a 14th century **Pedrão do Salado** portico commemorating a victory over the Moors. Behind the portico is the **Igreja de Nossa Senhora da Oliveira**, which was built in the 14th century on the site of a 10th century monastery. The church contains a 16th century Manueline tower and a humble 14th century Gothic chapel, as well as beautiful cloisters and a chapter house that are home to the **Museu Alberto Sampaio**. The museum (closed Mondays) contains a collection of azulejos, ceramics, sculptures, a beautiful silver bible, António Vaz paintings, artifacts from the structure's origins as a 10th century monastery, and a wide assortment of ecclesiastical items including a silver triptych altar piece said to have been captured during a Castillian battle. Also in the Largo area there are cafes, a few shops, the beautiful **Paços do Concehlo**, and the charming Pousada da Oliveira.

From the Largo da Oliveira you should turn left (north) and head up the cobblestone Rua de Santa Maria, one of the city's oldest and most interesting streets. While walking up the Rua de Santa Maria, take note of several ornate 14th century homes that can be identified by their unusual wood balconies and artistic iron grillwork. As you continue further north, you will pass next to an old stone structure called the **Casa dos Arco** (arch house) which is connected to an medieval granite arch overhead. A few steps more and you can enter the **Largo Conego José Gomes**. Have a look at the facade and the inner courtyard of the **Convento de Santa Clara** whose 17th century baroque structure now houses the town hall.

If you continue up Rua de Santa Maria towards the north end of town, you will pass a tree-lined park, **Largo Martins Sarmento**. This park is surrounded by the 17th century **Igreja de Carmo** on the right (east) side, and the house of archaeologist Martins Sarmento on the left (west) side.

A bit further up the street to the right (east) is the massive French designed 15th century **Paço dos Duques** (also known as Ducal Palace). Originally built for the Duke of Bragança, this palace was abandoned and then later restored as the official presidential residence in the north. The palace is also a museum (open daily) and has beautiful tapestries, sculptures, hand crafted wooden ceilings, furniture, and paintings (three of which are by Josefa D'Obidos), but it does not have a typical Portuguese design. In front of the palace is a 19th century statue of King Dom Afonso Henriques by famed Porto artist Soares dos Reis.

From the palace, you can't help but be drawn towards the massive 10th century **castelo** (closed Mondays), located on the northeast corner of town. There's a great view over the city from the castle. Its original structure was reinforced by Count Henriques, the father of Portugal's first king. There are seven towers and a large defensive wall that surrounds the keep. Just below the castle lies the tiny Romanesque **Igreja São Miguel do Castelo**, where King Dom Afonso Henriques is said to have been baptized.

After visiting the castle and church, I suggest returning to the southern end of town via a different set of streets. Bear right (west) when you reach the fork in the road at the top of **Largo Martins Sarmento**. This street, Rua das Trinas, leads into the **Largo Dr. Prego** plaza, and if you go straight through the plaza and onto Rua de Valdonas you will soon reach the large square known as **Largo João Franco**.

At the bottom (south end) of this large square you will find the beautiful 16th century renaissance **Igreja da Misericórdia**. Most notable is the beautiful organ in the church. Roughly behind the church on Rua Sapateira is one of prettiest houses in the city. The regal white walled and granite structure was the home of the Lobo Machado family back in the 18th century, and is not open to the public.

From the front of the Misericórdia church, walk west about two blocks until you leave the old town by crossing the north side of the **Largo do Toural** plaza. From this corner you can see the vast 14th century Gothic **Convento de São Domingos** whose cloister is now home to the **Museu de Martins Sarmento**. The museum (closed on Mondays) has a collection of archaeological and ethnological items ranging from prehistoric and Celtic artifacts to medieval weaponry.

To visit yet another impressive azulejos and marbled church, walk south on the **Largo do Toural** plaza. From here, pass the Turismo office again on Alameda da Resistencia Fascismo, and cross over to the 15th century **Igreja de São Fransisco**.

SPORTS & RECREATION
Horseback Riding
• **Casa de Sezim Horse Center**, *Guimarães, Tel. (053) 523-196*

BRAGA
The history of Braga goes back to at least the time of the Celtic settlement. The town was first known as Bracari, and when conquered by the Romans about 250 B.C. became known as Bracara Augusta. It was an important Roman merchant city because it was situated at the intersection of five important Roman roads. Many goods, such as ceramics and glassware, were imported from Egypt, Greece, and other parts of Europe.

Braga was later captured by Swabian troops in the 5th century and became their capital. After three centuries of conquer and occupation by the Visigoths and Moors, Braga reemerged as a Christian stronghold (about 1040). As a major religious center and seat of the archbishop, Braga became known as The Rome of Portugal. In the 16th century, Bishop Diogo de Sousa started to urbanize the city, and was responsible for many of the churches and other structures that adorn the city to this day.

Today, Braga is a major industrial city and a major center of Christianity. Other than a few ancient streets and the pretty gardens in the **Praça da República**, Braga is not a very pretty place. Most of the more than 75,000 residents of the city live in large unimpressive concrete block apartments that seem to be everywhere. Most are hard working middle-class factory employees from the leather, electronics, and garment industries that surround most of the city.

Braga has fine museums, religious buildings, and some good shopping possibilities, including a daily market in **Praça Comércio** and a Tuesday **mercado** (market) at **Largo da Feira**. You'll find a great selection of imperfect factory shoes at low prices.

ARRIVALS & DEPARTURES
By Air
The main airport servicing Braga is the Dr. Francisco Sá Carneiro airport just outside of Porto. From the airport, the easiest way to get to various destinations in this city is to rent a car or pre-arrange a transfer from your travel agent or tour operator. Those with minimal luggage looking to save a few dollars can take a taxi to Porto for about 575$00 and from there take a train or bus to Braga.

By Bus
• **Braga Main Bus Depot**, *Central de Camionagem, Tel. (053) 234-33*

By Car
The large commercial city of **Braga** is situated about 23 km northwest of Guimarães on Route N-101 north and 53 kilometers (33 miles) north-northeast of Porto.
• **Avis Rent a Car – Braga**, *Largo de Estação, Tel. (053) 725-20*

By Train
Trains from the São Bento rail station in Porto take you to Braga's main rail station on the Largo de Estação and tickets cost less than 725$00 a person. The main rail station in Braga is a 15 minute walk or a 465$00 taxi ride away from the heart of the old town.

ORIENTATION
While the city is quite big and has many different neighborhoods, the area of interest to tourists centers around a handful of streets that make up the bulk of the old town and surround the towering Sé Cathedral. The most obvious point of reference in Braga is the Sé Cathedral, and it can be seen from various locations in the center of the city.

GETTING AROUND TOWN

By Bus

Municipal buses are easy to find and utilize. However, you may not need to use them since the distances you will cover in the old section of Braga are short.

By Car

Finding street parking in Braga is all but impossible on weekdays, but there are several private and municipal parking lots that can be used for around 175$00 per hour or 1,650$00 per day. I suggest you park your car in one of these lots and use your feet to get around town. Traffic during rush hour can be terrible.

By Taxi

Taxis are easy to find, but are not usually necessary since the distances you are likely to cover are short.

WHERE TO STAY

Moderate

CASA DA PEDRA CAVALGADA, *N-101, Braga. Tel. (053) 245-96.*

A pretty and traditional stone Minho house, it has two private guest rooms with their own bathrooms, living room, fireplace and sitting room, and parking.

HOTEL CARANDA, *Ave. da Liberdade, 96. Tel. (053) 614-500.*

This modern 3 star hotel has 100 air conditioned, spacious rooms overlooking the main street in town. Facilities include restaurant, bar, cable TV, pool, and garage.

HOTEL TURISMO, *Pracenta João XXI. Tel. (053) 612-220.*

This 4 star, centrally located, hotel has 132 air conditioned comfortable rooms. The hotel staff is friendly, and facilities include a roof top pool, restaurant, café, bar, and TV.

Inexpensive

RESTHOTEL BRAGA, *N-14, Celeiros. Tel. (053) 673-865.*

This modern 2 star motel is just a few minutes away from town. It has 72 nice rooms with private bathrooms and TV, a bar, restaurant, and air conditioning.

PENSÃO SÃO JOÃO BAPTISTA, *Rua Monsenhor Airosa, 66. Tel. (053) 752-04.*

You will find a dozen small, but comfortable, rooms with TVs in this small inn.

WHERE TO EAT

Expensive

RESTAURANTE INACIO, *Campo das Hortas, 4. Tel. (053) 613-235.*

Excellent regional and international cuisine is served in this small and charming stone walled two story restaurant. The service is spotty, but there's plenty of atmosphere.

Moderate

CHURRASQUEIRA ANGOLANA, *Alameda do Fujacal, 96. Tel. (053) 612-127.*

This pretty little restaurant serves fine meat and seafood specialties, excellent house wine, and has impressive service. Try the veal dish called lombinhos de vitela.

Inexpensive

MAR E TERRE, *Rua Congregados, 105. Tel. (053) 730-79.*

This unassuming little combination restaurant and snack bar serves huge portions of very good meat and seafood dishes at great prices.

SEEING THE SIGHTS

Start your tour with the giant 11th century **Sé Primaz** cathedral. Situated on the site of the **Igreja de Santa Maria de Braga**, which was destroyed by the Moors some four centuries earlier, construction started in 1070 making this the oldest cathedral in Portugal. Since it has been rebuilt several times over the years, it has a varied mixture of Romanesque, Gothic, Renaissance, Baroque, and Manueline elements. The church still contains several Romanesque features including some windows, the naves, and the cloister's apse. Most of the other features were either altered or added in the later centuries.

While inside the church, don't overlook the fine high altar made from Anca stone, the gilded bronze Flemish tomb of Prince Afonso, the double 18th century pipe organs, the beautiful azulejos in the **Chapel of São Pedro de Rates**, and the impressive altars around the exterior cloister. Adjoining the Sé Primaz cathedral are several other chapels with impressive contents, such as the tombs in the Gothic **Capelo dos Reis** and **Capela da Glória**, as well as the impressive 16th century altar and ceiling in the **Capela de Nossa Senhora da Piedade**.

Inside the Sé Primaz's treasury is the **Museu de Arte Sacra de Sé Primaz** (closed Mondays), which houses a fine collection of sacred art objects including a 10th century ivory casket, 14th century Gothic chalice, items made of precious metals encrusted with rare gems, and some beautiful azulejos.

Across the street from the Sé Primaz cathedral is the **Antigo Paço Episcopal** palace, home to a 300,000 volume public library, the municipal archives, and the currently closed Museu do Dom Diego de Sousa, the future home of the city museum. The palace is comprised of several substructures built in the 14th, 16th, and 18th centuries. In the courtyard of the palace is the **Largo do Paço**, which surrounds the 17th century **Chafariz do Largo do Paço** fountain.

If you walk one block west of the palace, you can take a peek in the 18th century baroque **Câmara Municipal** (town hall). Of note are its beautiful facade and collection of paintings and azulejos. In front of the town hall is an 18th century baroque fountain in the form of a pelican.

A couple of streets further west on the Rua dos Biscainhos is the 17th century **Palácio dos Biscainhos** and its gardens. The palace grounds contain the **Biscainhos Museu de Etnografia, Historia, e Arte**. Inside this converted 17th century mansion (closed Mondays) you can see artifacts, artwork, azulejos, and furniture from the 17th-19th centuries. The mansion overlooks a tranquil well groomed garden.

There is also the **Museu Pio XII** in the eastern sector of town, off the **Campo de São Tiago**. An interesting little collection of Roman and Visigoth artifacts, as well as ecclesiastical items, can be found in the **Seminario de São Tiago** nearby.

SPORTS & RECREATION

Fishing
• **Braga Fishing Club**, *Rua dos Chaos, 112, Tel. (053) 260-60*

Horseback Riding
• **Hipico Horse Club of Braga**, *Rua de Santo André, 8, Tel. (053) 722-61*

Hunting
• **Cacadores Hunting Club**, *Braga, Tel. (053) 684-503*

Tennis
• **Braga Tennis Club**, *Rodovia Sports Complex, Tel. (053) 611-753*

BOM JESUS

The town of Bom Jesus is known for its lovely baroque church, Bom Jesus do Monte.

WHERE TO STAY

Expensive

CASTELO DO BOM JESUS, *Bom Jesus. Tel. (053) 676-566.*

This privately owned, ornate, nobleman's mansion has 10 nice guest rooms, a large pool, jacuzzi, farm, on site prehistoric megaliths, a winery, and beautiful azulejos.

Moderate

HOTEL DO ELEVADOR, *Bom Jesus. Tel. (053) 676-611.*

This 4 star hotel is quiet and friendly. There are 25 large and rooms decorated with antique furnishings. Facilities include restaurant, lounge, cable TV, and room service.

HOTEL DO PARQUE, *Bom Jesus. Tel. (053) 676-606.*

This beautiful mansion has been converted into a 4 star hotel with 50 deluxe rooms. Facilities include bar, park, TV, air conditioning, and handicapped access.

CASA DOS LAGOS, *Bom Jesus. Tel. 053) 676-738.*

Casa Dos Lagos is a converted 18th century manor house located in a peaceful setting with fine views of Braga. There are four large two bedroom apartments and one nice double room with private bathrooms. Facilities include bar, library, gardens, TV room, and parking.

APARTHOTEL MAE D'AGUA, *Bom Jesus, Tel. (053) 676-581.*

A bright and cheery modern hotel, Mae D'Agua has 30 large and comfortable one and two bedroom air conditioned apartments with hotel facilities including bar, restaurant, disco, barber, billiards, TV, direct dial phones, and parking. This is a great place for families.

SEEING THE SIGHTS

The baroque hilltop church of **Bom Jesus do Monte** is located 4 km from Braga, up hilly Route N-103-3 east. This 18th century church was constructed in neo-classical style by architect Carlos Amarante, and its simple interior was designed in the form of a Latin cross. The side of the church is surrounded by a peaceful park with benches, fountains, small chapels, and a man made lake. In front of the church is a set of unusual stairways and terraces down the hill (you can take a funicular back up).

Immediately in front of the church, start your descent from the **Terreiro de Moises** on the strange and mysterious granite **Stairway of the Three Virtues** (faith, hope, and charity). Continue down through the amazing baroque **Stairs of the Five Senses**. This stairway has statues that pour water from different body parts and are known as the fountains of touch, taste, smell, hearing, and sight. On each level of stairs there are shrines and chapels referring to differing scenes from the Passion of Christ. Most people believe that a mysterious power is present, and in fact, there is a small road near the church on which locals can show you a strange phenomenon: if you put your car in neutral, it will roll up hill.

If you continue further up N103-3, you will come to a beautiful view of the Braga region from the church lantern tower on the top of **Monte Sameiro**. After another 3 km further up the mountain road, turn on Route N-309 south to the excavated ruins of the Celt-Iberian walled city of **Citânia de Briteiros**, which dates back to before the 24th century B.C.

BARCELOS

Barcelos, a beautiful hilltop market town, rests at the foot of a 14th century arched bridge that crosses the Cávado River. The town was the 13th century home to the Bragança royal dynasty and today has beautiful old houses, palaces, museums, and churches. The 9,500 people who live here are friendly and always willing to point you in the right direction.

Barcelos is known as one of the major centers for the production of colorful hand painted pottery and crafts.

ARRIVALS & DEPARTURES
By Car
Barcelos is about 19 km southeast of Braga on Route N-205 east.

By Train
• **Barcelos CP Rail Station**, *Ave. Alcaide de Faria, Tel. (053) 811-234*

WHERE TO STAY
Moderate

QUINTA DE SANTA COMBA, *Lugar de Crujaes. Tel. (053) 832-101.*

This regal manor house and wine producing estate is located off Route N-204 in the village of Varzea about 5 km south of Barcelos. There are six good rooms with private bathroom. Facilities include winery, TV, horses, bikes, tennis, horses, and swimming pool.

ALBERGARIA CONDE DE BARCELOS, *Ave. Alcaides de Fari. Tel. (053) 811-602.*

This nice 4 star inn has 30 comfortable rooms. Facilities include restaurant, heating, radio, a TV room, bar, direct dial phones, and handicapped access.

CASA DO MONTE, *N-103, Barcelos. Tel. (053) 811-519.*

Casa do Monte is a charming country house surrounded by lots of trees and flowers a few minutes west of town. It has three guest rooms, a one bedroom, and a two bedroom apartment with private bathrooms, TV, bar, and other facilities.

Inexpensive

PENSÃO DOM NUNO, *Ave. Dom A. Periera, 76. Tel. (053) 815-084.*

This nice inn has comfortable rooms with private bathrooms and minimal services.

PENSÃO BAGOEIRA, *Ave. Dr. Sidonio Pais, 495. Tel. (053) 811-236.*

This clean and comfortable basic inn is near the fairgrounds. Six rooms without private bathroom are available. Facilities include a bar and restaurant. The inn is usually packed on market days.

WHERE TO EAT

Moderate

CEIA RESTAURANTE, *Rua Dr. F. Torres, 94. Tel. (053) 815-270.*

This nice clean family style restaurant offers pretty good fish and meat dishes in a friendly environment. The veal and lamb are fresh and well prepared.

Inexpensive

RESTAURANTE BAGOEIRA, *Ave. Sidonio Pais, 495. Tel. (053) 811-236.*

Great regional northern Portuguese cuisine is served in this funky little restaurant by a cast of merry staff. This is a great place to have lunch.

SEEING THE SIGHTS

From the central plaza of **Campo da República** you can see dramatic churches, stately buildings, and several streets such as Rua Dom António Barroso that are full of pottery shops, cafes, monuments, and medieval atmosphere. The 18th century church, **Igreja do Terco**, is just above the fairgrounds and is not to be missed. The church's interior is covered with original azulejo murals created by António de Oliveira Bernardes. The murals are adorned with incredible paintings, gold leaf woodwork, and unique painted vaulting. Also surrounding the fairgrounds are the lovely 18th century **Templo do Nosso Senhor da Cruz** and the solemn **Igreja da Misericórdia**.

The town's original keep, called the **Torre de Menagem**, *Largo do Porto Novo,* houses both the Turismo office and a small local crafts center. Nearby, in the **Largo do Municipal** plaza you can find a 13th century church, **Igreja Matriz** with an azulejo and baroque interior. In the **Cãmara Municipal** (city hall) you can visit a small regional museum of ceramics (closed Mondays).

Near the medieval bridge is the **Museu Archeological** (museum of archaeology), located within the ruins of the former 15th century residence of the Duke of Bragança, known as the **Paço dos Condos**.

SPORTS & RECREATION
Horseback Riding
• **Quinta Santa Comba**, *Barcelos, Tel. (053) 832-101*

SHOPPING
On Thursdays, the huge **Feira de Barcelos mercado** (market) takes over the **Campo da República** fairgrounds and offers shoppers items ranging from the famous local pottery to hand sewn leather saddles and live poultry. You can negotiate with the artisans who dress in regional peasant clothes.

One of the most common symbols on items sold here is the famed **Barcelos rooster** which commemorates the story of an unjustly accused thief. When he was about to be hung, he proclaimed his innocence by miraculously transforming the judge's roasted chicken lunch into a live crowing rooster.

ESPOSENDE & OFIR
The towns of Esposende and Ofir are separated by the mouth of an estuary of the Cávado River.

Esposende was once the Roman port town of Aquis Celnis. These days, the quiet fishing village still has a small, old town area and an understated beach. When wandering around Esposende, you can find typical scenes from the daily life of a medieval small town.

Ofir is on a small peninsula surrounded by the ocean on one side, and the river on the other. It has become a major beach resort area with several sports facilities, hotels, beach clubs, and restaurants. You'll find very little of the traditional village feeling that is so obvious across the water in Esposende. Most of the vacationers in Ofir stay in large hotels with pools, water sports, nightclubs, fancy restaurants, tennis, and other full service facilities.

ARRIVALS & DEPARTURES
By Car
Esposende and Ofir are about 14 km from Barcelos on Route N-103-1 east.

WHERE TO STAY
Expensive
HOTEL OFIR, *Ave. Sousa Martins, Ofir. Tel. (053) 981-383.*

This large 4 star hotel is situated right near the beach and offers 200 air conditioned rooms. Facilities include pool, tennis, disco, restaurant, sauna, and nearby golf.

Moderate
ESTALAGEM ZENDE, *N-13, Esposende. Tel. (053) 965-018.*

This is a 4 star inn with 25 great air conditioned rooms with private bath. Services include a good staff, bar, restaurant, cable TV, room service, handicapped access.

HOTEL NELIA, *Ave. Ribeiro, Esposende. Tel. (053) 961-244.*

A modern, 3 star, full service hotel, the Nelia has 42 small but good rooms with private bathrooms. Facilities include bar, restaurant, pool, squash, ping pong, and billiards.

HOTEL SAUVE MAR, *Ave Oliveira, Esposende. Tel. (053) 965-445.*

This reasonably nice 3 star ocean view hotel has 66 air conditioned, comfortable rooms with private bath. Facilities include bar, restaurant, pool, tennis, and parking.

Inexpensive
CASA DO MATINHO, *N-546, Forjaes. Tel. (053) 871-167.*

Two rooms with private bathrooms are available in this 18th century country house. The facilities are minimal, but it's a nice place about 11 km east of Esposende.

WHERE TO EAT
Inexpensive
RESTAURANTE DO RIO, *Ave. Dr. Manuel Pais, Fão. Tel. (053) 981-651.*

Large portions of local fish and meat dishes are served in this small, cozy corner restaurant and snack bar.

SEEING THE SIGHTS
There are a few old churches in **Esposende** including the beautiful baroque **Chapel of Our Lord of the Navigators**. This chapel has a beautiful arched ceiling of gold leaf and a number of medieval paintings. The **Praia de Sauve Mar** beach area is a stones throw away and can be reached by regular shuttle service from the center of town.

For the most part, **Ofir** offers little of cultural interest, but the nearby excavations at the Roman city of **Fão** are worth a look. The beach is the main reason people visit Ofir, and there is plenty of it to go around. Prices here tend to be a bit more reasonable than at the other regional resort areas such as Póvoa de Varzim and Espinho.

VIANA DO CASTELO & NEARBY BEACHES

The port city of Viana do Castelo is at the mouth of the Lima River. The rich history of Viana do Castelo is closely linked to the ocean, which has provided the town with successful international trade and shipbuilding industries since the 13th century. By the middle of the 16th century, local merchants and tradesman grew more prosperous and built many fine palaces and mansions that still grace the city and the outlying areas. Fortunately, many of the original structures still exist.

There are several shops that sell fine, locally embroidered table cloths and aprons.

ARRIVALS & DEPARTURES
By Car
Viana do Castelo is about 23 km north of Esposende on Route N-13 north.
• **Hertz Rent a Car**, *Ave. Conde de Carrera, Tel. (058) 822-250*

By Train
• **Viana do Castelo CP Rail station**, *Ave. dos Combatentes, Tel. (058) 822-296*

WHERE TO STAY
Expensive
HOTEL SANTA LUZIA, *Monte de Santa Luzia. Tel. (058) 828-889.*

Hotel Santa Luzia is a mansion that has been converted into a 4 star pousada with 55 art deco rooms with great panoramic views. Facilities include terraced gardens, pool, tennis, bar, and restaurant.

Moderate
CASA DOS COSTA BARROS, *Rua de São Pedro, 28. Tel. (058) 823-705.*

This 16th century converted manor house is located in the heart of the old town. It has 10 superior guest rooms with private bath, TV, heating, radio, and lots of antiques.

QUINTA DA BOA VIAGEM, *Além do Rio-Areosa. Tel. (058) 835-835.*

This wonderful yellow castle-like manor house and estate is about three km northeast of Viana do Castelo. The quinta has five separate one and two bedroom apartments with kitchens and bathrooms, a pool, billiards, bicycles, gardens, TV room, and parking.

QUINTA DO PAÇO D'ANHA, *Vila Nova de Anha. Tel. (058) 322-459*.

Located 3 km south of Viana do Castello off Route N-13, this wonderful 16th century manor house and wine producing estate has four two bedroom apartments with kitchens, horseback riding, gardens, bicycles, tennis, and parking.

CASA SANTA FILOMENA, *Estrada de Cabanas, Afife. Tel. (058) 981-619*.

Casa Santa Filomena is a typical stone farm house, about 15 km northeast from Viana, with five spacious guest rooms (some with private bathrooms) in a rustic and rural setting.

ALBERGARIA QUIM BARREIROS, *Vila Praia de Ancora. Tel. (058) 951-220*.

This is a good 4 star inn with 28 comfortable air conditioned rooms with private bathrooms. Facilities include bar, snack bar, TV, mini bar, and access to nice, nearby beaches.

Inexpensive

CASA DO PENEDO, *Lugar da Gaiteira, Afife. Tel. (058) 981-474*.

This traditional Minho stone farmhouse rents four rustic double rooms with semi private bathrooms. It's located on a hillside about 9 km northeast of Viana do Castelo.

RESIDENCIAL LARANJEIRA, *Rua General Luís Rego, 45. Tel. (058) 822-261*.

This nice 3 star basic inn, located in the heart of town, has 26 comfortable rooms with private bathrooms. Facilities include breakfast room, TV room, and parking.

PENSÃO MAGALHAES, *Rua M. Espregueira, 62. Tel. (058) 823-293*.

This pretty decent 2 star inn has double rooms that are reasonably comfortable. You can get rooms with or without a private bathroom. It's nothing special, but it's very cheap.

WHERE TO EAT

Moderate

RESTAURANTE TÍPICO OS 3 PORTES, *Beco dos Fornos, 7. Tel. (058) 829-928*.

This cozy and charming little restaurant is located near the Praça da República in a former 16th century bakery. Local folk dancing takes place at the restaurant on summer weekends.

RESTAURANTE DARQUEVILA, *Rua das Rosas, Darque. Tel. (058) 322-032.*

This is the place for the grilled fresh fish dinners and good service. It's located just south of Viana do Castelo in the town of Darque.

Inexpensive

RESTAURANTE MINHO, *Rua G. Coutinho, 107. Tel. (058) 823-261.*

Restaurante Minho is a simple and small restaurant specializing in regional fish and meat dishes.

SEEING THE SIGHTS

In the center of town is the 15th century **Chafariz** fountain in **Praça da República**, surrounded by fine examples of 16th century architecture. You can see the elaborate 16th century **Casa da Misericórdia** and its adjacent church. The balconies on Misericordia's facade are supported by arches and columns sculpted into statues of women and was originally designed by João Lopes. The interior's beautiful azulejos scenes from the bible were made in 1721 by António de Oliveira Bernardes.

Next to the Misericórdia is the restored 16th century Renaissance **Antiga Câmara Municipal** (old town hall) made with granite blocks. It has triple arched doors with the local coat of arms above the middle window. On Fridays, a charming local **mercado** (market) takes place a couple of blocks east of the old town hall off Rua da Palha.

If you follow the Rua Sacadura Cabral towards the river you will come across a 15th century Gothic church, **Igreja Matriz**. This church has fine examples of 16th and 17th century wood carvings and paintings. Another block towards the river is the charming Rua de São Pedro, with an abundance of impressive old houses.

If you double back to the **Praça da República** and turn left (west) onto Rua Manuel Espregueira, you will soon find the **Largo de São Domingos** and an 18th century palace that has been converted into the **Museu Municipal**. The interior of the palace has azulejo murals by Policarpo de Oliveira Bernardes (son of António) as well as 17th century ivory inlaid furniture, drawings by Soares dos Reis, 18th century pottery, fine oil paintings, Neolithic vases, massive Celtic and prehistoric statues, Roman coins, and amazing ceilings (closed on Mondays).

A few blocks up at the north edge of town on Ave. 25 de Abril you will find a funicular, which will take you up a hill called **Santa Luzia**. On this hill is the 19th century **Igreja de Santa Luzia**. The church contains a few frescoes and is of little interest, but the view from the top of its huge white dome is spectacular. Be advised that the walk up the 142 step narrow staircase to the small viewing platform is a bit scary.

One of the most exciting times to arrive in town is about the third weekend of August when the **Romaria de Nossa Senhoa da Agonia** festival takes place for a few days. This fun weekend event includes parades, folklore, fireworks, and a great carnival atmosphere.

Many people also come to Viana do Castelo for its nearby beaches and sports facilities. There are beautiful beaches south of town at **Praia do Cabedelo**, accessible by ferry from Viana do Castelo's river front dock or via the town's bridge. If you desire more isolated beaches you can take a nice drive up the coast to **Montedor**, **Afife**, **Moledo**, and **Vila Praia de Ancora**. These towns offer modest accommodations and restaurants near beaches that are sometimes deserted. Since few non-Portuguese tourists know about these towns, the prices are reasonable and rooms are usually available without advance booking.

SPORTS & RECREATION
• **Vela Club of Viana do Castelo**, *Viana do Castelo, Tel. (058) 276-52*

PONTE DE LIMA

Situated across an old Roman bridge on the Lima River is the beautiful town of Ponte de Lima. The area was inhabited by Celts and became an important center for trade under the Romans.

These days the town still maintains its historical ambiance. Although the number of specific attractions may seem few, the town possesses a unique old world charm which, in my opinion, is the main attraction.

ARRIVALS & DEPARTURES
By Car
Ponte de Lima is about 23 km northeast of Viana do Castelo on Route N-202 east.

WHERE TO STAY
Expensive
PAÇO DE CALHEIROS, *N-202, Calheiros. Tel. (058) 947-164.*
Located 7 km northeast of town, this is a wonderful converted 18th century mansion with 10 rooms with private bathroom. Facilities include bar, dining room, TV, pool, and horses.

Moderate
CASA DO BAGANHEIRO, N-201, *Queijada. Tel. (058) 941-612.*
This fine manor house, some 7 km southeast of town off Route N-201, has three deluxe rooms plus a two bedroom apartment, all with private

bath. The quinta is owned by a charming English speaking couple. Facilities include pool, lounge, TV, and library.

CONVENTO VAL DE PEREIRAS, *Arcozelo. Tel. (058) 742-161.*

This beautiful 14th century convent and manor house, located about 2 km northwest of town, offers 10 rooms with private bathrooms. Facilities include bar, dining room, pool, tennis, billiards, gardens, and lots of wonderful views of the mountains.

CASA DE MARTIN, *N-306, Calheiros. Tel. (058) 941-677.*

This nice manor house and estate is about 4 km north of town. It has 11 comfortable rooms in the main house and annex. Facilities include pool, tennis, and restaurant.

IMPÉRIO DO MINHO, *Ave. 5 de Outubro. Tel. (058) 943-654.*

The best hotel in town, this 4 star property has 50 rooms with private bathrooms, restaurant, shops, pool, air conditioning, TV, and nearby parking.

Inexpensive

CASA DO TAMANQUEIRO, *Lugar das Penas. Tel. (058) 941-432.*

This charming little 18th century stone Minho house has two bedrooms and a wood burning hearth. Located about 8 km northwest of town, this is perhaps the best small house available for families or two couples wanting a rustic setting near a small brook. A great place!

PENSÃO SÃO JOÃO, *Rua do Rosario. Tel. (058) 941-288.*

This is the best, inexpensive place to stay in town. There are about a dozen rooms with and without private bathrooms. Facilities include a bar, restaurant, and nearby parking.

WHERE TO EAT

Expensive

RESTAURANTE MADALENA, *Monte St. Madalena. Tel. (058) 941-239.*

This opulent mountain top restaurant offers fine regional cuisine with great service and an excellent panoramic view of the area. The people who eat here are well dressed.

Moderate

RESTAURANTE ENCANADA, *Ave. 25 de Abril. Tel. (058) 941-189.*

Restaurante Encanada is a good local restaurant near the river bank. They prepare regional, grilled shellfish and hearty local cuisine. The friendly staff speak some English.

Inexpensive

RESTAURANTE TULHA, *Rua Formosa. Tel. (058) 942-879.*

This friendly local eating establishment serves several fish and meat dishes, but they specialize in roasted meats. The portions are huge, and the service is good.

SEEING THE SIGHTS

Start at the foot of the arched Roman bridge and wander through the charming old town full of majestic streets and riverside avenues that were surrounded by the city's Roman walls.

Just off the Roman bridge is the town's keep. The keep doubles as an 18th century library, **Biblioteca Municipal**. From here, you can walk to the **Largo Camões** and sit by the fountain or at one of the nearby cafes to get a feel for the town. If you want to see the **Ponte de Lima** from an interesting perspective, walk on the pathway above parts of the Roman wall. At one time, this wall encircled the old town. A 15th century palace has been converted into the **Câmara Municipal** (town hall), and the 16th century church, **Igreja Matriz**, which has Romanesque, Renaissance, and Manueline elements.

In addition to wandering around the small stone lanes in the old town, I suggest a leisurely picnic on one of the benches below the trees on the unforgettable river front. After lunch, you can wander up to the ruins of the old **Torre de Menagem** keep, which was once a prison. Continue up the river front to captivating the **Igreja Santo António dos Frades**. Every fortnight, a Monday market rolls onto the banks of the river.

If you happen to be in the area on the third weekend of September, you can witness the **Feiras Novas**, a new fair with a market, live music in the streets, folklore, and fireworks.

Make sure to try one of the locally produced white wines before you leave this romantic little town. You will notice that most of the area's best accommodations are in converted manor houses (quintas) a few kilometers out of town.

PONTE DE BARCA

The quiet little town of Ponte de Barca is located on the banks of the Lima River and begins at the foot of a 15th century arched stone bridge.

ARRIVALS & DEPARTURES

By Car

Ponte de Barca is about 17 km northwest of Ponte de Lima off Route N-202 east.

WHERE TO STAY
Moderate
QUINTA DA PROVA, *N-202, Prova. Tel. (058) 421-63.*

This pretty little house is located just above the Lima River, opposite of town. The quinta rents three nice two bedroom apartments with kitchens.

TORRE DE QUINTELA, *N-101, Nogueira. Tel. (058) 422-38.*

This nice old manor house with a 16th century tower has three nice guest rooms with private bathrooms. It's located about 4 km southeast of town off Route N-101.

PAÇO VEDRO, *Paço Vedro. Tel. (058) 421-17.*

Located in the hamlet of Paço Vedro, this 18th century manor house has five good rooms with semi-private bathrooms. Facilities include bar and parking.

Inexpensive
PENSÃO SÃO FERNANDO, *Rua de Santo António. Tel. (058) 425-80.*

This is a clean and comfortable 2 star inn near the heart of town. It has 22 rooms with private bathrooms, and several facilities including telephones and TV in the rooms.

RESIDENCIAL OS POETAS, *Rua Dr. A. Cruz. Tel. (058) 435-78.*

The 10 heated, comfortable rooms in this little inn have private bathrooms. Facilities include cable TV, bar, breakfast room, telephone, and great local ambiance.

SEEING THE SIGHTS
The Lima River is the main attraction in this town and is fronted by a lovely riverside park called the **Jardim das Poetas**. Further along the river, there are many functioning antique watermills.

The town has a few interesting churches you may want to visit such as the **Igreja Matriz** with fine azulejos and wood work, the 18th century **Igreja da Misericórdia**, and the 17th century **Capela de Santo António**. In the center of the city is a beautiful pillory and public square dating back to the 16th century.

This peaceful agricultural area produces fine Vinho Verde white wines. A small local **mercado** (market) takes place in the town on most Wednesdays.

CAMINHA
Caminha is a lovely fishing town surrounded by both the Minho and Coura Rivers. A former Roman village, it was once a major medieval fortified town right in the path of the Spanish armies. These days the town

attracts mainly Spanish tourists on day trips to local beaches, as well as the old town.

ARRIVALS & DEPARTURES
By Car
Caminha is located about 28 km up the coast from Viana do Castelo on Route N-13 north.

WHERE TO STAY
Moderate
QUINTA DA GRAÇA, *Vilarelho. Tel. (058) 921-157.*
This 17th century ocean view house, just outside of town, has seven nice rooms with private bathrooms. Facilities include lounge, dining room, pool, gardens, and parking.

HOTEL PORTA DA SOL, *Ave. Marginal. Tel. (051) 795-377.*
This 3 star resort hotel has 93 air conditioned rooms with private baths. Facilities include restaurant, pool, sauna, tennis, squash, billiards, disco, TV, and minibar.

CASA DE ESTERIO, *Lugar de Esterio. Tel. (058) 921-356.*
Surrounded by gardens, this 18th century house has nice forest views. There is only one apartment for rent to those who call in advance. Facilities include kitchen and fireplace.

RESIDENCIAL ARCA NOVA, *Largo Sidonio Pais. Tel. (058) 922-780.*
This 3 star inn has 15 attractive, modern rooms with private bathroom near the river. Facilities include heating, TV, telephone, breakfast room, and parking.

Inexpensive
CASA DA ANTA, *Lugar da Anta-Lanhelas. Tel. (058) 921-434.*
Casa da Anta is a rustic 17th century stone Minho house, about 6 km northeast of town, that rents four nice rooms with private bathroom, a bar, TV, heating, restaurant, and wine cellar.

WHERE TO EAT
Expensive
RESTAURANTE REMO, *Sporting Clube. Tel. (058) 921-459.*
Remo is an impressive waterfront restaurant with an extensive wine list and a variety of regional Minho fish and meat dishes. Both the food and the views are special.

Moderate

VERSALHES, *Rua São João, 114. Tel. (058) 921-199.*

Located just off the Minho River, this is a great little fish and meat restaurant. The restaurant offers the best rock bass (Robalo) I have ever had.

ADEGA DO CHICO, *Rua Visconde de S. Rego. Tel. (058) 921-781.*

Adego do Chico is a small informal eating establishment with good, local atmosphere. They serve huge portions of the house codfish specialty, Bacalhau a Chico.

SEEING THE SIGHTS

You should wander past the beautiful old buildings that line the town's medieval main plaza, **Praça do Conselheiro Silva Torres**. Besides the central 16th century Chafariz fountain, you can see the beautiful 14th century **Torre do Relogio**, a clock tower which was part of the town's original fortifications. The clock tower's gate is embossed with the royal coat of arms of King Dom Afonso V.

Also in the plaza are the **Paços do Concelho**, 17th century town chambers with arcade and boxed wooden ceilings, and the 15th century Gothic **Casa dos Pitas** whose facade is adorned with battlements. Near the main plaza is a 17th century prison, the 16th century **Capela dos Mareantes** filled with azulejos, 16th century carvings and ex-votos in the renaissance church, **Igreja da Misericórdia**, and the 15th century Gothic and renaissance church, **Igreja Matriz**, with unusual carved Mudéjar wooden ceiling and fortified bell tower.

The town is quite interesting, and I suggest at least a half day here if you are within striking distance. If you have a little more time, you should visit the impressive little windmill and waterfall town of **Vilar de Mouros** which is only 6 km northeast of town.

SHOPPING

Make sure to keep your eyes open for the great handcrafted copper cookware produced and sold in small shops along Rua Ricardo Joaquim de Sousa.

VILA NOVA DE CERVEIRA

The small town of Vila Nova de Cerveira is located on the bank of the Minho River. The history of the small town goes back to the 13th century when it was fortified to ward off Spanish incursions. These days, a small ferry shuttles back and forth across the river to bring Spaniards and their cars across the border for day trips and shopping excursions into Portugal.

ARRIVALS & DEPARTURES

By Car

Vila Nova de Cerveira is about 9 km northeast of Caminha on Route N-13 north.

WHERE TO STAY

Expensive

POUSADA DE DOM DINIS, *Praça da Liberdade. Tel. (051) 795-604.*

This opulent, converted river front fortress is definitely the best place to stay in town. The 29 rooms are pretty comfortable and the public spaces are unforgettable. Facilities include bar, restaurant, TV, direct dial phones, and parking.

Moderate

ESTALAGEM DA BOEGA, *Gondarem. Tel. (051) 795-231.*

This full service, 4 star inn has 30 large, comfortable rooms 3 km south of town. Facilities include a bar, restaurant, pool, cable TV, river view park, and tennis.

Inexpensive

RESIDENCIAL MARINEL, *Ave. 25 de Abril. Tel. (051) 795-114.*

This clean and basic 10 room inn has minimal facilities. It's a good budget selection.

SEEING THE SIGHTS

There is a lovely 14th century fortress that has been converted into a nice **pousada**. The only other sights are an 18th century baroque church, **Igreja Matriz,** the 16th century **Capelas de São Roque** (chapels), and the 17th century **Igreja de Nossa Senhorha da Ajuda**. There are also a couple of small islands in the middle of the river that can be visited by boat, but finding someone to take you to them is difficult.

Vila Nova de Cerveira is a fairly nice stop, but other than the **pousada** there is no real reason to spend more than an hour or two here.

VALENÇA DO MINHO

Located near the border with Spain, this fortress-dominated walled city is strategically located on a hill overlooking the Minho River. Valença do Minho (Valença) was first founded in the 12th century as a defense post on the border, and was originally known as Contrasta.

ARRIVALS & DEPARTURES
By Car
Valença do Minho is located 20 km north of Vila Nova de Cerveira on Route N-13 north.

WHERE TO STAY
Expensive
POUSADA DE SÃO TEOTÓNIO, *Valença do Minho. Tel. (051) 824-020.*

This relatively new structure was built inside the fortress walls of the old town. It has 16 good double rooms with private bathroom, bar, restaurant, TV, and parking.

Moderate
LARA HOTEL, *Lugar de São Sebastião. Tel. (051) 824-348.*

This is a modern 3 star hotel with 53 good rooms, private bathrooms, swimming pool, bar, laundry, cable TV, breakfast room, direct dial phones, and lots of parking.

HOTEL VALENÇA DO MINHO, *Ave. Miguel Dantes-Troias. Tel. (051) 824-211.*

This is a good 3 star hotel with 36 air conditioned rooms with private bathrooms. Facilities include bar, restaurant, pool, TV, minibar, and handicapped access.

Inexpensive
RESIDENCIAL PONTE SECA, *Ave. Tito Fontes. Tel. (051) 225-80.*

This basic inn has simple heated rooms with or without private bathrooms.

SEEING THE SIGHTS
The old city of Valença is surrounded by a huge walled enclosure with five stone gates and two connected 17th century forts. Within the walls of the old city are cannons and watchtowers that face the Spanish city of **Tuy**.

This city of 2,700 residents is full of small pebbled lanes and old houses with azulejos-covered glass enclosed verandahs. As you wander through town, make an effort to see the medieval **Casa do Eirado**, the Romanesque 12th century **Igreja Matriz**, the beautiful altar and naves in the **Igreja de Santo Estavão**. This church also contains an original Roman mile marker in its courtyard.

For the best panoramic view of the area, walk to the vantage points above the ramparts. As with many of the northern towns, fine locally-produced handicrafts can be found in the small shops and at the local Wednesday **mercado** (market).

MONÇÃO

The small hamlet of Monção sits on the bank of the Minho River, and has a ferry that crosses the river into Spain (a bridge will be finished any time now). This border town was inhabited well before the Roman occupation, and you can still see the vestiges of the original fortifications.

In the 14th century, after Moncão's years of continued sieges and war, a local woman named Deu-la-Deu Martins single-handedly expelled the occupying Spanish troops by pelting them with small rolls of bread. You can still find the same kind of rolls on sale throughout the old town, and in fact the town erected a fountain and named Praça Deu-la-Deu in her honor.

ARRIVALS & DEPARTURES

By Bus
• **Monção Main Bus Depot**, *Antiga Estação, Tel. (051) 536-20*

By Car
Monção is 19 km northeast of Valença do Minho on Route N-101.

WHERE TO STAY

Moderate
QUINTA DO HOSPITAL, *N-202, Valinha. Tel. (051) 544-58.*

Quinta do Hospital is an impressive historic 18th century manor house 8 km east of Monção. It has five nice rooms with private bathroom. The facilities include bar, dining room, bikes, and TV.

CASA DE RODAS, *Lugar de Rodas. Tel. (051) 652-105.*

Located 1 km south of town off Route N-101A, this pleasant, converted 16th century manor house has three nice rooms and a one bedroom apartment, all with private bathroom.

ALBERGARIA ATLÂNTICO, *Rua General P. de Castro, 15. Tel. (051) 652-355.*

A good 4 star hotel in town, it has 24 comfortable rooms with private bathroom and friendly service. Facilities include bar, restaurant, cable TV, minibars, and parking.

Inexpensive
PENSÃO MANE, *Rua General P. de Castro, 5. Tel. (051) 652-490.*

This nice 3 star inn, located in the heart of town, has eight rooms with private bathrooms. Facilities include a restaurant, TV room, in room telephones, and nearby parking.

SEEING THE SIGHTS

The people of Monção (several are of Jewish descent) are traditional by nature, and can be seen in the small stone streets like Rua Direita on their way to the Thursday **mercado** (market). The town has several interesting sights to visit including a Romanesque church, **Igreja Matriz**, that has a beautiful monstrance; a 17th century church, **Igreja da Misericórdia**; a lookout with river views, **Miradouro dos Nerys**; and a local hot springs.

The town is located in a wine producing zone that is well known for Alvarinho wine varieties. If you drink wine, this wine must be tasted before leaving Monção.

MELGAÇO

Melgaço is a somewhat forgotten, wonderful border town loaded with character on the Minho River.

In 1170, King Dom Afonso I ordered the construction of a heavily fortified watchtower to be built on the site of a former Moorish lookout post. For the past 900 years, the impressive castle and massive circular wall have loomed high above on a hill above the old town. The streets that unfold beneath the castle are full of merchants, shepherds, and traditionally dressed local residents who can best be seen during the town's Friday mercado (market).

ARRIVALS & DEPARTURES
By Car

Melgaço is 33 km northeast of Monção on Route N-202 east.

WHERE TO STAY
Moderate

QUINTA DA CALÇADA, *Melgaço. Tel. (051) 425-47.*

This 17th century manor house has only one large one bedroom apartment with private bathroom and kitchen for rent from July 15 until September 30 each year.

PENSÃO BOAVISTA, *N-202, Peso. Tel. (051) 424-64.*

This is a better than average 3 star inn with 41 air conditioned guest rooms with private bathroom, pool, bar, restaurant, laundry, room service, cable TV, and telephone.

Inexpensive

PENSÃO FLÔR DO MINHO, *Rua Velha. Tel. (051) 429-05.*
A basic and clean 1 star inn with seven rooms and a good restaurant.

SEEING THE SIGHTS

The village is a wonder to walk through. Leave the castle and cross the **Alameda Inês Negra** and follow any of the small lanes. While you are strolling along, look inside the 13th century Romanesque church, **Igreja Matriz**, the beautiful porch on the 15th century **Igreja da Misericórdia**, and the many ancient alleys and walls throughout the old town.

While in Melgaço, try to take a beautiful half day ride to the small villages and remote country roads just south of town. A spa area called **Termas do Peso** is located about 4 km southwest of Melgaço in the town of **Peso**, and attracts many people for its curative waters and fine spa facilities. A kilometer or so to the east of town is the fine 13th century church, **Igreja de Nossa Senhora da Orada**.

PENEDA-GERÊS NATIONAL PARK

The mountain ranges of **Serra da Peneda**, **Serra do Soajo**, **Serra do Amarela**, and **Serra do Gerês** have been classified as the **Parque Nacional da Peneda-Gerês**. Founded in 1970, the park protects the delicate ecosystem of the 178,000 acres of pristine forests and rounded peaks. The park also contains several towns within its borders.

In prehistoric times, several settlements were located in the park area. There are several 5,000 year old dolmens that can be seen near **Soajo**, **Portos**, and **Tourém**. During the Roman era, a military road was constructed through the park linking Braga to Rome and is clearly demarcated by a number of Roman mile markers. About 17,000 residents live in the towns and rural farming communities scattered throughout the park.

ARRIVALS & DEPARTURES

By Car

The rustic and minimally-developed park can be reached from Melgaço, Arcos de Valdevez, Ponte de Barca, Braga, and Montalegre.

WHERE TO STAY

Expensive

POUSADA DE SÃO BENTO, *Caniçada. Tel. (053) 647-190.*
This hunting lodge/pousada has incredible views and 18 air conditioned rooms. Facilities include a pool, bar, fireplace, restaurant, tennis, and minibars.

Moderate

QUINTA DE GESTACOS, *Gerês. Tel. (053) 391-491.*

This rustic house, in the heart of the park, has six nice rooms with private bathrooms. Facilities include bar, heating, TV room, and a great scenic location.

QUINTA DAS GLICINIAS, *Vieira do Minho. Tel. (053) 648-436.*

Located off Route N-304 just a few minutes south of the park entrance near Gerês, this nice old stone Minho house has two traditional rooms with private bathrooms.

HOTEL DAS TERMAS, *Caldas do Gerês. Tel. (053) 391-143.*

If you like the idea of having access to a spa, this 2 star, 31 room hotel is a good choice. Facilities include spa, bar, restaurant, pool, mini golf, tennis, solarium, and parking.

ESTALAGEM SÃO BENTO, *São Bento da Porta Aberta. Tel. (053) 391-106.*

Located just off the Caldo River near Gerês, this great little 4 star inn has 25 good rooms with private bathrooms, bar, restaurant, TV, garage, and good service.

PENSÃO ABRIGO, *Castro Laboreiro. Tel. (051) 451-26.*

This comfortable and clean inn has 19 modest guest rooms with private bathrooms.

Inexpensive

HOTEL DO PARQUE, *Caldas do Gerês. Tel. (053) 675-548.*

This nice 2 star hotel, located near the spa, has 60 comfortable rooms and access to the spa. Facilities include bar, restaurant, pool, mini golf course, tennis, and a garage.

PENSÃO DA PONTE, *Rua da Boavista-Gerês. Tel. (053) 391-121.*

The rooms in this basic no-frills inn come with or without private bathrooms. There is also a restaurant.

SEEING THE SIGHTS

While it is possible to drive through several parts of the **park**, roads here range from acceptable to downright dangerous. The park is best enjoyed by horseback or by trekking through paths and roads. Those who come here to view the magnificent scenery also have a good chance of seeing wild horses, boars, eagles, owls, deer, mountain goats, and several other elusive creatures.

The park's oak forests are home to many rare, indigenous species of flora and fauna, some of which cannot be found anywhere else on Earth. There are also several waterfalls, vistas, paths lined by irises, and rivers that offer spectacular photo opportunities. Several dams were built on the rivers in the park and have created a series of man made trout filled lakes and lagoons. Fishing, swimming, and non-motorized water sports are permitted in some areas of the park. There are also facilities for mountaineers who wish to test their skills.

Be sure to see the 17th century spa at **Caldas do Gerês**, lookouts at **Bela Vista** and **Pedra Bela**, the **Ponte do Arado** waterfall, the high peak at **Carris**, the panoramic **Miradouro da Junceda** lookout, the ancient village of **Soajo**, the impressive 13th century castle of **Lindoso**, and massive castle at **Castro Laboreiro**.

PRACTICAL INFORMATION FOR THE COSTA VERDE

Casinos
• **Espinho Solverde Casino**, *Rua 19, Espinho, Tel. (02) 720-238*
• **Póvoa Do Varzim Sopete Casino**, *Avenida Braga, Póvoa Do Varzim, Tel. (052) 615-151*

Currency Exchange
Most of the banks in the Costa Verde will exchange foreign currency and travelers checks. Banking hours are from 8am until 3pm, Monday through Friday. Shops, restaurants, and hotel front desks usually offer lower exchange rates than banks.

Currency exchange machines are almost impossible to find this far north but you can find 24 hour ATM machines in the larger cities.

Emergency & Useful Phone Numbers
• **Emergency Assistance** (S.O.S.), *Tel. 115*
• **Braga's São Marcos Hospital**, *Largo Carlos Amarante, Tel. (053) 240-42*
• **Espinho Hospital**, *Corner of Ruas 35 & 28, Tel. (02) 721-141*
• **Guimarães Hospital**, *Ave. de Londres, Tel. (053) 512-612*
• **Vila do Conde Hospital**, *Praça Dr. A.J. d'Ameida, Tel. (052) 624-525*
• **Directory Assistance**, *Tel. 118*
• **Automobile Club of Portugal** *(emergency road services), Tel. (02) 830-1127*
• **Porto's Pedras Rubas Airport**, *14 km out of Porto, Tel. (02) 948-2141*
• **T.A.P.Airlines Porto**, *Praça M. Albuqurque, 105, Tel. (02) 600-5555*

Museums, Palaces, & Monuments
• **Amadeo Cardoso Museum/Albano Sardoeira Library**, *Convento de São Gonçalo, Amarante, Tel. (055) 423-663*. Contains collections of Cardoso,

Carneiro, Resende, Viana, and other famous artist's work. The museum also displays a collection of regional sculpture. Open 10am until 12:30pm and 2pm until 5pm, Tuesday through Sunday. Closed on Mondays and holidays.

- **Archaeological Museum of Barcelos**, *Largo do Municipal-Paço dos Condos, Barcelos, Tel. (053) 821-251.* Contains archaeological findings from the ruins of the medieval Ducal Palace. Open 10am until 12pm and 2pm until 5:30pm daily, October through March. Open 10am until 7pm daily, April through September.
- **Biscainhos Museum**, *Palácio dos Biscainhos-Rua dos Biscainhos, Braga, Tel. (053) 276-45.* Open 10am until 12:30pm and 2pm until 5:30pm, Tuesday through Sunday. Closed on Mondays and holidays.
- **Pio XII Museum**, *Seminario de São Tiago-Largo de Sant'Iago, Braga, Tel. (053) 233-70.* Contains collections of religious sculptures, Roman artifacts, and Visigoth artwork. Open 10am until 12pm and 3pm until 5pm, Tuesday through Sunday. Closed Mondays and holidays.
- **Sacred Art Museum (Museu de Sé Primaz)**, *Sé Primaz Cathedral, Braga, Tel. (053) 233-17.* Contains collections of jewelry, ancient ecclesiastical items, and paintings. Open 8:30am until 12:30pm and 1:30pm until 5:30pm, October through May. Open 8:30am until 6:30pm, June through September.
- **Ducal Palace-Paço dos Duques**, *Guimarães, Tel. (053) 412-273.* Contains a vast collection of 16th-18th century decorative and ornamental art. Open 10am until 5:30pm daily. Closed on holidays.
- **Alberto Sampaio Museum**, *Igreja N.S. da Oliveira-Largo de Oliveira, Guimarães, Tel. (053) 412-465.* Contains oil paintings by António Vaz as well as other Portuguese painters, ceramics, azulejos, royal clothing, sculptures, and baroque wooden items. Open 10am until 12:30pm and 2pm until 5:30pm, Tuesday through Sunday. Closed Mondays and holidays.
- **Martins Sarmento Museum**, *Rua de Paio Galvão, Guimarães, Tel. (053) 415-969.* Contains collections of artifacts from local excavations of Celtic settlements. Open 10am until 12pm and 2pm until 5pm, Tuesday through Sunday. Closed Mondays and holidays.
- **Póvoa de Varzim Museum of Ethnography**, *Rua Visconde de Azevedo, Póvoa de Varzim, Tel. (052) 622-200.* Contains collections of sacred art, ceramics, azulejos, and ethnographic items. Open 10am until 12:30pm and 2:30pm until 6pm, Tuesday through Sunday. Closed Mondays and holidays.
- **Viana do Castelo Museum (Museu da Cidade)**, *Largo de São Domingos, Viana do Castelo, Tel. (058) 242-23.* Contains a collection of local artifacts, paintings, and furniture. Open 9:30am until 12:30pm and

2pm until 5:30pm, Tuesday through Sunday. Closed Mondays and holidays.
• **Vila do Conde Sacred Art Museum**, *Igreja Matriz-Rua da Igreja, Vila do Conde, Tel. (052) 631-327.* Contains collections of ecclesiastical items, silverware, and rare books. Open 10am until 12pm and 4pm until 6pm, September through May. Open 3pm until 5pm, June through August.
• **House Museum of Teixeira Lopes**, *Rua Teixeira Lopes, 32, Vila Nova de Guia, Tel. (02) 301-224.* Contains collections of Teixeira Lopes and Diogo de Macedo sculptures, as well as paintings, stamps, porcelain, and tapestries from all over Portugal. Open 9am until 12:30pm and 2pm until 5:30pm, Tuesday through Saturday. Closed on Sundays, Mondays, and holidays.

Tourist Offices *(Turismos)*
• **Amarante Tourist Office**, *Rua Candido dos Reis, Tel. (058) 424-259*
• **Barcelos Tourist Office**, *Largo de Porto Nova, v(053) 811-882*
• **Braga Tourist Office**, *Ave. da Liberdade, 1, Tel. (053) 225-50*
• **Caminha Tourist Office**, *Rua R.J. Sousa, Tel. (058) 921-952*
• **Espinho Tourist Office**, *Corner of Ruas 6 & 23, Tel. (02) 720-911*
• **Esposende Tourist Office**, *Ave. Marginal, Tel. (053) 961-354*
• **Gerês Tourist Office**, *Ave. Alfonso da Costa, Tel. (053) 391-133*
• **Gondomar Tourist Office**, *São Cosme, Tel. (02) 083-0079*
• **Guimarães Tourist Office**, *Alameda da Resitencia, Tel. (053) 412-450*
• **Monção Tourist Office**, *Largo do Loreto, Tel. (051) 652-757*
• **Peneda-Gerês Park Information**, *Arcos de Valdevez, Tel. (058) 653-38*
• **Peneda-Gerês Park Information**, *Braga, Tel. (053) 613-166*
• **Peneda-Gerês Park Information**, *Caldas do Gerês, Tel. (053) 391-181*
• **Ponte de Lima Tourist Office**, *Praça da República, Tel. (058) 942-335*
• **Ponte de Barca Tourist Office**, *Largo da Misericórdia, Tel. (058) 428-99*
• **Póvoa de Varzim Tourist Office**, *Ave. M. de Albuquerque, Tel. (052) 614-609*
• **Viana do Castelo Tourist Office**, *Rua Hospital Velha, Tel. (058) 822-620*
• **Vila do Conde Tourist Office**, *Rua 25 de Abril, 103, Tel. (052) 642-700*
• **Vila Nova de Guia Tourist Office**, *Rua. A. Cabral, Tel. (02) 370-2559*
• **Valença Tourist Office**, Ave. de Espanha, *Tel.* (051) 233-74

Travel Agencies
• **Avic Travel**, *Rua G. P. de Castro, 28, Braga. Tel. (053) 251-66.* This is the Braga branch office of a good full service travel company that can book tickets, reserve hotel rooms, and suggest guided tours of the region.

• **Star**, *Ave. D. Henriques, 638, Guimarães. Tel. (053) 415-750.* This is a good full service branch office of a travel agency and tour operator with both reservation and ticketing capabilities in Guimarães.

• **Costa Verde Travel**, *Ave. da Liberdade, 44, Barcelos. Tel. (053) 815-155.* Costa Verde Travel is a friendly local travel agency that will be glad to assist you with all types of hotel, bus, train, airplane, resort, pousada, and car rental needs.

16. THE MONTANHAS

The **Montanhas**, the mountainous region, is in Portugal's remote northeast corner, and seldom visited by tourists. Comprised of large chunks of the **Trás-os-Montes**, **Beira Baixa**, and **Beira Alta** provinces, the **Montanhas** is full of rugged snow-capped mountains, dense pine forests, and huge boulder spiked valleys that dominate the landscape. The harsh climatic conditions create huge temperature fluctuations that range from well below freezing during the long winter nights up to searingly hot summer days. The area's traditional farmers struggle with terribly difficult conditions to raise livestock that produce some of Portugal's finest meats and cheeses. Many of the inhabitants still practice a lifestyle that dates back to the middle ages, and continue to produce most of their own wines, vegetables, and smoked meats.

Several of the villages in the Montanhas are full of centuries-old granite houses with small barns in their basements, three legged iron cauldrons above raging fireplaces in their living rooms, and almost no modern conveniences. Among the most impressive of the Montanhas's ancient and mysterious villages is **Monsanto** where traditional descendants of the original residents continue to live in small homes that have been built inside of, underneath, and between huge rocks.

It is not uncommon to see traditional festivals and ritual slaughters carried out in the village squares of these communities. Besides the largest mountains in Portugal, the **Serra da Estrêla**, travelers will find beautiful parks, rustic villages, pristine lakes, and many prehistoric vestiges scattered around the Montanhas. One of the country's oldest rituals takes place in the small villages in northern Montanhas. During the **Festas dos Rapazes**, young men dress up in bizarre masks and colorful costumes the last week of December and first week of January.

Other important sights include the medieval walled village of **Sortelha**, the rustic villages of the **Serra da Estrêla** mountains, the tiny city of **Miranda do Douro** that has its own dialect, the castle and church city of **Lamego**, the historic wine cities of **Viseu** and **Vila Real**, and the vast array of walled and castle-filled towns surrounding **Guarda**.

MONTANHAS

ARRIVALS & DEPARTURES

By Air

Since there are no international airports particularly close to this region, your best bet is to fly into Lisbon and drive or take mass transportation to reach your destination in the Montanhas. It can take as long as five hours. The airport Turismo office can give you current price and scheduling information on bus and train routes to and around this region.

By Bus

Bus service to the Montanhas is limited, but does exist. Service seems to be flux, so I recommend you contact a Turismo office or a bus company directly, either at the airport or in the city or town from which you'll be departing.

By Train

As with buses, train service is limited, but does exist. I recommend you contact a Turismo office or a ticket office for trains directly, either at the airport or in the city or town you will be departing from.

ORIENTATION

The Montanhas is the eastern half of northern Portugal. This is a large and sparsely populated region that reaches from the northern city of Bragança south 231 kilometers (143 miles) to the northern bank of the Tejo River near the city of Castelo Branco.

GETTING AROUND THE REGION

By Bus

There are bus stops and depots in over 40 towns and villages with main stations in Bragança, Guarda, Vila Real, Viseu, and Castelo Branco. It's probably more efficent to combine bus travel with train travel.

By Car

The Montanhas is by far the most difficult, and perhaps most dangerous, region in Portugal to drive around. There are only a few good highways here, and most of the region's narrow roads are poorly lit, not well maintained, and are subject to freezing rain and snow conditions throughout much of the winter. I do not recommend driving around this area in any season except for summer. Since so few people inhabit this region, rush hour is almost never a problem and street parking is readily available.

By Train

There are less than a dozen main rail lines in this region. Trains stop at larger cities such as Bragança, Guarda, Vila Real, Viseu, and Castelo Branco. To travel throughout this area, it is often necessary to combine travel on trains and buses.

MONTELEGRE

The small town of Montelegre is just south of the border with Spain. It is home to about 1,900 inhabitants who live in granite and whitewashed houses with red clay and tile roofs.

ARRIVALS & DEPARTURES

By Car

Montelegre is about 13 km east of the easternmost entry point for the Parque Nacional da Peneda-Gerês on Route N-308 west.

WHERE TO STAY

Inexpensive

PENSÃO FIDALGO, *Rua da Corujeira. Tel. (076) 524-62.*

This nice and comfortable 2 star inn, located in the heart of town, offers several nice rooms both with and without private bathrooms. The views from some rooms are great!

SEEING THE SIGHTS

The large turreted **castelo** dominating the north end of town was built by King Dom Dinis in the 13th century. The large keep was added later by King Dom Afonso III. The castle grounds are open to the public, and on a clear day provide a good panoramic view of the surrounding mountain ranges.

As you walk into town from the circular castle walls, several winding lanes make their way towards the main plaza of town, **Largo do Municipio**. You should make a point to stroll down the Rua Direita during shopping hours. Keep your eye out for local hand-woven baskets and the unique capes (*capas*) worn by the residents during the colder months. Montelegre is a great place to spend a couple of hours, but besides the castle and a nice Romanesque church known as the **Igreja de Santa Maria do Castelo**, there's little else to see.

EXCURSIONS & DAY TRIPS

The countryside is filled with nice walking paths that lead to small hamlets and prehistoric dolmens. In the **Serra do Barroso** mountains, about 26 km south of town (across the **Barragem de Paradela** dam) there are several small, primitive villages that are quite unusual.

The area produces a hearty wine, Vinho dos Mortos (Wine of the Dead), which is fermented in bottles buried underground. Towns such as **Vila da Ponte**, **Vilarinho Seco**, **Viveiro**, and **Dornelas** offer a glimpse into the old way of life in the mountains. If you are lucky, you'll run into a crowd watching an oxen fight known as a **Chega de Bois**. You should also try to visit the prehistoric fortress ruins of **Castro de Carvalhelhos**, near the sight of a thermal water spa station in **Carvalhelhos**.

CHAVES

Chaves is an historic and beautiful spa city. The area was once home to prehistoric settlements that left fine examples of Neolithic and Iron Age art throughout Chaves and the surrounding Trás-O-Montes subregion, including the many 2,000 year old granite pig sculptures (*berrões*).

In the 1st century, the Romans built the wonderful stone arched Trajan bridge and created the city of Aquae Flaviae on the sight of a hot thermal spring near the intersection of their two most important roads. Its strategic location on the banks of the Tâmega River (only 13 km south of the Spanish border) led to a vast history of conquer and occupation by the Suebians, Visigoths, Moors, and the Spanish. After its capture from the Moors in the 12th century, King Dom Afonso Henriques ordered the construction of defensive walls to help secure the area. The town was further strengthened in the 14th century with the additional fortifications of a massive turreted **castelo** (castle).

ARRIVALS & DEPARTURES

By Car

Chaves lies about 45 km southeast of Montalegre on Route N-103.

WHERE TO STAY

Expensive

HOTEL AQUAE FLAVIAE, *Praça do Brasil. Tel. (076) 267-11.*

This modern 4 star hotel with nice air conditioned rooms is located in central Chaves. Facilities include restaurant, pool, sauna, tennis, room service, TV, and handicapped access.

Moderate

QUINTA DA MATA, *N-213, Chaves. Tel. (076) 233-85.*

This wonderful 17th century manor house, 3 km southeast of town, has five great rooms with private bathrooms. Facilities include lounge, dining room, winery, sauna, horses, tennis, bicycles, nearby thermal springs, library, TV room, and parking.

QUINTA DE SANTA ISABEL, *Santo Estevão. Tel. (076) 218-18.*

This beautiful manor house is located on a wine producing estate 7 km northeast of Chaves off Route N-103. The house offers six fine rooms as well as one and two bedroom apartments with private bathrooms (some with kitchens). Facilities include TV room and parking.

ESTALAGEM SANTIAGO, *Rua do Olival. Tel. (076) 225-45.*

This friendly 4 star inn has 28 large and comfortable double rooms with private bathroom. Facilities include restaurant, bar, TV, and parking.

HOTEL TRAJANO, *Rua Candido dos Reis. Tel. (076) 332-415.*

This is a good 2 star hotel with 39 regionally styled rooms with private bathroom. Facilities include restaurant, bar, laundry, air conditioning, room service, and cable TV.

Inexpensive

GRANDE HOTEL DE CHAVES, *Rua 25 de Abril, 25. Tel. (076) 211-18.*

This friendly and reasonable 1 star hotel has 36 basic but comfortable rooms with and without private bathrooms. Facilities include a decent restaurant, bar, and TV room.

WHERE TO EAT

Moderate

RESTAURANTE LEONEL, *Campo da Roda. Tel. (076) 231-99.*

A nicely designed seafood and steak restaurant near the Aerodromo, it serves some of the best rice and seafood (arroz de marisco) in northern Portugal.

DIONISIOS, *Praça do Municipio. Tel. (076) 237-51.*

This simple little restaurant, near the castle, serves great fish and meat meals for reasonable prices. You can sit indoors in the dining room or at outdoor tables.

Inexpensive

O POTE, *Ave. Eng. Duarte Pacheco, 10. Tel. (076) 212-26.*

This nice regional restaurant, across the bridge, offers great meat dishes and huge daily specials. Try the wonderful roasted kid (cabrito a padeiro) if it's available.

SEEING THE SIGHTS

To begin your walking tour, first try to find parking near the large **Praça Luís de Camões** square. The center of this remarkable square contains a beautiful Manueline pillory, surrounded by several sights worth a good look. Behind the pillory is the oldest monument remaining in Chaves, the Romanesque church, **Igreja Matriz**.

Adjacent to the Igreja Matriz is the 17th century baroque **Igreja da Misericórdia**, with entrancing 18th century azulejos by Oliveira Bernardes and a gorgeous ceiling painted by Jerónimo Rocha Braga. Also in the same square you can visit the regional museum **Museu de Região Flaviense** (closed on Mondays), which contains a great assortment of prehistoric phallic sculptures and menhirs, Roman artifacts, and ancient coins.

Just behind these buildings near the old walls you can view the 14th century **castelo** (castle), of which little besides a nice garden and the spiked **Torre de Menagem** keep remains. The keep was used as the official residence of the first Duke of Bragança and now is home to the **Museu Militar** (Military Museum), which holds an assortment of weapons from ancient periods as well as more modern conflicts (closed on Mondays). A short trip to the terrace on top of the keep provides an excellent view over the beautiful houses and winding streets of the city.

The large spa complex just west of the **Praça Luís de Camões** is known as the **Estancia Termal** and is open from June through October. The hot thermal waters of the spa baths are said to help the treatment of internal organs, rheumatism, and nutritional disorders.

Walk to the riverside at the south edge of town to see the wonderful 1st century **Ponte Trajano** Roman bridge with its 16 arches and Roman mile markers. If you cross the bridge you can take a quick peek at the octagonal 18th century church, **Igreja da Madelena**, and cross back again.

Walking from the bridge towards the center of town via the Rua de Santo António, turn right (east) at the **mercado** (market). A block down you will find the 17th century **Forte de São Fransisco** (fortress). While walking through the charming streets in the old town, keep your eye out for the area's black pottery which is unique to this area.

You may also wish to sample the strong smoked ham (*presunto*), sausages (*enchidos*), and firewater (*aquardente*), which can be found in the shops and snack bars on Rua Direita as well as near **Praça do Brasil**. About 3 km northwest of Chaves are excellent examples of prehistoric *rupestre* art embedded into a large boulder known as the **Outeiro Machado**.

SPORTS & RECREATION
Horseback Riding
• **Quinta da Mata Horse Riding**, *Chaves, Tel. (076) 233-85*

BRAGANÇA

The royal city of Bragança is located on the banks of the Fervenca River and is dominated by a large citadel that encircles the picturesque medieval old town and a massive 12th century castle.

Originally a Spanish city, Bragança has been alternatively controlled by Romans, Moors, and finally the Portuguese Dukes of Bragança whose dynasty ruled Portugal until the proclamation of the republic in 1910. To this day, the ancestors of the royal family live in the area and are producing fine wines and hoping (in private) to one day regain both their throne and vast fortune that was confiscated during the revolution.

ARRIVALS & DEPARTURES

By Bus
• **Bragança Main Bus depot**, *Largo de Estação, Tel. (073) 228-70*

By Car
Bragança is 98 km northeast of Chaves on Route N-103 east. The trip can take up to three hours on this rugged mountain route.

By Train
• **Bragança CP Rail station**, *Largo de Estação, Tel. (073) 223-97*

WHERE TO STAY

Moderate
POUSADA DE SÃO BARTOLOMEU, *Estrada de Turismo. Tel. (073) 331-493.*

A nice pousada just out of town, it has 16 rustic rooms and great views of the castle. Facilities include a good restaurant, lounge with fireplace, tennis, and parking.

HOTEL BRAGANÇA, *Ave. Dr. Fancisco Sá Carneiro. Tel. (073) 331-579.*

This nice modern 3 star hotel has 42 clean and comfortable guest rooms with private bathroom. Facilities include restaurant, bar, cable TV, laundry, and parking.

Inexpensive
MOINHO DO CANICO, *N-103-Castrelos. Tel. (073) 235-77.*

This nice rustic stone house with a watermill is located on the banks of the Baceiro River about 12 km west of town. The house rents two nice guest rooms with private bathroom.

PENSÃO SÃO ROQUE, *Zona da Estacada, 26. Tel. (073) 381-481.*
This clean and simple inn has 30 or so comfortable guest rooms with private bathroom.

WHERE TO EAT
Expensive
POUSADA DE SÃO BARTOLOMEU, *Estrada de Turismo. Tel. (073) 331-493.*
Excellent regional cuisine is served in a relaxing environment with surprisingly good service. The chef creates several meat and fish specialties, including a wonderful trout dish called truta em escabeche.

Moderate
SOL NEVE, *Rua Loreto. Tel. (073) 244-13.*
This is a pretty good local restaurant and snack bar that serves huge portions of daily meat and fish specials with great salads. They serve the coldest beer in town.

SEEING THE SIGHTS
The citadel is located on the extreme southeastern edge of downtown and can be entered via the **Porta de Santo António** gate, which you'll pass through to enter the citadel. Once inside, you have entered a medieval town that has not changed much in several centuries. Small farmers' houses can be seen with an assortment of livestock roaming the premises.

The dominant structure in the old town is the **castelo** (open daily), where you can explore its towers, dungeon, cistern, battlements, drawbridge, and **Torre de Menagem**. This keep, once used to imprison Queen Dona Leonor, is home to the **Museu Militar** (Military Museum) with a permanent exhibition of 19th century weapons and artifacts (closed Thursdays). The top of the keep can be visited, and has a beautiful panoramic view over Bragança.

Also inside the citadel is the wonderful 13th century Romanesque **Domus Municipalis** building, used as a sort of town hall and meeting place. The building has a large cistern on the ground floor that stored the town's water during several major sieges. The next structure you will find in the citadel is the columned facade of the 18th century **Igreja de Santa Maria**, which contains an ornately painted vaulted ceiling. Be sure to look at the Iron Age granite boar (*porca da vila*) that has been used as a support for a Gothic pillory.

The small lanes south of the citadel near the riverfront, like Rua dos Fornos, were once home to the town's Jewish community (known as

Marranos) who were trying to flee the Inquisition in neighboring Spain. To the west of the citadel, follow Rua Serpa Pinto east down towards the heart of town to the peaceful square known as the **Praça São Vicente**, where you'll see the dramatic 17th century church, **Igreja da São Vicente**. Originally a Romanesque-style church, the facade and adjacent portico were added during its first complete renovation in the 17th century. The interior of the church is richly decorated with 17th century golden carvings and a strange 19th century depiction of Christ's ascension.

If you walk back towards the citadel and follow Rua Santo Condestavel north, you will soon come to the impressive Renaissance portal of the **Igreja de São Bento**. The church's fine interior boasts a beautiful ceiling, including rare Mudéjar woodwork above the chancel. All of these churches are difficult to gain access to. If you cannot find an open door, go over to the Turismo office on Ave. Cidade de Zamora and ask for the location of the keys.

From the **Praça São Vicente**, head down the Rua do Conselheiro Abilio Beco until you reach the old Episcopal Palace (**Antigo Paço Episcopal**). This 16th century palace is now home to the **Museu Regional do Abade de Baçal**. Inside the walls of this building (closed Mondays) you will find an amazing array of paintings, goldsmithery, decorative artwork, furniture, coins, antique clothing, ecclesiastical items, prehistoric stone pigs, and other important archaeological and ethnographic items collected by Abade de Baçal, the town's priest.

A bit further down the same road you will arrive at the **Praça da Sé**, dominated by the large 16th century **Sé Cathedral** which is worth a quick look. Behind the cathedral you can relax in the tranquil **Jardim António José Almeida** (public gardens).

EXCURSIONS & DAY TRIPS

Just above Bragança is the wonderful **Parque Natural de Montezinho**, with over 200,000 acres of prime park land within the **Serra de Coroa** and **Serra de Montezinho** mountain ranges. The park is dissected by several small roads (several are dirt roads) as well as the beautiful Onor and Tuela Rivers. These rivers have recently been used for kayac adventures, and provide much of the fresh fish used in the area's best restaurants.

Used mostly by local residents for weekend picnics and family hikes, the park contains a loose network of walking trails, trout streams, and small peasant villages like **Zeive** and **Labiados** that seem frozen in the middle ages. For details about hiking trails, camping, fishing, cabin rentals, stone home rentals in **Casas Abrigo**, and hunting, contact the Park office in Bragança, *Tel. (073) 287-34.*

MIRANDA DO DOURO

Dating back to the Roman era, this fortified town above the Douro River was finally liberated in 1385 by King Dom João I. Since Miranda do Douro is such an isolated town, many of the local residents still speak an unusual dialect called Mirandes.

ARRIVALS & DEPARTURES
By Car

Miranda do Douro is 102 km southeast of Bragança on Route N-218 south.

WHERE TO STAY
Moderate

POUSADA DE SANTA CATARINA, *Estrada da Barragem. Tel. (073) 422-55.*

This little pousada has 12 comfortable rooms, most of which have balconies that look over a large man-made lake. This is the best place to stay in the area.

Inexpensive

PENSÃO SANTA CRUZ, *Rua Abade de Baçal, 61. Tel. (073) 424-74.*

This nice 2 star inn and restaurant, located in the heart of the old town, has a dozen or so comfortable rooms with and without private bathrooms. It's a nice place to stay.

RESIDENCIAL PLANALTO, *Rua 1 de Maio. Tel. 073) 423-62.*

A surprisingly good, basic inn that offers over 40 clean and comfortable rooms with private bathroom. There are almost no facilities but it's close to everything.

WHERE TO EAT
Moderate

RESTAURANTE SANTA CRUZ, *Rua Abade de Baçal, 61. Tel. (073) 424-74.*

This great little family run restaurant serves hearty regional meats and stews that are only available in this area. The house wines are quite good as well.

SEEING THE SIGHTS

This small city unfolds below a 16th century cathedral set on the grounds of the citadel (which was blown up in the 18th century). Now about all that remains of the original castle is the **Torre de Menagem** keep, the **Porta da Traicão** (traitor's gate), and a few pieces of the fortified wall. The Sé Cathedral is open to the public and contains vaulted ceilings, the beloved hilarious 19th century statue of **Menino Jesus da Cartolinha** by artist Gregório Hernandez, a wonderful carved organ, beautiful gilded and carved altarpieces, and wooden stalls ornamented with beautiful 17th century paintings.

From the citadel area, stroll down the old medieval streets such as the **Rua Costanhila** which have beautiful 15th and 16th century houses. While walking through town, be sure to look in the small shops that sell the locally produced dark woolen carpets. When you reach the main square of town, **Praça Dom João III**, you can visit the **Museu da Terra de Miranda** (town museum) in the old town hall (*antiga casa da Câmara*) building. Here you can see a good collection of beautiful sacred art, prehistoric artifacts, unusual local costumes, and bizarre antique household items.

If you intend to dine in the area, make sure to try the very tender braised meat known as *posta a mirandesa*. A good place to find locally made goods and meats is at the daily market on Rua do Mercado.

For those of you who would like to explore this unusual little corner of the world, I suggest an early morning start. If you are a good driver, take route N-221 south to see the castle and town of **Mogodouro** amidst the fabulous **Serra de Mogadouro** mountains. You can also cross the border by car into Spain just past the **Barragem de Miranda** dam. Since this part of Portugal is quite remote, you may wish to return to Miranda do Douro for your overnight.

MIRANDELA

The wonderful walled town of Mirandela lies on the banks of the Tua River. This charming little secluded town has several interesting sights and is a nice place to visit.

ARRIVALS & DEPARTURES
By Car
Mirandela is about 76 km southwest of Bragança on Route IP-4 west.

WHERE TO STAY
Moderate
HOTEL MIRA TUA, *Rua da República, 20. Tel. (078) 224-04.*
This is a good 2 star hotel with 31 rooms with private bathrooms. Facilities include bar, restaurant, direct dial phones, TV room, safe deposit boxes, and nearby parking.

Inexpensive
PENSÃO PRAIA, *Largo 1 de Janeiro, 4. Tel. (078) 224-97.*
A cheap 1 star inn with a dozen or so basic rooms, some with private bathrooms. Besides a breakfast room, there are few facilities.

SEEING THE SIGHTS
The town's original fortress and castle are mostly in ruins, but you can still visit the fine 17th century **Câmara Municipal**, formerly the Palácio dos Tavoras manor house and the 17th century church, **Igreja Matriz**. Also worth seeing are the **Porta de Dom Dinis** gate in the old walls and the town's striking medieval **Ponte** (bridge) with its 17 arches, which was rebuilt atop the foundations of an older Roman bridge.

The town has an art museum, **Museu de Arte Moderna** (closed on Saturdays and Sundays). You'll find a rich collection of works by selected 20th century Portuguese artists as well as by local painter Armindo Texeira Lopes.

SHOPPING
The town is noted for producing quality woolen blankets that can be found in several small shops.

VILA REAL
The university city of Vila Real rests at the foot of both the Serra do Marão and Serra do Alvão mountain ranges. Originally part of a Roman region called Panóias, Vila Real became an important administrative town in the 15th century.

It is now home to 32,000 inhabitants who live just off the Corgo River. Although the city has grown to include industry and some modern suburbs, it still has a small town ambiance.

ARRIVALS & DEPARTURES
By Car
Vila Real is about 65 km southwest of Mirandela on Route IP-4 west.

By Train
• **Vila Real CP Rail station**, *Rua Miguel Bombarda, Tel. (059) 322-193*

WHERE TO STAY
Moderate
CASA AGRÍCOLA DA LEVADA, *Estrada do Circuito. Tel. (059) 322-190.*

This quiet farming house, just north of town near the river, makes its own provisions from the animals and fruits they raise. They offer four rooms with private bathrooms, a lounge, dining room, horses, boating, bicycles, and TV room.

HOTEL MIRACORGO, *Ave 1 de Maio, 76. Tel. (059) 250-01.*

This modern, 3 star river view hotel has 76 large air conditioned rooms. Facilities include restaurant, bar, room service, pool, sauna, TV, and handicapped access.

HOTEL CABANELAS, *Rua D. Pedro de Castro. Tel. (059) 323-154.*

This is a reasonably good 2 star hotel with 24 small double rooms. Facilities include bar, restaurant, heating, TV, direct dial phones, and parking.

QUINTA DE SÃO MARTINHO, *Estrada do Circuito. Tel. (059) 239-86.*

This rustic country house is located in a farming area close to the Solar de Mateus. The house offers a two bedroom apartment with kitchen, sitting room and private bathroom.

Inexpensive

CASA DA CRUZ, *N-304, Campea. Tel. (059) 979-422.*

Casa da Cruz is a typical 18th century stone house in the mountains with three nice double rooms that come with bathrooms and kitchens. It's located about 12 km northwest of Vila Real.

PENSÃO O VIZINHO, *Ave. Aureliano Barrigas. Tel. (059) 322-881.*

A decent, basic inn, it has 13 double rooms with and without private bathroom. Although there are few facilities, this is a good budget choice.

WHERE TO EAT

Moderate

RESTAURANTE ESPADEIRO, *Ave. Almeida Lucena. Tel. (059) 322-302.*

An impressive and cheerful restaurant, Restaurante Espadeiro prepares fine regional fish and meat dishes in front of its clients. Try the always fresh local river trout served here.

CHURRASCO, Rua António Azevedo, 24. Tel. (059) 322-313.

This little snack bar and restaurant specializes in roasted meats. The place is far from fancy, but with a little patience you'll be rewarded with great food.

SEEING THE SIGHTS

There are several buildings and churches worth seeing. Your best bet is to park as close as possible to the centrally located Avenida Carvalho

Araujo, home to several of the most interesting sights. On the avenue itself you can visit the 15th century Gothic **Sé Cathedral** (sometimes referred to as the **Igreja de São Domingos**), the 15th century **Casa de Diogo Cão** (the house of a famous Portuguese explorer), **Casa dos Marqueses de Vila Real** with its battlements and Manueline windows, and the Manueline Turismo building that is several centuries old.

Nearby, on the busy Rua 31 de Janeiro, you can visit the beautiful tiles of the baroque 18th century church, **Igreja dos Clérigos**, which has become known as the Capela Nova. Throughout the old part of town on streets such as Rua Serpa Pinto, Rua António de Azevedo, and Rua Teixeira de Sousa, you can find many fine examples of 17th century houses and impressive regal buildings.

The massive 18th century **Solar de Mateus** palace (open daily) can be reached by driving just 3 km east of the city to the village of **Mateus**. This Nicolau Nasoni designed baroque masterpiece includes several unusual towers, huge statues, impressive granite window moldings, and a bold whitewashed and granite block facade. The main section of the palace is set back behind two imposing side wings, and is entered by a huge grand staircase. The facade of the palace is fronted by a shallow pool containing a statue of a drowning naked lady. Connected to the left wing of the palace is the more impressive facade of a Nasoni designed baroque chapel. The interior includes 18th century furniture, remarkable wooden ceilings, a library full of rare editions, and several period paintings. The palace's formal gardens can also be viewed. You may recognize the palace from the label of **Mateus Rosé** wines.

Also worth a half-day trip from Vila Real is the **Parque Natural do Alvão**. This wonderful park is a protected area with waterfalls, trails, and local villages such as **Lamas de Olo**, **Galegos de Serra**, **Amal**, and **Ermelo**, which produce beautiful handcrafted wooden clogs and woolen capes.

For further details and trail maps, contact the park's main information offices in Vila Real on Rua Alves Torgo, 22 at Tel. (059) 241-38 or in Amarante area at Tel. (055) 382-09.

SPORTS & RECREATION
• **Casa Agrícola Levada Horse Riding**, *Vila Real, Tel. (059) 322-190*

EXCURSIONS & DAY TRIPS
Peso da Régua, also known as simply Régua, is a major Port wine producing and transportation city on the northern bank of the **Douro River**, about 24 km (14.5 miles) from Vila Real on Route IP-3 south (also called route N-2). This town is at the western border of the demarcated Port wine region, and has several wine tasting lodges that are open to the public for tastings and guided tours.

My favorite Port wine tours and tastings are held at the **Ramos Pinto** lodges (closed on Sundays). There is little else to do in town besides getting a bit smashed. If you know you're going to partake of the wine, go to Régua by public transportation (boat, bus, or train).

LAMEGO

The wealthy wine producing city of Lamego is near the Douro River, at the banks of the smaller Balsemão River and is surrounded by terraced agricultural fields. The city was once occupied by Roman, Swabian, Visigoth, and Moorish settlements.

Scattered throughout the city are several interesting granite mansions, small typical neighborhoods, and several beautiful historic buildings on wide avenues such as Avenida Dr. Alfredo de Sousa and the more commercial Rua Alexandre Hurculano.

ARRIVALS & DEPARTURES

By Car

Lamego is 11 km south of Peso da Régua on Route IP-3 south (also called Route N-2).

WHERE TO STAY

Moderate

QUINTA DA TIMPEIRA, *N-2, Lugar da Timpeira. Tel. (054) 628-11.*

Located about 3 km south of town off Route N-2A, this charming wine producing estate has five nice rooms with private bathrooms. Facilities include piano bar, fireside lounge, dining room, pool, billiards, tennis, bicycles, garden, TV, and wine cellar.

HOTEL PARQUE, *Parque N.S. de Remédios. Tel. (054) 621-06.*

This nice 2 star, 33 room hotel has great views over a church and the city. Facilities include a restaurant with panoramic views, bar, garden, TV, laundry, and handicapped access.

ALBERGARIA DO CERRADO, *Lugar do Cerrado. Tel. (054) 631-64.*

This modern comfortable inn has 30 air conditioned rooms (some with balconies) and is just east of town. Facilities include bar, restaurant, and handicapped access.

VILA HOSTILINA, *N-2, Lamego. Tel. (054) 623-947.*

This estate and 19th century house is located on a hilltop and offers eight rooms with private bathrooms, a fireside lounge, dining room, card room, sauna, tennis, pool, bicycles, health club, gardens, TV room, wine cellar, gardens, and a great view.

Inexpensive

PENSÃO SOLAR DO ESPÍRITO SANTO, *Rua Alexandre Hurculano. Tel. (054) 643-86.*

This pretty good, centrally located inn has 31 double and twin rooms with private bathrooms. Facilities include bar, heating, garage, TV, and handicapped access.

PENSÃO SOLAR, *Largo de Sé. Tel. (054) 620-60.*

Located near the cathedral, this clean and comfortable 2 star inn has 25 clean rooms with private bathrooms but few other facilities. It's close to everything.

WHERE TO EAT

Moderate

A MINHA, *Rua Alexendre Hurculano, 5. Tel. (054) 633-53.*

A Minha is a cozy, rustic restaurant that serves delicious locally produced meats in unusual dining rooms. The service is excellent, and the ambiance is great.

Inexpensive

COMBINADO, *Rua da Olaria, 89. Tel. (054) 629-02.*

This is a pretty good local fish and meat restaurant that serves up large portions of locally caught trout and other regional specialties. The prices are reasonable and the setting casual.

SEEING THE SIGHTS

The city rests at the base of two large hills. One of these hills is home to the ruins of a 13th century **castelo** (castle) and some stone houses, while the other hill is covered by a huge pinnacle and a 686 step staircase (covered with azulejos) that leads up to the imposing 19th century baroque **Santuario de Nossa Senhora dos Remidos** church. While the church's interior is nothing special, a stroll down the staircase is a great way to start your visit into the center of town. From the bottom of the staircase, walk straight down Ave. Dr. A. de Sousa and continue past the turnabout until you reach Ave. Visconde de Sousa. Stop at this street's Turismo office and ask for a local walking map.

A few more steps down Ave. Visconde de Sousa you will soon find the **Largo do Camões** plaza, dominated by the 12th century **Sé Cathedral**. Almost nothing is left from its Romanesque beginnings, but the lovely triple portico, 18th century organs, and beautifully carved choir chairs are worth noting. Across the plaza from the Sé is the **Antigo Paço Episcopal** (old Episcopal palace), which houses the **Museu Regional de Lamego**. The museum (closed Mondays) contains over 30 rooms filled with fine examples of baroque chapels, furniture, 16th century Belgian tapestries, statues, azulejos, sacred art, and many paintings including works by 16th century artist Vasco Fernandes.

Starting the last week of August, the **Festa de Nossa Senhora dos Remidos** (a festival) takes over town for three weeks. Events range from oxen-pulled processions to folklore expositions and huge rock concerts. Before leaving town, visit the **Caves Raposeira** winery, a few kilometers south of town off Route N-2. Here you can take a guided 20 minute tour of the facilities and sample some great sparkling wines for free.

VISEU

The enchanting city of **Viseu** stands at the bank of the **Pavia River**. With its roots going back to at least the Roman era, Viseu is an excellent place to wander back through time. The city became home to several masters of Portuguese art such as Vasco Fernandes and Gaspar Vaz who have left their mark in this city and all of Portugal.

This is a city with so much to see you should be sure to give yourself enough time. Viseu has been an important commercial city as far back as the 14th century when the Marranos (local Jewish merchants) forged the development unique trade methods. The local economy of Viseu and its 22,000 residents are heavily dependent on the Dão wine industry. These light and fruity wines are a staple of the country's diet, and excellent bottles are sold for as little as 250$00.

ARRIVALS & DEPARTURES
By Bus
• **Viseu Main Bus depot**, *Ave. Dr. António Almeida, Tel. (032) 412-337*

By Car
Viseu is 70 km from Lamego on Route IP-3 south (also called Route N-2).
• **Avis Rent a Car in Viseu**, *Hotel Grão Vasco, Tel. (032) 257-50*
• **Hertz Rent a Car in Viseu**, *Rua da Paz, 21, Tel. (032) 421-846*

By Train
• **Viseu CP Rail station**, *Ave. Capitão H. Ribeiro, Tel. (032) 423-100*

WHERE TO STAY
Moderate
HOTEL GRÃO VASCO, *Rua Gaspar Barreiros. Tel. (032) 423-512.*
This 4 star full service hotel near the Rossio offers 88 air conditioned

rooms with nice interiors. Facilities include bar, restaurant, pool, garden, and good service.

CASA DE REBORDINHO, *Rebordinho. Tel. (032) 461-258.*

This beautiful 17th century manor house and estate, 6 km south of Viseu off N-231, has four rooms with private bathrooms, lounge, TV room, a farm, and parking.

CASA DOS GOMES, *São João de Lourosa. Tel. (032) 461-341.*

An attractive 18th century granite house and farming estate, Casa Dos Gomes is about 5 km southeast of Viseu off Route N-231. There are seven nice rooms with private bathrooms, lounge, dining room, vineyards, pool, tennis, billiards, bicycles, library, TV room, and parking.

HOTEL MANA, *N-16, Via Cacador. Tel. (032) 479-243.*

Located about 3 km from Viseu, this modern 3 star hotel has 73 comfortable rooms. Facilities include bar, restaurant, pool, gym, TV, billiards, tennis, squash, and parking.

Inexpensive

RESTHOTEL VISEU, *Vernum-Campo. Tel. (032) 451-258.*

This nice new 2 star motel is a few kilometers out of town. It has 60 comfortable air conditioned rooms with private bathroom, bar, restaurant, TV, and parking.

RESIDENCAL DOM DUARTE, *Rua Alexandre Hurculano, 214. Tel. (032) 257-81.*

This pleasant, centrally located, basic inn has 18 comfortable but tacky rooms with private bathroom. The inn has a breakfast room and a TV room but is nothing special.

WHERE TO EAT

Moderate

RESTAURANTE TÍPICO O CORTICO, *Rua Agusta Hilario, 47. Tel. (032) 461-278.*

This excellent regional restaurant serves fine local meat dishes in a relaxing atmosphere. The old granite building is located in the heart of the old town.

RESTAURANTE A PARREIRA, *Ave. de Belgica, 2. Tel. (032) 417-94.*

This informal meat and seafood restaurant is located in an old stone house in the center of Viseu. The ambiance, service, and hearty dishes are among the best in town.

Inexpensive

RESTAURANTE CACIMBO, *Rua Alexandre Hurculano, 95. Tel. (032) 422-894.*

A down to earth eating establishment, it serves a limited selection of roasted meats and fried fish specialties. The large portions are very good.

SEEING THE SIGHTS

To begin your journey by foot through this amazing city, you must first find parking around the **Praça de República** square in the city's center (also called the **Rossio**). From the Rossio's statue of Prince Henry the Navigator, the first Duke of Viseu, you may wish to pop into the Turismo office – one block south on Avenida 25 de Abril and then half a block to the left (east) on Avenida Caloute Gulbenkian. While in the Turismo, ask for one of the great free town street maps in English.

As you walk back up the Ave. 25 de Abril towards the Rossio, you will first find the baroque 18th century **Igresa dos Terceiros de São Francisco**. This church's solemn interior contains beautiful azulejos and carefully carved and gilded pulpits. Upon exiting the church and walking a few steps north into the Rossio, notice the large azulejos mural of regional life by Joaquim Lopes. The 19th century **Câmara Municipal** (town hall) with its imaginative tile interior and the mastestic courtyard with its granite staircase can be visited across from the mural.

The Rossio extends up (northward) until it reaches the **Largo Major Teles** where you will find the lovely **Jardim das Maes**, adjacent to the **Casa-Museu de Almeida Moreira** (house and museum). The museum (closed Mondays) contains the private collections of furniture, ceramics, armor, and paintings.

From the museum, head up (north) on Rua Soar de Cima for a block or so until you have reached the massive 16th century **Porta do Soar de Cima** gate, built as the main entrance to the old town wall by King Alfonso V. As soon as you cross into the old town you are bombarded with immensely powerful facades and churches in every direction. As you make your way towards the heart of the old town, the **Praça da Sé** plaza, you will find yourself next to the whitewashed and granite facade of the beautiful 18th century **Igreja da Misericórdia**. The exterior of this church contains two large bell towers and a large portal that rests below a highly decorated baroque patio.

Directly across from the entrance to the Igreja de Misericórdia is the fantastic 12th century Romanesque **Sé Cathedral**. Rebuilt several times since its initial construction, the cathedral contains an odd assortment of elements including Gothic pillars, a vaulted stone block ceiling adorned with 16th century knot shaped tracery, a gilded 16th century baroque altarpiece, beautiful azulejos, and Renaissance cloisters. You can visit the chapter house of the cloisters, which contains the **Museu de Arte Sacra** (closed Sundays), with its several rare treasures and ecclesiastical items dating as far back as the 12th century.

Next to the Sé Cathedral, you will find yet another remarkable building known as the **Antigo Paço Episcopal dos Três Escaloes**. This granite 16th century former bishop's palace is now home to the wonderful **Museu de Grão Vasco**. Inside the three-floor museum (closed Mondays) you will find several rooms full of 16th century masterpieces by local artists such as Vasco Fernandes (Grão Vasco) and Gaspar Vaz, including the paintings moved here from the adjacent Sé Cathedral's original retable. Other rooms contain a selection of beautiful 13th through 19th century works – paintings, ceramics, sculptures, azulejos, carved ivory, furniture and tapestries.

From the left (west) side of the **Praça da Sé** plaza, take Rua Silva Gaio up past the northern edge of old town. After you have crossed the Ave. Emidio Navarro, you will soon find the beautiful **Porta dos Cavaleiros** which passes through the old town walls. Just west of the gate you'll see the ancient town well. Double back to the **Praça da Sé** and this time head south from the middle of the square and pass through the **Praça Dom Duarte** onto Rua Dom Duarte. On this street you can see the 14th century birthplace of King Dom Duarte, the medieval **Casa da Torre**, adorned with an unusual twin Manueline window.

From here you can follow Rua Dom Duarte south as it merges with Rua Direita and turn right (west) onto Rua Formosa, which leads you back past town's daily **mercado** (market). From the eastern edge of the market, you can also take a small walk up Rua Dr. Luís Ferreira to see some fine shops.

Return to the market, and turn right (west) onto Rua Formosa and follow it back to the Rossio. Before departing the city, you can stop by the tranquil **Parque Aquilino Ribeiro** park just below the Rossio for a restful stop or picnic. On Thursdays, the town hosts a large weekly **mercado** (market) in the north part of town below the riverside.

CARAMULO

The gorgeous spa town of Caramulo rests on a hill deep in the windswept Serra de Caramulo mountains and is surrounded by mountains, parks, gardens, pine forests, and hiking trails in every direction. Caramulo is primarily visited by local families in search of peaceful weekend outings.

ARRIVALS & DEPARTURES
By Car
Caramulo is 58 km southwest of Viseu. Although there are several scenic mountain approaches to the city, it is easiest to arrive by taking IP3 south from Viseu and connecting to Route N-230 west near Tondela.

WHERE TO STAY
Moderate
POUSADA DE SÃO JERÓNIMO, *Caramulo. Tel. (032) 861-291.*
This small and cozy pousada has six nice guest rooms with balconies, nice views, a relaxing lounge with fireplace, a good regional restaurant, good service, and a pool.

Inexpensive
PENSÃO SÃO CRISTÓVÃO, *Caramulo. Tel. (032) 861-394.*
This is a reasonable and simple 2 star inn with good rooms with and without private bathrooms in the heart of town. The inn is often closed during winter months.

SEEING THE SIGHTS
This quiet city is home to the **Fundação Abel de Lacerda** foundation (named for its benefactor, a local doctor), which maintains the city's two interesting museums (closed Mondays). The foundation's art museum boasts several collections of wonderful art. The most impressive of the museum's paintings consist of Portuguese masterworks by Vasco Fernandes (Grão Vasco), Eduardo Nery, Frei Carlos, and Amadeu de Sousa Cardoso, while its European collection includes modern paintings by Dali, Picasso, Miro, Chagall and Leger.

Also included in the foundation's collection is a vast array of ceramics, tapestries, statues, jewelry, and furniture. The adjacent museum contains an assortment several dozen classic cars and motorcycles, including a rare vintage 1911 Rolls Royce, a mint 1898 Hurtu, and the world's only remaining Pegaso.

EXCURSIONS & DAY TRIPS
Most visitors come to picnic and to take short drives or hikes to the panoramic plateaus and small mountaintop villages. The most accessible of these vistas can be reached by taking Route N-230-3 south for about 3 km; turn left at the sign for the dramatic **Cabeço da Neve** lookout. If you prefer to hike, go back to Route N-230-3 south and continue another half mile or so to the marked path for **Caramulinho**. This 45 minute hike leads to an impressive view over several mountain ranges.

MANGUALDE
The quaint town of Mangualde is also a lively commercial town of 9,000 residents. It has managed to preserve its small, but delightful, old section of stone lanes and tiny granite houses that seem to be lost in time.

ARRIVALS & DEPARTURES
By Car
Mangualde lies 17 km southeast of Viseu on Route IP-5 east.

WHERE TO STAY
Moderate
CASA DAS MESQUITELA, *Mesquitela. Tel. (032) 614-210.*

This wonderful 16th century manor house has six luxuriously furnished guest rooms with private bathroom. It's located about 4 km southeast of Mangualde near Route N-16. This truly remarkable inn also has a period dining room that serves regional cuisine.

CASA DE QUINTELA, *Quinta de Azzura. Tel. (032) 622-936.*

Located 5 km northeast of Mangualde off IP-5A, this large granite 16th century manor house has five nice guest rooms with private bathroom. Facilities include dining room, lounge, pool, tennis, trails, TV room, gardens, library, and parking.

HOTEL SENHORA DO CASTELO, *Monte Senhora do Castelo. Tel. (032) 611-608.*

This large 3 star hotel with 85 air conditioned rooms is not far from Mangualde's center. Facilities include bar, grill room, restaurant, pools, sauna, cable TV, and billiards.

ESTALAGEM CASA DE AZURARA, *Rua Nova, 78. Tel. (032) 612-010.*

This nice 4 star inn, located near the heart of Mangualde, has 15 comfortable rooms with private bathroom, bar, restaurant, air conditioning, TV, and kitchen facilities.

Inexpensive
ESTALAGEM CRUZ DA MATA, *Lugar da Cruz da Mata. Tel. (032) 611-945.*

This reasonably good inn has 19 basic twin and double guest rooms with private bathroom, bar, restaurant, room service, heating, laundry, and good service.

SEEING THE SIGHTS
Mangualde boasts several beautiful churches, including the medieval 13th century **Igreja Matriz** with its fine paintings and eerie courtyard, and the 18th century **Igreja das Almas** with its ornate altar. The most impressive structure is the wonderful 18th century noble residence known as the **Palácio dos Condes de Anadia** – still privately owned. The opulent house (closed Mondays) contains a vast assortment of bizarre scenic azulejos, beautiful period furnishings, portraits of the Count of Anadia and his family, beautiful ceilings, and several regal rooms.

There are also several smaller houses in the old quarter that are emblazoned with bold coats of arms. Mangualde provides an excellent base from which to explore the wonderful **Serra da Estrêla** mountain range just 21 km away.

SERRA DA ESTRÊLA

The remarkable **Parque Nacional da Serra da Estrêla's** mountain range is Portugal's highest range. In addition to the peaks, its rugged glacier-carved valleys, pristine lakes, and rivers with watermills make this area an irresistible attraction (often closed during winter).

Although seldom seen by non-Portuguese visitors, the Serra da Estrêla offers a vast array of activities and sights including downhill skiing, fishing, trekking, thermal water spas, regional country fairs, and peaceful villages dotted with historical monuments.

Many of the local inhabitants are engaged in traditional tending of large goat and sheep herds that provide the area with an abundance of excellent wool and the raw materials that are magically transformed into the soft and tasty Queijo da Serra. You should not leave the region before sampling this tasty cheese.

ARRIVALS & DEPARTURES
By Car

Take route N-232 south from Mangualde for 21 km to the park.

WHERE TO STAY/WHERE TO EAT
Expensive

POUSADA DE SÃO LOURENÇO, *Penhas Douradas. Tel. (075) 982-450.*

This lovely chalet pousada, 14 km west of Manteigas, has 22 rooms with private bathroom and great views. Facilities include a lounge with fireplace and restaurant.

POUSADA DE SANTA BÁRBARA, *Oliveira do Hosipital. Tel. (038) 522-52.*

This nice 16 room (some with balcony) pousada is located just west of the Serra da Estrêla range in Oliveira do Hospital. Facilities include bar, restaurant, pool, tennis.

Moderate

CASA DA CAPELA, *Rio Torto. Tel. (038) 464-23.*

This ornate 18th century mansion and chapel, located off Route N-17 about 7 km west of Gouveia, has a great two bedroom apartment with kitchen and fireplace for rent.

QUINTA DA PONTE, *Faia-Guarda. Tel. (071) 961-26.*

This nice 18th century manor house is near the Mondego River a few kilometers northwest of Guarda, near the village of Faia. They offer five rooms and five one bedroom apartments with private bathrooms, lounge with fireplace, dining room, pool, billiards, and parking.

CASA DAS TILIAS, *São Romano, Seia. Tel. (038) 200-55.*

This peaceful estate and 19th century manor house next to a stream is in the hamlet of São Romão about 2 km south of Seia off Route N-231. The pleasant house offers six nice rooms with private bathrooms, lounge, breakfast room, bicycles, and gardens.

QUINTA DO PINHEIRO, *Cavadoude. Tel. (071) 961-62.*

This dramatic 17th century stone manor house is approximately 15 km northwest of Guarda off Route N-16 near the town of Porto da Carne. The house has six great rooms with antiques and private bathrooms, a lounge, TV room, bicycles, billiards, and parking.

CASA DE SÃO ROQUE, *Rua de Santo António, 63. Tel. (075) 981-125.*

This charming house in the center of Manteigas rents six nice guest rooms with private bathrooms. The owners are quite friendly and speak some English.

CASA GRANDE, *Paços de Serra. Tel. (038) 433-41.*

This impressive 18th century manor house is about 9 km north of Gouveia off Route N-17. There are two rooms and three rustic apartments with kitchen and private bathrooms for rent.

HOTEL TURISMO DA COVILHÃ, *Covilhã. Tel. (075) 323-843.*

This new hotel has 60 large air conditioned rooms. Facilities include bar, restaurant, squash, TV, disco, sauna, and minibars.

ESTALAGEM DE SEIA, *Ave. Dr. A. Costa, Seia. Tel. (038) 226-66.*

This nice 3 star inn with 35 comfortable guest rooms with private bath is not far from the city's center. Facilities include bar, restaurant, pool, billiards, heating, and TV room.

HOTEL CAMELO, *Rua 1 de Maio, Seia. Tel. (038) 225-10.*

This nice 3 star hotel, with 66 double rooms with private bathrooms, is located in the heart of town. Facilities include bar, restaurant, tennis, billiards, TV, mini bars, and parking.

HOTEL DE MANTEIGAS, *Caldas de Manteigas. Tel. (075) 982-400.*

This reasonably good full service hotel, near the spa, has 26 barren rooms with private bathroom. Facilities include bar, restaurant, tennis, sauna, gym, and garage.

HOTEL DE GOUVEIA, *Ave. 1 de Maio-Gouveia. Tel. (038) 428-90.*

This is a clean and basic 2 star hotel with 31 clean rooms with private bathroom. Facilities include bar, snack bar, restaurant, heating, direct dial phones, TV, and good service.

Inexpensive

CASA DO PONTE, *Alvoco de Serra. Tel. (038) 933-51.*
This granite house, in front of the Alvoco stream, is about 24 km from Seia off Route N-231. Six rustic rooms with private bathroom are available for rent. Minimal facilities.

SEEING THE SIGHTS

As you enter the Serra da Estrêla area from the quaint city of **Gouveia**, you will be immersed in the beauty of the mountains. The peaceful town of Gouveia is one of the Serra's bases for the production of woolen clothing, and contains the beautiful azulejos covered **Igreja de Matriz**.

Nearby is the small **Museu Municipal de Arte Moderno Abel Manta**, *Rua Direita, 45* (closed Mondays), exhibiting several paintings from its namesake as well as ceramics, weapons, and local artifacts. The town also contains the **park information office**, *Rua dos Bombeiros Voluntarios, 8, Tel. (038) 242-11*, which can give you free park maps and help with trail and hiking information.

From Gouveia, Route N-232 twists and turns south and then east past the Mondego River and the huge **Penhas Douradas** peak during its dramatic 39 km journey towards the most famous city in the area, **Manteigas**. This stunning city of 3,500 people is filled with beautiful 17th century whitewashed and granite houses with handcarved wooden balconies. After a stroll through town you can take Route N-338 south about 5 km to the spa complex at **Caldas de Manteigas**, whose hot sulphur thermal springs are known to ease the pain of those suffering from rheumatism, respiratory, and muscular diseases.

From the bridge spanning the **Zêzere** River at Caldas de Manteigas, you can take a small and curvy dirt road east for 7 km or so to see the **Poço do Inferno** waterfall. You may wish to have a brief rest near the waterfall, and then backtrack to Route N-338 south and follow it about 14 km south along the glacier-formed Zêzere River basin until you have reached the intersection at Nave de Santo António. From here you can either exit the mountains via **Covilhã**, or if you have a few more hours before sunset (do not attempt to drive in the Serra da Estrêla at night!), you can see more of the area by turning right (west) onto Route N-339.

After about 4 km on route N-339 west, stop at **Covão do Boi** to see wonderful granite sculptures whose origins are a mystery. A few more kilometers up Route N-339, you will find an access road on the left to the snow-capped **Torre**, the largest peak in the range with a ski area and panoramic views over the melted snow pools that feed the Zêzere River.

After you have returned to Route N-339, continue past the beautiful **Lagoa Comprida** lake and down into the valley past the quaint traditional villages of **Sabugueiro**, **Aldeia da Serra**, and **Seia**. At this point, consider ending your first day on the Serra de Estrêla roads and check into your hotel (see *Where to Stay* above; you should reserve your room far as in advance as possible).

If you enjoy the area, on your next day you might consider taking Route N-231 south from Seia to Pedras Lavradas, which in turn connects to Route N-230 east past the lovely spa town of **Unhais de Serra** and on to the city of **Covilhã**.

GUARDA

The historic city of Guarda rests at the eastern foot of the Serra da Estrêla mountains. Since its settlement by the Romans, this strategic city has been the guardian of the mountains since it was first fortified by the Visigoths, captured by the Moors, and finally liberated and further strengthened by the Portuguese in the 12th century.

The town lacks any real beauty, but there are two good excursions from Guarda: The Southern & Northern Castle Circles.

ARRIVALS & DEPARTURES
By Bus
• **Guarda Main Bus depot**, *Ave. Coronel Caravalho, Tel. (071) 227-20*

By Car
Guarda is 96 km southeast of Viseu off Route IP-5 east.

By Train
• **Guarda CP Rail station**, *5 km from town, Tel. (071) 211-565*

WHERE TO STAY
Moderate
SOLAR DE ALARCÃO, *Rua Dr. Miguel de Alarcao, 25. Tel. (071) 243-92.*

This nice, centrally located, 17th century manor house rents three rooms with private bathroom. Facilities include bar, TV and video room, garden, library, and parking.

HOTEL TURISMO, *Ave. Coronel O. de Carvalho. Tel. (071) 222-05.*

This pleasant hotel has 105 comfortable rooms in a relatively peaceful area of town. Facilities include bar, restaurant, pool, disco, TV, parking, and some shops.

RESIDENCIAL FILIPE, *Rua Vasco de Gama, 9. Tel. (071) 212-659.*

This is a pretty good 25 room establishment near in the heart of town. You'll find friendly service and a bar, restaurant, direct dial phones, and TV.

Inexpensive

PENSÃO ALIANCA, *Rua Vasco de Gama, 8. Tel. (071) 212-135.*

This nice and comfortable 3 star inn, located in the heart of town, offers 29 rooms with private bathroom, a restaurant, bar, TV room, direct dial phones, and parking.

SEEING THE SIGHTS

The 12th century **Torre de Menagem** keep, and a few remaining gates that pass through wall segments known as the Torre dos Ferreiros, Porta de Erva, and the Porta d'el Rei, are about all that remains of the city's ruined castle. Below the castle you will find the **Praça Luís de Camões** square, home to several bold 16th and 18th century noblemen's houses emblazoned with coats of arms.

Also in the square is the massive **Sé Cathedral**. The cathedral's construction began in 1390, and its original Gothic design was considerably altered by Diogo Boitac with Manueline finishing by the time of completion in 1541. Besides the dominant Gothic and Manueline portals and beautiful granite Manueline window, the towers and buttresses of the Sé are a bit overbearing. The solemn vaulted interior includes 16th century statues and an altarpiece created by Jean de Roen, as well as Renaissance portals leading to the Pinas family chapel and its Gothic family tomb carved of solid granite. Next door to the Sé is a beautiful facade and tile courtyard of the 17th century manor house known as the **Solar de Alarcao**, *Rua D. Miguel de Alarcão, 25.*

Also worth visiting are the nearby 18th century **Chafariz de Santo António** fountain, the 17th century baroque **Igreja da Misericórdia** across from the Torre dos Ferreiros tower, and next door at the **Museu Regional de Viseu** (closed Mondays) in a 17th century mansion at *Rua General Alves Rocadas, 30,* which showcases a collection of 16th through 20th century paintings, sculptures, armory, and assorted artifacts. A short walk in the small streets like Rua Direita, Rua Fransisco de Passos, and Rua dos Clérigos will reveal even more interesting 15th through 18th century houses with unusual doors and windows.

There's a daily **mercado** (market) in the southeastern corner of town, just off Rua Dom Nuno Alvares Pereira, and a huge Wednesday **mercardo** (market) in the fairgrounds by Ave. Monsenhor Mendes do Carmo.

EXCURSIONS & DAY TRIPS

The Southern Castle Circle

Owing to its prime defensive importance, the area surrounding Guarda is filled with several fortified cities worth visiting. A full day of hopping from one impressive castle to another is a great experience.

There are two separate circles and each take a full day. If you don't have two full days, I recommend the southern circle. You can do this as day trips from Guarda or you can stay in places along the circles. At the end of each circle, I suggest a number of places you can stay along each route.

To see the wonderful villages of the southern circle of castles, depart from Guarda on Route N-18 south for about 18 km, until you can turn left on a small road towards **Comeal da Torre**. A minute or two down the road, you can see a bizarre Roman structure known as **Centum Cellas**. This unusual pink granite tower has been a matter of controversy among leading archaeologists who have been debating its origins and purpose. The upcoming excavation of the surrounding area may provide some answers.

From the tower, head back to Route N-18 south for another 4 km or so until you can turn left on Route N-345 east for half a mile to **Belmonte**. This wonderful small city is dominated by the impressive walls (and a beautiful Manueline window) and keep of a **castelo** (castle), which dates back to the King Dom Dinis I reign in the 13th century.

DISCOVERER OF BRAZIL

*Belmonte is the birthplace of Pedro Alvares Cabral, the discoverer of Brazil. In fact, the town named its main square, **Praça Pedro Alvares Cabral**, in his honor. He brought back with him a large 15th century cross that is located just outside the town walls.*

Adjacent to the castle is the remarkable 14th century Romanesque church, **Igreja de São Tiago**, whose beautiful interior contains the remnants of its original frescoes and the stone tombs of local hero Cabral and his mother. Although a new modern city has emerged, the medieval old town has managed to keep most of its original charm.

Belmonte is also home to the ancestors of Jewish settlers who were forced to flee from Spain during large anti-semitic riots in the 14th century. Although they were resigned to live in a separate area called the **Judiara** (Jewish quarter), they integrated into the social and commercial society of Belmonte. When the Inquisition was brought to Portugal in 1496, the king ordered the forceful conversion of Jews to Christianity. Many of these **Marranos**, as they are called in Portugal, secretly practiced their faith even though they attended regular services at Igreja de São Tiago. The Jewish community today has its own synagogue, and Marranos still live within the old Judiaria section of town beside the castle.

From Belmonte, go back to Route N-18 south for about 27 km through Fundão, and continue on Route N-18 south for another 9 km until you can make a left turn onto Route N-239 east; go another 37 km to the turn-off for the incredible mountain village of **Monsanto**. Of all the villages and castles in this region, Monsanto is by far the loveliest. The winding approach to town brings you past the post office and a newly built ultra-modern pousada. Park here as the road becomes perilously narrow beyond this point. The village has not changed very much in the centuries since its pre-Roman occupation.

The shy and traditional residents of Monsanto live in granite houses that are under, on top of, and between huge boulders. Most of these unusual folks still practice a way of life that has all but vanished from western Europe. The small stone patio on the main road just before the pousada is the sight of monthly communal pig slaughters that are horrific.

There are several ornate residences with small window gardens and patios, and a beautiful Romanesque bell tower. As you walk through the stone lanes you will notice that the older peasant population maintain working barns in the basements of their houses and gated chicken coups, using the boulders as ceilings. If you're lucky enough to befriend one of the locals, they may show you how they use the region's famous three-legged iron fire-blasted cauldrons to prepare the heartiest meals I have ever seen.

High atop the rocky mountain perch at the end of town lies the fog-enshrouded ruins of a once important defensive castle. The exhilarating walk up the rugged path is best enjoyed on clear, sunny days since the view is dramatic.

After your visit to Monsanto, take Route N-239 west for 7 km until you can turn right onto Route N-332 north. In about 16 km you will reach the ruined castle of **Penamacor**. The town has been home to a castle since the 9th century, but it has been sacked several times since. Most of the current wall fragments and the Torre de Menagem (a tower) dates back to the 16th century. The town has several fine 16th and 17th century granite houses that are concentrated around the streets radiating from the main square, **Praça 25 de Abril**. Also worth noting is the beautiful 18th century **Câmara Municipal** (town hall), and the imposing 16th century church, **Igreja da Misericórdia**. The nearby **Serra da Malcata** mountain park is a great place to watch wildlife.

From Penamacor, continue up Route N-332 north, now merged with Route N-233 north, for about 6 km, until you can bear left onto Route N-233 north. Stay on Route N-233 for about 27 km until you come to the town of **Sabugal**. Dominating the small town is a large, restored 13th century pentagonal keep and its massive fortified walls. The sleepy town offers little else worth noting with the exception of the vast panoramic views of the nearby **Côa River** from the ramparts.

After a brief stopover at Sabugal, take Route N-233 south for 12 km until you reach Terreiro das Bruxas, and turn right onto Route N-18-3 west for 8 km until you reach the town of Santo Amaro, where you will find signs for the haunting walled city of **Sortelha**. After Monsanto, this is the second most impressive castle village in the region. Although seemingly deserted, several people still live in the 20 or so granite houses in the old part of town. These homes are entered via a massive Gothic portal in the large fortified wall, which also surrounds a partially ruined 12th century castle.

A beautiful old church and pillory are close to the castle, while several gardens stretch between the ivy covered rustic village houses. Not much really happens here anymore, since the majority of the town's inhabitants have moved into more comfortable dwellings in the newer section of town outside the walls.

Return to **Santo Amaro** and visit the large ruins of a spa hotel, the **Aguas Radium**. This once grand hotel is scheduled to become a major golf and spa resort, but the stone cutters and woodcrafters have not done much in the past two years to rebuild the bizarre structure. I won't hold my breath.

From Santo Amaro, take Route N-18-3 west for about 20 km until you can bear right onto IP-2 north and return to Guarda. You should be able to do this circle in time to be back in Guarda for dinner.

WHERE TO STAY
Moderate
POUSADA DE MONSANTO, *Monsanto. Tel. (077) 344-71.*

This brand new pousada has 10 designer double rooms with bizarre modern furnishings. Facilities include a nice bar, good restaurant, and some parking.

Inexpensive
ESTALAGEM VILA RICA, *Penamacor. Tel. (077) 343-11.*

This nice little old farmhouse offers 10 spacious and comfortable rooms with private bathroom. Facilities include bar, regional restaurant, library, and parking.

HOTEL BELSOL, *N-18, Belmonte. Tel. (075) 912-207.*

This good 2 star hotel has 39 clean and comfortable rooms a few kilometers out of town at Quinta do Rio. Facilities include bar, restaurant, TV, direct dial phones, and parking.

CASA DO PATIO, *Sortelha. Tel. (071) 681-13.*

This nice rustic house outside of the town wall rents one nice room and a huge two bedroom apartment with kitchen, sitting room, TV, and fireplace. Minimal facilities.

CASA DO VENTO QUE SOA, *Sortelha. Tel. (071) 681-82.*
This is an old basic granite house within the old city walls. The house can be rented by the day or week and has several basic and traditional bedrooms as well as a kitchen.

The Northern Castle Circle

To visit the villages of the northern circle, you must start out early in the morning. Your best bet is to start from Guarda on Route N-16 north for 23 km to the cheese producing city of **Celorico da Beira**. This small city has a wonderful walled castle, a beautiful Mannerist church, and a peaceful main square that is home to a large cheese market that is in business every two weeks on Fridays.

From Celorico de Beira, take the small unnamed road leading south for about 11 km (past the quaint village of Cortico de Serra) until you reach **Linhares**. This wonderful 15th century walled village is located high in the mountains and is a great place to wander around. The town contains several straw covered lanes, an ancient pillory, beautiful period houses, two Gothic and Romanesque keeps, and massive fortified walls that once surrounded the original castle.

After visiting Linhares, take the same small road back up for a couple of kilometers until you reach a left side turn-off, which will take you 5 km west to Route N-17 north. From there, you can go back through Celorico de Beira on your way to Route N-102 north. After roughly 18 km along Route N-102 north, you should take a left at the intersection onto Route N-226 north and drive for 4 km until your see the massive castle above the village of **Trancoso**. It was in this lovely village during the 13th century that King Dom Dinis met and soon after married his 12 year old bride, Queen Isabel. The town became one of Queen Isabel's wedding presents and is watched over by a massive citadel and strong fortified walls.

From Transcoso, continue up Route N-226 north for 7 km until you can bear right onto Route N-229-1 north. Drive about 32 km to the small town of **Penedono**. The town's 1,000 residents live on a hilltop beneath the shadow of the remarkable 15th century triangle shaped castle of the knight, Alvaro Coutinho. The wonderfully-preserved turreted walls and towers provide great panoramic views over the mountains.

From Penedono, you bear right onto Route N-331 west for 25 km until you can turn right onto Route N-102 south, and follow it 8 km south to the abandoned village and ruined castle at **Marialva**. Although nobody lives here anymore, you can still stroll down the unpaved lanes to see the 15th century Manueline **Igreja Matriz**, the remaining towers from the 13th century castle, and several empty houses. This is a great place to relax.

From Marialva, head back to Route N-102 and this time head north for about 20 km until you can bear right onto Route N-222 east; go for 14 km until you find another ruined castle amidst the village of **Castelo Melhor**. Only a couple of hundred residents remain in this small village, which has a dramatic medieval wall. From Castelo Melhor, drive down Route N-222 south as it merges with (and is renamed) Route N-332 south for 21 km to **Castelo Rodrigo**. This fortified village, with its shrinking population of about 240 traditional dwellers, contains the ruins of a once grand castle. The castle was destroyed by angry town residents who did not approve of the Count of Castelo Rodrigo's decision to side with Philip of Spain during his efforts to conquer Portugal.

After you have visited Castelo Rodrigo, continue on Route N-332 south for about 22 km until you reach the wonderful border town of **Almeida**. Although the site of several conflicts throughout the centuries, the town still stands within the six-sided, star-shaped walls of a frontier castle last modified in the 18th century.

The town itself is quite lively, and has three original entry gates, several ornate houses, the original 18th century barracks that at one point held over 250,000 troops, several small gardens, and the area's only pousada. After walking through town, head back on Route N-332 south for another 13 km until you can turn west onto Route N-16 west (the service road of IP-5), drive for about 17 km or so until you find **Castelo Mendo**. This small hilltop settlement of stone houses is surrounded by a partially ruined defensive wall. The town itself contains the fine 17th century **Igreja Matriz** and an unusual pillory. The town is crowned by the ruins of a castle and a church.

From here you can return to Guarda via Route N-16 west for 30 km.

WHERE TO STAY
Expensive
POUSADA DA S. DAS NEVES, *Almeida. Tel. (071) 542-83.*

This new pousada has great views of the old town and castle. The pousada offers 21 good air conditioned rooms and a bar, restaurant, TV, heating, and parking.

Moderate
HOTEL MIRA SERRA, *IP-5, Celorico de Basto. Tel. (071) 733-82.*

This nicely furnished and welcoming 3 star hotel has 42 comfortable rooms with private bathroom. Facilities include bar, restaurant, disco, TV, and a garage.

Inexpensive
PENSÃO FIGUEIRENSE, *Castelo Rodrigo. Tel. (071) 325-17.*
This nice inn has 16 comfortable rooms a few kilometers away from town at Figueira da Castelo Rodrigo. Facilities include bar, restaurant, TV room, garden, and parking.

FUNDÃO & ALPEDRINHA
The charming city of **Fundão** is full of fruit trees and flowers. It lies at the starting point of the wonderful Serra da Gardunha mountains.

The quaint town of **Alpedrinha** is a wonderful little agricultural community with several old palácios (mansions) and a variety of great manor houses and fine inns to stay in.

ARRIVALS & DEPARTURES
By Car
Fundao is about 59 km from Guarda and Alpedrinha is another 11 km further south, both on Route N-18 south.

WHERE TO STAY
Moderate
CASA DOS MAIS, *Fundão. Tel. (075) 521-23.*
A beautiful 18th century manor house and gardens set in the Praça da Municipio of peaceful Fundão with 6 great rooms with private bathroom, a TV room, and library.

ESTALAGEM DA NEVE, *Fundão. Tel. (075) 522-15.*
A good 4 star inn on Rua de São Sebastião which offers rooms with private bathrooms, air conditioning, pool, bar, restaurant, cable TV, minibars, and parking.

HOTEL SAMASA, *Fundão. Tel. (075) 712-99.*
A modern multilevel hotel on Rua Vasco de Gama which offers 50 air conditioned rooms with private bath. Facilities include lounge, minibar, TV, and parking.

CASA DA COMENDA, *Alpedrinha. Tel. (075) 571-61.*
A fortified 17th century stone house in the center of town which offers 4 rooms with private bathrooms, a garden, lounge, TV room, pool, billiards, and parking

CASA DE BERREIRO, *Alpedrinha. Tel. (075) 571-20.*
A uniquely designed manor house on Ave. Paço Vieira with great views which offers 6 rooms with private bathroom, lounge, dining room, bicycles, and TV room.

Inexpensive
ESTALAGEM SÃO JORGE, *Alpedrinha. Tel. (075) 571-54.*
A nice 4 star inn located in the heart of town at Largo da Misericórdia which offers rooms with private bathroom, a bar, restaurant, TV room, and parking.
PENSÃO TAROUCA, *Fundão. Tel. (075) 521-68.*
A clean and basic 2 star inn located in Rua 25 de Abril which offers rooms with and without private bathroom. Very few facilities, but close to everything.

SEEING THE SIGHTS
The heart of town, **Praça do Municipo**, is lined by the main streets of Ave. da Liberdade and Rua 5 de Outobro where you can find good shopping and dining. Make sure to view the extraordinary azulejos-covered **Igreja Matriz**. Be sure to try the wonderful fresh fruits that are locally grown.

The mountain view lanes off the central **Largo da Misericórdia** in the center of town offer several sights worth seeing, including the 18th century **Chafariz de Dom João** fountain, the simple **Igreja Matriz**, the **Paços do Concelho** town hall and museum, a fine furniture workshop, and a few interesting lanes with curious inhabitants. On the first Sunday of each month, the town hosts a **mercado** (market).

CASTELO BRANCO
Once a grand border town crowned by a massive castelo (castle), this city has grown into a modern commercial center full of broad avenues, good shopping and dining possibilities, and a few interesting attractions. Unfortunately there is little left of its castle, which dates back to Roman times.

During the Napoleonic war in the early 18th century, the French invaded, occupied, and looted much of the city and its treasures.

ARRIVALS & DEPARTURES
By Car
Castelo Branco is on Route N-18 about 48 km south of Fundão.
• **Europcar in Castelo Branco**, *Praça R. da Leonor, 13, Tel. (072) 262-04*

By Train
• **Castelo Branco CP Rail station**, *Ave. D. Nuno Alvares, Tel. (072) 222-83*

WHERE TO STAY
Moderate
HOTEL RAINHA D. AMELIA, *Rua de Santiago, 15. Tel. (072) 326-315.*

This modern and comfortable 64 room air conditioned hotel is in the new part of the city. Facilities include bar, restaurant, cable TV, minibar, and lots of parking.

RESIDENCIAL ARRAIANA, *Ave. 1 de Maio, 18. Tel. (072) 216-34.*

A clean and centrally located inn, it has several basic and comfortable rooms with private bathrooms. Facilities include a bar, TV, direct dial phone, and minibar.

Inexpensive
PENSÃO MARTINHO, *Alameda da Liberdade, 41. Tel. (072) 217-06.*

This basic and clean inn offers cheap accommodations in somewhat comfortable rooms that come with or without private bathroom. Minimal facilities.

WHERE TO EAT
Moderate
RESTAURANTE PRAÇA VELHA, *Praça Luís de Camões. Tel. (072) 286-330.*

This charming eating establishment, with an exposed beam and granite interior, serves upscale clientele a vast selection of local meat dishes. Great service.

SEEING THE SIGHTS
The most impressive sight in town is the **Museu Fransisco Tavares Proenca** housed in the old Episcopal Palace (Antigo Paço Episcopal), *Rua de Frei Bartolomeu da Costa.* Inside the museum (closed Mondays), you can view a vast collection of Roman artifacts, ancient coins, weaponry, 16th century Flemish tapestries, 17th century Portuguese furniture, sacred art, 16th century paintings, weaving implements, and a beautiful collection of locally-made colchas (linen bedspreads hand embroidered with silk designs). Next to the museum are the **Jardim do Antigo Paço Episcopal** gardens, with 18th century sculptures, carefully pruned trees, and several small ponds.

A nice walk is through the old town via the quaint Rua dos Ferreiros and onward past the old town's nice main **Praça Luís de Camões**, lined by the remarkable 16th century **Câmara Municipal** (town hall) and several ornate mansions. From here you can stroll past several shops and restaurants on Rua de Santa Maria. At the end of the street, bear right and follow the Rua do Arressario up and around to the grounds of the **Igreja de Santa Maria do Castelo**.

From here you can view the scant remains of the former castle and walk up the staircase to the lovely **Miradouro de São Gens** promenade, where you can see the beautiful panoramic views over both the old and the new city. On your way back through town you can window-shop for a fine bedspread to take home with you.

PRACTICAL INFORMATION FOR THE MONTANHAS

Currency Exchange

Many of the banks in the Montanhas will exchange foreign currency and travelers checks. Some tourist shops, restaurants, and hotel front desks offer you a rather poor exchange rate. Banking hours are from 8am until 3pm, Monday through Friday.

Currency exchange machines are almost impossible to find this far north but you can still locate 24-hour ATM machines in large cities.

Emergency & Useful Phone Numbers

- **Emergency Assistance** (S.O.S.), *Tel. 115*
- **Castelo Branco Hospital**, *Ave. Pedro Cabral, Tel. (072) 322-133*
- **Guarda Hospital**, *Rua Dr. F. Prazeres, Tel. (071) 222-133*
- **Automobile Club of Portugal** (Emergency road services), *Tel. (02) 830-1127*
- **Directory Assistance**, *Tel. 118*
- **Porto's Pedras Rubas Airport** (14 km out of Porto), *Tel. (02) 948-2141*
- **T.A.P.Airlines Porto**, *Praça M. Albuqurque, 105, Tel. (02) 600-5555*

Museums, Palaces, & Monuments

- **Abade de Baçal Museum**, *Rua do Conselheiro Abilio Beca, 27, Bragança, Tel. (073) 232-42*. Contains a collection of sacred art, furniture, archaeological findings, tapestry, and 17th-18th century paintings. Open 9am until 12pm and 2pm until 5pm, Tuesday through Sunday. Closed on Mondays and holidays.
- **Abel de Lacerda Foundation Art Museum**, *Caramulo, Tel. (032) 861-270*. Contains collections of paintings by Portuguese masters including Sousa-Cardosa, Vasco Fernandes, Eduardo Nery, and Eduardo Viana as well as works by Chagall, Dali, Leger, and Miro. There are

also examples of tapestries, jewelry, and ceramics. Open 10am until 1pm and 2pm until 6pm daily.

- **Abel de Lacerda Foundation Automobile Museum**, *Caramulo, Tel. (032) 861-493.* Contains collections of several dozen classical cars from the 19th and 20th century. Open 10am until 1pm and 2pm until 6pm daily.
- **Fransisco Tavares Proenca Museum**, *Rua de Frei Bartolomeu da Costa, Castelo Branco, Tel. (072) 242-77.* Contains a collection of Roman artifacts, coins, 16th century Flemish tapestries, 16th century Portuguese paintings, and a display of local colchas bedspreads. Open 10am until 12pm and 2:30pm until 5pm, Tuesday through Sunday. Closed on Mondays and holidays.
- **Castle Tower and Miltary Museum of Bragança**, *Torre de Menagem, Bragança, Tel. (073) 223-78.* The original keep of Bragança's castle and a collection of weapons and artifacts from previous centuries. Open 10am until 12pm and 2pm until 5pm daily.
- **Francisco Tavares Proenca Museum**, *Paço Episcopal, Rua Bartolomeu Costa, Castelo Branco, Tel. (072) 242-77.* Contains collections of 16th century Flemish tapestries, 17th century Portuguese furniture, locally embroidered bedspreads, antique coins, ceramics, and artifacts. Open 10am until 12pm and 2:30pm until 5pm, Tuesday through Sunday. Closed on Mondays and holidays.
- **Regional Museum of Chaves**, *Praça de Camões, Chaves, Tel. (076) 219-66.* Contains a vast collection of archaeological findings from pre-Roman through modern eras, 19th and 20th century paintings, and locally made handicrafts. Open 9:30am until 12:30pm and 2pm until 5pm, Tuesday through Friday. Open 2pm until 4:30pm, Saturday and Sunday. Closed on Mondays and holidays.
- **Castle Keep and Military Museum of Chaves**, *Praça de Camões, Chaves, Tel. (076) 219-66.* Contains a vast collection of military objects including weapons from the 12th century and more recent military displays. Open 9:30am until 12:30pm and 2pm until 5pm, Tuesday through Friday. Open 2pm until 4:30pm, Saturday and Sunday. Closed on Mondays and holidays.
- **Abel Manta Modern Art Museum**, *Rua Direita, 45, Gouveia, Tel. (038) 431-55.* Contains collections of Abel Manta paintings as well as ceramics, modern art, some antique weapons, and local archaeological items. Open 10am until 12:30pm and 2pm until 5pm, Tuesday through Sunday. Closed on Mondays and holidays.
- **Guarda Regional Museum**, *Rua Gen. Alves Rocadas, 30, Guarda, Tel. (071) 213-460.* Contains a collection of 16th-20th century paintings, sculptures, weapons, and archaeological finds from all over the

region. Open 10am until 12:30pm and 2pm until 5:30pm, Tuesday through Sunday. Closed Mondays and holidays.

- **Lamego Town Museum**, *Largo de Camões, Lamego, Tel. (054) 620-08*. Contains collections of 16th century Flemish tapestries, antique jewelry, metal sculptures, scared art, furniture, and 16th-20th century Portuguese paintings. Open 10am until 12:30pm and 2pm until 5pm, Tuesday through Sunday. Closed on Mondays and holidays.
- **Terra de Miranda Museum**, *Praça Dom João III, Miranda do Douro, Tel. (073) 421-64*. Contains collections of local festival costumes, archaeological findings, furniture, ceramics, weapons, handicrafts, and other regional artifacts. Open 10am until 12pm and 2pm until 5pm, Tuesday through Sunday. Closed on Mondays and holidays.
- **Mateus Manor House Museum**, *Solar de Mateus, Mateus-Vila Real, Tel. (059) 323-121*. A regal 18th century manor house and chapel that contains vast collections of antique furniture, paintings, documents, sculpture, jewelry, porcelain, and gardens. Open 10am until 1pm and 2pm until 5pm, daily from October through April. Open 9am until 1pm and 2pm until 8pm, daily from May through September.
- **Almeida Moreira House & Museum**, *Rua Soar de Cima, Viseu, Tel. (032) 423-769*. Open 10am until 12:30pm and 2pm until 5:30pm, Tuesday through Sunday. Closed on Mondays and holidays.
- **Grão Vasco Museum**, *Paço dos 3 Escaloes, Viseu, Tel. (032) 422-049*. Contains a large collection of paintings from Vasco Fernandes (Grão Vasco) as well as other 16th-20th century paintings, furniture, ceramics, and sacred art. Open 9:30am until 12:30pm and 2pm until 5pm, Tuesday through Sunday. Closed on Mondays and holidays.
- **Sacred Art Museum of Viseu**, *Sé Cathedral-Adro da Sé, Viseu, Tel. (032) 422-984*. Contains a collection of paintings, jewelry, and assorted sacred art items. Open 10am until 12pm and 2pm until 5pm, Monday through Saturday. Closed on Sundays and holidays.

Tourist Offices *(Turismos)*

- **Belmonte Tourist Office**, *Praça Pedro Cabral, Tel. (075) 911-48*
- **Bragança Tourist Office**, *Ave. Cidade de Zamora, Tel. (073) 282-73*
- **Castelo Branco Tourist Office**, *Alameda da Librdade, Tel. (072) 210-02*
- **Covilhã Tourist Office**, *Praça do Municipo, Tel. (075) 221-70*
- **Chaves Tourist Office**, *Rua de Santo António, Tel. (076) 210-29*
- **Fundão Tourist Office**, *Ave. de Liberdade, Tel. (075) 527-70*
- **Gouveia Tourist Office**, *Ave. dos Bombeiros, (Tel. 038) 421-85*
- **Guarda Tourist Office**, *Praça de Luís Camões, Tel. (071) 222-51*
- **Lamego Tourist Office**, *Ave. Visconde Teixeira, Tel. 054) 620-05*
- **Manteigas Tourist Office**, *Rua Dr. G. de Carvalho, Tel. (075) 981-129*
- **Miranda do Douro Tourist Office**, *Largo do Men. Jesus, Tel. (073) 421-32*

- **Moncovo Tourist Office**, *Rua Manuel Seixas, Tel. (079) 222-89*
- **Penamacor Tourist Office**, *Praça 25 de Abril, Tel. (090) 341-06*
- **Seia Tourist Office**, *Praça do Mercado, Tel. (038) 222-72*
- **Vila Real Tourist Office**, *Ave. Carvalho Araujo, Tel. (059) 322-819*
- **Viseu Tourist Office**, *Ave. Calouste Gulbenkian, Tel. (032) 279-94*
- **Serra da Estrêla Park Info-Viseu**, *Rua dos B. Voluntarios, Tel. (038) 242-11*

Travel Agencies

- **Novo Mundo Travel**, *Ave. João da Cruz, 5, Tel. (073) 226-36.* This full service branch travel agency in central Bragança has expertise in booking accommodations, tickets, and specialty excursions throughout Portugal.
- **Intercontinental Travel and Tours**, *Rua Direita, 150, Tel. (076) 214-83.* This friendly and reliable Chaves branch travel agency and tour operator has full service booking and ticketing facilities for all sorts of travel needs.
- **Abreu Tours**, *Ave. Calouste Gulbenkian, Tel. (032) 423-545.* This is the Viseu office of a major tour company and travel agent, and has computerized central reservations systems and good rates at a large assortment of resorts.

17. THE PLANÍCIES

The **Planícies**, the Plains region, is the largest region in Portugal, roughly one-third of Portugal's land mass, and consists of the entire **Alto Alentejo** province, as well as most of the **Ribatejo** and **Baixa Alentejo** provinces. The majority of this agricultural and historic region is covered with cork and olive fields, as well as prehistoric megaliths, cave drawings, and opulent cathedrals.

Due to the extremely long growing season, the plains produce most of the country's food supply. Although the region has some fine Atlantic coastline just north of the Algarve and many rivers filled with fish, it is primarily an arid region. A controversial project is currently underway to create a massive man made lake-reservoir near the Spanish border to solve water supply problems, but it means submerging thousands of acres worth of historic sights. The landscape also includes mountain ranges, including the unspoiled beauty of the **Serra dos Ossa**. The Planícies is known for raising Lusitanian horses and purebred bulls for Portugal's non-lethal bullfights.

This region is very rich in history and culture. The friendly peasants who ride their oxen and donkeys down the region's small rural highways are happy to stop and talk to locals and tourists alike. Besides the wonderful handmade ceramics and tapestries created by local artisans, the Planícies produces several varieties of table wines that are quite enjoyable and inexpensive.

While all of this region is worth exploring, the most impressive stops include the perfectly preserved mountain village of **Monsaraz**, the endless wonders in the incredible city of **Évora**, the 15th century **Convento de São Paulo** in **Redondo**, the ancient fortress towns of **Marvão** and **Elvas**, the world famous artisans of **São Pedro do Corval**, **Portalegre**, and **Arraiolos**, the wine producing villages around **Cartaxo**, the quaint traditional fishing settlement of **Escaropim**, the historic old sections of **Castelo de Vide**, and the beaches of **Milfontes**, **Porto Corvo**, and **Santo André**. And don't forget to take in a bullfight.

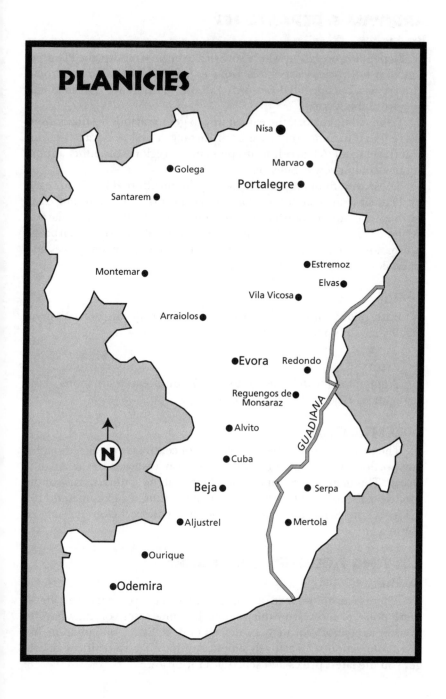

ARRIVALS & DEPARTURES

By Air

Depending on exactly where you wish to begin your trip, the Planicíes region is most easily accessible from either the Portela International Airport just outside of downtown Lisbon, or the Faro International Airport in the Algarve.

From either airport, the easiest way to get to various destinations in this region is to either rent a car or pre-arrange a reserved transfer from your travel agent. A taxi ride to any point in this region from either airport will be prohibitively expensive.

Those with minimal luggage looking for an affordable way to reach the Planicíes can take a bus from either airport to the relevant city's downtown area, and transfer to public transportation systems to take you to your destination in the Planicíes. The Turismo office in either airports' international arrivals areas will be happy to give you current prices and schedules on all regional buses and trains.

By Bus

Buses, along with trains, go to over 73 different destinations. You will usually have to go to Beja, Évora, or Santarém first.

By Train

Trains, along with buses, go to over 73 different destinations in the Planicíes via Beja, Évora, or Santarém.

ORIENTATION

The Planicíes covers the western side of central Portugal, although a tiny portion of the region extends all the way eastward to the Atlantic Ocean. This giant agricultural region begins at the southern bank of the river near the town of Constância and moves south 244 kilometers (151 miles) to the Serra do Caldeirão mountain range below the city of Mértola.

GETTING AROUND THE REGION

By Bus

There is an abundance of daily scheduled services that cover almost every point of interest in this region. In some cases you may have to transfer at centrally located bus depots in Beja, Évora, or Santarém, but these connections are relatively simple. Any local Turismo office can help get you the latest prices and schedules for buses.

By Car

Since much of this region is covered by a few toll highways and many superb no-toll roads, driving around here is easy and enjoyable. This is the best region in the country to drive through, and the local government has recently spent billions of escudos to improve pavements, signs, and even added new roads. Other than in Beja, Évora, Estremoz, and Santarém, rush hours are not a major problem and street parking is possible to find with some effort.

By Train

There is an abundance of daily scheduled services on regional and commuter trains and cover almost every point of interest in this region. In some cases, you may have to transfer trains in the centrally located, main rail stations in Beja, Évora, or Santarém, but these connections are relatively simple. Any local Turismo office can help get you the latest prices and schedules for the trains.

SANTARÉM

The city of Santarém rests above the Tejo River and the fertile plains that make up much of the Planícies region. It is the district capital of Ribatejo province and its 21,000 inhabitants are typically preoccupied with the vast number of agricultural, gastronomic, bullfighting, and horsemanship events for which the city has become famous.

The history of Santarém goes back to the days when barbarians roamed through Europe. After the city was captured from the Moors in 1147 by King Dom Afonoso Henriques, Santarém remained an important agricultural and commercial city. It has been home to several royal parliaments (cortes) and historical events. During the Napoleonic wars, Santarém was occupied by the French troops who destroyed and pillaged several of the town's most important structures, but fortunately several fine sights still remain fairly intact.

ARRIVALS & DEPARTURES

By Bus
• **Santarém Main Bus Depot**, *Rua Duarte Periera, Tel. (043) 220-01*

By Car
Take the A-1 Highway north from Lisbon for 72 km.

By Train
• **Santarém CP Rail station**, *2 km northwest of town, Tel. (043) 333-180*

WHERE TO STAY
Expensive
QUINTA DE VALE DE LOBOS, *Azoia de Baixo, Santarém. Tel. (043) 429-264.*

This lovely 19th century manor house and estate is about 6 km north of town off Route N-3. The historic inn offers four nice rooms and two one bedroom apartments with private bathrooms. Facilities include bar, library, pool, hunting, trails, and parking.

Moderate
QUINTA DE SOBREIA, *Vale de Figueira. Tel. (043) 420-221.*

This inviting manor house on a farm is located about 16 km north of Santarém on Route N-365 near the peaceful village of Vale de Figueiro. The inn has three nice guest rooms with private bathroom, bar, pool, bicycles, library, TV, and parking.

Inexpensive
RESIDENCIAL VICTORIA, *Rua Visconde de Santarém, 21. Tel. (043) 225-73.*

Located in a good part of Santarém, this nice and friendly small inn has a dozen or so clean and comfortable guest rooms with private bathrooms. If you're willing to pay a bit extra, you can get a balcony. Facilities include breakfast room and nearby parking.

WHERE TO EAT
Moderate
PORTAS DO SOL, *Jardim de Portas do Sol. Tel. (043) 295-20.*

This beautiful and casual little restaurant, near the castle's belvedere, has a patio area surrounded by gardens. The friendly and helpful staff provide some insight on which regional dish is the best of the day. A great place to eat and relax.

SEEING THE SIGHTS
The best way to start your trip through Santarém is to look for the municipal parking area on the city's centrally located Rua Serpa Pinto. After securing your car, walk up Rua Serpa Pinto a couple of blocks until you find yourself at the beautiful **Praça Sá da Bandeira** plaza. Your first stop: the imposing 17th century **Nossa Senhorha da Conceição**, a Jesuit seminary church, with a bold baroque whitewashed and granite block exterior.

Inside this wonderful building, once the site of a royal palace, you will find impressive azulejos-covered hallways, 18th century frescoes, niches filled with interesting statues of Jesuits, several gilt wood altars, and a large 18th century marble-encrusted high altar. From the mosaic-paved plaza in front of the church, continue up through the **Largo Piedade** and turn right onto Rua 31 de Janeiro to stroll through the tranquil **Jardim do República** (gardens).

From here you can continue up the Rua 31 de Janeiro to view the Gothic 13th century **Igreja de Santa Clara** and the nearby panoramic **São Bento Miradouro** lookout. If you double back to the western edge of the garden, you can turn up Rua Cidade da Covilhã for a block or so and visit the azulejos-covered public **mercado** (market), which is the perfect place to buy small quantities of local produce, meats, bread, and cheeses, that can be used for a picnic. Head back to the **Praça Sá da Bandeira** and this time follow Rua Capelo Ivens, with its many shops, down through town. You may want to pop in to the Turismo office at # 63 for a free local map.

From Rua Capelo Ivens, turn left (east) onto Rua 1 de Dezembro for a couple of blocks until you can turn left into the quaint **Praça Visconde Serra Pillar** square and bear right to visit the 16th century **Igreja da Marvila**. The church, whose original construction actually dates back to the 12th century, contains an impressive Manueline portal and has 17th century azulejos covering its walls.

From the Marvila church, bear right for a block or so to Rua Coselheiro Figueiredo Leal, where you'll find the 13th century Romanesque **São João de Alporão** church that is now home to the city's archaeological museum (closed Mondays). The museum features a somewhat disorganized clutter of ancient pottery, coats of arms, coins, azulejos, sculptures, and the tomb of Duarte de Menses, whose tooth is all that remained of him after he was killed battling the Moors in the 15th century. Across from the church you can see the **Torre das Cabacas** bell tower, built in the 15th century and adorned by several large clay pots known as cabacas.

From the tower, head back to the Rua 1 de Dezembro and take a left turn to reach the **Largo Pedro Alvares Cabral**. Here you'll find the 14th century Gothic **Igreja de Nossa Senhora da Graça**, which has a large Rosé window carved from a single block of stone, a beautiful interior containing ornate tombs, and fine azulejos panels. From the church, you can head back to the Torre das Cabacas and turn right onto Ave 5 de Outubro, which ends at the old citadel's walls and the **Portas do Sol** gardens. The gardens provide a beautiful place to sit on a bench and enjoy a picnic while looking down onto the Tejo River and the plains unfolding before you. If you didn't stop at the market for picnic supplies, try lunch on the patio of the lovely Portas do Sol restaurant.

You can watch a bullfight here if one is scheduled during your visit; check with the local Turismo. In terms of other events, each October the city is the host of a huge 10 day gastronomic festival, where you can stroll from one booth to another tasting cuisines from all over Portugal.

EXCURSIONS & DAY TRIPS

There are several cities along both the western and eastern banks of the **Tejo River** that can all be visited in one long day. What follows is an easy to follow circular itinerary that will take you south and west of Santarém to **Cartuxa** and **Azambuja** on one side of the Tejo River, and then up the other bank of the river through **Benavente, Salverra de Magos**, and **Almeirim** and finally back to Santarém. I strongly recommend this day trip to these great little traditional towns. Accommodations are almost non-existent in these towns, so staying in Santarém is your best bet.

Cartaxo is 15 km southwest of Santarém on Route N-3 south. Cartaxo produces some of my favorite Portuguese white wines and would be of particular interest to wine lovers. These wines are premiered yearly at the area's famed **Feira do Santos** festival in November.

The town offers visitors a few interesting sights within easy walking distance from the main plaza, **Largo Vasco de Gama**. Among my favorite things to do are the arts and crafts exhibits at the small museum in the Largo Vasco de Gama and the 15th century Manueline cross in the portico at **Igreja Matriz** in **Largo João Baptista**.

On the outskirts of town off Rua José Ribeiro da Costa you will find the **Quinta das Pratas**, home to the beautiful and wonderful **Museu Rural e do VInho**, a rural life and wine museum. The exhibits are located in impressive traditional buildings that are part of a beautiful 50 acre farm (closed on Mondays).

Several wineries are based around town, most notably the **Quinta da Fonte Bela** cellars a few minutes east. I recommend a stop in **Cãmara Municipal** on the **Praça 15 de Dezembro** for a map of the local wineries. Cartuxa is also close to the traditional fishing village of **Palhota**, just a few kilometers south of town on the Tejo River.

The once sleepy agricultural town of **Azambuja** lies about 13 km south of Cartuxa on Route N-3. The town can also be reach by train, Azambuja CP Rail station, *Largo dos Combatentes, Tel. (063) 431-57*. The town has become a base for industries such as automobile manufacturing, but it still offers some interesting sights.

The town is also home to a festive and colorful fair, **Feira de Maio**, held the end of May. During the fair, the yard that surrounds the fine Manueline pillory of the **Igreja Matriz** on **Largo do Adro** becomes a makeshift bullring, and the streets of town are full of young people trying to out run the bulls. The small streets such as Rua do Espírito Santo and

Rua Eng. Moniz da Maia are full of old world ambiance and a few shops that sell the locally-produced wines and baskets made from corn husks.

Azambuja also has a small museum of African art, *Rua Victor Cordon, 69* (closed on weekends). Stroll down to the **Largo dos Combatentes da Grade Guerra** and go inside the train station to see some wonderful azulejos panels. A few minutes east of town along the river, you can visit the quaint fishing village of **Lezirão**, while a short drive north of town will lead you to **Manique do Intendente** and its outrageous 18th century palace, **Palácio Pina Manique**.

On the way to **Benavente**, stop in the small hamlet of **Santo Estevão**, which can be reached from Azambuja by following Route N-3 south for about 11 km, turning onto the A-1 highway south and crossing the bridge from Vila Franca de Xira to Route N-10 east. From Route N-10, continue for 26 km or so and exit on Route N-119 north, where you'll turn off in 2 km or so to the left for the cute settlement at Santo Estevão. The scenic bull-raising hamlet of **Santo Estevão** contains many colorfully dressed campinos (herdsmen) who live a traditional way of life, the Portuguese equivalent to our cowboys. You can visit a working farm estate in this area, **Monte dos Condes**, where time seems to have stood still.

The drive on Route N-118-1 north from Santo Estavão to the bull breeding town of **Benavente** is a bit rough, but the sights are worth the bumps on this 15 km drive. Most of the land along the way belongs to family-owned stud farms as well as a few melon plantations.

In **Benavente**, stroll down the open streets and stop to view the 17th century **Igreja da Misericórdia**, *Rua da Misericórdia*. While in the church, look for its particularly unique azulejos. Rua da Misericórdiaon is a lovely street and will lead you to the **Largo do Municipio** where you will find a rebuilt 16th century pillory. Continue to the beautiful Sorraia riverfront, and then back through town until you reach Rua Luís de Camões, home to the **Museu Municipal de Dr. António Gabriel**. The museum contains an assortment of unusual items including 19th century photography, antique postcards, and lots of items that relate to life in the region. While walking around the streets in town, keep your eye out for shops that sell the linen stockings worn by many townspeople. The town is at its best during the annual **Fiera do Sardinhas** in June, when free grilled sardines and wine is served to all.

The former royal hunting village of **Salvaterra de Magos** is located about 6 km north of Benavente on Route N-118 north. Agriculture and livestock production are still the dominant economic bases of this town, and the local acorn-fed pork is the best in the country. From the 13th through 19th centuries, the town was inhabited by several members of the royal family who built several massive structures in town and practiced the art of hunting and falconry.

Although most of the original royal palace was destroyed by the 1755 earthquake, you can still visit the multiple arched falconry, the fine **capela** (chapel) and parts of the kitchen just off the **Largo dos Combatentes**. In the 18th century, a new palace was built, and can still be seen at the edge of town. Also worth a visit is the 18th century **Igreja da Misericórdia**, and its beautiful azulejos-covered interior. The town hosts a few yearly bullfights at its large bullring, and each year in June there are bull runs and folklore displays during the local **Fandango** festival.

For me, the highlight of a visit here is a stop at the river front settlement of **Escaropim**, about 3 km north of town, where wildly painted fishermen's houses rest on stilts at the water's edge. Nearby, at the beach, **Praia Doce**, you can enjoy a nice summer swim.

In **Salvaterra de Magos**, you'll find a cute little house off Route N-114 east near the Magos reservoir with rooms for rent. The moderately priced **Casa do Granho**, Granho Novo, *Tel. (063) 585-16,* has a nice apartment with two beds, two sofa beds, a kitchen and private bathroom.

Located about 28 km away from Salvaterra de Magos on Route N-118 north is the lovely village of **Almeirim**. Situated just across the Tejo River bridge from Santarém, this town has a rich tradition of royalty, artisans and folklore. The town has lovely gardens and produces a fruity white wine often served with slices of the fabled Almeirim melon.

In the center of town is the lovely **Praça da República** square, a great place to start a short walking tour of town. Make sure to stop in at the 16th century whitewashed and granite **Igreja Matriz**, *Rua Conde de Tiapa*, the Moorish **Fonte de São Roque**, *Rua de São Roque*, and the **Casa do Povo**, *Rua de Coruche*, which houses a small ethnological museum. Just out of town off Route N-118 south is the lovely **Quinta da Alorna**, a 19th century horse farm and manor house that produces great wines. They'll be happy to sell you their wine directly from the caves.

ALPIARÇA, CHAMUSCA, & GOLEGÃ

Alpiarça, **Chamusca**, and **Golegã** are north of Santarém along the Tejo River. You could visit these towns as a day trip from Santarém or stay in one of two places in the small town of Azinhaga that I recommend.

WHERE TO STAY
Moderate
CASA DA AZINHAGA, *Rua da Misericórdia, Azinhaga. Tel. (049) 951-46.*

This beautiful 18th century nobleman's manor house in the village of Azinhaga has seven rooms and suites with private bathrooms, a lounge, dining room, billiards, bicycles, boating, fishing, TV room, and parking.

CASA DE S.ANTÓNIO DE AZINHAGA, *Rua Nova de Santo António, Azinhaga. Tel. (049) 951-62.*
This relaxing manor house in the peaceful village of Azinhaga offers travelers three nice guest rooms with private bathrooms. Facilities include library, fireside lounge, dining room, TV room, and parking.

SEEING THE SIGHTS

The quiet town of **Alpiarça** is near the eastern bank of the Tejo River about 10 km east of Santarém. The surrounding area is loaded with archaeological findings that date back to prehistoric times. Primarily a wine producing town, Alpiarça hosts an enchanting wine festival, **Feira do Vinho**, on the last weekend of every March. On the edge of town, there is a wonderful museum, **Casa dos Patudos** (closed Mondays and Tuesdays), which is housed in the elegant former mansion of local art collector, diplomat, and philanthropist José Relvas on the appropriately named Rua José Relvas. The beautiful museum contains a fine collection of 16th century paintings, ceramics, sculptures, azulejos, Arraiolos rugs, pottery, and other rare items. The town also has a beautiful 19th century church called **Igreja de Santo Eustaquio** that has some unusual paintings.

An old fishing village known as the **Porto do Patacão de Cima** can be found just northwest of town at the Tejo River.

The tranquil village of **Chamusca** is also on the eastern bank of the Tejo River some 16 km up from Alpiarça on Route N-118 north. There are several interesting sites in this town, and you can purchase quality handmade leather goods and beautifully painted ceramics.

The town features several pretty little plazas, including the **Largo Sacadura Cabral**, with a mosaic-filled park and bandstand, the **Largo da Misericórdia**, home to the 17th century **Igreja da Misericórdia** full of gilt woodwork and azulejos, the **Largo Vasco de Gama** which is dominated by the 16th century Gothic **Igreja Matriz**, and the **Largo 25 de Abril** and the adjacent **Parque Municipal** (park and gardens), which contains the **Traditional Rural House** and **Museu Municipal** archaeological museums.

Above all, the town presents a good opportunity to hunt for unusual handicrafts. During the town's wonderful **Festa da Ascensão** (Ascension Day Festival), you can witness several bullfights and the running of the bulls that goes on for about a week.

The famous horse breeding town of **Golegã** is situated directly across the Tejo River from Chamusca (on the western side), about 31 km northeast of Santarém. The town is known primarily for the yearly **Feira Nacional da Cavalo** (National Horse Fair), consisting of races, parades, feasts, and bull runs during the first two weeks of November.

While in town, make sure to visit the 16th century Manueline church with an incredible doorway, **Igreja Matriz**, *Rua do Campo*. Also well worth a stop is the fantastic **Museu de Carlos Relvas**, *Rua José Farinha Relvas*, a photography museum in the ornate palatial mansion of the 19th century photographer Carlos Relvas. Nearby on the **Largo da Imaculada Conceição** is the wonderful **Museu de Mestre Martins Correia**, a museum of the Mestre Martins Correia's modern sculptures and paintings (closed Mondays).

The nearby village of **Azinhaga**, about 8 km away on Route N-365 south just off the Almonda River, is a great place to see traditional rural life. Few tourists get here, but your efforts will be rewarded with excellent ancient mansions, churches, manor houses, and beautiful farms.

CONSTÂNCIA

The historic town of Constância is located on a small hill at the confluence of the Tejo and Zêzere Rivers just northeast of Golegã. The heart of the town can be found at the lovely Praça Alexandre Herculano square.

ARRIVALS & DEPARTURES

By Car

From Golegã, take Route N-365 north for about 7 km and then turn onto Route N-3 east for another 11 km.

WHERE TO STAY

Moderate

QUINTA DE SANTA BÁRBARA, *Constância. Tel. (049) 992-14.*

This beautiful 17th century manor house is 1 km east of town and has six great rooms with private bathroom, bar, billiards, pool, dining room, library, trails, and horse riding.

CASA O PALÁCIO, *Rua F. Falcão, Constância. Tel. (049) 992-24.*

This nice antique noble mansion is located on the Tejo River in the old part of town. The inn offers four double rooms with private bathroom, bar, gardens, TV room, and parking.

SEEING THE SIGHTS

The center of town and the main square is **Praça Alexandre Herculano**, where a central pillory and ornate facades can be seen. From the square, walk up the Rua Luís de Camões towards the **Galeria**, with a restored traditional house that you can visit. Just off the Galeria, turn on Rua da Barca and see the remains of the old city walls and a house where poet Luís de Camões once lived. Throughout town, there are great parks and gardens, including the **Jardim de Horta Camoniano** off Ave. das Forças Armadas at the edge of town, and the nearby riverfront **Parque de Merendas**, where you can enjoy a picnic or just sit and watch the rivers collide.

The town offers several nice churches to visit, including the 17th-century **Igreja Matriz**, with its José Malhoa fresco, and the **Igreja da Misericórdia** that has beautiful azulejos and a gilt wood altar. On Easter Monday, the fishermen of Constância gather to celebrate the **Festa do Senhora da Boa Viagem**, when the boats are blessed and the residents parade down the old town streets with marching bands.

SPORTS & RECREATION
Horseback Riding
• **Quinta Santa Bárbara**, *Constância, Tel. (049) 992-14*

SHOPPING
The town has a great reputation for locally-made handicrafts including dolls and wooden models of the traditional river boats. Theses items can be found in the small shops throughout town.

EXCURSIONS & DAY TRIPS
The romantic **Castelo do Almourol** is the most amazing castle in all of Portugal, and is perched on a small island in the Tejo River about 4 km southwest of Constância. Built in 1171 on the grounds of an even older Roman fortress, this massively fortified 11 tower castle can be reached by ferry row boat (in high season) from the northern bank of the river for about 350$00. Check with the people at Constáncia's Cãmara Municipal (town hall), *Tel. (049) 992-05*, for more specific ferry information.

Although abandoned since the 14th century, Almourol is in surprisingly good condition, and the view from above the towering square keep is impressive. Every person that I have told to visit this castle has returned home and thanked me.

ABRANTES
The quaint town of Abrantes rests on a hill above the banks of the Tejo River.

ARRIVALS & DEPARTURES
By Car
Abrantes is 13 km from Constância on Route N-3 east.

WHERE TO STAY

Moderate

QUINTA DOS VALES, *N-118, Tramagal. Tel. (041) 073-63.*

This country inn and horse stable offers six nice rooms with private bathrooms 10 km west of town and across the river. Facilities include lounge, dining room, TV room, library, gardens, horse back riding, and parking.

HOTEL TURISMO, *Largo de Santo António. Tel. (041) 212-71.*

This is a good 3 star hotel above the river. It has 41 rooms with private bathroom. Facilities include bar, restaurant, air conditioning, tennis, pool, TV, and parking.

Inexpensive

PENSÃO CENTRAL, *Praça Raimundo Soares, 15. Tel. (041) 224-22.*

This clean and basic inn has 14 reasonably comfortable rooms with and without private bathrooms. There are almost no facilities, but it is the only budget choice.

WHERE TO EAT

Inexpensive

RESTAURANTE CRISTINA, *N-3, Rio de Moinhos. Tel. (041) 981-77.*

A homey and simple restaurant, a few kilometers west of town, it serves huge portions of locally raised meat and fish dishes with friendly service. The ambiance is great.

RESTAURANTE LIRIOS, *Praça da Batalha, 31. Tel. (41) 221-42.*

This nice family-owned restaurant near the center of town offers several regional meat and fish specialties at very good prices. The desserts are great.

SEEING THE SIGHTS

The ruins of a 14th century **castelo** (castle) – of which little remains except the keep – overlooks the town. Inside the castle walls (closed Mondays) you can view the 15th century **Igreja de Santa Maria do Castelo** that now houses the **Museu de Lope de Almeida** (closed Mondays). The museum contains collections of Roman statues, Spanish-Arab tiles, ceramics, old manuscripts, 16th century paintings, and ornate tombs. From the top of the keep you can look out over the town and the beautiful olive trees that line the banks of the river. The town can be reached by leaving the castle keep and strolling past the ancient maze-like alleys.

With much of its economy coming from agriculture, Abrantes is home to the Victor Guedes company, which produces a limited quantity of traditionally harvested extra, extra virgin olive oil under the Gallo brand name. If you love cooking, you'll want to bring home some of their amazing Azeite Novo olive oil, which can match any famous Italian brand at a quarter of the price.

One place well worth visiting in Abrantes is the 16th-century **Igreja da Misericórdia** with Gregório Lopes paintings. The town's most interesting attractions include the streets, gardens, and residents themselves who seem to show great interest and curiosity in visitors.

CASTELO DE VIDE

The spa town of Castelo de Vide rests on a hill in the Serra de São Mamede mountains.

ARRIVALS & DEPARTURES

By Bus
• **Castelo de Vide Main Bus stop**, *Rua de Bartolomeu Santa, no phone*

By Car
From Abrantes, cross the river and follow Route N-118 east for about 68 km until you reach the town of Alpalhão and can turn off onto Route N-246 east for about another 16 km.

By Train
• **Castelo de Vide CP Rail station**, *4 km northeast of town, Tel. (045) 916-63*

WHERE TO STAY

Moderate
QUINTA DA BELA VISTA, *Póvoa-Meadas. Tel. (045) 981-25.*

This charming 19th century country inn is on a farm about 14 km north of town. It has four great guest rooms with private bathroom, bar, restaurant, pool, tennis, billiards, air conditioning, TV room, bicycles, trails, and parking. This is a great little inn.

ALBERGARIA JARDIM, *Rua Sequeira Sameiro, 6. Tel. (045) 912-17.*

This attractive and beautifully furnished 4 star inn has 43 guest rooms with private bathroom, and is located in a great part of town. Facilities include a bar, restaurant, and TV room.

HOTEL SOL E SERRA, *Estrada São Vicente. Tel. (045) 913-37.*

This large and comfortable 3 star hotel is located near a park. It has 50 air conditioned rooms, all with private bathroom. Facilities include bar, restaurant, pool, TV room, and parking.

Inexpensive

CASAL DOS LILASES, *Castelo de Vide. Tel. (045) 912-50.*

This fairly comfortable country house offers five rustic rooms with semi-private bathrooms, but has almost no facilities. It's located on a small farm about a 2 km south of town.

PENSÃO CASA DO PARQUE, *Ave. de Aramenha, 37. Tel. (045) 912-50.*

This well furnished and comfortable inn has good rooms with private bathrooms.

SEEING THE SIGHTS

This cute little town with rows of whitewashed houses rests below a 12th century fortified **castelo** (castle) whose original tower looms above its defensive walls. Besides visiting the tower for a good view of the town's flower-lined alleys, you can visit the 17th century **Igreja de Nossa Senhora da Alegria** with its impressive azulejos inside the compound.

Below the castle, the town's lovely streets and plazas await your visit. The town's medieval Jewish section, known as the **Judiaria**, is where local Jewish residents (known as Marranos) were forced to live apart from their Christian neighbors before the Inquisition; during the Inquisition they were forced to convert. There is a small and unassuming 14th century rabbi's house and temple on Rua da Judiaria that can be visited, as well a small handicrafts shop and studio located in the former town jail.

Just below the Judiaria is the town's famed 16th century baroque **Fonte da Vila** (town fountain), spewing a constant stream of unfiltered mineral water said to cure several internal ailments. From the fountain, proceed towards the heart of town, the **Praça Dom Pedro V** square, which is surrounded by fine examples of 17th and 18th century structures. Among the buildings worth viewing in this square are the 17th century **Torre Palácio**, the 17th century **Câmara Municipal** (town hall), and the lovely **Igreja de Santa Maria** (church).

MARVÃO

The medieval walled village of Marvão is located on top of a cliff in the Serra de São Mamede mountain range near the Spanish border. It is one of the most dramatic fortified towns in Portugal.

ARRIVALS & DEPARTURES

Marvão is about 13 km southeast of Castelo de Vide on a hairpin-turn access road off Route N-246-1.

WHERE TO STAY
Expensive
POUSADA DE SANTA MARIA, *Rua 24 de Janeiro. Tel. (045) 932-02.*
Two typical adjoining homes were converted into this beautiful pousada. The inn offers 28 well appointed rooms and one suite with traditional furnishings. Facilities include lounges with fireplaces, bar, restaurant, air conditioning, cable TV, and parking.

Inexpensive
ESTALAGEM DOM DINIS, *Rua Dr. António M. Magalhaes. Tel. (45) 932-36.*
This nice and rustic traditional inn has 15 comfortable rooms (some with views) with and without private bathrooms, a bar, and a restaurant.

Alternative Lodgings
Inexpensive and moderately priced nice local rustic apartments and houses can be rented by the night or by the week by contacting the **Turismo** office, *Rua Dr. António Matos Magalhaes, Tel. (045) 932-26.* The quality varies greatly from one house to another.

WHERE TO EAT
Moderate
POUSADA DE SANTA MARIA, *Rua 24 de Janeiro. Tel. (045) 932-02.*
Although I don't usually recommend hotel restaurants, this pousada offers great regional cuisine in a wonderfully relaxing setting. The rabbit (*coelho*) is amazing.

SEEING THE SIGHTS
If you're driving, leave your car in the demarcated parking area. Follow Rua do Espírito Santo past an assortment of Renaissance and Gothic whitewashed houses with balconies and go to the bold **castelo** (castle). After passing through a series of gates, you can walk up the staircase to enter the 13th century keep. From atop the castle it is easy to view all of tiny Marvão and its massive defensive fortifications, which include watchtowers that seem to barely cling to the top of the cliffs.

Besides the castle and several picturesque lanes, the village offers few attractions. You can visit the **Igreja de Santa Maria** (church) just below the castle at the **Largo do Municipio**, which contains the small **Museu Municipal** with a few interesting exhibits of traditional life in town including costumes and local artifacts. While you're wandering around, make sure to stop in at the Pousada de Santa Maria, *Rua 24 de Janeiro*, for a great meal or a nice cold beer.

After walking around the half dozen or so lanes dissecting the village, follow the access road back down the hill for a hundred yards or so to stop at the Gothic 15th century **Igreja de Nossa Senhora da Estrêla**, which features unusual azulejos and a nice altar.

PORTALEGRE

The bustling city of **Portalegre** rests at the western foot of the Serra de São Mamede mountains. Known primarily for its tapestries and silk weaving, Portalegre can seem somewhat disappointing after visiting the beautiful small villages in the surrounding area.

ARRIVALS & DEPARTURES

By Bus

• **Portalegre Main Bus Depot**, *Rua N. Alvares Pereira, Tel. (045) 227-23*

By Car

Portalegre is about 21 km from Marvão. Take Route N-359 south then turn onto Route N-246 south, which will take you right into town.

By Train

• **Portalegre CP Rail station**, *11 km south of town, Tel. (045) 961-21*

WHERE TO STAY

Expensive

POUSADA FLÔR DA ROSA, *Flôr da Rosa, Crato. Tel. (045) 997-210, Fax (045) 997-212. US & Canada bookings with Marketing Ahead, Tel. 800/ 223-1356. Low season rack rates from 23,000$00, double room, BP; high season rack rates from 28,000$00, double room, BP. All major credit cards accepted.*

This deluxe government owned hotel is a restored 14th century Gothic monastery. There are 24 individually designed air conditioned rooms, in a newly constructed wing, with sophisticated Memphis style designer furnishings, ultra-modern decorative arts and lighting fixtures, hand carved wooden ceilings and floors, private marble bathrooms, remote control satellite televisions, mini-bar, mini-safe, direct dial telephones, executive desks, large closets, and in many cases even large patios.

You will be amazed by the interior's unique mixture of medieval architectural elements and ultra modern interior design features. The public rooms in the pousada include a fine regional restaurant, a quiet bar and reading room full of plush designer sofas, amazing restored cloisters, an outdoor swimming pool and sun deck, and even a small historical museum. The staff of hard working area residents provide polite and friendly service. This pousada is located near Crato, a 20 minute drive from Portalegre, amidst tranquil farmlands in the north central section of the Planicíes region.

Selected as one of my *Best Places to Stay* (see Chapter 10 for more details).

Moderate

QUINTA DAS VARANDAS, *Serra de São Mamede. Tel. (045) 288-83. Year round rack rates from 15,750$00, double room, BP. Cash only - No credit cards accepted.*

This tranquil manor house and estate is about 5 km from town off Route N-246-2. There are five rooms with private bathrooms, a lounge, dining room, pool, TV room, beautiful formal gardens, horse riding, fountains, fine antiques, and parking.

QUINTA DA FONTE FRIA, *Serra-Portalegre. Tel. (045) 275-75. Year round rack rates from 16,000$00, double room, BP. Cash only - No credit cards accepted.*

This is a nice country inn located 3 km out of town. The inn rents three large and comfortable three bedroom apartments with kitchens and private bathrooms. Facilities include bar, pool, trails, library, TV room, and parking.

HOTEL DOM JOÃO III, *Ave. de Liberdade. Tel. (045) 211-92. Year round rack rates from 17,500$00, double room, CP. Cash only - No credit cards accepted.*

The Dom João is a large and functional 3 star hotel in the heart of Portalegre with 56 comfortable rooms (some with park views), a bar, restaurant, pool, disco, TV room, and parking.

Inexpensive

PENSÃO ALTO ALENTEJO, *Rua 19 de Junho, 59. Tel. (045) 222-90. Year round rack rates from 12,500$00, double room, CP. Cash only - No credit cards accepted.*

This nice and comfortable inn is located in the heart of the old town. It has 15 guest rooms with and without private bathrooms. There are almost no facilities, but it is close to everything.

WHERE TO EAT

Moderate

O ABRIGO, *Rua de Elvas, 74. Tel. (45) 227-78. No dress code. Most major credit cards accepted.*

O Abrigo is a charming and little cork-lined restaurant in the heart of the old town. This casual place serves hearty regional cuisine with nice and friendly service. Expect to spend around 2,100$00 a person here.

SEEING THE SIGHTS

The best way to wander through the city is to park your car in the municipal parking areas off Rua 1 de Maio in the southwestern part of town. From here you can walk through the old town walls and over to the **Largo de Sé** plaza. You can't help but be drawn towards the bold marble columns and strange pinnacles of the 16th century **Sé Cathedral**, which contains some beautiful chapels filled with fine altarpieces, 16th century azulejos, and paintings.

The plaza is also home to **Museu Municipal** which is housed in a former 16th century seminary (closed Tuesdays). The museum contains a vast assortment of sacred art, including beautiful 16th century gold and silver church plates, a 15th century gilded wood Spanish Pieta, a wonderful 17th century silver and ebony tabernacle, altarpieces, ivory statues, and other ecclesiastical art. The museum also contains collections of ceramics, silver snuff boxes, furniture, 17th century china, Arraiolos rugs, and paintings by Abel Santos.

From the **Largo de Sé** plaza, head up Rua de São Vicente for a block or so until you find the beautiful 17th century **Abrancalhas** (Yellow Palace), which has an elaborate facade complete with highly decorative wrought iron grillwork. From the palace, continue uptown on Rua da Figueira for a block or so until bearing right (east) to connect to Rua Luís de Camoes, where you can stroll past some wonderful houses and shops. Continue in the same direction through the old town walls and find more good shopping along Rua 5 de Outubro. A few blocks further up you can turn right (east) to reach a former 17th century Jesuit seminary, *Rua Guilherme Gomes Fernandes, 26*, where you can take a 20 minute guided tour (10am and 4pm weekdays) of its famous **Fabrica Real de Tapisseria** tapestry workshop. If you have a several thousand extra dollars, you can commission a beautiful tapestry here, but it may take a few years to complete.

From the tapestry factory, continue east along the same street until you come to the beautiful **Parque Miguel Bombarda**. After a brief stroll through the park and gardens, you should make your way back downtown to the old part of the city. This time from the Sé Cathedral you should head left (east) down the charming Rua 19 de Junho to view some great old houses. Turn left (east) which will lead you out of the town walls and down to the **Praça da República**. At the end of the square, bear right (south) onto Rua José Regio. You can visit the 18th century mansion of this famed early 20th century poet and novelist that houses the **Museu de**

José Regio. The museum (closed Mondays) contains many pieces of religious art and local artifacts collected by its famous namesake.

SPORTS & RECREATION
Hunting
• **Herdade do Carrascal**, *Portalegre, Tel. (045) 228-56*

EXCURSIONS & DAY TRIPS
The beautiful little town of **Crato** has fine examples of 16th century mansions and churches just off its main square including the remarkable **Varanda do Grão Prior**. You may also want to stop by its small museum, **Museu Municipal**, *Rua 5 de Outobro* (closed on Mondays), which exhibits interesting local art and handicrafts. Crato is on Route N-119 west, 20 km from Portalegre. Just a few kilometers north of Crato is the hamlet of **Flor da Rosa** where a unique new pousada in the remains of a 14th century monastery has recently opened its doors to the public.

From Crato, take Route N-363 west for about 6 km to reach a large prehistoric dolmen about a kilometer before the town of **Aldeia da Mata**. This is one of over 20 stone age monuments in the area, and is difficult to reach since there's no sign marking the dirt access road that cuts through a massive bull farm.

From the dolmen, return to Crato and turn south onto Route N-245 south for about 12 km to reach the wonderful equestrian breeding town of **Alter do Chão**. The heart of town is the mosaic square, **Praça da República**, which is centered around a pentagonal 14th century **castelo** (castle). The castle's **Torre de Menagem** keep has a great panoramic view.

The square also contains a regal 16th century marble column-lined fountain. Just a few kilometers out of town, on the unnamed road towards Reguengo, you can visit 18th century royal stud farms and an equestrian museum of the **Coudelaria de Alter Real**. The beautiful and well disciplined horses that are trained and bred here are highly prized and bring huge prices at the annual Couldelaria horse auction on April 25th. The day after the auction is the town's wonderfully amusing festival, **Festa da Nossa senhora da Alegria**.

ELVAS
Elvas is an intriguing fortified border city.

ARRIVALS & DEPARTURES
By Bus
• **Elvas Main Bus Depot**, *Praça da República, Tel. (068) 622-144*

By Car

Elvas is located about 58 km southeast of Portalegre on Route N-246 south.

By Train

• **Elvas CP Rail Station**, *Rua de Campo Maior, Tel. (068) 622-816*

WHERE TO STAY

Moderate

POUSADA DE SANTA LUZIA, *Ave. de Badajoz. Tel. (068) 622-128, Fax (068) 622-127. US & Canada bookings with Marketing Ahead, Tel. 800/ 223-1356. Low season rack rates from 12,000$00, double room, CP high season rates from 16,500$00, double room, CP. All major credit cards accepted.*

This pleasant country inn is just outside of the town walls. The pousada's 24 rooms and one suite offer typical regional furniture, televisions, mini-bars, and private bathrooms. Facilities include a good restaurant, bar, central air conditioning, a garden, and parking.

HOTEL D. LUIS, *Ave. de Badajoz. Tel. (068) 622-758, Fax (068) 620-733. Year round rack rates from 17,500$00, double room, CP. Most major credit cards accepted.*

This is a good 3 star hotel facing the aqueduct outside of the walls of Elvas. It has 90 air conditioned rooms with television, mini-bar, and private bathroom. Facilities include bar, restaurant, and parking.

MONTE DA AMOREIRA, *Sao Bras. Tel. (068) 624-687, Fax (068) 624-683. Year round rack rates from 13,000$00, double room, CP. Cash only - No credit cards accepted.*

This quaint farm house and estate, off Route N-514 about 7 km west of town, has seven rooms with semi-private bathrooms, lounge, hunting, TV room, and parking.

Inexpensive

ESTALAGEM DON SANCHO II, *Praca da República, 20. Tel. (068) 626-684, Fax (068) 624-717. Year round rack rates from 8,500$00, double room, CP. Cash only - No credit cards accepted.*

This is a well located 4 star inn near the Turismo with 26 comfortable rooms with private bathrooms, a bar, restaurant, TV room, and nearby parking.

PENSÃO QUINTA DAS AGUIAS, *Ave. de Badajoz. Tel. (068) 622-340. Year round rack rates from 6,900$00, double room, EP. Cash only - No credit cards accepted.*

This clean and basic inn offers several simple rooms with and without private bathrooms.

WHERE TO EAT

Moderate

O AQUEDUTO, *Ave da Piedade. Tel. (068) 623-676. No dress code. Cash only - No credit cards accepted.*
This nice and friendly regional restaurant serves great meat and seafood specialities. The food is rather good, the service is prompt, and the average bill here is usually less than 1,950$00 a person plus wine.
CHURRASQUEIRA ALENTEJANA, *Rua da Cadeia. Tel. (068) 622-471. No dress code. Cash only - No credit cards accepted.*
This nice and simple barbecue and roasted meat restaurant is located near the Praca da República. It serves huge portions of tasty meat dishes served in a casual ambiance. Expect to spend around 1,500$00 a person.

SEEING THE SIGHTS

As the perimeter road turns toward the southern sector of the old town, you will pass the beautiful 16th century **Aqueducto da Amoreiras**. The massive aqueduct system of three and four story arches still brings fresh water into the town's fountains from a source some seven km away.

The area around this aqueduct hosts the town's large weekly regional **mercado** (market), which is held each Monday and is well worth the visit. After passing under the aqueduct, bear left and pass the pousada to access the **Portas de Olivenca** town gates, from which Rua de Olivenca proceeds into the **Praça da República** square in the heart of town. After you have found parking (not always so easy), your first stop should be at the local Turismo office on the southern side of the square for a large and detailed walking map.

If you walk a block or so west on Rua de Cadeia, which is just behind the Turismo, you can see the massive **Torre de Fernandina** tower. Walk back to the Praça da República, and as you cross the square, the Câmara Municipal (town hall) will be on your left. In front of you on the northern side you can visit the **Igreja de Nossa Senhora da Assuncão**. This Manueline 16th century cathedral was built on the site of the town's ruined 13th century Gothic **Sé Cathedral** and its exterior contains a beautiful Manueline main portal topped by a Rosé colored window, a pyramid shaped bell tower, and some nice iron grillwork. Inside the vaulted interior you will see several examples of 18th century azulejos, a fine 18th century organ, and lots of marble.

Behind the cathedral, you will find the medieval **Largo do Dr. Santa Clara** plaza, home to the octagonal shaped 16th century Renaissance **Igreja de Nossa Senhora da Consolacão**. Here you'll see an inspiring dome-topped interior, covered with unique azulejos bearing lace and flower motifs and several nice paintings above the altars.

The plaza itself is a great sight as it is loaded with attractions. The plaza's central 16th century Manueline **pelourinho** (pillory) is spiked with iron hangman's hooks and is surrounded by the church, several regal homes, and two massive towers from the town's old defensive walls. The towers are bridged by a wonderful gate that rests below an ornate Moorish loggia.

As you pass under the gate and onto **Largo da Alacova**, bear left and then right onto the charming Rua das Beatas that will take you towards the old **castelo** (castle). The castle grounds (closed Thursdays) dates back to Moorish times and contains a small exhibit inside of the former governor's house. If you walk the ramparts, you will see a wonderful view of the city. Follow the old town walls back down in either direction to reach the **Porta de Olivenca** gate.

If you're in Portugal during the third week of September, you may want to visit this city during its annual **Festa do Senhora da Piedade** and **Feira de São Mateus** festivals.

VILA VIÇOSA

The former royal town of Vila Viçosa lies on the side of a hill. In the 15th century, the town grew in prominence as it became the residence to the dukes of Bragança and so became home to the kings of Portugal. Now that the kings are gone, Vila Viçosa remains as a living museum.

ARRIVALS & DEPARTURES
By Bus
• **Vila Viçosa Main Bus Stop**, *Rua André Pereira, no phone.*

By Car
Vila Viscosa is about 33 km from Elvas, and about 5 km southeast of Borba (see *Excursions & Day Trips* below). Take Route IP-7 east to Borba and then turn onto Route N-255 south for about 5 km.

WHERE TO STAY
Expensive
CASA DE PEIXINHOS, *Vila Viçosa. Tel. (068) 984-72.*
This is a delightful 17th miniature century castle located on a farming estate. It has six great rooms with private bathrooms, bar, restaurant, gardens, bicycles, TV room, trails, library, and parking.

Moderate
CASA DOS ARCOS, *Vila Viçosa. Tel. (068) 985-18.*

This 18th century manor house, in the heart of town, rents four guest rooms and two studio apartments with private bathrooms, kitchens, bar, TV room, and parking.

WHERE TO EAT
Inexpensive
RESTAURANTE FRAMAR, *Praça da República. Tel. (068) 988-82.*

This is a pretty good regional restaurant, located in the heart of town, that serves reasonably priced large portions of local specialties in a nice dining room.

SEEING THE SIGHTS

As you enter town you are drawn to the huge 16th century **Paço Ducal** palace, which is entered from behind the large statue of King João IV on his horse in the **Terreiro do Paço** square. You can visit more than 50 beautifully furnished rooms located in both wings (closed Sundays and Mondays) of the royal residence constructed by Dom Jaime I, the 4th duke of Bragança. The 45 minute tour of exhibits include Arraiolos carpets, frescoed ceilings, azulejos, armor, massive kitchens, 19th century royal portraits by Malhoa and Sousa Pinto, classical furniture, ceramics, a gallery full of paintings by King Carlos, jewelry, a 17th century holy cross studded with thousands of diamonds and rubies, and over 75 royal coaches from the 17th through 19th centuries.

The plaza also contains several somber, beautiful churches including the 16th century **Convento das Chagas**, which has some royal tombs, and the 17th century **Igreja de Santo Agostinho** with royal tombs made from solid marble. A bit further up Rua de Duque D. Jaime above the northern edge of the plaza are the medieval **Porta da Vila** old town gate, and the 16th century Manueline **Porta dos Nos** town gate with a sculptured knot motif.

The first local residence of the dukes of Bragança was the moated 13th century **castelo** (castle) reached by walking south on the Avenida Duque de Bragança through the heart of town until you can see the large 16th century pillory. The castle, entered via a drawbridge, housed the royal family members until the Paço Ducal was completed.

Inside the castle (closed Mondays) you can visit the keep, home to a collection of artifacts from the prehistoric through the Roman eras. There is also a tour through the ramparts, dungeon, and living quarters of the castle. A cluster of old houses and the 15th century **Igreja da Nossa Senhora da Conceição** are also within the castle compound.

EXCURSIONS & DAY TRIPS

The town of **Borba** is about 5 km north of Elvas on Route N-255. Every inch of the area surrounding this town seems to be filled with huge marble quarries, and every house, office building, and bathroom in the area is crammed full of the stuff. Much of this marble ends up North America as so-called Italian Carrera marble.

The town once was dominated by a medieval castle, but almost nothing remains of it. While passing through the town you should visit the **Praça da República**, the town's main square, and from there visit the modest 15th century **Igreja de Nossa Senhora das Neves** and see its fine paintings; the frescoes and marble interior of the vaulted 17th century Renaissance church, **Igreja de São Bartolomeu**; the 17th century **Cãmara Municipal** (town hall); and the 18th century marble **Fonte das Bicas** fountain. I also recommend a quick drive over to a museum, **Museu de Ceramica** (closed on Mondays) at **Quinta dos Lobos**.

Before leaving town, try to taste an old bottle of hearty red Borba wine. The best bottles have a label made of real cork.

REDONDO

The friendly rural town of Redondo rests near the foot of the peaceful Serra de Ossa mountain range and is conveniently located in the middle of the region's most important tourist sights. I like to stay here because it is just 20 minutes away from Évora, Estremoz, Vila Viçosa, Monsaraz, and several other great towns: the perfect base for day trips throughout the entire area.

This quiet town is oriented around a beautiful central plaza known as the Praça da República, where local farmers can be seen chatting with businessmen dressed in full length wool capes in front of the lovely 18th century Cãmara Municipal (town hall). The Turismo office is located in the town hall.

ARRIVALS & DEPARTURES

By Car

Redondo is about 18 km southwest of Vila Viçosa on Route N-254. Parking is no problem.

WHERE TO STAY

Expensive

HOTEL CONVENTO DE SÃO PAULO, *Aldeia da Serra, Redondo. Tel. (066) 999-100, Fax (066) 999-104. US and Canada bookings with Alta Tours, Tel. 800/338-4191. Low season rack rates from 18,000$00, double room,*

BP; high season rack rates from 28,500$00, double room, BP. All major credit cards accepted.

This is a remarkable medieval convent on a huge rural estate that has been converted into one of the country's best and most memorable deluxe accommodations. The hotel has 21 super deluxe rooms with air conditioning, private marble bathrooms, remote control satellite televisions, complimentary buffet breakfast and evening tea service, and more charm than is possible to describe.

Facilities include a superb restaurant, an art gallery/bar, an outdoor pool, formal gardens, nearby hiking trails, a 400 year old chapel, room service, 50,000 historic azulejos, amazing cloisters, countless rare antiques, and plenty of free parking. Off-season rates are extremely reasonable.

Selected as one of my *Best Places to Stay* (see Chapter 10 for more details).

Moderate

QUINTA DA TALHA, *N-524, Redondo. Tel. (066) 999-468. Year round rack rates from 15,500$00, double room, CP. Cash only - No credit cards accepted.*

This rustic farming estate in the Serra de Ossa area offers houses with four good rooms, private bathrooms, a lounge, dining room, and vineyards.

Inexpensive

PENSÃO BASTIÃO, *Rua Manuel J. da Silva. Tel. (066) 991-02. Year round rack rates from 13,000$00, double room, EP. Cash only - No credit cards accepted.*

This clean, small 2 star establishment has several basic rooms with private bathroom. There are almost no facilities in the inn except for a bar.

WHERE TO EAT

HOTEL CONVENTO DE SÃO PAULO, *Aldeia da Serra, Redondo. Tel. (066) 999-100. Dress code is casual but neat. All major credit cards accepted.*

The Gothic dining room at this superb hotel is a magnificent place to enjoy a gourmet dinner. As you sit below an original frescoed ceiling depicting the heavens above, you will be presented a large menu with over 35 different dishes including delicious salads, amazing shrimp crepes, cream of leak and almond soup, gazpacho, lobster salad, dogfish in coriander sauce, filet of grouper, filet of sole, roasted duck, veal Stroganoff, pork cutlets with fine herbs, roast leg of lamb, steak in pepper sauce, chicken baked with pine nuts, and much more.

The service here is outstanding, and you can have a wonderful three course meal for as little as 3,450$00 a person plus wine. Highly Recommended.

SEEING THE SIGHTS

A walk through the town's central streets will lead you through several ancient gates and towers which were part of Redondo's defensive walls and ruined castle, including the **Porta da Ravessa** gate, the **Porta do Sol** gate, the **Postigo de Relogigo** clock and bell tower gate, and the towering **Torre de Menagem** keep. Nearby you can wander through several beautiful ancient lanes and stone paved streets, such as the Rua do Castelo, to view the town's impressive whitewashed and blue-bordered homes. There are also a couple of wonderfully decorated churches in the heart of town, including the 16th century whitewashed and granite **Igreja de Nossa Senhora da Anunciacão**, and the nearby 16th century somber **Igreja da Misericórdia**.

At the edge of town there is the wonderful little **Pirraca** earthenware shop and studio (follow the blue Artisanato sign), which has some of the finest and least expensive hand painted casserole dishes and pitchers in Portugal. The town is also well known for its fine wines, including the inexpensive *Porta da Ravessa* brand (produced by the **Cooperativa de Redondo** winery, which may be visited on the outskirts of town).

Looking out over the wonderful sights in and around Redondo is the magnificent 16th century **Convento de São Paulo**, about 8 km up route N-381 north just after the village of **Aldeia de Serra** at the base of the majestic **Serra de Ossa** mountains. This wonderful convent, situated on hundreds of acres of beautiful land, has been restored into what has become the most impressive hotel in Portugal. Its original azulejos-lined walls, marble floors, ceiling frescoes, fine furniture, deluxe public rooms, opulent guest rooms and fine regional restaurant are among the finest in Europe. Even if you are not a guest, ask for the friendly English-speaking manager (Mr. José Almeida) and he will be glad to show you around. Try to stay here a few days; it is an experience you will not forget.

ESTREMOZ

The historic town of Estremoz was home to a number of Portuguese kings and queens and a castle. Estremoz has seen much of the country's history unfold within its defensive walls.

ARRIVALS & DEPARTURES
By Bus
• **Estremoz Main Bus Depot**, *Rossio, Tel. (068) 222-82*

By Car

Estremoz is about 26 km northwest of Redondo on Route N-381 north.

WHERE TO STAY
Expensive

POUSADA RAINHA SANTA ISABEL, *Largo Dom Dinis. Tel. (068) 332-075, Fax (068) 332-079. US & Canada bookings with Marketing Ahead, Tel. 800/223-1356. Low season rack rates from 23,000$00, double room, BP; high season rack rates from 28,000$00, double room, BP. All major credit cards accepted.*

After undergoing some major enhancements, this pousada, once a 13th century royal palace and castle, has become one of the most popular government owned hotels in Portugal. Inside the hotel, you will find 23 large period rooms with antique furnishings, azulejos, marble accented private bathrooms, remote control satellite television, unusual four poster beds, rare regional artwork, mini-bar, direct dial telephones, and lots of medieval ambiance.

Facilities include a new outdoor swimming pool, inner courtyards, gardens, a full service bar, a well known gourmet restaurant, a series of sitting rooms full of monastic furnishings, and free parking.

Moderate

HOSPEDARIA D. DINIZ, *Rua 31 de Janeiro, 46. Tel. (068) 332-717, Fax (068) 226-10. Low season rack rates from 10,000$00, double room, EP; high season rack rates from 12,500$00, double room, EP. Most major credit cards accepted.*

For my money, this is certainly the best place to stay in Estremoz. While much less expensive than some other choices I recommend, no other area hotel or inn can compare with the level of personalized service and welcoming ambiance that this cute, family-managed property has to offer.

Located just off the main town square, the Hospedaria features eight spacious rooms with remote control air conditioning, private marble bathrooms, satellite color televisions with infrared headsets (so as not to disturb your partner when viewing late at night), extremely comfortable beds, nice modern furnishings, and small terraces. While there are few extra services here, everything you need from restaurants to laundry facilities are just steps away. Highly Recommended.

MONTE DOS PENSAMENTOS, *Estrada Estação do Ameixal. Tel. (068) 223-75. Year round rack rates from 17,500$00, double room, CP. Cash only - No credit cards accepted.*

This 19th century country inn is 2 km out of town, and is owned by a charming older English women. The inn has four nice rooms with private bathrooms, a bar, pool, TV room, library, traditional regional furnishings, garden, bicycles, and parking.

POUSADA DO SÃO MIGUEL, *Sousel. Tel. (068) 551-155. US & Canada bookings with Marketing Ahead, Tel. 800/223-1356. Low season rack rates from 22,000$00, double room, CP; high season rack rates from 16,500$00, double room, CP. All major credit cards accepted.*

This modern pousada on a hilltop is about 16 km northwest of Estremoz near the hunting area of Sousel. Special services for sportsmen as well as tourists are available at this 28 room inn. Facilities include bar, restaurant, air conditioning, TV, kennels, and parking.

Inexpensive

PENSÃO CARVALHO, *Largo da República, 27. Tel. (068) 227-12. Year round rack rates from 17,500$00, double room, CP. Cash only - No credit cards accepted.*

This clean and basic 2 star inn is located in the heart of the lower town. There are 15 clean guest rooms with and without private bathrooms and almost no facilities.

WHERE TO EAT

Expensive

RESTAURANTE AGUIAS D'OURO, *Rossio Marquês de Pombal. Tel. (068) 228-36. No dress code. Most major credit cards accepted.*

Winner of many prestigious awards for their superb regional cuisine, this small second floor restaurant is the best in Estremoz. The small white stucco dining rooms have a few tables each where local businessmen, well traveled visitors, and hard working locals come for long, relaxing meals. The menu includes a wonderful fisherman's soup, seafood crepes, rice with tamboril, melon with ham, stuffed partridge, grilled swordfish, acorda, filet of sole, beef steak with pepper sauce, roast suckling pig, and many other area favorites.

Expect to spend about two hours, and around 2,250$00 per person for a great dinner. Highly Recommended.

POUSADA RAINHA SANTA ISABEL, *Largo Dom Dinis. Tel. (068) 226-18. Dress code is semi-formal. All major cards accepted.*

This nicely decorated and somewhat formal restaurant has a heavy old world ambiance complete with red velvet furnishings, waiters in black tie, and classical music. This is a good place to go if you wish to splurge on dishes like lamb chops with fresh mint sauce, filet of local trout, seafood cataplana, roasted chicken, veal kebabs in mint sauce, shrimp in herbed butter, cod fish with spinach and melted cheese, pork with clams, rabbit with red peppers, and many others.

Make sure to call in advance for reservations, and expect to pay about 3,750$00 per person plus wine for lunch or dinner.

Moderate

RESTAURANTE OITO, OITO, OITO, *Avenida Tomaz Alcaide, 14. Tel. (068) 333-584. No dress code. Cash only - No credit cards accepted.*

While it may be a bit hard to find, this small Chinese restaurant near the city's theater offers a great selection of tasty Asian favorites. The interior is typical of any other Chines restaurant, and the staff are extremely nice to all who enter their doors. The extensive menu (good for eat-in and for take-out) features won ton soup, egg rolls, fried rice with shrimp, sweet and sour chicken, vegetarian chop suey, shrimp with chili sauce, beef with orange sauce, fish with bamboo shoots and bean sprouts, lamb with oyster sauce, and many others. My dinner cost only 1,150$00 and was delicious. Highly Recommended.

RESTAURANTE ARLEQUIM, *Rua Dr. G. Resende, 15. Tel. (068) 237-26. No dress code. Cash only - No credit cards accepted.*
This friendly and simple restaurant near the Rossio offers hearty regional cuisine prepared with fresh local produce and presented by nice staff. Expect to pay around 1,350$00 a person.

SEEING THE SIGHTS

To begin exploring the upper portion of town, drive up through the massive 14th century gateway to the castle area known as the **Largo Dom Dinis** plaza and leave your car near the pousada in the parking lot. The first stop on your walking tour is the 13th century **Torre de Menagem** keep, topped by a ring of pointed merlons. Inside the keep you can visit its octagonal room and the rooftop observation deck.

The adjacent former royal armory of the ruined palace is home to the delightful **Pousada da Rainha Santa Isabel**, which must be visited to view its elegant decor and fine stairways. Steps away from the pousada is the 17th century **Capela da Rainha Santa** chapel, covered in lovely azulejos panels showing various scenes from the life of the late Queen Isabel who died in Estremoz in 1336. Also worth a peek inside is the 16th century **Igreja dae Santa Maria** church, filled with locally mined marble and unusual primitive paintings.

Other impressive sights in this plaza include the Gothic vaulted loggia of the 13th century **Paços de Audiencia**, which was the former audience gallery of King Dom Dinis, and the **Museu Municipal** museum (closed Mondays) located in a 17th century alms house. The museum has traditional furniture, ceramics, clay dolls, azulejos, and 20th century paintings.

Below the Largo Dom Dinis plaza is the lower and somewhat more modern part of town. A small road winds its way down to the town's central **Rossio do Marquis de Pombal** square. The square contains a nice Manueline pillory, the 18th century former **Convento de Congregados de São Filipe de Nery** whose wonderful azulejos-covered interior houses the **Câmara Municipal** (town hall), and the **Museu Rural de Casa do Povo de Santa Maria** museum (closed Mondays), which houses a strange collection of local handicrafts and artifacts, and several cafés.

Each Saturday morning, a large regional produce **mercado** (market) takes place in this square; every day there are a handful of kiosks selling ceramics and handmade leather goods. Estremoz is well known for its wonderful clay figurines, water pitchers, and pottery that can also be found in small shops near the central square.

NIGHTLIFE & ENTERTAINMENT

Although Estremoz is not a major night life center, there are a few noteworthy places to meet the locals and sip on cool drinks. The younger set seems to head for places like the cavernous **Bar Reguengos**, *Rua Serpa Pinto,* where students watch sporting events on their large screen television, or play pool while munching down hamburgers and Budweiser beer.

There are the more laid-back pubs like the **Bar Dado** and **Symphonia**, *Rua 31 de Janeiro,* that serve local and imported beers and have a friendly crowd. On Saturday nights after 2:00am when the above bars close down, some folks head for the rowdy subterranean **Subsolo** disco on the edge of town along the road towards Arcos.

SPORTS & RECREATION
Fishing & Hunting
• **Pousada São Miguel**, *Sousel, Tel. (068) 551-160*

ÉVORA MONTE

The tiny, sleepy village of Évora Monte lies peacefully below a castle on a large hill. Its one and only main road is filled with charming village houses painted in traditional whitewash with blue borders.

ARRIVALS & DEPARTURES
By Car

Évora Monte is 12 km southwest of Estremoz on Route N-18 south.

WHERE TO STAY

Inexpensive

MONTE DA FAZENDA, *Évora Monte, Tel. (068) 951-72.*

This is a very rustic farm house just outside of town on a difficult dirt road. The family that operates the house as an inn offers two basic rooms with private bathroom. Facilities include a bar, pool, TV room, billiards, library, hunting, horseback riding, and parking.

SEEING THE SIGHTS

A large reconstructed **castelo** (castle) has been here since Roman times, although the current structure bears little resemblance to its original design. The current castle, with towered ramparts and a 16th century **Torre de Menagem** (tower), loom high above the surrounding plains of olive and orange trees.

At night the castle is brightly lit up and can be seen from far away. The town's beautiful 16th century church, **Igreja da Misericórdia**, is on the main street.

SPORTS & RECREATION

Hunting & Horseback Riding

• **Monte da Fazenda**, *Évora Monte, Tel. (068) 951-72*

ÉVORA

The incredibly beautiful walled city of Évora sit on a hill in the heart of a vast plain. Of all the wonderful sights in Portugal, Évora is the one place I find myself returning to on every trip to Portugal. After more than 20 visits to this historical city of 45,000 inhabitants, I always find new sights to explore. The area around Évora has been inhabited since prehistoric times, as is evident by the megaliths located a few minutes out of town in places like Guadalupe.

The city retains several reminders of the Roman occupation since the 1st century B.C., followed by the Visigoths and then the Moors, who left their mark as well. The city came under Christian control in 1165 after a bold attack by local hero Geraldo Sem-Pavor (Gerald the Fearless) and his local outlaw forces, and was given its first official charter by King Dom Afonso Henriques. Évora became home to several kings and royal families in the 12th–16th centuries, and they filled the town with many ornate palaces and churches that still grace every corner.

As numerous politicians, artists, poets, religious leaders and scholars poured into Évora, its 16th century university was established and the city flourished to become an important center for Portugal's Renaissance.

With the Spanish occupation of Portugal in 1580, Évora lost much of its prominence and slowly faded out of the limelight.

ARRIVALS & DEPARTURES

By Air

Since Évora is almost equidistant from both Lisbon and Faro, to travel directly here you can fly into either Lisbon's Portela airport or Faro's newly enlarged airport.

By Bus

Most buses from within Portugal stop off at the city's main bus depot located inside the city walls.

•**Évora Main Bus Depot**, *Rua da República, Tel. (066) 221-21*

By Car

Évora is about 44 km southwest of Estremoz on Route N-18 south.

By the time you read this section, there will be a new toll motorway from Lisbon to Évora, and another new toll motorway from Faro to Évora. These motorways will be the best ways to reach the city. The names and prices of the roads had not be decided by press time, so check with any Turismo office for the latest information.

•**Hertz Rent a Car in Évora**, *Rua de Isabel, 7, Tel. (066) 217-67*

By Train

Those coming to Évora by rail will find frequently scheduled local and express trains from both Lisbon and Faro. Trains arrive into Évora's downtown rail station just outside of the old city walls.

•**Évora CP Rail Station**, *Rua da República, Tel. (066) 221-25*

ORIENTATION

The compact walled city of Évora rests on a softly rising hill surrounded by the vast cork tree dotted plains of the Planicíes region. It is about 151 kilometers (94 miles) east of Lisbon, and some 213 kilometers (132 miles) north of Faro.

This beautiful city is covered with countless small winding lanes that in many cases were built during Roman, Moorish, or medieval eras, and can be confusing to navigate through. My best advice is to pop inside the Turismo office off the main square, Praça de Giraldo, and get an inexpensive walking map or booklet that notes all the major landmarks to help you get around.

GETTING AROUND TOWN

By Car

Finding parking in Évora is not too difficult since there are a new series of parking lots. They charge around 165$00 per hour and 1,450$00 per day. Since the streets are rather narrow and it's not uncommon for trucks to block downtown lanes for long periods of time as they unload merchandise, I suggest parking your car in one of these lots and walk.

By Taxi

Taxis are easy to find, but are not necessary since the distances you will cover are rather short.

By Bus

Municipal buses are also easy to both find and utilize, but will not be necessary since the distances you will cover in town are short.

WHERE TO STAY

Expensive

POUSADA DOS LÓIOS, *Largo Conde de Vila Flor. Tel. (066) 240-51, Fax (066) 272-48. US & Canada bookings with Marketing Ahead, Tel. 800/ 223-1356. Low season rack rates from 23,000$00, double room, BP; high season rates from 28,000$00, double room, BP. All major credit cards accepted.*

This beautiful, deluxe, and historic 32 room government owned inn is located amidst the cloisters of a 15th century monastery next to a Roman temple in the heart of town. This fantastic pousada is unfortunately sold out on many nights. Facilities include bar, gourmet regional restaurant, swimming pool, and parking.

Selected as one of my *Best Places to Stay* (see Chapter 10 for more details).

Moderate

O'EBORNESE, *Largo da Misericordia. Tel. (066) 220-31. Year round rack rates from 14,500$00, double room, CP. Most major credit cards accepted.*

This pleasant and well located 16th century manor house has been converted into a good 3 star bed and breakfast inn with 25 comfortable rooms with private bathrooms. The inn offers a lounge, breakfast room, terrace, and nearby public parking.

ESTALAGEM MONTE DAS FLORES, *Estrada das Alcacovas. Tel. (066) 254-90, Fax (066) 275-64. Cash only - No major credit cards accepted.*

This charming farm house and stables offers 17 traditionally decorated rooms with private bathrooms and television just a few minutes outside of town. Facilities include bar, lounge, dining room, TV room, gardens, horse riding, and free parking.

EVORA HOTEL, *N-114, Évora. Tel. (066) 734-800, Fax (066) 734-806. Year round rack rates from 17,500$00, double room, CP. Most major credit cards accepted.*

Évora Hotel is an modern new business hotel a few minutes west of town that lacks any real charm or good service. The property offers 114 air conditioned rooms with private bathrooms, mini-bar, terraces, and modern furnishings. Facilities include a swimming pool, bar, restaurant, business meeting rooms, and free parking.

CASA DE SAM PEDRO, *Quinta de Sam Pedro. Tel. (066) 221-38, Fax (066) 221-26. Year round rack rates from 14,250$00, double room, CP. Cash only - No credit cards accepted.*

This is a charming 18th century manor house some 5 km north of town near the hamlet of Monte de Oliveirinha. It has three fine bedrooms with private bathrooms, lounge, dining room, antique laden public rooms, library, bicycles, and parking.

CASA DE SÃO TIAGO, *Largo Alexandre Hurculano, 2. Tel. (066) 226-86, Fax (066) 600-0357. Year round rack rates from 14,300$00, double room, CP. Cash only - No credit cards accepted.*

This typical whitewashed old house, in the heart of town, has six good rooms with private bathrooms, a fireside lounge, dining room, TV room, library, and parking.

ESTALAGEM POKER, *N-114, Évora. Tel. (066) 337-21, Fax (066) 337-10. Year round rack rates from 13,600$00, double room, EP. Most major credit cards accepted.*

A cute and modern little 4 star inn located a couple of minutes west of town. It has 15 comfortable double rooms with private bathrooms, bar, restaurant, snack bar, TV, air conditioning, pool, tennis, and parking.

HOTEL PLANACIE, *Rua Miguel Bombarda, 40. Tel. (066) 240-26, Fax (066) 298-80. US and Canada bookings with Best Western, Tel. 800/528-1234. Year round rack rates from 15,250$00, double room, BP. Most major credit cards accepted.*

This older 3 star hotel, in the heart of Évora, has 33 basic and somewhat comfortable rooms with private bathrooms, direct dial telephones, and televisions. The hotel is in need of some renovations, but its ever friendly staff make it a good place to stay. Facilities include a bar, restaurant, and central air conditioning

Inexpensive

RESIDENCIAL DIANA, *Rua Diogo Cao, 2. Tel. (066) 220-08. Year round rack rates from 8,650$00, double room, CP. Cash only - No credit cards accepted.*

This old house in the heart of town has been converted into a pleasant inn. The dozen or so rooms offer private bathrooms and are comfortably furnished. Facilities include bar, restaurant, TV room, and safe deposit boxes.

PENSÃO POLICARPO, *Rua Freiria de Baixo,16. Tel. (066) 224-24. Year round rack rates from 8,250$00, double room, CP. Cash only - No credit cards accepted.*

This quaint family owned inn, located in a great part of town, has 24 rooms both with and without private bathrooms. See a few rooms before selecting yours as they are not all alike. Very few facilities except a breakfast room.

QUINTA DA NORA, *Estrada dos Canaviais. Tel. (066) 298-10. Year round rack rates from 9,995$00, double room, CP. Cash only - No credit cards accepted.*

Quinta da Nora is a rustic farm house whose absentee owners offer five traditionally furnished rooms with private bathrooms. The house is just a few minutes northwest of town on a farming estate. Facilities include pool, bicycles, TV room, and parking.

WHERE TO EAT
Expensive
POUSADA DOS LÓIOS, *Largo Conde de Vila Flor. Tel. (066) 240-51. Dress code is jacket preferred. All major credit cards accepted.*

Simply the most elegant place to eat in all of Évora! Although rather expensive and somewhat formal, this amazingly ornate restaurant serves fine regional cuisine with a special flare. Try the unforgettable borrego assado no forno (oven roasted lamb). A typical four course meal here costs around 4,250$00.

COZINHA DE SANTO HUMBERTO, *Rua da Moeda, 39. Tel. (066) 242-51. Dress code is smart casual. Most major credit cards accepted.*

This wonderful restaurant is located just off the Praca do Giraldo in a converted wine cellar. Superb regional cuisine is served in a great setting with fine service. The excellent food here has won several Portuguese gold medals. Try anything the staff suggest and expect to spend around 3,450$00 a person.

Moderate
RESTAURANTE FIALHO, *Travessa das Mascarenhas, 16. Tel. (066) 230-79. No dress code. Most major credit cards accepted.*

This is a well known and long established family owned regional restaurant with exposed beam ceilings and lots of atmosphere. The fine chefs specialize in locally raised pork, lamb, and fish specialties that are prepared with great flair. A great meal here will set you back about 1,950$00 a head plus wine.

RESTAURANT TIPICO GUIAO, *Rua da República, 81. Tel. (066) 230-71. No dress code. Most major credit cards accepted.*

This small and charming little restaurant near the bottom of the Praca do Giraldo offers great food at reasonable prices. If you are ready for some of the best affordable regional cuisine in Évora, this is the place to go. Try the great trout here and expect to spend less than 1,400$00 each.

SEEING THE SIGHTS

As you come into Évora you will notice a road known as the Estrada da Circunvalação that fully circles the walled town. The easiest way to find parking is to take a left at that circular road and another left to enter town at the posted pousada exit. After going up the small street for a block, you will intersect with the Rua de Colegio, where you can find a municipal parking lot and another parking lot next to the university.

With your back to the edge of town, walk right down the Rua do Colegio and continue for a block as it bends towards the left to meet with Largo Duques de Cadaval. The large structure you will see on your left is the 14th century **Palácio dos Duques de Cadaval**. This former royal residence is flanked by two large towers, one of which was originally part of Évora's defensive walls. The palace's **Torre das Cinco Quinas** tower houses a small museum (closed Mondays) that has Flemish bronze tombs, paintings, sculptures, and historical documents.

A small road leads uphill from the palace past a quaint sculpture garden and onto the wonderful **Largo do Conde de Vila Flôr** square. The most obvious attraction in the square is the mystical granite and marble columned **Templo Romano** temple, which dates back to the 2nd century during Évora's Roman occupation. Surrounding the temple are several impressive buildings.

Just across from the temple is the magnificent 15th century Gothic **Igreja de São João Evangelista** (also known as the **Igreja dos Lóios**, closed Mondays), which was built on the site of a former Moorish castle. As you pass through the church's original Gothic portal you will be lead into a beautiful vaulted interior that boasts intricate 18th century azulejos by famed master craftsman António de Oliveira Bernardes and the eerie tombs of the noble Melo family.

The church's adjacent cloisters now contain the elaborate **Pousada dos Lóios**, by far the most impressive place to stay in town. The pousada must be visited to see its lovely chapter house doorway, Renaissance gallery, Manueline columns, and fine furnishings. On the end of the square is the former 17th century bishop's palace, housing the **Museu de**

Évora. This wonderful museum (closed Mondays) contains a vast assortment of Roman, medieval, Manueline, and Moorish-Portuguese sculptures. There are also several exhibits of 16th century Portuguese and Flemish paintings, archaeological findings, furniture, ceramics, jewelry and fine azulejos.

As you pass the museum, you will find yourself on the **Largo do Marquêsde Marialva**, which is dominated by the huge Gothic 12th century **Sé Cathedral** (closed Mondays). Topped with an octagonal dome, the cathedral's facade contains massive granite block towers. Under these towers, a Gothic portal is supported by marble columns sculpted with figures of the Apostles. Inside, while walking within the vaulted interior, notice the Gothic Rosé windows, the baroque chapel, the hand carved choir stalls in the coro alto, and the Renaissance chapel portal designed by Nicolas Chanterene. If you buy tickets, you can also visit the fantastic 14th century sculpture- and tomb-filled cloisters, as well as the **Museu de Arte Sacra**, featuring several fine religious pieces, including a bizarre 13th century ivory Virgin that opens up to show scenes from her life. Other exhibits include a 17th century reliquary cross, studded with over a thousand precious stones, a piece of wood from the cross that Jesus died on, jewelry, furniture, sculpture, and more.

After visiting the cathedral, head down the Rua 5 de Octubro towards the city's central square known as the **Praça de Giraldo**. Besides being home to Évora's helpful Turismo office, the plaza's fountain is also the gathering place for local students and workers alike. Several shops, cafés, and banks line the square, but don't expect the 24 hour currency conversion machine to be working.

At this point you may want to stop at the square's **Café Arcadia** for a great torta with a café or galão. At the top of the square is the whitewashed facade of the 16th century **Igreja de Santo Antão**. If you're in town for shopping, head up past the church and browse in the windows along Rua João de Dues where lace, clothing, and shoe shops are in abundance. From the Praça de Giraldo's opposite end, continue your tour by taking Rua da República a few blocks down to the 15th century Gothic **Igreja de São Fransisco**. This unusual church contains a huge vaulted interior with both baroque and Renaissance elements, including a beautiful gilt wood baroque altar in the lateral chapel.

The most unusual sight is the adjacent **Capela dos Ossos** (chapel of bones), lined with a collection of neatly arranged bones and skulls belonging to former monks. Its rather amusing welcoming epitaph loosely translates to "our bones are waiting for your bones." Entrance to the chapel of bones is extra, and photographers must pay a small fee to take pictures inside. If you're lucky, the **Museu do Artesanato** handicrafts museum and shop just across the street will be open.

As you exit the church, the city's bustling covered **mercados** (markets) await your visit just steps away across the **Praça 1 de Maio**. Its two separate buildings house several dozen vendors selling cheeses, fresh produce, fish, and my favorite item, the hot peppers and piri-piri hot sauce sold by a man with a huge red nose (probably the effect of too much piri-piri). Why not buy some bread, queijo de cabra (goat cheese), and tomatoes for a great picnic lunch?

A few ceramics merchants sell colorful items directly in front of the marketplace. Behind the markets, you can stop for a picnic in the lovely **Jardim Público**. At the edge of the gardens stands the impressive 15th century **Palácio de Dom Manuel**, which boasts a series of Mudéjar archways and beautiful windows.

From the gardens, walk up the Rua da República that passes the back of the Igreja de São Fransisco, and turn right onto the **Largo da Graça**. The plaza is home to the 16th century Renaissance **Igreja da Nossa Senhora da Graça**. The structure's unusual columned granite facade is topped by spear carrying statues that seem ready to leap up and chase you away.

From the front of the church, walk up the narrow steps of the small **Travessa da Caraca** and turn right onto the **Largo de Alvaro Velho** plaza, which has a great blacksmith shop and is surrounded by stores with cheap shoes and clothing. From the left side of the end of the plaza, go up the Rua da Misericórdia to view the 16th century **Igreja da Misericórdia** featuring 18th century azulejos. On the same street you will also find the 15th century Manueline **Casa Sor** mansion, adorned with arches and a large spire. At the end of the street, a right turn onto the peaceful **Largo das Portas de Moura** square and a spherical Renaissance fountain will lead you to several beautiful old whitewashed and yellow bordered houses, including the wonderful 16th century cone top and arched facade of the elegant **Casa Cordovil** house.

Return back up the plaza and make a wide right turn onto Rua Conde de Serra da Tourega, near the front of the two large stone towers from the medieval town walls. This street will take you to the **Largo do Colegio** university area, where you can view the 15th century **Paço des Condes de Basto** and the 16th century **Igreja de Espírito Santo**. At this point you have seen most of Évora's sights and beautiful streets. You can proceed to your car, just steps away, or enjoy a fine dinner at one of several great restaurants.

If you are departing town, make sure to turn left on the Estrada da Circunvalacão to see the 16th century arched **Aqueduto da Agua da Prata** aqueduct just moments away. If you're in town on the second Thursday of the month, a huge regional **mercado** (market) takes over several acres of land just outside the walls in the **Rossio São Brás** square.

In the general area of Évora, you can visit several prehistoric monuments. The Turismo sells a useful pamphlet on this subject called *Roteiro do Megalitismo* at their office in the Praça do Giraldo square. The most famous of these sights is called the **Menhir Os Almendres**, located near the town of **Guadalupe** 9 km west of Évora off route N-114 west. Other impressive sights include the **Zambujeiro** dolmen, located near the village of **Valverde** 11 km southwest of Évora off route N-380 south, and the **Anta do Silval** stones located near the town of **Valeira** 11 km northwest of Évora on route N-114-4 north.

For details of these and other prehistoric sights, contact the Turismo offices in Évora and Montemor-O-Novo.

NIGHTLIFE & ENTERTAINMENT

Since Évora is home to several thousand university students, there are many fine bars, pubs, and dance clubs throughout the city. The best place to get up-to-date information on the club scene is to ask any of the younger staff at the Pousada dos Lóios. You can get a drink at the bar of the pousada, and, after leaving a good tip, ask the bartender to suggest a few spots. Bring your map and ask about **Amas do Cardeal**, **Xeque Mate**, and **Club 16**, and see what else they suggest.

SPORTS & RECREATION

Bicycling
· **Évora Bicycle Rentals**, *Évora, Tel. (066) 761-453*

Horseback Riding
· **Monte das Flores**, *Évora, Tel. (066) 254-90*

EXCURSIONS & DAY TRIPS

A nice day trip from Évora is to the wonderful little town of **Arraiolos**. Take Route N-114-4 west for 11 km and connect to Route N-370 north for another 11 km or so. Above town, you can visit the fortified walls of a 13th century **castelo** (castle) built by King Dom Dinis. This castle circles around the 16th century whitewashed and azulejos-covered convent, **Convento dos Lóios**.

The small town below the convent and castle ruins has been the center of production for beautiful hand-embroidered carpets. Many traditionally dressed local women can be seen on the porches of their homes weaving these colorful carpets. During the Age of Discoveries, the Portuguese began returning from India and Arabia with elaborate rugs. At some point in the 17th century, the local residents of this town began imitating several patterns and weaving techniques that eventually evolved into today's unique styles. Several local companies now offer these carpets at somewhat reasonable prices (about 25,000$00 per square meter). An exhibit of these carpets can be viewed at the town hall on **Praça Lima de Brito**, the main square of town. Make sure to see the 16th century **Antigo Paços do Concelho** (town hall and prison), the spiraled 16th century pillory with hangman's hooks, the old ruined **castelo**, and the lovely stone fountain known as the **Fonte de Pedra**.

For those interested in outdoor activities, there is hunting, fishing and horseback riding. Call **Herdade dos Coelheiros**, *Arraiolos, Tel. (066) 471-31*, if you are interested in hunting. For those interested in horseback riding or fishing, call **Herdade das Lages**, *Arraiolos, Tel. (066) 462-21*.

MONSARAZ

Situated on a hilltop about a half hour drive southeast of Évora, the wonderful mountain top walled city of Monsaraz is one of the best sights in the entire region. The tiny town has not changed much for several centuries, and the people live in houses built by their ancestors. Even the door locks, hinges, and knockers are hundreds of years old.

Other than electricity and TV, the only other modern convenience Monsaraz has accepted is a traveling salesman who each fortnight drives his minivan to the center of town and sells a selection of household goods to the villagers. The town itself is strictly off limits to cars, and several locals use oxen and donkeys as their preferred mode of transportation.

ARRIVALS & DEPARTURES
By Car

To get here from Évora, take Route N-18 east for about 16 km until it connects to Route N-256 east. Travel on Route N-256 for another 21 km to the city of Reguengos de Monsaraz. Follow the signs to Monsaraz, known locally as the Estrada de Monsaraz, through several small hamlets before the twisting access road runs past numerous cork and olive trees, then upward towards the towering medieval walls that completely surround Monsaraz.

WHERE TO STAY
Moderate

QUINTA HORTA DA MOURA, *Reguengos de Monsaraz. Tel. (066) 550-100, Fax (066) 550-108. Low season rack rates from 15,000$00, double room, BP; high season rack rates from 16,500$00, double room, BP. Most major credit cards accepted.*

This is a charming refined country inn and farming estate just below the mountain and castle of Monsaraz. This great hotel offers a truly stress free environment and a great place to use as a base as you explore the entire region.

The inn's traditional white and blue structures are surrounded by herds of sheep, fruit trees, prehistoric megaliths, Roman wells, vineyards, tennis courts, an equestrian center and riding academy, winery, patios, and a delightful swimming pool with a sun terrace. Inside this architectural masterpiece you'll find relaxing lounges, a fine game room with a great billiard table, a bar, and wine cellars.

The accommodations consist of 26 air conditioned rooms, junior suites, and a separate little self-contained house, all with air conditioning, heating, satellite television, huge private bathrooms, and mini-bar. Most of the units also have working fireplaces, patios, living rooms, local artwork, and handicrafts.

Selected as one of my *Best Places to Stay* (see Chapter 10 for more details).

ESTALAGEM DE MONSARAZ, *Monsaraz. Tel. (066) 551-12, Fax (066) 551-01. Year round rack rates from 12,850$00, double room, CP. Most major credit cards accepted.*

This quaint old inn is just outside the walls of town, and is owned by a young couple. There are eight well decorated and comfortable rooms and suites with private bathrooms, plus one apartment. Facilities include rustic lounge, a great regional restaurant, swimming pool, available excursions, Roan relics, antiques, and parking. Highly Recommended.

Inexpensive

CASA DE DOM NUNO, *Rua Direita. Tel. (066) 551-46. Year round rack rates from 8,750$00, double room, EP. Cash only - No credit cards accepted.*

This typical rustic village house with exposed beams and regional furniture has six rooms with semi-private bathrooms in the heart of town. No facilities except a bar.

WHERE TO EAT

Moderate

QUINTA HORTA DA MOURA, *Monsaraz. Tel. (066) 552-41. Dress code is smart casual. Most major credit cards accepted.*

This fine inn's beautiful dining room serves the freshest possible local game and produce including their own homemade cheese, olives, and jams. Ludi, the English speaking owner, will enchant you with her professional staff's delightful meals. A great dinner here will cost around 2,175$00 a person plus wine.

ESTALAGEM DE MONSARAZ, *Largo de Sao Bartolomeu. Tel. (066) 551-12. Dress code is smart casual. Most major credit cards accepted.*

The favored spot for visiting Spanish vacationers, the inn's dining room offers a daily selection of well prepared regional dishes served in an ambiance loaded with charm. The salads are great here, but the daily specials are the way to go. Expect the bill to average around 1,500$00 a head for a delicious lunch or dinner.

CASA DO FORNO, *Travessa da Sanabrosa. Tel. (066) 551-90. Dress code is smart casual. Cash only - No credit cards accepted.*

This friendly regional restaurant has a wonderful window-lined dining room that shows off the splendid countryside. The selection of regional specialties includes fine roasted lamb, pork, and occasionally rabbit. My last meal here cost me 1,650$00.

SEEING THE SIGHTS

The best way to tour Monsaraz is by foot. Leave your car at the parking lot in front of the **Estalagem de Monsaraz** inn at the right border of the village. From here you can walk through the town's walls and up **Rua Direita**, the village's main street. There are about four streets that run the length of town (only six blocks long) and they all offer great photo opportunities and historical sights. Every whitewashed and iron grilled house offers a different glimpse into why the local residents prefer to keep medieval ways of life in their small corner of the world.

As you walk through the stone lanes of town, you will pass by dozens of 16th century homes with delicate iron grill patios. At the **Largo Dom Nuno Alveres Pereira** (the only square in town), you will find the beautiful 18th century sphere topped pillory. Surrounding the square, you can visit several buildings including the 16th century former prison and town hall known as the **Paços do Concelho** (closed Tuesdays), which houses a wonderful ancient fresco depicting the judgment of good and evil. There are also several other churches and chapels that can be entered.

At the end of the plaza you can walk to the ruins of a 13th century **Castelo** (castle), which includes the massive **Torre de Menagem** keep and a small bullring that may date back to Roman times. The views from the castle's walls out over the plains are amazing, with vistas of clay, vineyards, cork trees, sheep and olive trees.

If you want a truly unforgettable experience, call the **Quinta Horta da Moura** a few days in advance and arrange a horseback or carriage ride up the mountain to the castle. Just tie up your horse to the castle walls and have a nice walk through town. A few minutes from the base of town you can see several Roman wells, megaliths, and monoliths including the **Menhir do Outeiro**, the **Menhir da Bulhoa**, the **Cromlech do Xerez**, and the **Antas do Olival da Pega**. Although these prehistoric sights are just minutes away, you may wish to ask the Turismo office at the pillory square in Monsaraz for specific instructions on how to reach their dirt access roads, which are not always marked.

On the way out of town on the Estrada de Monsaraz towards **Reguengos de Monsaraz**, you will pass three important stops. First there are the local pottery artisans, whose colorful hand painted bowls and pitchers are found inside the rustic studio/showrooms in the village of **São Pedro do Corval** 9 km west of Monsaraz.

A few km further west is the wonderful artist cooperative known as **T.E.A.R.**, which sells and exhibits fine iron work, traditional ceramics, wood work, tapestries, miniatures and other handicrafts. The artists can be found throughout the building in the process of creating their unique crafts. Do not miss this place! Also along this same road you will find the **Cooperativa de Reguengos** wine company, which makes a good local wine known as *Terras del Rei*.

SPORTS & RECREATION
Horseback Riding & Jeep Safaris
• **Horta da Moura**, *Monsaraz, Tel. (066) 552-06*

EXCURSIONS & DAY TRIPS
The castle town of **Portel** can be reached by taking Route N-256 west for 21 km from Reguengos de Monsaraz and connecting to IP-2 south for about another 22 km. This agricultural town produces excellent fresh goat and sheep milk cheeses that are sold throughout the region.

Of particular interest to visitors are the huge walls and **Torre de Menagem** keep at the medieval **castelo** (castle), the 16th century church, **Igreja de Espírito Santo**, the old public **Chafriz** fountains, and several azulejos churches such as the 18th century **Igreja da Misericórdia**, a short walk away from the town's central square, **Praça D. Nuno Alvares Pereira**. Near the entrance to town you can also visit an ancient convent, **Convento de Capuchos**.

Horseback riding is available in several neighboring farm houses, referred to as **Herdades**. The Turismo office at the **Cãmara Municipal** on the central square can provide you with a free list of places.

The sleepy fortified town of **Viana do Alentejo** lies on the plains about 28 km from Portel on Route N-384 west. This remarkable town is dominated by the defensive walls and towers of a 14th century **castelo** (castle). There is a great path atop the walls.

In the 15th century, several structures including a pillory, the buttress and the turret facade of the gothic church, **Igreja Matriz,** were added within the fortifications. The church was designed by Diogo de Arruda and among its many splendid elements are a large Manueline portal, azulejos-covered walls, carved columns, and an elaborate crucifix.

ALVITO

Alvito is a remarkably peaceful old fortified town. Until recently, it had been a stop-over point for supplies before continuing to the beautiful Odivelas and Alvito Barragems (dams that create lakes) just minutes out of town.

ARRIVALS & DEPARTURES
By Car

Alvito lies about 10 km from Viana do Alentejo on Route N-257 south.

WHERE TO STAY
Expensive

POUSADA DO CASTELO ALVITO, *Castelo de Alvito. Tel. (084) 483-83.*

This wonderfully deluxe pousada offers 20 great rooms with private bathrooms and a hard working staff. Facilities include a bar, regional restaurant, pool, air conditioning, hunting excursions, garden, chapel, TV, and parking.

Moderate

QUINTA DOS PRAZERES, *Largo das Alcacarias. Tel. (084) 481-70.*

This cute and comfortable rustic country inn sometimes serves as a lodge for the sportsmen who frequent the area. The inn offers six nice rooms with semi-private bathrooms. Facilities include fishing and hunting excursions, boats, bar, dining room, barbecue, pool, bicycles, gardens, and lots of parking.

SEEING THE SIGHTS

Recently, the town's wonderful turreted 15th century Gothic, Manueline, and Mudéjar styled **castelo** (castle), along with its fine gardens and square **Torre de Menagem** keep, has been remarkably transformed into a deluxe pousada (see above). The inn will undoubtedly bring more foreigners within the town's lanes, lined with ancient rustic homes with fine Manueline windows and doorways, adorned by incredible door knockers.

The town also has a 13th century church, **Igreja Matriz**, a well-used pillory, and some small gardens. This is a great place that has yet to see many tourists – get here soon!

MOURA

The regal former spa town of Moura is situated amidst the ruins of a 13th century castelo (castle). According to local legend, a 12th century Moorish princess named Saluquia jumped off the castle after mistakenly opening the doors of town to advancing Christian troops disguised as her future husband and his friends.

ARRIVALS & DEPARTURES

By Car

Moura is 57 km southeast of Alvito on Route N-258 east.

WHERE TO STAY

Moderate

HOTEL DE MOURA, *Praça Gago Coutinho, 1. Tel. (085) 224-95.*

This old world hotel is in the process of restoring its 37 grand rooms. The hotel has gardens, terraces, azulejos, and turn of the century furnishings. Facilities include bar, snack bar, restaurant, TV, disco, and parking.

SEEING THE SIGHTS

Below the ruins of Moura's 13th century castelo, you can visit a 13th century **Convento do Carmo** and its amazing frescoed chancel ceiling. Then walk around and down past the famed hot springs next to the **Jardim Santiago** (gardens) into the heart of the old town.

The old town is made up of several sections including the beautiful **Mouraria** (Moorish quarter) that contains many original Moorish houses with Arab chimneys and unusual azulejos. In the town's central **Largo de Santa Clara** plaza is the wonderful Gothic and Manueline church, **Igreja de São João**, with its amazing portal and 17th century azulejos.

SERPA

Serpa is an old Moorish walled city with a castle, archaeological museum, and a 13th century church.

ARRIVALS & DEPARTURES

By Bus

• **Serpa Main Bus Stop**, *Rua Soldado, no phone.*

By Car

Serpa is 28 km southwest of Moura on Route N-255 south.

WHERE TO STAY

Moderate

POUSADA DE SÃO GENS, *Alto de São Gens. Tel. (084) 537-24.*
This cute little hilltop pousada, a few minutes south of town, offers 16 nice air conditioned rooms with private bathrooms, bar, restaurant, pool, and parking.

Inexpensive

CASA DE SÃO BRÁS, *São Brás. Tel. (084) 902-72.*
This relaxing, rustic farm house, a few minutes south of town near the village of São Brás, has a few nice guest rooms with private bathrooms. Facilities include bar, TV room, Video room, pool, tennis, trails, gardens, horse riding, and parking.

SEEING THE SIGHTS

The most dramatic attraction in town may very well be the **Castelo de Serpa** castle, whose keep (closed Mondays) is home to the **Museu de Arqueologia**, a museum of local prehistoric and Roman artifacts.

Near the castle you can visit the 13th century Gothic church, **Igreja da Santa Maria**, and a beautiful clock tower. The only other sights of interest are the old town's lovely winding lanes like the Rua da Parreira, the small but imaginative **Jardim Botánico** gardens, the impressive 11th century aqueduct, and the ethnological museum **Museu de Etnologia** (closed Mondays) on the **Largo do Corro** plaza. The museum displays a series of exhibitions dedicated to the methods of production of Serpa's local handicrafts.

A wonderful waterfall called **Pulo do Lobo** is located 17 km south of town on the road that goes past São Brás. Ask directions from someone in town, though, as it is easy to get lost along the dirt stretch of this road.

SPORTS & RECREATION

Horseback Riding

• **Casa de São Brás**, *Serpa, Tel. (084) 902-72*

BEJA

The historic city of Beja was originally the Roman city of Pax Julia, and continued to flourish under Visigoth and Moorish civilizations. Today, Beja is an important agricultural trade center for the area's vast supply of wheat and olive oil and offers several interesting attractions. It's a good stop over point from Évora to the Algarve.

ARRIVALS & DEPARTURES

By Bus
• **Beja Main Bus Depot**, *Rua Cidade de São Paulo, Tel. (084) 240-44*

By Car
Beja can be reached by taking Route N-260 west for 29 km from Serpa.
• **Europcar Rent a Car in Beja**, *Rua Angola, Centro Carmo, Tel. (084) 328-128*

By Train
• **Beja CP Rail Station**, *2 km northeast of town, Tel. (084) 325-056*

WHERE TO STAY

Expensive
POUSADA DE SÃO FRANCISCO, *Beja. Tel. (084) 328-441, Fax (084) 329-143. US & Canada bookings with Marketing Ahead, Tel. 800/223-1356. Low season rack rates from 23,000$00, double room, BP; high season rack rates from 28,000$00, double room, BP. All major credit cards accepted.*

Located just one block from the center of the city, this dramatic new pousada has been built inside a massive 13th through 17th century monastery complete with cloisters, chapels, and a richly decorated chapter house. This ultra-deluxe government owned hotel has 34 large air conditioned rooms and one suite, all with private marble bathrooms, remote control satellite television, mini-bar, large desks, direct dial telephones, and beautiful modern furnishings.

The pousada also has a Manueline main entrance hall, several opulent private business meeting rooms, a superb regional restaurant, a quiet bar, an outdoor swimming pool surrounded by a beautiful courtyard garden, an outdoor tennis court, several former chapels converted into sitting rooms, richly decorated art exhibition areas, terraces, and some of the most impressive lounges imaginable. Highly Recommended.

Inexpensive
RESIDENCIAL CRISTINA, *Rua de Mértola, 71. Tel. (084) 323-036. Year round rack rates from 13,500$00, double room, CP. Cash only - No credit cards accepted.*

This clean and comfortable modern hotel has 31 large guest rooms with private bathrooms. Facilities include bar, direct dial phones, TV, and nearby parking.

WHERE TO EAT

Expensive

POUSADA DE SÃO FRANCISCO, *Beja. Tel. (084) 328-441. Dress code is smart casual. All major credit cards accepted.*

Located off the central cloister of Pousada De São Francisco, this is one of the city's best gourmet restaurants. Designed to take full advantage of the bold Manueline stonework that laces the ceiling, the pousada's restaurant is well worth the money. There are several dozen white linen tables that seat a total of 150 fortunate patrons in a luxurious ambiance, and the service is quite good.

The menu includes many delicious specialties such as cream of carrot soup, fish pate, chicken salad with pineapple, seafood stew, vegetable kebobs, poached salmon, duck in orange sauce, pork tenderloin in chili sauce, vegetarian tart, rack of lamb, lamb stew, cod fish sautéed in olive oil with white wine, and some serious desserts and wines. Open daily for lunch and dinner, you should expect to spend around 3,650$00 per person for a three course meal.

Moderate

RESTAURANTE ALENTEJANO, *Largo dos Duques de Beja, 6. Tel. (084) 238-49. No dress code. Most major credit cards accepted.*

Perfectly situated in the historic center of Beja, this is the oldest and most famous restaurant in the city. The simple azulejos-lined dining room is rather traditional, and provides the perfect setting for a relaxing regional meal. Dishes may include homemade soup, fried hake with potatoes, cod fish in special sauce, filet of sole, grilled chicken, pork cutlets, lamb steaks, beefsteak with mushrooms, assorted omelets, grilled shrimp, and many daily specials. A full meal will set you back around 1,800$00 per person.

Inexpensive

TEM AVOND, *Rua Alexandre Hurculano, 25a. Tel. (084) 328-956. No dress code. Cash only - No credit cards accepted.*

This simple family run restaurant, in the heart of the old town, offers some of the best affordable dinners in Portugal. The cramped 30 seat dining room is always packed (except Saturday when it is closed) with hungry students who know the food is simply outstanding. On my last visit here the menu offered grilled filet of sole with broccoli and carrots, shrimp omelets, pork chops, veal cutlets in wine sauce, entrecote, roasted chicken, and many other local staples. A great dinner here including wine will set you back less than 1,050$00 per person, but get here before 8:30pm to avoid the line. Highly Recommended.

SEEING THE SIGHTS

The old section of the city is dominated by a large **castelo** (castle) that was rebuilt by King Dom Dinis in the 13th century on the site of a Roman structure. This elaborately decorated castle is surrounded by a crenelated defensive wall incorporating several towers. Inside the castle's merlon-topped **Torre de Menagem** keep, you can climb up a winding stairway to reach its Gothic windows and lookout which present a great view over the area. Additional buildings within the compound have been converted into a military museum, with several weapons ranging from spears to shotguns. Near the castle you can also visit the 15th century Visigothic **Igreja de Santo Amaro**, which contains a museum of Visigoth artifacts (closed Mondays).

From the castle you can walk a block down and bear left to get to the **Praça da República** square. While strolling through the square you will notice the 16th century **Igreja da Misericórdia**, worth a quick visit, and take Rua dos Infantes down a couple of blocks until reaching the heart of the old town at the central **Largo dos Duques de Beja** square.

In the squre you'll find the former 15th century **Convento de Nossa Senhora de Conceição**. The convent was once home to the infamous 17th century nun named Mariana Alcoforado, who supposedly wrote the *Cartas Portuguesas* (Five Love Letters of a Portuguese Nun) to a French knight named Chamilly whom she fell in love with during his posting to Beja. Although the letters were widely published in France, they have never been authenticated and some doubts remain as to their true origins. The convent itself is quite beautiful as it contains marble and gilt chapels, cloisters covered with Moorish azulejos, an incredible chapter house, and many paintings enclosed under an elaborate pinnacle roof.

The convent now contains the **Rainha Leonor Museu Regional de Beja** (closed Mondays), which has vast collections of Roman artifacts, 17th century azulejos, and fine Spanish and Portuguese paintings from the 15th through the 18th centuries. Across the from the museum you will see the beautiful facade and bell tower of the Gothic 16th century **Igreja de Santa Maria**, whose azulejos-covered interior is an impressive sight.

About 9 km southwest of Beja off route N-18 west are the ruins of a 1st century Roman villa at **Pisões**. Recently, excavation has uncovered a mosaic floor of tiny green stones that form unusual patterns.

NIGHTLIFE & ENTERTAINMENT

This mid-sized city has an active nightlife thanks in part to the university students that start the weekend on Thursday nights. Among the best places to grab a cup of strong coffee is the **Esplanada de Capitel** outdoor café off the Rua Alexandre Hurculano. The crowd starts leaving this café around 11:00pm and many head for the simple but fun **Cafe Lumiar**, *Rua Dom Alfonso Henriques, 3*. Others walk over to the split level **Ritual** club, *Rua do Moleda, 9*.

Those into dancing will enjoy **Os Infantes**, *Rua dos Infantes, 14*, a three floor dance club. The crowd, aged 17 to 25, dances to flamenco music mixed with house music. After 2:00am, everyone heads for the **República de Alcohol** just outside the city center.

MÉRTOLA

The quiet riverfront town of Mértola rests above western bank of the Guadiana River.

ARRIVALS & DEPARTURES

By Car

Mértola is approximately 53 km southeast of Beja on Route N-122 south.

WHERE TO STAY

Inexpensive

CASA JANELAS VERDES, *Rua Dr. Manuel F. Gomes. Tel. (086) 621-45*.

This rustic house, in the old part of town near the river, offers three double rooms with private bathrooms. Facilities include lounge, patio, TV room, and parking.

PENSÃO BEIRA RIO, *Rua Dr. Afonso Costa, 18. Tel. (086) 623-40*.

This nice and basic inn is nothing fancy, and has guest rooms that share bathrooms.

SEEING THE SIGHTS

Most of this border town's visitors come to see the ruins of its Moorish 13th century **Castelo** (castle); the vaulting and ancient marble columns of the 11th century **Igreja Matriz**, which has retained some of the features from its Moorish Alhomad mosque origins; the **Museu Arqueológico** on Rua da República with its Moorish pottery and local artifacts; and the famous endangered black storks, who reside around the river.

I like Mértola for the river fishing and boat excursions, which are offered on the beautiful Guadiana River.

PRACTICAL INFORMATION FOR THE PLANÍCIES

Currency Exchange

Most of the banks in the main towns of the Planícies will exchange foreign currency and travelers checks without hesitation. Banking hours are from 8am until 3pm, Monday through Friday only. In most cities, restaurants and hotel front desks provide these services, but give you a rather poor exchange rate.

Electronic 24 hour exchange booths can be found in **Évora**, but they tend to be out of order.

Emergency & Useful Phone Numbers

- **Emergency Services** (S.O.S.), *Tel. 115*
- **Directory Assistance**, *Tel. 118*
- **Arraiolos Hospital**, *Largo do Matadouro Velho, Tel. (066) 422-70*
- **Estremoz Health Center**, *Rossio Marquis de Pombal, Tel. (068) 222-27*
- **Évora Hospital**, *Largo Senhor da Pobreza, Tel. (066) 250-01*
- **Golegã Hospital**, *Rua José Relvas, Tel. (049) 943-69*
- **Redondo Health Center**, *Rua do Castelo, 17, Tel. (066) 991-68*
- **Vila Viçosa Hospital**, *Rua Câmara Pereira, Tel. (068) 981-86*
- **Automobile Club of Portugal – Lisbon**, *Tel. (01) 942-5095*
- **Lisbon's Portela Airport**, *Tel. (01) 802-060*
- **TAP at Lisbon Airport**, *Tel. (01) 386-0480*

Museums & Castles

- **D. Lope de Almeida Museum**, *Igreja de Santa Maria do Castelo, Abrantes, Tel. (042) 223-26*. Contains collections of local Roman artifacts, Moorish tiles, sculptures, paintings, ceramics, and other ethnographic items such as historic books and documents. Open 10am until 12pm and 2pm until 5pm, Tuesday through Sunday. Closed on Mondays and holidays.
- **Casa dos Patudos Museum**, *Town Hall, Alpiarça, Tel. (043) 543-90*. Contains the collection of local politician José Relvas including 16th century Portuguese paintings, ceramics, Arraiolos carpets, azulejos, and furniture. Open 10am until 12:30pm and 2pm until 5pm, Wednesday through Sunday. Closed on Mondays and Thursdays.
- **Museum of Azambuja**, *Rua Victor Cordon, 69, Azamuja, Tel. (063) 422-58*. Contains a collection of African art from former Portuguese colonies. Open 10am until 12pm and 2pm until 5pm, Monday through Friday. Closed on Saturdays, Sundays, and holidays.

- **Beja Castle and the Military Museum of the Baixo Alentejo**, *Castelo de Beja, Beja, Tel. (084) 221-52.* The castle contains a tower and several other old buildings and exhibits include collections of various military weapons, uniforms, flags, and devices. Open 10am until 1pm and 2pm until 6pm daily, April through September. Open 9am until 12pm and 1pm until 4pm daily, October through May. Closed on holidays.
- **Municipal Museum (of Queen Leonor) of Beja, Convento de Nossa Senhora da Conceição**, *Largo da Conceição, Beja, Tel. (084) 233-51.* Contains a vast collection of Roman artifacts, 16th century Chinese porcelain, 15th-17th century paintings, marble statues, and azulejos. Open 10am until 1pm and 2pm until 5pm, Tuesday through Sunday. Closed on Mondays and Holidays.
- **Municipal Museum (of Queen Leonor) of Beja- Visigothic Section, Igreja de Santo Amaro**, *Castelo de Beja, Beja, Tel. (084) 233-51.* Contains a collection of 7th-9th century Visigothic artifacts. Open 10am until 1pm and 2pm until 5pm, Tuesday through Sunday. Closed on Mondays and Holidays.
- **Dr. António Lourenço Municipal Museum**, *Rua Luís de Camões, Benavente, Tel. (063) 524-66.* Contains a collection of 19th century photography, antique postcards, regional clothing, weapons, African art, ceramics, and local artifacts. Open 9am until 12:30pm and 2pm until 5pm, Tuesday through Friday. Open 2pm until 6pm, Saturday and Sunday. Closed on Mondays and holidays.
- **Rural Museum and Wine Museum of Cartaxo**, *Quinta das Pratas, Cartaxo, Tel. (043) 702-372.* This large historic farming estate contains exhibits on rural life and agricultural products such as wines, grains, olive oil, horses, and bulls. Open 10:30am until 12:30pm and 3:30pm until 5:30pm, Tuesday through Sunday. Closed on Mondays and holidays.
- **The Museums of Chamusca**, *Chamusca, Tel. (049) 760-176.* A series of five separate museums that consist of the following: a traditional rural house in the Parque Municipal; an ethnology section at Carregueira; an archeology section in the Parque Municipal; a music section at the Coreto da Vila, and a funerary section at the Cemetario Municipal. Open from 9am until 12:30pm and 2pm until 5:30pm daily.
- **Municipal Museum of Crato**, *Rua 5 de Outubro, Crato, Tel. (045) 971-61.* Contains collections of local artifacts, ceramics, furniture, sacred art, and crafts. Open 10am until 12pm and 3pm until 7pm, Tuesday through Sunday. Open 3pm until 6pm, Sunday. Closed on Mondays and holidays.

- **António Pires Ethnological Museum**, *Rua dos Apostolos, Elvas, Tel. (068) 624-02.* Contains collections of pre-historic through Moorish era artifacts, ceramics, painting, crafts, sacred art, and other regional items. Open 9am until 12:30pm and 2pm until 5:30pm, Tuesday through Sunday. Closed on Mondays and holidays.
- **Municipal Museum of Estremoz**, *Largo Dom Dinis, Estremoz, Tel. (068) 227-83.* Contains collections of local artifacts, crafts, ceramics, local clay dolls, and furniture. Open 10am until 12pm and 2pm until 6pm, Tuesday through Sunday. Closed on Mondays and holidays.
- **Casa do Povo Rural Museum**, *Rossio de Marquêsde Pombal, 89, Estremoz, Tel. (068) 225-38.* Contains collections of local and regional crafts. Open 10am until 1pm and 3pm until 5pm, Tuesday through Sunday. Closed on Mondays and holidays.
- **Évora Sacred Art Museum**, *Igreja das Merces, Rua Raimundo, Évora, Tel. (066) 226-04.* Contains collections of religious objects, 17th century jewelry, and paintings. Open 10am until 12:30pm and 2pm until 5pm, Tuesday through Sunday. Closed on Mondays and holidays.
- **Sé Cathedral Sacred Art Museum**, *Sé Cathedral, Largo de Sé, Évora, Tel. (066) 269-10.* Contains the cathedral's treasures including a 13th century folding ivory Virgin, a precious stone studded reliquary, a piece of the True Cross, furniture, and jewelry. Open 9am until 12pm and 2pm until 4:30pm, Tuesday through Sunday. Closed on Mondays.
- **Town Museum of Évora**, *Largo do Conde de Vila Flôr, Évora, Tel. (066) 226-04.* Contains a large selection of Roman through Manueline era sculptures, 16th and 17th century paintings, local artifacts, jewelry, ceramics, azulejos, and furniture. Open 10am until 12:30pm and 2pm until 5:30pm, Tuesday through Sunday. Closed on Mondays and holidays.
- **Évora Toy Museum**, *Jardim Público-Parque Infantil, Évora, Tel. (066) 217-89.* Contains a historical collection of antique and more recent toys. Open 10am until 12pm and 2pm until 5pm, Monday through Friday. Closed on Saturdays, Sundays, and holidays.
- **Mestre Martins Correira Museum**, *Largo da Imaculada Conceição, Golegã, Tel. (049) 94387.* Contains paintings and sculptures of the museum's namesake. Open 11am until 12:30pm and 3pm until 6pm, Tuesday through Sunday. Closed on Mondays.
- **Municipal Museum of Marvão**, *Igreja de Santa Maria, Largo do Municipio, Marvão, Tel. (045) 932-26.* Contains collections of local artifacts, documents, sacred art, and weapons. Open 9am until 12:30pm and 2pm until 5:30pm daily.
- **José Régio Museum**, *Rua José Régio, Portalegre, Tel. (045) 236-25.* Contains a collection of local sacred art and regional crafts. Open

9:30am until 12:30pm and 2pm until 6pm, Tuesday through Sunday. Closed on Mondays and holidays.

• **Museum of Portalegre**, *Rua José Maria da Rosa, Portalegre, Tel. (045) 216-16*. Contains collections of ceramics, sacred art, Arraiolos carpets, and furniture. Open 9:30am until 12:30pm and 2pm until 6pm, Wednesday through Monday. Closed on Tuesdays and holidays.

• **Santarém Archaeological Museum**, *Igreja de São João de Alporão, Largo Eng. Zeferino Sarmento, Santerém, Tel. (043) 226-45*. Contains a collection of local archaeological items from many eras. Open 9am until 12pm and 2pm until 5pm, Tuesday through Sunday. Closed on Mondays and holidays.

• **Castle Keep and Serpa Archaeological Museum**, *Castelo de Serpa, Serpa, Tel. (084) 903-51*. Contains archaeological findings from prehistoric through Roman eras. Open 9am until 12:30pm and 2pm until 5:30pm, Tuesday through Sunday. Closed on Mondays and holidays.

• **Serpa Ethnological Museum**, *Largo do Corro, Serpa, Tel. (084) 903-51*. Contains workshops dedicated to local crafts and ethnological items. Open 9am until 12:30pm and 2pm until 5:30pm, Tuesday through Sunday. Closed on Mondays and holidays.

• **Castle of Vila Viçosa**, *Castelo de Vila Viçosa, Vila Viçosa, Tel. (068) 981-28*. Contains a collection of furniture, painting, and artifacts from prehistoric through Roman eras. The facility also houses royal family archives. Open 9:30am until 1pm and 2pm until 5pm, Tuesday through Sunday. Closed on Mondays and holidays.

• **Museum of the Bragança Family Ducal Palace**, *Paço Ducal, Vila Viçosa, Tel. (068) 986-59*. Contains a huge assortment of Arraiolos carpets, paintings, ceramics, a 17th century diamond and ruby holy cross, azulejos, jewelry, weapons, rare books, musical archives, classical furniture, and the royal coach collection. Open 9:30am until 1pm and 2pm until 5pm, Tuesday through Sunday. Closed on Mondays and holidays.

Tourist Offices *(Turismos)*

• **Arraiolos Tourist Office**, *Praça Lima e Brito, Tel. (066) 42-105*
• **Borba Tourist Office**, *Praça de República, Tel. (068) 941-13*
• **Chamusca Tourist Office**, *Largo 25 de Abril, Tel. (049) 760-566*
• **Constância Tourist Office**, *Rua Eng. Vicente Castro, Tel. (049) 992-05*
• **Estremoz Tourist Office**, *Largo da República, Tel. (068) 225-38*
• **Évora Tourist Office**, *Praça do Giraldo, Tel. (066) 226-71*
• **Monsaraz Tourist Office**, *Largo D. Nunes Pereira, Tel. (066) 551-36*
• **Portel Tourist Office**, *Praça D. Nuno A. Pereira, Tel. (066) 623-35*
• **Redondo Tourist Office**, *Praça da República, Tel. (066) 996-60*

• **Santarém Tourist Office**, *Rua Pedro de Santarém, Tel. (043) 263-18*
• **Vila Viçosa Tourist Office**, *Praça da República, Tel. (068) 983-06*

Travel Agencies

• **Turalentejo**, *Rua Miguel Bombarda, Évora, 78, Tel. (066) 227-17*. A good travel agency in Évora that books excursions, hotels, cars and tickets.
• **Alegretur**, *Rua do Comércio, 43, Portalegre, Tel. (045) 242-40*. A Portalegre based travel agency that offers all types of reservation services.
• **Omnitur**, *Rua Serpa Pinto, 77, Santarém, Tel. (043) 264-89*. A full service travel agency in Santarém that can also exchange currency.

18♦ THE ALGARVE

The **Algarve** is the southernmost region in mainland Portugal and is drenched with sunshine for almost the entire year. It is surrounded by a series of mountain ranges to its north and an abundance of sand dunes and cliffs along the beaches to the west and south. The windswept southern coastline has become the most visited region in the entire country.

The Algarve's hundreds of hotels, ocean side apartments, deluxe villas, golf courses, tennis schools, water sport facilities, casinos, restaurants, and night clubs have been a huge tourism magnet for Portugal for the last 20 years or so. Vacationing English, German, Scandinavian, and Dutch tourists have swamped many of the area's beaches for the past 20 years resulting in a huge amount of ocean front development. Although most of the Algarve's beautiful coastline has been overdeveloped and is now crammed with one hotel after the other, several small fishing villages and inland towns remain secluded and full of their original historic and traditional character.

Most visitors seem determined to spend their days on the vast assortment of sandy beaches (most are topless) and their nights hopping between the many pubs and loud discos in the packed resort areas of **Albufeira**, **Praia da Rocha**, and **Vilamoura**. When you have had enough time on the beaches, I suggest that you visit a few less commercialized areas such as the fishing village of **Olhão**, the charming towns of **Silves** and **Tavira**, the photogenic cliffs near **Praia do Vau** and **Armação de Pêra**, the beach islands off of **Faro** and **Olhão**, the giant Saturday outdoor market in **Loulé** (open until midnight), the historic village of **Sagres**, and the absolutely magnificent unspoiled beaches and mountains along the **Costa Vicentina** near the charming village of **Carrapateira**.

The destinations covered in this chapter begin with the northwestern and western Algarve attractions, and continue east towards the Spanish border.

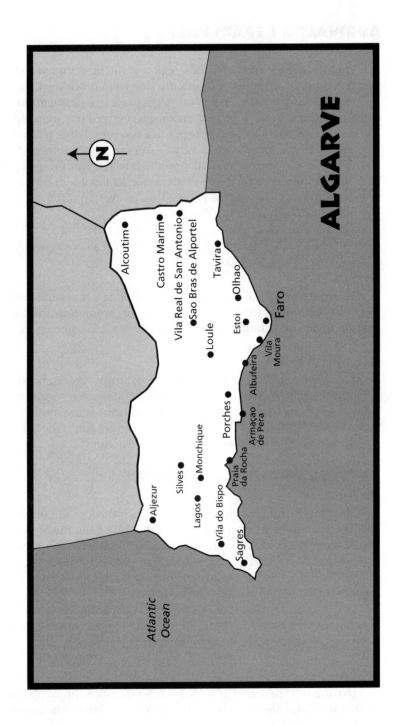

ARRIVALS & DEPARTURES

By Air

The only airport servicing this region is the modern Faro International Airport which is just a 10 minute ride from downtown Faro.

From the airport, the easiest way to get to various destinations in this region is to either rent a car, pre-arrange a reserved transfer from your travel agent, or take a somewhat expensive taxi ride. Those with minimal luggage seeking a more affordable way to reach the resorts and major towns within the Algarve can take public bus #16 from the airport to Faro's main bus depot on the Avenida da República and transfer to one of several frequent buses that proceed on to over 43 different Algarve destinations for around 550$00 a person.

The Turismo office in the airport's international arrivals area can give you current scheduling and price information on all area buses.

By Bus

Those arriving from Lisbon can take advantage of several daily non-stop air conditioned express buses that depart from downtown Lisbon and go directly to Albuferia and Faro for under 2,500$00 a person.

ORIENTATION

The Algarve is Portugal's southern most province and borders the Atlantic Ocean to its west and south. This medium sized region of sandy white beaches and massive hotel complexes begins at the foothills of the Serra do Caldeirão mountain range and continues south for as much as 47 kilometers (28 miles) before reaching the ocean.

GETTING AROUND THE REGION

By Bus

Most locals and tourists without their own cars use the much better and faster commuter bus system, rather than the train. Buses stop off at almost every beach area, resort, market town, and city in the Algarve. All you have to do is ask any Turismo office, or just keep your eyes open for one of hundreds of well marked bus stops and read the signs to find out the schedule and destinations covered.

In the unlikely event that you need to reach a tiny village or remote area not covered by normal buses, you may have to transfer at either Faro, Portimão, Sagres, or Albufeira to different, local bus company.

By Car

Driving in this region is a fairly easy task since the roads are well maintained. The Algarve is home to a new, super-fast toll motorway that runs parallel to the ocean, and east to west from the Spanish border all the way to Albufeira. Another major road is the rapid, non-toll N-1 highway.

Since this area includes the residences of many local workers and foreign expatriates, the rush hours, 7:00am until 9:30am and 4:30pm until 8:15pm, create horrific traffic conditions on almost every road. Also keep in mind that street parking is difficult to find in many resort areas and cities, but the local government has added lots of free or reasonably priced parking areas near the most popular beaches.

By Train

While there are trains that service the Algarve, most locals and tourists without their own cars tend to use the much better and faster commuter bus system. If you really need to use the train, CP rail line #314 offers slow and infrequent service between the largest cities along the Algarve's coast at reasonable prices.

ODECEIXE

Odeceixe is a charming little beach front community in the Algarve's western coastal area. The town consists of a few hundred whitewashed and red roofed houses surrounded by farms and pine forests.

The village itself rests on the river and retains a sleepy and inviting atmosphere in the months before and after summer. As the summer approaches, hundreds of younger Dutch and German tourists trample through town on their way to the beautiful sandy **Praia de Odeceixe** beach a mile or so out of town. During these months, you can see a huge assortment of VW vans with peace sign bumper stickers blasting reggae music near the beach. Several locals have told me they actually depart the town in July and August. In the off season, the town is quiet.

Accommodations in town and around the beach consist of a series of private houses that offer guest rooms without private bathrooms, and a campsite that gets full during the summer.

WHERE TO STAY

Inexpensive

HOSPEDARIA CLAUDIO, *Rua da Correio, Aljezur. Tel. (082) 941-17, Fax (082) 944-83. Year round rack rates from 6,500$00, double room. Cash only - No credit cards accepted.*

This is a nice white four story modern inn near the entrance to the town of Odeceixe. It has 18 clean and comfortable rooms with and without private bathrooms, balconies, and large nice windows. Facilities here include a restaurant, mountain bicycles, and nearby parking. It's a good budget choice.

ALJEZUR & THE BEACHES OF THE COSTA VICENTINA

The town lies below a ruined hilltop 10th century Moorish castle on a small plain off the Ribeira de Aljezur River within the Espinhaco de Ção foothills. Much of the Moorish section of town was destroyed by the infamous 1755 earthquake that rocked Portugal, but many buildings still maintain the traditional whitewashed and blue-bordered facade.

ARRIVALS & DEPARTURES

By Car

Aljezur is about 14 km from Odeceixe on Route N-120 south.

WHERE TO STAY

Moderate

CASA FAJARA, *Sítio do Rio, Carrapateira. Tel. (082) 971-19, Fax (082) 971-86. Low season rack rates from 6,500$00, double room, EP; high season rack rates from 10,000$00, double room, EP. Cash and travelers checks only - No credit cards accepted.*

Casa Fajara is the only small charming rural inn in the Parque Natural Costa Vincentina. This exceptional and surprisingly affordable bed and breakfast inn is located near the ocean about 13 miles southwest of Aljezur.

The inn has nine double rooms with private bathrooms, comfortable beds, direct dial telephone, individually controlled heating systems, large private terraces overlooking a 600 hectare lush valley, and exposed beam ceilings in some cases.

The inn features a huge self-catering professionally equipped kitchen for use by guests, its own nearby regional restaurant serving delicious steaks and freshly caught seafood, a well maintained outdoor swimming pool and sun deck, a fire-side television lounge, a game room and library with a massive snooker table, private stables with rides on Luso-Arabian horses to the awesome cliffs and coastline, a tennis court, countless hiking trials through unspoiled landscape, guided day trips to superb fishing spots for catching sea bream, jeep safaris, and a location that is perfect for some of the most amazing car and/or bicycle rides to a series of secluded white sand beaches.

During the day most guests either relax by the pool, take a four minute walk down to the amazingly beautiful Praia da Bordeira in the Parque Natural da Costa Vincentina, or drive a few minutes away to explore several traditional fishing villages lined with antique whitewashed houses.

Selected as one of my *Best Places to Stay* (see Chapter 10 for more details).

Inexpensive

HOSPEDARIA DE S. SEBASTIÃO, *Rua 25 de Abril, Aljezur. Tel. (082) 980-52. Year round rack rates from 5,500$00, double room. Cash only - No credit cards accepted.*

For those who wish to stay in the heart of Aljezur, this nice and comfortable inn and restaurant offers several medium sized rooms with air conditioning, private bathrooms, television, and nice windows looking out over the town.

WHERE TO EAT

Moderate

O SITO DO RIO, *Praia Bordeira, Carrapateira. Tel. (082) 971-19. No dress code. Most major credit cards accepted.*

This outstanding restaurant is located just a minute away from the awesome virgin beach at Praia de Bordeira and is a real gem! Set amidst an exposed beam chapel style ceiling and full of antique cooking instruments, this great restaurant is the best in the Costa Vincentina area.

The regional menu includes items made with vegetables grown in their own gardens and features a daily selection of dishes such as homemade pate, tomato soup, cucumber salad, Russian salad, prawns in garlic, pork kebabs in ginger sauce, marinated lamb chops, grilled chicken in hot sauce, roasted freshly caught fish with potatoes, white bream grilled with veggies, and many others. Expect to pay around 1,950$00 for a wonderful three course meal. Highly Recommended.

SEEING THE SIGHTS

The town's 17th century church, **Igreja Matriz** is about the only other specific attraction worth noting besides a pretty windmill known as the **Moinho do Rogil**, about 8 km north of town in the hamlet of **Rogil**. Aljezur's Turísmo office on the central **Largo do Mercado** plaza can provide lists of private homes offering rooms, campsites (full of Germans and Dutch during the summer), and local maps.

Most visitors to the Aljezur come here to go to a series of dramatic beaches, which are just a short drive away along the truly awesome **Parque Natural de Costa Vicentina** along a long strip of windswept Atlantic coastline. Further down the coast are small unmarked dirt roads (ask a local for directions) that head around the mountains and onwards to some of the world's most breathtaking and secluded sandy cove beaches. The government has created this park to protect the abundant wildlife and seashore of this magnificent zone from any further development. The beaches are often full of nude sunbathers and surfers.

Among the most impressive local beaches in the Aljezur area are the nearby wide and sandy **Praia da Amoreira** and the adjacent **Praia de Monte Clerigo**, about seven km northwest of town, and the huge windswept beaches below the cliffs at **Praia da Arrifana** 11 km southwest of town. Another beautiful day trip I strongly suggest would be to drive 30 km down Route N-268 south to the village of **Carrapateira**, where you can visit the ancient **Igreja e Fortaleza da Carrapateira** (church and fortress) and then continue to the fishing havens and sand dune beaches at **Praia da Bordeira**. From Praia da Bordeira, you can take a small coastal road south a few minutes to the cliffs and beaches at the wonderful nude beach at **Praia do Amado**.

VILA DO BISPO

Vila do Bispo is a cute little town with few attractions except for a few windmills and nice nearby beaches.

ARRIVALS & DEPARTURES
By Car
Vila do Bispo is about 30 km from Aljezur on Route N-268 south (bear right off Route N-120 south at Alfambras).

WHERE TO STAY
Inexpensive
PENSÃO MIRA SAGRES, *Rua do Hospital, 3. Tel. (082) 661-60. Year round rack rates from 7,500$00, double room, CP. Cash only - No credit cards accepted.*

This basic 2 star inn offers four rooms with shared bathroom. There aren't many facilities.

SEEING THE SIGHTS
The famed 18th century church, **Igreja Matriz**, is heavily decorated with fine azulejos, and contains a small **Museu de Atre Sacra** (sacred art museum) and the garden-lined ruins of an old fortress. Also about 5 km south of town are the **Grutas de Monte Frances** (grottoes), full of unusual stalagmites and stalactites. About 4 km east of town is the 13th century Romanesque **Capilla de Nossa senhore da Guadalupe** chapel.

Vila do Bispo is probably best known as an access point for a few nice beaches where you can go swimming, surfing, and fishing. Of these local sandy beaches, the finest are about 5 km northwest of town at **Praia do**

Castelejo and **Praia de Barriga**, which can be reached by small roads from town that are not well maintained. Accommodations include a couple of basic small inns, houses that rent rooms, and a huge campground.

SAGRES & NEARBY COASTAL BEACHES

The fishing village of Sagres rests on cliffs above the ocean and has little of historical significance left since the 1755 earthquake destroyed most of its original structures.

It was in this town that Prince Henry the Navigator founded his famous School of Navigation in the 15th century. The school became a major center for the study of navigation, cartography, and astronomy enabling its members to begin a series of expeditions to Africa and beyond. This period would become known as the Age of Discoveries. Among the more famous students, according to legend, were Christopher Columbus, Vasco de Gama, Pedro Alvares Cabral, and Fernão de Megellan.

The school was also responsible for the design and construction of a new type of sailing vessel known as a caravel. These ships were able tack very tightly (almost able to sail towards the direction of the wind). Most of the school was unfortunately destroyed by Sir Francis Drake in the 16th century.

ARRIVALS & DEPARTURES
By Car
Follow Route N-258 south from Vila do Bispo for about 8 km and the road will pass Sagres.

WHERE TO STAY
Expensive
FORTALEZA DO BELICHE, *Sagres. Tel. (082) 641-24, Fax (082) 642-25. US & Canada bookings with Marketing Ahead, Tel. 800/223-1356. Low season rack rates from 10,500$00, double room, CP; high season rates from 14,500$00, double room, CP. All major credit cards accepted.*

Overlooking the ocean, this awesome old fortress, about 5 km away from central Sagres, has been beautifully converted by the government into an annex for the larger Pousada do Infante. There are only four beautiful rooms with ocean views and private hand painted tile bathrooms, vaulted ceilings, unusual hardwood furnishings, individual heating systems, and lots of charm. Facilities include bar, restaurant, air conditioning, a chapel, a wonderful inner courtyard terrace, a TV room, and parking. Highly Recommended.

POUSADA DO INFANTE, *Sagres. Tel. (082) 642-22, Fax (082) 642-25. US & Canada bookings with Marketing Ahead, Tel. 800/223-1356. Low season rack rates from 23,000$00, double room, BP; high season rates from 28,000$00, double room, BP. All major credit cards accepted.*

This is a nice fortress-like pousada built in 1960 that offers 38 nice rooms and one suite with private bathrooms, direct dial telephones, remote control satellite television, mini-bar, and in most cases fine balconies with views out to sea. Facilities include bar, restaurant, air conditioning, pool, tennis, TV, and parking.

Moderate

APARTHOTEL NAVEGANTE, *Sítio da Baleeira, Sagres. Tel. (082) 643-54, Fax (082) 643-60. Low season rack rates from 6,000$00, one bedroom apartment, per night, EP; high season rack rates from 15,000$00, one bedroom apartment, per night, EP. Most major credit cards accepted.*

This is a nice modern apartment-hotel next to the pousada and above the ocean with 55 one bedroom ocean view apartments with air conditioning, private bathroom, kitchen, satellite television, direct dial telephone, and balconies. There is also a restaurant, squash courts, direct beach access, business meeting rooms, and two nice outdoor swimming pools.

RESIDENCIAL D. HENRIQUE, *Praça de República, Sagres. Tel. (082) 620-000, Fax (082) 620-001. Low season rack rates from 4,000$00, double room, EP; high season rack rates from 10,000$00, double room, EP. Cash only - No credit cards accepted.*

Located just above the ocean off Sagres' main square, this nice family run 18 room hotel offers a series of nice modern accommodations with either land or ocean views. Rooms have air conditioning and balconies in most cases (higher rates apply for these rooms), private bathrooms, television, comfortable furnishings, and large closets. There is also a restaurant, bar, and plenty of parking.

DON TENORIO APARTHOTEL, *Sagres. Tel. (082) 643-66, Fax (082) 643-65. Low season rack rates from 7,000$00, studio apartment, per night, EP; high season rack rates from 16,000$00, one bedroom apartment, per night, EP. Most major credit cards accepted.*

Located just a few minutes walk from the heart of Sagres, this modern 4 story apartment-hotel has 40 studio and one bedroom pool-view apartments with small kitchenettes, private bathrooms, simple furnishings, cable television, and direct dial telephones. Facilities include a restaurant, a bar, a business meeting room, a large outdoor freshwater swimming pool, and free parking.

WHERE TO EAT
Expensive
VILA VELHA, *Sagres. Tel. (082) 647-88. Dress code is semi-formal. All major credit cards accepted.*

When you are in the mood for a more elegant gourmet meal, try this converted villa with terrace that is among the most beautiful interior and exterior dining spaces in the eastern Algarve. The menu includes smoked serrano ham, broiled prawns in two sauces, fried mushrooms in garlic, French onion soup, shrimp soup, sirloin steak with bacon, mixed grill, herbed lamb cutlets, rice with duck, filet of sole, prawn curry, fish stew with noodles, vegetarian chile, noodles with creamy spinach sauce, roasted rabbit, filet mignon with wild mushrooms, and house style crepes. Dinner will set you back at least 2,350$00 a person plus wine. Reservations are suggested at least one day in advance; the restaurant is closed on Mondays. Highly Recommended.

Moderate
O TELHEIRO DO INFANTE, *Praia da Maréta, Sagres. Tel. (082) 641-79. Dress code is smart casual. All major credit cards accepted.*

Located just on the edge of Sagres' main Praia da Maréta beach, this duplex seafood restaurant, terrace snack bar, oyster bar, and more dressy dining room is a great place to enjoy fine steak and seafood meals. The menu features escargot, mixed salads, fish soup, mixed omelets, grilled sea bass, fried hake filet, veal steak, oysters, pork chops, char-broiled chicken, baked king crab, and beef steak with pepper sauce. A dinner should cost about 1,800$00 a person plus wine.

FORTALEZA DO BELICHE, *Sagres. Tel. (082) 641-24. Dress code is smart casual. Most major credit cards accepted.*

Situated within the walls of an old fortress about 5 km out of Sagres, this nice and intimate regional restaurant is a real treat. About 40 fortunate patrons dine in this ocean view restaurant beneath a vaulted ceiling dotted by medieval chandeliers and tile murals. You'll enjoy such treats as fish soup, vegetable soup, grilled sardines, assorted omelets, burgers, pork chops with pineapple, beef steak, roasted turkey with cream, poached fish plates, and more. Reservations are advised at least six hours in advance.

Inexpensive
ROSA DOS VENTOS, *Praça da República, Sagres. Tel. (082) 644-80. No dress code. Cash only - No credit cards accepted.*

This small whitewashed bar and restaurant, in the heart of town's main square, is my favorite place for a casual meal in Sagres. You'll sit in one of a dozen or so small, handmade wooden tables surrounded by photos and paintings of local scenery. The menu includes grilled tuna steak, filet of hake, calamari, pork chops, veal steak, fried chicken, and many other daily specials. Dinner will set you back only 1,350$00 or so a person. Highly Recommended.

RESTAURANTE A SAGRES, *Stio do Tunel, Sagres Tel. (082) 641-71. No dress code. Cash only - No credit cards accepted.*

This small roadside snack bar and restaurant, just outside of the center of Sagres, has a small indoor dining room and outdoor terrace and serves up tasty simple meals such as grilled sardines, tuna sandwiches, cheese burgers, vegetable soup, rice with octopus, spaghetti Bolognese, grilled swordfish and more. The price is around 1,375$00 per person for lunch and dinner.

SEEING THE SIGHTS

The main square in town is called the **Praça de República** and is home to a few bars, restaurants, newsstands, rental rooms, and souvenir shops. Also on the square is the **Turinfo** private tourist information center, where you can rent mountain bicycles and arrange special jeep safaris, boat rides, donkey rides, and all sorts of interesting excursions. The village is made up of a few streets full of small restaurants and bars that run between the town's small main square and a fishing harbor that brings in most of the Algarve's highly prized lobsters. Outside of town there are many new condo, villa, and resort developments that are beginning to chip away at Sagres' once charming atmosphere. Additional plans are underway to build one of Europe's largest aquariums just alongside the area where the pousada now rests.

From the back of the main square you can take a road leading just south of town onto a small peninsula. You can enter the ruins of the once important 15th century **Fortaleza de Sagres** fortress (which unfortunately has been partially rebuilt using ugly modern cement). Inside the fortress (free admission) are nice scenic wall and cliff-top walks, the remains of an original compass-point map made of pebbles known as the **Rosa dos Ventos**, and a small restored 14th century chapel called the **Capelo da Nossa Senhora da Graca**.

Besides the fortress, the only other attractions in Sagres itself are the fine beaches, such as **Praia da Maréta** just across from the village. Other nice beaches for wind surfing, fishing, and sunbathing include **Praia da Baleeira**, **Praia do Martinal**, and **Praia do Ingrina**, which are a bit east of the town's harbor. The undertow at any of these area beaches is quite strong, so I recommend extreme caution.

About 6 km northwest of Sagres is another peninsula called the **Cabo de São Vicente**. This rugged and photogenic area is Europe's most southwestern point and was once thought of as *O Fim do Mundo* (The End of the Earth). The Romans believed that this was the point where the sun sank into the sea. The cape was later named for Saint Vincent, whose body arrived here by ship in the 8th century. The saint became the focal point for a Christian shrine and a 16th century monastery that now lies in ruins.

Atop the cape's sparsely vegetated cliffs, you can visit the large **Farol** (lighthouse) on the site of Prince Henry's former residence. The long windy isolated beach of **Praia de Beliche** is located just west of the cape near a highly secret electronic intelligence gathering post with large antennas, and nearby is the **Fortaleza do Beliche** seaside fortress, now a pousada annex and good restaurant.

NIGHTLIFE & ENTERTAINMENT

Since the town attracts a younger blend of international tourists, the small village has several fun cafés, bars, and clubs to visit in the summer season. I recommend you try walking through the village and peek inside the ocean front **Last Chance Saloon** and the **Rosa dos Ventos** bar near the main square.

For those of you who want to party all night, try the **Clube Caravelo** disco located a few minutes north of town.

SALEMA

Salema has recently developed into a small resort community of villas and apartments on the slopes of cliffs and hills that meet the ocean at the beautiful beach, **Praia do Salema**.

Although several foreigners inhabit this area, the ocean front village seems to have kept its original ambiance. On any given day, several local fishermen still work hard to get a good day's catch.

ARRIVALS & DEPARTURES

By Car

Salema is about 8 km southeast of Vila do Bispo just south of Route N-125 east.

WHERE TO STAY

Moderate

ESTALAGEM INFANTE DO MAR, *Salema. Tel. (082) 654-43*.

This nice 4 star local inn, above the ocean on a cliff, has 30 comfortable double rooms with private bathrooms. Many of the room have balconies overlooking the ocean. Facilities include a bar, restaurant, pool, TV room, direct dial phones, and parking.

SALEMA PRAIA CLUB, *Salema. Tel. (082) 652-52.*

This modern English-managed resort community has villas, apartments, and townhouses for rent. Facilities include a bar, restaurant, pool, tennis, and parking.

SEEING THE SIGHTS

There are no specific attractions in the village, but it is a great place to relax. A nice 18 hole golf course called **Parque da Floresta Golf** is just minutes away from town.

BURGAU

While the town is fairly tranquil, it has already started to undergo a transformation into a resort community and is well on its way to losing much of its original charm.

The village lies below shrub covered hills and is made up of a few stone streets that ramble past a small main square. English tourists tend to select Burgau as one of their bases in the Algarve, and have built many villa and condo properties around the village area.

ARRIVALS & DEPARTURES
By Car

Burgau is about 8 km from Salema off Route N-125 east.

WHERE TO STAY
Moderate

CASA GRANDE, *Burgau. Tel. (082) 651-68.*

This is an amusing inn run by an English women that was converted from an old house. Some rooms have semi-private bathrooms. It's located on the way to Luz.

WHERE TO EAT
Moderate

RESTAURANTE ANCORA, *Burgau. Tel. (082) 691-02.*

This ocean view fish and regional cuisine restaurant, near town, offers huge portions of freshly caught local fish prepared to order.

SEEING THE SIGHTS

The beach area remains the main attraction of town. There are several small bars and water sports rental facilities, including the **Beach Bar**, where you can arrange waterskiing, wind surfing, boat rentals, and rent chairs.

SPORTS & RECREATION
Horseback Riding
· **West Algarve Horse Center**, *Praia do Burgau*, Tel. (082) 691-02

LUZ

I once liked this area, but am now disgusted by what massive development by English and Portuguese construction companies has done to the place. The beach is still fairly nice, but the town offers little of interest besides shops, pub-style bars, and some decent restaurants.

Other than the nearby scuba, golf, and windsurfing facilities, I don't see the attraction of staying here. Many of the villa and timeshare properties are not up to par with the rest of the resorts on the Algarve. If you get stuck staying here, you may wish to head east to the more peaceful beaches of Porto do Mós which tend to attract a more local crowd.

ARRIVALS & DEPARTURES
By Car
Luz is about 5 km from Burgau off Route N-125 east.

WHERE TO STAY
Moderate
THE OCEAN CLUB, *Praia da Luz*. Tel. (082) 789-763.

This is one of the better villa and apartment complexes in Luz. They rent nicely furnished inland, as well as oceanview villas and apartments, with hotel facilities and nearby pools.

RESIDENCIAL VILAMAR, *Estrada de Burgau, Luz*. Tel. (082) 789-541.

This nice 3 star, 15 room inn, not far from the beach, has good guest rooms with private bathrooms, bar, restaurant, tennis, gardens, TV room, and parking.

LUZ BAY CLUB, *Praia da Luz*. Tel. (082) 789-640.

This is a huge villa complex where most units are crammed next to each other. They rent decent apartments and fairly comfortable villas that are not far from the ocean.

WHERE TO EAT
Moderate
RESTAURANTE O ANTÓNIO, *Porto de Mós*. Tel. (082) 763-560.

This nice beach front grill room and restaurant has a great outdoor dining area a few kilometers east of Luz at the beach of Porto de Mós. They serve great linguado (sole).

SPORTS & RECREATION
Sailing
· **Luz Bay Sailing Club**, *Praia da Luz,* Tel. *(082) 789-640*

Scuba Diving
· **Sea Sports Scuba Center**, *Praia da Luz,* Tel. *(082) 789-538*

Tennis
· **Luz Bay Tennis Club**, *Praia da Luz,* Tel. *(082) 789-640*

Wind Surfing
· **Luz Bay Windsurfing**, *Praia da Luz,* Tel. *(082) 789-640*

LAGOS & NEARBY COASTAL BEACHES
Unlike many oceanfront areas, Lagos does not depend solely on tourists for its economy, and there are many sights worth visiting while you are here.

The city was first founded by the Carthaginians sometime before the 3rd century B.C. and was home to later Roman and Moorish trading settlements. After the Christians took control of the area in the 13th century, Lagos became a prominent commercial city and its wide harbor became a Maritime base for exploration during the 15th century's Age of Discoveries.

In 1576, the city became the capital of the Algarve and remained prosperous until 1755 when the massive earthquake destroyed most of the city and its historical structures. Fortunately, several ancient remnants of this delightful city can still be found in both the old quarter of town and in assorted other locations.

ARRIVALS & DEPARTURES
By Bus
· **Lagos Main Bus Depot**, *Rua Vasco da Gama,* Tel. *(082) 763-014*

By Car
Lagos is on the ocean about 10 km from Luz on Route N-125 east.
· **Avis Rent a Car in Lagos**, *Largo Portas de Portugal,* Tel. *(081) 763-691*

By Train
· **Lagos CP Rail Station**, *just across the bridge,* Tel. *(082) 762-987*

WHERE TO STAY
Expensive
HOTEL DE LAGOS, *Rua Nova da Aldeia. Tel. (082) 769-970.*

This large, 4 star modern hotel with beautiful gardens is located above the center of town. It has 318 nice air conditioned rooms. Facilities include bar, restaurant, snack bar, shops, pools, nearby golf, tennis, TV, shuttle buses to a beach club, and parking.

HOTEL GOLFINHO, *Praia de Dona Ana. Tel. (082) 769-900.*

This is a good ocean view, 4 star hotel with 262 comfortable rooms (many are water view) located just outside of town. Facilities include bar, restaurant, snack bar, pool, bowling, nearby golf, air conditioning, shops, billiards, TV, disco, baby-sitting, beach, and parking.

Moderate
QUINTA DA ALFARROBEIRA, *Meia Praia. Tel. (082) 798-424.*

This lovely stone and whitewashed country inn and estate is located close to the ocean. It has two large guest rooms and a nice apartment, all with private bathrooms. Facilities include bar, terraces, gardens, pool, nearby golf and horses, and parking.

MEIA PRAIA BEACH CLUB, *Meia Praia. Tel. (082) 769-980.*

This nice family apartment-hotel complex, just east of town near the ocean, offers 77 comfortable apartments with kitchen and TV. Facilities include bar, pool, billiards, game room, direct dial phones, nearby golf, and lots of parking.

CASA DO PINHÃO, *Praia do Pinhão. Tel. (082) 762-371.*

This charming cliffside house, slightly west of town just above the ocean, rents three nice rooms with private bathrooms. Facilities include bar, terrace, TV room, and parking.

HOTEL MARINA SÃO ROQUE, *Meia Praia. Tel. (082) 763-761.*

This 3 star hotel, not far from the beach area, is a good value. It has 27 double rooms at lower rates than most area hotels. Facilities include bar, restaurant, pool, squash, billiards, TV, air conditioning, direct dial phones, nearby golf, and parking.

ALBERGARIA MARINA RIO, *Ave. dos Descobrimentos. Tel. (082) 769-859.*

This clean and comfortable ocean front inn, near the heart of Lagos, has 36 air conditioned double rooms with private bathrooms, bar, TV room, radio, and parking.

Inexpensive
PENSÃO RUBI MAR, *Rua da Barroca, 70. Tel. (082) 763-165.*

This small centrally located inn has nine nice rooms (some with views) with and without private bathroom. There are almost no facilities besides the complimentary breakfast.

PENSÃO DONA ANA, *Praia de Dona Ana. Tel. (082) 762-322.*

This clean and comfortable inn is located above a great beach. It has 11 rooms with and without private bathrooms and almost no facilities except a breakfast room.

WHERE TO EAT
Expensive

RESTAURANTE ALPRENDE, *Rua António B. Viana, 17. Tel. (082) 762-05.*

This luxurious seafood restaurant offers a huge menu of Portuguese cuisine mixed with continental flare. The intimate setting makes for great ambiance.

DOM SEBASTIÃO, *Rua 25 de Abril, 22. Tel. (082) 762-795.*

This wonderful relaxing establishment offers fine seafood and regional meat dishes served in either its dining rooms, or outside on the terrace. Try the grilled fish: it is the finest in the Algarve. Reservations are necessary.

Moderate

O GALEÃO, *Rua da Laranjeira, 1. Tel. (082) 763-909.*

This remarkably good restaurant offers continental and regional cuisine served from its amazingly active open kitchen. It's a lot of fun to people watch in this place.

Inexpensive

RESTAURANTE PIRI-PIRI, *Rua Afonso D'Almeida, 10. Tel. (082) 763-803.*

This narrow little restaurant serves an assortment of well prepared regional meals at quite reasonable prices. This is one of the best casual places to eat in town.

SEEING THE SIGHTS

The best way to explore the many sights in the city is to park your car somewhere off the picturesque seafront Ave. dos Descobrimentos, perhaps near the **Praça da República** square. Just off the east side of the plaza on Rua da Senhora da Graça you can visit the remaining arcades of the former **Casa de Afândega** custom house, which hosted a **Mercado de Escravos** (slave market) where ships returning from 15th century African expeditions sold their cargo of captured humans.

On the other side of the plaza you can view the solemn interior and Manueline windows of the 15th century church, **Igreja da Santa Maria**. From the front of the church, walk up the Rua Henriques Correira Silva (which then becomes Rua de São Gonçalo) until the next corner, where you will see the beautiful baroque 18th century **Igreja de Santo António**. The inside of this church is filled with fantastic wooden animals and cherubs covered in pure Brazilian gold, vaulted ceilings, and fine azulejos. Adjacent to the church you really should visit the **Museu Municipal de José Formosinho** (closed Mondays), which contains a vast assortment of local artifacts including Roman mosaics, 16th century ceramics, replicas of Algarve style chimneys, the 16th century charter of Lagos, and lots of other unusual paintings, embroideries, and sculptures.

From the museum, walk a bit further up Rua de São Gonçalo until you can make the next right (east) turn, which leads you across town on Rua Candido dos Reis past several interesting shops. At the end of this street you will find the **Praça Luís de Camões** plaza, and a right turn from this plaza onto Rua Garrett will lead you directly onto the main **Praça Gil Eanes** square with its somewhat tasteless statue of King Dom Sebastião. From the front of the Câmara Municipal (town hall), turn left (east) onto Rua das Portas de Portugal which leads you back to the seafront.

If you happen to be in town on Saturday morning, you may wish to pop into the **Mercado** (market), just to your left (east) on this part of Ave. dos Descobrimentos. In any case, you can head back west along the seafront for several blocks to reach the harbor and its 17th century **Forte Ponta da Bandeira** fortress (closed Mondays) and the old town walls across the street.

Of course, many people visiting Lagos are not at all interested in historical sights and fine architecture. Most tourists come here to visit the beautiful local beaches and coves which are just outside of town, while others arrive in town to use the famed Frank Pennink designed 18 hole **Palmares Golf** course on **Meia Praia** beach.

Just south of Lagos, follow the coastal road towards Sagres (starting from the fortress) to the carved stone stair paths to reach some impressive beaches, beginning with the rather small **Praia do Pinhão** just west of town. The most dramatic sandy beaches are the beautiful rock coves at **Praia de Dona Ana** and **Praia do Camilo** which offer extremely nice swimming areas.

At the nearby seaside resort of **Ponta da Piedade**, you can walk down near the lighthouse to view some beautiful ocean caves and boulders that have been formed by the ocean's waves. If you prefer a larger and less dramatic sandy beach, you can go in the opposite direction to find **Meia Praia** just to the southeast of town.

NIGHTLIFE & ENTERTAINMENT

A resort city this large tends to have lots of nightlife, and Lagos is no exception. To start off your night you can head for a good bar like **Roskos**, *Rua Candido dos Reis*, **Lords Tavern**, *Rua Antontio C. Santos*, or **Zanzibar**, *Rua 25 de Abril*.

After 11pm rolls around, you can head to one of the larger clubs like **Mullens**, *Rua Candido dos Reis*, or **Phoenix**, *Rua 5 de Outubro*.

SPORTS & RECREATION

Fishing
· **Surfpesca Fishing Ltd.**, *Lagos, Tel. (082) 573-54*

Water Skiing
· **Meia Praia Water-ski School**, *Meia Praia, Tel. (082) 314-910*

ALVOR & NEARBY COASTAL BEACHES

The hotel-packed resort area of Alvor is a nice little port town on the banks of the Alvor River estuary. Alvor area attracts mostly bus groups to the massive hotels owned by the Salvor company, the several modern tower hotels, infamous timeshare properties, and massive English villa complexes. A mixture of bars and restaurants serve the nearby tourist developments.

ARRIVALS & DEPARTURES

By Car
Alvor is about 17 km past Lagos off Route N-125 east.

WHERE TO STAY

Expensive
HOTEL ALVOR PRAIA, *Praia dos Três Irmãos. Tel. (082) 458-900.*

This nice ocean view 5 star resort hotel has 201 comfortable air conditioned rooms. Facilities include bar, restaurant, snack bar, pools, shops, nearby golf, tennis, billiards, disco, sauna, TV, minibars, direct dial phones, and parking.

PENINA GOLF HOTEL, *Penina-Alvor. Tel. (082) 411-093.*

This great 5 star golf resort and hotel, a few kilometers away from town, has 192 nice air conditioned rooms, a bar, restaurant, shops, pool, golf courses, tennis, billiards, children's park, baby-sitting, sauna, TV, minibars, gardens, and parking.

Moderate

QUINTA NOVA, *Alvor. Tel. (082) 458-812.*

One of the better large apartment and villa complexes, Quinta Nova has over 400 units with kitchens and TV. Facilities include market, car rental, pools, tennis, nearby golf.

HOTEL DOM JOÃO III, *Praia de Alvor. Tel. (082) 459-135.*

This is a pretty good 4 star air conditioned family hotel with 220 air conditioned rooms, many facing the ocean. Facilities include bar, restaurant, snack bar, pools, billiards, TV, nearby golf and tennis, direct dial phones, and parking.

CLUB ALVOR FERIAS, *Praia do Alvor. Tel. (082) 459-230.*

This is a small complex of one, two, and three bedroom apartments with kitchens. Facilities include bar, restaurant, pool, air conditioning, sauna, tennis, shops, billiards, and parking.

TORRALTA APARTMENT TOWERS, *Praia do Alvor. Tel. (082) 459-211.*

This massive complex of several unimpressive towers offers hundreds of tourist apartments near the beach. Facilities include market, pools, and nearby golf.

HOTEL DELFIM, *Praia dos Três Irmãos. Tel. (082) 458-970.*

This huge and somewhat tasteless hotel is behind the Alvor Praia. I don't like this place but many people get stuck here. Facilities include bar, restaurant, pool, air conditioning, nearby golf and tennis, and parking.

SEEING THE SIGHTS

Besides the 16th century Manueline church, **Igreja Matriz**, several old houses, and a few cute streets, there is little else of interest here besides the nearby sports facilities. This includes several fishing, waterskiing, and tennis facilities as well as the 9 and 18 hole Henry Cotton designed courses at the **Penina Golf Clube** and nearby **Alto Golf** complex.

There are three beaches in the area: **Praia de Alvor** and **Praia dos Três Irmãos**, which are near the Salvor company properties, and **Praia Torralta**, which is close to some modern tower hotels, infamous time-share properties, and massive English villas. Although these are nice beaches, you can certainly find nicer spots in other parts of the Algarve.

SPORTS & RECREATION

Fishing

· **Hotel Alvor Praia Fishing**, *Alvor, Tel. (082) 458-900*

Horseback Riding

· **Fernando dos Santos Stables**, *Alvor, Tel. (082) 202-11*

Tennis
• **Hotel Alvor Praia Tennis Club**, *Alvor, Tel. (082) 458-900*

Water Skiing
• **Torralta Water-ski Center**, *Alvor, Tel. (082) 459-511*

Wind Surfing
• **Hotel Alvor Praia Windsurfing**, *Alvor, Tel. (082) 458-900*
• **Torralta Wind Surfing**, *Alvor, Tel. (082) 459-511*

PRAIA DA ROCHA

The heavily developed town of Praia da Rocha is centered on a wide beach and has its fair share of colorful dramatic cliffs and ocean rocks that are famous in the Algarve.

The long sandy beach and bustling resort area offers many hotels, clubs, and restaurants that line the Ave. Tomas Cabreira, which separates the town from the beach area.

ARRIVALS & DEPARTURES
By Car
Praia da Rocha is about 7 km east of Alvor along a small, unnamed coastal road at the edge of the bay of Portimão.

WHERE TO STAY
Expensive
HOTEL ORIENTAL, *Ave. Tomas Cabreira. Tel. (082) 413-000.*

This beautiful Moorish palace-style 4 star hotel has 85 beautiful deluxe air conditioned apartments on a cliff just off the beach. Facilities include a bar, café, pool, billiards, sauna, direct dial phones, and parking. Great service and views.

HOTEL BELA VISTA, *Ave. Tomas Cabreira. Tel. (082) 240-55.*

This wonderful Moorish-style mansion hotel, just off the ocean, is filled with fine antiques and azulejos. The hotel has 25 nice double rooms, a bar, and restaurant.

HOTEL ALGARVE, *Ave. Tomas Cabreira. Tel. (082) 415-001.*

This deluxe ocean view hotel tends to attract an older crowd. Once the best hotel in town with 220 air conditioned rooms with balconies, it still offers great service. Facilities include bar, restaurant, minibars, pool, shops, beach, sauna, health club, tennis, and parking.

Moderate

CASA TRÊS PALMEIRAS, *Praia do Vau. Tel. (082) 401-275.*

This nice oceanview country inn is located on a cliff and offers its guests five comfortable guest rooms with private bathrooms, a bar, TV room, pool, garden, and parking.

HOTEL AVENIDA PRAIA, *Ave. Tomas Cabreira. Tel. (082) 417-740.*

This comfortable and reasonably priced 3 star hotel, across from the ocean, has 61 air conditioned double rooms with private bathrooms. Facilities include bar, disco, sun deck, and direct dial phones. Nothing special, but a good value.

APARTHOTEL PRESIDENTE, *Praia do Vau. Tel. (082) 417-507.*

One of the best apartment-hotel complexes in the area, this modern hotel offers 107 ocean view one and two bedroom apartments with kitchens, balconies and TVs next to a great beach. Facilities include bar, restaurant, shops, pool, tour desk, and parking.

CLUB PRAIA DA ROCHA, *Ave. das Com. Lusiadas. Tel. (082) 412-912.*

This huge and relatively unappealing apartment complex offers 600 or so one and two bedroom units with kitchens just outside of the downtown area. Facilities include bar, restaurant, shops, pool, tennis, squash, billiards, baby-sitting, gym, and parking.

Inexpensive

PENSÃO SOLAR PENGUIM, *Rua António Feu. Tel. (082) 243-08.*

This nice converted mansion, on a cliff near the ocean, has 13 comfortable rooms with private bathrooms. Almost no facilities, but still a good choice.

PENSÃO PRAIA DO VAU, *Praia do Vau. Tel. (082) 253-12.*

This clean and comfortable 2 star basic inn, not far from the ocean, has 21 double rooms with private bathrooms and minimal facilities. Nothing special, but good for budget travelers.

WHERE TO EAT

Moderate

SAFARI, *Rua António Feu. Tel. (082) 235-40.*

This great little ocean view restaurant specializes in fresh fish and regional cuisine with a somewhat African atmosphere. The outdoor terrace is the best in town.

DON PEPE, *Rua Eng. Fransisco Bivar. Tel. (082) 414-721.*

This great Spanish restaurant in the Club Vila Rosa complex serves the best paella (Spanish rice and seafood) in the Algarve. It's a great place with good service.

FORTALEZA DE SANTA CATARINA, *Ave. Tomas Cabreira. Tel. (082) 220-66.*

Inside the walls of an old fort, you will find this nice ocean view restaurant serving excellent seafood dishes at good prices. The ambiance is remarkable.

Inexpensive

FU HUA, *Ave. Tomas Cabreira. Tel. (082) 852-05.*

This small casual Chinese restaurant in the Pimenta building prepares pretty good Hunan style dishes with surprisingly friendly service.

RIO A VISTA, *Rua António Feu. Tel. (082) 251-95.*

This is a pretty good casual Italian restaurant and pizzeria that prepares the best pizza in town. I should mention that Portuguese pizza is a bit unusual, but it is good.

SEEING THE SIGHTS

A nice walkway runs the width of town, starting from the **Forteleza de Santa Catarina** fortress (now home to a Café and restaurant). The walkway has lots of bars and small oceanview cafes. The town maintains a steady year-round flow of tourists from all over the world, many of whom go to the **Casino de Alvor**, which is actually here in Praia da Rocha.

The least crowded and most impressive beaches lies just west of town at **Praia do Vau**. This is a great place to relax, sunbathe, and enjoy fine cuisine in all price ranges. If you are looking for a busy and attractive resort area where all types of people gather, this is the place for you.

NIGHTLIFE & ENTERTAINMENT

The night starts off with drinks on the ocean front cafes and bars, and then the crowds move on to **Bacchus** off Ave. Marginal and finally on to **Coconuts**, *Rua Bartolomeu Diaz.*

PORTIMÃO

This bustling, dynamic city rests at the mouth of a large bay formed by the Arade River. It has been a fishing port since before the Roman era. The town is reliant on the worldwide export of locally caught and canned sardines, and has grown to become the largest city in the Algarve.

ARRIVALS & DEPARTURES

By Car

Portimão is a few kilometers from Praia da Rocha on Route N-124 north.

By Train
· **Portimão CP Rail Station**, *Rua Infante Henrique, Tel. (082) 230-56*

WHERE TO STAY
Moderate
HOTEL GLOBO, *Rua 5 de Outubro, 26. Tel. (082) 416-350.*

This nice and friendly 3 star hotel is just a few blocks from the harbor. It has 71 rooms with private bathrooms, a bar, restaurant, billiards, disco, baby-sitting, TV, and parking.

VILA ROSA DE LIMA, *Portimão. Tel. (082) 411-097.*

Located a few kilometers northwest of town off Route N-125A, this nice rustic inn has four good guest rooms with private bathrooms, TV room, pool, gardens, and parking.

RESIDENCIAL MIRA-FOIA, *Rua V. Vaz de Vacas, 33. Tel. (082) 417-852.*

This clean and comfortable inn is located in the heart of town, and has 32 rooms with private bathrooms. Facilities include bar, minibars, TV, direct dial phones, and parking.

Inexpensive
RESIDENCIAL O PATIO, *Rua Dr. J. V. Mealha, 3. Tel. (082) 242-88.*

This cute little 2 star inn has 17 guest rooms with private bathroom. O Patio is located near the Turismo in a tranquil atmosphere. It's a great budget selection, although with few facilities.

WHERE TO EAT
Moderate
AVOZINHA, *Rua do Capote, 7. Tel. (082) 229-22.*

This is an excellent award winning seafood restaurant that serves the finest cataplana (seafood stew) I have ever had in the area. Reservations are recommended.

Inexpensive
FLÔR DE SARDINHA, *Cais de Lota. Tel. (082) 248-62.*

This nice and simple outdoor fish restaurant, near the harbor and fish market, serves some of the best grilled sardines you can imagine in a very casual atmosphere.

SEEING THE SIGHTS
The city was destroyed by the 1755 earthquake, so many of its earlier buildings were lost. The most picturesque part of town is the harborside

off Ave. Louis de Camões, where fishing boats unload their daily catch. The fish is then transported to the frantic **Lota** fish market. Several casual and inexpensive restaurants line the harbor and serve great grilled sardines to hungry residents and visitors alike on small outdoor tables.

There are a few other sights in town worth a quick peek, including the mosaic-lined **Praça 1 de Dezembro** plaza, the 18th century **Câmara Municipal** (town hall), and a couple of churches. The only other activity I can recommend is shopping. The price of most items are reasonable compared to stores in nearby resort areas. Portimão is home to many boutiques, shopping centers, antique shops, and a large monthly outdoor **mercado** (market) on the first Monday. Across the bay you can see the 16th century **Fortaleza de São João** fort, standing guard over the small sister city of **Ferragudo**.

SPORTS & RECREATION
Fishing
• **Capemar Game Fishing Center**, *Portimão, Tel. (082) 258-66*

MONCHIQUE
Set in the rainy, wooded Serra de Monchique volcanic mountains is the busy market town of Monchique. This pretty town is is filled with camellias and is known for spicy presunto hams and strong eucalyptus oils that are pressed locally.

ARRIVALS & DEPARTURES
By Car
Monchique is 23 km from Portimão on Route N-266 north.

WHERE TO STAY
Moderate
ESTALAGEM ABRIGO DA MONTANHA, *Estrada da Foia. Tel. (082) 921-31.*

This great 4 star inn has several nice rooms with private bathroom and views. Facilities include bar, restaurant, pool, gardens, and parking.

ALBERGAIA DO LAGEADO, *Caldas de Monchique. Tel. (082) 926-16.*

This comfortable inn, near the center of town, has 20 good rooms with private bathrooms. Facilities include bar, restaurant, gardens, pool, and parking.

ESTALAGEM MON-CICUS, *Estrada de Foia. Tel. (082) 926-50.*

This pretty and pleasant 3 star inn has 10 comfortable rooms with private bathroom. Facilities include bar, restaurant, sauna, gardens, and parking.

Inexpensive

PENSÃO BICA-BOA, *Rua da Saboia-Foia. Tel. (082) 922-71.*
This friendly little inn and restaurant has six rooms both with and without private bathroom. Facilities include TV room, splash pool, gardens, and parking.

WHERE TO EAT
Moderate

TERESHINA, *Estrada da Foia. Tel. (082) 923-92.*
This wonderful regional restaurant offers superb meat and fish specialties served either in their dining room or on a nice patio. The views are also great.

RESTAURANTE CENTRAL, *Caldas de Monchique. Tel. (082) 922-03.*
This restaurant serves several good regional dishes including the locally made presunto ham. The prices are good, but don't expect great service.

Inexpensive

RESTAURANTE CHARETTE, *Rua Samora Gil. Tel. No phone.*
This simple and unpretentious restaurant, located in the heart of town, offers large portions of pretty good local dishes at remarkably affordable prices.

PARAISO DA MONTAHA, *Estrada da Foia. Tel. (082) 921-50.*
This large regional restaurant serves roasted meat and chicken specials. Try the spicy piri-piri chicken with a half bottle of house wine. Expect a short line on weekends.

SEEING THE SIGHTS

In town, there are few sights worth noting besides the beautiful portal and azulejos-covered interior of the 16th century Manueline **Igreja Matriz** church and the crumbling ruins of the 17th century monastery, **Mosterio de Nossa Senhora do Desterro**. The most impressive sights around town are the views from nearby mountain peaks, from which you can see all the way down the western Algarve coastline. The best of these dramatic lookouts is the 2,960 foot high peak at **Monte Foia**, reached by taking Route N-266-3 west for a few kilometers past cork, pine, and eucalyptus forests.

On the way back to the coast you will first pass through the old spa town of **Caldas de Monchique**. It is here that the hot volcanic *nascentes termais* (thermal waters) from the mountains spring up and are utilized and bottled by the local **Termas das Caldas de Monchique** spa (open June through October). Many people including former kings have bathed in the heavy mineral waters of this town to relieve rheumatism and digestive tract problems. The town's main square is dominated by several old buildings, including a former casino that is now home to a wonderful handicrafts center selling everything from pottery and handmade fabrics to the strong local brandy. The town is quite pleasant, and long walks around the flower-covered outskirts of town can be quite enjoyable.

SILVES

The beautiful and historic walled city of Silves stands at the confluence of the Odelouca and Arade Rivers. It was once an important Moorish stronghold and the rich regional capital city of Xelb until it was savagely attacked by the Crusaders in 1189 and finally conquered in the 13th century.

ARRIVALS & DEPARTURES
By Car
Silves can be reached from Monchique by taking Route N-266 south for about 15 km and connecting to Route N-124 east for another 10 km or so.

By Train
• **Silves CP Rail Station**, *2 km south of town, Tel. (082) 442-310*

WHERE TO STAY
Moderate
QUINTA DA FIUEIRINHA, *Silves. Tel. (082) 442-671.*
This nice rustic farming estate and country inn, a few kilometers east of town, has three comfortable apartments (one is a one bedroom and two are three bedrooms) with kitchens in a tranquil setting of fruit trees and flowers. Facilities include pool, and parking.

ALBERGARIA SOLAR DOS MOUROS, *Horta do Porchino Santo. Tel. (082) 443-106.*
This clean and comfortable inn has 22 guest rooms with private bathrooms. Facilities include a bar, restaurant, air conditioning, direct dial phones, TV, and parking.

Inexpensive
RESIDENCIAL SOUSA, *Rua Samora Barros, 17. Tel. (082) 442-502.*
This clean and basic inn, near the heart of town, has several decent rooms with private bathrooms, heating, TV room, breakfast room, and nearby parking.

WHERE TO EAT

Moderate

MARISQUEIRA RUI, *Rua Com. Vilarhino. Tel. (082) 442-682.*

This is the most famous seafood restaurant in this part of the Algarve. Even though this simple restaurant is packed during lunch and dinner, it's worth the wait.

SEEING THE SIGHTS

The town is dominated by a wonderfully restored Moorish **castelo** (castle) surrounded by a ring of massive crenelated sandstone towers and defensive walls. Now the walls have been converted into a wonderful panoramic walkway and encircle a tranquil garden that rests above two large cisterns.

Below the castle you can enter the town to see the Gothic 13th century cathedral **Sé da Santa Maria**, constructed on the sight of an important Moorish mosque. The interior of the cathedral still contains a few original Mosque vestiges as well as several tombs of the Crusaders, while its exterior features Gothic towers and gargoyles. At one point the body of King Dom João II was buried here as well, but was later moved to the monastery at Batalha. Silves is also home to the **Museu Arqueológico**, *Rua das Portas de Loulé*, (closed Sundays) which offers visitors a great collection of prehistoric, Arabic, and early Portuguese artifacts.

The town also contains a busy little daily produce **mercado** (market) just off the riverfront a few blocks west of the ancient bridge, which is a great place to pick up supplies for picnics (closed Sundays). On the riverfront itself you will find several small outdoor restaurants offering grilled fish.

As you depart the city, head towards the edge of town on Route N-124 east and take a peek at the 16th century carved **Cruz de Portugal** cross. Each June the amusing **Festa do Cerveja do Silves** national beer festival takes over the castle and can be heard for miles around. It is a great chance to experience the micro breweries' products, which are hard to find in normal shops.

CARVOEIRO

The heavily developed cliffside beach town of Carvoeiro has somehow managed to save a small amount of its former fishing village ambiance despite the continual overbuilding of villas, condos, timeshare complexes, and resorts. It is the small sandy **Praia do Carvoeiro** beach and the adjacent cliffs, beches, and caves around the town that attract hundreds of tourists daily to sunbathe, swim, and fish.

ARRIVALS & DEPARTURES
By Car
Carvoeiro is 10 km south of Silves on Route N-124-1 south via the wine producing town of Lagoa.

WHERE TO STAY
Expensive
HOTEL ALMANSOR, *Vale Corvo-Carvoeiro. Tel. (082) 358-026.*

This huge ocean view, 4 star resort hotel was built on the side of a cliff just outside of town. It has 293 nice air conditioned rooms, many with oceanviews and balconies. Facilities include bar, restaurants, coffee shops, pool, beach, billiards, game room, minibars, TV, tennis, nearby golf, and parking.

APARTMENTOS CRISTAL, *Carvoeiro. Tel. (082) 358-601.*

One of the best apartment hotel complexes in the area, it has 100 air conditioned apartments near the ocean with kitchens and TV. Facilities include bar, restaurant, shops, pool, tennis, billiards, sauna, baby-sitting services, minibars, nearby golf, and parking.

Moderate
HOTEL DOM SANCHO, *Largo da Praia Carvoeiro. Tel. (082) 357-301.*

This friendly 4 star beach-view hotel is located on the main square in town. The 51 comfortable air conditioned rooms make this small hotel a real winner. Facilities include bar, restaurant, pools, terrace, minibars, TV, beach, nearby golf, and lots of parking.

APARTMENTOS SOLFERIAS, *Sitio do Mato Serrão. Tel. (082) 357-403.*

This good 4 star apartment hotel is near both the beach and town. It has several dozen comfortable air conditioned apartments, some accommodating up to eight people. Facilities include bar, restaurant, pools, terrace, minibars, TV, beach, tennis, billiards, safe deposit boxes, gardens, nearby golf, parking.

WHERE TO EAT
Moderate
RESTAURANTE TEODOROS, *Rampa da Encarnado. Tel. (082) 357-864.*

This beautiful ocean view restaurant offers fine seafood dishes and great service in an artistic, air conditioned setting above the ocean. Ask for a table on the patio.

SEEING THE SIGHTS

The town fans out from its relaxing beachfront **Largo da Praia** plaza and leads up several streets lined with cafes, bars, and ice cream parlors. I really like the laid-back ambiance here, and I come here often in the months of May and June before the beach becomes a zoo.

Just 2 km east of town off the coastal road you can visit the beautiful **Algar Seco** sea rock formations. There's a rock carved step pathway to caverns and wave pounded caves that are truly dramatic. There are lots of boat excursions to beaches that are inaccessible by land, so the police suspect drug smugglers operate here often. Your car may very well be stopped by heavily armed police with drug sniffing dogs on your way out of town.

SPORTS & RECREATION
Golf

The town boasts two great 18 hole golf courses: the Ron Fream designed **Quinta do Gramacho** course at the Carvoeiro Country Club; and the Dave Thomas designed course at **Vale de Milho**.

Sailing
• **Carvoeiro Club Sailing Dept.**, Carvoeiro, Tel. (082) 357-266

Tennis
• **Carvoeiro Tennis Club**, Carvoeiro, Tel. (082) 357-847

ARMAÇÃO DE PÊRA

The resort town and fishing village of Armação de Pêra has a long 15 km sandy beach, said to be the largest in the Algarve. All along the beach you'll find a series of informal grilled fish restaurants and bars. In town, there are over two dozen small bars and dining establishments scattered on the narrow cobblestone roads that extend from the beach.

ARRIVALS & DEPARTURES
By Car

Armação de Pêra is about 15 km from Carvoeiro just off Route N-125 east.

WHERE TO STAY
Very Expensive

VILA VITA PARC, *Alporchinos, Armação de Pêra. Tel. (082) 315-310, Fax (082) 315-333. US & Canada bookings with Leading Hotels of the World,*

Tel. 800/223-6800. Low season rack rates from 26,000$00, double room, BP; high season rack rates from 56,400$00, double room, BP. All major credit cards accepted.

Vila Vita Parc is the most luxurious hotel along the southernmost coast of Portugal. This outstanding 5 star property, on 18 acres of tropical gardens, is a magnificent example of Moorish influenced Algarvian architecture.

The hotel contains 182 of the most lavishly decorated and spacious rooms, junior suites, and memorable one and two bedroom suites found in both the main building, a separate residence wing, and 30 lavish villas. All accommodations have private marble and hand painted tile bathrooms with dual basins, individually controlled air conditioning and heating systems, handsome bleached pine furnishings, terra cotta flooring embellished with either tapestries or azulejos murals, remote control color satellite televisions, direct dial telephones, a fully stocked mini-bar, hair dryer, make-up mirrors, mini-safe, giant closets, and magnificent private ocean or garden view terraces.

Vila Vita has an impressive array of world class services and facilities including a complimentary full American buffet breakfast served daily, several different restaurants, lounges with live music, five massive freshwater heated indoor and outdoor swimming pools that are fed by cascading water falls, a fully equipped heath club, sauna and steam rooms, five outdoor tennis courts, an indoor racquetball court, a full service Vital Center spa with a full range of optional natural health and beauty treatments, a unisex beauty salon, business meeting and reception rooms, boutiques, a nine hole par three pitch and put golf course, mini-golf, mountain bicycles, hundreds of comfortable lounge chairs with sun umbrellas, 24 hour room service, snack and natural juice bars, cobblestone walking paths, plenty of free secure parking, a daily schedule of exciting activities, and of course a fantastic secluded white sand cove beach.

During the high season there are also supervised children's programs each day, a water sports center featuring everything from para-sailing to water-skiing, dozens of interesting optional excursions including yacht cruises and jeep safaris, live entertainment nightly, a discotheque, special buffet dinners with exotic themes, organized walking tours of the cliffs that straddle the ocean, water aerobics classes, and much more.

Selected as one of my *Best Places to Stay* (see Chapter 10 for more details).

VILALARA HOTEL AND SPA, *Armação de Pêra. Tel. (082) 314-910, Fax (082) 314-956. US & Canada bookings with Lumina Tours, Tel. 514/858-1586. Low season rack rates from 25,000$00, double room, BP; high season rack rates from 48,000$00, double room, BP. All major credit cards accepted.*

This outstanding 5 star hotel and spa is situated just above a remarkable semi-private sandy cove beach. The property features 89 massive junior suites and several fully equipped apartments that are housed in a series of beautifully designed low rise wings.

Each unit has giant, dual basin marble bathrooms, air conditioning systems, remote control satellite televisions, in-room radios, tropical rattan furnishings, mini-bar, direct dial telephone, mini-safe, huge closets, hand painted tile decorations, and balconies that overlook the ocean or swimming pools in many cases. Vilalara's deluxe one, two, and three bedroom apartments also include fully stocked kitchens, ensuite bathrooms, opulent living rooms, and full hotel services.

The entire complex is surrounded by lavishly manicured gardens that surround a unique state of the art Thalosso therapy spa, currently ranked among the best in all of Europe. Additionally, there are six beautiful outdoor fresh and salt water swimming pools, several patios overlooking the ocean and the flowering gardens, a half dozen tennis courts, a fully equipped health club, a complete children's activities program in the summer, room service, a superb beach with water sports, complimentary sauna and steam baths, a billiard room, walking trails, and much more.

The cuisine is served at three different restaurants including a special dietetic dining room. There are also snack bars, game rooms, lounges, meeting rooms, and a particularly good room service menu.

Selected as one of my *Best Places to Stay* (see Chapter 10 for more details).

Expensive

HOTEL VIKING, *Praia Senhora da Rocha. Tel. (082) 314-876. Year round rack rates from 17,500$00, double room, CP. Most major credit cards accepted.*

This modern, ocean front, 4 star resort hotel has 184 large and comfortable air conditioned rooms, many with ocean views and balconies. Facilities include bar, restaurant, pools, sauna, health club, beach, billiards, TV, mini-bars, direct dial phones, and parking.

HOTEL GARBE, *Ave. Marginal. Tel. (082) 312-187. Year round rack rates from 21,750$00, double room, CP. Most major credit cards accepted.*

Once the best hotel in the area, this large 140 air conditioned room hotel attracts an older crowd. Facilities include bar, restaurant, pool, beach, TV, and parking.

Moderate

CASA DE BELA MOURA, *Alporchinos. Tel. (082) 313-422. Year round rack rates from 18,000$00, double room, BP. Most major credit cards accepted.*

This country inn hotel offers eight nice rooms with private bathrooms. Facilities include bar, patio with barbecue, TV room, pool, sun deck, gardens, and parking.

VILA SENHORA DA ROCHA, *Praia Senhora da Rocha. Tel. (082) 312-349. Year round rack rates from 19,500$00, per apartment, per night, CP. Most major credit cards accepted.*

This huge cliff-top complex rents one, two, and three bedroom apartments and villas near the ocean. Facilities include bar, restaurant, pools, tennis, and parking.

WHERE TO EAT
Expensive
ALADDIN GRILL, *Vila Vita Parc, Alporchinos. Tel. (082) 315-310. Dress code is jacket preffered. All major credit cards accepted.*

While this superb hotel offers several fine restaurants, the Aladdin Grill dining room is the best place to eat in town. The dining area is a circle surrounding an open grill and kitchen area. The 20 or so elegantly set tables are set among Moorish arches and a stained glass moon-roof that make you feel as though you've been invited to dinner by a Sultan.

The huge menu includes salads made at your table, duck terrine with chutney, smoked salmon and trout, shrimp marinated in garlic, Sevruga and Beluga caviar, gazpacho, vegetable consommé with brandy, grilled lobster, prawns with spicy sauce, filet of sole, grilled swordfish, T-bone steaks, veal cutlets, entrecote with Bernaise sauce, pork medallions in herb sauce, and many daily specials. Expect dinner to cost around 6,750$00 a person plus wine.

SEEING THE SIGHTS
Although much of the coast in this area seems to have a resort or villa built above it, the semi-private sandy cove beaches near Vila Vita Parc and Vilalara are worth the effort to reach by a stunning cliff-top walkway. You might also consider a short drive to visit the famous beaches west of town, like **Praia Senhora da Rocha** near the village of **Alporchinos** or a bit further west at **Praia Marinha**.

SPORTS & RECREATION
Scuba Diving
• **Algarve Diving Center**, *Armação de Pera, Tel. (082) 313-203*

ALBUFEIRA & NEARBY BEACH TOWNS
The resort city and party town of Albufeira is nestled within a series of small hills right on the coast. When my friends ask me for the most

outrageous place in Europe to spend their summer vacation, I send them here.

The town was first inhabited by the Romans who called the town Baltum. Soon after, the Moors arrived, built defensive fortresses and renamed the town Al-Buhena (the castle of the sea). Finally, it was captured by the Christians in 1191 and renamed slightly to Albufeira.

Most of town's historical buildings were devastated by the 1755 earthquake and the huge tidal waves that followed. The city still contains many winding mosaic roads, whitewashed buildings, and stone cut stairways whose design can certainly be attributed to the city's former Moorish roots.

In the early 1960s, Albufeira was discovered again, this time by mostly English and some German tourists in search of an inexpensive resort area to develop in southern Europe. This was the beginning of what eventually would turn the Algarve into a major tourist destination.

ARRIVALS & DEPARTURES

By Air
The main airport servicing Albufeira is the Faro International Airport about 38 kilometers east of here.

From the airport, the easiest way to get to Albufeira is to either rent a car, pre-arrange a transfer from your travel agent, or take a taxi ride for around 5,575$00. Those with minimal luggage looking to save a few dollars getting into town can hop on public bus #16 and for 150$00 a person to Faro's main bus depot on the Avenida da República where they can then transfer to a regional bus that stops in downtown Albufeira for around 675$00 a person.

By Bus
The bus depot is just a few minutes walk north of the town center.
• **Albufeira Main Bus Depot**, *Ave. da Liberdade, Tel. (089) 543-01*

By Car
Depending on where you are coming from, you can take either the new toll IP-1 motorway or the slower N-125 coastal highway and get off at the exit for Albufeira's "Centro" (downtown). Albufeira is about 16 km from Armação de Pera off Route N-125 east.
• **Hertz Rent a Car in Albufeira**, *Hotel Tropical, Tel. (089) 512-920*

By Train
The train station is actually a suburban train station 7 km north Albufeira in the village of Ferrerias. From the train station you can take

a local shuttle bus into the heart of town.
•**Albufeira CP Rail Station**, *7 km north of town, Tel. (089) 571-616*

ORIENTATION

The Algarve's extremely popular oceanside resort town of Albufeira sits on a series of superb white sandy Atlantic Ocean beaches about 31 kilometers (19 miles) west of Faro, and some 267 kilometers (166 miles) south-southeast of Lisbon.

The town is spread out over several adjacent cliffs that rise up over the nearby beaches and its suburbs extend a few kilometers inland. Packed with hundreds of hotels and time share complexes, the town of Albufeira was completely reconstructed after the great earthquake of 1755. It now boasts a few large public squares that feed into rambling lanes which in turn head down towards the crowded beaches. No matter where you are in town, the ocean is easily found and getting lost is never an issue.

The town of Albufeira is also part of a larger local zone known as the municipality of Albufeira which includes other adjacent resort villages such as Praia da Oura, Montechoro, Aries de São João, Praia da Galé, and Praia da Falésia.

GETTING AROUND TOWN

By Bus

The downtown area has no public bus service. The only bus you may need to use are those to Praia da Oura, Montechoro, Aries de São João, Praia da Galé, or Praia da Falésia. Local commuter buses will get you to these and many other nearby destinations for around 275$00 a person, and can be found at either the town's main bus depot off the Avenida da Liberdade, or at one of several other well marked bus stops.

By Car

These days there are plenty of metered street parking spots available downtown for around 120$00 per hour. The local government has also added lots of free or reasonably priced parking areas near the most famous beaches. Keep in mind that local rush hours, from 7:00am until 9:30am and 4:30pm until 8:15pm, create horrific traffic conditions on most area roads.

By Taxi

Taxis are an inexpensive way to get around Albufeira. The average ride anywhere in the downtown area should cost no more than 495$00. Since downtown Albufeira is rather compact, you may never actually need to use a taxi unless you are staying in a different resort village. Typical fares to Praia da Oura, Montechoro, Aries de São João, Praia da Galé, and Praia da Falésia range from 925$00 to 1,450$00 each way.

WHERE TO STAY
Expensive

SHERATON ALGARVE, *Praia da Falésia. Tel. (089) 501-999, Fax (089) 501-950. US & Canada bookings with Sheraton Luxury Collection, Tel. 800/325-3535. Low season rack rates from 27,000$00, double room, BP; high season rack rates from 45,500$00, double room, BP. All major credit cards accepted.*

An eight minute drive from downtown Albufeiria, this is a great place to stay. The Sheraton is a modern, Moorish hotel decorated with rare multicolored marbles, peaceful inner courtyards, beautiful hand painted azulejos, cascading fountains, lush semi-tropical gardens, regal tapestries, and fine paintings.

There are 215 spacious ocean or garden-view rooms and suites that all feature marble bathrooms, air conditioning systems, custom designed hardwood furnishings, hand painted tile murals, remote control satellite television, executive desks, terra cotta tile floors, mini-bar, walk-in closets, direct dial telephones, mini-safe, and huge terraces.

There is an extensive array of services and facilities including a 9 hole par 33 golf course and academy, huge indoor and outdoor swimming pools, three tennis courts, a fully equipped health club, sauna, Jacuzzi, massage and spa treatments, a business center, car rental and excursion desks, boutiques, a beauty salon, a wine shop, a newsstand and tobacconist, 24 hour room service, a high season children's activities program, and business meeting rooms. The property's beach is a four minute hike and has a private beach club with water sports. The resort also has multiple restaurants and bars.

Selected as one of my *Best Places to Stay* (see Chapter 10 for more details).

VILA JOYA, *Praia da Gale. Tel. (089) 591-839. Year round rack rates from 27,500$00, double room, BP. Most major credit cards accepted.*

This wonderful deluxe German operated exclusive ocean view inn has 13 of the most incredible rooms you can imagine. Facilities include bar, gourmet restaurant, air conditioning, pool, sun deck, nearby golf and horses, terraces, beach, and parking.

HOTEL SOL E MAR, *Rua José Bernadino de Sousa. Tel. (089) 586-721, Fax (089) 587-036. Low season rack rates from 12,000$00, double room, BP; high season rack rates from 18,000$00, double room, BP. All major credit cards accepted.*

This is the only hotel situated directly above the main beach, so it tends to sell out well in advance during much of the year. The Sol e Mar is a good 4 star property with dramatic ocean views from all 74 rooms that come complete with terraces, private bathrooms, air conditioning, cable television, mini-bar, direct dial phone, small refrigerators, and reasonably nice furnishings. Facilities include bar, restaurant, baby-sitting, direct beach access, sun umbrellas and lounge chairs, a snack bar, and nearby parking.

CLUB MED (da Balaia), *Praia Maria Luísa. Tel. (089) 586-681. Year round rack rates from 39,500$00, double room, AI. Most major credit cards accepted.*

This all inclusive resort offers its combination of both single and married guests 320 air conditioned rooms near the ocean. No minimum length of stay is required. Facilities include bars, restaurants, pool, golf, tennis, archery, windsurfing, and parking.

Moderate

HOTEL CERRO ALAGOA, *Via Rapida. Tel. (089) 588-261. Year round rack rates from 19,750$00, double room, CP. Most major credit cards accepted.*

This large and modern 4 star hotel, just a few minutes walk from the beach, has 310 comfortable air conditioned rooms with balconies. Facilities include bar, restaurants, pool, sauna, beach bus, billiards, cable TV, mini-bars, safe, shops, health club, and parking.

FALÉSIAHOTEL, *Praia da Falésia. Tel. (089) 501-237. Year round rack rates from 21,500$00, double room, BP. Most major credit cards accepted.*

This modern 4 star hotel, near the ocean, has 169 air conditioned rooms with balconies. Facilities include bar, restaurant, pools, sauna, tennis, beach bus, TV, and parking.

HOTEL MONTECHORO, *Rua Dr. F. S. Carneiro. Tel. (089) 589-423. Year round rack rates from 22,750$00, double room, BP. Most major credit cards accepted.*

This huge 4 star resort hotel has 362 large air conditioned rooms (many with balconies) just a few minutes inland from the heart of town in the Montechoro area. Facilities include bars, restaurants, pools, sauna, squash, tennis, TV, and parking.

HOTEL ROCAMAR, *Largo Jacinto D'ayat. Tel. (089) 586-990, Fax (089) 586-998. Low season rack rates from 10,000$00, double room, CP; high season rack rates from 14,000$00, double room, CP. Most major credit cards accepted.*

This modern 3 star ocean front hotel on the western side of town is a good value for the money. All 91 rooms feature large balconies, private bathrooms, direct dial telephones, air conditioning, and either city or ocean views. There is also a good restaurant, a nice staff, and a friendly, relaxed ambiance.

ESTALAGEM DO CERRO, *Rua B-Cerro da Piedade. Tel. (089) 586-191. Year round rack rates from 19,750$00, double room, CP. Most major credit cards accepted.*

This nice inn, a few minutes away from town in the Cerro da Piedade area, has 85 clean and comfortable rooms with private bathrooms. Facilities include bar, restaurant, pool, sauna, health club, TV, kitchens, and parking.

APARTAMENTOS PATIO DA ALDEIA, *Areias de São João. Tel. (089) 589-231. Year round rack rates from 21,000$00, per apartment, per night, EP. Most major credit cards accepted.*

This is one of the best small apartment complexes in town. The hotel offers 70 garden apartments and villas with kitchens in a quiet location not far from the beach. Facilities include bar, pool, gym, air conditioning, direct dial phones, and parking.

APARTHOTEL ALMAR, *Cerro de Alagoa. Tel. (089) 586-265. Year round rack rates from 19,000$00, per apartment, per night, EP. Most major credit cards accepted.*

This comfortable apartment complex, near the edge of town, has 44 studio and one bedroom terrace apartments with kitchens, bar, water sports, pools, and parking.

Inexpensive

ALFAGAR, *Semina. Tel. (089) 514-960. Year round rack rates from 16,750$00, per apartment, per night, EP. Most major credit cards accepted.*

This 210 room apartment complex, a few minutes out of town near Praia do Santo Elalia beach, offers comfortable accommodations above the ocean cliffs. Facilities include bar, restaurant, pools, market, billiards, tennis, TV, beach bus, and parking.

CLUB PRAIA DA OURA, *Praia da Oura. Tel. (089) 589-135. Year round rack rates from 15,750$00, double room, EP. Most major credit cards accepted.*

This massive and ugly 579 room time share apartment hotel, near the beach, is usually filled to the brim with English tourists. I don't really like this place very much.

RESIDENCIAL POLANA, *Rua Candido dos Reis, 32. Tel. (089) 587-168. Low season rack rates from 7,000$00, double room; high season rack rates from 8,500$00, double room. Cash only - No credit cards accepted.*

This modern and clean 2 star inn has a dozen or so guest rooms with private bathrooms. This is one of the few decent, cheap establishment in the center town.

RESIDENCIAL LIMAS, *Rua da Liberdade, 27. Tel. (089) 514-025. Year round rack rates from 13,250$00, double room, EP. Most major credit cards accepted.*

This reasonably nice and well located 3 star inn is located near the heart of town. The 11 rooms come with or without private bathrooms and are a real bargain, but there are no facilities.

WHERE TO EAT
Expensive
RESTAURANTE TIPICO A RUINA, *Largo Cais Herculano. Tel. (089) 512-094. Dress code ranges from casual to smart casual depending on what level you dine in. Cash only - No credit cards accepted.*

This three floor restaurant, in a beautiful oceanside mansion above the town's beach, has opulent dining rooms with vaulted stone and hand painted tile ceilings, ground level outdoor tables, and a great roof top al fresco terrace. Although the prices depend on what section you choose to dine in, their extensive menu includes excellent dishes like fish chowder, grilled sardines, grilled salmon, filet of sole, entrecote, fried calamari, grilled shrimp, fresh hake, stuffed lobster, beef steak, pork chops, and many daily specials. A formal dinner in the more dressy dining room will cost around 3,250$00, while a simple grilled fish meal on the terrace is about half the price. Highly Recommended.

RESTAURANTE O PENADO, *Rua Latina Coelho, 15. Tel. Unlisted. Most major credit cards accepted.*

With its prime location near the esplanade in the old fisherman's district on the west end of town, this superb seafood restaurant is one of my favorites. The sun drenched interior has nice tiles and checkerboard linens with enough room for about 44 lucky patrons. The menu is extensive and includes freshly caught fish and Portuguese meat dishes such as smoked ham, shrimp cocktail, salmon pate, grilled sardines, Asian styled shrimp and vegetables, mixed acorda, grilled chicken, stewed rabbit, pork filet, grilled entrecote, broiled sole, lobster, and much more. Dinner will set each person back around 2,650$00 plus wine. Highly Recommended.

CABAZ DA PRAIA, *Praça Miguel Bombarda. Tel. (089) 512-173. Dress code is smart casual. Most major credit cards accepted.*

This nice Portuguese restaurant serves regional cuisine on a wonderful patio above the beach. The large menu includes many unusual meat and seafood dishes. Expect to spend around 4,100$00 a person.

Moderate
EL BOLERO STEAKS AND MEXICO, *Rua São Goncalo de Lagos, 17. Tel. (089) 515-959. Dress code is casual. Most major credit cards accepted.*

Situated near the fishermen's beach, this is a good Mexican grill house with a faux adobe interior that serves up spicy gazpacho, Mexican bean soup, guacamole, chili con carne, Caesar salad, nachos, potato skins, taco salads, enchiladas, burritos, chicken tacos, buffalo wings, veggie combos, shrimp fajitas, and thick steaks. Dinner here will set you back around 1,950$00 a person plus drinks.

BAMBOO, *Rua Alves Correria, 7. Tel. (089) 515-922. No dress code. Cash only - No credit cards accepted.*

For my money, this is the best Chinese/Thai restaurant in town. Situated just a block from the main square, you can order well prepared food. You can eat in or take out such delicacies as shark fin soup, won ton soup, hot and sour soup, egg rolls, fried rice with shrimp, vegetable lo mein, curried chicken, sweet and sour pork, spare ribs, Peking duck, beef chop suey, fish with lemon sauce, steak with oyster sauce, and more. Your meal should cost around 1,750$00 a person.

Inexpensive

TONY'S PIZZARIA, *Rua Candido dos Reis, 7. Tel. (089) 514-075. No dress code. Cash only - No credit cards accepted.*

Located just a block or so away from the main square in town, this is the best pizzeria in the Algarve. You can sit inside or on their amusing terrace and select from a full range of delicious Italian items including garlic bread, minestrone soup, green lasagna, cannelloni, tuna salad, mixed salad, chicken salad, calzones, and over a dozen types of large pizzas. Total cost, per person, usually averages less than 1,550$00.

SOTAVENTO, *Rua São Gonzales de Lagos, 16. Tel. (089) 512-719. No dress code. Most major credit cards accepted.*

This simple indoor/outdoor restaurant and café, a block behind the fishermen's beach, serves good and affordably priced fish and meat dishes. You'll find vegetable soup, fish soup, mixed salad, boiled shrimp, grilled prawns, clams with garlic, tuna steak, beef steak with pepper sauce, burgers, spaghetti Bologense, lamb chops with mint sauce, all sorts of omelets, and more on the menu. A good lunch or dinner can cost as little as 1,100$00 per person.

MINAR, *Travessa Cais Herculano. Tel. (089) 513-196. No dress code. Most major credit cards accepted.*

This great little tandoori restaurant, near the fishermen's beach, offers a vast assortment of traditional Indian food that ranges from mild to extremely hot. A meal will set you back around 1,950$00 a person.

SEEING THE SIGHTS

To begin with, the town centers around a large and active square known as the **Largo Eng. Duarte Pacheco**, which is the sight of several handicraft kiosks and is itself surrounded by countless popular cafés, pubs, gift shops, and restaurants. A series of little arched lanes and charming streets merge off this square and are all worth strolling along. From the edge of this square, walk two blocks west to intersect with the main street through the town called Rua 5 de Outubro which will take you to several eating establishments, gift shops, boutiques, bars and the main **Turísmo** tourist information center.

As you walk south on this main street you will come to a tunnel cut through a small mountain, which then leads directly under the **Praça da República** square and on to the large cliff-bordered **Praia de Albufeira** town beach. On hot summer days, as many as 15,000 people can be seen packed closely together (many are half naked) in pursuit of each other's attention at this beach. Lounge chairs and umbrellas are available for a small fee.

Just a few hundred yards further along the coast on the eastern end of downtown Albfureira, there are a few dozen motorized fishing boats that continue to be based at both the **Praia dos Barcos** (boat beach) and **Praia dos Pescadores** (fisherman's beach) just below the **Largo Cais Herculano** plaza. While the fishing industry still makes a contribution to the local economy, as is evident by the former fish **mercado** (market) just above fisherman's beach, these days I would hesitate to describe this city as a fishing village. From the paths just above these beaches, it is possible to hike for several kilometers along the dramatic cliff-top walk.

You can visit the ruins of a Moorish **castelo** (castle) behind the city, the lovely 18th century neo-classical **Igreja Matriz** off the Rua Miguel Bombarda, the fortified **Câmara Municipal** (town hall) near the beach off Rua Bernardo de Sousa, a wonderfully quaint former fisherman's district off the Rua Latino Coelho on the west side of town, the small **Praça das Touros** bullring on the north side of the city with bullfights every Saturday evening, and a few remaining sections of the **Vila Velha** (old town), which can be seen off the Rua do Cemiteiro Velha. I should warn you about the obnoxious hard selling time share salesmen who hawk free gift offers around town if you spend an hour at one of those presentations. Don't fall into their trap!

Since the municipality of **Albufeira** extends for several kilometers along the coastline and inland areas, many local beaches and hotels are actually not in the town center itself but are still advertised as being in Albufeira. To the west of town are the less crowded rock cove beach areas of **Praia de São Rafael**, **Praia do Castelo**, and **Praia da Galé**. To the east of town you can visit a series of other beaches, such as the over-developed **Praia da Oura**, **Praia Maria Luísa**, and **Praia do Balaia**, the quaint fishing beach at **Olhos d'Água**, or the long sandy beach of **Praia da Falésia**. In this general area you will find several sports and family activity facilities, including water parks, tennis complexes, and golf courses.

NIGHTLIFE & ENTERTAINMENT

Since Albufeira is the biggest party town in the Algarve, its aggressive nightlife scene is varied and a big part of the town's appeal to younger tourists. Bars on the main square (Largo Eng. Duarte Pacheco) like the famous **Sir Harry's** offer live music and happy hours.

As the night wears on, several more downtown bars such as the **Zanzibar** on Rua Miguel Bombarda, the **Classic Bar** on Rua Candido dos Reis, and **Steps Bar** on Rua J.P. Samora are also worth a try. The action really picks up after 11pm when thousands of well dressed night crawlers hop over to Avenida Sa Carneiro (known locally as "The Strip") just off Praia da Oura to places like **The Garage**, **La Bamba**, and **Liberto's**.

A bit later on the crowds start heading for the multilevel **Kiss Disco** and the Brazilian influenced live music venue called the **Montinho** that are both in the Montechoro area, as well as the **IRS** disco near the Albufeira bullring which all offer dancing with somewhat reasonable cover charges until 4am. For real night owls, the new **Kadoc** mega-disco way out on the EN-1 towards Loulé stays open on weekend nights with up to 7,000 party animals until around sunrise, much later than most other venues in the Algarve.

SPORTS & RECREATION

Scuba Diving
• **Atlantic Diving Club**, *Albufeira, Tel. (089) 513-642*

Tennis
• **Hotel Alfamar Tennis Club**, *Albufeira, Tel. (089) 501-351*
• **Hotel Montechoro Tennis Club**, *Albufeira, Tel. (089) 589-423*

Wind Surfing
• **Hotel Alfamar Wind Surfing Club**, *Albufeira, Tel. (089) 501-351*
• **Hotel Montechoro Wind Surfing**, *Albufeira, Tel. (089) 589-423*

VILAMOURA

Vilamoura is an impressive small city centered around golf courses and an extensive marina lined with water view cafes, boutiques, and restaurants that tend to cater to a more upscale and older crowd.

ARRIVALS & DEPARTURES

By Car
Vilamoura is located about 24 km from Albufeira off Route N-125 east.

WHERE TO STAY

Expensive

VILAMOURA MARINOTEL, *Vilamoura Marina. Tel. (089) 389-988.*
This 5 star hotel is located in front of the town's marina. The 385 air conditioned rooms (many have ocean views) offer superb comfort. Facilities include bars, gourmet restaurants, shops, pool, sauna, sun deck, health club, nearby tennis and golf, minibars, direct dial phones, TV, and lots of parking.

HOTEL ATLANTIS, *Vilamoura Beach. Tel. (089) 389-977.*
This is a good resort hotel near the beach. It has 313 comfortable rooms, bars, restaurants, air conditioning, pools, sun deck, beach, health club, nearby golf and tennis, sauna, shops, TV, handicapped facilities, direct dial phones, and parking.

HOTEL DOM PEDRO, *Vilamoura. Tel. (089) 389-650.*
This is a good 4 star hotel, not far from the beach, is starting to show signs of aging. Facilities in this 261 room hotel include bar, restaurants, air conditioning, pools, sun deck, nearby golf and tennis, sauna, billiards, squash, TV, and parking.

Moderate

HOTEL AMPALIUS, *Vilamoura Beach. Tel. (089) 388-008.*
This is a wonderfully friendly family 4 star hotel on the beach. There are 357 large air conditioned ocean view rooms. Facilities include bar, restaurants, pools, health club, nearby golf and tennis, beach, children's park, shops, TV, minibars, and parking.

ALDEIA DO MAR, *Vilamoura. Tel. (089) 302-635.*
This nice villa and apartment complex, in the heart of town, has 70 villas and 192 apartments with kitchens, and sleep up to six people. Facilities include bar, restaurant, pools, shops, nearby golf and tennis, TV, handicapped facilities, and parking.

ESTALAGEM DA CEGONHA, *Vilamoura. Tel. (089) 302-577.*
This nice old 4 star inn, near the horseback riding center, has 10 comfortable rooms. Facilities include bar, restaurant, pool, horseback riding, nearby golf, and parking.

MOTEL DO GOLF, *Vilamoura Golf Course. Tel. (089) 302-092.*
This warm and friendly motel is on the golf course, can use some renovation. Facilities include bar, restaurant, pool, sun deck, air conditioning, and parking.

Inexpensive

PENSÃO MIRAMAR, *Rua G. Velho, 8, Quarteira. Tel. (089) 315-225.*
This reasonably good 3 star inn, near the heart of Quarteira, has 18

guest rooms with private bathrooms. There are no real facilities besides the breakfast room.

WHERE TO EAT
Moderate
A MARGARIDA, *Vilamoura Marina. Tel. (089) 312-168.*

This great restaurant has a great view of the marina. It serves fine fresh meat and seafood dishes by a staff of friendly English speaking waiters. Try the grilled espadarte (swordfish).

RESTAURANTE CANTON, *Vilamoura. Tel. (089) 314-772.*

This casual Chinese restaurant, near the cinema, serves good Cantonese cuisine at great prices. Lets face it, we all need a break from local cuisine now and again.

SEEING THE SIGHTS
On the northeast edge of town, a Roman village known as **Cerro da Vial** has been excavated. The ruins can be viewed on site and at the local **Museu de Cerro da Vial**. There's a casino, appropriately enough, called **Vilamoura Casino**. I like this town a lot, but it is completely artificial by nature. This is a good place if you want to spend your vacation in a resort area; it is located close enough to take day trips to anywhere in the Algarve.

The nearby overbuilt city of **Quarteira** offers little of interest besides its Wednesday regional **mercado** (market) off Rua Vasco da Gama, and the oceanview promenade adjacent to Ave. Infante Sagres.

SPORTS & RECREATION
Boating
• **Vilamoura Marina Yacht Center**, *Vilamoura Marina, Tel. (089) 302-925*

Golf
Designed in the 1970's and financed by rich multinational oil companies, Vilamoura contains several large 9 and 18 hole golf courses designed by Frank Pennink, Robert Trent Jones, and Joseph Lee.

Horseback Riding
• **Vilamoura Horse Center**, *Vilamoura, Tel. (089) 301-577*

Sailing
• **Vilamoura Sailing Club**, *Vilamoura Marina, Tel. (089) 313-933*

Tennis
· **Vilamoura Tennis Center**, *Vilamoura, Tel. (089) 380-088*

LOULÉ

The fascinating town of Loulé has several enchanting sights and one of the best regional Saturday markets in the country.

ARRIVALS & DEPARTURES
By Car
Loulé lies some 13 km northeast of Vilamoura on Route N-396 north.

WHERE TO STAY
Moderate
QUINTA DA VAREZA, *Querenca-Loulé. Tel. (089) 414-443*.

This charming country inn is on a tranquil farming estate about 10 km north of Loulé. It has nine nice guest rooms with private bathrooms. Facilities include bar, pool, tennis, billiards, horse riding, gardens, library, winery, jeep safaris, and parking.

HOTEL LOULÉ JARDIM, *Praça Manuel Arriaga. Tel. (089) 413-096*.

This nice and well located 3 star hotel has 52 comfortable rooms. Facilities include bar, pool, air conditioning, TV, direct dial phones, and parking.

Inexpensive
PENSÃO IBERICA, *Ave. Marcal Pacheco, 157. Tel. (089) 414-100*.

This clean and comfortable 3 star basic inn has over 40 good guest rooms with private bathrooms. Facilities include breakfast room, TV room, and parking.

WHERE TO EAT
Moderate
O AVENIDA, *Ave. J. da Costa Mealha. Tel. (089) 621-06*.

This great little regional restaurant, in the heart of town, offers simple but delicious meat and fish plates at reasonable prices. The place gets packed on market days.

SEEING THE SIGHTS
Be sure to visit the defensive walls and towers of the large medieval Moorish **castelo** (castle). Its walls have been converted into a great walking path with panoramic views. The walls also surround the castle's small

museum, **Museu Municipal**, which displays local art and artifacts (closed Mondays). Near the museum is the 12th century Gothic **Igreja Matriz**. This church contains wonderful altars and azulejos. There are also several charming streets throughout town that are full of cafes and local crafts-men hard at work.

The best time to visit Loulé is during the huge weekly regional **mercado** (market). The mercado is open every Saturday until midnight. Although you may get stuck in some serious traffic, a trip to the Algarve is simply incomplete without an excursion to the Saturday mercado. Loulé celebrates the annual **Carnival** in late February with a variety of parades and costume parties.

ALMANCIL & THE GOLF RESORTS

The quiet town of Almancil offers little of interest other than a few charming crafts shops and good restaurants. The reason most people come to this village is to spend time at major resorts known for their golf and tennis facilities and to have access to some nice beaches. The hotels, villas, and apartment complexes in these resorts are almost all deluxe and exclusive. Many seasonal inhabitants own their own villas, and you can see the Porches and Ferraris slipping past heavily secured driveways.

ARRIVALS & DEPARTURES
By Car

From Loulé, take Route N-125-4 south for about 7 km and connect to Route N-125 west for another 4 km.

WHERE TO STAY
Expensive

HOTEL QUINTA DO LAGO, *Quinta do Lago. Tel. (089) 396-666.*

This is a deluxe, 141 room, 5 star hotel and golf resort that primarily attracts a middle aged upscale clientele looking for great accommodations with golf facilities near the beach. Facilities include bars, restaurants, pool, sauna, terrace, nearby private beach, golf, health club, air condition-ing, shops, minibars, billiards, TV, and lots of parking.

HOTEL DONA FILIPA, *Vale do Lobo. Tel. (089) 394-141.*

This is an exclusive 5 star golf and tennis resort located just off the beach. This deluxe property has 147 air conditioned rooms with balco-nies, a bar, restaurants, pool, terrace, golf, tennis, beach, shops, baby-sitting, TV, minibars, and parking.

VALE DO LOBO VILLAS, *Vale do Lobo. Tel. (089) 393-939.*

This is an impressive resort community of 1,000 apartments and private villas with kitchens and TVs set among the hills near area golf courses. Facilities include maid service, bar, restaurants, pools, sauna, tennis, golf, health club, shops, and parking.

Moderate

QUINTA DAS ROCHAS, *Almancil. Tel. (089) 393-165.*

A wonderful bed and breakfast inn with six spacious rooms with private bathrooms and cable TV not far from the ocean. Facilities include bar, bicycles, and parking.

DUNAS DOURADAS VILLAS, *Almancil. Tel. (089) 396-297.*

This is a small complex of luxury two and three bedroom townhouses and villas. Facilities include bar, restaurant, pools, tennis, nearby health club and golf, shops, private beach, front desk, TV, and parking.

VILAR DO GOLF, *Quinta do Lago. Tel. (089) 396-615.*

This English operated villa and apartment complex has 180 apartments and villas. Facilities include bar, restaurant, pools, tennis, golf, shops, and parking.

VALE DE GARRÃO, *Almancil. Tel. (089) 394-593.*

This 4 star apartment and villa complex, near the golfing areas, offers 103 apartments and villas. Facilities include bar, restaurant, pool, tennis, and parking.

Inexpensive

PENSÃO SANTA TERESA, *Rua do Comércio, 13. Tel. (089) 395-525.*

This clean and comfortable 3 star inn, in downtown Almancil, has just about the only budget accommodations in the area. They have 22 rooms with private bathrooms.

WHERE TO EAT

Moderate

O TRADICIONAL, *Almancil. Tel. (089) 399-093.*

This converted old farmhouse offers great French-Portuguese cuisine in a casual country setting. It's a great spot to have dinner after a long day of golf.

PEQUENO MUNDO, *Almancil. Tel. (089) 399-866.*

This charming restaurant set in an old house filled with antiques serves international cuisine. The English and Portuguese chefs prepare fine dinners.

SEEING THE SIGHTS

Just east of town you can visit the remarkable Romanesque **Igreja de São Lourenço**. The church features incredibly ornate 18th century azulejos created by Policarpo de Oliviera Bernardes, son of the master craftsman António de Oliveira Bernardes, whose famous work adorns the churches of Évora and Barcelos.

SPORTS & RECREATION

The most famous golf and tennis hot spots are the **Vale do Lobo** and **Quinta do Lago** resorts just south of town near the ocean. These well marketed areas are packed with upscale British, German, and Scandinavian vacationers. Golfing here is serious business, and most of these ocean view courses are more expensive than their equivalent course would be back home.

There are also several sand dune beaches, a large tennis center, and a horseback riding complex in the vicinity.

Golf

Among the most famous golf courses in the area are the ocean view 9 hole courses at **Vale de Lobo Golf**, designed by Henry Cotton, and the several tranquil 9 hole William Mitchell and Joe Lee designed courses at **Quinta do Lago Golf** and **San Lorenzo Golf**.

Horseback Riding
• **Quinta dos Amigos Horse Club**, *Almancil, Tel. (089) 394-536*
• **Quinta da Lago Horse Center**, *Vale de Lobo, Tel. (089) 396-902*

Sailing
• **Vale de Lobo Sailing Club**, *Vale de Lobo, Tel. (089) 394-444*

Tennis
• **Roger Taylor Tennis Center**, *Vale de Lobo, Tel. (089) 304-145*

FARO

Faro is the waterfront capital city of the Algarve. Even though Faro is home to southern Portugal's international airport, this remarkable city is seldom visited by the thousands of daily arrivals who tend to immediately depart to the more fashionable resort areas.

This large city was in Moorish hands until its capture in 1249 by King Dom Afonso III and his Christian forces. Many of Faro's original structures were destroyed by the 1755 earthquake but several historic sights are still standing throughout the old sections of town.

ARRIVALS & DEPARTURES

By Air

The main airport servicing Faro is simply called the Faro International Airport and is located about 7 km east of the city center.

From the airport, the easiest way to get to the city is to take a taxi for around 1,100$00. Those with minimal luggage looking to save a few dollars getting into town can hop on public bus # 16 and for about 150$00 a person. Ask the driver to let you off at the Jardim Manuel Bivar stop near the harbor's docks.

By Bus

The main bus depot is on Avenida da República near the harbor.
• **Faro Main Bus Depot**, *Avenida da República, no phone*

By Car

You can take either the new toll IP-1 motorway or the slower N-125 coastal highway and get off at the exit for Faro's centro (downtown). Faro is located 13 km from Almancil on Route N-125 east.
• **Europcar Renta a Car in Faro**, *Faro Airport, Tel. (089) 818-726*

By Train

The train station is at Largo da Estação just off Avenida da República near the harbor.
• **Faro CP Rail Station**, *Largo da Estação, Tel. (089) 822-769*

ORIENTATION

The large sprawling city of Faro is located on the southern coast of Portugal, about 298 kilometers (185 miles) south-southeast of Lisbon.

The western boundry of Faro is a series of Atlantic Ocean beaches and proceeds inland for a few kilometers until it finally peters out. The city is divided into a series of different neighborhoods that include a somewhat dirty harbor and beach front, a pedestrian only retail shopping district, a downtown core loaded with modern office buildings, and an industrial park area with several large factories.

Since almost all of the city's most charming quarters are located within a few blocks of the harbor, and the ocean is visible from these small sections, getting lost is not normally a problem.

GETTING AROUND TOWN

By Bus

Although public buses connect just about every point in Faro, there is normally no need to use them since most visitors prefer to walk around town. Bus system maps can be found at the main Turismo office in the Jardim Manuel Bivar gardens near the harbor, and bus tickets cost about 150$00 per person.

By Car

Since finding parking in Faro is usually difficult, navigating around the narrow downtown streets is stressful, and traffic jams are a common occurrence, I do not recommend using your car to explore this city.

In the event that you have rented a car and have it during your stay, I suggest parking it at the airport (ask the company you rented from if they will let use their airport parking lot for free) and pick the vehicle up when you are ready to leave the city. There are also a number of hotel and private parking garages that can be used for around 1,950$00 a day.

By Taxi

Taxis are an effective and inexpensive way to get around Faro. The average ride anywhere in the downtown area should cost no more than 595$00 and all the drivers know how to avoid traffic jams.

A taxi is usually vacant when the "Taxi" light on top of the cab is illuminated. You can flag them in much the same way you would at home, or you can go to one of many taxi lines and wait your turn.

Since downtown Faro is rather compact, you may never actually need to use a taxi unless your feet get too tired from walking around all day.

WHERE TO STAY

Expensive

LA RESERVE, *Santa Bárbara de Nexe. Tel. (089) 904-74.*

This exclusive and deluxe apartment hotel, about 15 km northwest of Faro off Route N-125 west, offers 20 double air conditioned ocean view suites, bar, gourmet restaurant, pool, tennis, shops, minibars, TV, and parking.

Moderate

HOTEL EVA, *Ave. de República. Tel. (089) 803-354.*

This modern ocean view, air conditioned 4 star hotel has 150 rooms. Facilities include disco, piano bar, restaurant, roof top pools, TV, direct dial phones, and parking.

CASA DE LUMENA, *Praça Alexandre Hurculano. Tel. (089) 801-990.*

This charming old mansion offers 12 nice guest rooms with private bathrooms in the heart of town. Facilities include bar, restaurant, and nearby parking.

HOTEL FARO, *Praça Francisco Gomes. Tel. (089) 803-276.*
This large 3 star hotel on the harbor offers 52 reasonable rooms. Facilities include bar, restaurant, terrace, air conditioning, direct dial phones, and parking.
ESTALAGEM AEROMAR, *Praia de Faro. Tel. (089) 817-542.*
This nice ocean view 4 star inn has 23 good rooms on Faro's beach island. Facilities include bar, restaurant, shops, billiards, TV room, direct dial phones, and parking.

Inexpensive
PENSÃO O FARÃO, *Largo da Madelena, 4. Tel. (089) 823-356.*
This nice and centrally located 3 star inn has 30 rooms with private bathrooms, a bar, restaurant, TV room, terrace, and telephones.
APARTMENTOS VITORIA, *Rua Serpa Pinto, 58. Tel. (089) 806-583.*
This nice and modest apartment building in the heart of the city offers 12 clean and basic one bedroom apartments with kitchens. There are no facilities but it is close to everything.
PENSÃO MADELENA, *Rua Consel, Bivar, 109. Tel. (089) 805-806.*
This clean and basic 2 star inn, located in the heart of town, has 20 or so guest rooms with and without private bathroom. It's not a bad choice but nothing special.

WHERE TO EAT
Expensive
CIDADE VELHA, *Rua Domingos Guiero. Tel. (089) 271-45.*
This wonderful French influenced Portuguese restaurant is located in an historic building in the old section of town. The meat and fish dishes are among the best in the Algarve.

Moderate
DOS IRMÃOS, *Largo Terrio do Bispo, 13. Tel. (089) 823-337.*
This well established seafood restaurant specializes in regional fish meals cooked to perfection. The ambiance here is old world, and they have a massive menu.

SEEING THE SIGHTS
You will find that parking near the **Doca de Recreio** (docks) is an easy task. To begin your walking tour, start at the **Praça D. Fransisco Gomes** plaza. As you walk through the **Jardim Manuel Bivar** (gardens), you might want to stop in at one of the small outdoor cafes. As you leave the southern end of the garden, first stop off at the Turismo just off the corner of Rua da Misericórdia and pick up a free city map of attractions.

A few steps back down from the Turismo is the 18th century **Arco da Vila** town gate, which leads to the Rua do Municipo and into the **Cidade Velha** (old town) section of Faro. As you enter the old walled area, you will soon find yourself at the **Largo da Sé** plaza which is dominated by the ancient **Sé Cathedral**. This beautiful azulejos-filled cathedral was built on the site of the city's former mosque; it was rebuilt once again after the 1755 earthquake damaged it severely.

Directly across the plaza you can also view the ornate 18th century **Paço Episcopal** (bishop's palace), which backs onto the medieval ramparts of the old town. Behind the Sé, walk down Rua Dominingos Guieiro to reach the Praça **Afonso III**. The clositers of this 16th century **Convento de Nossa Senhora da Assuncão** have become home to the town's **Museu Arqueológico e Lapidar Infante Dom Henrique**. This unusual archaeology museum (closed Saturdays and Sundays) contains local Roman and Moorish artifacts, as well as fine paintings and azulejos. In the convent's chapel there are additional collections of sculptures and antique furnishings. After strolling down the stone lanes of this part of the city, you can depart via the **Arco da Porta Nova** town gate (where you can see the water) and follow the Rua Com. Francisco Manuel back to the dockside gardens.

Follow the Rua D. Francisco Gomes from the northern end of the garden until it merges with the Rua de Santo António, the city's main commercial street where you'll find a variety of boutiques. From this street, turn right onto Rua Pe da Cruz to enter the **Museu de Etnografia Regional** (museum of ethnography). Inside this museum (closed Saturdays and Sundays) you will find collections of paintings, photographs, models of traditional cottages, handicrafts and fishing methods.

From the museum, continue down the same street until it ends at the **Largo do Pe da Cruz** plaza, where you can see the magnificent 17th century **Igreja de Pe da Cruz** with impressive frescoes and elegant paintings. Now head back to the Praça D. Francisco Gomes' northern edge and follow the Rua Conselheiro Bivar up for a few blocks before turning right onto the Rua de São Pedro. At the end of this street you'll enter the **Largo de São Pedro** plaza. The plaza's main sight is the richly decorated 16th century **Igreja de São Pedro**.

A block straight ahead from the front of the church is another large plaza known as the **Largo do Carmo**. From this plaza you'll see the massive bell towers of the baroque 18th century **Igreja de Nossa Senhora da Carmo**. The church has a strange **Capela dos Ossas** (chapel of bones) which is covered with skeletal remains of former monks (closed Saturdays and Sundays). Once again it is time to head back to the dock area. This time I suggest a final stop at the city's famous **Museu Maratimo de Admiral Ortigão**, a maritime museum at the northern edge of the docks behind the Hotel Eva in the port captain's offices. You can see a vast collection of miniature scale models of historic and traditional Portuguese ships.

The beaches around Faro also are worth some consideration. Although the quality of the water here may be questionable, you can at least get a nice tan. The closest beach to town is an island called **Praia de Faro**, which is packed during the summer. It can be reached by ferry from the terminal in front of the Cidade Velha area, where you can also catch high season ferry service to the better and somewhat developed **Ilha da Culatra** and **Ilha Deserta** island beaches in the Ria Formosa natural park area (see Olhão below).

NIGHTLIFE & ENTERTAINMENT

Most of Faro's best nightspots can be found along the Rua do Prior. There are several different types of bars, pubs, and clubs that fill up on weekend nights. I suggest you start at the infamous **Adega dos Argos** where the patrons sing along to old songs. From here you can peek inside the more aggressive hot spots such as the **Chaplin Bar** and **Megahertz**, but expect to pay a cover charge. The more upscale tourists tend to go to the Hotel Eva to dance in the **Sheherazade Club.**

SPORTS & RECREATION
Sailing
• **Ginásio Sailing Clube**, *Doca de Faro, Faro, Tel. (089) 823-434*

OLHÃO & THE COASTAL ISLANDS

The picturesque town of Olhão is situated on a river estuary, separated from the ocean by a series of salt marshes and small islands known officially as the Parque Natural da Ria Formosa.

This old Moorish city still makes much of its livelihood from the fishing industry. The Moorish design of the town's many whitewashed cube-shaped houses is based on the typical style of North African coastal communities that local merchants have been trading with since the 16th century.

ARRIVALS & DEPARTURES
By Car
Olhão is about 9 km from Faro on Route N-125 east.

By Train
• **Olhão CP Rail Station**, *Ave. dos Combatentes, Tel. (089) 705-378*

WHERE TO STAY

Moderate

HOTEL RIA SOL, *Rua General H. Delgado, 37. Tel. (089) 705-276.*

This modern and comfortable 2 star hotel has 52 nice double rooms in the heart of town. Facilities include bar, breakfast room, TV room, and nearby parking.

Inexpensive

PENSÃO BELA VISTA, *Rua Teofilo Braga, 65. Tel. (089) 702-538.*

This fairly nice 2 star inn with a tranquil courtyard, in the heart of town, has about nine guest rooms with and without private bathrooms. There are almost no facilities except a TV.

SEEING THE SIGHTS

There are only a few attractions in the town itself. There's a nice harbor, a tranquil riverside park (**Parque de Joaquim Lopes municipal gardens**) with pleasant cafes, a nearby riverfront morning seafood and produce mercado (market – daily except Sunday), the small **Museu Municipal** (closed Sundays) with a few local artifacts and fossils on the **Largo da Lagoa**, and several meandering stone streets off the Ave. da República.

The best view of Olhão can be seen from atop the towers of the delightful 17th century **Igreja Matriz** in the heart of town.

EXCURSIONS & DAY TRIPS

The reason most visitors come to this area is to catch the local ferry service that runs from the dock near the gardens to a couple of long sandy beach islands at the edge of the **Parque Natural da Ria Formosa**. The ferry ride to the beaches, cafes, and rental cottages on **Ilha da Armona** takes 20 minutes and costs about 380$00 round-trip, with service several times daily year round.

The longer 50 minute ride to the fishing villages and beaches on the **Ilha da Culatra** costs about 500$00 round-trip with service several times each day. Your best bet is to wait until you have reached the more promising beach area of **Farol** to disembark. Accommodations on these islands are extremely limited, so plan to return to the mainland by sundown.

ESTÓI & THE COUNTRYSIDE

This sleepy town has a series of quaint streets full of traditional whitewashed homes and baroque buildings around squares such as the

Largo da Liberdade. The town is quite relaxing and has several nice bed and breakfast inns.

ARRIVALS & DEPARTURES
By Car
Estói can be reached by taking Route N-2-6 north from Olhão for about 10 km.

WHERE TO STAY
Moderate
MONTE DO CASAL, *Cerro do Lobo, Estói. Tel. (089) 951-03, Fax (89) 913-41. Low season rack rates from 12,480$00, double room, BP; high season rack rates from 24,240$00, double room, BP. Most major credit cards accepted.*

Monte do Casal is a magnificent 18th century farmhouse that has been converted into a truly magical deluxe country hotel just a 3 minute drive from Estói. The owner and manager, Bill Hawkins, greets every guest personally, and then heads for the kitchen to prepare some of the finest meals I have had in Portugal.

The hotel has 13 spacious and beautifully furnished air conditioned rooms and suites with private bathrooms, direct dial telephones, and in most cases private terraces. The property also features a superb gourmet restaurant, an opulent bar, a large heated outdoor swimming pool and sun deck, an outdoor tennis court, and several sitting rooms with fireplaces.

Another advantage to this inn is the close proximity by car to the country's best 18 hole championship golf courses and countless miles of pristine secluded sandy beaches. I give Monte do Casal my highest recommendation, and am sure that you will love this place as much as I do. Selected as one of my *Best Places to Stay* (see Chapter 10 for more details).

POUSADA DE SÃO BRAS, *São Bras de Alportel. Tel. (089) 842-306. US & Canada bookings with Marketing Ahead, Tel. 800/223-1356. Low season rack rates from 12,000$00, double room, CP; high season rates from 16,500$00, double room, CP. All major credit cards accepted.*

This newly renovated, government owned, hilltop country inn is located on a bluff above the town of São Bras de Alportel. It has 24 rooms with private bathrooms, television, comfortable furnishings, and great views. Facilities include bar, restaurant, pool, tennis, and parking.

WHERE TO EAT
MONTE DO CASAL, *Cerro do Lobo, Estói. Tel. (089) 951-03. Open daily for lunch and dinner. Dress code is smart casual. Most major credit cards accepted.*

After my last two truly incredible meals at this superb inn's restaurant, I am convinced that Monte do Casal is one of Portugal's best restaurants. You'll be seated at a stunningly set table in one of a series of garden terraces or intimate dining rooms, surrounded by dramatic exposed wooden beams and traditional Algarvian split bamboo ceilings, white stucco walls lined by fine works of art, Portuguese cooking instruments, and large wood burning fireplaces. Within seconds, one of the restaurants friendly waiters will present you with as many as three different menus that feature an outstanding selection of simply delicious daily specials and innovative seasonal a la carte dishes that are beyond comparison.

European trained master chef Bill Hawkins and his assistant chef Paula Matias have been working together for over a decade creating their unique fusion of internationally inspired gourmet cuisine based on choice cuts of prime meats, freshly caught local seafood, locally grown vegetables, and a vast array of rare spices that are blended together in perfect harmony.

You'll have to make an unusually difficult choice between such sumptuous dishes as smoked quail mousse in creamy horseradish sauce, crab croquettes in tartar sauce garnished with gerkins and capers, tender prawns in white wine with garlic and oyster sauce served on Chinese noodles, an awesome ragout of onions and mushrooms topped with slices of delicious smoked local goat cheese, cream infused tomato basil soup, curried cauliflower soup, smoked swordfish and salmon served with gravalax, pan fried fillet steak with garlic butter, Asian flavored tender slices of roasted duck breast, chicken Louise with chestnut stuffing, fillet of lamb in a dry white Madeira wine and rosemary sauce, beef Stroganoff, salmon baked with spinach in a delicate hand rolled puff pastry, giant grilled tiger prawns with leeks and vegetable rosti in a rich Champagne sauce, seafood Monte do Casal with prawns and langoustines topped with a rich reduction of fish broth and heavy cream, several vegetarian items including Thai spiced stir-fry or over-stuffed green peppers with saffron rice, and amazing desserts such as iced coffee soufflés and homemade almond ice cream.

Make sure to ask George to recommend one of their many affordably priced Portuguese wines, or have a cocktail from their full selection of top shelf liquors and single malt Scotches.

Expect to pay around 4,950$00 per person (plus wine) for a three course gourmet lunch or dinner. Reservations are recommended at least a day in advance if possible. With this small establishment's remarkably welcoming atmosphere, fine staff of dedicated young professionals, and unparalleled cuisine, it easily deserves my absolute highest recommendation.

SEEING THE SIGHTS

From **Largo da Liberdade**, follow the Rua da Jardim for a block or so until passing through a pink and green gateway that leads towards the wonderfully ornate 18th century **Palácio do Visconde de Estói**. The palace formerly belonged to the various Dukes of Estói, but these days it keeps changing hands every few years. While the palace is still not open to the public, the adjacent terraced gardens (closed Sundays and Mondays) are full of mermaid fountains, hand painted antique azulejos, and blossoming fruit trees, and is well worth the effort to wander through. The town offers little else in the way of attractions, besides pleasant little squares and parks and the regional mercado (market) on the second Sunday of each month.

A mile or so west of Estói you should stop at the remarkable Roman ruins of **Milreu**. Originally this 2nd century hamlet was known as Ossonoba. The site was first found in 1876, and minimal excavation led to the uncovering of a Roman villa, courtyard, mosaics, baths, columns, mausoleums, and a converted temple that some say may be the oldest Christian church in the world. The ruins are sometimes closed on Mondays and are always free to enter.

EXCURSIONS & DAY TRIPS

The quaint countryside market towns to the north and east of Estói are well worth a visit. I strongly suggest the 8 km trip to Route N-2 north to visit the pleasant village of **São Bras de Alportel**. Visit the beautiful old **Igreja Matriz** (church) and the stately home that houses the **Museu Etnografico**, a museum of traditional Algarvian costumes (closed on Mondays). There is also a regional **mercado** (market) in the town's center on every Saturday.

Another old fashioned local town, **Moncarapacho** is about 13 km away from Estói on Route IP-1 east. You can stroll through the quaint streets and if you are lucky enough to arrive on the first Sunday of the month you can follow the hordes of local country folk towards the huge produce, handicrafts, and livestock **mercado** (market).

TAVIRA

This delightful small city has a rich history that dates back thousands of years before successive Greek, Roman, and Moorish occupations. The Moors were conquered in 1242 by Christian forces under the command of Dom Paio Peres Correia as revenge for the murders of seven knights of the St. James order. During the 1755 earthquake several of the most important structures in town, including the castle and old seven arch Roman bridge, were heavily damaged.

Tavira has been built around both sides of the Sequa and Gilão Rivers. These rivers merge under their lovely bridges and are lined by beautiful homes with balconies. Many ornate churches, palaces, regal pastel colored homes, and ramparts can be seen along many of the old winding streets. Today, Tavira's economy depends on a combination of local fishing and nearby beach front resort developments that have thus far spared the historic parts of town.

ARRIVALS & DEPARTURES
By Car
Tavira is about 29 km from Olhão on Route N-125 east.

By Train
• **Tavira CP Rail Station**, *Rua da Liberdade, Tel. (081) 223-54*

WHERE TO STAY
Moderate
QUINTA DO CARACOL, *Tavira. Tel. (081) 224-75.*
This wonderful former farming estate has been converted into a fabulous bed and breakfast inn with seven apartments with kitchens. Facilities include bar, pool, gardens, tennis, bicycles, and a great barbecue area. Near the train station.

EUROTEL TAVIRA, *Tavira. Tel. (081) 324-324.*
This modern 3 star hotel has 80 air conditioned rooms with balconies just outside of town. Facilities include bar, restaurant, pool, tennis, billiards, TV room, and parking.

HOTEL GOLDEN DUNA, *Cabanas. Tel. (081) 204-81.*
This nice hotel and villa complex, near the beach, has 147 rooms in either its main hotel or in one of several cabana villas at land's edge. Facilities include pool.

PEDRAS DEL RAINHA, *Cabanas. Tel. (081) 201-81.*
This large cabana complex has hundreds of adjacent one to four bedroom cabanas with kitchens. The rooms surround a central recreation complex. Facilities include bar, restaurant, shops, pool, bicycles, tennis, disco, baby-sitting, and phones.

ESTALAGEM OASIS, *Manta Rota. Tel. (081) 951-660.*
This nice and friendly 4 star inn is located near the beach and has 20 rooms with private bathroom. Facilities include bar, restaurant, gardens, sun deck, TV, and parking.

PEDRAS D'EL REI, *Santa Luzia. Tel. (081) 325-352.*
This huge low end cabana complex has hundreds of cabanas with kitchens and small beds for rent. It's a good value for families on tight

budgets. The complex is not very appealing to people wanting any form of luxury or peace. Facilities include bar, restaurant, shops, pool, barbecue, bicycles, tennis, baby-sitting, and phones.

Inexpensive

RESIDENCIAL PRINCESSA DO GILÃO, *Rua Borda da Agua de Aguiar. Tel. (081) 226-65.*

This nice 2 star inn, just across the river from the mercado, offers 22 rooms with and without private bathrooms and nice views.

RESIDENCIAL LAGOA, *Rua Almirante Candido dos Reis, 34. Tel. (081) 222-52.*

This nice and basic 2 star inn has 16 guest rooms with and without private bathrooms. It's a good budget choice.

WHERE TO EAT

Moderate

O CANECÃO, *Rua José P. Padinha, 162. Tel. (081) 819-21.*

This wonderful harbor front restaurant with huge picture windows serves the finest cataplana (seafood stew) in the Algarve. One order is enough for three people.

RESTAURANTE IMPERIAL, *Rua José P. Padinha, 24. Tel. (081) 222-34.*

This fine seafood and meat restaurant on the harbor serves well prepared, freshly caught grilled and fried fish dishes including Tavira'a famed bife de atum (tuna steak).

Inexpensive

RESTAURANTE BICA, *Rua A. Can. dos Reis, 24. Tel. (081) 222-82.*

This good and reasonably priced casual seafood restaurant in the Residencial Lagoa offers huge portions of the day's catch. A great budget choice.

SEEING THE SIGHTS

Upon arriving in the downtown area, your best bet is to park in the central riverside **Praça da República** square and walk up the main street of Rua da Liberdade until you can turn right onto Rua D. Paio Peres Correia. At the next corner you again turn right, this time onto the Calçãda D. Paio Peres Correira where you will find yourself next to the somber **Igreja de Santiago**. From here can't help but notice the bell and clock towers above the 13th century **Igreja de Santa Maria do Castelo**, built on the site of a former mosque and housing the tomb of Dom Paio Peres Correia.

Nearby are the ancient ramparts and ruins of the town's 13th century **castelo** (castle). The small lanes that cross through this side of town feature several interesting churches and palatial buildings including the **Convento de Nossa Senhora de Graça** off the quaint **Largo de Postigo** (plaza), the **Palácio da Galeria** (palace) and park on Calçãda de D. Ana, and the remarkable Renaissance 16th century **Igreja da Misericórdia** near the riverfront.

After returning to the **Praça da República**, stroll down the Rua José Pires Padinha and adjacent Rua do Cais, which are surrounded by a wonderful riverfront garden esplanade. You will pass the daily morning fish mercado (market) and several good restaurants before reaching the docks where you can see the fishermen unload squid and fish into crates. After a look around the dockside, you may want to cross the modernized Roman bridge to the other side of town, where you can see women hanging their laundry out on the panoramic Rua de Borda de Agua da Asseca just in front of the riverside. If you venture inward on the Rua 5 de Outubro and turn left, you'll come across even nicer plazas and old churches.

SPORTS & RECREATION
Horseback Riding
• **Eurotel Horse Center**, *Tavira, Tel. (081) 220-41*

EXCURSIONS & DAY TRIPS
The town of Tavira is close to some fine sandy beaches on the tip of **Ilha de Tavira** which can be reached during the summer by a 15 minute ferry trip from the town's fishing docks or from nearby **Quatro Aguas**. The ride costs about 200$00 round-trip. Although there are bars, restaurants, and a campsite on the island, you may find that the best accommodations are back on the mainland.

Additional sandy islands with dune beaches can be reached by rowboat or shuttle service from the appropriately named and overbuilt resort area of **Cabanas** and the lovely traditional village of **Cacela** to the east, and **Pedras D'el Rei** (Santa Luzia) to the west. Long sandy stretches of beach can be accessed directly by car (without ferry and shuttle service) a bit further east of town at **Manta Rota** and **Alagoa**.

MONTE GORDO
This is the first reasonable beach area that Spaniards pass when entering the Algarve, and many of them seem to just settle here for their vacations. There are also a few older English, Dutch, and German visitors. For some reason the town's hotels are often packed.

ARRIVALS & DEPARTURES
By Car
Monte Gordo is about 22 km from Tavira on Route N-125 east.

WHERE TO STAY
Expensive
HOTEL DOS NAVEGADORES, *Rua Gonçalo Velho. Tel. (081) 512-490.*

This large and modern 3 star hotel near the beach has 344 air conditioned rooms with balconies. Facilities include bar, restaurant, pool, health club, squash, and parking.

HOTEL ALCAZAR, *Rua de Cueta. Tel. (081) 512-184.*

This modern 4 star hotel, a few blocks from the ocean, has 95 large air conditioned rooms. Facilities include bar, disco, restaurant, pool, billiards, TV, and parking.

Moderate
VASCO DE GAMA HOTEL, *Ave. Infante Dom Henrique. Tel. (081) 423-22.*

This good, beach front 3 star hotel has 165 air conditioned rooms. Facilities include bar, disco, restaurant, pool, tennis, water sports facilities, billiards, TV, and parking.

HOTEL CASABLANCA INN, *Rua 7. Tel. (081) 444-45.*

This nice and friendly 3 star hotel has 42 comfortable double rooms near the beach and casino. Facilities include bar, restaurant, pool, sun deck, and TV room.

APARTHOTEL ATLÂNTICO, *Ave. Infante Dom Henrique. Tel. (081) 511-040.*

This large ocean front apartment complex has 88 one bedroom units that include kitchens and ocean view balconies. Facilities include bar, restaurant, shops, and parking.

Inexpensive
ALBERGARIA MONTE GORDO, *Ave. Infante Dom Henrique. Tel. (081) 421-24.*

This good and reasonably priced 4 star inn near the ocean offers 25 double rooms with private bathrooms, a bar, restaurant, TV room, and nearby parking.

WHERE TO EAT
Inexpensive
MOTA, *Praia do Monte Gordo. Tel. (081) 426-50.*

This good and reasonably priced casual outdoor restaurant offers everything from salads and burgers to freshly caught local seafood. This is a great place for a quick bite.

SEEING THE SIGHTS
The town has a long sandy beach known as the **Praia de Monte Gordo** and a decent water view **casino**. The nicest beach in the area can be found a few km west at Praia Verde.

VILA REAL DE SANTO ANTÓNIO
The pleasing little border town of Vila Real de Santo António is located at the mouth of the Guadiana River. This port city had been devastated by a huge tidal wave and was completely rebuilt by the Marquês de Pombal in 1774 in less than six months.

The town used to serve as the primary border crossing point for excursions to and from Ayamonte, Spain by ferry and train. Today, a more rapid highway and bridge system allows people with cars to bypass the ferry and avoid town.

ARRIVALS & DEPARTURES
By Car
Vila Real de Santo António is located 4 km from Monte Gordo at the end of Route N-125 east.

WHERE TO STAY
Moderate
HOTEL GUADIANA, *Ave. de República, 92. Tel. (081) 511-482.*

This good, 2 star hotel has 37 fairly comfortable rooms with private bathrooms in the heart of town. Facilities include bar, restaurant, minibars, TV, and parking.

HOTEL APOLO, *Ave. Bomb. Portugueses, (081) 512-448.*

This clean and basic 2 star hotel has 42 double rooms with private bathrooms. Facilities include bar, restaurant, TV room, direct dial phones, and parking.

WHERE TO EAT
Moderate
CAVES DO GAUDIANA, *Ave. de República, 90. Tel. (081) 444-98.*

This huge seafood restaurant is in an old building on the river front. This restaurant serves well prepared locally caught fish and has a vast menu of reasonably priced selections.

SEEING THE SIGHTS
There are several interesting old riverfront mansions to see, as well as the **Museu de Manuel Cabanas** of wood carvings (closed Mondays) on the mosaic-lined **Praça Marquês de Pombal** square. All that said, the city offers a nice place to spend a few hours wandering around, but an overnight here is unnecessary.

The towns surrounding the Portuguese side of the Guadiana River border are worth a nice day trip. There are boats that take excursions to the quaint town of **Foz de Odeleite** (contact the Turismo office on Praça Marquêsde Pombal for booking details and schedules), with lunch included.

You can also drive on route N-122 north up the riverside for 5 km to the fortress town of **Castro Marim** and onward another 31 km or so to the inviting rural village of **Alcoutim**.

PRACTICAL INFORMATION FOR THE ALGARVE

Casinos
• **Casino do Alvor**, *Praia da Rocha, Tel. (82) 231-41*
• **Casino de Vilamoura**, *Vilamoura, Tel. (89) 302-997*
• **Casino de Monte Gordo**, *Monte Gordo, Tel. (81) 512-224*

Currency Exchange
Most banks throughout the Algarve will exchange foreign currency and travelers checks without hesitation. Banks are open from 8am until 3pm, Monday through Friday. Private exchange booths, shops, restaurants, and hotel front desks usually have lower exchange rates.

In the more popular tourist areas and big towns you may be able to find a 24 hour ATM or currency exchange machine.

Emergency & Useful Phone Numbers
• **Emergency assistance** (S.O.S.), *Tel. 115*
• **Aljezur Health Center**, *Igreja Nova, Tel. (082) 981-13*

- **Lagos Hospital**, *Rua do Castelo, Tel. (082) 630-34*
- **Faro Hospital**, *Rua Leão Pinedo, Tel. (089) 220-11*
- **Faro International Airport**, *Faro, Tel. (089) 818-221*
- **TAP Airlines in Faro**, *Rua D Francisco Gomes, Tel. (089) 803-249*
- **Automobile Club of Portugal in Lisbon**, *Tel. (01) 942-5095*

Museums

- **Roman Excavations at Milreu**, *Estoi, Tel. (089) 916-20.* This is a series of unearthed ruins from the 1st century Roman village of Ossonoba. Open by appointment 10am until 12pm and 2pm until 5pm, Tuesday through Sunday. Closed on Mondays and holidays.
- **Infante D. Henrique Archaeological Museum**, *Largo Dom Afonso III, Faro, Tel. (089) 822-042.* Contains collections of local archaeological findings, ceramics, paintings, sculptures, furniture, glassware, azulejos, and jewelry. Open 9am until 12pm and 2pm until 5pm, Monday through Friday. Closed on Saturdays and Sundays.
- **Regional Ethnography Museum of Faro**, *Rua Pe da Cruz, 4, Faro, Tel. (089) 276-10.* Contains collections of paintings, handicrafts, folklore, and scale models of boats. Open 9:30am until 12:30pm and 2:30pm until 4:30pm, Monday through Friday. Closed on Saturdays, Sundays, and holidays.
- **Admiral Ortigão Maritime Museum**, *Harbor Master's Office, Faro, Tel. (089) 803-601.* Contains exhibits on local fishing, and scale models of famous vessels. Open 10am until 11am and 2:30pm until 4:30pm daily.
- **José Formosinho Municipal Museum**, *Igreja de Santo António, Rua General Alberto Silveira, Lagos, Tel. (082) 762-301.* Contains local prehistoric and Roman artifacts, 16th century clothing, ceramics, cork carvings, 17th century embroidery, sacred art, and sculptures. Open 9:30am until 12:30pm and 2pm until 5pm, Tuesday through Sunday. Closed on Mondays and holidays.
- **Olhão Municipal Museum and Library**, *Largo da Lagoa, 3, Olhão, Tel. (089) 705-301.* Contains collections of local fossils, artifacts, handicrafts, and numismatics. Open 2pm until 6pm, Monday through Friday. Open 10am until 12pm and 2pm until 6pm, Saturday. Closed on Sundays and holidays.
- **António Bentes Museum of Costumes**, *Rua Dr. José Dias Sancho, 59, São Brás de Alportel, Tel. (089) 842-618.* A collection of typical Algarvian costumes. Open 10am until 1pm and 2pm until 5:30pm, Wednesdays only during winter. Open 10am until 1pm and 2pm until 6pm, daily during summer. Closed Thursdays until Tuesday during winter.
- **Municipal Museum of Archaeology**, *Rua das Portas de Loulé, 14, Silves, Tel. (082) 444-832.* Contains a collection of prehistoric through 17th

century archaeological findings. Open 10am until 12:30pm and 2:30pm until 6pm daily.

- **Roman Ruins of Cerro da Vial**, *Cerro da Vilamoura, Vilamoura, Tel. (089) 312-153.* An excavated Roman town and archaeological museum with many artifacts. Open 10am until 5pm, daily during winter. Open 10am until 8pm, daily during summer.
- **Manuel Cabanas Municipal Museum**, *Praça Marquêsde Pombal, Vila Real de Santo António, Tel. (081) 511-030.* Contains a collection of antique wood engravings. Open 11am until 12pm and 3pm until 7pm, Tuesday through Sunday during winter. Open 4pm until 8pm and 9pm until 11pm, Tuesday through Sunday during summer. Closed on Mondays and holidays.

Tourist Offices *(Turismos)*

- **Albufeira Tourist Office**, *Rua 5 de Outubro, Tel. (089) 512-144*
- **Aljezur Tourist Office**, *Largo do Mercado, Tel. (082) 982-29*
- **Armação de Pêra Tourist Office**, *Ave. Marginal, Tel. (082) 312-145*
- **Faro Tourist Office**, *Rua da Misericórdia , 8, Tel. (089) 803-667*
- **Faro Tourist Office**, *Faro Airport, Tel. (089) 818-582*
- **Lagos Tourist Office**, *Largo Marquês Pombal, Tel. (082) 630-31*
- **Loulé Tourist Office**, *Edifício de Castelo, Tel. (089) 639-00*
- **Monte Gordo Tourist Office**, *Ave. Marginal, Tel. (081) 444-95*
- **Olhão Tourist Office**, *Largo da Lagoa, Tel. (089) 713-936*
- **Portimão Tourist Office**, *Largo 1 de Dezembro, Tel. (082) 236-95*
- **Praia da Rocha Tourist Office**, *Ave. Marginal, Tel. (082) 222-90*
- **Sagres Tourist Office**, *Promontorio de Sagres, Tel. (082) 641-25*
- **Silves Tourist Office**, *Rua 25 de Abril, Tel. (082) 422-255*
- **Tavira Tourist Office**, *Praça da República, Tel. (081) 225-11*
- **Vila Real de S. A. Tourist Office**, *Posta de Turismo, Tel. (081) 432-72*

Travel Agencies

- **Algarve Marina Tours**, *Vilamoura Marina, Tel. (089) 302-772.* This friendly and well established full service travel agency can book bus tours, villas, apartments, boat excursions, train and airplane tickets, and provides other services.
- **RN Tours**, *Ave. 25 de Abril, 210, Albufeira, Tel. (089) 554-26.* The Albufeira branch office of a national travel company offering bus tours, reservations, ticketing, and discounts at major area hotels.
- **Top Tours**, *Estrada Praia da Rocha, Praia da Rocha, Tel. (082) 417-552.* This Praia da Rocha based branch of a good travel agency can help book all types of tours, hotels, rental cars, airfare, bus and train tickets, and more.

DICTIONARY
& USEFUL PHRASES

NUMBERS

zero	0
um,uma	1
dois	2
Três	3
quatro	4
cinco	5
seis	6
sete	7
oito	8
nove	9
dez	10
onze	11
doze	12
treze	13
catorze	14
quinze	15
dezaseis	16
dezassete	17
dezoito	18
dezanove	19
vinte	20
vinte e um	21
vinte e dois	22
trinta	30
quarenta	40
cinquenta	50
sessenta	60
setenta	70
oitenta	80
noventa	90
cem	100
cem e um	101

cem e dois	102
duzentos	200
quinhentos	500
mil	1000
mil e quinhentos	1500
dois mil	2000
um Milhão	1,000,000

DAYS OF THE WEEK

Segunda-feira	Monday
Terça-feira	Tuesday
Quarta-feira	Wednesday
Quinta-feira	Thursday
Sexta-feira	Friday
Sábado	Saturday
Domingo	Sunday

MONTHS OF THE YEAR

Janeiro	January
Fevereiro	February
Março	March
Abril	April
Maio	May
Junho	June
Julho	July
Agosto	August
Setembro	September
Outubro	October
Novembro	November
Dezembro	December

SEASONS OF THE YEAR

Inverno	Winter
Primavera	Spring
Verão	Summer
Outono	Fall

COLORS

branco	white
negro	black
azul	blue
verde	green
encarnado	red
amarelo	yellow
prata	silver
ouro	gold

TIME

dia	day
meio-dia	noon
tarde	afternoon
noite	night
meia-noite	midnight
ontem	yesterday
hoje	today
logo a tarde	this afternoon
logo a noite	this evening
Amanhã	tommorow
agora	now
cedo	early
mais tarde	later
velho	old
novo	new
minuto	minute
hora	hour
semana	week
mes	month
ano	year

USEFUL WORDS

sim	yes
Não	no
Está bem	okay

bom	good
mau	bad
entrada	entrance
Saída	exit
aberto	open
fechado	closed

GREETINGS

Olá	hello
como Está ?	how are you?
chamo-me...	my name is..
adeus	good bye
faz favor	please
obrigado	thank you (masculine)
obrigada	thank you (feminine)
muito obrigado	thanks a lot (masculine)
muito obrigada	thanks a lot (feminine)
de nada	you're welcome
desculpe	sorry
com Licença	excuse me
bom dia	good morning
boa tarde	good afternoon
boa noite	good evening
senhora	Mrs.
menina	Ms.
senhor	Mr.
Médico	Dr.
senhoras	women
homens	men

Descriptions

pequeno	small
grande	big
menos	less
mais	more
perto	close
longe	far
quente	hot

frio	cold
belo	beautiful
feio	ugly
este	this
esse	that
preco	price
barato	cheap
caro	expensive

QUERIES

quando?	when?
como?	how?
quanto?	how much?
que?	what?
onde?	where?
Porquê?	why?
Não entendo	I don't understand

DIRECTIONS

esquerda	left
direita	right
sempre em frente	directly ahead

TRANSPORTATION

Automóvel	car
autocarro	bus
comboio	train
Avião	airplane
metro	subway
fluvial	ferry
taxi	taxi
Estação	station
aeroporto	airport
primeira classe	first class
segunda classe	second class
ida e volta	round trip
bilhete	ticket
bilheteira	ticket office
bagagem	luggage
estrada	road
ponte	bridge
portagem	toll booth

garagem	garage
gasolina	gasoline
sem chumbo	unleaded gas

SERVICES

posta da policia	police station
Médico	doctor
hospital	hospital
Farmácia	pharmacy
correio	post office
banco	bank
Cãmbio	exchange
hotel	hotel
restaurante	restaurant
casa de banho	bathroom
telefone	telephone

ACCOMMODATIONS

quinta	manor house or estate
pousada	government-owned inn
hotel	hotel
pousada de juventude	hostel
estalagem	quality inn
residencial	budget inn
albergaria	minor hotels
Pensão	boarding house
apartamentos	apartments
vila	villa
campismo	camp site
quarto simple	single room
quarto duplo	double room
quarto com banho	room with private bath
quarto com dois camas	room with 2 beds
air condicionado	air conditioning
aquecimento	heating
lavandaria	laundromat

Televisão	TV
chave	key
Câmbio	exchange
gerente	manager

SPORTS & ENTERTAINMENT

Ténis	tennis
golfe	golf
piscina	pool
bowling	bowling
barcos	boats
canoagem	canoeing
squash	squash
Ténis de mesa	ping pong
equitacão	horse riding
sala de bilhar	billiard room
pesca	fishing
bicicletas	bicycles
Caça	hunting
sauna	sauna
termas	spa
Ginásio	health club
Solário	solarium
casino	casino
cinema	movie theater
Praça de touros	bullfighting ring

SIGHTS

cidade	city
aldeia	village
centro da cidade	city center
rossio	town's main square
Praça	square
largo	plaza
Câmara municipal	town hall
museu	museum
igreja	church
convento	convent
Sé	cathedral
mosteiro	monastery

capela	chapel
claustro	cloister
fonte, chafariz	fountain
pelourinho	pillory
torre	tower
cruz	cross
anta	megalith
castelo	castle
torre de menagem	castle keep
Palácio , Paço	palace
fortaleza	fortress
azulejo	glazed tile
festa	festival
mercado	market
feira	fair
artesanato	handicraft shop
antigo	ancient
floresta	forest
lago	lake
barragem	dam
aqueduto	aqueduct
praia	beach
esplanada	seaview prominade
miradouro	scenic lookout
grutas	caves

BEVERAGES

garrafa	bottle
Café , bica	espresso
Café com leite	coffee with milk
Galão	Café au lait
Chá	tea
leite	milk
sumo	juice
cerveja	beer
vinho tinto	red wine
vinho branco	white wine
agua	water
agua com gas	water with bubbles
agua sem gas	mineral water without bubbles
gelo	ice

FOOD

ementa	menu
empregado	waiter
carta de vinhos	wine list
conta	the bill
pequeno Almoço	breakfast
Almoço	lunch
jantar	dinner
faca	knife
garfo	fork
colher	spoon
Xícara	cup
prato	plate
uma dose	one portion
meia dose	half portion
vegitariano	vegetarian
Pão	bread
mantiega	butter
sal	salt
pimenta	pepper
piri-piri	medium hot sauce
Açúcar	sugar
azeite	olive oil
azeitonas	olives
vinagre	vinegar
sopa	soup
fruta	fruit
salada	green salad
salada mista	mixed salad
ovos	eggs
ovos mexidos	scrambled eggs
ovos estrelados	fried eggs
omelete, omoleta	omelet
bacon	bacon
hamburguesa	hamburger
prego no Pão	steak sandwich
batatas fritas	french fries
sande	sandwich
sande mista	ham and cheese sandwich
tosta	grilled sandwich
Pastéis	filled dumplings
Pastéis de queijo	cheese filled fried dumpling
Pastéis de carne	meat-filled fried dumpling
sobremesa	dessert
bolo	pastry
torta	tart
gelado	ice cream
chocolate	chocolate
arroz doce	rice pudding
pudim flan	flan
carne	meat
bife	steak
lombo	fillet
Leitão	roasted pig
porco	pork
vitela	veal
pato	duck
fiambre	ham
presunto	smoked ham
Chouriço	smoked sausage
tripas	tripe
borrego	lamb
coelho	rabbit
peru	turkey
frango	chicken
peixe	fish
bacalhau	cod
atum	tuna
linguado	flounder
pescada	hake
truta	trout
robalo	bass
espadarte	swordfish
tamboril	monkfish
cherne	turbot
peixe-espada	scabbard fish
Salmão	salmon
carpa	carp
sardinhas	sardines
mariscos	seafood
Camarões	shrimp
gambas	prawns

lagosta	lobster
lagostins	crayfish
caranguejos	crabs
polvo	octopus
lulas	squid
vieiras	scallops
Amêijoas	cockles
ostras	oysters
Mexilhões	mussels
legumes	vegatables
arroz	rice
cebolas	onions
pimentos	peppers
batatas	potatoes
cenouras	carrots
espinafres	spinach
congumelos	mushrooms
pepino	cucumber
alho	garlic
Feijão	beans
alface	lettuce
frutas	fruits
laranja	orange
bananas	bananas
Limão	lemon
Melão	melon
melancia	watermelon
morango	strawberry
Ananás	pineapple
cerejas	cherries
pera	pear
Pêssego	peach
uvas	grapes
Maça	apple
ameixas	plums
tangerina	tangerine
toranja	grapefruit
queijo	cheese
queijo de cabra	goat cheese
queijo de ovelha	sheep cheese
queijo de vaca	cow cheese
quiejo da serra	sheep cheese

COOKING METHODS

grelhado	grilled
no forno	oven baked
assado	roasted
fumado	smoked
cozido	boiled
frito	fried
estufado	stewed
nas brasas	braised
no espeto	on a spit
bem passado	well done
Médio	medium done
mal passado	rare

COMMON QUESTIONS

Fala Inglês?
> Do you speak English?

Onde é a Turismo?
> Where is the tourist office?

Como Sé chama?
> What is your name?

Como Está ?
> How are you?

Que horas São?
> What time is it?

Pode ajuda-me?
> Can you please help me?

Pode indicar-me a....?
> Can you direct me to......?

Qual é a estrada para....?
> Which is the road towards....?

Onde é a parragem do autocarro?
> Where is the bus stop?

Onde é a casa de banho?
> Where are the bathrooms?

Quanto custa?
> How much does it cost?

Como Sé chama isto?
> What is this called?

Aceitam Cartão credito?
> Do you take credit cards?

Aceitam travelers checks?
>Do you accept travelers checks?

Tem quartos livres?
>Are there any rooms available?

Qual o Número de telefone?
>What is the phone number?

Qual o Endereço?
>What is the address?

Quando abrem?
>When do you open?

Quando fecham?
>When do you close?

Quando fica pronto?
>When will it be ready?

Onde é a Estação de ?
>Where is the train station?

A que horas sai o autocão?
>What time does the bus leave?

Quando parte o ultimo comboio?
>When does the last train depart?

Por favor, chama-me um taxi?
>Can you please call a taxi for me?

INDEX

THINGS CHANGE!

Phone numbers, prices, addresses, quality of food, etc, all change. If you come across any new information, we'd appreciate hearing from you. No item is too small! Write us at:

Portugal Guide
Open Road Publishing, P.O. Box 20226
Columbus Circle Station, New York, NY 10023

Or drop us an E-mail note at: Jopenroad@aol.com